1 MONTH OF
FREE
READING

at
www.ForgottenBooks.com

By purchasing this book you are eligible for one month membership to ForgottenBooks.com, giving you unlimited access to our entire collection of over 1,000,000 titles via our web site and mobile apps.

To claim your free month visit:
www.forgottenbooks.com/free1305214

ISBN 978-0-428-72661-4
PIBN 11305214

This book is a reproduction of an important historical work. Forgotten Books uses
state-of-the-art technology to digitally reconstruct the work, preserving the original format
whilst repairing imperfections present in the aged copy. In rare cases, an imperfection in
the original, such as a blemish or missing page, may be replicated in our edition. We do,
however, repair the vast majority of imperfections successfully; any imperfections that
remain are intentionally left to preserve the state of such historical works.

Foreign-Language and English Dictionaries In the Physical Sciences and Engineering

A Selected Bibliography 1952 to 1963

United States Department of Commerce

National Bureau of Standards

Miscellaneous Publication 258

ABBREVIATIONS USED FOR NAMES OF LANGUAGES

AF	AFRIKAANS	IA	INTERLINGUA
AL	ALBANIAN		IRISH (SEE GAELIC)
AM	AMERICAN	IT	ITALIAN
	ANNAMESE (SEE	JA	JAPANESE
	VIETNAMESE)	KO	KOREAN
AR	ARABIC	LA	LATIN
AZ	AZERBAIJANI	LI	LITHUANIAN
BR	BURMESE		MALAY (SEE
BU	BULGARIAN		INDONESIAN)
CH	CHINESE	MO	MONGOLIAN
CR	CROATIAN	NO	NORWEGIAN
CZ	CZECH	PL	POLISH
DA	DANISH	PO	POLYGLOT
DU	DUTCH	PR	PORTUGUESE
EN	ENGLISH	RO	ROMANIAN
EO	ESPERANTO	RU	RUSSIAN
ES	ESTONIAN	SC	SERBOCROATIAN
FI	FINNISH	SL	SLOVAK
FR	FRENCH	SV	SLOVENIAN
GA	GAELIC	SP	SPANISH
GE	GERMAN	SW	SWEDISH
GR	GREEK	TH	THAI
HE	HEBREW	TU	TURKISH
HI	HINDI	UK	UKRAINIAN
HU	HUNGARIAN	VI	VIETNAMESE
IC	ICELANDIC	WE	WELSH
IN	INDONESIAN	WR	WHITE RUSSIAN

Foreign-Language and English Dictionaries In the Physical Sciences and Engineering

A Selected Bibliography 1952 to 1963

Tibor W. Marton

National Bureau of Standards Miscellaneous Publication 258

Issued July 24, 1964

Contents

Library of Congress Catalog Card Number: 64–60041

FOREIGN-LANGUAGE AND ENGLISH DICTIONARIES

IN THE PHYSICAL SCIENCES AND ENGINEERING:

A SELECTED BIBLIOGRAPHY 1952 TO 1963

Tibor W. Marton

ABSTRACT

The bibliography lists over 2800 unilingual, bilingual,
and polyglot dictionaries, glossaries and encyclopedias
in the physical sciences, engineering and technology
published during the past twelve years. The majority of
the titles cited have English as the source or target
language, or are dictionaries giving definitions in
English.   The bibliographic entries are arranged in 49
subject classes; within each subject, the entries are
listed alphabetically by language, and within each
language group by author. Forty-seven foreign languages
are represented in the compilation. Lists of abbreviations and reference sources, and detailed author,
language, and subject indexes complement the publication.

1. INTRODUCTION

The rapid pace of technological progress in the United States, th Soviet Union, the United Kingdom, West Germany, France, Japan, and man other countries throughout the world has quickened interest in scientifi and engineering terminology. Even the less developed countries, wanti to keep abreast of the scientific literature of the technologicall advanced nations, have substantially increased their lexicographic effort

The publishing of glossaries and dictionaries, responding to th law of supply and demand, has been further stimulated by four majo factors: 1) the obsolescence of a fast-developing technology, 2) th interdisciplinary character of modern science, 3) the need for quic dissemination of scientific and technical information, and 4) th corresponding need for standardization of national and internationa terminology.

The proliferation of technical dictionaries and encyclopedias i turn has increased the need for up-to-date bibliographic aids designed t guide the literature searcher and user to the best and latest languag tools. While a few excellent bibliographies have been published in th last decade (e.g., the compilations of UNESCO, Zaunmüller, Malclès), non has been geared to the specific requirements of the American specialist With this in mind, the compiler has attempted to provide an up-to-dat bibliography oriented toward the American user. The by-product of a acquisition program aimed at the expansion of the technical dictionar collection of the National Bureau of Standards Library, the compilation comprises unilingual defining glossaries, dictionaries, encyclopedias and bi- or multilingual dictionaries in the physical sciences and technology listed in a subject-language arrangement.

Within the limits set by time and budget, considerable effort was made to locate and peruse as many entries as possible; however, the compilation does not claim to be all-inclusive. The compiler will welcome suggestions for information on important publications which may have been overlooked.

Selection criteria. The chronological scope -- the past twelve years -- was chosen because bibliographic coverage of the field is quite adequate up to the early 1950's.

The principal criterion for the selection of entries -- although evaluation per se was not intended -- was the usefulness of the cited worl to the English-speaking scientific community within the range expressed by the title: physical sciences and engineering. The biological sciences and their applied fields (medicine, agriculture, etc.) were excluded unless there was an overlap between the physical and biological disciplines, e.g., biophysics, biochemistry, radiology, agricultural machinery.

As a rule, <u>general</u> language dictionaries and encyclopedias (English or foreign) were not included, although most of the reputable compilations in this category list a fair proportion of scientific and technical terms; the large number of such dictionaries would have considerably increased the size of the publication. In any case, this category can easily be located in the better-known reference books, publishers' catalogs, etc. (See Bibliographic References, pp.167-9).

In view of the English-language orientation of this compilation, the second major criterion for the inclusion of bilingual and polyglot dictionaries was that English be either the source language or one of the target languages. Unilingual defining dictionaries in languages other than English were included only if their subject areas were marked by a scarcity of bilingual or multilingual titles, and if they met the additional criteria of quality, comprehensiveness, or special interest in the physical sciences and/or technology (e.g., Metrology, Engineering Standards, Cryogenics, Superconductivity). Interlingual and polyglot dictionaries <u>lacking English</u> as one of the languages (e.g., a German-French geophysics dictionary or a Russian-Chinese-Japanese technical dictionary) were excluded, however valuable in other respects.

<u>Literature search</u>. An extensive search was made of the relevant literature, including specialized, national and international bibliographies, publishers' catalogs and announcements, and serials in this field. Emphasis was placed on significant titles issued in the past twelve years. A few exceptions were made to this chronological scope in order to include earlier titles outstanding for their excellence or pertinence to their particular subject.

The literature search was not extended to locate a significant portion of glossaries in textbooks, monographs, handbooks, serials, etc. Pertinent lists of terms in publications of these types were included only if they came easily to the compiler's attention. One of the reasons for not covering fully these glossaries -- aside from the size of the task -- is that the better ones in these categories are often incorporated into a major compilation.

<u>Subject analysis</u>. This aspect presented minor problems. Some dictionaries have titles that are not self-explanatory or fully descriptive of their contents; a substantial number cover more than one major subject class and express such multiple coverage in the title; others comprise a whole range of subjects without expressing all of them in the main title. For the convenience of the reader, it was decided that dictionaries listing terms in two or three distinct technical fields would be entered under <u>each</u> major topic; those referring to more than three subjects would be printed under general and comprehensive designations such as Materials, Science, Technology.

<u>Production</u>. The processing technique developed out of a modest effort to explore the possibilities offered by mechanized handling of a medium-sized but rather complex bibliography. For the benefit of those

interested in the mechanization aspects, it is perhaps appropriate to touch upon the main features of the system adopted: key-punched cards, machine sorting by subject and language code, tabulating, and photographically reduced offset printing.

Ten columns were reserved for five 2-digit codes on each punched card: three codes for subjects, one for language, and one for card identification, leaving the rest of the punched card for the text of the entry Card sets having two or, less frequently, three subject affiliations were mechanically duplicated, sorted and listed in the appropriate subject class. For 2800 individual entries with approximately 40 per cent subject duplication, about 10,000 cards had to be keypunched, interpreted, sorted, and tabulated. In the final printout, of course, the code designations were suppressed.

Programming and computer treatment were considered but abandoned in the early stages of planning because of limited project funds and time, and because of the complexity of a task involving the permutation and alphabetization of over 2800 entries representing 49 subject areas and 48 languages. Permuted title printout (Keyword-in-Context) was also rejected for obvious reasons: the keywords in the various languages would be scattered all over the alphabet (e.g., Chemistry, Chimie, Kemia, Khimiia, Quimica), thus defeating the very purpose of the KWIC arrangement. The additional listing of all entries by language, though easily feasible with machine sorting and tabulating, was given up due to practical considerations, i.e., the almost double printing costs.

It may be worthwhile here to point out some of the advantages of the selected system: it facilitates error correction and updating for possible future cumulation or rearrangement; it requires no manual retyping of entries to be listed in more than one place in the bibliography; it lends itself to the production of special printouts for specific requests, such as listings by languages or by author.

Arrangement. The main body of the bibliography covers 49 major subject areas in the physical sciences, engineering and technology listed in alphabetical order. Each subject area is subdivided by language groups, also arranged alphabetically. Within each language group, the entries are arranged alphabetically by author or title.

Entries. Most entries in this bibliography consist of individual or corporate author(s), original title, abbreviated translation of foreign titles, imprint, Library of Congress card number, and approximate number of terms contained in the dictionary.

Author(s). Since dictionaries and encyclopedias are often the result of cooperative effort, and also for the sake of brevity, designations such as "editor", "compiler", etc. have been omitted throughout. If more than two personal authors are involved, only the name of the senior author is listed, followed by an "et al" notation. In general, preference was given to individual compilers over corporate author(s). In cases in

4

which no individual or corporate author was cited, the entry was listed by title. Finally, if the corporate author was the same as the publisher, the publisher's name was omitted in the imprint.

Titles of entries. As a rule, titles are given in the vernacular to insure accurate and easy identification. For the same reason, abbreviations or omission of parts of original titles are sparingly used, even if the original title is in English. However, English translations of foreign-language titles (appearing in parentheses following the original title) are abbreviated in accordance with the List of Abbreviations on pp. 162-6. The Library of Congress transliteration system for Slavic languages and romanization system for Oriental languages have been used throughout.

Abbreviations and symbols. Translated titles, language information, publishers' names, etc. have been abbreviated in accordance with the Lists of Abbreviations. The adoption of abbreviations, especially in the translated titles, reduced very considerably the length of the entries and therefore, the number of cards to be punched, handled, and tabulated. It is hoped that this minor inconvenience to the reader will be understood.

The names of languages have been abbreviated to a two-letter mnemonic symbol, e.g., EN(glish), FR(ench), RU(ssian), JA(panese). (See List of Language Abbreviations, p. 162). The asterisk (*) preceding the language abbreviation means the language into which the dictionary translates. Thus, the abbreviated translation of a "two-way" title, e.g., a German-English, English-German dictionary, appears in the compilation as:

(*GE*EN D).

A "one-way" glossary, e.g., an English-Russian glossary, is listed as:

(EN*RU GL).

Defining dictionaries published exclusively in foreign languages are identified by an abbreviated note following the translated title: "RU DEFS", or "GE DEFS", etc., meaning that the terms are defined in Russian or German, not in English.

Imprint and Other Data. The original title and its abbreviated translation are followed by the series statement and edition statement wherever applicable, place of publication, publisher's name, date of publication, pages or number of volumes, Library of Congress card number whenever available, and, when known, the number of terms contained in the dictionary. EXAMPLE:

PALOTAS, L. ET AL. MÜSZAKI MECHANIKA. (ENG.MECH. D, *HU*EN*GE*RU) (MUSZ. ERT. SZ, NO.4) ED2. BUDAPEST, TERRA, 1959. 167P. 59-40060. 1200T.

This bibliographic citation sequence is the same throughout, although some of the elements may be missing, depending on the publication itself or on its availability for inspection.

Various editions. In the case of several editions of the same title, usually the latest available edition has been listed. In view of the practice of certain publishers of calling a slight re-manipulation of the original work a "new" or subsequent edition, it is suggested that the reader using this bibliography for acquisition purposes compare the various editions carefully. Naturally, an attempt was made to locate and inspect all cited dictionaries, at least in the libraries of the Greater Washington area, or to obtain detailed bibliographic information on elusive entries by corresponeence. However, these efforts were not always successful; as a result, some titles lack complete bibliographic information.

Glossaries in serials and monographs. For the relatively few entries representing glossaries published in serials, the names of periodicals have been abbreviated in accordance with the <u>Chemical Abstracts List of Periodicals</u> and the <u>Publications and Report Manual</u> of the National Bureau of Standards. Glossaries appearing as a part or appendix in monographs are so identified in the bibliographic citation.

Type font. The limitations of available key-punching and tabulating equipment necessitated some departures from the typeset bibliographic format. Another aspect of these limitations is the substitution of commas for apostrophes in Western languages and for apostrophe-like symbols in the romanization systems for Oriental languages and in the transliteration systems for Slavic languages.

Indexes. It was decided not to employ serial numbers for entry identification; such numbers offer no clue to the subject or author of an entry and involve a great deal of scanning time. Furthermore, the very nature of the bibliography's arrangement (by subject and language within the subject) facilitates location of the desired entry and encourages browsing. For ease of perusal, dictionaries which cover terms in two or three distinct technical fields are listed under each <u>major</u> subject class in the bibliography; however, in the author and language indexes, page references are <u>only</u> to the entry under the major subject class to avoid duplication of look-up.

Author index. In order to facilitate location of the entries in library catalogs and publishers' announcements, etc. -- especially for the purpose of acquisition and/or inspection -- an Author Index is supplied on pp.170-9. However, since various reference tools, publishers' lists and library catalogs may use different cataloging and bibliographic systems, the reader is cautioned to consider carefully alternate choices of entry.

Language index. A detailed Language Index is provided on pp.180-3 indicating page and subject references for uni- and bilingual entries. Index references for languages contained in the <u>polyglot</u> dictionaries include -- in addition to page and subject -- the symbol PO and the first word of the entry. For entries in <u>English</u>, <u>French</u>, <u>German</u>, and <u>Russian,</u> the index gives only page references due to the fact that these

6

languages are represented in all subject fields and in all polyglot sections; the perusal of a detailed index for this group of languages would be too laborious and time-consuming for the reader.

Subject index. In addition to the broad classes of subjects in the physical sciences, engineering, and technology which form the very structure of the bibliography and are listed in the table of contents, a detailed Subject Index is provided on pp. 184-9 for readers interested in specific, narrower topics. These index entries include subject groups at the lower hierarchical level, such as names of materials (e.g., Glass, Rubber, Steel) or instruments (e.g., Oscilloscope, Microscope, Potentiometer).

Acknowledgments. It is a great pleasure to acknowledge the encouragement given to the project from its inception to completion by Miss Sarah Ann Jones, Chief Librarian of the National Bureau of Standards.

It goes without saying that a compilation of this nature would not have been possible without the generous help of many specialists; the bibliography has been strengthened through the assistance and counsel of many scientists, librarians, linguists and translators in the Washington area. To all of these, I wish to express my sincere gratitude.

Invaluable help in locating, romanizing and translating Chinese, Japanese, and Korean titles was given by Dr. Osamu Shimizu, Miss Joan Wu, and Mr. Chi Wang, all of the Library of Congress.

The compiler is particularly indebted to the following staff members of the National Bureau of Standards: Dr. Don I. Mittleman, Chief of the Computation Laboratory, and Mr. William W. Youden of the Information Technology Division, for helpful comments and advice on the technique chosen for production; Mr. Kermit Nelson of the Computation Laboratory for his tireless efforts to improve the key-punching and tabulating operations; Mr. John E. Carpenter, Chief of the Publications Section, for suggestions on printing and distribution aspects; Mr. Conrad F. Peters, Chief of the Graphic Arts Section, and staff members in that section, for assistance in the preparation of the manuscript-printout for photo-offset printing. Special thanks are due to Miss Stella J. Pridgen and Mrs. Natalie J. Goldenberg of the Library of the National Bureau of Standards for the valiant service rendered in the seemingly endless and arduous task of searching, typing, proofreading, supervision of tabulating operations, and general editorial work.

1.1. ABBREVIATIONS USED FOR NAMES OF LANGUAGES*

AF	....	AFRIKAANS	IA	.... INTERLINGUA
AL	....	ALBANIAN		IRISH (SEE GAELIC)
AM	....	AMERICAN	IT	.... ITALIAN
	ANNAMESE (SEE		JA	.... JAPANESE
		VIETNAMESE)	KO	.... KOREAN
AR	....	ARABIC	LA	.... LATIN
AZ	....	AZERBAIJANI	LI	.... LITHUANIAN
BR	....	BURMESE		MALAY (SEE
BU	....	BULGARIAN		INDONESIAN)
CH	....	CHINESE	MO	.... MONGOLIAN
CR	....	CROATIAN	NO	.... NORWEGIAN
CZ	....	CZECH	PL	.... POLISH
DA	....	DANISH	PO	.... POLYGLOT
DU	....	DUTCH	PR	.... PORTUGUESE
EN	....	ENGLISH	RO	.... ROMANIAN
EO	....	ESPERANTO	RU	.... RUSSIAN
ES	....	ESTONIAN	SC	.... SERBOCROATIAN
FI	....	FINNISH	SL	.... SLOVAK
FR	....	FRENCH	SV	.... SLOVENIAN
GA	....	GAELIC	SP	.... SPANISH
GE	....	GERMAN	SW	.... SWEDISH
GR	....	GREEK	TH	.... THAI
HE	....	HEBREW	TU	.... TURKISH
HI	....	HINDI	UK	.... UKRAINIAN
HU	....	HUNGARIAN	VI	.... VIETNAMESE
IC	....	ICELANDIC	WE	.... WELSH
IN	....	INDONESIAN	WR	.... WHITE RUSSIAN

---

*This list is repeated inside the front and back
cover for convenience of the user.

8

2. Bibliography

Pages 11 to 161

2.1. LIST OF SUBJECT AREAS USED IN THE BIBLIOGRAPHY

ABBREVIATIONS AND ACRONYMS
AEROSPACE SCIENCE AND ENGINEERING
ASTRONOMY AND ASTROPHYSICS
AUTOMATION AND AUTOMATIC CONTROL
AUTOMOTIVE ENGINEERING AND
    INDUSTRY
CARTOGRAPHY, GEODESY AND
    SURVEYING
CHEMISTRY AND CHEMICAL
    ENGINEERING
CIVIL ENGINEERING AND BUILDING
    INDUSTRY
COMPUTERS, DATA PROCESSING AND
    INFORMATION RETRIEVAL
CRYSTALLOGRAPHY AND MINERALOGY
DOCUMENTATION AND BIBLIOGRAPHY
ELECTRICAL AND ELECTRONIC
    ENGINEERING
FOOD CHEMISTRY, RESEARCH AND
    TECHNOLOGY
FUELS (SOLID, LIQUID AND GAS)
GEOLOGY
GEOPHYSICS AND PHYSICAL
    GEOGRAPHY
HYDRAULIC ENGINEERING
INDUSTRIAL ENGINEERING AND
    MANAGEMENT
INSTRUMENTATION AND METROLOGY
MACHINERY AND TOOLS
MATERIALS TESTING AND INDUSTRIAL
    PRODUCTS
MATHEMATICS (PURE AND APPLIED)
MECHANICAL ENGINEERING

METALLURGY AND METALLOGRAPHY
METEOROLOGY
MILITARY SCIENCE AND ENGINEERING
MINING ENGINEERING
NAVAL SCIENCE AND ENGINEERING
NUCLEAR PHYSICS AND ENGINEERING
OCEANOGRAPHY AND HYDROLOGY
OPTICS AND SPECTROSCOPY
PAINTS, DYES AND PROTECTIVE
    COATINGS
PAPER CHEMISTRY AND TECHNOLOGY
PETROLEUM CHEMISTRY, ENGINEERING
    AND GEOLOGY
PHOTOGRAPHY AND CINEMATOGRAPHY
PHYSICS
PLASTICS AND POLYMERS
PRINTING TECHNOLOGY AND INDUSTRY
RAILROAD ENGINEERING
REFRIGERATION, CRYOGENICS,
    HEATING, AND AIR CONDITIONING
SANITARY ENGINEERING
SCIENCE AND RESEARCH
STATISTICS (MATHEMATICAL AND
    APPLIED)
TECHNOLOGY AND INDUSTRY
TELECOMMUNICATION ENGINEERING
TEXTILE CHEMISTRY, ENGINEERING
    AND INDUSTRY
TRAFFIC ENGINEERING AND
    TRANSPORTATION
WELDING RESEARCH AND
    TECHNOLOGY
WOOD RESEARCH AND TECHNOLOGY

ABBREVIATIONS AND ACRONYMS

BULGARIAN

FURNESS, K.Z. BULGARIAN ABBREVIATIONS, A SELECTIVE LIST. WASHINGTON, U.S. LIBR. CONGR, 1961. 326P. 61-60056. 3600T.

CZECH

CACEK, K. AND KRATKY, M. SLOVNIK ANGLO-AMERICKYCH TECHNICKYCH ZKRATEK. (D. OF EN/AM TECH. ABBRS, CZ DEFS) PRAGUE, SNTL, 1961. 191P. 61-46640. 3500T.

HORECKY, P.L. CZECH AND SLOVAK ABBREVIATIONS, A SELECTIVE LIST. WASHINGTON, U.S. LIBR. CONGR, 1956. 164P 56-60067. 3500T.

ENGLISH

AMERICAN SOCIETY FOR TESTING/MATERIALS. TENTATIVE ABBREVIATIONS OF TERMS RELATING TO PLASTICS. (D1600-61T) ASTM STDS, PT.9. 791-3. PHILADELPHIA, 1961. 60T.

AMERICAN SOCIETY OF HEATING, REFRIGERATING AND AIR-CONDITIONING ENGINEERS. ASHRAE GUIDE AND DATA BOOK. (STD. ABBR/SYMBOLS FOR PIPING, DUCTWORK, HEAT/VENT/REFRIG, PP.855-62, 400T) NEW YORK, 1961. V.1, 880P. 62-1033.

AMERICAN SOCIETY OF MECHANICAL ENGINEERS. ABBREVIATIONS FOR USE ON DRAWINGS. (ASA Y1.2, PROP. AM. STD) NEW YORK. 29P. 2300T. (IN PREP)

AMERICAN SOCIETY OF MECHANICAL ENGINEERS. ABBREVIATIONS FOR USE IN TEXT. (ASA Y1.1. PROP. AM. STD) NEW YORK. 24P. 1700T. (IN PREP)

AMERICAN STANDARDS ASSOCIATION. LETTER SYMBOLS FOR ACOUSTICS. (Y10.11) NEW YORK, 1959.

AMERICAN STANDARDS ASSOCIATION. LETTER SYMBOLS FOR AERONAUTICAL SCIENCES. (Y10.7) NEW YORK, 1954.

AMERICAN STANDARDS ASSOCIATION. LETTER SYMBOLS FOR CHEMICAL ENGINEERING. (Y10.12) NEW YORK, 1961.

AMERICAN STANDARDS ASSOCIATION. LETTER SYMBOLS FOR HEAT AND THERMODYNAMICS. (Y10.4) NEW YORK, 1957.

AMERICAN STANDARDS ASSOCIATION. LETTER SYMBOLS FOR HYDRAULICS. (Y10.2) NEW YORK, 1958.

AMERICAN STANDARDS ASSOCIATION. LETTER SYMBOLS FOR METEOROLOGY. (Y10.10) NEW YORK, 1953.

AMERICAN STANDARDS ASSOCIATION. LETTER SYMBOLS FOR PETROLEUM RESERVOIR ENGINEERING AND ELECTRIC LOGGING. (Y10.15) NEW YORK, 1958.

AMERICAN STANDARDS ASSOCIATION. LETTER SYMBOLS FOR RADIO. (Y10.9) NEW YORK, 1953.

AMERICAN STANDARDS ASSOCIATION. LETTER SYMBOLS FOR ROCKET PROPULSION. (Y10.14) NEW YORK, 1959.

ATLANTIC REFINING CO. DICTIONARY OF ABBREVIATIONS PECULIAR TO THE OIL INDUSTRY. DALLAS, 1963. 62P. 63-5675. 2000T.

BRACKEN,J.A. GLOSSARY OF TELEPHONE ABBREVIATIONS. TELEPHONY, V.150, NO.17-18, FF, (1956) 1150T.

BRITISH STANDARDS INSTITUTION. GLOSSARY OF TERMS RELATING TO TIMBER AND WOODWORK. (B.S. 565) LONDON, 1963. 104P. 750T. 70 ABBR.

BRITISH STANDARDS INSTITUTION. LETTER SYMBOLS, SIGNS AND ABBREVIATIONS. PT.1. GENERAL. (B.S. 1991, AMEND. PD 2241-1955, PD 2707-1957, PD 3920-1960) LONDON, 1954-60. 48P. 500T.

BRITISH STANDARDS INSTITUTION. LETTER SYMBOLS, SIGNS AND ABBREVIATIONS. PT.2 CHEMICAL ENGINEERING, NUCLEAR SCIENCE AND APPLIED CHEMISTRY. (B.S. 1991) LONDON, 1961. 48P. 550T.

BRITISH STANDARDS INSTITUTION. LETTER SYMBOLS, SIGNS AND ABBREVIATIONS. PT.3. FLUID MECHANICS. (B.S. 1991) LONDON, 1961. 36P. 400T.

BRITISH STANDARDS INSTITUTION. LETTER SYMBOLS, SIGNS AND ABBREVIATIONS. PT.4. STRUCTURES, MATERIALS AND SOIL MECHANICS. (B.S. 1991) LONDON. 1961. 52P. 500T.

BRITISH STANDARDS INSTITUTION. LETTER SYMBOLS, SIGNS AND ABBREVIATIONS. PT.5. APPLIED THERMODYNAMICS. (B.S. 1991) LONDON, 1961. 32P. 320T.

BRITISH STANDARDS INSTITUTION. LIST OF COMMON NAMES AND ABBREVIATIONS FOR PLASTICS. (B.S.3502) LONDON, 1962. 7P.

BUTTRESS, F.A. WORLD LIST OF ABBREVIATIONS OF SCIENTIFIC, TECHNOLOGICAL AND COMMERCIAL ORGANIZATIONS. ED2. NEW YORK, HAFNER, 1960. 300P. 60-2449. 2500T.

COPE, S.T. GLOSSARY OF ABBREVIATIONS FOR NAMES OF ... ORGANISATIONS... (IN) THE TELECOMMUNICATIONS INDUSTRY. ED2. GREAT BADDOW, ESSEX, MARCONI,S WIRELESS TELEGRAPH CO, 1957. 38P. 57-43854. 800T.

DE SOLA, R. ABBREVIATIONS DICTIONARY... NEW YORK, DUELL, SLOAN/PEARCE, 1958. 177P. 58-5564. 9600T.

FAWCETT, F.D. CYCLOPAEDIA OF INITIALS AND ABBREVIATIONS. LONDON, BUSINESS PUBL, 1963.

ABBREVIATIONS AND ACRONYMS

ENGLISH

GALE RESEARCH CO. ACRONYMS DICTIONARY, A GUIDE TO ALPHABETIC DESIGNATIONS, CONTRACTIONS, AND INITIALISMS ...DETROIT, 1960. 211 P. 60-10869. 12000T.

GALE RESEARCH CO. CODE NAMES DICTIONARY. DETROIT, 1963. 555P. 7500T.

GOLDSTEIN, M. DICTIONARY OF MODERN ACRONYMS AND ABBREVIATIONS. INDIANAPOLIS, SAMS, 1963. 158P. 63-17022.

GREEN, A.R. ELECTRONIC TERMINOLOGY...ABBREVIATIONS... HILVERSUM, OCECO, 1950. 64P. 53-37520. 1600T.

INSTITUTE OF RADIO ENGINEERS. STANDARDS ON ABBREVIATIONS OF RADIO-ELECTRONIC TERMS. (51 IRE 21.S1) PROC. IRE, V.39, 397-400 (1951) 180T.

INSTITUTE OF RADIO ENGINEERS. STANDARDS ON GRAPHICAL AND LETTER SYMBOLS FOR FEEDBACK CONTROL SYSTEMS. (55 IRE 26.S1) PROC. IRE, V.43, 1608-9 (1955) 10T.

INSTITUTE OF RADIO ENGINEERS. STANDARDS ON LETTER SYMBOLS AND MATHEMATICAL SIGNS. (REPRINTED, 57 IRE 21.S1) PROC. IRE V.45, 1140-7 (1957) 400T.

INSTITUTE OF RADIO ENGINEERS. STANDARDS ON LETTER SYMBOLS FOR SEMICONDUCTOR DEVICES. (56 IRE 28.S1) PROC. IRE, V.44, 934-7 (1956) 70T.

INSTITUTE OF RADIO ENGINEERS. STANDARDS ON NAVIGATION AIDS, DIRECTION FINDER MEASUREMENTS. (ABBRS/DEFS,PP. 1350-2) (59 IRE 12.S1) PROC. IRE, V.47, 1349-71 (1959) 30T.

JACOBS, H. AND WHITNEY, E.E. MISSILE AND SPACE PROJECTS GUIDE. NEW YORK, PLENUM, 1962. 235P. 62-13473.

MAYBERRY, G. A CONCISE DICTIONARY OF ABBREVIATIONS. NEW YORK, TUDOR, 1961. 159P. 61-9227.

MILEK, J.T. STANDARDS AND SPECIFICATIONS, DOCUMENTATION SYMBOLS AND ABBREVIATIONS. LOS ANGELES, STANDARDS, 1961- 1V. LL. 61-3463.

NATIONAL ELECTRICAL MANUFACTURERS ASSOCIATION. EIA-NEMA STANDARDS ON LETTER SYMBOLS AND ABBREVIATIONS FOR SEMICONDUCTOR DATA SHEETS AND SPECIFICATIONS. (RS-245/NEMA SK-53) NEW YORK, 1961. 8P. 150T.

OCECODE. NAVIGATION ELECTRONICS (LAND, SEA, AIR, SPACE) HILVERSUM, 1962. 282P.

REDMAN, H.F. AND GODFREY, L.E. DICTIONARY OF REPORT SERIES CODES. NEW YORK, SPEC.LIBR.ASSOC, 1962. 656P. 12500T.

SCHWARTZ, R.J. THE COMPLETE DICTIONARY OF ABBREVIATIONS. NEW YORK, CROWELL, 1955. 211P. 55-5843. 25000T.

TABLES, FORMULAS, ABBREVIATIONS AND SYMBOLS USEFUL TO THE INSULATION ENGINEER. INSULATION (LIBERTYVILLE) V.8, NO.6, 4-14 (1962) 300T.

U.S. FEDERAL AVIATION AGENCY. CONTRACTIONS. WASHINGTON, 1959. 132P. 59-64199.

U.S. JOINT CHIEFS OF STAFF. JCEC. STANDARD ABBREVIATIONS. (JANAP I69) WASHINGTON, 1953. 1V. LL.54-61379

WILKES, I. BRITISH INITIALS AND ABBREVIATIONS. LONDON, HILL, 1963. P. 3500T.

WITTY, M.B. ET AL. DICTIONARY OF AERONAUTICS, MISSILES AND ROCKETS ABBREVIATIONS, SIGNS, SYMBOLS AND TABLES. NEW YORK, SETI, 1963. 352P.

WITTY, M.B. ET AL. DICTIONARY OF ARCHITECTURAL ABBREVIATIONS, SIGNS, SYMBOLS AND TABLES. NEW YORK, SETI, 1963. 416P.

WITTY, M.B. ET AL. DICTIONARY OF ASTRO-PHYSICS ABBREVIATIONS. NEW YORK, SETI, 196 .

WITTY, M.B. ET AL. DICTIONARY OF AUTOMOTIVE ENGINEERING ABBREVIATIONS. NEW YORK, SETI, 196 .

WITTY, M.B. ET AL. DICTIONARY OF BIO-CHEMISTRY ABBREVIATIONS. NEW YORK, SETI, 196 .

WITTY, M.B. ET AL. DICTIONARY OF BIO-PHYSICS ABBREVIATIONS. NEW YORK, SETI, 196 .

WITTY, M.B. ET AL. DICTIONARY OF CARTOGRAPHY AND TOPOGRAPHY ABBREVIATIONS, SIGNS AND SYMBOLS. NEW YORK, SETI, 196 .

WITTY, M.B. ET AL. DICTIONARY OF CHEMICAL ABBREVIATIONS, SIGNS, SYMBOLS AND TABLES. NEW YORK, SETI, 1961. 416P.

WITTY, M.B. ET AL. DICTIONARY OF CHEMICAL ENGINEERING ABBREVIATIONS, SIGNS AND SYMBOLS. NEW YORK, SETI, 1963. 384P.

WITTY, M.B. ET AL. DICTIONARY OF CIVIL ENGINEERING ABBREVIATIONS, SIGNS, SYMBOLS AND TABLES. NEW YORK, SETI, 1963. 352P.

WITTY, M.B. ET AL. DICTIONARY OF COMMUNICATIONS ABBREVIATIONS, SIGNS, SYMBOLS AND TABLES. NEW YORK, SETI, 1963. 384P.

WITTY, M.B. ET AL. DICTIONARY OF COMPUTERS AND CONTROLS ABBREVIATIONS, SIGNS AND SYMBOLS. NEW YORK, SETI, 196 .

ABBREVIATIONS AND ACRONYMS

ENGLISH

WITTY, M.B. ET AL. DICTIONARY OF ELECTRICAL ABBREVIATIONS, SIGNS AND SYMBOLS. NEW YORK, SETI,1963. 320P.

WITTY, M.B. ET AL. DICTIONARY OF ELECTRONICS ABBREVIATIONS, SIGNS, SYMBOLS AND TABLES. NEW YORK, SETI, 1963. 416P.

WITTY, M.B. ET AL. DICTIONARY OF ENGINEERING SIGNS AND SYMBOLS. NEW YORK, SETI. 1963. 352P.

WITTY, M.B. ET AL. DICTIONARY OF ENVIRONMENTAL ENGINEERING ABBREVIATIONS, SIGNS, SYMBOLS AND TABLES. NEW YORK, SETI, 196 . 320P.

WITTY, M.B. ET AL. DICTIONARY OF GEOLOGY AND MINERALOGY ABBREVIATIONS, SIGNS AND SYMBOLS. NEW YORK, SETI, 196 . 192P.

WITTY, M.B. ET AL. DICTIONARY OF HUMAN ENGINEERING ABBREVIATIONS. NEW YORK, SETI, 196 .

WITTY, M.B. ET AL. DICTIONARY OF INDUSTRIAL ENGINEERING ABBREVIATIONS, SIGNS AND SYMBOLS. NEW YORK, SETI, 1963. 224P.

WITTY, M.B. ET AL. DICTIONARY OF MANAGEMENT AND ENGINEERING ECONOMICS ABBREVIATIONS, SIGNS, SYMBOLS AND TABLES. NEW YORK, SETI, 196 . 192P.

WITTY, M.B. EL AL. DICTIONARY OF MARINE ENGINEERING AND NAVAL ARCHITECTURE ABBREVIATIONS, SIGNS AND SYMBOLS. NEW YORK, SETI, 196 . 256P.

WITTY, M.B. ET AL. DICTIONARY OF MATERIALS ABBREVIATIONS. NEW YORK, SETI, 196 .

WITTY, M.B. ET AL. DICTIONARY OF MECHANICS AND MECHANICAL ENGINEERING ABBREVIATIONS. NEW YORK, SETI, 1963. 384P.

WITTY, M.B. ET AL. DICTIONARY OF METALLURGICAL ABBREVIATIONS. NEW YORK, SETI, 196 .

WITTY,M.B. ET AL. DICTIONARY OF METEOROLOGY, ASTRONOMY AND OCEANOGRAPHY ABBREVIATIONS, SIGNS, SYMBOLS, AND TABLES. NEW YORK, SETI, 196 . 256P.

WITTY, M.B. ET AL. DICTIONARY OF MILITARY SCIENCE ABBREVIATIONS, SIGNS AND SYMBOLS. NEW YORK, SETI, 196 .

WITTY, M.B. ET AL. DICTIONARY OF NAVIGATION ABBREVIATIONS, SIGNS AND SYMBOLS. NEW YORK, SETI, 196 .

WITTY, M.B. ET AL. DICTIONARY OF NUCLEAR ABBREVIATIONS, SIGNS, SYMBOLS AND TABLES. NEW YORK, SETI, 1963. 192P.

WITTY, M.B. ET AL. DICTIONARY OF PHYSICS AND MATHEMATICS ABBREVIATIONS, SIGNS, SYMBOLS AND TABLES. NEW YORK, SETI, 1963. 288P.

WITTY, M.B. ET AL. DICTIONARY OF PLASTICS AND CERAMICS, SIGNS, SYMBOLS AND TABLES. NEW YORK, SETI, 196 . 192P.

WITTY, M.B. ET AL. DICTIONARY OF SANITARY ENGINEERING ABBREVIATIONS, SIGNS, SYMBOLS AND TABLES. NEW YORK SETI, 196 . 192P.

WITTY, M.B. ET AL. DICTIONARY OF THERMODYNAMICS ABBREVIATIONS. NEW YORK, SETI, 196 .

WOOLAM, W.G. SHIPPING TERMS AND ABBREVIATIONS, MARITIME, INSURANCE, INTERNATIONAL TRADE. CAMBRIDGE, MD. CORNELL MARITIME, 1963. 144P. 62-22181. 2200T.

FINNISH

POROILA, E.E. ENGLANTILAIS-SUOMALAINEN, SUOMALAIS-ENGLANTILAINEN SOTILASLYHENNESANASTO. (*FI*EN GL. OF MIL. ABBR) HELSINKI, 1954. 133P. 63-331.

FRENCH

BAUDRY, H. NOUVEAU DICTIONNAIRE D.ABREVIATIONS D.A. FRANCAISES ET ETRANGERES...(D. OF ABBRS, FR. DEFS) LA CHAPELLE-MONTLIGEON (ORNE), 1956. 418P. A56-5893. 10000T.

BODSON,G. DICTIONNAIRE DES TERMES RECENTS, SYMBOLES ET ABBREVIATIONS ARCHITECTURE, ART DE CONSTRUIRE, GENIE CIVIL. (ARCHIT, BLDG,CIVIL ENG. T. SYMBOLS,ABBREV, FR DEFS) PARIS, GIRARDOT, 1952. 244P.

DUSNICKIS, I. AND CHAUMELLE, P. DICTIONNAIRE TECHNIQUE ANGLAIS-FRANCAIS, CHAUFFAGE INDUSTRIEL. (*EN*FR IND. HEATING D) PARIS. DUNOD, 1954. 143P. A54-4039. 6000T.

ORGANIZATION FOR EUROPEAN ECONOMIC COOPERATION. GLOSSAIRE DE SYMBOLES ET D.ABREVIATIONS. (GL. OF SYMBOLS/ABBRS, *FR*EN) ED2. PARIS, 1956. 238P. 4500T.

GERMAN

DEUTSCHE NORMENAUSSCHUSS. (DNA) ABKUERZUNGEN TECHNISCH-WISSENSCHAFTLICHER ORGANISATIONEN DES AUSLANDES UND IHRER VEROEFFENTLICHUNGEN. (ABBR. OF TECH/SCI. ORG. IN FOR. COUNTRIES... GE DEFS) BERLIN,1961. 14P.

EITZEN, K.H. GERMAN-ENGLISH, ENGLISH-GERMAN MILITARY DICTIONARY... 2000 ABBR... ED4. NEW YORK, PRAEGER, 1957. 549P. 56-13090. 10000T.

13

ABBREVIATIONS AND ACRONYMS

GERMAN

GREISER, M. LEXIKON DER ABKUERZUNGEN... (D. OF ABBRS, GE DEFS) ED2. OSNABRUECK, FROMM, 1955. 271P. 55-23756.

SPILLNER, P. AND GOETTLING, H. BUCH DER ABKUERZUNGEN. (BOOK OF ABBR, GE DEFS) BAMBERG, BUCHNERS, 1952. 159P. A53-1567.

HEBREW

EBEN-SHOSHAN, A. YALKUT ROSHE-TEVOT VE-KITSURIM. (LIST OF' INITIALS/ABBR, HE DEFS) JERUSALEM,' 1952. 52P. 55-49446.

HUNGARIAN

BAKO, E. HUNGARIAN ABBREVIATIONS, A SELECTIVE LIST. WASHINGTON, U.S. LIBR. CONGR, 1961. 146P. 61-60004. 2700T.

RANKI, A. TERMESZETTUDOMANYI ES MUSZAKI ROVIDITESEK, JELEK, JELOLESEK. (SCI-TECH. ABBRS, SYMBOLS/ NOTATIONS, HU DEFS) ED2. BUDAPEST, TANKONYVKIADO, 1959. 126P. 60-37679.

ITALIAN

TRAMONTI, N. DIZIONARIO DELLE SIGLE E DELLE ABBREVIAZIONI. (D. OF ACRONYMS/ABBRS, IT DEFS) ED3. BUSTO ARSIZIO, 1957. 330P. A58-5061.

JAPANESE

JAPAN. MINISTRY OF EDUCATION. JAPANESE SCIENTIFIC TERMS, LIBRARY SCIENCE. (*JA*EN) TOKYO, DAINIPPON TOSHO, 1958. 307P. J60-77. 2600T. 150 ABBR; EN*JA.

KOGYO KYOIKU KENKYUKAI. ZUKAI KOGYO YOGO JITEN. (ILLUS. MIN.D, *JA*EN) TOKYO, 1961. 446P. J62-1110. 45000T. 330 ABBR.

KUMURA, H. KOKUGAKU JITEN. (AERON. D, *EN*JA) TOKYO, CHIJIN, 1959. 792P. J59-187. 3500T.

POLISH

WOJCICKA, J. POLISH ABBREVIATIONS, A SELECTIVE LIST. ED2. WASHINGTON, U.S. LIBR. CONGR, 1957. 164P. 57-60055. 2500T.

ZIMNICKI, H. SLOWNIK ELEKTRYĆZNY POLSKO-ANGIELSKI. (PL*EN ELEC. ENG. D) WARSAW, WYDAW. NAUK-TECH, 1962. 372P. 62-46681. 24000T.

POLYGLOT

ALLERDING, J.E. GERMAN AND FRENCH ABBREVIATIONS AND TERMS USED IN SERIAL PUBLICATIONS AND IN BIBLIOGRAPHICAL CITATIONS. SPEC. LIBR, V.43, 358-63 (1952) 220T.

BORISOV, V.V. ET AL. SLOVAR INOSTRANNYKH VOENNYKH SOKRASHCHENII. (D.OF FOR. MIL. ABBRS, RU DEFS) MOSCOW, VOENIZDAT, 1961. 895P. 62-38360.

CSIKOLY, . NYOLCNYELVU CIMFELVETELI KEZISZOTAR. (8-LANG. CATALOGING D/ABBR) BUDAPEST, ORSZ. MUSZ. KONYVTAR, 1954. 41P.

FROES, H.P. DICIONARIO INTERNACIONAL DE ABREVIATURAS. (INTL. D. OF ABBRS, PR DEFS) RIO DE JANEIRO, GRAFICA.MUNIZ, 1961. 597P. 62-51488.

GOEDECKE, W. AMERIKANISCHE, DEUTSCHE, ENGLISCHE UND FRANZOESISCHE KURZWOERTER UND ABKUERZUNGEN VON FACHAUSDRUECKEN, MASSEINHEITEN UND FACHORGANISATIONEN DES NACHRICHTENWESENS UND VERWANDTER GEBIETE. (TELECOMMUN/ABBR, *GE*AM/EN*FR) BERLIN, TECHNIK, 1958. 116P. 61-45256. 3300T.

GOEDECKE, W. KURZWOERTER UND ABKUERZUNGEN DES NACHRICHTENWESENS... (TELECOMMUN. ABBR, *GE*EN*FE) BERLIN VEB, 1963. 116P.

GOEDECKE, W. TECHNISCHE ABKUERZUNGEN. DEUTSCH-ENGLISCH-FRANZOESISCH... FUNKTECHNIK, FERNSEHEN... KERNTECHNIK... ELEKTROTECHNIK... (TECH. ABBRS, *GE*EN*FR, TELECOMMUN, NUCL/ELEC. ENG) WIESBADEN, BRANDSTETTER, 1961. 288P. 63-29594. 5000T.

HUNGARY, MAGYAR TUDOMANYOS AKADEMIA. KONYVTAR. ABBREVIATURAE CYRILLICAE. (CYRILLIC ABBRS, *BU*RU*SC*UK *WR*EN*GE*HU) BUDAPEST, 1961. 138P. 63-6205.

HUNGARY, MAGYAR TUDOMANYOS AKADEMIA . KONYVTAR. INDEX ACRONYMORUM SELECTORUM. BUDAPEST, 1962. 278P. 10000T.

HUNGARY, MAGYAR TUDOMANYOS AKADEMIA . KONYVTAR. VOCABULARIUM ABBREVIATURARUM BIBLIOTHECARII. BUDAPEST, 196 - .

INTERNATIONAL ELECTROTECHNICAL COMMISSION. SYMBOLES LITTERAUX INTERNATIONAUX UTILISES EN ELECTRICITE. (INTL. LETTER SYMBOLS IN ELEC, FR EN SP) ED3. GENEVA, 1953. 15P. 54-43816.

INTERNATIONAL ORGANIZATION FOR STANDARDIZATION. FUNDAMENTAL QUANTITIES AND UNITS OF THE MKSA SYSTEM AND QUANTITIES AND UNITS OF SPACE AND TIME. (R31-PT1) GENEVA, 1957.

INTERNATIONAL ORGANIZATION FOR STANDARDIZATION. QUANTITIES AND UNITS OF HEAT. (SIMILAR TO ASA Y10.4) (R31-PT6) GENEVA, 1960.

14

ABBREVIATIONS AND ACRONYMS

POLYGLOT

INTERNATIONAL ORGANIZATION FOR STANDARDIZATION. QUANTITIES AND UNITS OF MECHANICS. (SIMILAR TO ASA Z10.3) (R31-PT3) GENEVA, 1960.

INTERNATIONAL ORGANIZATION FOR STANDARDIZATION. QUANTITIES AND UNITS OF PERIODIC AND RELATED PHENOMENA (R31-PT2) GENEVA, 1958.

INTERNATIONAL TELECOMMUNICATION UNION. CODES ET ABREVIATIONS A L'USAGE DES SERVICES INTERNATIONAUX DE TELECOMMUNICATIONS. (CODES/ABBRS, INTL TELECOMMUN, FR EN SP) GENEVA, 1958. 312P.

INTERNATIONALE ABKUERZUNGEN AUF DEM GEBIETE DER ELEKTROTECHNIK. (INTL. ELEC. ENG. ABBR) BUL. ASSOC. SUISSF ELEC, V.46,1037 (1955) 60T.

KERKHOF, H. AND GRAS, M. FACHWOERTERBUCH DER FERNMGLDETECHNIK UND ELEKTRONIK. (TELECOMMUN/ELECTRON D) V.1. LEXIKON ENGLISH-AMERIKANISCHER ABKUERZUNGEN. (GL. OF EN/AM ABBRS, *EN*GE*FR) HAMM, WESTF. GROTE, 1956. 264P. 57-23532. 7500T.

MORAN, L. CZECH, POLISH, AND RUSSIAN BOOK TRADE TERMS AND ABBREVIATIONS. SPEC.LIBR.V.49, 246-52 (1958) 200T.

MORAVEK, E. AND BERNATH-BODNAR, E. VERZEICHNIS UNGARISCHER FACHAUSDRUECKE UND ABKUERZUNGEN AUS DEM BUCH-UND BIBLIOTHEKSWESEN... (BOOK/LIBR.T/ABBR, HU*EN*FR*GE) VIENNA, OESTERR.NATL.-BIBL. 1958. 61P. 59-52242.

NENRYO KYOKAI. KOKUSU BUKAI. KOKUSU KOGYO YOGO-SHU. (COKE IND. D, JA*EN*GE) TOKYO, SHIGEN SHIMPO, 1958. 148P. J62-971. 2000T. 300ABBR.

ORNE, J. LANGUAGE OF THE FOREIGN BOOK TRADE, ABBREVIATIONS, TERMS, PHRASES. ED2. (*CZ*DA*DU*EN*FR*GE*IT *PL*PR*RU*SP*SW) CHICAGO, AM. LIBR. ASSOC, 1962. 213P. 61-12881. 16000T.

PURASUCHIKKUSU YOGO JITEN. (PLAST. D, EN*JA*GE) TOKYO, KOGYO CHŌSA KAI, 1959. 756+70+530+25P. 6500T. 1200 EN*JA ABBR.

SOME COMMON ABBREVIATIONS USED IN AERONAUTICS. (EN*FR*GE*SP) INTERAVIA, V.13, 610-1 (1958) 120T.

UNION.OF INTERNATIONAL ASSOCIATIONS. INTERNATIONAL INITIALESE, INDEX TO INTERNATIONAL ABBREVIATIONS IN CURRENT USE. ED2. BRUSSELS, 1963. 50P.

PORTUGUESE

VALLANDRO, L. DICIONARIO INGLES-PORTUGUES... TERMOS TECNICOS E CIENTIFICOS... ABREVIATURAS... (EN*PR TECH/SCI. D/ABBR) RIO DE JANEIRO, GLOBO, 1954. 1135P. 54-44677.

RUSSIAN

AKADEMIIA NAUK SSSR. INDEX OF ABBREVIATED AND FULL TITLES OF SCIENTIFIC AND TECHNICAL PERIODICAL LITERATURE. (UKAZATEL SOKR. I POLN. NAZV. NAUCH/TEKH. LIT) TRANSL. BY WRIGHT-PATTERSON AFB, OHIO, 1960. 247P. 60-60261. 1800T.

AKADEMIIA NAUK SSSR. KOM. TEKH. TERM. OSNOVNYE BUKVENNYE OBOZNACHENIIA V ASTRONOMII. (BASIC LETTER SYMBOLS IN ASTRON, RU DEFS) (SB. REK. BUKV. OBOZN, NO.1) MOSCOW, 1959. 17P. 6 23829.

BLUVSHTE.IN, V.O. ET AL. SLOVAR ANGLIISKIKH I AMERIKANSK'IKH SOKRASHCHENII. (D. OF EN/AM ABBRS, RU DEFS) ED3. MOSCOW, GOS. IZD. INOSTR/NATS. SLOV, 1957. 767P. 57-36383. 31000T.

FISHER, E.L. ABBREVIATIONS OF RUSSIAN SCIENTIFIC SERIAL PUBLICATIONS. AM. DOC, V.10, 192-208 (1959) 200T.

FISHER, E.L. SOKRASHCHENIIA, RUSSIAN ABBREVIATIONS FOR BIBLIOGRAPHIC SEARCH. SPEC. LIBR. V.49, 365-70 (1958) 240T.

GWIRTSMAN,J.J. ABBREVIATIONS IN RUSSIAN ABSTRACT JOURNALS COVERING CHEMISTRY AND RELATED FIELDS. J. CHEM. DOC, V.3, 44-59 (1963) 700T.

INSTITUT ZUR ERFORSCHUNG DER UDSSR. SPISOK RUSSKIKH SOKRASHCHENII, PRIMENIAEMYKH V SSSR. (LIST OF USSR ABBRS) MUNICH, 1954. 304P. 54-41132. 8000T.

KRAMER, A. AND E. ABBREVIATIONS AND SYMBOLS IN SOVIET SCIENTIFIC AND TECHNICAL LITERATURE. TRENTON, N.J. 1960. 12P. 60-9262. 500T.

MIKHAILOV, V.V. AND MELNIKOVA, M.M. ANGLO-RUSSKII SLOVAR PO ELEKTROKHIMII I KORROZII. (EN*RU ELECTROCHEM/ CORR. D) MOSCOW, VINITI, 1963. 234P. 63-59367. 20000T. 450 ABBR.

NEISWENDER, R. GUIDE TO RUSSIAN REFERENCE AND LANGUAGE AIDS. (ABBR. SOVIET PUBL, PP.69-73, 70T) NEW YORK, SPEC. LIBR. ASSOC. 1962. 92P. 62-21081.

ROSENBERG, A. RUSSIAN ABBREVIATIONS, A SELECTIVE LIST. ED2. WASHINGTON, U.S. LIBR. CONGR, 1957. 513P. 57-60063. 3000T.

RUSSIAN-ENGLISH GLOSSARY OF ABBREVIATIONS OCCURRING IN PHYSICS LITERATURE...NEW YORK, INTERLANGUAGE DICT, 1960. 64P. 60-3086. 1500T.

SLOVAR SOKRASHCHENII RUSSKOGO IAZYKA. (RU ABBR. D, RU DEFS) MOSCOW, 1963. 486P. 12500T.

U.S. DEPT. OF THE ARMY. GLOSSARY OF SOVIET MILITARY AND RELATED ABBREVIATIONS. (TM30-546) WASHINGTON, 1957. 178P. 58-61484. 5400T.

ABBREVIATIONS AND ACRONYMS

RUSSIAN

U.S. DEPT. OF THE ARMY. SOVIET MILITARY SYMBOLS. (TM30-547) WASHINGTON, 1958. 217P. 59-62261.

U.S. LIBRARY OF CONGRESS. GLOSSARY OF UNITS AND MEASURES, ENGLISH-RUSSIAN, RUSSIAN-ENGLISH. (OTS-61-31103) WASHINGTON, 1961. 531P. 2600T.

VASILEV, A.A. AND NIKOLAEV, N.I. ANGLO-RUSSKII AVIATSIONNYI SLOVAR. (EN*RU AVIATION D) MOSCOW, VOENIZDAT, 1963. 544P. 20000T. 2400 ABBR.

WITTY, M.B. POLON, D.D. ET AL. THE RUSSIAN ELECTRONICS DICTIONARY OF TERMS, ABBREVIATIONS AND TABLES. *RU*EN (IN PREP) 20000T.

SERBO-CROATIAN

PLAMENATZ, I.P. YUGOSLAV ABBREVIATIONS, A SELECTIVE LIST. ED2. WASHINGTON, U.S. LIBR. CONGR, 1962. 198P. 62-60076. 3200T.

SPANISH

CASTILLA,S SPANISH AND ENGLISH TECHNICAL DICTIONARY.(V.1, EN*SP, 1611P, 150000T. V.2, SP*EN, 1137P. 120000T.) NEW YORK, PHIL. LIBR, 1958. 58-2320.

COSTA RICA. MINISTERIO DE RELACIONES EXTERIORES. SIGLAS INTERNACIONALES... (INTL ABBRS, SP DEFS) SAN JOSE, COSTA RICA, IMPR. NACL, 1954. 23P. 56-34855.

SWEDISH

ROTH, N. FOERKORTNINGSLEXIKON. (ABBR. D, SW DEFS) STOCKHOLM, WAHLSTROEM/WIDSTRAND, 1960. 251P. 62-43980.

TURKISH

TURKEY. ERKANSHARBIYEI UMUMIYE RIYASETI. RESMI AMERIKAN ASKERI KISALTMALARI VE TURKCE MUKABILLERI. (AM MIL. ABBR, TU DEFS) ANKARA, BASIMEVI, 1955. 49P. 59-47624. 1500T.

AEROSPACE SCIENCE AND ENGINEERING

DUTCH

ROSKAM,P. LUCHTVAARTTECHNISCH WOORDENBOEK, ENGELS-NEDERLANDS. (AERON.D, EN*DU) HAARLEM, STAM,1952. 225P.

STRABEL, A. VLIEGTUIG, AUTOMOBIEL, MOTORRIJWIEL. (FLYING/MOTORING D, *DU*EN) HILVERSUM, OCECO, 1954. 145P. 1600T.

ENGLISH

ADAMS, F.D. AERONAUTICAL DICTIONARY. WASHINGTON, U.S. NATL. AERON/SPACE ADMIN, 1959. 199P. 60-60459. 4000T.

ALLEN, W.H. DICTIONARY OF SPACE TERMS. WASHINGTON, U.S. NATL. AERON/SPACE ADMIN. (IN PRESS)

ALLEN, W.H. AND MULCAHY, B.A. SHORT GLOSSARY OF SPACE TERMS. WASHINGTON, U.S. NATL. AERON/SPACE ADMIN, 1962. 57P. 62-61784. 440T.

AMERICAN ROCKET SOCIETY. MISSILE GLOSSARY. NEW YORK, 1958.

AMERICAN STANDARDS ASSOCIATION. LETTER SYMBOLS FOR AERONAUTICAL SCIENCES. (Y10.7) NEW YORK, 1954.

AMERICAN STANDARDS ASSOCIATION. LETTER SYMBOLS FOR ROCKET PROPULSION. (Y10.14) NEW YORK, 1959.

ASHBROOK, J. ET AL. GLOSSARY OF ASTRONOMICAL TERMS FOR THE DESCRIPTION OF SATELLITE ORBITS. CAMBRIDGE, MASS, ASTROPHYS. OBS, SMITHSONIAN INST, 1957. 16P.

ASTROLOG, CURRENT STATUS OF U.S. MISSILE AND SPACE PROGRAMS PLUS ALL ORBITING SATELLITES. MISSILES/ROCKETS, V.12, NO.1, 25-32 (1963) 150T.

BANCROFT, R.W. AND CLAMANN, H.G. A GLOSSARY OF TERMS RELATED TO THE HUMAN FACTOR IN SPACE TRAVEL. AIR UNIV.QUART.REV. V.10, 147-52 (1958)

BARRY, W.S. THE LANGUAGE OF AVIATION. LONDON, CHATTO/WINDUS, 1962. 197P. 63-34656.

BECKFORD, L.L. AN A.B.C. OF AERONAUTICS. NEW YORK, PITMAN, 1957. 113P. 58-735.

BESSERER, C.W. AND H.C. GUIDE.TO THE SPACE AGE. ENGLEWOOD CLIFFS, N.J, PRENTICE-HALL, 1959. 320P. 59-15719. 5500T.

BIZONY, M.T. ET AL. THE SPACE ENCYCLOPAEDIA, A GUIDE TO ASTRONOMY AND SPACE RESEARCH. ED2. NEW YORK, DUTTON, 1960. 288P. 61-3750. 2500T.

BRITISH STANDARDS INSTITUTION. GLOSSARY OF AERONAUTICAL TERMS. (B.S.185, SECT. 1-15) LONDON, 1962. 18P. 300T.

AEROSPACE SCIENCE AND ENGINEERING

ENGLISH

CAIDIN, M. THE MAN-IN-SPACE DICTIONARY, A MODERN GLOSSARY. NEW YORK,DUTTON, 1963. 224P. 63-14274. 1900T.

GAYNOR, F. AEROSPACE DICTIONARY. NEW YORK, PHIL. LIBR, 1960. 260P. 60-16202. 2000T.

GENTLE, E.J. AND CHAPEL, C.E. AVIATION AND SPACE DICTIONARY. ED4. LOS ANGELES, AERO, 1961. 444P. 61-15652. 8000T.

GOLDSWORTHY, H.E. GLOSSARY OF OBSERVER TERMS. (NO.APG/SAR/497-A) EGLIN AFB, FLA. 1955. 7P.

GUIDED MISSILE ENCYCLOPEDIA, 1ST ANNUAL. MISSILES/ROCKETS, V.2, NO.2, 123-64. (1957) 30T.

HEFLIN, W.A. AEROSPACE GLOSSARY. MAXWELL AFB, ALA, AIR UNIV, 1959. 115P. 60-60268.

HEFLIN, W.A. INTERIM GLOSSARY, AEROSPACE TERMS. MAXWELL AFB, ALA, AIR UNIV, 1958. 35P. 58-61455. 500T.

HEFLIN, W.A. ET AL. THE UNITED STATES AIR FORCE DICTIONARY. MAXWELL AFB, AIR UNIV, 1956. 578P. 56-61737. 16500T.

HERRICK, J.W. AND BURGESS, E. ROCKET ENCYCLOPEDIA, ILLUSTRATED. LOS ANGELES, AERO, 1959. 607P. 59-8488.

HERRICK, S. ET AL. ASTRODYNAMICAL NOTATION AND USAGE. (ASTRODYN REPT. NO.10) LOS ANGELES, CALIFORNIA UNIV, 1960. 18P.

HIGHLAND,J.H. AUDELS ENCYCLOPEDIA OF SPACE SCIENCE... NEW YORK, AUDEL, 1963. 4V. 1004P. 63-3655.

IATA TRAFFIC GLOSSARY. AIR TRANSP, V.27, 42-3 (1955) 130T.

INSTRUMENT SOCIETY OF AMERICA. GLOSSARY OF TERMS FOR FLIGHT TESTING INSTRUMENTATION. (BASED ON AIA-ARTC REPT.16) (IN PREP)

JACOBS, H. AND WHITNEY, E.E. MISSILE AND SPACE PROJECTS GUIDE. NEW YORK, PLENUM, 1962. 235P. 62-13473.

LEAVITT, W. ET AL. THE SPACE FRONTIER, WITH ASTRONAUTICS GLOSSARY. WASHINGTON, NATL. AVIATION EDUC. COUNCIL, 1961. 32P. 62-1349.

MCLAUGHLIN, C. SPACE AGE DICTIONARY. PRINCETON, N.J, VAN NOSTRAND, 1959. 128P. 59-14613. 600T.

MADRID, D.C. GLOSSARY OF ASTRONAUTICS TERMINOLOGY. IRE TRANS. S.E.T. V.5, 73-5 (1959)

MERRILL, G. ET AL. DICTIONARY OF GUIDED MISSILES APD SPACE FLIGHT. PRINCETON, N.J, VAN NOSTRAND, 1959. 688P. 59-10112. 8400T.

MILITARY ASTRONAUTICS GLOSSARY. AIR FORCE MAG, V.41,157-67 (1958) 200T.

MISSILE AND SPACE GLOSSARY. AIR FORCE SPACE DIG, V.43, 148-52 (1960) AND V.44, 164-6 (1961)

NAYLER, J.L. DICTIONARY OF AERONAUTICAL ENGINEERING. NEW YORK, PHIL.LIBR, 1959. 318P. 59-4976.

NEWELL, H.E. GUIDE TO ROCKETS, MISSILES, AND SATELLITES. ED2. NEW YORK, WHITTLESEY, 1961. 95P. 61-17343.

NEWSWEEK. WORDS OF THE SPACE AGE, AN ABRIDGED GLOSSARY, NEW YORK, 1961. 28P..

NORTHROP AIRCRAFT, INC. DEFINITIONS OF OPERATIONAL RANGE AND ALTITUDE PERFORMANCE FOR THE SM-62A. (REPT. NO. NAI-55-1007) HAWTHORNE, CALIF, 1955. 3P.

OCECODE. NAVIGATION ELECTRONICS (LAND, SEA, AIR, SPACE) HILVERSUM, 1962. 282P.

RACKER, J. TECHNICAL WRITING TECHNIQUES FOR ENGINEERS. (GL, PP.129-234, 1130T) ENGLEWOOD CLIFFS, N.J, PRENTICE-HALL, 1960. 234P. 60-16623.

SELL,S BRITISH AVIATION. LONDON, BUSINESS DICT, 1961- . (ANNUAL) VAR. PP. 57-22102. 600T.

SOME COMMON ABBREVIATIONS USED IN AERONAUTICS. (EN*FR*GE*SP) INTERAVIA, V.13, 610-1 (1958) 120T.

SPITZ, A.N. AND GAYNOR, F. DICTIONARY OF ASTRONOMY AND ASTRONAUTICS. PATERSON, N.J, LITTLEFIELD/ADAMS, 1960. 439P. 61-65363. 2000T.

STILTZ, H.L. AEROSPACE TELEMETRY. (GL,PP. -) ENGLEWOOD CLIFFS, N.J, PRENTICE-HALL, 1961. 505P. 61-15664.

STRAUBEL, J.H. ET AL. SPACE WEAPONS, A HANDBOOK OF MILITARY ASTRONAUTICS. (GL. PP.205-26) NEW YORK, PRAEGER, 1959. 245P. 59-7882.

SWANBOROUGH, F.G. TURBINE-ENGINED AIRLINERS OF THE WORLD. LOS ANGELES, AERO, 1963. 130P.

THADDEUS, P. GLOSSARY OF TERMS FREQUENTLY USED IN SPACE PHYSICS. NEW YORK, AM. INST. PHYS, 1963. 18P. 110T.

U.S. AIR FORCE. ARDC. VOCABULARY FOR CURRENT ARDC TECHNICAL EFFORTS. WASHINGTON, 1960. 159P. 60-64594. 5000T.

AEROSPACE SCIENCE AND ENGINEERING

ENGLISH

U.S. AIR FORCE MISSILE TEST CENTER. MISSILE GLOSSARY. PATRICK AFB, FLA, 1958.

U.S. DEPT. OF THE AIR FORCE. GLOSSARY OF OBSERVER TERMS. (AF MANUAL 50-26) WASHINGTON, 1956. 83P. 56-62003.

U.S. DEPT. OF THE AIR FORCE. GLOSSARY OF STANDARDIZED TERMS. ADMINISTRATIVE PRACTICES. (MANUAL AFM 11-1) WASHINGTON, 1959- 1 V. LL. 59-60487.

U.S. DEPT. OF THE AIR FORCE. INTERIM AEROSPACE TERMINOLOGY REFERENCE, ADMINISTRATIVE PRACTICES. (AF PAMPHLET 11-1-4) WASHINGTON, 1959. 75P. 60-60256. 700T.

U.S. FEDERAL AVIATION AGENCY. CONTRACTIONS. WASHINGTON, 1959. 132P. 59-64199.

U.S. FEDERAL AVIATION AGENCY. GLOSSARY OF AIR TRAFFIC CONTROL TERMS. WASHINGTON, 1962. 13P. 80T.

U.S. WHITE SANDS MISSILE RANGE. TELEMETRY STANDARDS (IRIG-106-60) (GL, 16P) NEW MEXICO, 1960.

WITTY, M.B. ET AL. DICTIONARY OF AERONAUTICS, MISSILES AND ROCKETS ABBREVIATIONS, SIGNS, SYMBOLS AND TABLES. NEW YORK, SETI, 1963. 352P.

WITTY, M.B. POLON, D.D. ET AL. THE AMERICAN DICTIONARY OF AERONAUTICS, MISSILES, ROCKETS, AND SPACE TERMS. NEW YORK, SETI. 416P. (IN PREP)

WORLD MISSILE/SPACE ENCYCLOPEDIA, 6TH ANNUAL. MISSILES/ROCKETS, V.11, NO.5, 41-112 (1962) 250T.

WORLD MISSILE/SPACE ENCYCLOPEDIA, 7TH ANNUAL. MISSILES/ROCKETS, V.13, NO.5, 36-153 (1963) 400T.

FRENCH

CHALMETTE, M. ENGLISH-FRENCH VOCABULARY OF AERONAUTICAL TERMS. LONDON, AIRCRAFT ENG, 1952. 36P. 52-41476.

DICTIONNAIRE TECHNIQUE ANGLAIS-FRANCAIS, AERONAUTIQUE ET MOTEURS. (EN*FR D. OF AERON/MOTORS) BOIS-COLOMBES (SEINE) HISPANO-SUIZA, 1952. 356P.

HENRY, L. DICTIONNAIRE AERO-TECHNIQUE ANGLAIS-FRANCAIS.... (EN*FR AERON. D) PARIS, PETIT, 1963. 584P.

HUMBERT, S. AVIATION ENGLISH... (V.1 FR*EN, 257P. V.2 EN*FR, 223P) PARIS, DUNOD, 1955. 56-28848.

NORTH ATLANTIC TREATY ORGANIZATION. AGARD. GLOSSAIRE DES TERMES COURAMMENT EMPLOYES EN MEDECINE AERONAUTIQUE, FRANCAIS-ANGLAIS ET ANGLAIS-FRANCAIS. (GL. OF... AVIATION MED, *FR*EN) LONDON, NATO-AGARD 1959. 30P. 61-1191. 600T.

SOCIETY OF BRITISH AIRCRAFT CONSTRUCTORS. ENGLISH-FRENCH TRANSLATIONS OF AERONAUTICAL TERMS AND UNITS. LONDON, 1952. 5P.

GERMAN

CESCOTTI, R. LUFTFAHRT-DEFINITIONEN, ENGLISCH-DEUTSCH, DEUTSCH-ENGLISCH. (GL. OF AERON. DEFS,*EN*GE) MUNICH, REICH, 1956. 270P. 57-2237. 2500T.

CESCOTTI, R. LUFTFAHRT-WOERTERBUCH, DEUTSCH-ENGLISCH, ENGLISCH-DEUTSCH. (AVIATION D, *GE*EN) ED2. MUNICH, REICH, 1957. 448P. 60-24363. 5500T.

DARCY, H.L. ET AL. AIR TECHNICAL DICTIONARY, GERMAN-ENGLISH. NEW YORK, DUELL, SLOAN/PEARCE, 1960. 312P. 60-16109. 30000T.

DARCY, H.L. ET AL. LUFTFAHRTTECHNISCHES WOERTERBUCH... (AIR TECH. D, V.2, EN*GE, IN PREP) BERLIN, DE GRUYTER, 1962. 62-33521. 30000T.

FACHWOERTERBUCH FUER DIE ZIVILLUFTFAHRT. (EN*GE D. OF CIVIL AVIATION) EQ2. FRANKFURT/MAIN, BUNDESANSTALT FLUGSICHERUNG, 1954. 200P.

GARTMANN, H. ECON WELTRAUM ABC. (AEROSPACE ABC, GE DEFS) DUESSELDORF, ECON, 1958. 231P. 59-42649.

LEIDECKER, K.F. GERMAN-ENGLISH TECHNICAL DICTIONARY OF AERONAUTICS, ROCKETRY, SPACE NAVIGATION... NEW YORK, VANNI, 1950-51. 2V. 968P. 50-14702.

LUETCKE, E. ABC DES LUFTVERKEHRS. (AIR TRAFFIC ABC, GE DEFS) HAMBURG, 1955.

OPPERMANN, A. AERONAUTICAL ENGLISH. TECHNISCHES TASCHENWOERTER-'UND HANDBUCH DER LUFTFAHRT. (*GE*EN AVIATION D) ED2. MUNICH, OPPERMANN, 1958-60. 1170P. 59-541. 30000T. SUPPL.1, 1960.

GREEK

AEROPORIKA NEA. ENGLISH-GREEK DICTIONARY OF TECHNICAL AND AERONAUTICAL TERMS. ED2. ATHENS, 1950. 144P. 4800T.

ITALIAN

BUIATTI, N. TERMINOLOGIA AERONAUTICA ANGLOAMERICANA. (EN/AM IT D. OF AERON) ROME, ARTE DELLA STAMPA, 1955. 196P. A56-5789. 5500T.

JAPANESE

AERONAUTICAL TERMS. (JA*EN) TOKYO, 1952. 76P. 2450T.

(AERON. D, *EN*JA) TOKYO, CHIJIN, 1959. 792P. J59-187. 3500T.

POLISH

LOW O LOTNICTWIE...(1000 AERON. WORDS, PL DEFS) WARSAW, MIN. OBRONY NAR, T.

ENCYKLOPEDIA. (AERON. D, PL DEFS) WARSAW, PANSTW. WYDAW. TECH, 1961. 531P.

LY SLOWNIK ASTRONAUTYCZNY. (ASTRONAUTICS D, PL DEFS) WARSAW, WIEDZA 24766.

POLYGLOT

ENCH AND SPANISH TRANSLATIONS OF DEFINITIONS IN THE IATA TRAFFIC GLOSSARY. , V.17, 55-64 (1953) 130T.

ERONAUTICS, *EN*FR*GE*IT*PR*SP. NEW YORK, ELSEVIER. 800P. 6500T. (IN PREP)

D AERONAUTICAL MULTILINGUAL DICTIONARY,*EN*DU*FR*GE*IT*RU*SP*TU. NEW YORK, 7. 3000T.

TICAL MULTILINGUAL DICTIONARY. SUPPL. 1. (*EN*FR*GE*SP*GR*IT*DU*RU*TU) 4P. 58-9477. 1300T.

ORGANIZATION. LEXICO DE TERMINOS USADOS EN AVIACION CIVIL INTERNACIONAL, OF INTL. CIVIL AVIATION, SP EN FR) MONTREAL, 1953. 204P. 54-18476. 1500T.

ORGANIZATION. LEXICON OF TERMS USED IN CONNEXION WITH INTERNATIONAL CIVIL 1952. 197P. 52-30278. 1500T.

R*IT) (SCHLOMANN,S ILLUSTRIERTE TECHNISCHE WOERTERBUECHER, V.17) MUNICH, P. 57-27427.

NICA DEI RAZZI E D.ASTRONAUTICA. (D. OF ROCKETS/ASTRONAUTICS *IT*EN*FR , 1955. 107P. A57-3506. 1400T.

ON AND AIR TRAFFIC CONTROL. (*EN*FR*GE*SP) INTERAVIA, V.13, 607-10 (1958)

D IN AERONAUTICS. (EN*FR*GE*SP) INTERAVIA, V.13, 610-1 (1958) 120T.

LIST OF TERMS ON THE PEACEFUL USES OF OUTER SPACE. (*FR*EN*SP) NEW YORK,

EDESUGY.PT.2, HAJOZAS, REPULES, POSTA ES CSOVEZETEKES SZALLITAS. (D. OF EUMATIC TRANSP,*HU*EN*GE*RU) (MUSZ. ERT. SZ, NO.8) BUDAPEST, TERRA, 1960.

PORTUGUESE

L DE ENGENHARIA CIVIL. VOCABULARIO DE ESTRADAS E AERODROMOS. (ROAD/AIRPORT 62.

ERONAUTICAL VOCABULARY, (PR*EN) PRESIDIO OF MONTEREY, 1953. 12P. 53-61214.

RUSSIAN

.TERM. TERMINOLOGIIA AERODINAMICHESKOGO RASCHETA SAMOLETA. (AERODYN. FOR .REK.TERM, NO.17) MOSCOW, 1954. 20P. 55-36936. 60T.

.TERM. TERMINOLOGIIA AVIATSIONNYKH SILOVYKH USTANOVOK. (AIRPLANE ENG,RU DEFS) 1954. 24P. 57-29694. 70T.

.TERM. TERMINOLOGIIA ELEKTROOBORUDOVANIIA SAMOLETOV. (AIRPLANE ELEC. , NO.25) MOSCOW, 1954. 35P. 55-15035. 170T.

.TERM. TERMINOLOGIIA KISLORODNOGO I VYSOTNOGO OBORUDOVANIIA SAMOLETOV. E EQUIP, RU DEFS) (SB.REK,TERM, NO.26) MOSCOW, 1954. 17P. 56-24001. 50T.

.TERM. TERMINOLOGIIA KONSTRUKTSII I PROCHNOSTI SAMOLETA. (AIRPLANE SB.REK.TERM, NO.18) MOSCOW, 1954. 55-32306. 200T.

.TERM. TERMINOLOGIIA KONSTRUKTSII TURBOREAKTIVNYKH, TURBOVINTOVYKH I IGN OF TURBOJET, TURBOPROP/PISTON ENG, RU DEFS) (SB.REK.TERM, NO.19) . 120T.

.TERM. TERMINOLOGIIA TEORII I KHARAKTERISTIK AVIATSIONNYKH GAZOTURBINNYKH HEORY/CHAR. OF GAS TURBINE ENG/TURBINES...RU DEFS) (SB.REK.TERM, NO.24) . 80T.

RUSSIAN

AKADEMIIA NAUK SSSR. KOM.TEKH.TERM. TERMINOLOGIIA UPRAVLENIIA, REGULIROVANIIA I AVTOMATIKI AVIADVIGATELEI. (GUIDANCE, CONTROL/AUTOM. OF AIRPLANE ENG, RU DEFS) (SB.REK.TERM, NO.28) MOSCOW,] 20P. 55-35584. 40T.

AKADEMIIA NAUK SSSR. KOM.TEKH.TERM. TERMINOLOGIIA VOZDUSHNYKH VINTOV I VERTOLETOV. (PROPELLERS/ HELICOPTERS, RU DEFS) (SB.REK.TERM, NO.20) MOSCOW, 1954. 36P. 58-19856. 160T.

AKADEMIIA NAUK SSSR. KOM.TEKH.TERM. TERMINOLOGIIA ZHIDKOSTNYKH RAKETNYKH DVIGATELEI. (LIQUID-FUEL ROCKET ENG, RU DEES) (SB.REK.TERM, NO.16) MOSCOW, 1953. 25P. MIC 56-4252. 70T.

BURIAKOV, IU. ET AL. ANGLO-RUSSKII AVIATSIONNYI SLOVAR. (EN*RU AVIATION D) MOSCOW, VOENIZDAT, 1963. 544P. 63-58318.

CHIROKOV, K.V. AND SUPRUN, . ANGLO-RUSSKII AEROKOSMICHESKII SLOVAR. (EN*RU AEROSPACE D) MOSCOW, VOENIZDAT, 1963.

DARCY, H.L. ET AL. LUFT- UND RAUMFAHRTTECHNISCHES WOERTERBUCH, RUSSISCH-ENGLISCH. (AEROSPACE D, *RU BERLIN, DE GRUYTER. 600P. (IN PREP)

DREMICHEV, I.D. AND GRECHKIN, V.P. ANGLO-RUSSKII SLOVAR PO REAKTIVNOMU ORUZHIIU. (*EN*RU D. OF ROCKE WEAPONS) MOSCOW, VOENIZDAT, 1960. 383P. 61-29176. 7500T.

DUBOSHIN, V.N. AND KOTOV, V.S. ANGLO-RUSSKII AVIATSIONNYI SLOVAR. (EN*RU AVIATION D) ED. 2. MOSCOW, GITTL, 1950. 456P. 20000T.

GLOSSARY OF RUSSIAN TERMS ASSOCIATED WITH GUIDED MISSILES, EARTH SATELLITE, SPACE VECHICLE AND OTHER RELATED SUBJECTS... WASHINGTON, 1958. 42P. 61-40335.

KONARSKI, M.M. HANDBOOK FOR AIR FORCE AND CIVIL AVIATION INTERPRETERS (RUSSIAN) V.1, ELEMENTARY. NEW YORK, PERGAMON, 1963. 150P.

KONARSKI, M.M. RUSSIAN-ENGLISH DICTIONARY OF MODERN TERMS IN AERONAUTICS AND ROCKETRY. NEW YORK, PERGAMON, 1962, 515P. 62-16918. 14500T.

KOTIK, M.G. ANGLO-RUSSKII SLOVAR PO AEROGIDRODINAMIKE. (EN*RU D. AEROHYDRODYN. D) MOSCOW, FIZMATGIZ 1960. 457P. 61-30949. 13000T.

KRAMER, A.A. RUSSKO-ANGLIISKI SLOVAR PO RAKETNOI TEKHNIKE I BALLISTICHESKIM SNARIADAM. (RU*EN ROCKE BALLISTIC MISSILE D) TRENTON, N.J, 1960. 240P. 61-23952. 10000T.

MURASHKEVICH, A.M. ANGLO-RUSSKII SLOVAR PO RAKETNOI TEKHNIKE. (EN*RU ROCKET D) MOSCOW, FIZMATGIZ, 19 231P. 59-18428. 5000T.

NIKITIN, S.M. AND KHRUSHCHEV, IU.I. ANGLO-RUSSKII SLOVAR PO AVIATSIONNYM I RAKETNYM BAZAM. (EN*RU D. AIR/ROCKET BASES) MOSCOW, VOENIZDAT, 1962. 335P. 62-65970. 8000T.

ROSENBERG, A. RUSSIAN-ENGLISH GLOSSARY OF GUIDED MISSILE, ROCKET, AND SATELLITE TERMS. WASHINGTON, LIBR. CONGR. 1958. 352P. 58-60055. 4800T.

SUDZILOVSKII, G.A. ET AL. ANGLO-RUSSKII SLOVAR PO PROTIVOVOZDUSHNOI I PROTIVORAKETNOI OBORONE. (EN* OF ANTI-AIRCRAFT/ANTI-MISSILE DEFENSE) MOSCOW, VOENIZDAT,1961. 720P. 62-34518. 27000T.

U.S. AIR TECHNICAL INTELLIGENCE CENTER. RUSSIAN-ENGLISH GLOSSARY,AERONAUTICAL AND MISCELLANEOUS TERMS. WRIGHT-PATTERSON AFB, OHIO, 1956. VAR. P. 57-61417. 30000T.

VASILEV, A.A. AND NIKOLAEV, N.I. ANGLO-RUSSKII AVIATSIONNYI SLOVAR. (EN*RU AVIATION D) MOSCOW, VOENIZDAT, 1963. 544P. 20000T. 2400 ABBR.

VVEDENSKII, B.A. ET AL, FIZICHESKII ENTSIKLOPEDICHESKII SLOVAR. (ENCYCL. D. OF PHYS, RU DEFS) MOSCO SOV. ENTSIKL, 1960- . 4V. 61-29525.

SPANISH

. HAMMOND, C.W. GLOSSARY OF AVIATION TERMS, ENGLISH-SPANISH. AUSTIN, TEXAS UNIV, 1958. 116P.

INTER-AMERICAN DEFENSE BOARD. DICCIONARIO DE TERMINOS MILITARES PARA LAS FUERZAS ARMADAS, INGLES-ESP (EN*SP MIL.D) ED2. WASHINGTON, 1957. 245P. 58-20616.

LIZARRAGA, F. DICCIONARIO TECNICO, INGLES-ESPANOL Y ESPANOL-INGLES, PARA USO DE LOS EJERCITOS DE TIE MAR Y AIRE. (*SP*EN MIL.D, LAND/SEA/AIR) MADRID, BIBLIOG. ESP, 1953. 706P. 54-33732.

MANGOLD, W. TERMINOLOGIA MILITAR-NAVAL-AEREA. (POCKET MANUAL OF MIL.T... LAND, SEA/AIR,*SP*EN) MADRI MANGOLD, 1955. 191P. 55-1306. 3000T.

ROBAYO, LIA. SPANISH-ENGLISH, ENGL-ISH-SPANISH TECHNICAL, LEGAL, AND COMMERCIAL DICTIONARY. MONTREAL, DICT. PUBL, 1952. 334P. 52-13398.

SELL,L.L. ENGLISH-SPANISH COMPREHENSIVE TECHNICAL DICTIONARY OF AIRCRAFT, AUTOMOBILE, ELECTRICITY, R TELEVISION, PETROLEUM,STEEL PRODUCTS... NEW YORK, MCGRAW-HILL, 1960. 1079P. 61-3462. 525000T.

SELL,L.L. ESPANOL-INGLES DICCIONARIO TECNICO COMPLETISIMO DE AERONAUTICA, AUTOMOVILES,FERROCARRILES, CARRETERAS, ELECTRICIDAD, ELECTRONICA, RADIO, TELEVISION...(SP*EN TECH. D) NEW YORK, MCGRAW-HILL, 194 1706P. 61-4329. 700000T.

AEROSPACE SCIENCE AND ENGINEERING

SPANISH

AIR COMMAND AND STAFF COLLEGE. GLOSSARY OF U.S. AIR FORCE TERMS, ENGLISH-SPANISH. MAXWELL AFB, ALA, 27P. 55-12650.

AIR FORCE SCHOOL FOR LATIN AMERICA. DICCIONARIO AERONAUTICO. (AERON.D, EN*SP) (HSLAUSAF 129) ALBROOK CANAL ZONE, 1961. 437P. 62-64446.

SWEDISH

LIUS, S. BALLOON, FLYING-MACHINE, HELICOPTER... ALMQUIST/WIKSELL, STOCKHOLM, 1960. 396P. A61-2766.

ASTRONOMY AND ASTROPHYSICS

CHINESE

-KUO K,O HSUEH YUAN. PIEN I CHU. (ACAD. SINICA. BUR. COMPIL/TRANSL) T,IEN WEN HSUEH MING TZ,U. ON. T, CH EN) SHANGHAI, COMMERCIAL, 1952. 61P. C59-1213.

-KUO K,O HSUEH YUAN. PIEN I CH,U PAN WEI YUAN HUI. (ACAD. SINICA. COMM. PUBL/TRANSL) T,IEN WEN MING TZ,U. (ASTRON. T, EN CH) PEKING, SCIENCE 1956. 61P. C59-3213.

DUTCH

LA, E. AND PRAAG, H. ENCYCLOPEDIE VAN HET HEELAL. (ENCYCL. OF THE UNIVERSE, DU DEFS) ZEIST, ND, HAAN, 1960. 251P. 61-33463.

ENGLISH

OOK, J. ET AL. GLOSSARY OF ASTRONOMICAL TERMS FOR THE DESCRIPTION OF SATELLITE ORBITS. CAMBRIDGE, ASTROPHYS. OBS, SMITHSONIAN INST, 1957. 16P.

RER, C.W. AND H.C. GUIDE TO THE SPACE AGE. ENGLEWOOD CLIFFS, N.J, PRENTICE-HALL, 1959. 320P. 719. 5500T.

Y, M.T. ET AL. THE SPACE ENCYCLOPAEDIA, A GUIDE TO ASTRONOMY AND SPACE RESEARCH. ED2. NEW YORK, N. 1960. 288P. 61-3750. 2500T.

LIN, K.L. GLOSSARY OF TERMS FREQUENTLY USED IN RADIO ASTRONOMY. NEW YORK, AM, INST, PHYS, 1962. 28P.

NT, R.A. THE ABC,S OF ASTRONOMY, AN ILLUSTRATED DICTIONARY. GARDEN CITY, N.Y, DOUBLEDAY, 1962. 61-5048.

R, F. AEROSPACE DICTIONARY. NEW YORK, PHIL. LIBR, 1960. 260P. 60-16202. 2000T.

LINGER, A. MODERN SCIENCE DICTIONARY... PALISADE, N.J, FRANKLIN, 1959. 784P. 59-2320. 14500T.

CK, S. ET AL. ASTRODYNAMICAL NOTATION AND USAGE. (ASTRODYN REPT. NO.10) LOS ANGELES, CALIFORNIA 1960. 18P.

, J.N. SCIENTIFIC TERMINOLOGY. NEW YORK, RINEHART, 1953. 231P. 52-13874.

R, C.M. ASTRONOMY POCKET CRAMMER. GARDEN CITY, N.Y, DOUBLEDAY, 1963. 159P. 63-5856.

TT, W. ET AL. THE SPACE FRONTIER, WITH ASTRONAUTICS GLOSSARY. WASHINGTON, NATL. AVIATION EDUC. IL, 1961. 32P. 62-1349.

ARY ASTRONAUTICS GLOSSARY. AIR FORCE MAG, V.41,157-67 (1958) 200T.

N, J.R. ET AL. THE HARPER ENCYCLOPEDIA OF SCIENCE. NEW YORK, HARPER, 1962. 4V. 62-14541. 4000T.

N, R.R. ASTRONOMY FOR THE NON-ASTRONOMER. IRE TRANS. S.E.T.-6, NO.1, 13-6 (1960) 130T.

X, L. ET AL. THE LAROUSSE ENCYCLOPEDIA OF ASTRONOMY. ED2. LONDON, PUTNAM, 1962. 512P.

, A.N. AND GAYNOR, F. DICTIONARY OF ASTRONOMY AND ASTRONAUTICS. PATERSON, N.J, LITTLEFIELD/ADAMS, 439P. 61-65363. 2000T.

E, O. AND ZEBERGS, V. ASTRONOMY OF THE 20TH CENTURY. (GL, PP.515-25, 150T) NEW YORK, MACMILLAN, 544P. 62-21206.

AIR FORCE. ARDC. A GLOSSARY OF SOME ASTRONOMICAL TERMS AND SYMBOLS. TULLAHOMA, TENN, ARNOLD ENG. OP. CENTER, 1958. 15P. 60T.

, M.B. ET AL. DICTIONARY OF ASTRO-PHYSICS ABBREVIATIONS. NEW YORK, SETI, 196 .

, M.B. ET AL. DICTIONARY OF METEOROLOGY, ASTRONOMY AND OCEANOGRAPHY ABBREVIATIONS, SIGNS, SYMBOLS, ABLES. NEW YORK, SETI, 196 . 256P.

FRENCH

ONNAIRE DES SCIENCES MATHEMATIQUES, ASTRONOMIE, PHYSIQUE, CHIMIE. (D. OF MATH, ASTRON, PHYS, CHEM, FS) PARIS, SEGHERS, 1962. 336P.

ASTRONOMY AND ASTROPHYSICS

FRENCH

RUDAUX, L. ET AL. ASTRONOMIE, LES ASTRES, L.UNIVERS. (ASTRON, STARS, UNIVERSE, FR DEFS) PARIS, LAROUSSE, 1956. 503P. 58-26777.

GERMAN

FLUEGGE, S. ET AL. HANDBUCH DER PHYSIK. (ENCYCL. OF PHYS) V.46, KOSMISCHE STRAHLUNG 1. (COSMIC RAYS 1, *GE*EN GL, PP.316-33, 550T) BERLIN, SPRINGER, 1961. 333P. A56-2942.

FLUEGGE, S. ET AL. HANDBUCH DER PHYSIK. (ENCYCL. OF PHYS) V.50, ASTROPHYSIK 1, STERNOBERFLAECHEN-DOPPELSTERNE. (ASTROPHYS. 1, STELLAR SURFACES-BINARIES, *GE*EN GL, PP.432-58, 700T) BERLIN, SPRINGER, 1958. A56-2942.

FLUEGGE, S. ET AL. HANDBUCH DER PHYSIK. (ENCYCL. OF PHYS) V.51, ASTROPHYSIK 2, STERNAUFBAU. (ASTROPHYS. 2, STELLAR STRUCT, *GE*EN GL, PP.786-830, 1200T) BERLIN, SPRINGER, 1958. 831P. A56-2942.

FLUEGGE, S. ET AL. HANDBUCH DER PHYSIK. (ENCYCL. OF PHYS) V.52, ASTROPHYSIK 3, DAS SONNENSYSTEM. (ASTROPHYS. 3, THE SOLAR SYSTEM, *GE*EN GL, PP.565-601, 1000T) BERLIN, SPRINGER, 1959. 601P. A56-2942.

FLUEGGE, S. ET AL. HANDBUCH DER PHYSIK. (ENCYCL. OF PHYS) V.53, ASTROPHYSIK 4, STERNSYSTEME. (ASTROPHYS. 4, STELLAR SYSTEMS,*GE*EN GL, PP.538-65, 850T) BERLIN, SPRINGER, 1959. 565P. A56-2942.

FLUEGGE, S. ET AL. HANDBUCH DER PHYSIK. (ENCYCL. OF PHYS) V.54, ASTROPHYSIK 5, VERSCHIEDENES. (ASTROPHYS. 5, MISC, *GE*EN GL, PP.289-308, 500T) BERLIN, SPRINGER, 1962. 308P. A56-2942.

FRANKE, H. ET AL. LEXIKON DER PHYSIK. (PHYS. ENCYCL, GE DEFS) STUTTGART, FRANCKH, 1959. 2V. 1687P. 59-34885.

HOERNER, S. AND SCHAIFERS, K. MEYERS HANDBUCH UEBER DAS WELTALL. (HANDBOOK OF UNIVERSE, GE DEFS) MANNHEIM, BIBLIOG. INST, 1960. 369P.

LEIDECKER,K.F. GERMAN-ENGLISH TECHNICAL DICTIONARY OF AERONAUTICS, ROCKETRY, SPACE NAVIGATION... NEW YORK,VANNI, 1950-51. 2V. 968P. 50-14702.

STUMPFF, K. ASTRONOMIE. (ASTRON. D, GE DEFS) FRANKFURT/MAIN, FISCHER, 1957. 345P. 1000T.

WEIGERT, A. AND ZIMMERMANN, H. BROCKHAUS ABC DER ASTRONOMIE. (ABC OF ASTRON, GE DEFS) ED2. LEIPZIG, BROCKHAUS, 1962. 408P.

POLYGLOT

ARAKI, T. GENDAI TEMMONGAKU JITEN. (ASTRON. D, JA GE EN) TOKYO, KOSEISHA, 1959. 4+14+2+730P. J61-1040.

CHUNG-KUO K,O HSUEH YUAN. PIEN I CH,U PAN WEI YUAN HUI. (ACAD. SINICA. COMM. PUBL/TRANSL). T,IEN WEN HSUEH MING TZ,U. (RU*EN*CH ASTRON. T) PEKING, SCIENCE, 1958. 176P. C59-1261.

KLECZEK, J. ASTRONOMICAL DICTIONARY. (*EN*RU*GE*FR*IT*CZ) NEW YORK, ACAD, PRESS, 1961. 972P. 62-2177. 11000T.

THEWLIS, J. ET AL. ENCYCLOPAEDIC DICTIONARY OF PHYSICS, GENERAL, NUCLEAR, SOLID STATE,MOLECULAR,CHEMICAL, METAL AND VACUUM PHYSICS, ASTRONOMY, GEOPHYSICS, BIOPHYSICS AND RELATED SUBJECTS, EN DEFS. MULTILINGUAL GL, *CH*FR*GE*JA*SP. NEW YORK, PERGAMON, 1961-63. 9V. 60-7069. 15000T.

RUSSIAN

AKADEMIIA NAUK SSSR. KOM. TEKH. TERM. OSNOVNYE BUKVENNYE OBOZNACHENIIA V ASTRONOMII. (BASIC LETTER SYMBOLS IN ASTRON, RU DEFS) (SB. REK. BUKV. OBOZN, NO.1) MOSCOW, 1959. 17P. 60-23829.

CHIROKOV, K.V. AND SUPRUN, . ANGLO-RUSSKII AEROKOSMICHESKII SLOVAR. (EN*RU AEROSPACE D) MOSCOW, VOENIZDAT, 1963.

EMIN, I. ET AL. RUSSIAN-ENGLISH GLOSSARY OF NAMED EFFECTS, LAWS, AND REACTIONS AND MISCELLANEOUS TERMS IN PHYSICS, MATHEMATICS AND ASTRONOMY. NEW YORK, INTERLANG. DICT, 1962. 22P. 62-51916. 2000T.

KRAMER, A.A. RUSSKO-ANGLIISKI SLOVAR PO ASTRONOMII. (RU*EN D. OF ASTRON) TRENTON, N.J, 1962. 191P. 62-66573. 10000T.

TRIFONOVA, N.F. ET AL. ANGLO-RUSSKII ASTROGEOFIZICHESKII SLOVAR. (EN*RU ASTRON/GEOPHYS,D) MOSCOW, FIZMATGIZ, 1962. 512P. 63-40099. 16000T.

U.S. LIBRARY OF CONGRESS. GLOSSARY OF LUNAR TERMS, ENGLISH-RUSSIAN, RUSSIAN-ENGLISH. (OTS-61-11163) WASHINGTON, 1960. 65P. 1200T.

SPANISH

COSTA, L. DICCIONARIO DE GEOCOSMOGRAFIA. (GEOCOSMOGRAPHY, SP DEFS) LIMA, 1961. 539P. 62-1172.

AUTOMATION AND AUTOMATIC CONTROL

DUTCH

STICHTING STUDIECENTRUM VOOR ADMINISTRATIEVE AUTOMATISERING VERKLARENDE WOORDENLIJST.(D. OF OFFICE AUTOM, DU*EN) AMSTERDAM, 1960. 136P.

AUTOMATION AND AUTOMATIC CONTROL

ENGLISH

AEROSPACE INDUSTRIES ASSOCIATION. STANDARD GYRO TERMINOLOGY. (REPT. EETC-5) WASHINGTON, 1960. 10P. 80T.

AMERICAN INSTITUTE OF ELECTRICAL ENGINEERS. DEFINITIONS OF ELECTRICAL TERMS. COMMUNICATION. (GR-65,ASA C42.65) NEW YORK, 1957. 128P. 1800T.

AMERICAN INSTITUTE OF ELECTRICAL ENGINEERS. DEFINITIONS OF ELECTRICAL TERMS. INDUSTRIAL CONTROL EQUIPMENT. (GR-25, ASA C42.25) NEW YORK, 1956. 24P. 220T.

AMERICAN INSTITUTE OF ELECTRICAL ENGINEERS. DICTIONARY OF SWITCHING THEORY TERMS. (PRELIM. DRAFT, CP-60-1225) NEW YORK, 196 .

AMERICAN INSTITUTE OF ELECTRICAL ENGINEERS. SPECIFICATION STANDARDS FOR ELECTROHYDRAULIC FLOW CONTROL SERVOVALVES. (AIEE 59-357) NEW YORK, 1959. 30P. 100T.

AMERICAN SOCIETY OF MECHANICAL ENGINEERS. AUTOMATIC CONTROL TERMINOLOGY. (ASME STD NO. 105) NEW YORK, 1954. 23P. 70T.

AMERICAN SOCIETY OF MECHANICAL ENGINEERS. DIAPHRAGM-ACTUATED CONTROL VALVE TERMINOLOGY. (ASME STD. NO.112) NEW YORK, 1961. 14P. 62-1921.

AMERICAN STANDARDS ASSOCIATION. COMMUNICATIONS GLOSSARY, DRAFT. NEW YORK, 1962. 44P. 400T.

AMERICAN STANDARDS ASSOCIATION. STANDARD DEFINITIONS AND TERMINOLOGY FOR RELAYS. (C83.16-1959) NEW YORK, ELECTRONIC IND. ASSOC. 1959. 29P. 380T.

AMERICAN STANDARDS ASSOCIATION. TERMINOLOGY FOR AUTOMATIC CONTROL. (ASA-C85.1) NEW YORK, AM. SOC. MECH. ENG, 1963. 45P. 600T.

BELL TELEPHONE LABORATORIES, INC. GERMAN STANDARDS, CONTROL ENGINEERING TERMS. (TRANSL, TR D-54, DIN-19226, 1954) MURRAY HILL, N.J, 1957.

BERKELEY, E.C. AND LOVETT, L.L. GLOSSARY OF TERMS IN COMPUTERS AND DATA PROCESSING. ED5. NEWTONVILLE, MASS, BERKELEY, 1960. 90P. 61-4747. 900T.

BIBBERO, R.J. DICTIONARY OF AUTOMATIC CONTROL. NEW YORK, REINHOLD, 1960. 282P. 60-14156. 560T.

BRITISH STANDARDS INSTITUTION. GLOSSARY OF TERMS USED IN AUTOMATIC CONTROLLING AND REGULATING SYSTEMS. (B.S.1523) SECT. 2, PROCESS CONTROL, 1960. 24P. SECT. 3, KINETIC CONTROL, 1954. 24P. SECT.5, COMPONENTS OF SERVO-MECHANISMS. 32P. LONDON, 1954-1960. 330T.

BRITISH STANDARDS INSTITUTION. GLOSSARY OF TERMS USED IN AUTOMATIC DATA PROCESSING. (B.S.3527) LONDON, 1962. 132P. 1500T.

DATA PROCESSING EQUIPMENT ENCYCLOPEDIA. DETROIT, GILLE, 1961. 2V. 61-15132.

GENERAL ELECTRIC CO. REGULATING AND D-C CONTROL SYSTEM TERMINOLOGY AND DEFINITIONS. (GE 2654, IE 1099) SCHENECTADY, N.Y, 1956.

GOODWIN, K.E. AND GINDER, C.E. NOMA GLOSSARY OF AUTOMATION TERMS. WILLOW GROVE, PA. NATL. OFFICE MANAGEMENT ASSOC, 1961. 88P. 61-2548. 550T.

INSTITUTE OF RADIO ENGINEERS. STANDARDS ON GRAPHICAL AND LETTER SYMBOLS FOR FEEDBACK CONTROL SYSTEMS. (55 IRE 26.S1) PROC. IRE, V.43, 1608-9 (1955) 10T.

INSTITUTE OF RADIO ENGINEERS. STANDARDS ON INDUSTRIAL ELECTRONICS, DEFINITIONS... (55 IRE 10.S1) PROC. IRE, V.43, 1069-72 (1955) 70T.

INSTITUTE OF RADIO ENGINEERS. STANDARDS ON TERMINOLOGY FOR FEEDBACK CONTROL SYSTEMS. (55 IRE26.S2) PROC. IRE, V.44, 107-9 (1956) 40T.

INTERNATIONAL BUSINESS MACHINES CORP. GLOSSARY FOR DATA PROCESSING MACHINES. WASHINGTON, 1959. 14P.

KELLEY, D.X. GLOSSARY OF ELECTRONIC DATA PROCESSING TERMINOLOGY. BEDFORD, MASS. C.W. ADAMS. 1962. 8P. 40T.

MCCRACKEN, D.D. ET AL. PROGRAMMING BUSINESS COMPUTERS. (GL, PP.469-87, 400T) NEW YORK, WILEY, 1959.

MINNEAPOLIS-HONEYWELL REGULATOR CO. AUTOMATION DICTIONARY. PHILADELPHIA,(N.D) 19P. 100T.

MORGAN, R.E. ET AL. DEFINITIONS OF MAGNETIC AMPLIFIERS. TRANS. AM. INST. ELEC. ENG, V.77, PT.1, 429-32 (1958) 40T.

MURPHY, E.A. JR. DO YOU TALK COMPUTERESE. PHILADELPHIA, MINN.-HONEYWELL REGULATOR, 1960. 22P. 90T.

NATIONAL ELECTRIC MANUFACTURES ASSOC. DEFINITIONS FOR INDUSTRIAL AUTOMATIC SYSTEMS. (AS 1-1961) NEW YORK, 1961. 10P. 90T.

PRUDENTIAL INSURANCE CO. OF AMERICA. INTRODUCTION TO ELECTRONIC COMPUTERS, GLOSSARY. NEW YORK, 195 .

U.S. INTERAGENCY AUTOMATIC DATA PROCESSING COMMITTEE. ADP GLOSSARY (PRELIM.DRAFT) 1961. 213P. 1400T.

WILMOT, E.DE B. GLOSSARY OF TERMS USED IN AUTOMATIC DATA PROCESSING. LONDON, BUSINESS PUBL. 1960. 36P.

AUTOMATION AND AUTOMATIC CONTROL

ENGLISH

WITTY, M.B. ET AL. DICTIONARY OF COMPUTERS AND CONTROLS ABBREVIATIONS, SIGNS AND SYMBOLS. NEW YORK, SETI, 196 .

GERMAN

VEREIN DEUTSCHER MASCHINENBAUANSTALT. OELHYDRAULIK- UND PNEUMATIK-KATALOG 1962 (OIL HYDRAULICS/PNEUMATI CATALOG, GE DEFS) WIESBADEN, KRAUSSKOPF,1962. 130P.

POLYGLOT

AKADEMIIA NAUK SSSR. KOM.TEKH.TERM. TERMINOLOGIIA RELE. (D. OF RELAYS, RU*EN*FR*GE) (SB.REK.TERM. NO.. MOSCOW, 1958. 42P. 59-45194. 180T.

BOUSEK, J. PRIRUCNI TECHNICKY SLOVNIK V (5) JAZ ... PRO OBOR PRUMYSLOVEHO MERENI A AUTOMATICKE REGULACI (D. OF IND. METROL/AUTOM. CONTROL, CZ EN FR GE RU) PRAGUE, MATICE HORNICKO-HUTNICKA, 1955. 210P.

CLASON, W.E. ELSEVIER.S DICTIONARY OF AUTOMATIC CONTROL, *EN/AM*FR*GE*RU. NEW YORK, ELSEVIER, 1963. 211P. 63-16075. 2600T.

CLASON, W.E. ELSEVIER.S DICTIONARY OF AUTOMATION, COMPUTERS, CONTROL AND MEASURING. *EN/AM*DU*FR*GE*IT *SP. NEW YORK, ELSEVIER, 1961. 848P. 60-53482. 3400T.

CONTROL GEAR GLOSSARY. (*EN*FR*GE*IT*SW) ELEC. TIMES, LONDON, V.137, NO.3, 97-8 (1960) 100T.

DORIAN, A.F. SIX-LANGUAGE DICTIONARY OF AUTOMATION, ELECTRONICS AND SCIENTIFIC INSTRUMENTS...(*EN*FR*GI *IT*RU*SP) ENGLEWOOD CLIFFS, N.J. PRENTICE HALL, 1962. 732P. 63-5414. 5500T.

DORIAN, A.F. SIX-LANGUAGE DICTIONARY OF ELECTRONICS, AUTOMATION, AND SCIENTIFIC INSTRUMENTS. (EN*FR*GE*IT*RU*SP) ENGLEWOOD CLIFFS, N.J. PRENTICE-HALL, 1963. 732P. 63-510. 5500T.

FRIGYES, A. ET AL. IRANYITASTECHNIKA. (AUTOM. D. *HU*EN*GE*RU) (MUSZ. ERT. SZ, NO.19) BUDAPEST, TERI 1962. 135P. 1100T.

HELLSTROEM, G. AND KARLQVIST, O. ORDLISTA INOM OMRADET DATE- OCH BERAEKNINGSMASKINER. (GL. OF DATA PROCESS/COMP. SW*EN*GE) KONTORSVAERLDEN (STOCKHOLM) NO.12 (1956) AND NO.1 (1957) 7P. 110T.

HOLMSTROM, J.E. MULTILINGUAL DICTIONARY OF DATA PROCESSING.*GE*EN*FR*RU*SP. (TRANSL.OF DRAFT STD. BRIT. DEFS. FOR AUTOM. DATA PROCESS/B.S.3527) ROME, PROV.INTL.COMP.CENTRE, 1959. 250P. 1500T. SUPPL. 1/2, 196

INTERNATIONAL ELECTROTECHNICAL COMMISSION. INTERNATIONAL ELECTROTECHNICAL VOCABULARY. (IEC-50-GR-15) SWITCHBOARDS AND APPARATUS FOR CONNECTION AND REGULATION. *FR*EN*DU*GE*IT*PL*SP*SW. ED2. GENEVA, 195` 75P. 250T.

INTERNATIONAL ELECTROTECHNICAL COMMISSION. INTERNATIONAL ELECTROTECHNICAL VOCABULARY. (IEC-50-GR-16) PROTECTIVE RELAYS. *FR*EN*DU*GE*IT*PL*SP*SW. ED2. GENEVA, 1956. 56P. 200T.

INTERNATIONAL ELECTROTECHNICAL COMMISSION. MEZHDUNARODNYI ELEKTROTEKHNICHESKII SLOVAR. (INTL. ELECTROTECH. VOC) (IEC 50-GR-16) RELEINAIIA ZASHCHITA. (PROTECTIVE RELAYS,*RU*EN*DU*FR*GE*IT*PL*SP*S ED2. MOSCOW, FIZMATGIZ, 1960. 115P. 200T.

KAWECKI, J. PODRECZNY SLOWNICZEK AUTOMATYKA. (AUTOM.D, PL*EN*FR*GE*RU) PRZEGLAD TECH. V.82, I-XIV (196 650T.

KHRAMOI, A.V. RUSSKO-ANGLO-NEMETSKO-FRANTSUZKII SLOVAR TERMINOV PO AVTOMATICHESKOMU UPRAVLENIIU. (*RU *FR*GE D. OF AUTOM. CONTROL) MOSCOW, AKAD. NAUK, SSSR, 1963. 205P. 3100T.

LEIPZIG. INSTITUT FUER ENERGETIK. EINHEITLICHE BEGRIFFE DER ENERGIEWIRTSCHAFT. DDR. (D. OF STD, ELEC ENG. T, AL BU CZ GE HU PL RO RU) LEIPZIG, GRUNDSTOFFIND, 1961-- . 62-44979.

VOCABULAIRE TRILINGUE DE LA REGULATION AUTOMATIQUE. (GE EN FR AUTOM. GL) MESURES/CONTROLE IND, V.22, 137-8 (1957)

RUSSIAN

AKADEMIIA NAUK SSSR. KOM. TEKH. TERM. TERMINOLOGIIA OSNOVNYKH PONIATII AVTOMATIKI. (BASIC CONCEPTS I AUTOM, RU DEFS) (SB. REK. TERM, NO.35) MOSCOW,1954. 22P. 55-35588. 40T.

AKADEMIIA NAUK SSSR. KOM.TEKH.TERM. TERMINOLOGIIA PO STRUKTURNOMU ANALIZU I SINTEZU RELEINO-KONTAKTNYK SKHEM. (D. OF STRUCT,ANAL/SYNTH.OF RELAY-CONTACT SYSTEMS, RU DEFS) (SB.REK.TERM. NO.8) MOSCOW, 1953. 2 54-27905. 50T.

AKADEMIIA NAUK SSSR. KOM.TEKH.TERM. TERMINOLOGIIA UPRAVLENIIA, REGULIROVANIIA I AVTOMATIKI AVIADVIGATELEI. (GUIDANCE, CONTROL/AUTOM. OF AIRPLANE ENG, RU DEFS) (SB.REK.TERM, NO.28) MOSCOW, 195 20P. 55-35584. 40T.

BERG, A.I. AND TRAPEZNIKOV, V.A. AVTOMATIZATSIIA PROIZVODSTVA I PROMYSHLENNAIA ELEKTRONIKA... (IND. AUTOM/ELECTRON. ENCYCL, RU DEFS) MOSCOW, SOV. ENTSIKL, 1962- . 63-32131.

CLASON, W.E. ELSEVIER.S DICTIONARY OF AUTOMATION, COMPUTERS, CONTROL AND MEASURING. RUSSIAN SUPPL, NEW YORK, ELSEVIER, 1962. 90P. 3400T.

KHRAMOI, A.V. AND ZHURKINA, E.G. RUSSKO-ANGLIISKII I ANGLO-RUSSKII SLOVAR PO AVTOMATICHESKOMU REGULIROVANIIU I UPRAVLENIIU. (*RU*EN D. OF AUTOM. CONTROL-IFAC) MOSCOW, AKAD. NAUK, SSSR, 1960. 91P. MIC 61-7392. 1600T.

AUTOMATION AND AUTOMATIC CONTROL

RUSSIAN

PTASHNYI, L.K. ANGLO-RUSSKII SLOVAR PO AVTOMATIKE I KONTROLNO-IZMERITELNYM PRIBORAM. (EN*RU D. OF AUTOM/INSTR) MOSCOW, GITTL, 1957. 379P. 58-30223. 12000T.

SWEDISH

SVERIGES STANDARDISERINGSKOMMISSION. DATAMASKINER ORDLISTA. (COMP. GL, SW DEFS) (SWEDISH STD, SEN-0116) STOCKHOLM, 1961.

AUTOMOTIVE ENGINEERING AND INDUSTRY

BULGARIAN

LOKOV, D. TERMINOLOGIIA PO MOTOTSIKLETIZM. (MOTORCYCLES, BU DEFS) SOFIA, MED. FIZKULT, 1957. 62P. 0-22935. 240T.

DANISH

HANNIBAL, A. AUTOMOBILORDBOG, ENGELSK, AMERIKANSK, DANSK. (*DA*EN AUTO. D) COPENHAGEN, IVAR, 1958. 122P. A58-6073. 6000T.

DUTCH

TRABEL, A. VLIEGTUIG, AUTOMOBIEL, MOTORRIJWIEL. (FLYING/MOTORING D, *DU*EN) HILVERSUM, OCECO, 1954. 45P. 1600T.

ENGLISH

AKER, J.S. ET AL. DICTIONARY OF HIGHWAY TRAFFIC. EVANSTON, ILL. NORTHWESTERN UNIV, 1960. 304P. 60-4093.

OCIETY OF AUTOMOTIVE ENGINEERS. DEFINITIONS OF HEAT-TREATING TERMS,PP.79-81. SAE HANDBOOK, NEW YORK,1961. 14P. 120T.

OBOLT, W.K. AND PURVIS, J. MOTOR SERVICES NEW AUTOMOTIVE ENCYCLOPEDIA. CHICAGO, GOODHEART-WILLCOX, 1962. AR. P.

ITTY, M.B. ET AL. DICTIONARY OF AUTOMOTIVE ENGINEERING ABBREVIATIONS. NEW YORK, SETI, 196 .

FRENCH

ICTIONNAIRE TECHNIQUE ANGLAIS-FRANCAIS, AERONAUTIQUE ET MOTEURS. (EN*FR D. OF AERON/MOTORS) OIS-COLOMBES (SEINE) HISPANO-SUIZA, 1952. 356P.

RANCE. AMBASSADE. U.S. INDUSTRIE AUTOMOBILE, AMERICAIN-FRANCAIS. (AUTO. IND. AM*FR GL) WASHINGTON, 1953. 45P. 2800T.

RANCE. AMBASSADE. U.S. INDUSTRIE AUTOMOBILE, FRANCAIS-AMERICAIN. (AUTO. IND. FR*AM GL) WASHINGTON, 1953. 75P. 3500T.

UERBER,R. DICTIONNAIRE DE L,AUTOMOBILE. (AUTO. D, FR DEFS) 1956.

GERMAN

E VRIES, L. AND JOERGENSEN,O.M. FACHWOERTERBUCH DES KRAFTFAHRZEUGWESENS UND VERWANDTER GEBIETE... (*GE EN D. OF AUTO/ALLIED IND) WIESBADEN, BRANDSTETTER, 1957. 471P. 58-16234. 8000T.

CHNAUBERT, K. KRAFTFAHRTECHNISCHES LEXIKON...(AUTO. GL, GE DEFS) HANOVER, DEGENER, 195 . 225P. 56-18789. 300T.

ANNER,G. LEXIKON DER KRAFTFAHRT. (AUTO. D, GE DEFS) MUNICH, 1953.

ITALIAN

UTOMOBILE CLUB DI MILANO. DIZIONARIO TECNICO AUTOMOBILISTICO. (AUTO. D, IT DEFS) MILAN, 1957.

ALAMANTE, M. DIZIONARIO DELL, AUTOMOBILE. (AUTO. D, IT DEFS) MILAN, 1952. 309P. A52-3401.

JAPANESE

UTOMOBILE RESEARCH INSTITUTE. ILLUSTRATED DICTIONARY OF AUTOMOBILE TERMINOLOGY. (EN*JA) TOKYO, OKUMURA, 953. 196P.

APANESE STANDARDS ASSOCIATION. AUTOMOBILE TERMINOLOGY. (*JA*EN) TOKYO, 1954. 179P.

IYAMOTO, T. ILLUSTRATED JAPANESE-ENGLISH DICTIONARY OF AUTOMOBILES AND BICYCLES. (*JA*EN) (TRANS. OF NION TECHNIQUE DE L.AUTOMOBILE, DU MOTOCYCLE ET DU CYCLE. LEXIQUE ILLUSTRE DE L.AUTOMOBILE) TOKYO, OMU, 953. 187P.

ESAKA, M. JAPANESE ENGLISH STANDARD TERMINOLOGY OF AUTOMOBILES. (*JA*EN) TOKYO, AUTO. ENG. CO, 1957. 71P.

POLISH

DEBSKI, K. SLOWNIK SAMOCHODOWY ANGIELSKO-POLSKI. (EN*PL AUTO. D) WARSAW, PANSTW. WYDAWN. TECH, 1960. 409P. 61-28685.

GOLEBIEWSKI, T. ET AL. SLOWNIK ENCYKLOPEDYCZNY TRANSPORTU SAMOCHODOWEGO. (ENCYCL. D. OF AUTO. TRANSP, PL DEFS) WARSAW, WYDAWN. KOMUNIKACJI I LACZNOSCI, 1962. 295P. 63-39143.

POLYGLOT

ACADEMY OF THE HEBREW LANGUAGE, JERUSALEM. MILON LE-MUNAHE HA-MEKHONIT. (AUTO. T, *HE*EN*FR*GE) JERUSALEM, 1955. 220P. 57-55578.

AUTO-MOTO SAVEZ HRVATSKE. RJECNIK AUTOMOBILSKIH IZRAZA... (AUTO. D, CR EN FR GE IT) ZAGREB, 1954. 80P. 56-19220. 350T.

BOSCH, R. KRAFTFAHRTECHNISCHES TASCHENBUCH. (AUTO. HANDBOOK, GL, PP.372-93, GE*EN*FR*IT) ED2. STUTTGAF BOSCH, 1959.

BUECKEN, F.J. VOCABULARIO TECNICO PORTUGUES-INGLES-FRANCES-ALEMAO... APENDICE DE TERMOS AUTOMOBILISTIC((TECH. D, PR*EN*GE, WITH APPENDIX OF AUTO. T) ED4. SAO PAULO, MELHORAMENTOS, 1961. 600P. 62-3680. 45000T.

BUNJES, W. MOTOR CARS, *EN/AM*FR*GE*SP. NEW YORK, ELSEVIER. (IN PREP)

CALZADA,R. MOTORISTS 5 LANGUAGE GUIDE... (EN FR GE IT SP) LONDON, RENOWN, 1952. 48P. 52-38529. 1000T.

CHUNG-KUO K.O HSUEH YUAN. PIEN I CH.U PAN WEI YUAN HUI. (ACAD. SINICA. COMM. OF PUBL/TRANSL) CHAN HSII CH.I CH.E P.EI CHIEN T.UNG I MING CH.ENG. (AUTO PARTS D, CH RU EN) 3V. PEKING. 1957. C58-5180.

DIERFIELD, B.R. MOTOR DICTIONARY. V.4, SP EN PR. ED3. ZURICH, SCIENTIA, 1959. 227P. (EARLIER ED, V.1-3, *GE*FR*EN)

JUNCKERS SPRACHFUEHRER FUER KRAFTFAHRER... (MOTORING PHRASEBOOK, GE*EN*FR*IT*SP) BERLIN, JUNCKER, 1957. 4V. IN 1. 383P. A58-3291.

LE GRAIN, R. ILLUSTRATED LEXIKON OF THE MOTOR CAR. (FR EN GE IT SP) PARIS, 1953. 221P.

SCHUURMANS-STEKHOVEN, G. ET AL. ELSEVIER,S AUTOMOBILE DICTIONARY, *EN*FR*GE*IT*JA*PR*RU*SP. NEW YORK, ELSEVIER, 1960. 946P. 59-8946. 5200T.

SHELL INTERNATIONAL PETROLEUM CO. INTERNAL COMBUSTION ENGINE. (TECH T,*EN/AM*DU*FR*GE*IT*PR*RU*SP) NEW YORK, ELSEVIER, 1961. 278P. 60-53498. 1200T.

SIMIC, D. ILUSTROVANI AUTOMOBILSKI RECNIK... (ILLUS. AUTO. D, SC EN FR GE IT) SARAJEVO, SVJETLOST, 196(165P. 61-41969. 1000T.

UNION TECHNIQUE DE L,AUTOMOBILE, DU MOTOCYCLE ET DU CYCLE. LEXIQUE ILLUSTRE DE L,AUTOMOBILE...(ILLUS. AUTO. D, FR EN GE IT SP) ED.5. PARIS, S.N.E.E.P. 1958. 245P. 59-35328. 16000T.

VAN RENSSEN,S. TECHNISCH WOORDENBOEK VOOR DE AUTOMOBIEL EN MOTORRIJWIELBRANCHE. (4-LANG. AUTO. D, *DU *EN*FR*GE) ED3. ANTWERP, 1959. 208P.

VARGA, J. ET AL. VIZGEPEK, BELSO EGESU MOTOROK. (D. OF HYDR/INTERN. COMB. ENGS, *HU*EN*GE*RU) (MUSZ. ERT. SZ. NO.20) BUDAPEST, TERRA, 1962. 138P. 62-66313. 1100T.

PORTUGUESE

LINS, P. DICIONARIO DE TERMOS TECNICOS DE AUTOMOBILISMO...(*PR*EN AUTO. D) RIO DE JANERIO, IRMAOS DI GIORGIO, 1954. 203P. 57-35660. 6800T.

RUSSIAN

AKADEMIIA NAUK SSSR. KOM.TEKH.TERM. PORSHNEVYE DVIGATELI VNUTRENNEGO SGORANIIA... (INTERNAL COMBUSTION PISTON ENG, RU DEFS) (SB.REK.TERM, NO.50) MOSCOW, 1959. 13P. 60-21844. 60T.

AKADEMIIA NAUK SSSR. KOM.TEKH.TERM. TERMINOLOGIIA KONSTRUKTSII TURBOREAKTIVNYKH, TURBOVINTOVYKH I PORSHNEVYKH DVIGATELEI. (DESIGN OF TURBOJET, TURBOPROP/PISTON ENG, RU DEFS) (SB.REK.TERM, NO.19) MOSCOW, 1954. 27P. 55-35582. 120T.

AKADEMIIA NAUK SSSR. KOM.TEKH.TERM. TERMINOLOGIIA PO AVTOMOBILIAM. (AUTO, RU DEFS) (SB.REK.TERM, NO.37 MOSCOW, 1954. 40P. 55-38830. 120T.

AKADEMIIA NAUK SSSR. KOM.TEKH.TERM. TERMINOLOGIIA PORSHNEVYKH DVIGATELEI VNUTRENNEGO SGORANIIA. (INTE COMBUSTION PISTON ENG, RU DEFS)(SB.REK.TERM, NO.34) MOSCOW, 1954. 58P.55-36951. 160T.

AKADEMIIA NAUK SSSR. KOM. TEKH. TERM. TERMINOLOGIIA TOPLIVA OLIA DVIGATELEI VNUTRENNEGO SGORANIIA (FUELS FOR INTERNAL COMBUSTION ENG, RU DEFS)(SB. REK. TERM, NO.44) MOSCOW, 1957. 28P. 57-45392. 100T.

GOLD, B.V. AND KUGEL, R.V. ANGLO-RUSSKII AVTOTRAKTORNYI SLOVAR. (EN*RU AUTO. D) ED.2. MOSCOW, GITTL, 1957. 831P. 58-29087. 35000T.

AUTOMOTIVE ENGINEERING AND INDUSTRY

SPANISH

AUTOMOTIVE EXPORT BLUE GUIDE. LIMA AUTOMOTIVE D, *SP*EN, PP 1-362. NEW YORK, BLUE GUIDES, 1962-- VAR. P. 62-52144. 18000T.

CARTOGRAPHY, GEODESY, AND SURVEYING

CHINESE

CHUNG-KUO K,O HSUEH YUAN. PIEN I CH,U PAN WEI YUAN HUI. (ACAD. SINICA. COMM. OF PUBL/TRANSL) TZU JAN TI LI MING TZ,U. TI HSING CHIH PU. (PHYS. GEOG. T, TOPOGRAPHY SECT, CH EN) PEKING, SCIENCE, 1958. 61P. C59-1274.

ENGLISH

AMERICAN SOCIETY OF CIVIL ENGINEERS. DEFINITIONS OF SURVEYING, MAPPING, AND RELATED TERMS... (ASCE MANUALS OF ENG, NO.34) NEW YORK, 1954. 202P. 55-14234.

GOODSON, J.B. AND MORRIS, J.A. A CONTOUR DICTIONARY...ED3. LONDON, HARRAP, 1960. 64P. 61-500.

SHENKLE, W. GLOSSARY OF PHOTOGRAPHIC AND RECONNAISSANCE TERMS. (WADC TECH. NOTE NO.56-510) WRIGHT-PATTERSON AFB, OHIO, 1956. 61P.

WITTY, M.B. ET AL. DICTIONARY OF CARTOGRAPHY AND TOPOGRAPHY ABBREVIATIONS, SIGNS AND SYMBOLS. NEW YORK, SETI, 196 .

FINNISH

PALMERLEE, A.E. AND SMITH, T.R. A FINNISH-ENGLISH GLOSSARY OF MAP TERMS. LAWRENCE, UNIV. KANSAS, 1959. 49P. 59-3156.

FRENCH

BROMMER, S. LEXIQUE ANGLAIS-FRANCAIS DES TERMES APPARTENANT AUX TECHNIQUES EN USAGE A L,INSTITUT GEOGRAPHIQUE NATIONAL. PT.2 REPRODUCTION ET TIRAGES... (EN*FR D. OF CARTOGR, MAP PRINTING...) PARIS, INST. GEOG. NATL, 1958. 103P. 60-40583. 3900T.

FRANCE. INSTITUT GEOGRAPHIQUE NATIONAL. LEXIQUE ANGLAIS-FRANCAIS DES TERMES APPARTENANT AUX TECHNIQUES EN USAGE A L,INSTITUT GEOGRAPHIQUE NATIONAL. (EN*FR GEOG. D) ED2. PARIS, 1961.   V. 62-66757.

HUDON, C. PILOTAGE ET HYDROGRAPHIE,GLOSSAIRE ANGLAIS-FRANCAIS,BT-105. (PILOTING/HYDR, EN*FR GL) OTTAWA, DEPT. SECY.STATE, 1962. 48P. 1200T.

THUILLIER, R. LEXIQUE ANGLAIS-FRANCAIS DES TERMES APPARTENANT AUX TECHNIQUES EN USAGE A L,INSTITUT GEOGRAPHIQUE NATIONAL. PT.1 GEODESIE ET NIVELLEMENT, TOPOGRAPHIE... (EN*FR D.OF GEOD, SURV, TOPOGR) PARIS, INST. GEOG. NATL. 1958. 278P. 60-40583. 5100T.

GERMAN

U.S. AERONAUTICAL CHART PLANT. GLOSSARY OF CARTOGRAPHIC TERMS, GERMAN-ENGLISH. WASHINGTON, 1951. 54P. 51-61571.

ITALIAN

GASPARRELLI, L. ET AL. MANUALE DEL GEOMETRA AD USO DEGLI ALLIEVI DEGLI ISTITUTI TECNICI PER GEOMETRI... STUDENTS,S HANDBOOK/D. FOR SURV, IT DEFS) ED10. MILAN, HOEPLI, 1956. 1503P. A57-6940.

MONACO, S. BREVE VOCABOLARIO DI TERMINI TOPOGRAFICI... (*IT*EN D. OF TOPOGR) FLORENCE, IST. GEOG. MIL, 1954. 63P. 56-45313.

JAPANESE

.S. ARMY MAP SERVICE, FAR EAST. DICTIONARY OF MAPPING TERMS, JAPANESE-ENGLISH, ENGLISH-JAPANESE. 1959. 64P. 60-60115.

POLYGLOT

HUNG-KUO K,O HSUEH YUAN. PIEN I CH,U PAN WEI YUAN HUI. (ACAD. SINICA. COMM. OF PUBL/TRANSL) TS,E LIANG SUEH MING TZ,U. (SURVEYING T, CH EN GE) PEKING,SCIENCE, 1956. 206P. C58-5145.

NTERNATIONAL FEDERATION OF SURVEYORS. DICTIONNAIRE MULTILINGUE DE LA FEDERATION DES GEOMETRES. (*FR*GE EN SURVEYORS D) AMSTERDAM, ARGUS, 1963. 500P.

NTERNATIONAL HYDROGRAPHIC BUREAU. GLOSSARY OF CARTOGRAPHIC TERMS AND MANUAL OF SYMBOLS AND ABBREVIATIONS SED ON THE LATEST NAVIGATION CHARTS... (*EN*FR+21 LANG) ED3. MONACO, 1951. 188P. SUPPL. 1956.

NTERNATIONAL HYDROGRAPHIC BUREAU. HYDROGRAPHIC DICTIONARY. (*EN*FR*DA*DU*PR*SP*IT*NO*SW*GE) ED2. MONACO, 951. 89+89P. 52-65869.

NTERNATIONAL SOCIETY FOR PHOTOGRAMMETRY. MULTI-LINGUAL DICTIONARY FOR PHOTOGRAMMETRY... (*EN*FR*GE*IT*PL SP*SW) 7V. AMSTERDAM, ARGUS, 1961.

ESTERREICHISCHE GESELLSCHAFT FUER PHOTOGRAMMETRIE. PHOTOGRAMMETRISCHES WOERTERBUCH. (PHOTOGRAMMETRIC D, GE*EN*FR*IT*PL*SP*SW) VIENNA. 100P. 5000T. (IN PREP)

27

POLYGLOT

REDEY, I. ET AL. ALTALANOS GEODEZIA. (D. OF GEOD. HU*EN*GE*RU) (MUSZ. ERT. SZ, NO. 13) BUDAPEST, TERRA, 1961. 216P. 61-31346. 1200T.

SZTOMPKE, W. SLOWNIK GEODEZYJNY W 5 JEZYKACH... (D. OF GEOD, *PL*EN*FR*GE*RU) WARSAW, PANST. PRZED. WYDAW. KARTOGR. 1954. 525P. 55-34784. 4800T.

RUSSIAN

AKADEMIIA NAUK SSSR. KOM.TEKH.TERM. TERMINOLOGIIA PO VOZDUSHNOMU FOTOGRAFIROVANIIU. (AERIAL PHOT, RU DEFS) (SB. REK. TERM. NO.29) MOSCOW, 1954. 29P. 59-53689. 120T.

GALPERIN, G.L. AND GOSPODINOV, G.V. ANGLO-RUSSKII SLOVAR PO KARTOGRAFII, GEODEZII I AEROFOTOTOPOGRAFII. (EN*RU D. OF CARTOGR,GEOD/AERIAL PHOTOTOPOGR) MOSCOW, FIZMATGIZ, 1958. 546P. 59-45138. 8000T.

GOTSKII, M.V., ANGLIISKIE MORSKIE POSOBIIA I KARTY. (EN*RU D. OF NAVAL MANUALS/MAPS, PP. 195-230, 4000T) MOSCOW, MORSK. TRANSP, 1958. 258P. 59-42465.

U.S. AERONAUTICAL CHART AND INFORMATION CENTER. GLOSSARY OF GEODETIC TERMS, RUSSIAN-ENGLISH. ST. LOUIS, MO, 1959. 66P.

U.S. DEPT. OF THE ARMY. SOVIET TOPOGRAPHIC MAP SYMBOLS. (TM 30-548) (RU EN D/ABBRS, PP.91-101) WASHINGTON, 1958. 104P. 58-62387.

SLOVAK

SLOVENSKA AKADEMIA VIED. ZEMEMERACSKA TERMINOLOGIA. (D. OF SURV, SL DEFS) BRATISLAVA, 1958. 52P. 59-22602.

SPANISH

STOWARZYSZENIE NAUKOWO-TECHNICZNE GEODETOW POLSKICH. SLOWNIK GEODEZYJNY W 5 JEZYKACH, POLSKIM, ROSYJSKIM, NIEMIECKIM, ANGIELSKIM, FRANCUSKIM. WKLADKA HISZPANSKA. (5-LANG. GEOD. D. SP SUPPL) WARSAW, PPWK, 1961.

CHEMISTRY AND CHEMICAL ENGINEERING

AFRIKAANS

SUID-AFRIKAANSE AKADEMIE VIR WETENSKAP EN KUNS. LYS SKEIKUNDIGE TERME, ENGELS-AFRIKAANS. (EN*AF D. OF CHEM) PRETORIA, 1955. 157P. 56-28677.

ARABIC

UNITED ARAB REPUBLIC. SCIENTIFIC TERMS. SER. 1, EN*AR. CAIRO, SCI. COUNCIL, 1961. 435P. NE 62-1569.

CHINESE

CHI-HSUAN, C. PRACTICAL CHEMICAL DICTIONARY. (*EN*CH) HONG KONG, COMMERICIAL. 1960. 1111P.

CHUNG-KUO K,O HSUEH YUAN. PIEN I CHU. (ACAD. SINICA. BUR. COMPIL/TRANSL) HUA HSUEH HUA KUNG SHU YU. (CHEM/CHEM. ENG. T, CH EN) PEKING, 1955.

CHUNG-KUO K,O HSUEH YUAN. PIEN I CHU. (ACAD. SINICA BUR. COMPIL/TRANSL) KAO FEN TZU HUA .HSUEH HUA KUNG SHU YU. (HIGH POLYMER CHEM/CHEM. ENG. T, EN CH) PEKING, SCIENCE, 1957. 35P. C59-706.

CHUNG-KUO K,O HSUEH YUAN. PIEN I CH,U PAN WEI YUAN HUI. (ACAD. SINICA. COMM. OF PUBL/TRANSL) KAO FEN TZU HUA HSUEH MING TZ,U. (HIGH POLYMER CHEM, CH EN) PEKING, 1956.

CHUNG-KUO K,O HSUEH YUAN. PIEN I CH,U PAN WEI YUAN HUI. (ACAD. SINICA COMM. OF PUBL/TRANSL) YING HAN WU CHI HUA HO WU MING TZ,U. (EN CH INORG. COUMPOUNDS D) PEKING, SCIENCE, 1959. 174P. C59-2295.

HSUEH, SHUO-JEN. HUA HSUEH TA TZ,U T,IEN. (CHEM. D, CH EN) TAIWAN, LI-JENG BOOKS, 1959. 972+139P. C62-4017.

KUO LI PIEN I KUAN. T,AI-PEI. (NATL. INST. OF TRANSL) HUA HSUEH MING TZ,U. (CHEM. T, EN CH) TAIPEI, CHENG-CHUNG BOOK STORE, 1960. 401P. C61-1985.

LIU, CHANG-CHI. HSI YAO TA TZ,U TIEN. (WESTERN DRUGS D, CH DEFS) HONG KONG, PRACTICAL PRESS, 1959. VAR. P. C62-4015.

ROSE, A. AND E. HUA HSUEH YAO P,IN TZ,U TIEN HSU PIEN. (ROSE,S CONDENSED CHEM. D, CH EN) ED4. SHANGHAI, NEW ASIA, 1955. 456P. C58-5861.

YANG, PAO CHANG. HUN HSUEH HUN KUNG MING TZ,U HUI PIEN. (CHEM/CHEM. ENG. D, EN CH) HONG KONG, PRACTICAL SCI/ENG, 1961. 1458P. C63-951.

CZECH

FURCH, J. SEZNAM ANGLICKO-CESKYCH HORNICKYCH VYRAZU. (EN*CZ MIN. GL) PRAGUE, MAT. HORN-HUTN, 1952. 430P.

RUZICKA, J. ET AL. CHEMICKY PRIRUCNI SLOVNIK. (D. OF CHEM, CZ DEFS) PRAGUE,SNTL, 1953. 328P. 55-22618

DUTCH

DUIJN, C. FOTOGRAFISCHE CHEMICALIEN... (PHOT. CHEM, DU DEFS) ED2. DOETINCHEM, MISSET, 1955. 208P. 59-49361.

ENGLISH

AMERICAN INSTITUTE OF CHEMICAL ENGINEERS. CHEMICAL ENGINEERING THESAURUS... NEW YORK, 1961. 175P. 61-66804.

AMERICAN INSTITUTE OF ELECTRICAL ENGINEERS. DEFINITIONS OF ELECTRICAL TERMS. ELECTROCHEMISTRY AND ELECTROMETALLURGY. (GR-60. ASA C42.60) NEW YORK, 1956.30P. 300T.

AMERICAN PETROLEUM INSTITUTE. GLOSSARY OF TERMS USED IN PETROLEUM REFINING. ED2. NEW YORK, 1962.

AMERICAN SOCIETY FOR TESTING/MATERIALS. ASTM STANDARDS ON SOAPS AND OTHER DETERGENTS... DEFINITIONS OF TERMS. ED9. PHILADELPHIA, 1960. 272P. 61-16067.

AMERICAN SOCIETY FOR TESTING/MATERIALS. DEFINITIONS OF TERMS RELATING TO ATMOSPHERIC SAMPLING AND ANALYSIS. (D1356-60) ASTM STDS, PT. 10, 1681-6. PHILADELPHIA, 1961. 100T.

AMERICAN SOCIETY FOR TESTING/MATERIALS. STANDARD DEFINITIONS OF TERMS RELATING TO ADHESIVES. (D907-60) ASTM STDS,PT.6. 504-12. PHILADELPHIA 1961. 180T.

AMERICAN SOCIETY FOR TESTING/MATERIALS. STANDARD DEFINITIONS OF TERMS RELATING TO MAGNESIUM OXYCHLORIDE AND MAGNESIUM OXYSULFATE CEMENTS. (C376-58) ASTM STDS, PT.4, 416-7. PHILADELPHIA, 1961. 20T.

AMERICAN SOCIETY FOR TESTING/MATERIALS. STANDARD DEFINITIONS OF TERMS RELATING TO PAINT, VARNISH, LACQUER AND RELATED PRODUCTS (D16-59) ASTM STDS, PT.8, 1133-8. PHILADELPHIA, 1961. 120T.

AMERICAN SOCIETY FOR TESTING/MATERIALS. TENTATIVE DEFINITIONS OF TERMS AND SYMBOLS RELATING TO ABSORPTION SPECTROSCOPY. (E131-62T) ASTM STDS, SUPPL, PT.7, 280-2. PHILADELPHIA, 1962. 50T.

AMERICAN SOCIETY FOR TESTING/MATERIALS. TENTATIVE DEFINITIONS OF TERMS RELATING TO CELLULOSE AND CELLULOSE DERIVATIVES. (D1695-60T) ASTM STDS, PT.6, 1182-7. PHILADELPHIA, 1961. 150T.

AMERICAN SOCIETY FOR TESTING/MATERIALS. TENTATIVE DEFINITIONS OF TERMS RELATING TO DENSITY AND SPECIFIC GRAVITY OF SOLIDS, LIQUIDS, AND GASES. (E12-61T) ASTM STDS, PT.4, 1627-30. PHILADELPHIA, 1961. 10T.

AMERICAN SOCIETY FOR TESTING/MATERIALS. TENTATIVE DEFINITIONS OF TERMS AND SYMBOLS RELATING TO EMISSION SPECTROSCOPY. (E135-60T) ASTM STDS, PT.7, 1597-1600. PHILADELPHIA, 1961. 70T.

AMERICAN SOCIETY FOR TESTING/MATERIALS. TENTATIVE DEFINITIONS OF TERMS RELATING TO SOAPS AND OTHER DETERGENTS. (D459-58T) ASTM STDS, PT.10, 1137-9. PHILADELPHIA, 1961.60T.

AMERICAN STANDARDS ASSOCIATION. LETTER SYMBOLS FOR CHEMICAL ENGINEERING. (Y10.12) NEW YORK, 1961.

ANDERSON, E. ET AL. PERFUME GLOSSARY. ED3. LONDON, FRAGRANCE BUR, 1959. 54P.

BALLENTYNE, D.W.G. AND WALKER, L.E.Q. A DICTIONARY OF NAMED EFFECTS AND LAWS IN CHEMISTRY, PHYSICS, AND MATHEMATICS. ED2. NEW YORK, MACMILLAN, 1961. 234P. 61-1620. 1200T.

BENNETT, H. ET AL. THE CHEMICAL FORMULARY... NEW YORK, VAN NOSTRAND, 1933-1961. 11V. (INDEX TO V.1-10, 1958) 33-36898. 50000T.

BENNETT, H. CONCISE CHEMICAL AND TECHNICAL DICTIONARY. ED2. NEW YORK, CHEMICAL, 1962. 1039P. 62-4271. 60000T.

BENNETT, H. ET AL. NEW FORMULAS FOR PROFIT... CLEVELAND, WORLD, 1957. 674P. 57-4308.

BLACKSHAW, H. AND BRIGHTMAN, R. DICTIONARY OF DYEING AND TEXTILE PRINTING. NEW YORK, INTERSCIENCE, 1961. 221P. 61-65748. 2000T.

BRITISH STANDARDS INSTITUTION. GLOSSARY OF PAINT TERMS. (B.S.2015) LONDON, 1953. 44P. 300T.

BRITISH STANDARDS INSTITUTION. GLOSSARY OF TERMS RELATING TO GAS CHROMATOGRAPHY. (B.S. 3282) LONDON, 1963. 11P. 40T.

BRITISH STANDARDS INSTITUTION. LETTER SYMBOLS, SIGNS AND ABBREVIATIONS. PT.2 CHEMICAL ENGINEERING, NUCLEAR SCIENCE AND APPLIED CHEMISTRY. (B.S. 1991) LONDON, 1961. 48P. 550T.

BRITISH STANDARDS INSTITUTION. RECOMMENDED COMMON NAMES FOR PESTICIDES. (B.S.1831) LONDON, 1961. 52P. 120T. SUPPL,1962. 7P. 10T.

BRITISH STANDARDS INSTITUTION. RECOMMENDED NAMES FOR CHEMICALS USED IN INDUSTRY. (B.S.2474, AMEND. PD2440) LONDON, 1954-56. 64P. 2000T.

CAHN, R.S. AN INTRODUCTION TO CHEMICAL NOMENCLATURE. LONDON, BUTTERWORTHS, 1959. 96P. 60-3121.

CHEMICAL SOCIETY, LONDON. HANDBOOK FOR CHEMICAL SOCIETY AUTHORS. LONDON, 1960. 224P. A61-1835.

CLARK, G.L. ET AL. THE ENCYCLOPEDIA OF CHEMISTRY. NEW YORK, REINHOLD, 1957. 1037P. 57-7142. 3000T. SUPPL, 1958. 330P.

CLARK, G.L. ET AL. THE ENCYCLOPEDIA OF SPECTROSCOPY. NEW YORK, REINHOLD, 1960. 787P. 60-53028.

CHEMISTRY AND CHEMICAL ENGINEERING

ENGLISH

CROSLAND, M.P. HISTORICAL STUDIES IN THE LANGUAGE OF CHEMISTRY. CAMBRIDGE, HARVARD UNIV. PRESS, 1962. 406P. 62-53151.

DE NAVARRE, M.G. INDUSTRIAL ENCYCLOPEDIA OF COSMETIC MATERIAL TRADE NAMES. NEW YORK, MOORE, 1957. 369P. 57-2553.

EVANS, R.S. A DICTIONARY OF PH APPLICATIONS. LONDON, HERBERT, 1957. 78P.

FLECK, H.R. SYNTHETIC DRUGS... LONDON, CLEAVER-HUME, 1955. 380P. A56-3392.

FLOOD, W.E. THE DICTIONARY OF CHEMICAL NAMES. NEW YORK, PHIL. LIBR, 1963. 238P. 63-5578. 1800T.

FREEMAN, M. PRACTICAL AND INDUSTRIAL FORMULARY. NEW YORK, CHEMICAL, 1962. 297P. 62-5090.

GALLANT, R.A. THE ABC,S OF CHEMISTRY. GARDEN CITY, N.Y, DOUBLEDAY, 1963. 88P. 62-7526.

GILMAN, A.F. JR. A DICTIONARY OF CHEMICAL EQUATIONS. ED9. CHICAGO, ECLECTIC, 1961. 880P. 62-524.

GREENBERG, L.A. ET AL. HANDBOOK OF COSMETIC MATERIALS... NEW YORK, INTERSCIENCE, 1954. 455P. 54-7989. 1000T.

HACKH, I.W. AND GRANT, J. CHEMICAL DICTIONARY. ED4. NEW YORK, MCGRAW-HILL, 1963. (IN PREP) 80000T.

HAYNES, W. CHEMICAL TRADE NAMES AND COMMERCIAL SYNONYMS, A DICTIONARY OF AMERICAN USAGE. ED2. PRINCETON, N.J. VAN NOSTRAND, 1955. 466P. 55-9902. 20000T.

HEILBRON, I. AND BUNBURY, H.M. DICTIONARY OF ORGANIC COMPOUNDS... ED4. LONDON, EYRE/SPOTTISWOODE, 1953. 4V. 3095P. 54-930.

HENDERSON, J.G. AND BATES, J.M. METALLURGICAL DICTIONARY. NEW YORK, REINHOLD, 1953. 396P. 53-12371.4000T.

HONIG, J.M. ET AL. THE VAN NOSTRAND CHEMIST,S DICTIONARY. NEW YORK, VAN NOSTRAND, 1953. 761P. 53-10098. 10000T.

INFORMATION FOR INDUSTRY, INC. PRINCIPAL CHEMICAL AND CHEMICALLY RELATED TERMS USED IN U.S. PATENTS... WASHINGTON, SPARTAN, 1962. 80P. 62-22338.

INFORMATION FOR INDUSTRY, INC. VOCABULARY OF PRINCIPAL MAJOR TERMS USED IN THE UNITERM INDEX TO CHEMICAL PATENTS. WASHINGTON, 1962. UNPAGED. 62-52469.

INTERNATIONAL UNION OF PURE AND APPLIED CHEMISTRY. NOMENCLATURE OF ORGANIC CHEMISTRY, 1957. LONDON, BUTTERWORTHS, 1958. 92P. 59-3118.

INTERNATIONAL UNION OF PURE AND APPLIED CHEMISTRY. A PROPOSED INTERNATIONAL CHEMICAL NOTATION... NEW YORK LONGMANS, GREEN, 1958. 165P. 58-59970.

INTERNATIONAL UNION OF PURE AND APPLIED CHEMISTRY. RULES FOR I.U.P.A.C. NOTATION FOR ORGANIC COMPOUNDS. NEW YORK, WILEY, 1962. 107P. 62-4916.

JACOBSON, C.A. AND HAMPEL, C.A. ENCYCLOPEDIA OF CHEMICAL REACTIONS. NEW YORK, REINHOLD. 8V. 1946-59. 46-822.

JOHNSTON, H.W. A SHORT DICTIONARY OF TERMS USED MAINLY IN PEST CONTROL. WELLINGTON, IMP. CHEM. IND, 1959. 13P. 60-45385.

JOSEPHY, E. RADT,F, ET AL. ELSEVIER,S ENCYCLOPEDIA OF ORGANIC CHEMISTRY. NEW YORK, ELSEVIER, 1940-56, BERLIN, SPRINGER, 1959- . 14V, SEVERAL SUPPL. (IN PROGR)

KINGZETT,S CHEMICAL ENCYCLOPAEDIA... ED8. LONDON. BAILLIERE, TINDALL/COX, 1952. 1186P. 52-3303.

KIRK, R.A. AND OTHMER, D.F. ENCYCLOPEDIA OF CHEMICAL TECHNOLOGY. ED2. NEW YORK, INTERSCIENCE, 1963- (ED2, 18V, IN PREP) 63-14348.

LENNOX-KERR, P. INDEX TO MAN-MADE FIBRES OF THE WORLD. MANCHESTER, ENG, MAN-MADE TEXTILES, 1961. 117P. 62-51652.

MARK, H.F. AND GAYLORD, N.G. ENCYCLOPEDIA OF POLYMER SCIENCE AND TECHNOLOGY. NEW YORK, INTERSCIENCE. (IN PREP)

MARTIN, J.H. AND MORGANS, W.M. GUIDE TO PIGMENTS AND TO VARNISH AND LACQUER CONSTITUENTS. NEW YORK, CHEMICAL, 1959. 111P. 54-42002. 1500T.

MAXWELL, I.R. ET AL. THE INTERNATIONAL ENCYCLOPEDIA OF PHYSICAL CHEMISTRY AND CHEMICAL PHYSICS. NEW YORK 1960--V.1- (SEVERAL V. IN PREP)

MELLAN, I. DICTIONARY OF POISONS. NEW YORK, PHIL. LIBR, 1956. 150P. 56-59060.

MELLAN, I. AND E. ENCYCLOPEDIA OF CHEMICAL LABELING. NEW YORK, CHEMICAL, 1961. 111P. 61-66272.

MERRIMAN, A.D. A DICTIONARY OF METALLURGY. LONDON, MACDONALD/EVANS, 1958. 401P. 59-480. 4000T.

MIALL, L.M. A NEW DICTIONARY OF CHEMISTRY. ED3. NEW YORK, INTERSCIENCE, 1961. 593P. 62-2038. 4800T.

CHEMISTRY AND CHEMICAL ENGINEERING

ENGLISH

MODERN DRUG ENCYCLOPEDIA AND THERAPEUTIC INDEX. ED8. NEW YORK, DRUG PUBL, 1961. 1649P. 34-12823.

MOORE,H.C. DICTIONARY OF PLANT FOODS. PHILADELPHIA, 1955. 111P. 55-4492.

PATAI, S. GLOSSARY OF ORGANIC CHEMISTRY, INCLUDING PHYSICAL ORGANIC CHEMISTRY. NEW YORK, INTERSCIENCE, 1962. 227P. 62-12995. 700T.

PATTERSON, A.M. ET AL. THE RING INDEX...ED2. WASHINGTON, AM. CHEM. SOC, 1960. 1425P. A61-610.

PATTERSON, A.M. WORDS ABOUT WORDS, A COLLECTION OF NOMENCLATURE COLUMNS. WASHINGTON, AM. CHEM. SOC, 1957 86P. 57-59079.

PETROLEUM EDUCATIONAL INSTITUTE. ILLUSTRATED PETROLEUM DICTIONARY AND PRODUCTS MANUAL. LOS ANGELES, 1962. 754P. 62-18323. 10000T.

THE PHARMACOPEIA OF THE U.S.A. ED16. WASHINGTON, U.S. PHARM. CONV, 1960. 1148P. 35-37146.

POSER, C.M. AND OSBOURN, V. THE INTERNATIONAL DICTIONARY OF DRUGS USED IN NEUROLOGY AND PSYCHIATRY. SPRINGFIELD, ILL, THOMAS, 1962. 157P. 62-17611.

ROSE, A. AND E. THE CONDENSED CHEMICAL DICTIONARY. ED6. NEW YORK, REINHOLD, 1961. 1256P. 61-14790. 18000T.

SISLEY,J.P. AND WOOD,P.J. ENCYCLOPEDIA OF SURFACE-ACTIVE AGENTS... (TRANSL. OF INDEX DES HUILES SULFONEES ET DETERGENTS MODERNES) NEW YORK, CHEMICAL, 1952. 540P. 52-12985.

SNELL, F.D. AND C.T. DICTIONARY OF COMMERCIAL CHEMICALS. ED3. PRINCETON, N.J. VAN NOSTRAND, 1962. 714P. 62-3474. 3000T.

STECHER, P.G. ET AL. THE MERCK INDEX OF CHEMICALS AND DRUGS, AN ENCYCLOPEDIA FOR CHEMISTS, PHARMACISTS... ED7. RAHWAY, N.J, MERCK, 1960. 1641P. 60-S088.

STEWART, J.R. AND SPICER, F.E. AN ENCYCLOPEDIA OF THE CHEMICAL PROCESS INDUSTRIES. NEW YORK, CHEMICAL, 1956. 820P. 56-2478. 4000T.

SURREY, A.R. NAME REACTIONS IN ORGANIC CHEMISTRY. ED2. NEW YORK, ACADEMIC, 1961. 278P. 54-7611. 120T.

THORPE, J.F. ET AL. DICTIONARY OF APPLIED CHEMISTRY. ED4. NEW YORK, LONGMANS, GREEN, 1937-56. 12V. 37-28650.

TULI, G.D. AND SONI, P.L. THE LANGUAGE OF CHEMISTRY, CHEMICAL EQUATIONS... ED12. DELHI, PREMIER, 1962. 76P. 5A63-21.

UVAROV, E.B. AND CHAPMAN, D.R. A DICTIONARY OF SCIENCE... BALTIMORE, PENGUIN, 1959. 239P. 60-2541. 3500T

WHEELER, T.S. AND GOWAN, J.E. NAME INDEX OF ORGANIC REACTIONS. NEW YORK, INTERSCIENCE, 1960. 293P. 60-14001.

WHITE, J.H. A REFERENCE BOOK OF CHEMISTRY. LONDON, UNIV. LONDON PRESS, 1960. 302P. 61-66498. 3000T.

WINBURNE,J. A DICTIONARY OF AGRICULTURAL AND ALLIED TERMINOLOGY. EAST LANSING, MICH. STATE UNIV.PRESS, 1962. 905P. 62-9169. 30000T.

WITTY, M.B. ET AL. DICTIONARY OF BIO-CHEMISTRY ABBREVIATIONS. NEW YORK, SETI, 196 .

WITTY, M.B. ET AL. DICTIONARY OF CHEMICAL ABBREVIATIONS, SIGNS, SYMBOLS AND TABLES. NEW YORK, SETI, 1961. 416P.

WITTY, M.B. ET AL. DICTIONARY OF CHEMICAL ENGINEERING ABBREVIATIONS, SIGNS AND SYMBOLS. NEW YORK, SETI, 1963. 384P.

WOLDMAN, N.E. ENGINEERING ALLOYS. ED4. NEW YORK, REINHOLD, 1962. 62-19661. 35000T.

ESPERANTO

DUNCAN, D. ENGLISH-ESPERANTO CHEMICAL DICTIONARY. LONDON, BRIT.ESPERANTO ASSOC. 1956. 56P. 2800T.

FINNISH

KARAMAKI,E.M. KEMIALLISTA TAVARAOPPIA, KANSAINVALISEN TULLITARIFFIJA TILASTONIMIKKEISTON MUKAAN... (CHEM. D, FI DEFS) HELSINKI, SOEDERSTROEM, 1962. 695P.

FRENCH

BADER, O. AND THERET, M. DICTIONNAIRE DE METALLURGIE. (MET.D, *EN*FR) PARIS, EYROLLES, 1961. 701P. A62-812. 1400T.

CHARLES, V. VOCABULAIRE DU METALLURGISTE... (MET. GL, FR DEFS) PARIS, GAUTHIER-VILLARS, 1956. 166P. 57-22265. 1700T.

CORNUBERT, R. DICTIONNAIRE CHIMIQUE ANGLAIS-FRANCAIS... (EN*FR CHEM. D) ED3. PARIS, DUNOD, 1963. 223P. 63-28251.

FRENCH

DE VRIES, L. FRENCH-ENGLISH SCIENCE DICTIONARY... ED3. NEW YORK, MCGRAW-HILL, 1962. 655P. 61-17943. 53000T.

DURIEZ,M. AND ARRAMBIDE,J. LIANTS HYDROCARBONES, MORTIERS ET BETONS BITUMINEUX. (HYDROCARB. BONDING AGENTS, MORTARS/BIT, CONCRETE,FR DEFS) PARIS, DUNOD,1954. 728P.

DUVAL, C. ET AL. DICTIONNAIRE DE LA CHIMIE ET DE SES APPLICATIONS. (D. OF CHEM/APPL, FR DEFS) ED2. PARIS, PRESSES SCI. INTL, 1959. 1330P. 61-4817.

GRANDERYE, L.M. DICTIONNAIRE DE CHIMIE. (CHEM. D, FR DEFS) PARIS, DUNOD, 1962. 655P. 63-26949.

INTERNATIONAL UNION OF PURE AND APPLIED CHEMISTRY, MANUAL OF PHYSICO-CHEMICAL SYMBOLS AND TERMINOLOGY. (EN*FR) LONDON, BUTTERWORTHS, 1959. 27P. 60-4395.

INTERNATIONAL UNION OF PURE AND APPLIED CHEMISTRY. NOMENCLATURE OF INORGANIC CHEMISTRY... (EN*FR, 1957 REPT) LONDON, BUTTERWORTHS, 1959. 93P. 60-1567.

LEXIQUE TECHNIQUE DES PRODUITS CHIMIQUES. (D. OF CHEM, FR DEFS) ED14. PARIS, ROUSSET, 1960. 2V. 1360P. 62-28010.

MENSIER,P.H. DICTIONNAIRE DES HUILES VEGETALES. (VEGETABLE OILS D, FR DEFS) PARIS, LECHEVALIER, 1957. 763P.

PATTERSON, A.M. A FRENCH-ENGLISH DICTIONARY FOR CHEMISTS. ED2. NEW YORK, WILEY, 1954. 476P. 54-.661. 42000T.

PROULX, G. ELECTROCHIMIE ET ELECTROMETALLURGIE, GLOSSAIRE ANGLAIS-FRANCIS, BT-48. (ELECTROCHEM/ ELECTROMET, EN*FR GL) OTTAWA, DEPT. SECY. STATE, 1956. 21P. 500T.

QUERE, H. AND BENAMOU, M. VOCABULAIRE TECHNIQUE ANGLAIS-FRANCAIS DE LA CHIMIE DU PETROLE. (EN*FR D. OF PETROL. CHEM) PARIS, DUNOD, 1957. 122P. 58-2855. 300T.

ROUSSET, H. (CHAPLET,A. PSEUD) DICTIONNAIRE DES PRODUITS CHIMIQUES COMMERCIAUX ET DES DROGUES INDUSTRIELLES. (D. OF COM. CHEM/ DRUGS, FR. DEFS) ED5. PARIS, DUNOD, 1957. 564P.

UVAROV, E.B. ET AL. DICTIONNAIRE DES SCIENCES... (SCI.D, FR DEFS) PARIS, PRESSES UNIV. FRANCE, 1956. 325P. 58-2097. 3500T.

GERMAN

BABEL, E. ET AL. ABC DER ANSTRICHSTOFFE UND ANSTRICHTECHNIK. (ABC OF PAINT TECH,GE DEFS) ED3. LEIPZIG, FACHBUCHVERLAG, 1960. 394P.

BERGWEIN,K. FACHWOERTER DER KOSMETIK MIT GRUND- UND HILFSSTOFFEN FUER DIE KOSMETISCHE INDUSTRIE. (COSMETICS IND.T, GE DEFS) 1957.

BLASBERG-LEXIKON FUER KORROSIONSSCHUTZ UND MODERNE GALVANOTECHNIK. (ANTI-CORROSION/METAL-PLATING D, GE DEFS) ED3. SAULGAU, WUERTTEMBERG, LEUZE, 1960. 366P. 500T.

BODENBENDER,H.G. CHEMISCH-TECHNISCHES SPEZIAL-LEXIKON...(CHEM. D, GE DEFS) BERLIN, CHEM/TECH, 1952. 396P

DETTNER, H.W. FACHWOERTERBUCH FUER DIE METALLOBERFLAECHENVEREDELUNG... (*GE*EN D. OF MET. FINISHING) BERLIN, SIEMENS, 1960. 391P. A60-5542. 8500T.

DE VRIES, L. ET AL. GERMAN-ENGLISH SCIENCE DICTIONARY... ED3. NEW YORK, MCGRAW-HILL, 1959. 592P. 59-9412 40000T.

DEVRIES, L. ET AL. WOFRTERBUCH DER CHEMIE. (CHEM. D, V.1, GE*EN, V.2, EN*GE) WEINHEIM, CHEMIE. (IN PREP)

DYCKERHOFF, H. WOERTERBUCH DER PHYSIOLOGISCHEN CHEMIE FUER MEDIZINER. (PHYSIOL. CHEM. FOR PHYSICIANS, G DEFS) BERLIN, DE GRUYTER, 1955. 175P. A55-3360.

ELMER, T.H. GERMAN-ENGLISH DICTIONARY OF GLASS, CERAMICS, AND ALLIED SCIENCES. NEW YORK, INTERSCIENCE 1963. 304P. 63-17477. 21000T.

ERNST, A. AND NEUMANN, L. AUSKUNFTSBUCH FUER DIE CHEMISCHE INDUSTRIE. (CHEM. IND. ENCYCL, GE DEFS) ED1 BERLIN, DE GRUYTER, 1954. 1386P. 54-3312.

ERNST, R. AND ERNST VON MORGENSTERN, I. CONCISE GERMAN-ENGLISH CHEMICAL DICTIONARY... NEW YORK, CROWEL 1961. 727P. 61-17109. 36000T.

ERNST, R. AND ERNST VON MORGENSTERN, I. DICTIONARY OF CHEMISTRY, INCLUDING CHEMICAL ENGINEERING AND FUNDAMENTALS OF ALLIED SCIENCES. (V.1 GE*EN, 727P, 45000T. V.2, *EN*GE, 1056P, 65000T) WIESBADEN, BRANDSTETTER, 1961-63. 62-4596.

FOERST, W. ULLMANN,S ENZYKLOPAEDIE DER TECHNISCHEN CHEMIE. (ULLMANN,S ENCYCL. OF CHEM. ENG, GE DEFS) ED MUNICH, URBAN/ SCHWARZENBERG, 1955-- . (IN PROGR)

FROMHERZ, H. AND KING, A. ENGLISCHE UND DEUTSCHE CHEMISCHE FACHAUSDRUECKE... (GE*EN CHEM.T) ED4. WEINHEIM, CHEMIE, 1963. 616P. 10000T.

CHEMISTRY AND CHEMICAL ENGINEERING

GERMAN

BAEGELE,G. DAS KLEINE LEXIKON DER CHEMIE. (CHEM.D,GE DEFS) STUTTGART, UNION DEUT. VERLAGSGES, 1952.
184P. 53-27014.

HUNNIUS, C. PHARMAZEUTISCHES WOERTERBUCH. (PHARM.D, GE DEFS) ED3. BERLIN, DE GRUYTER, 1959. 731P.
59-5762.

IRION,H. DROGISTEN-LEXIKON... (PHARM. D, GE DEFS) BERLIN, SPRINGER, 1955. 2V. IN 3. 56-26688.

IVANOVSKY, L. WACHS ENZYKLOPAEDIE. (WAX ENCYCL, GE DEFS) AUGSBURG, CHEM.IND, 1954-- 2V. 54-28895.

JANSEN, H. AND MACKENSEN, L. RECHTSCHREIBUNG DER TECHNISCHEN UND CHEMISCHEN FREMDWOERTER...(ORTHOGRAPHY
OF TECH/CHEM.WORDS OF FOR. ORIGIN, GE DEFS) DUESSELDORF, VDI, 1959. 267P. 61-40164. 10000T.

OGLIN, W. KURZES HANDBUCH DER CHEMIE... (HANDBOOK OF CHEM, GE DEFS) GOETTINGEN, VANDENHOECK/RUPRECHT,
1951-54. 4V.IN 3. 52-30552.

RETSCHMER, R. TEXTILFAERBEREI UND ANGRENZENDE GEBIETE. ENGLISCH-DEUTSCH, DEUTSCH-ENGLISCH. (TEXTILE
DYEING..., *GE*EN D) BERLIN, TECHNIK, 1961. 181P. 4600T.

LEIBIGER, O.W. AND LEIBIGER, I.S. GERMAN-ENGLISH AND ENGLISH-GERMAN DICTIONARY FOR SCIENTISTS. ANN
ARBOR, MICH, EDWARDS, 1959. (REPR) 741P.

MERZ, O.A. DEUTSCH-ENGLISCHES UND ENGLISCH-DEUTSCHES FACHWOERTERBUCH FUER FACHAUSDRUECKE AUS DEM LACK-
UND FARBENGEBIET. (*GE*EN D. OF LACQUER/PAINT) ED2. STUTTGART, WISSENSCHAFTLICHE-VERLAG,1954. 351P.
55-22330. 4400T.

NEVILLE, H.H. AND JOHNSTON, N.C. A NEW GERMAN-ENGLISH DICTIONARY FOR CHEMISTS. PRINCETON, N.J,
VAN NOSTRAND, 1964. 330P. 40000T.

PATTERSON, A.M. A GERMAN-ENGLISH DICTIONARY FOR CHEMISTS. ED3. NEW YORK, WILEY, 1959. 541P. 59000T.

ROEMPP, H. CHEMIE LEXIKON. (ENCYCL. OF CHEM, GE DEFS) ED5. STUTTGART, FRANCKH, 1962. 3V. 63-29758.
29000T.

TECHNOLOGICAL DICTIONARY FOR INDUSTRIES CONSUMING DYESTUFFS AND TEXTILE AUXILIARIES. PT.1, EN*GE, 627P.
PT.2, GE*EN, 489P. FRANKFURT, FARBWERKE HOECHST, 1952.

VEREIN DEUTSCHER EISENHUETTENLEUTE. STAHLEISEN-WOERTERBUCH, DEUTSCH-ENGLISCH, ENGLISCH-DEUTSCH. (*GE*EN
IRON/STEEL D) ED2. DUESSELDORF, STAHLEISEN, 1962. 338P. 63-34657.

HEBREW

VAAD HA-LASHON HA-IVRIT BE-ERETS-YISRAEL. MUNAHE KHIMIYAH. (CHEM. T, HE*EN) JERUSLAEM, 1950/51. 11P.
56-55635.

HINDI

AUSHAL, S.C. CHEMICAL ENGINEERING, ENGLISH-HINDI DICTIONARY. ALLAHABAD, HINDI SAHITYA SAMMELAN, 1950.
00T.

AUSHAL, S.C. FERMENTATION TECHNOLOGY, ENGLISH-HINDI DICTIONARY. ALLAHABAD, HINDI SAHITYA SAMMELAN,
950. 600T.

AUSHAL, S.C. MINERAL OILS AND BY-PRODUCTS, ENGLISH-HINDI DICTIONARY. ALLAHABAD, HINDI SAHITYA SAMMELAN,
950. 350T.

AUSHAL, S.C. OILS, FATS, AND WAXES, ENGLISH-HINDI DICTIONARY. ALLAHABAD, HINDI SAHITYA SAMMELAN, 1950.
00T.

AUSHAL, S.C. SUGAR TECHNOLOGY, ENGLISH-HINDI DICTIONARY. ALLAHABAD, HINDI SAHITYA SAMMELAN, 1950. 900T.

ALAVIYA, B.K. BIOCHEMISTRY, ENGLISH-HINDI DICTIONARY. ALLAHABAD, HINDI SAHITYA SAMMELAN, 1950. 6000T.

ARMA, P. GAS, GAS INSTRUMENTS AND DISTILLERY, ENGLISH-HINDI DICTIONARY. ALLAHABAD, HINDI SAHITYA
AMMELAN, 1950.

INDONESIAN

INDONESIAN CHEMICAL NOMENCLATURE. DJAKARTA, COUNCIL FOR SCI. INDONESIA, 1957. 35P. 58-27790.

INTISARI TATANAMA. KIMIA ANORGANIK DAN KIMIA ORGANIK BESERTA KAMUS ISTILAH KIMIA... (INORG/ORG. CHEM. D)
JAKARTA, DINAS PENERBITAN BALAI PUSTAKA, 1956. 99P. 2000T.

ITALIAN

GHINA, L. DIZIONARIO TECNICO ITALIANO-INGLESE CON PARTICOLARE RIFERIMENTO ALLA INDUSTRIA CHIMICA. (IT*EN
ECH/CHEM.D) FLORENCE, VALLECCHI, 1961. 431P. A61-3420. 12000T.

ARBONI, P. NUOVISSIMA ENCICLOPEDIA DI. CHIMICA E MERCEOLOGIA... (ENCYCL.OF CHEM/CHEM.PROD, IT DEFS)
ILAN, GOERLICH, 1959. 1072P. 60-42521. 2000T.

APASOGLI, E. DIZIONARIO DELLA CHIMICA MODERNA. (D. OF MODERN CHEM, IT DEFS) FLORENCE, CYA, 1955. 427P.
6-42621.

33

CHEMISTRY AND CHEMICAL ENGINEERING

ITALIAN

UVAROV, E.B. ET AL. DIZIONARIO DELLE SCIENZE. (SCI. D, IT DEFS) MILAN, 1957.

JAPANESE

CHIYODA KAKO KENSETSU GIJUTSUBU. SEKIYU KAGAKU YOGO JITEN. (PETROL. CHEM. D, EN*JA) TOKYO, SEKYU KOGYO JIHYO, 1960. 106P. 1200T.

HASHIMOTO, Y. EI-WA WA-EI SHIN KAGAKU YOGO JITEN. (NEW *EN*JA CHEM. D, EN*JA, 10000T. JA*EN, 45000T) TOKYO, SANKYO, 1957. 484P. J61-833.

INOUE, T. ET AL. IWANAMI,S DICTIONARY OF PHYSICS AND CHEMISTRY. (*JA*EN) TOKYO, IWANAMI,1953. 1475+66+121P.

INSTITUTE OF CHEMICAL EDUCATION IN UNIVERSITIES. STUDENTS, DICTIONARY OF CHEMICAL TERMS. (EN*JA) TOKYO, KYORITSU, 1956. 268P.

ISHII, Y. KAGAKU, RIKAGAKU, KOGYOKAGAKU, NETSU, NENSHO KANKEI EI-WA JUKUGO JITEN. (SCI, PHYS, CHEM, IND CHEM.TECH.D, EN*JA) OSAKA, NENRYO OYOBI NENRYOSHA, 1958. 464P. J62-27. 35000T.

ISHIBASHI, K. SEKIYU KAGAKU JITEN. (PETROL.CHEM.D,*JA*EN) TOKYO, NIKKAN KOGYO SHIMBUNSHA, 1958. 245+46P. J62-1537. 3000T.

JAPAN. MINISTRY OF EDUCATION. JAPANESE SCIENTIFIC TERMS, CHEMISTRY, (*JA*EN) TOKYO, NANKODO, 1955. 457P. 6600T.

MATSUDA, M. NEW ENGLISH-JAPANESE CHEMICAL DICTIONARY. (EN*JA) TOKYO, KEIBUNSHA, 1961. 1120P. J62-74. 20000T.

NEW ENGLISH-JAPANESE DICTIONARY FOR CHEMISTS. TOKYO, 1958. 653P.

NIPPON GAKUJUTSU SHINKOKAI. DAI 120 (SENSHOKU KAKO) IINKAI. SENI SENSHOKU KAKO JITEN. (TEXTILE DYE/FINISH. D, *JA*EN) TOKYO, NIKKAN KOGYO SHIMBUNSHA, 1962. 605+39P, J63-101. 3900T.

RIKAGAKU JITEN. (JA*EN D. OF PHYS/CHEM) TOKYO, FUZAMBO, 1959. 938P.

SHIN·KAGAKU JITEN. (CHEM. D, *JA*EN) TOKYO, NIKKAN KOGYO SHIMBUNSHA, 1958. 1137+204P. J58-4075. 20000T.

SOCIETY OF CHEMICAL ENGINEERS, JAPAN. DICTIONARY OF CHEMICAL ENGINEERING... (JA EN) TOKYO, MARUZEN, 1953. 243P.

SODA, T. KAGOBUTSU JITEN. (CHEM. COMPOUND D. *JA*EN) TOKYO, KYORITSU, 1954. 456+28+38P. J59-324. 7000T.

TSUDA, M. ET AL. DICTIONARY OF CHEMICAL PRODUCTS. (JA EN) TOKYO, DOBUNKAN, 1954. 1090P.

POLISH

BANKOWSKI, Z. AND RADZIWILL, K. SLOWNIK CHEMICZNY ANGIELSKO-POLSKI. (EN*PL CHEM. D) WARSAW, PANSTW. WYDAW. TECH, 1957. 838P. 58-15224. 42000T.

MIODUSZEWSKI, F. SLOWNIK CHEMICZNO-FARMACEUTYCZNY ANGIELSKO-POLSKI I POLSKO-ANGIELSKI. (*PL*EN CHEM/ PHARM.D) (V.1 EN*PL, 347P, V.2 PL*EN, IN PREP) WARSAW, PANSTW. ZAKLAD WYDAW. LEK, 1956-   . 58-30603. 13000T.

POLYGLOT

CARRIERE, G. DETERGENTS, A GLOSSARY OF TERMS USED IN THE DETERGENTS INDUSTRY... (FK*EN/17LANG) NEW YOR ELSEVIER, 1960. 141P. 60-16596. 260T.

CENTRE DE DOCUMENTATION SIDERURGIQUE. DICTIONNAIRE SIDERURGIQUE. (MET.D, CZ EN FR GE IT PR RU SP SW) PARIS, 1953.

CHUNG-KUO K,O HSUEH YUAN. PIEN I CHU. (ACAD. SINICA. BUR. COMPIL/TRANSL) O CHUNG YING HUA HSUEH HUA KUNG SHU YU. (RU*CH*EN CHEM/CHEM. ENG. T) PEKING, 1955. 771P. C58-5278.

CHUNG-KUO K,O HSUEH YUAN. PIEN I CH,U PAN WEI YUAN HUI. (ACAD. SINICA. COMM. OF PUBL/TRANSL) O CHUNG YI WU CHI HUA HO WU MING TZ,U. (RU*CH*EN INORG. COMPOUNDS D) PEKING, SCIENCE, 1956. 120P. C58-5258.

CHUNG-KUO K,O HSUEH YUAN. PIEN I CH,U PAN WEI YUAN HUI. (ACAD. SINICA. COMM. OF PUBL/TRANSL) O CHUNG YING YU·CHI JAN LIAO MING TZ,U. (RU*EN*CH ORG. DYE T) PEKING, SCIENCE, 1956. 233P. C58-5804.

CLASON, W.E. DICTIONARY OF CHEMICAL ENGINEERING. (*EN/AM*FR*SP*DU*GE)NEW YORK, ELSEVIER. (IN PREP)

CLASON, W.E. DICTIONARY OF SCIENTIFIC APPARATUS. (*EN/AM*DU*FR*GE*IT*SP) NEW YORK, ELSEVIER. (IN PREP)

CLASON, W.E. ELSEVIER,S DICTIONARY OF METALLURGY,*DU*EN*FR*GE*IT*SP) NEW YORK, ELSEVIER. 102P. (IN PREP

CLEVELAND, F.F. ET AL. DICTIONARIO MULTILINGUAL PRO LE SPECTROSCOPIA. (PO SPECTRY. D, IA*EN*GE*IT*PR*RU *SP) NEW YORK, STORM, (IN PREP) 1500T.

34

POLYGLOT

COUNCIL OF EUROPE. GLOSSARY IN FIVE LANGUAGES OF PRINCIPAL PHARMACEUTICAL TERMS. (EN FR GE IT DU) STRASBOURG, 1962. 144P. 350T.

CSUROS, Z. ET AL. KEMIA. (CHEM. D,*HU*EN*GE*RU) (MUSZ. ERT. SZ. NO,17-18) BUDAPEST, TERRA, 1961. 403P. 62-66364. 2500T.

FOUCHIER, J. AND BILLET, F. CHEMICAL DICTIONARY.(*EN*FR*GE) ED2. AMSTERDAM, NETHERLANDS UNIV.PRESS, 1961. 3V.IN 1. 1295P. 62-456. 8000T.

GUIDE DE LA CHIMIE. PT.2. NOMENCLATURE DES PRODUITS, CHIMIQUES, NEGOCIANTS. (FR*EN*GE GL. OF CHEM. PROD) PARIS, COLMA, 1954. 786P. 52-29793.

HAFERKORN, R. ET AL. SCIENCA KAJ TEKNIKA TERMINARO,DESTINATA POR KOMPLEMENTI LA PLENAN VORTARON. (SCI/ TECH. T. EO*EN*FR*GE) PARIS, SENNACIECA ASOCIO TUTMONDA, 1956. 248P. 6000T.

HAKKO KOGYO GYO JITEN HENSHU IINKAI. HAKKO YOGO JITEN. (FERMENTATION D, *JA*EN*GE) TOKYO, GIHODO, 1960. 4+372P. J61-629.

HASHIMOTO, Y. TECHNICAL DICTIONARY OF CHEMICAL TERMS...(*JA*GE*EN) TOKYO, JAPAN LIBR. BUR, 1954. 404P. 2000T.

HEINIGE,A. INDEX INTERNATIONALIS PHARMACEUTICUS... (INTL. PHARM. INDEX) PRAGUE, STATNI ZDRAV. NAKL, 1958. 867P. 60-23379.

HUANG, CHEN-HSUN. K,O HSUEH CHI SHU MING TZ,U CHIEH SHIH. (SUGAR CHEM/TECH, CH EN RU) PEKING, 1958. 85P. C59-1206.

INOUE, T. ET AL. IWANAMI RIKAGAKU JITEN. (PHYS/CHEM. D, *JA*EN*FR*GE) ED2. TOKYO, IWANAMI, 1958. 1744P.

INTERNATIONAL ELECTROTECHNICAL COMMISSION. INTERNATIONAL ELECTROTECHNICAL VOCABULARY. ELECTROCHEMISTRY AND ELECTROMETALLURGY, *FR*EN*DU*GE*IT*PL*PR*SP*SW. (IEC-50-GR-50) ED2. GENEVA, (IN PREP)

INTERNATIONAL ENCYCLOPEDIA OF CHEMICAL SCIENCE. (*EN*FR*GE*RU*SP) PRINCETON, N.J, VAN NOSTRAND, 1964. 1331P. 64-1619.

KAGAKU DAIJITEN. (CHEM. ENCYCL, JA*EN*GE) TOKYO, KYORITSU,1960- . J61-355.

KAGAKU JITEN. (CHEM.D, *JA*EN*GE) TOKYO, MARUZEN, 1954. 797P. 4800T.

KAGAKU YOGO JITEN. (CHEM. D, *JA*EN*GE) TOKYO GIHODO, 1958. 650P. J58-4114. 8000T.

MARTINENGHI, G.B. MANUALE PER L,INDUSTRIA ED IL COMMERCIO DEGLI OLII, GRASSI E DERIVATI. (OILS, FATS/ DERIV, IT EN GE D) MILAN, MANFREDI, 1956. 237P. 56-45552.

NAKAYAMA, H. AND IWAMI, H. VOCABULARY OF COMMON GERMAN CHEMICAL TERMS. (GE*EN*JA) TOKYO, DAIGAKU, 1956. 86P.

RAAFF, J.J. INDEX VOCABULORUM QUADRILINGUIS, VERF EN VERNIS... (PAINT/VARNISH D, DU EN FR GE) THE HAGUE, VER.VERNIS/VERFFABRIKANTEN, 1958. 898P. 59-27978. 2300T.

SANTHOLZER, R. AND KORINSKY, J. PETIJAZYCNY SLOVNIK, BARVY, LAKY, POVRCHOVA, UPRAVA, KOROSE. (PAINT, LACQUER/VARNISH CORR D, CZ*EN*FR*GE*RU) ED2. PRAGUE, SNTL, 1956. 436P. 60-37933. 2900T.

SCHLOMANN, A. ET AL. ILLUSTRIERTE TECHNISCHE WOERTERBUECHER. V.2. ELEKTROTECHNIK UND ELEKTROCHEMIE. (ELEC. ENG/ELECTROCHEM, *GE*EN*FR*IT*RU*SP) ED2. BERLIN, OLDENBOURG, 1957. 1304P. 10700T.

SHUNG-MING, W. RUSSIAN-CHINESE-ENGLISH TECHNICAL AND CHEMICAL VOCABULARY. PEKING, ACAD. SINICA, 1961. 279P.

SINDICATO VERTICAL DE INDUSTRIAS QUIMICAS. ANUARIO DE LA INDUSTRIA QUIMICA ESPANOLA. (YEARBOOK OF SP CHEM IND,*FR*EN*GE*SP) BARCELONA, 1953. 737P.

SOBECKA, Z. STEPHEN, H. ET AL. DICTIONARY OF CHEMISTRY AND CHEMICAL TECHNOLOGY, EN*GE*PL*RU. NEW YORK, PERGAMON, 1962. 724P. 62-11564. 12000T.

STOECKHERT, K. KUNSTSTOFF-LEXIKON. (PLAST. D, GE*EN*FR*IT*SP) ED3. MUNICH, HANSER, 1961. 408P. 62-58103.

TEKNISKA NOMENKLATURCENTRALEN. (CORROSION D,SW DEFS, *EN*GE GL) STOCKHOLM,INGENIOERSVETENSKAPSAKADEMIEN, 1957. 72P. 140T.

TEKNISKA NOMENKLATURCENTRALEN. PAINTS AND VARNISHES GLOSSARY. (SW*EN*GE) (TNC PUBL. NO.14) STOCKHOLM, 196 . (REV. ED. IN PREP)

VOTOCEK, E. SESTIJAZYCNY CHEMICKY SLOVNIK... (CHEM. D, CZ*EN*FR*GE*IT*LA) ED2. PRAGUE, TECH. VED. VYDAV, 1952. 685P. 53-21037.

WITTFOHT, A.M. PLASTICS LEXICON, PROCESSING AND MACHINERY, IN GERMAN, ENGLISH, FRENCH, ITALIAN, SPANISH AND DUTCH. NEW YORK, ELSEVIER, 1963. 216P. 1200T.

CHEMISTRY AND CHEMICAL ENGINEERING

RUSSIAN

AKADEMIIA NAUK SSSR. KOM. TEKH. TERM. TERMINOLOGIIA FIZIKO-KHIMICHESKOGO ANALIZA. (PHYSICO-CHEM. ANAL. RU DEFS) (SB. REK. TERM. NO.6) MOSCOW. 1951. P. 54-35373.

AKADEMIIA NAUK SSSR. KOM. TEKH. TERM. TERMINOLOGIIA KHIMICHESKOI TEKHNOLOGII VODY. IDUSHCHEI NA PITANIE PAROVOZNYKH KOTLOV. (CHEM PREP. OF WATER FOR LOCOMOTIVES. RU DEFS) (BIUL. NO.62) MOSCOW. 1952. 240T.

AKADEMIIA NAUK SSSR. KOM. TEKH. TERM. TERMINOLOGIIA PO KORROZII I ZASHCHITE METALLOV. (CORR/ANTI-CORR. OF MET. RU DEFS) (SB. REK. TERM. NO.4) MOSCOW. 1951. 42P. 54-35127.

AKADEMIIA NAUK SSSR. KOM.TEKH.TERM. TERMINOLOGIIA VODOPODGOTOVKI DLIA PAROVYKH KOTLOV. (WATER PROCESS. FOR STEAM BOILERS. RU DEFS) (SB. REK. TERM. NO.38) MOSCOW. 1956. 38P. 56-46923. 250T.

CALLAHAM. L.I. AND UVAROV. E.V. RUSSIAN-ENGLISH CHEMICAL AND POLYTECHNICAL DICTIONARY. ED2. NEW YORK. WILEY. 1962. 892P. 62-18989. 70000T.

CARPOVICH. E.A. AND V.V. RUSSIAN-ENGLISH CHEMICAL DICTIONARY... ED2. NEW YORK. TECH. DICT. 1963. 352P. 63-4199. 25000T.

DERUGUINE. T. RUSSIAN-ENGLISH DICTIONARY OF METALLURGY AND ALLIED SCIENCES. NEW YORK. UNGAR. 1962. 470P. 61-13632. 12000T.

GERTSFELD. K.M. ANGLO-RUSSKII KHIMIKO-TEKHNOLOGICHESKII SLOVAR. (EN*RU D. OF PURE/APPL. CHEM) ED3. MOSCOW. FIZMATGIZ. 1960. 706P. 61-43272. 30000T.

GWIRTSMAN.J.J. ABBREVIATIONS IN RUSSIAN ABSTRACT JOURNALS COVERING CHEMISTRY AND RELATED FIELDS. J. CHEM. DOC. V.3. 44-59 (1963) 700T.

HOSEH. M. RUSSIAN-ENGLISH DICTIONARY OF CHEMICAL AND TECHNICAL TERMS(TENT.TITLE). NEW YORK. REINHOLD. (IN PREP)

JABLONSKI. S. RUSSIAN DRUG INDEX. WASHINGTON. U.S. DEPT. HEW. 1961. 106P. 61-61056.

KEDRINSKII. V.V. ANGLO-RUSSKII SLOVAR PO KHIMII I PERERABOTKE NEFTI. (EN*RU D.OF PETROL. CHEM/REFINING) LENINGRAD. GOSTOPTEKHIZDAT. 1962. 910P. 62-49596. 35000T.

KNUNIANTS.'I.L. ET AL. KRATKAIA KHIMICHESKAIA ENTSIKLOPEDIIA. (CONCISE CHEM. ENCYCL. RU DEFS) MOSCOW. SOV. ENTSIKL. 1961-62. 4V. 62-49800. 5000T.

MACANDREW. A.R. GLOSSARY OF RUSSIAN TECHNICAL TERMS USED IN METALLURGY. NEW YORK. VARANGIAN. 1953. 127P. 53-2032. 6000T.

MIKHAILOV. V.V. AND MELNIKOVA. M.M. ANGLO-RUSSKII SLOVAR PO ELEKTROKHIMII I KORROZII. (EN*RU ELECTROCHEM CORR. D) MOSCOW. VINITI. 1963. 234P. 63-59367. 20000T. 450 ABBR.

SHISHAKINA. A.I. AND SHVARTSMAN. E.M. KRATKII ANGLO-RUSSKII SLOVAR DLIA KHIMIKOV. (EN*RU D. FOR CHEM) ALMA-ATA. KAZAKH. GOS. UCHEB. PED. IZD. 1960. 97P. 62-32615. 2000T.

TERENTEV. A.P. NOMENKLATURA ORGANICHESKIKH SOEDINENII...(NOMENCL. OF ORG. COMPDS. RU DEFS) MOSCOW. AKAD NAUK SSSR. 1955. 302P. 56-35466.

SLOVAK

SLOVENSKA AKADEMIA VIED. TERMINOLOGIA ANORGANICKEJ A FYZIKALNEJ CHEMIE. (INORG/PHYS. CHEM. SL DEFS) BRATISLAVA. 1956. 176P. 59-19566.

SLOVENSKA AKADEMIA VIED. TERMINOLOGIA ORGANICKEJ CHEMIE. (ORG. CHEM. D. SL DEFS) BRATISLAVA. 1958. 146P. 58-49090.

SLOVENSKA AKADEMIA VIED. TERMINOLOGIA SILIKATOVEHO PRIEMYSLU. (SILICATE IND. SL DEFS) BRATISLAVA. 1955. 53P. 61-45600.

SPANISH

BARCELO. J.R. DICCIONARIO TERMINOLOGICO DE QUIMICA. (D. OF CHEM. SP DEFS) BARCELONA. SALVAT. 1959. 718P A60-3955.

BOEHME. E.T. VOCABULARIO TECNICO INDUSTRIAL. ESPANOL-INGLES. INGLES-ESPANOL PARA LAS INDUSTRIAS DE JABONES. DETERGENTES. GLICERINAS. PERFUMES Y COSMETICOS. (*SP*EN D. OF SOAPS. DETERGENTS. GLYCERINES. PERFUMES AND COSMETICS) HAVANA. 1959. 199P. 59-46920.

CHABAS LOPEZ. J. DICCIONARIO INGLES-ESPANOL DE TERMINOLOGIA QUIMICA. FARMACEUTICA Y BIOQUIMICA. (EN*SP D OF CHEM.PHARM/ BIOCHEM) BARCELONA. RAUTER. 1955. 180P.

DELORME. J.M. FORMULAS Y PROCEDIMENTOS DE LA INDUSTRIA QUIMICA MODERNA EN GRANDE Y PEQUENA ESCALA. (FORM PROCESS. FOR CHEM. IND. SP DEFS) MADRID. STUDIUM. 1958. 748P. A59-1875.

DICCIONARIO ESPANOL DE ESPECIALIDADES FARMACEUTICAS. (PHARM. D. SP DEFS) SAN SEBASTIAN. 1958. 1772P.

GOLDBERG. M. SPANISH-ENGLISH CHEMICAL AND MEDICAL DICTIONARY... NEW YORK. MCGRAW-HILL. 1952. 609P. 51-12609. 30000T.

CHEMISTRY AND CHEMICAL ENGINEERING

SPANISH

MOLINA FONT,J. SPANISH-ENGLISH CHEMICAL,COMMERCIAL, INDUSTRIAL AND PHARMACEUTICAL DICTIONARY. LONDON, BAILEY, 1957. 192P.

MORAGAS DE MONTIS, G.F. ENCICLOPEDIA DE LA QUIMICA... (ENCYCL. OF CHEM, SP DEFS) BARCELONA, DE GASSO, 1960. 571P. 62-34121.

ROSE, A. ET AL. DICCIONARIO DE QUIMICA Y DE PRODUCTOS QUIMICOS... (*SP*EN D. OF CHEM/CHEM PROD) BARCELONA, OMEGA, 1959. 995+130P. 61-33121. 16000T.

UVAROV, E.B. ET AL. DICCIONARIO DE CIENCIAS... (SCI. D, SP DEFS) MADRID, DOSSAT, 196 .

SWEDISH

TEKNISKA NOMENKLATURCENTRALEN. ORGANISK KEMISK NOMENKLATUR... (ORG. CHEM. NOMENCLATURE, SW DEFS) (TNC PUBL. 32) STOCKHOLM, SEELIG, 1960. 48P. 62-67756.

CIVIL ENGINEERING AND BUILDING INDUSTRY

AFRIKAANS

SUID-AFRIKAANSE AKADEMIE VIR WETENSKAP EN KUNS. LYS BOUTERME. (CONSTR.T,*AF*EN) PRETORIA,1952,182P.

CHINESE

CHUANG, C. CHIEN CHU KUNG CH,ENG MING TZ,U HUI PIEN. (EN CH CONSTRUCTION ENG) HONG KONG, PRACTICAL SCIENCE, 1961. 251P. C62-4150. 17000T.

CHUNG-KUO K,O HSUEH YUAN. PIEN I CHU. (ACAD. SINICA. BUR. OF COMPILATIONS/TRANSL) CHIEH KOU KUNG CH,ENG MING T,ZU. (STRUCT. ENG. T, CH EN) PEKING, 1954.

CHUNG-K,O HSUEH YUAN. PIEN I CH,U PAN WEI YUAN HUI. (ACAD. SINICA. COMM. OF PUBL/TRANSL) T,IEH TAO YU KUNG LU KUNG CH,ENG MING TZ,U. (R.R./HIGHWAY ENG. T, CH EN) PEKING, SCIENCE, 1956. 218P. C58-5143.

CHUNG-KUO K,O HSUEH YUAN. PIEN I CHU. (ACAD. SINICA. BUR. OF COMPILATIONS/TRANSL) T,U JANG HSUEH MING TZ,U. (SOIL SCI. T, CH EN) PEKING, 1955. 43P. C59-1227.

CHUNG-KUO K,O HSUEH YUAN. PIEN I CH,U PAN WEI YUAN HUI. (ACAD. SINICA. COMM. OF PUBL/TRANSL) YING HAN CHIEN CHU KUNG CH,ENG MING TZ,U. (EN CH ARCHIT. ENG. T) PEKING, SCIENCE, 1958. 251P. C60-1621.

KUO LI PIEN I KUAN. (NATL. INST. OF TRANSL) T,U·JANG HSUEH MING TZ,U. (SOIL SCI. T, EN CH) TAIPEI, 1953. 25P. C59-1273.

KUO LI PIEN I KUAN, TAI-PEI. (NATL. INST. OF TRANSL) TU MU KUNG CHENG MING TZ,U. (EN CH CIV. ENG. D) TAIPEI, 1959. 3+380P. C62-4020.

CZECH

SEIDLOVA,L. ANGLICKE TEXTY PRO FAKULTU INZENYRSKEHO STAVITELSTVI. (EN*CZ CIVIL ENG. TEXTBOOK/GL) PRAGUE, SNTL, 1957. 135P.

SYROVY, B. ARCHITEKTURA, NAUCNY SLOVNIK. (D. OF ARCHIT, CZ DEFS) PRAGUE, SNTL, 1961. 238P. 61-48128.

DANISH

BREDSDORFF, R. BYGGE-ORDBOG, DANSK-ENGELSK, ENGELSK-DANSK. (*DA*EN D.OF BLDG) COPENHAGEN, NYT NORDISK, 1960. 240P. 60-33092.

ENGLISH

AMERICAN HOME ECONOMICS ASSOCIATION. HANDBOOK OF HOUSEHOLD EQUIPMENT TERMINOLOGY. WASHINGTON, 1959. 34P. 60-70228.

AMERICAN SOCIETY FOR TESTING/MATERIALS. STANDARD DEFINITIONS OF TERMS RELATING TO BITUMINOUS WATERPROOFING AND ROOFING MATERIALS. (D1079-54) ASTM STDS, PT.4,1244-5. PHILADELPHIA, 1961. 20T.

AMERICAN SOCIETY FOR TESTING/MATERIALS. STANDARD DEFINITIONS OF TERMS RELATING TO CERAMIC WHITEWARES AND RELATED PRODUCTS. (C242-60) ASTM STDS, PT.5, 556-8. PHILADELPHIA, 1961. 60T.

AMERICAN SOCIETY FOR TESTING/MATERIALS. STANDARD DEFINITIONS OF TERMS RELATING TO CONCRETE AND CONCRETE AGGREGATES. (C125-58) ASTM STDS, PT.4, 646-7. PHILADELPHIA, 1961. 10T.

AMERICAN SOCIETY FOR TESTING/MATERIALS. STANDARD DEFINITIONS OF TERMS RELATING TO GYPSUM. (C11-60) ASTM STDS, PT.4, 350-1. PHILADELPHIA, 1961. 20T.

AMERICAN SOCIETY FOR TESTING/MATERIALS. STANDARD DEFINITIONS OF TERMS RELATING TO LIME.(C51-47)ASTM STDS, PT.4, 282-3. PHILADELPHIA, 1961. 20T.

AMERICAN SOCIETY FOR TESTING/MATERIALS. STANDARD DEFINITIONS OF TERMS RELATING TO MAGNESIUM OXYCHLORIDE AND MAGNESIUM OXYSULFATE CEMENTS. (C376-58) ASTM STDS, PT.4, 416-7. PHILADELPHIA, 1961. 20T.

AMERICAN SOCIETY FOR TESTING/MATERIALS. STANDARD DEFINITIONS OF TERMS RELATING TO MATERIALS FOR ROADS A
PAVEMENTS. (D8-55) ASTM STDS, PT.4, 655-7. PHILADELPHIA, 1961. 40T.

AMERICAN SOCIETY FOR TESTING/MATERIALS. STANDARD DEFINITIONS OF TERMS RELATING TO NATURAL BUILDING STON
(C119-50) ASTM STDS, PT.5, 775-7. PHILADELPHIA, 1961. 30T.

AMERICAN SOCIETY FOR TESTING/MATERIALS. STANDARD DEFINITIONS OF TERMS AND SYMBOLS RELATING TO SOIL
MECHANICS. (D653-60) ASTM STDS, PT.4, 1402-19. PHILADELPHIA, 1961. 380T.

AMERICAN SOCIETY FOR TESTING/MATERIALS. STANDARD DEFINITIONS OF TERMS RELATING TO STRUCTURAL CLAY TILE.
(C43-55) ASTM STDS, PT.5, 115-6. PHILADELPHIA, 1961. 40T.

AMERICAN SOCIETY FOR TESTING/MATERIALS. STANDARD DEFINITIONS OF TERMS RELATING TO STRUCTURAL SANDWICH
CONSTRUCTIONS. (C274-53) ASTM STDS, PT.5, 1067. PHILADELPHIA, 1961. 10T.

AMERICAN SOCIETY FOR TESTING/MATERIALS. STANDARD DEFINITIONS OF TERMS RELATING TO THERMAL INSULATING
MATERIALS. (C168-56) ASTM STDS, PT.5, 991-4. PHILADELPHIA, 1961. 30T.

AMERICAN SOCIETY FOR TESTING/MATERIALS. STANDARDS IN BUILDING CODES, SPECIFICATIONS, METHODS
OF TEST, DEFINITIONS. ED2. PHILADELPHIA, 1963. 1282P. 63-5674.

AMERICAN SOCIETY FOR TESTING/MATERIALS. TENTATIVE DEFINITIONS OF TERMS RELATING TO ASBESTOS-CEMENT AND
RELATED PRODUCTS. (C460-60T) ASTM STDS, PT.5, 38-40. PHILADELPHIA, 1961. 50T.

AMERICAN SOCIETY FOR TESTING/MATERIALS. TENTATIVE DEFINITIONS OF TERMS RELATING TO CERAMIC WHITEWARES AN
RELATED PRODUCTS. (C242-60T) ASTM STDS, PT.5, 559-62. PHILADELPHIA, 1961. 110T.

AMERICAN SOCIETY FOR TESTING/MATERIALS. TENTATIVE DEFINITIONS OF TERMS RELATING TO CONDITIONING. (E41-
60T) ASTM STDS, PT.4, 1624-6. PHILADELPHIA, 1961. 40T.

AMERICAN SOCIETY FOR TESTING/MATERIALS. TENTATIVE DEFINITIONS OF TERMS RELATING TO FIRE TESTS OF BUILDI
CONSTRUCTION AND MATERIALS. (E176-62T) ASTM STDS, PT.5, 150-1. (1962 SUPPL) PHILADELPHIA, 1963. 20T.

AMERICAN SOCIETY FOR TESTING/MATERIALS. TENTATIVE DEFINITIONS OF TERMS RELATING TO SOIL DYNAMICS. (D170
60T) ASTM STDS, PT.4, 1396-401. PHILADELPHIA, 1961. 60T.

AMERICAN SOCIETY OF HEATING, REFRIGERATING AND AIR-CONDITIONING ENGINEERS. ASHRAE GUIDE AND DATA BOOK.
(GL.OF PHYS/HEAT/VENT/REFRIG/AIR COND. T.IN TEXT,PP.845-54, 400T) NEW YORK, 1961. V.1. 880P. 62-1033.

AMERICAN SOCIETY OF HEATING, REFRIGERATING AND AIR-CONDITIONING ENGINEERS. ASHRAE GUIDE AND DATA BOOK.
(STD. ABBR/SYMBOLS FOR PIPING, DUCTWORK, HEAT/VENT/REFRIG, PP.855-62, 400T) NEW YORK, 1961. V.1, 880P.
62-1033.

AUDELS DO-IT-YOURSELF ENCYCLOPEDIA... NEW YORK, AUDEL, 1959. 2V. 1012P. 60-338.

BERRY, E. AN ILLUSTRATED DICTIONARY OF PLUMBING TERMS. LONDON, TECH.PRESS, 1960. 244P. 61-3609.

BRIGGS, M.S. EVERYMAN,S CONCISE ENCYCLOPEDIA OF ARCHITECTURE. NEW YORK, DUTTON, 1959. 372P. 59-5837.

BRITISH STANDARDS INSTITUTION. GLOSSARY OF GENERAL BUILDING TERMS (B.S.3589) LONDON, 1963. 32P. 400T.

BRITISH STANDARDS INSTITUTION. GLOSSARY OF HIGHWAY ENGINEERING TERMS. (B.S.892) LONDON, 1954. 72P.
750T.

BRITISH STANDARDS INSTITUTION. GLOSSARY OF TERMS APPLICABLE TO ROOF COVERINGS. (B.S.2717) LONDON, 1956.
36P. 280T.

BRITISH STANDARDS INSTITUTION. GLOSSARY OF TERMS FOR CONCRETE AND REINFORCED CONCRETE. (B.S.2787, AMEND
PD3811) LONDON, 1956-60. 40P. 550T.

BRITISH STANDARDS INSTITUTION. GLOSSARY OF TERMS FOR STONE USED IN BUILDING. (B.S.2847) LONDON, 1957.
40P. 450T.

BRITISH STANDARDS INSTITUTION. GLOSSARY OF TERMS RELATING TO THERMAL INSULATION. (B.S. 3533) LONDON,
1962. 24P. 130T.

BRITISH STANDARDS INSTITUTION. LETTER SYMBOLS, SIGNS AND ABBREVIATIONS. PT.4. STRUCTURES, MATERIALS AND
SOIL MECHANICS. (B.S. 1991) LONDON. 1961. 52P. 500T.

BRITISH STANDARDS INSTITUTION. MODULAR CO-ORDINATION IN BUILDING. (B.S.2900, PT.1, GL) LONDON, 1957.
12P. 40T.

BURKE,.A.E. ET AL. ARCHITECTURAL AND BUILDING TRADES DICTIONARY. CHICAGO, AM. TECH. SOC, 1955. 377P.
56-433.

CLAUSEN,C.F. AND DERNSNAH,W.R. CEMENT PLANT GLOSSARY. PIT/QUARRY, V.48, 112-26 (1956) 500T.

A COMPLETE DIRECTORY OF CERAMIC MATERIALS...CERAM. IND, V.74, 111-70 (1960) (REPR. BY INTL. COOP. ADMIN
WASHINGTON) 1960. 43P. 60-61806. 500T.

DEL VECCHIO, A. DICTIONARY OF MECHANICAL ENGINEERING. NEW YORK, PHIL. LIBR, 1961. 346P. 60-13664.
2500T.

ENGLISH

HORNBOSTEL, C. MATERIALS FOR ARCHITECTURE, AN ENCYCLOPEDIC GUIDE. NEW YORK, RHEINHOLD, 1961. 610P. 61-13206.

KAY, N.W. THE MODERN BUILDING ENCYCLOPAEDIA...NEW YORK, PHIL. LIBR, 1955. 768P. 56-58099.

LIPOWSKY, B. AND BERSTEN, M. A PICTURE DICTIONARY AND GUIDE TO BUILDING AND CONSTRUCTION TERMS. NEW YORK, ARCO, 1960. 27P. 60-12986.

MCLERRAN, J.H. GLOSSARY OF PEDOLOGIC (SOILS) AND LANDFORM TERMINOLOGY FOR SOIL ENGINEERS. (HIGHWAY RESEARCH BOARD. SPEC. REPT. NO.25) WASHINGTON, 1957. 32P. 57-61134.

MOSES, G.L. GLOSSARY OF INSULATION ENGINEERING TERMS. INSULATION (LIBERTYVILLE) V. 8, NO. 6, 15-8(1962) 200T.

OSBORNE, A.L. A DICTIONARY OF ENGLISH DOMESTIC ARCHITECTURE. NEW YORK, PHIL. LIBR, 1956. 111P. 57-926.

POWDRILL, E.A. VOCABULARY OF LAND PLANNING. LONDON, ESTATES GAZ, 1961. 97P.

SAYLOR, H.H. DICTIONARY OF ARCHITECTURE. NEW YORK, WILEY, 1952. 221P. 52-8260.

SCOTT, J.S. A DICTIONARY OF CIVIL ENGINEERING. HARMONDSWORTH, MIDDLESEX, PENGUIN, 1958. 415P. 58-4451.

SIEGELE, H.H. BUILDING TRADES DICTIONARY... CHICAGO, DRAKE, 1959. 380P. 59-16934.

SOIL SCIENCE SOCIETY OF AMERICA. SOIL DEFINITIONS. MADISON, WIS, 195 .

TABLES, FORMULAS, ABBREVIATIONS AND SYMBOLS USEFUL TO THE INSULATION ENGINEER. INSULATION (LIBERTYVILLE) V.8, NO.6, 4-14 (1962) 300T.

U.S. DEPT. OF AGRICULTURE. YEARBOOK OF AGRICULTURE, SOILS. (GL, PP. 751-70) WASHINGTON, 1957. 784P.

U.S. SOIL CONSERVATION SERVICE. NATIONAL CATALOG OF PRACTICES AND MEASURES USED IN SOIL AND WATER CONSERVATION. WASHINGTON, 1959. 11P. 59-64226. 130T.

WITTY, M.B. ET AL. DICTIONARY OF ARCHITECTURAL ABBREVIATIONS, SIGNS, SYMBOLS AND TABLES. NEW YORK, SETI, 1963. 416P.

WITTY, M.B. ET AL. DICTIONARY OF CIVIL ENGINEERING ABBREVIATIONS, SIGNS, SYMBOLS AND TABLES. NEW YORK, SETI. 1963. 352P.

FRENCH

BARBIER, M. ET AL. DICTIONNAIRE TECHNIQUE DU BATIMENT ET DES TRAVAUX PUBLICS. (BLDG/PUBL. WORKS D, FR DEFS) PARIS, EYROLLES, 1963. 146P. NUC64-1336.

BODSON ,G. DICTIONNAIRE DES TERMES RECENTS, SYMBOLES ET ABBREVIATIONS ARCHITECTURE, ART DE CONSTRUIRE, GENIE CIVIL. (ARCHIT. BLDG,CIVIL ENG. T. SYMBOLS,ABBREV, FR DEFS) PARIS, GIRARDOT, 1952. 244P.

BUCKSCH, H. DICTIONNAIRE POUR LES TRAVAUX PUBLICS, LE BATIMENT ET L.EQUIPEMENT DES CHANTIERS DE CONSTRUCTION. ANGLAIS-FRANCAIS. (D. OF CIVIL ENG. CONSTR. MACH/ EQUIP,*EN*FR) PARIS, EYROLLES, 1960-62. 2v. 62-6556.

LA CONSTRUCTION DES ROUTES, GLOSSAIRE ANGLAIS-FRANCAIS, BT-88. (ROAD BLDG, EN*FR GL) OTTAWA, DEPT. SECY. STATE, 1960. 31P. 650T.

DURIEZ ,M. AND ARRAMBIDE,J. LIANTS HYDROCARBONES, MORTIERS ET BETONS BITUMINEUX, (HYDROCARB. BONDING AGENTS, MORTARS/BIT, CONCRETE,FR DEFS) PARIS, DUNOD,1954. 728P.

FERGUSON, C.E. A GLOSSARY OF GENERAL SOIL SCIENCE, ENGLISH-FRENCH, FRENCH-ENGLISH. WASHINGTON, AGENCY FOR INTL. DEVELOPMENT, 1962. 95P. 63-60304.

FRANCE. AMBASSADE. U.S. INDUSTRIE DU BATIMENT, AMERICAIN-FRANCAIS. (BLDG.IND, AM*FR GL) WASHINGTON, 1953. 135P. 2800T.

LOZET, J. PETIT DICTIONNAIRE DE PEDOLOGIE. (D. OF SOIL SCI, EN*FR) BRUSSELS, MIN. COLONIES, 1954. 169P. 56-45477.

LE MENUISIER DE BATIMENT... GLOSSAIRE FRANCAIS-ANGLAIS ET ANGLAIS-FRANCAIS, BT-14. (BLDG. CARPENTER, *FR*EN GL) OTTAWA, DEPT. SECY. STATE, 1954. 18P. 200T.

MOREAU, J. DICTIONNAIRE TECHNIQUE AMERICAIN-FRANCAIS DE CONSTRUCTION,BATIMENT ET TRAVAUX PUBLICS. (EN*FR D.OF BLDG.IND/ PUBLIC WORKS) PARIS, DUNOD, 1960. 190P. 61-2619. 5700T.

PLAISANCE, G. AND GAILLEUX, A. DICTIONNAIRE DES SOLS. (D. OF SOILS, FR DEFS) PARIS, MAISON RUSTIQUE. 1958. 604P. 62-25442. 15000T.

PROULX, G. LA CONSTRUCTION DES ROUTES, GLOSSAIRE ANGLAIS-FRANCAIS, BT-40. (ROAD BLDG, EN*FR GL) OTTAWA, DEPT. SECY. STATE, 1955. 39P. 1000T.

PROULX, G. MATERIEL ET ENGINS DE CHANTIERS, GLOSSAIRE ANGLAIS-FRANCAIS, BT-41. (FIELD MATER/EQUIP, EN*FR GL) OTTAWA, DEPT. SECY. STATE, 1956. 89P. 1300T.

CIVIL ENGINEERING AND BUILDING INDUSTRY

FRENCH

ROWE, R.S. FRENCH-ENGLISH TRANSLATION GUIDE FOR RIVER AND HARBOR ENGINEERING. PRINCETON, N.J, PRINCETON UNIV, 1954. 90P. 54-6521. 2000T.

UNITED NATIONS. LISTE DE TERMES RELATIFS A LA CONSTRUCTION ET A LA CIRCULATION ROUTIERS. (ROAD BLDG/ TRAFFIC ENG,FR*EN GL)(BUL.NO.109) NEW YORK,195 .

L.URBANISME, GLOSSAIRE ANGLAIS-FRANCAIS, BT-85. (URBAN DEVELOP, EN*FR GL) OTTAWA, DEPT. SECY. STATE, 1960. 51P. 1000T.

GERMAN

BUCKSCH, H. WOERTERBUCH FUER INGENIEURBAU UND BAUMASCHINEN...(*GE*EN D. OF CIVIL ENG/CONSTR. MACH) (V.1. GE*EN, 512P. V.2. EN*GE, 436P) ED2. WIESBADEN, BAUVERLAG, 1958. 59-31910. 18000T.

GRAF, O. ET AL. DAS KLEINE LEXIKON DER BAUTECHNIK. (GL. OF CIVIL ENG, GE DEFS) ED2. STUTTGART, UNION VERLAG, 1959. 809P.

HAEHNLE, O. BAUSTOFF LEXIKON. (BLDG. MATER. D, GE DEFS) STUTTGART, DEUT. VERLAGSANSTALT, 1961. 424P. 63-26787.

PROBST, E. DER BAUSTOFFUEHRER...(BLDG. MATER. GUIDE, GE DEFS) ED4. WIESBADEN, BAUVERLAG, 1954. 512P. A55-8125.

PROBST,E. HANDBUCH DER BETONSTEININDUSTRIE... (CONCRETE D, GE DEFS) ED7. BERLIN, MARHOLD, 1962. 667P. 62-67686.

ROWE, R.S. GERMAN-ENGLISH TRANSLATION GUIDE FOR RIVER AND HARBOR ENGINEERING. PRINCETON, N.J, PRINCETON UNIV, 1953. 96P. 52-12056.

RUECKERT,O. GLOSSARIUM DER BAUFORMEN. (BLDG.GL, GE DEFS) STUTTGART, 1955.

SAENDIG,J. ZIEGELEILEXIKON, HANDBUCH FUER DIE GESAMTE BAUKERAMISCHE INDUSTRIE. (BRICKMAKING D, GE DEFS) WIESBADEN, SAENDIG, 1959.

SAUTTER,L. DAS GROSSE ABC DES BAUENS. (LARGE ABC OF BLDG, GE DEFS) BRAUNSCHWEIG, SCHLOESSER, 1953.2V.LL. A53-5589.

STEGMAIER, W. KERAMISCHES FACHWOERTERBUCH... (CERAMIC GL, V.1, EN*GE 292P. V.2, GE*EN, P) BONN, DEUT. KERAM. GES, 1954-- . 56-36503. 3000T.

WANDERSLEB,H. HANDWOERTERBUCH DES STAEDTEBAUES, WOHNUNGS-SIEDLUNGSWESENS. (CITY/DWELLING PLANNING D, GE DEFS) 3V. STUTTGART,KOHLHAMMER,195 .

HINDI

INDIA. MINISTRY OF EDUCATION. LIST OF TECHNICAL TERMS IN HINDI, TRANSPORT, HIGHWAY ENGINEERING. DELHI, MANAGER OF PUBL, 1959. 140P.

ROORKEE ENGINEERING COLLEGE. BUILDINGS, PLASTERS, HYDRAULICS, REINFORCED CONCRETE... DICTIONARY. (EN*HI) ALLAHABAD, HINDI SAHITYA SAMMELAN, 1950.

JAPANESE

DOBOKU SHIKEN MONDAI KENKYUKAI. (CIV. ENG. EXAM. BOARD) DOBOKU YOGO JITEN. (CIV. ENG. D, JA EN) TOKYO, 1960. 336P. J61-1052.

JAPAN. MINISTRY OF EDUCATION. ARCHITECTURE, DWELLING TERMS. (JA*EN) TOKYO, 1952. 10P. 300T.

JAPAN. MINISTRY OF EDUCATION. ARCHITECTURE, STRUCTURE TERMS. (JA*EN) TOKYO, 1952. 62P. 1800T.

JAPAN. MINISTRY OF EDUCATION. GLOSSARY OF ARCHITECTURAL MATERIALS. (JA*EN) TOKYO, 1952. 31P. 1500T.

JAPAN. MINISTRY OF EDUCATION. JAPANESE SCIENTIFIC TERMS, ARCHITECTURE. (*JA*EN) TOKYO, ARCHIT. INST. JAPAN, 1955. 360P. 5000T.

JAPAN. MINISTRY OF EDUCATION. JAPANESE SCIENTIFIC TERMS, CIVIL ENGINEERING. (*JA*EN) TOKYO, JAPAN SOC. CIV. ENG, 1954. 395P. 5000T.

JAPAN. MINISTRY OF EDUCATION. VOCABULARY OF BUILDING MATERIALS. (JA*EN) TOKYO, 1951. 47P. 1330T.

JAPAN. MINISTRY OF EDUCATION. VOCABULARY OF CEMENT. (EN*JA) TOKYO, 1950. 10P. 230T.

JAPAN. MINISTRY OF EDUCATION. VOCABULARY OF HIGHWAYS. (EN*JA) TOKYO,1950. 6P. 120T.

JAPANESE STANDARDS ASSOCIATION. JAPANESE ENGINEERING TERMS, PLUMBING, HEATING, AND VENTILATION...(*JA*EN TOKYO, 1955. 176P.

KONDO, Y. KONKURITO JITEN. (CONCRETE D, *JA*EN) TOKYO, NIHON SEMENTO GIJUTSU KYOKAI, 1959. 254P. J61-1447.

KUBOTA, T. KENCHIKU JUTSUGO JITEN. (BLDG. D, *JA*EN) TOKYO, OMU, 1956. 386P. J62-158. 2000T.

JAPANESE

SUDO, M. JAPANESE-ENGLISH ARCHITECTURAL DICTIONARY. TOKYO, RIKO TOSHO, 1958. 165P.

TOKYO ENGINEERING INSTITUTE. PRACTICAL ENGLISH-JAPANESE DICTIONARY OF ARCHITECTURAL TERMS. TOKYO, KOGAKU, 1956. 214P.

TOKYO ENGINEERING INSTITUTE. PRACTICAL ENGLISH-JAPANESE DICTIONARY OF CIVIL ENGINEERING TERMS. TOKYO, KOGAKU, 1956. 250P. 6000T.

TSUGAWA, T. ENGLISH-JAPANESE DICTIONARY OF ARCHITECTURAL TERMS. TOKYO, SAGAMI, 1955. 360P.

NORWEGIAN

NORWAY. RADET FOR TEKNISK TERMINOLOGI. CONCRETE TECHNOLOGY. (RTT-1) (NO DEFS) OSLO, 1958. 11P.

POLISH

ZBOINSKI, A. SLOWNIK INZYNIERYJNO-BUDOWLANY ANGIELSKO-POLSKI Z INDEKSEM TERMINOW POLSKICH. (*EN*PL D. OF BLDG/CIVIL ENG) WARSAW, PANSTW. WYDAW. TECH, 1959. 833P. 60-37128. 37000T.

POLYGLOT

BARDET, G. PETIT GLOSSAIRE DE L,URBANISTE EN 6 LANGUES. (URBAN DEVELOP, 6-LANG D) PARIS, 195 . 150P.

BAZANT, Z. ET AL. SLOVNIK STAVEBNE MECHANIKY A PRIBUZNYCH OBORU V PETI RECICH. (D. OF STRUCT. MECH, *CZ *EN*FR*GE*RU) PRAGUE, CESKOSLOV. AKAD. VED, 1953. 251P. 54-42992. 1900T.

BELLIENI, L. AND TESSARI, B. PICCOLA ENCICLOPEDIA DEL MURATORE. (MASON,S ENCYCL, IT*EN*FR*GE) VICENZA, TIP. OPERAI, 1953. 254P. A53-8374.

BUNDESANSTALT FUER STRASSENBAU. STRASSENBAU-FACHWOERTER. (ROADBLDG.D, GE*EN*FR) COLOGNE-RADERTHAL,1955. 79P. 59-40629.

CHUNG-KUO K,O HSUEH YUAN. PIEN I CH,U PAN WEI YUAN HUI. (ACAD. SINICA. COMM. OF PUBL/TRANSL) CHI SHUI P,AI SHUI KUNG NUAN T,UNG FENG KUNG CH,ENG MING TZ,U. (DRAINAGE, HEATING/VENTILATION ENG. T, RU EN CH) PEKING, SCIENCE, 1957. 154P. C58-5311.

ELSEVIER,S DICTIONARY OF SOIL MECHANICS. NEW YORK, 1964. 380P. 3000T. (IN PREP)

FEDERATION INTERNATIONALE DE LA PRECONTRAINTE. 7-LANGUAGE DICTIONARY OF REINFORCED CONCRETE. (*FK*EN*GE *SP*IT*RU#DU) AMSTERDAM, STUVO, 1962. UNPAGED.

HYOJUN GAKUJUTSU YOGO JITEN HENSHU IINKAI. SHINKYU EI-DOKU TAISHO HYOJUN GAKUJUTSU YOGO JITEN. (*JA*EN *GE SCI. D, CIV. ENG) TOKYO, SEIBUNDO-SHINKOSHA, 1962. 508P. J63-168.

INTERNATIONAL COMMISSION ON IRRIGATION AND DRAINAGE. MULTILINGUAL DICTIONARY ON IRRIGATION AND DRAINAGE. (*EN*FR*GE) NEW DELHI, 1960- . (IN PROC) 800P. 10000T.

INTERNATIONAL COMMISSION ON LARGE DAMS. DICTIONNAIRE TECHNIQUE DES BARRAGES. (D. OF DAMS, *FR*EN*GE*IT*PR *SP) ED2. PARIS, 1960. 380P. 61-805. 5800T.

INTERNATIONAL COMMISSION ON LARGE DAMS. TEKHNICHESKII SLOVAR PO PLOTINAM NA 11 IAZYKAKH. (DAM BLDG. IN 11 LANG, RU EN BU SP IT GE PL PR RO CZ FR) MOSCOW, 1962. 379P.

INTERNATIONAL SOCIETY OF SOIL MECHANICS AND FOUNDATION ENGINEERING. TECHNICAL TERMS...USED IN SOIL MECHANICS AND FOUNDATION ENGINEERING. (*EN*FR*GE*PR*SP*SW) ED2. ZURICH, 1954. 103P. 54-4683. 1200T.

JACKS, G.V. ET AL. MULTILINGUAL VOCABULARY OF SOIL SCIENCE.(*FR*EN*DU*GE*IT*PR*SP*SW) ED2. ROME, FAO (UN) 1960. 428P. 60-50105. 340T.

KAUFFMANN, F. DICTIONNAIRE TECHNIQUE DES MATERIELS AGRICOLES ET DE TRAVAUX PUBLICS. (MACH. IN AGRIC/ PUBL. WORKS, FR*EN*GE*SP D) PARIS, G.E.P, 1953. 446P.

KONO, K. NEW DICTIONARY OF CIVIL ENGINEERING AND ARCHITECTURE... (*JA*EN*FR*GE) TOKYO, KEIBUNSHA, 1956. 513P.

LANG, O. ET AL. FUENF SPRACHEN WOERTERBUCH FUER DIE KAELTE- UND KLIMATECHNIK, HEIZUNG UND LUEFTUNG. (5- LANG,D. OF REFRIG, AIR COND, HEAT/VENT, GE*EN*FR*IT*SP) HAMBURG, LINDOW, 1959. 588P. A60-1971.

LEKSIKON GRADEVINARSTVA. (CIV. ENG. D, *SC*EN*FR*GE) BELGRADE, 1962. 1054P.

PALOTAS, L. ET AL. EPITOANYAGOK. (D. OF BLDG. MATER, HU*EN*GE*RU) (MUSZ. ERT. SZ, NO.1) BUDAPEST, TERRA, 1958. 174P. 59-20131. 1100T.

PALOTAS, L. ET AL. TARTOSZERKEZETEK. (D. OF SUPPORTING STRUCT, HU*EN*GE*RU) (MUSZ. ERT. SZ, NO.14) BUDAPEST, TERRA, 1961. 190P. 62-46390. 1100T.

PERMANENT INTERNATIONAL ASSOCIATION OF NAVIGATION CONGRESSES. DICTIONNAIRE TECHNIQUE ILLUSTRE...(ILLUS. TECH. D, *FR*EN*DU*GE*IT*SP) CH. 5. MATERIAUX. (MATER) BRUSSELS, 1951.204P.

PERMANENT INTERNATIONAL ASSOCIATION OF NAVIGATION CONGRESSES. DICTIONNAIRE TECHNIQUE ILLUSTRE... (ILLUS. TECH. D, *FR*EN*DU*GE*IT*SP) CH. 6. CONSTR. PLANT/METHODS. BRUSSELS, 1959. 237P. 58-16041. 3000T.

POLYGLOT

PERMANENT INTERNATIONAL ASSOCIATION OF ROAD CONGRESSES. DICTIONNAIRE TECHNIQUE ROUTIER EN 8 LANGUES. (D. OF ROAD T, *FR*EN*DA*DU*GE*IT*RU*SP) ED3. PARIS. (IN PREP)

PLAISANCE, G. LEXIQUE PEDOLOGIQUE TRILINGUE. (SOILS GL, FR EN GE) PARIS, S.E.D.E.S.1958. 357P. A59-1516.

SAITO, K. KYORITSU KENCHIKU JITEN. (BLDG.D,*JA*EN*GE) TOKYO, KYORITSU,1959. 533P. J61-1502. 8000T.

SHNEIDER, M.E. AND DENISOV, N.IA. SLOVAR TEKHNICHESKIKH TERMINOV PO MEKHANIKE GRUNTOV I FUNDAMENTOSTROENIIU... (RU VERSION OF THE INTL.SOC.OF SOIL MECH.AND FOUNDATION ENG.D. *RU*EN*FR*GE*PR*SP* SW) MOSCOW, FIZMATGIZ, 1958. 139P. 59-20756. 1200T.

SPIWAK, H.J. INTERNATIONAL GLOSSARY OF TECHNICAL TERMS USED IN HOUSING AND TOWN PLANNING, EN FR GE IT SP ED2. AMSTERDAM, INTL. FED/HOUSING/TOWN PLANNING, 1951. 144P. 53-39800.

STEINE UND ERDEN. BAUSTOFF-LEXIKON... (BLDG. MATER. D, *GE*EN*FR*SP) WIESBADEN, KRAUSSKOPF, 1962. 320P. 6000T.

SUENSON, E. BETONTEKNISKE FAGUDTRYK. (D. OF CONCRETE TECH, *EN*DA*FR*GE*NO*SW) COPENHAGEN, DANSK INGENIOERFORENING, 1954. 192P. A54-5536.

SZECHY, K. AND KEZDI, A. ALAGUTAK,' ALAPOZAS, FOLDMUVEK, TALAJMECHANIKA. (D.OF TUNNELS, FOUNDATION ENG, EARTH WORKS, SOIL MECH, HU*EN*GE*RU) (MUSZ. ERT. SZ, NO.10) BUDAPEST, TERRA, 1960. 252P. 1400T.

VAN MANSUM, C.J. ELSEVIER,S DICTIONARY OF BUILDING CONSTRUCTION. (*EN/AM*DU*FR*GE) NEW YORK, ELSEVIER, 1959. 482P. 58-59508. 8500T.

VICENZA. SCUOLA PROFESSIONALE EDILE ANDREA PALLADIO. PICCOLO VOCABOLARIO DEL MURATORE NELLE LINGUE ITALIANA,FRANCESE,INGLESE,TEDESCA. (MASON,S VOC,IT*EN*FR*GE) VICENZA, TIP/OPERAI, 1953. A53-8372. 500T.

VISSER, A.D. DICTIONARY OF SOIL MECHANICS (EN*DU*FR*GE) NEW YORK, ELSEVIER. 380P. 3000T. (IN PREP)

ZBOINSKI, A. AND TYSZYNSKI, L. DICTIONARY OF ARCHITECTURE AND BUILDING TRADES. (*EN*GE*PL*RU) NEW YORK PERGAMON, 1963. 491P. 63-22975. 8000T.

ZLATOVSKII, G.M. DICTIONNAIRE TRILINGUE DES ESSAIS DES MATERIAUX DE CONSTRUCTION. (D.OF MATER. TESTING,*F *EN*GE) ED4. PARIS, RILEM, 1956. 451P. 3000T.

PORTUGUESE

PORTUGAL. LABORATORIO NACIONAL DE ENGENHARIA CIVIL. VOCABULARIO DE ESTRADAS E AERODROMOS. (ROAD/AIRPORT D, PR DEFS) ED4. LISBON, 1962.

VASCONCELLOS, S. DE. VOCABULARIO ARQUITETONICO. (GL. OF ARCHIT, PR DEFS) BELO HORIZONTE, UNIV. MINAS GERAIS, 1961. 66P. 62-32084.

RUSSIAN

AKADEMIIA NAUK SSSR. KOM.TEKH.TERM. GIDROMEKHANIKA, VOLNOVOE DVIZHENIE ZHIDKOSTI, STROITELNAIA MEKHANIKA, TERMINOLOGIIA (FLUID MECH, WAVE MOTION OF FLUIDS/STRUCT. MECH, RU DEFS) (SB. REK. TERM. NO.58. MOSCOW, 1962. 85P. 63-40826.

AKADEMIIA NAUK SSSR. KOM.TEKH.TERM. TERMINOLOGIIA TEORII UPRUGOSTI, ISPYTANII I MEKHANICHESKIKH SVOISTV MATERIALOV I STROITELNOI MEKHANIKI. (THEORY OF ELASTICITY, TESTING/ MECH. PROP. OF MATER/STRUCT. MECH, R DEFS) (SB.REK.TERM,NO.14) MOSCOW) 1952. 78P. 54-35126.

AKADEMIIA NAUK SSSR. TOLKOVYI SLOVAR PO POCHVOVEDENIIU. FIZIKA, MELIORATSIIA I MINERALOGIIA POCHV. (D. OF SOIL PHYS, IMPROVEMENT/MINERAL, RU DEFS) MOSCOW, 1960. 144P. 800T.

AKADEMIIA STROITELSTVA I ARKHITEKTURY SSSR. TERMINY PO STROITELSTVY I ARKHITEKTURE NA ANGLIISKOM I RUSSKO IAZYKAKH. (EN*RU GL. OF BLDG/ARCHIT) MOSCOW, 1958. 95P.

AMBURGER, P.G. ANGLO-RUSSKI STROITELNYI SLOVAR. (EN*RU D. OF CIVIL ENG) ED3. MOSCOW, FIZMATGIZ, 1961. 599P. 62-41262. 30000T.

GERWICK, B.C, JR. AND PETERS, V.P. RUSSIAN-ENGLISH DICTIONARY OF PRESTRESSED CONCRETE AND CONCRETE CONSTRUCTION. NEW YORK, GORDON/BREACH. (IN PREP) 9000T.

KHAIKIN, IA.B. AND ORNATSKII, N.V. ANGLO-RUSSKII SLOVAR DOROZHNIKA. (EN*RU D. OF ROAD BLDG) MOSCOW, AVTOTRANSIZDAT, 1956. 319P. 57-29754. 16000T.

KHAIKIN, IA.B. AND SKRAMTAEV, B.G. ANGLO-RUSSKII SLOVAR PO TSEMENTU I BETONU. (EN*RU D. OF CEMENT/ CONCRETE) MOSCOW, GOSSTROIIZDAT, 1959. 283P. 60-30414. 16000T.

PUSHKAREV, V.I. AND SHCHEGOLEVA, A.M. ANGLO-RUSSKII I RUSSKO-ANGLIISKII ARKHITEKTURNOSTROITELNII SLOVAR. (*EN*RU D. OF ARCHIT/BLDG) KIEV, GOSSTROIIZDAT, 1961. 841P. 61-47210.

ROWE, R.S. RUSSIAN-ENGLISH TRANSLATION GUIDE FOR RIVER AND HARBOR ENGINEERING. PRINCETON, N.J, PRINCETO UNIV. 1954. 96P. 53-12066.

VOLODIN, N.V. ANGLO-RUSSKII VOENNO-INZHENERNYI SLOVAR. (EN*RU MIL. ENG. D) MOSCOW, VOENIZDAT, 1962. 783P. 63-56315. 33000T.

CIVIL ENGINEERING AND BUILDING INDUSTRY

SLOVAK

SALINGS, S. AND FIGUS, V. STAVEBNICKY NAUCNY SLOVNIK. (BLDG. D, SL DEFS) BRATISLAVA, SLOV. VYDAV. TECH. LIT, 1961-- . 63-26791.

SPANISH

GUINLE, R.L. MODERN SPANISH-ENGLISH, ENGLISH-SPANISH TECHNICAL AND ENGINEERING DICTIONARY...NEW YORK, DUTTON, 1959. 311P. 15000T.

ROBB, L.A. ENGINEERS DICTIONARY, SPANISH-ENGLISH AND ENGLISH-SPANISH. ED2. NEW YORK, WILEY, 1956. 664P. 56-4369. 30000T.

SALAZAR-PACHECO, S. TECHNICAL ENGLISH, CIVIL ENGINEERING AND AGRICULTURE. MEXICO, IMPR. ACOSTA, 1956. 225P.

U.S. BUREAU OF PUBLIC ROADS. TECHNICAL GLOSSARY OF HIGHWAY, BRIDGE, AND SOILS ENGINEERING TERMS. SPANISH-ENGLISH, ENGLISH-SPANISH. CHICAGO, GILLETTE, 1955. 317P. 55-4633. 20000T.

ZURITA RUIZ, J. DICCIONARIO DE LA CONSTRUCCION. (D. OF CONSTR, SP DEF) BARCELONA, CEAC, 1955. 192P. A56-2980.

COMPUTERS, DATA PROCESSING, AND INFORMATION RETRIEVAL

CZECH

URADRO NORMALISACI VACLAVSKE NAMESTI. DIGITAL AND ANALOGOUS COMPUTERS, TERMINOLOGY. (CZECHOSLOV. STD, CSN-01 6928, CZ DEFS) PRAGUE, 195 .

DUTCH

STICHTING STUDIECENTRUM VOOR ADMINISTRATIEVE AUTOMATISERING VERKLARENDE WOORDENLIJST.(D. OF OFFICE AUTOM, DU*EN) AMSTERDAM, 1960. 136P.

ENGLISH

AMERICAN STANDARDS ASSOCIATION. COMMUNICATIONS GLOSSARY, DRAFT. NEW YORK, 1962. 44P. 400T.

AMERICAN STANDARDS ASSOCIATION. DATA PROCESSING STANDARDS, COMPUTER NOMENCLATURE. NEW YORK. 1800T. (IN PREP)

ASSOCIATION FOR COMPUTING MACHINERY. FIRST GLOSSARY OF PROGRAMMING TERMINOLOGY. NEW YORK, 1954. 25P. 260T.

BELL TELEPHONE LABORATORIES. GLOSSARY. MURRAY HILL, N.J, 1960. 21P. 120T.

BERKELEY, E.C. AND LOVETT, L.L. GLOSSARY OF TERMS IN COMPUTERS AND DATA PROCESSING. ED5. NEWTONVILLE, MASS, BERKELEY, 1960. 90P. 61-4747. 900T.

BERLIN, R. ET AL. A DICTIONARY OF SWITCHING THEORY TERMS. NEW YORK, AM.INST.ELEC.ENG, 1960. 43P.

BORMANN, W.O. GLOSSARY-TERMS USED IN COMPUTER PROGRAMMING AND ENGINEERING. POUGHKEEPSIE,N.Y. IBM, 1960. 28P.

BRITISH STANDARDS INSTITUTION. GLOSSARY OF TERMS RELATING TO AUTOMATIC DIGITAL COMPUTERS. (B.S.2641, AMEND.PD2719-195) LONDON,1955. 16P.

BRITISH STANDARDS INSTITUTION. GLOSSARY OF TERMS USED IN AUTOMATIC DATA PROCESSING. (B.S.3527) LONDON, 1962. 132P. 1500T.

DATA PROCESSING EQUIPMENT ENCYCLOPEDIA. DETROIT, GILLE, 1961. 2V. 61-15132.

EASTWOOD, D.E. SHARE GLOSSARY OF TERMS. MURRAY HILL,N.J. BELL TEL.LABS, 1960. 11P.

ELLSWORTH, L. BASIC IBM APPLIED PROGRAMMING TEACHING GLOSSARY. NEW YORK, IBM, 1960. 3P.

FOX, P. GLOSSARY OF TERMS FREQUENTLY USED IN PHYSICS AND COMPUTERS. NEW YORK, AM.INST. PHYS, 1962. 24P. 180T.

GLOSSARY OF COMPUTER TERMS. SYLVANIA TECH. V.12, 106-8 (1959) 100T.

GOODWIN, K.E. AND GINDER, C.E. NOMA GLOSSARY OF AUTOMATION TERMS. WILLOW GROVE, PA. NATL. OFFICE MANAGEMENT ASSOC, 1961. 88P. 61-2548. 550T.

GREMS, M. GLOSSARY OF COMPUTER AND PROGRAMMING TERMINOLOGY. WHITE PLAINS, N.Y. IBM, 1960. 43P.

GREMS, M. ET AL. IBM GLOSSARY FOR INFORMATION PROCESSING. PRELIM.ED. WHITE PLAINS, N.Y, IBM, 1961. 83P. 950T.

HANNUM, D.E. GLOSSARY FOR DATA TRANSMISSION STUDY GROUP. DOWNEY, CALIF, NORTHROP AVIATION, 195 . 26P. 190T.

HERRON, R.M. GLOSSARY OF TERMS. WHITE PLAINS, N.Y, IBM, 1960. 24P.

COMPUTERS, DATA PROCESSING, AND INFORMATION RETRIEVAL

ENGLISH

HOLMES, J.F. COMMUNICATIONS DICTIONARY, A COMPILATION OF THE TERMS USED IN ELECTRONIC COMMUNICATIONS AND DATA PROCESSING. NEW YORK. RIDER, 1962. 88P. 62-13397.

INSTITUTE OF RADIO ENGINEERS. PROPOSED STANDARD DEFINITIONS, ABBREVIATIONS AND SYMBOLS FOR ANALOG COMPUTERS. (60 IRE 8.8 PS1) 39P. (IN PREP)

INSTITUTE OF RADIO ENGINEERS. STANDARDS ON ELECTRON DEVICES, DEFINITIONS OF TERMS RELATED TO STORAGE TUBES. (56 IRE 7.S1) PROC.IRE, V.44, 521-2 (1956) 30T.

INSTITUTE OF RADIO ENGINEERS. STANDARDS ON ELECTRONIC COMPUTERS, DEFINITIONS OF TERMS. (56 IRE 8.S1) PROC. IRE, V.44, 1166-73 (1956) 2000T.

INSTITUTE OF RADIO ENGINEERS. STANDARDS ON INFORMATION THEORY, DEFINITIONS OF TERMS. (58 IRE 11.S1) PROC. IRE V.46, 1646-8 (1958) 30T.

INSTITUTE OF RADIO ENGINEERS. STANDARDS ON STATIC MAGNETIC STORAGE, DEFINITIONS OF TERMS. (59 IRE 8.S1) PROC. IRE, V.47, 427-30 (1959) 60T.

INTERNATIONAL BUSINESS MACHINES CORP. GLOSSARY FOR DATA PROCESSING MACHINES. WASHINGTON, 1959. 14P.

INTERNATIONAL BUSINESS MACHINES CORP. GLOSSARY FOR INFORMATION PROCESSING. (REF.MANUAL) NEW YORK, 1962. 97P.

KELLEY, D.X. GLOSSARY OF ELECTRONIC DATA PROCESSING TERMINOLOGY. BEDFORD, MASS. C.W. ADAMS. 1962. 8P. 60T.

MCCRACKEN, D.D. ET AL. PROGRAMMING BUSINESS COMPUTERS. (GL, PP.469-87, 400T) NEW YORK, WILEY, 1959.

MACK, J.D. AND TAYLOR, R.S. A SYSTEM OF DOCUMENTATION TERMINOLOGY. (GL,PP.15-26, 150T) IN/ SHERA,J.H. ET AL. DOCUMENTATION IN ACTION. NEW YORK, REINHOLD, 1956. 471P. 56-12913.

MACKAY, D.M. THE NOMENCLATURE OF INFORMATION THEORY. IRE TRANS. INFORM. THEORY, PP. 9-21 (FEB. 1953) 70T.

MANDL, M. FUNDAMENTALS OF DIGITAL COMPUTERS (GL, PP.279-89) ENGLEWOOD CLIFFS, N.J. PRENTICE-HALL, 1958. 297P. 58-14304. 150T.

MOORE BUSINESS FORMS, INC. DATA PROCESSING TERMS. NIAGARA FALLS, N.Y. 1962. 15P. 110T.

MORDY, D.L. GLOSSARY OF PROGRAMMING AND COMPUTER TERMINOLOGY. NEW YORK, IBM, 1960. 28P.

MURPHY, E.A. JR. DO YOU TALK COMPUTERESE. PHILADELPHIA, MINN.-HONEYWELL REGULATOR, 1960. 22P. 90T.

NATIONAL CASH REGISTER CO. BANK TERMINOLOGY. DAYTON, OHIO, 1954. 44P.

PERRY, O.W. GLOSSARY OF COMPUTER AND PROGRAMMING TERMS. POUGHKEEPSIE, N.Y. IBM, 1959. 40P.

PERRY, J.W. AND KENT, A. DOCUMENTATION AND INFORMATION RETRIEVAL... (GL, PP.136-50, 200T) CLEVELAND, WEST. RESERVE UNIV, 1957. 156P. 57-10828.

PROGRAMMERS GLOSSARY FOR NAREC. NAV. RES.ELECTRON. COMP.BULL,NO.37 (1961).

PRUDENTIAL.INSURANCE CO. OF AMERICA. INTRODUCTION TO ELECTRONIC COMPUTERS, GLOSSARY. NEW YORK, 195 .

RCA SERVICE CO. LANGUAGE AND SYMBOLOGY OF DIGITAL COMPUTER SYSTEMS. (GL,PP.72-108, 700T) CAMDEN, N.J. 1959. 114P. 60-4305.

RAND CORP. GLOSSARY OF DATA PROCESSING TERMINOLOGY. SANTA MONICA, CALIF. 1959. 12P.

ROTH, G.D. A BRIEF GLOSSARY OF DATA PROCESSING TERMS. WHITE PLAINS. N.Y. IBM, 1959. 6P.

SAMS(HOWARD W) AND CO. POCKET DICTIONARY OF COMPUTER TERMS. INDIANAPOLIS, 1962. 96P. 62-20911.

SANDIA CORP. GLOSSARY OF TERMS.(1542 ADP SYST) ALBUQUERQUE, N.M. 1960. 5P. 14T.

SPERRY RAND CORP. SYSTEMS DESIGN AND PROGRAMMING TERMINOLOGY, GLOSSARY. PHILADELPHIA, REMINGTON-RAND, 1960. 23P.

U.S. AGRICULTURAL STABILIZATION AND CONSERVATION SERVICE. GLOSSARY OF ADP TERMINOLOGY. WASHINGTON,1960. 47P.

U.S. BUREAU OF THE BUDGET. AUTOMATIC DATA PROCESSING GLOSSARY. WASHINGTON, 1963. 62P. 63-60813.

U.S. DEPT. OF LABOR. OCCUPATIONS IN ELECTRONIC DATA-PROCESSING SYSTEMS. WASHINGTON, 1959. 44P. 100T.

U.S. INTERAGENCY AUTOMATIC DATA PROCESSING COMMITTEE. ADP GLOSSARY (PRELIM.DRAFT) 1961. 213P. 1400T.

VITRO CORP. OF AMERICA. ELECTRONIC DIGITAL COMPUTER SURVEY FOR THE USAF, GLOSSARY.

WAGNER, F.S,JR. DICTIONARY OF DOCUMENTATION TERMS. AM.DOC,V.11, 102-19 (1960) 500T.

WAGNER, F.S,JR. DICTIONARY OF DOCUMENTATION TERMS. CLARKWOOD, TEXAS, CELANESE CORP. AM, 1959. 31P. 500T.

COMPUTERS, DATA PROCESSING, AND INFORMATION RETRIEVAL

ENGLISH

ARHEIT, I.A. INDEX ORGANIZATION FOR INFORMATION RETRIEVAL. (GL,PP.35-49 T) WASHINGTON, IBM, 1960. 52P.

EIK, M.H. GLOSSARY OF COMPUTER ENGINEERING AND PROGRAMMING TECHNOLOGY. (BRL REPT. NO 1115, PP.1089-116)
.S. ABERDEEN PROVING GROUND, 1961. 1131P. 400T.

ILMOT, E.DE B. GLOSSARY OF TERMS USED IN AUTOMATIC DATA PROCESSING. LONDON, BUSINESS PUBL. 1960. 36P.

ITTY, M.B. ET AL. DICTIONARY OF COMPUTERS AND CONTROLS ABBREVIATIONS, SIGNS AND SYMBOLS. NEW YORK,
ETI, 196 .

FRENCH

OMMISSARIAT GENERAL DU PLAN D.EQUIPEMENT ET DE LA PRODUCTIVITE. TERMINOLOGIE DE L.EXPLOITATION
LECTRONIQUE DES INFORMATIONS... (EN*FR T.IN ELECTRON.INFORM.RETR) PARIS, IMPR. NATL, 1959. 26P. 220T.

GERMAN

ASTEN, R. DEUTSCH-ENGLISCHES WOERTERBUCH FUER ELEKTRONISCHE RECHENAUTOMATEN...(*GE*EN D.OF ELECTRON.
OMP) WUERZBURG, TRILTSCH, 1957. 39P. 500T.

AUER,F.L. AND HEINHOLD,J. FACHBEGRIFFE DER PROGRAMMIERUNGSTECHNIK. (PROGRAMMING T, GE DEFS) ED2. MUNICH,
LDENBOURG, 1962. 52P.

RAHEIM, H. BENENNUNGEN VON LOCHKARTEN. (PUNCHED-CARDS, GE DEFS) NACHR.DOK,V.8, 94-7 (1957) 40T.

LEKTRONISCHE RECHNER. ANGLOAMERIKANISCHE FACHWOERTER. (EN*GE COMPUTER T) ELEKTRON. RUNDSCHAU,V.11,310-13
1957) 400T.

AGNER, S.W. BEGRIFFSBESTIMMUNGEN. (INFORM. PROCESS, GE DEFS) STEINBUCH, 1961. 19P. 300T.

JAPANESE

APANESE INDUSTRIAL STANDARDS COMMITTEE. GLOSSARY OF TERMS RELATING TO DIGITAL COMPUTERS. (JIS Z 8111)
OKYO, 1961. 12P.

POLYGLOT

IKELE, E. ET AL. HANDBUCH DER LOCHKARTEN-ORGANISATION... (HANDBOOK OF PUNCHED CARD TECH, GL, GE*EN*FR
50T) ED2. FRANKFURT/MAIN, AGENOR, 1957. 240P.

LASON, W.E. ELSEVIER.S DICTIONARY OF AUTOMATION, COMPUTERS, CONTROL AND MEASURING, *EN/AM*DU*FR*GE*IT
SP. NEW YORK, ELSEVIER, 1961. 848P. 60-53482. 3400T.

EUTSCH-FRANZOESISCH-ENGLISCH FACHWOERTER-VERZEICHNIS. LOCHKARTEN.(GE FR EN PUNCHED CARD D) FRANKFURT/
AIN, AGENOR, 1957. 16P.

EINHOLD, J. FACHBEGRIFFE DER PROGRAMMIERUNGSTECHNIK, WOERTERVERZEICHNIS FUER DIE PROGRAMMIERUNG VON
IGITAL-RECHENANLAGEN...(GL. OF DIGIT. PROG, GE*EN*DU*FR*SW) MUNICH, OLDENBOURG, 1959. 37P. 180T.

ELLSTROEM, G. AND KARLQVIST, O. ORDLISTA INOM OMRADET DATE- OCH BERAEKNINGSMASKINER. (GL. OF.DATA·
ROCESS/COMP, SW*EN*GE) KONTORSVAERLDEN (STOCKHOLM) NO.12 (1956) AND NO.1 (1957) 7P. 110T.

OLMSTROM, J.E. MULTILINGUAL DICTIONARY OF DATA PROCESSING,*GE*EN*FR*RU*SP. (TRANSL.OF DRAFT STD. BRIT.
EFS. FOR AUTOM. DATA PROCESS/B.S.3527) ROME, PROV.INTL.COMP.CENTRE, 1959. 250P. 1500T. SUPPL. 1/2, 196 .

OLMSTROM, J.E. MULTILINGUAL TERMINOLOGY OF INFORMATION PROCESSING, PROV.DRAFT. (*GE*EN*FR*RU*SP) ROME,
ROV.INTL.COMP.CENTRE, 1959. 392P.

IRSCHSTEIN,G. AND UHLEIN,E. TERMINOLOGIE DER LOCHKARTENTECHNIK. (PUNCHED CARDS T, GE DU EN FR SW)
RANKFURT/MAIN, DEUT. GES, DOK, 1962. 83P.

RISTOUFEK, K. AND SVORODA, F. VYZNAMOVY SLOVNIK VYRAZU Z OBORU STROJU NA ZPRACOVANI INFORMACI. (D.OF
NFORM.PROCESS.MACH, *CZ*EN*GE*RU) REPR.FROM/STROJE ZPRAC.INFORM,SB.NO.6, 295-327 (1958). PRAGUE,
E&KOSLOV.AKAD.VED,1958. 33P. 180T.

RUSSIAN

KADEMIIA NAUK SSSR. KOM.TEKH.TERM. TERMINOLOGIIA VYCHISLITELNYKH MASHIN I PRIBOROV. (COMP/INSTR,RU DEFS)
SB.REK.TERM.NO.42) MOSCOW,1957. 15P. 58-33626.

KADEMIIA NAUK SSSR. KOM.TEKH.TERM. TERMINOLOGY OF COMPUTER MACHINES AND INSTRUMENTS. (JPRS/NY-328)
RANSL.OF ABOVE ENTRY) NEW YORK, U.S. JPRS, 1958. 16P. 58-61620.

LASON, W.E. ELSEVIER.S DICTIONARY OF AUTOMATION, COMPUTERS, CONTROL AND MEASURING. RUSSIAN SUPPL,
EW YORK, ELSEVIER, 1962. 90P. 3400T.

AMONOV, E.I. OSNOVNAIA TERMINOLOGIIA I TEKHNIKA AVTOMATICHESKIKH TSIFROVYKH MACHIN. (BASIC T/DEFS. OF
UTOM.COMP, RU DEFS) VYCHISL. TEKH, V.4, 140-50 (1958)

EIDENBERG, V.K. AND LOSEVA, T.S. ANGLO-RUSSKII SLOVAR PO VYCHISLITELNOI TEKHNIKE. (EN*RU D.OF COMP.
ECH) MOSCOW, AKAD.NAUK SSSR,1958. 93P. MIC 61-7384. 2700T.

COMPUTERS, DATA PROCESSING, AND INFORMATION RETRIEVAL

SWEDISH

SVERIGES STANDARDISERINGSKOMMISSION. DATAMASKINER ORDLISTA. (COMP. GL, SW DEFS) (SWEDISH STD, SEN-0116) STOCKHOLM, 1961.

CRYSTALLOGRAPHY AND MINERALOGY

CHINESE

BRADLEY, J.E.S. AND BARNES, A.C. CHINESE-ENGLISH GLOSSARY OF MINERAL NAMES. NEW YORK, CONSULTANTS BUR, 1963. 120P. 63-20001.

CHUNG-KUO K,O HSUEH YUAN. PIEN I CHU. (ACAD. SINICA. BUR. OF COMPILATIONS/TRANSL) YEH SHIH HSUEH MING TZ,U. (PETROL. T, CH EN) PEKING, 1954. 107P. C58-5636.

KUO LI PIEN KUAN. (NATL. INST. OF TRANLS) K,UANG YEH KUNG CH,ENG MING TZ,U. (MINERAL. ENG. T, CH EN) TAIPEI, CHENG-CHUNG BOOK STORE, 1960. 73P. C61-1986.

ENGLISH

CHAMBERS MINERALOGICAL DICTIONARY. NEW YORK, CHEMICAL, 1957. 47P. 59-2964. 1400T.

COPELAND, L.L. ET AL. THE DIAMOND DICTIONARY. LOS ANGELES, GEMOL.INST.AM, 1960. 317P. 60-51947. 2400T.

CROSBY, J.W. A DESCRIPTIVE GLOSSARY OF RADIOACTIVE MINERALS. PULLMAN, WASHINGTON STATE COLL, 1955. 148P. 400T.

FRONDEL, J.W. AND FLEISCHER, M. GLOSSARY OF URANIUM-AND THORIUM-BEARING MINERALS. ED3. WASHINGTON, U.S. GEOL. SURV, 1955. 169+209P.

HEY, M.H. AN INDEX OF MINERAL SPECIES AND VARIETIES ARRANGED CHEMICALLY. ED2. LONDON, BRITISH MUSEUM, 1955. 728P. 57-532.

SHIPLEY, R.M. DICTIONARY OF GEMS AND GEMOLOGY. ED5. LOS ANGELES, GEMOL. INST. AM, 1951. 261P. 6500T.

WITTY, M.B. ET AL. DICTIONARY OF GEOLOGY AND MINERALOGY ABBREVIATIONS, SIGNS AND SYMBOLS. NEW YORK, SETI, 196 . 192P.

FRENCH

RUDLER, G. AND ANDERSON, N.C. COLLINS FRENCH GEM DICTIONARY, ENGLISH-FRENCH, FRENCH-ENGLISH. LONDON, COLLINS, 1952. 760P.

GERMAN

EHLERS,K. NOMINA DER KRISTALLOGRAPHIE UND MINERALOGIE... (CRYST/MINERAL. D, GE DEFS) HAMBURG, BOYSEN-MAASCH, 1952. 166P. 52-65044.

FLUEGGE, S. ET AL. HANDBUCH DER PHYSIK. (ENCYCL. OF PHYS) V.7, PT.1, KRISTALLPHYSIK 1. (CRYSTAL PHYS. 1, *GE*EN GL, PP.666-87, 750T) BERLIN, SPRINGER, 1955. 687P. A56-2942.

FLUEGGE, S, ET AL. HANDBUCH DER PHYSIK. (ENCYCL. OF PHYS) V.7, PT.2, KRISTALLPHYSIK 2. (CRYSTAL PHYS. 2, *GE*EN GL, PP.254-73, 650T) BERLIN, SPRINGER, 1958. 273P. A56-2942.

FLUEGGE, S. ET AL. HANDBUCH DER PHYSIK. (ENCYCL. OF PHYS) V.25/1, KRISTALLOPTIK, BEUGUNG. (CRYSTAL OPTICS, DIFFRACTION, *GE*EN GL, PP.574-92, 500T) BERLIN, SPRINGER, 1961. 592P. A56-2942.

FLUEGGE, S. ET AL. HANDBUCH DER PHYSIK. (ENCYCL. OF PHYS) V.32, STRUKTURFORSCHUNG. (STRUCT. RES,*GE*EN GL, PP.643-60, 600T) BERLIN, SPRINGER, 1957. 663P. A56-2942.

JAPANESE

KINOSHITA, K. COLOURED ILLUSTRATIONS OF ECONOMIC MINERALS. (*JA*EN) OSAKA, HOIKUSHA, 1957. 255P. 300T.

KINOSHITA, K. DICTIONARY OF RECENT MINERALOGICAL TERMS... (EN*JA). TOKYO, KAZAMA SHOBO, 1954. 922P. 18000T.

KINOSHITA, K. KOBUTSU GAKUMEI JITEN. (MINERAL D, EN*JA) TOKYO, KAZAMA, 1960. 1002P. J61-12. 15000T.

KUME, T. HOSEKI, KIKINZOKU JITEN. (JEWELS/PRECIOUS MET.D, EN*JA) TOKYO, KAZAMA SHOBU, 1957. 353+105P. J59-145. 3800T.

MASUTOMI, K. GENSHOKU GANSEKI ZUKAN. (ILLUS. ROCK D, *JA*EN) OSAKA, HOIKUSHA, 1960. 158P. J62-1180. 500T.

POLYGLOT

CHUNG-KUO K,O HSUEH YUAN. PIEN I CH,U PAN WEI YUAN HUI. (ACAD. SINICA. COMM. OF PUBL/TRANSL) K,UANG WU HSUEH MING TZ,U. (MINERAL T, RU EN CH) PEKING, SCIENCE, 1957. 279P. C58-5287.

INTERNATIONAL UNION OF CRYSTALLOGRAPHY. INTL.TABLES FOR X-RAY CRYSTALLOGRAPHY. (D. CRYST, V.1, *EN*FR*GE *RU*SP... PP.554-8, 150T) BIRMINGHAM,ENG. KYNOCH, 1952. V.1. 558P. 53-868.

INTERNATIONAL UNION OF CRYSTALLOGRAPHY. INTL. TABLES FOR X-RAY CRYSTALLOGRAPHY. (D.CRYST,V.2, *EN*FR*GE *RU*SP... PP.433-44, 500T) BIRMINGHAM,ENG. KYNOCH, 1959. V.2. 444P. 53-868.

46

CRYSTALLOGRAPHY AND MINERALOGY

POLYGLOT

NATIONAL UNION OF CRYSTALLOGRAPHY. INTL.TABLES FOR X-RAY CRYSTALLOGRAPHY. (D.CRYST,V.3, *EN*FR*GE
P... PP.339-54. 700T) BIRMINGHAM,ENG. KYNOCH, 1962. V.3. 362P. 53-868.

MZHAN, O.E. ET AL. PIATIIAZYCHNYI SLOVAR MINERALOGICHESKIKH NAZVANII. (5-LANG. MINERAL D. EN GE FR
) MOSCOW, FIZMATGIZ, 1962. 347P. 63-44287. 25000T.

RUSSIAN

MIIA NAUK SSSR. KOM. TEKH. TERM. TERMINOLOGIIA SISTEM RAZRABOTKI MESTOROZHDENII TVERDYKH POLEZNYKH
AEMYKH PODZEMNYM SPOSOBOM. (WORKING SYST. FOR UNDERGROUND MIN, RU DEFS) (SB. REK.TERM. NO.51)
W, 1959. 13P. 60-30443. 90T.

SPANISH

VO, P. AND CHICARRO, F. DICCIONARIO DE GEOLOGIA Y CIENCIAS AFINES. (D. OF GEOL/ RELATED SCI, SP
BARCELONA, LABOR, 1957. 2V. 1685P. 57-45178. 14000T.

,R.F. COLLINS SPANISH GEM DICTIONARY, SPANISH-ENGLISH, ENGLISH-SPANISH. LONDON, COLLINS, 1957. 768P.

DOCUMENTATION AND BIBLIOGRAPHY

ENGLISH

CAN STANDARDS ASSOCIATION. BASIC CRITERIA FOR INDEXES. (ASA Z39.4-1959) NEW YORK,1959.

N, D.M. GLOSSARY OF TERMS FOR MICROPHOTOGRAPHY AND FOR REPRODUCTION MADE FROM MICRO-IMAGES.
OLIS, NAT,L. MICROFILM ASSOC, 1962. 50P.

F.C. THE BOOKMAN,S CONCISE DICTIONARY. NEW YORK, PHIL.LIBR, 1956. 318P. 57-678. 9000T.

LEY, E.C. AND LOVETT, L.L. GLOSSARY OF TERMS IN COMPUTERS AND DATA PROCESSING. ED5. NEWTONVILLE,
BERKELEY, 1960. 90P. 61-4747. 900T.

R,J. ABC FOR BOOK-COLLECTORS. ED3. LONDON, MERCURY, 1961. 208P. 62-39954.

PROCESSING EQUIPMENT ENCYCLOPEDIA. DETROIT, GILLE. 1961. 2V. 61-15132.

AN KODAK CO. GLOSSARY OF TERMS FOR THE MINICARD SYSTEM. ROCHESTER, N.Y. 195 .

TER, G.A. AN ENCYCLOPEDIA OF THE BOOK TERMS USED IN PAPER-MAKING, PRINTING, BOOKBINDING...
LAND, WORLD, 1960. 484P. 61-2811.

, M. ET AL. IBM GLOSSARY FOR INFORMATION PROCESSING. PRELIM.ED. WHITE PLAINS, N.Y. IBM. 1961. 83P.

D, L.M. THE LIBRARIANS GLOSSARY... ED2. LONDON, GRAFTON, 1959. 332P. 59-2822.

NATIONAL BUSINESS MACHINES CORP. GLOSSARY FOR INFORMATION PROCESSING. (REF.MANUAL) NEW YORK, 1962.

U, T. ENCYCLOPAEDIA OF LIBRARIANSHIP. ED2. LONDON, BOWES, 1961. 397P.

J.D. AND TAYLOR, R.S. A SYSTEM OF DOCUMENTATION TERMINOLOGY. (GL,PP.15-26, 150T) IN/ SHERA,J.H. ET
DOCUMENTATION IN ACTION. NEW YORK, REINHOLD, 1956. 471P. 56-12913.

Y, D.M. THE NOMENCLATURE OF INFORMATION THEORY. IRE TRANS. INFORM. THEORY, PP. 9-21 (FEB. 1953) 70T.

, J.W. AND KENT, A. DOCUMENTATION AND INFORMATION RETRIEVAL... (GL, PP.136-50, 200T) CLEVELAND,
RESERVE UNIV, 1957. 156P. 57-10828.

N, H.F. AND GODFREY, L.E. DICTIONARY OF REPORT SERIES CODES. NEW YORK, SPEC.LIBR.ASSOC, 1962. 656P.
T.

, J.H. ET AL. ENCYCLOPEDIA OF LIBRARY SCIENCE AND DOCUMENTATION. NEW YORK, INTERSCIENCE. (IN PREP)

R, R.S. GLOSSARY OF TERMS FREQUENTLY USED IN SCIENTIFIC DOCUMENTATION. NEW YORK, AM. INST. PHYS,
16P. 100T.

CK, H. GLOSSARY OF TERMS USED IN MICROREPRODUCTION. HINGHAM,MASS, NATL. MICROFILM ASSOC, 1955. 88P.

DEPT. OF DEFENSE. GLOSSARY OF PHOTOGRAPHIC TERMS, INCLUDING DOCUMENT REPRODUCTION. (TM11-411)
NGTON, 1961. 128P. 62-60293. 2500T.

RY, B.C. GLOSSARY OF CURRENT TERMINOLOGY, PP.27-46, 300T. IN/ RANGANATHAN, S.R. DEPTH
IFICATION AND REFERENCE SERVICE... DELHI, INDIAN LIBR.ASSOC, 1953. 444P. 53-12382.

R, F.S,JR..DICTIONARY OF DOCUMENTATION TERMS. CLARKWOOD, TEXAS, CELANESE CORP. AM, 1959. 31P. 500T.

R, F.S,JR. DICTIONARY OF DOCUMENTATION TERMS. AM.DOC,V.11, 102-19 (1960) 500T.

IT, I.A. INDEX ORGANIZATION FOR INFORMATION RETRIEVAL. (GL,PP.35-49 T) WASHINGTON, IBM, 1960. 52P.

DOCUMENTATION AND BIBLIOGRAPHY

FRENCH

COMMISSARIAT GENERAL DU PLAN D.EQUIPEMENT ET DE LA PRODUCTIVITE. TERMINOLOGIE DE L.EXPLOITATION
ELECTRONIQUE DES INFORMATIONS... (EN*FR T.IN ELECTRON.INFORM.RETR) PARIS, IMPR. NATL, 1959. 26P. 220T.

GERMAN

DRAHEIM, H. BENENNUNGEN VON LOCHKARTEN. (PUNCHED-CARDS, GE DEFS) NACHR.DOK,V.8, 94-7 (1957) 40T.

GROSS, O. FACHAUSDRUCKE DES BIBLIOTHEKSWESENS UND SEINER NACHBARGEBIETE. (*GE*EN D.OF LIBR.T) ED2.
HAMBURG, EBERHARD STICHNOTE, 1952. 163P. 53-15675.

HILLER, H. WOERTERBUCH DES BUCHES. (PRINTING D, GE DEFS) ED2. FRANKFURT/MAIN, KLOSTERMANN, 1958. 332P.

KIRCHNER, J. ET AL. LEXIKON DES BUCHWESENS. (ENCYCL. OF BOOKS/PRINTING, GE DEFS) STUTTGART, HIERSEMANN,
1952-56. 4V. 53-17416.

MARTIN, W. KLEINES FREMDWOERTERBUCH DES BUCH-UND SCHRIFTWESENS. (FOR. T. IN BUOK/PRINTING IND, GE DEFS)
LEIPZIG, HARRASSOWITZ, 1959. 169P. 59-30052.

HEBREW

WELLISCH, H. THE SPECIAL LIBRARY, MANAGEMENT AND ORGANIZATION. (*HE*ÈN GL) TEL AVIV, HISTADRUT, 1962.
205P.

HINDI

GOUR, P.N. PUSTAKALAYA VIJNANA KOSU. (LIBR. GL, *HI*EN) 1961. 256P. SA62-668.

ITALIAN

GAMBIGLIANI-ZOCCOLI, B. DIZIONARIO DI TERMINOLOGIA BIBLIOGRAFICA... (*IT*EN D. OF BIBL) PT.1, EN*IT
/LA RICERCA SCIENTIFICA.V.26, 655-63 (1956) MONTHLY THROUGH V.27, 2610-5 (1957). PT.2 IT*EN/V.27, 2907-12
THROUGH V.27, 3761-5 (1957) (INCOMPL)

JAPANESE

JAPAN. MINISTRY OF EDUCATION. JAPANESE SCIENTIFIC TERMS, LIBRARY SCIENCE. (*JA*EN) TOKYO, DAINIPPON
TOSHO, 1958. 307P. J60-77, 2600T. 150 ABBR, EN*JA.

POLISH

PRZYBYLSKI, E.S. A DICTIONARY OF SELECTED BIBLIOGRAPHICAL TERMS, BOOKTRADE TERMS, AND PLACE NAMES IN
POLISH. LEXINGTON, UNIV. KENTUCKY LIBRS, 1955. 36P. 55-62450.

POLYGLOT

AIKELE, E. ET AL. HANDBUCH DER LOCHKARTEN-ORGANISATION... (HANDBOOK OF PUNCHED CARD TECH, GL, GE*EN*FR
450T) ED2. FRANKFURT/MAIN, AGENOR, 1957. 240P.

ALLERDING, J.E. GERMAN AND FRENCH ABBREVIATIONS AND TERMS USED IN SERIAL PUBLICATIONS AND IN
BIBLIOGRAPHICAL CITATIONS. SPEC. LIBR, V.43, 358-63 (1952) 220T.

CSIKOLY, . NYOLCNYELVU CIMFELVETELI KEZISZOTAR. (8-LANG. CATALOGING D/ABBR) BUDAPEST, ORSZ. MUSZ.
KONYVTAR, 1954. 41P.

DANMARKS BIBLIOTEKSSKOLE. BIBLIOTEKSGLOSER, DANSK-ENGELSK-FRANSK-TYSK.(LIBR.GL, DA*EN*FR*GE) COPENHAGEN,
DANSK BIBL.KONTOR, 1962. 29P. 300T.

DUBUC, M.R. AND GUENTHER, A. DOCUMENTATION TERMINOLOGY. (FR AND GE TRANSL.OF EN GL. BY MACK, J.D. AND
TAYLOR, R.S.) REV.DOC. V.25, NO.2, 37-44 (1958). 70T.

HERTZBERGER, M. DICTIONNAIRE A L.USAGE DE LA LIBRAIRIE ANCIENNE. (DA DU EN FR GE IT SP SW D. OF MEDIEVAL
/ANCIENT LIBR) PARIS, LIGUE INTL. LIBR.ANCIENNE, 1956. 1200T.

HOLMSTROM, J.E. MULTILINGUAL TERMINOLOGY OF INFORMATION PROCESSING, PROV.DRAFT. (*GE*EN*FR*RU*SP) ROME,
PROV.INTL.COMP.CENTRE, 1959. 392P.

HUNGARY. MAGYAR TUDOMANYOS AKADEMIA. KONYVTAR. ABBREVIATURAE CYRILLICAE. (CYRILLIC ABBRS, *BU*RU*SC*UK
*WR*EN*GE*HU) BUDAPEST, 1961. 138P. 63-6205.

HUNGARY. MAGYAR TUDOMANYOS AKADEMIA . KONYVTAR. VOCABULARIUM ABBREVIATURARUM BIBLIOTHECARII. BUDAPEST,
196 - .

INTERNATIONAL FEDERATION FOR DOCUMENTATION. UNIVERSAL DECIMAL CLASSIFICATION. TRILINGUAL ABRIDGED ED,
*GE*EN*FR. (FID PUBL.277, B.S. 1000B) LONDON. BRIT.STDS.INST, 1958. 518P.

INTERNATIONAL FEDERATION FOR DOCUMENTATION. VOCABULARIUM DOCUMENTATIONIS (DOC. GL) THE HAGUE. (IN PREP)

INTERNATIONAL POLYGLOT VOCABULARY OF ARCHIVES. UNESCO BULL. LIBR, V.11, 57 (1957)

KHAVKINA, L.B. ET AL. SLOVARI BIBLIOTECHNO-BIBLIOGRAFICHESKIKH TERMINOV... (D. OF LIBR. T, *EN*RU*GE*FR)
MOSCOW, VSESOIUZ.KNIZHN.PALATA, 1952. 234P. 53-25638.

DOCUMENTATION AND BIBLIOGRAPHY

POLYGLOT

KRISTOUFEK, K. AND SVOBODA, F. VYZNAMOVY SLOVNIK VYRAZU Z OBORU STROJU NA ZPRACOVANI INFORMACI. (D.OF INFORM.PROCESS.MACH, *CZ*EN*GE*RU) REPR.FROM/STROJE ZPRAC.INFORM,SB.NO.6, 295-327 (1958). PRAGUE, CESKOSLOV.AKAD.VED,1958. 33P. 180T.

MACK, J.D., DUBUC, M.R. AND GUENTHER, A. DOCUMENTATION TERMINOLOGY, *EN*FR*GE. (FID 307) THE HAGUE, INTL.FED.DOC, 1958. 8P. 70T.

MAMIYA, F. A COMPLETE DICTIONARY OF LIBRARY TERMS... *EN*GE*FR*CH*JA. TOKYO, JAPAN LIBR. BUR, 1952. 645P. 10000T.

MORAN, L. CZECH, POLISH, AND RUSSIAN BOOK TRADE TERMS AND ABBREVIATIONS. SPEC.LIBR.V.49, 246-52 (1958) 200T.

MORAVEK, E. AND BERNATH-BODNAR, E. VERZEICHNIS UNGARISCHER FACHAUSDRUECKE UND ABKUERZUNGEN AUS DEM BUCH- UND BIBLIOTHEKSWESEN... (BOOK/LIBR.T/ABBR. HU*EN*FR*GE) VIENNA, OESTERR.NATL.-BIBL. 1958. 61P. 59-52242.

NADVORNIK, M. ET AL. SLOVNIK KNIHOVNICKYCH TERMINU V SESTI JAZYCICH... (D. OF LIBR. T, CZ RU PL GE EN FR) PRAGUE, (OLOMOUC) STATNI PED NAKL, 1958. 632P. 59-30054. 2500T.

ORNE, J. LANGUAGE OF THE FOREIGN BOOK TRADE. ABBREVIATIONS, TERMS, PHRASES. ED2. (*CZ*DA*DU*EN*FR*GE*IT *PL*PR*RU*SP*SW) CHICAGO, AM. LIBR. ASSOC, 1962. 213P. 61-12881. 16000T.

PIPICS,Z. DICTIONARIUM BIBLIOTHECARII PRACTICUM. (LIBR. PRACT D, HU*EN/ 18 LANG) BUDAPEST, KULTURA, 1963. 317P. 300T.

SCHLEMMINGER, J. FACHWOERTERBUCH DES BUCHWESENS, DEUTSCH, ENGLISCH, FRANZOESISCH... (D. OF BOOK T, *GE*EN *FR) ED2. DARMSTADT, STOYTSCHEFF, 1954. 367P. A56-2927. 6000T.

SENALP, L. AND THOMPSON, A. DORT DILDE KUTUPHANECILIK TERIMLERI SOZLUGU. (TU TRANSL. OF VOC. BIBL, TU*EN*FR*GE) ANKARA. TUERK TARIH KURUMU BASIMEVI, 1959. 379P. 60-33751. 2500T.

THOMPSON, A. ET AL VOCABULARIUM BIBLIOTHECARII. (EN*FR*GE*RU*SP) ED2. PARIS, UNESCO, 1962. 627P. 63-1650. 2800T.

TURNER, M.C. THE BOOKMAN,S GLOSSARY. (FOREIGN BOOK TRADE T, *DA*FR*GE*IT*RU*SP, PP.181-203) ED4. NEW YORK, BOWKER, 1961. 212P. 61-13239. 1100T.

UNITED NATIONS. TITLES OF NON-GOVERNMENTAL ORGANIZATIONS. (*EN*FR*SP) (TERMINOLOGY BULL. NO.140, ADD.2) NEW YORK, 1958.

VON OSTERMANN, G.F. MANUAL OF FOREIGN LANGUAGES... (130 LANG) ED4. NEW YORK, CENTRAL BOOK, 1952. 414P. 52-2409.

WIECKOWSKA, H. AND PLISZCZYNSKA, H. PODRECZNY SLOWNIK BIBLIOTEKARZA. (LIBR. GL, *PL*EN*FR*GE*RU) WARSAW, PANSTW. WYDAW. NAUK, 1955. 309P. 55-39069. 3000T.

RUSSIAN

AKADEMIIA NAUK SSSR. INDEX OF ABBREVIATED AND FULL TITLES OF SCIENTIFIC AND TECHNICAL PERIODICAL LITERATURE. (UKAZATEL SOKR. I POLN. NAZV. NAUCH/TEKH. LIT) TRANSL. BY WRIGHT-PATTERSON AFB, OHIO, 1960. 247P. 60-60261. 1800T.

ELIZARENKOVA,T.P. ANGLO-RUSSKII SLOVAR KNIGOVEDCHESKIKH TERMINOV. (EN*RU LIBR.SCI.T) MOSCOW, SOV. ROSSIIA, 1962. 510P. 63-36755.

FISHER, E.L. ABBREVIATIONS OF RUSSIAN SCIENTIFIC SERIAL PUBLICATIONS. AM. DOC, V.10, 192-208 (1959) 200T.

FISHER, E.L. SOKRASHCHENIIA, RUSSIAN ABBREVIATIONS FOR BIBLIOGRAPHIC SEARCH. SPEC. LIBR, V.49, 365-70 (1958) 240T.

GWIRTSMAN,J.J. ABBREVIATIONS IN RUSSIAN ABSTRACT JOURNALS COVERING CHEMISTRY AND RELATED FIELDS. J. CHEM, DOC. V.3, 44-59 (1963) 700T.

KRASSOVSKY, D.M. A GLOSSARY OF RUSSIAN TERMINOLOGY USED IN BIBLIOGRAPHIES AND LIBRARY SCIENCE. LOS ANGELES, UNIV. CALIF. LIBR, 1955. 19P.

NEISWENDER, R. GUIDE TO RUSSIAN REFERENCE AND LANGUAGE AIDS. (GL OF RU BIBLIOG/BOOK-TRADE T, PP.74-84, 800T) NEW YORK, SPEC.LIBR.ASSOC, 1962. 92P. 62-21081.

SARINGULIAN, M.KH. ET AL. ANGLO-RUSSKII BIBLIOTECHNO-BIBLIOGRAFICHESKII SLOVAR. (EN*RU D. OF LIBR/ BIBL. T) MOSCOW, VSESOIUZ. KNIZH. PALATA, 1958. 284P. 59-363300. 11000T.

SHAMURIN, E.I. SLOVAR KNIGOVEDCHESKIKH TERMINOV DLIA BIBLIOTEKAREI,BIBLIOGRAFOV... (D. OF LIBR. SCI, RU DEFS) MOSCOW, SOV. ROSSIIA, 1958. 340P. 59-36469. 4500T.

SPANISH

BUONOCORE, D. DICCIONARIO DE BIBLIOTECOLOGIA... (LIBR. SCI. D, SP DEFS) SANTA FE, ARGENTINA, CASTELLVI, 1963. 336P. 63-49887. 2250T.

IGUINIZ, J.B. LEXICO BIBLIOGRAFICO. (BIBL. D, SP DEFS) MEXICO, INST. BIBL. MEX, 1959. 307P. 60-35566.

49

ELECTRICAL AND ELECTRONIC ENGINEERING

CHINESE

FAN, FENG-YUAN. WU—HSIEN-TIEN TA TZ,U-TIEN. (ELECTRON. D, EN CH) SHANGHAI, K,O HSUEH SHU PAO
SHE, 1952. 491P.

HSUAN FENG CH,U PAN SHE, TAI-PEI. WU HSIEN TIEN TA TZ,U TIEN. (ELECTRON D, CH EN) TAIPEI, 1956. 491P.
C62-1107.

KUO LI PIEN I KUAN. (NATL. INST. OF TRANSL) T,IEN CHI KUNG CHENG MING TZ,U. (ELEC. ENG. T, EN CH)
TAIPEI, CHENG-CHUNG BOOKS, 1962. 464P. C63-22.

DUTCH

STRABEL, A. ET AL. TECHNISCHE ENCYCLOPEDIE VOOR RADIO, TELEVISIE, RADAR, ELECTRONICA... (RADIO,TV,RADAR,
ELECTRON.D, DU DEFS) AMSTERDAM, STRENGHOLT, 1954. 320P. A55-1123.

ENGLISH

AEROSPACE INDUSTRIEV ASSOCIATION. SPECIFICATION NAS 710, RESISTORS, VARIABLE, PRECISION. WASHINGTON,
1955. 40T.

AMERICAN INSTITUTE OF ELECTRICAL ENGINEERS. DEFINITIONS OF ELECTRICAL TERMS. COMMUNICATION. (GR-65,AS,
C42.65) NEW YORK, 1957. 128P. 1800T.

AMERICAN INSTITUTE OF ELECTRICAL ENGINEERS. DEFINITIONS OF ELECTRICAL TERMS. ELECTRIC WELDING AND
CUTTING. (GR-50, ASA C42.50) NEW YORK, 1958. 12P. 100T.

AMERICAN INSTITUTE OF ELECTRICAL ENGINEERS. DEFINITIONS OF ELECTRICAL TERMS. ELECTROBIOLOGY, INCLUDING
ELECTROTHERAPEUTICS (GR-80,ASA C42.80) NEW YORK, 1957. 13P. 120T.

AMERICAN INSTITUTE OF ELECTRICAL ENGINEERS. DEFINITIONS OF ELECTRICAL TERMS. ELECTROCHEMISTRY AND
ELECTROMETALLURGY. (GR-60, ASA C42.60) NEW YORK, 1956.30P. 300T.

AMERICAN INSTITUTE OF ELECTRICAL ENGINEERS. DEFINITIONS OF ELECTRICAL TERMS. ELECTROMECHANICAL DEVICES,
(GR-45, ASA C42.45) NEW YORK, 1959. 15P. 150T.

AMERICAN INSTITUTE OF ELECTRICAL ENGINEERS. DEFINITIONS OF ELECTRICAL TERMS. ELECTRON DEVICES. (GR-70,
ASA C42.70) NEW YORK, 1957. 29P. 300T.

AMERICAN INSTITUTE OF ELECTRICAL ENGINEERS. DEFINITIONS OF ELECTRICAL TERMS. GENERAL... (FUNDAMENTAL/
DERIVED) TERMS. (GR-05, ASA C42.05) NEW YORK. (IN PREP)

AMERICAN INSTITUTE OF ELECTRICAL ENGINEERS. DEFINITIONS OF ELECTRICAL TERMS. GENERATION, TRANSMISSION AI
DISTRIBUTION. (GR-35, ASA C42.35) NEW YORK, 1957. 38P. 350T.

AMERICAN INSTITUTE OF ELECTRICAL ENGINEERS. DEFINITIONS OF ELECTRICAL TERMS. ILLUMINATING ENGINEERING.
(GR-55, ASA C42.55) NEW YORK, 1956. 14P. 120T.

AMERICAN INSTITUTE OF ELECTRICAL ENGINEERS. DEFINITIONS OF ELECTRICAL TERMS. INDUSTRIAL CONTROL
EQUIPMENT. (GR-25, ASA C42.25) NEW YORK, 1956. 24P. 220T.

AMERICAN INSTITUTE OF ELECTRICAL ENGINEERS. DEFINITIONS OF ELECTRICAL TERMS. INSTRUMENTS, METERS AND
METER TESTING. (GR-30, ASA C42.30) NEW YORK, 1957. 39P. 400T.

AMERICAN INSTITUTE OF ELECTRICAL ENGINEERS. DEFINITIONS OF ELECTRICAL TERMS. MINING. (GR-85,ASA C42.8
NEW YORK, 1956. 12P. 90T.

AMERICAN INSTITUTE OF ELECTRICAL ENGINEERS. DEFINITIONS OF ELECTRICAL TERMS. MISCELLANEOUS. (GR-95, AS
C42.95) NEW YORK, 1957. 17P. 170T.

AMERICAN INSTITUTE OF ELECTRICAL ENGINEERS. DEFINITIONS OF ELECTRICAL TERMS. RADIOLOGY. (GR-75, ASA
C42.75) NEW YORK (IN PREP)

AMERICAN INSTITUTE OF ELECTRICAL ENGINEERS. DEFINITIONS OF ELECTRICAL TERMS. ROTATING MACHINERY. (GR-1
ASA C42.10) NEW YORK, 1957. 34P. 320T.

AMERICAN INSTITUTE OF ELECTRICAL ENGINEERS. DEFINITIONS OF ELECTRICAL TERMS. SWITCHGEAR.
(GR-20, ASA C42.20) NEW YORK, 1956. 38P. 400T.

AMERICAN INSTITUTE OF ELECTRICAL ENGINEERS. DEFINITIONS OF ELECTRICAL TERMS. TRANSFORMERS, REGULATORS,
REACTORS AND RECTIFIERS. (GR-15, ASA C42.15) NEW YORK, 1958. 34P..320T.

AMERICAN INSTITUTE OF ELECTRICAL ENGINEERS. DEFINITIONS OF ELECTRICAL TERMS. TRANSPORTATION. (GR-40,
GENERAL,ASA C42.40/GR-41, AIR, ASA C42.41/ GR-42, LAND, ASA C42.42/ GR-43, MARINE, ASA C42.43) NEW YOR
1956. 42P. 4Z0T.

AMERICAN INSTITUTE OF ELECTRICAL ENGINEERS. DICTIONARY OF SWITCHING THEORY TERMS. (PRELIM. DRAFT,
CP-60-1225) NEW YORK, 196 .

AMERICAN INSTITUTE OF ELECTRICAL ENGINEERS. SPECIFICATION STANDARDS FOR ELECTROHYDRAULIC FLOW CONTROL
SERVOVALVES. (ATEE 59-357) NEW YORK, 1959. 30P. 100T.

AMERICAN SOCIETY FOR TFSTING/MATERIALS. TENTATIVE DEFINITIONS OF ELECTRICAL TERMS. (D1711-60T) ASTM
STDS, PT.11, 1368-9. PHILADELPHIA, 1961. 10T.

ELECTRICAL AND ELECTRONIC ENGINEERING

ENGLISH

AMERICAN SOCIETY FOR TESTING/MATERIALS. TENTATIVE DEFINITIONS OF TERMS RELATING TO ELECTROPLATING. (B374-62T) ASTM STDS, PT.2, SUPPL.203-12. PHILADELPHIA, 1962. 250T.

AMERICAN SOCIETY FOR TESTING/MATERIALS. TENTATIVE DEFINITIONS OF TERMS RELATING TO UNINSULATED METALLIC ELECTRICAL CONDUCTORS.(B354-62T) ASTM STDS, PT.2, SUPPL.250-1. PHILADELPHIA, 1962. 40T.

AMERICAN SOCIETY OF MECHANICAL ENGINEERS. AUTOMATIC CONTROL TERMINOLOGY. (ASME STD NO. 105) NEW YORK, 1954. 23P. 70T.

AMERICAN STANDARDS ASSOCIATION. AUTOMATIC NULL-BALANCING ELECTRICAL MEASURING INSTRUMENTS. (C39.4-1956) NEW YORK, 1956. P.

AMERICAN STANDARDS ASSOCIATION. COMMUNICATIONS GLOSSARY, DRAFT. NEW YORK, 1962. 44P. 400T.

AMERICAN STANDARDS ASSOCIATION. DIRECT ACTING ELECTRICAL RECORDING INSTRUMENTS. (C39.2-1953) NEW YORK, 1953. P.

AMERICAN STANDARDS ASSOCIATION. ELECTRICAL INDICATING INSTRUMENTS. (C39.1-1951) NEW YORK, 1951. P.

AMERICAN STANDARDS ASSOCIATION. QUANTITIES AND UNITS USED IN ELECTRICITY. (C61.1-1961) NEW YORK, 1961. 2P.

AMERICAN STANDARDS ASSOCIATION. STANDARD DEFINITIONS AND TERMINOLOGY FOR RELAYS. (C83.16-1959) NEW YORK, ELECTRONIC IND. ASSOC, 1959. 29P. 380T.

AMERICAN STANDARDS ASSOCIATION. TERMINOLOGY FOR TRANSFORMERS, REGULATORS, AND REACTORS. (C57.12.80) NEW.YORK, 1958.

BATTEY, E.W. AND LINFORD, A. INSTRUMENT ENCYCLOPEDIA. (GL, PP.1-28) LONDON, HERBERT, 1958. 292P. 58-44430. 1340T.

BEAM, R.E. A DICTIONARY OF ELECTRONIC TERMS. CONCISE DEFINITIONS OF WORDS USED IN RADIO, TELEVISION, AND ELECTRONICS. ED7. CHICAGO, ALLIED·RADIO, 1963. 88P. 63-5264.

BELL TELEPHONE LABORATORIES, INC. GERMAN STANDARDS, CONTROL ENGINEERING TERMS. (TRANSL, TR D-54, DIN-19226, 1954) MURRAY HILL, N.J, 1957.

BELL TELEPHONE LABORATORIES. GLOSSARY. MURRAY HILL, N.J, 1960. 21P.

BERLIN, R. ET AL. A DICTIONARY OF SWITCHING THEORY TERMS. NEW YORK, AM.INST.ELEC.ENG, 1960. 43P.

BRITISH STANDARDS INSTITUTION. GLOSSARY OF TERMS FOR ELECTRICAL CHARACTERISTICS OF RADIO RECEIVERS. (B.S. 2065) LONDON, 1954. 42P. 150T.

BRITISH STANDARDS INSTITUTION. GLOSSARY OF TERMS USED IN ELECTRICAL ENGINEERING. (B.S.205, PTS.1-8, AMEND. PD1653-1953, PD2187-1955, PD2188-1955) LONDON, 1943-1955. 186P. 1700T.

BRITISH STANDARDS INSTITUTION. GLOSSARY OF TERMS USED IN ILLUMINATION AND PHOTOMETRY. (B.S. 233) LONDON, 1953. 20P. 110T.

BRITISH STANDARDS INSTITUTION. GLOSSARY OF TERMS USED IN INDUSTRIAL HIGH-FREQUENCY INDUCTION AND DIELECTRIC HEATING. (B.S.2759) LONDON, 1956. 16P. 90T.

BRITISH STANDARDS INSTITUTION. GLOSSARY OF TERMS USED IN TELECOMMUNICATION (INCL.RADIO/ELECTRON) ED3. (B.S.204 AMEND. 1, PD4694, 30T) LONDON, 1960. 352P. 3500T.

BRITISH STANDARDS INSTITUTION. GUIDE TO TERMS USED IN A.C. POWER SYSTEM STUDIES. (B.S. 2658) LONDON,1956. 32P. 80T.

BRITISH STANDARDS INSTITUTION. TYPES OF ENCLOSURE OF ELECTRICAL APPARATUS. (B.S. 2817. PT.1,GL) LONDON, 1957. 12P. 40T.

CARTER, H. DICTIONARY OF ELECTRONICS. NEW YORK, PITMAN, 1960. 377P. 62-51362. 3000T.

CODLIN, E.M. AND MOORE, C.K. LIST OF RECENTLY-COINED TERMS IN ELECTRONICS... LONDON, ASLIB, 1960. 14P.

COOKE, N.M. AND MARKUS, J. ELECTRONICS AND NUCLEONICS DICTIONARY... NEW YORK, MCGRAW-HILL, 1960. 543P. 60-10605. 13000T.

COYNE TECHNICAL DICTIONARY OF 4000 TERMS USED IN TELEVISION, RADIO, ELECTRICITY AND ELECTRONICS.. CHICAGO, COYNE ELEC/TV SCHOOL, 1955. 152P. 55-14738. 4000T.

EDISON ELECTRIC INSTITUTE. GLOSSARY OF ELECTRIC UTILITY TERMS, FINANCIAL AND TECHNICAL. (PUBL. NO.61-31) NEW YORK, 1961. 80P.

EDISON ELECTRIC INSTITUTE. GLOSSARY OF ELECTRIC UTILITY TERMS, FINANCIAL AND TECHNICAL. NUCLEAR SUPPL. (PUB. NO.61-49) NEW YORK, 1961. 13P.

GENERAL ELECTRIC CO. REGULATING AND D-C CONTROL SYSTEM TERMINOLOGY AND DEFINITIONS. (GE 2654, IE 1099) SCHENECTADY, N.Y, 1956.

ENGLISH

GLOSSARY OF COMPUTER TERMS. SYLVANIA TECH. V.12, 106-8 (1959) 100T.

GRAF, R.F. HOWARD W. SAMS MODERN DICTIONARY OF ELECTRONICS... INDIANAPOLIS, SAMS,1962. 370P. 61-18659. 10000T.

GRAHAM, F.D. AUDELS NEW ELECTRIC SCIENCE DICTIONARY... NEW YORK, AUDEL, 1963. 555P. 64-590. 9000T.

GREEN, A.R. ELECTRONIC TERMINOLOGY...ABBREVIATIONS... HILVERSUM, OCECO, 1950. 64P. 53-37520. 1600T.

GUNDERSEN, J.L. RELIABILITY GLOSSARY. ED2. DOWNEY, CALIF, AUTONETICS, 1962. 73P. 63-916.

HANDEL, S. A DICTIONARY OF ELECTRONICS. BALTIMORE, PENGUIN, 1962. 383P. 62-52677. 5000T.

ILLUMINATING ENGINEERING SOCIETY. IES LIGHTING HANDBOOK. (NOMENCLATURE, CH.3, PP.3-21) ED3. NEW YORK, 1959. 250T.

INSTITUTE OF RADIO ENGINEERS. IRE DICTIONARY OF ELECTRONICS TERMS AND SYMBOLS... NEW YORK, 1961. 225P. 61-1732. 3700T.

INSTITUTE OF RADIO ENGINEERS. INDEX TO IRE STANDARDS ON DEFINITIONS OF TERMS, 1942-57. (58 IRE 20.S1) PROC. IRE, V.46, 449-76 (1958) 4000T.

INSTITUTE OF RADIO ENGINEERS. STANDARDS ON ABBREVIATIONS OF RADIO-ELECTRONIC TERMS. (51 IRE 21.S1) PROC. IRE, V.39, 397-400 (1951) 180T.

INSTITUTE OF RADIO ENGINEERS. STANDARDS ON CIRCUITS, DEFINITIONS OF TERMS FOR LINEAR PASSIVE RECIPROCAL TIME INVARIANT NETWORKS. (60 IRE 4.S2) PROC. IRE, V.48, 1608-10 (1960)30T.

INSTITUTE OF RADIO ENGINEERS. STANDARDS ON CIRCUITS, DEFINITIONS OF TERMS FOR LINEAR SIGNAL FLOW GRAPHS. (60 IRE 4.S1) PROC. IRE, V.48, 1611-2 (1960) 30T.

INSTITUTE OF RADIO ENGINEERS. STANDARDS ON CIRCUITS, DEFINITIONS OF TERMS IN THE FIELD OF LINEAR VARYING PARAMETER AND NONLINEAR CIRCUITS. (53 IRE 4.S1) PROC. IRE, V.42,554-5 (1954) 20T.

INSTITUTE OF RADIO ENGINEERS. STANDARDS ON ELECTRON DEVICES, DEFINITIONS OF SEMICONDUCTOR TERMS. (54-IRE 7.S2) PROC. IRE, V.42, 1505-8 (1954) 100T.

INSTITUTE OF RADIO ENGINEERS. STANDARDS ON ELECTRON DEVICES, DEFINITIONS OF TERMS RELATED TO MICROWAVE TUBES (KLYSTRONS, MAGNETRONS/TRAVELING WAVE TUBES) (56 IRE 7.S1) PROC. IRE, V.44. 346-50 (1956) 80T.

INSTITUTE OF RADIO ENGINEERS. STANDARDS ON ELECTRON DEVICES, DEFINITIONS OF TERMS RELATED TO PHOTOTUBES. (54 IRE 7.S1) PROC.IRE, V.42, 1276-7 (1954) 10T.

INSTITUTE OF RADIO ENGINEERS. STANDARDS ON ELECTRON TUBES, DEFINITIONS OF TERMS. (57 IRE 7.S2) PROC. IRE, V.45, 983-1010 (1957) 800T.

INSTITUTE OF RADIO ENGINEERS. STANDARDS ON ELECTRON TUBES. TR AND ATR TUBE DEFINITIONS. (56 IRE 7.S3) PROC. IRE, V.44, 1037-9 (1956) 50T.

INSTITUTE OF RADIO ENGINEERS. STANDARDS ON ELECTROSTATOGRAPHIC DEVICES. (60 IRE 28.S2) PROC. IRE, V.49, 619-21 (1961) 20T.

INSTITUTE OF RADIO ENGINEERS. STANDARDS ON GRAPHICAL AND LETTER SYMBOLS FOR FEEDBACK CONTROL SYSTEMS. (55 IRE 26.S1) PROC. IRE, V.43, 1608-9 (1955) 10T.

INSTITUTE OF RADIO ENGINEERS. STANDARDS ON GRAPHICAL SYMBOLS FOR ELECTRICAL DIAGRAMS. (54 IRE 21.S1) PROC. IRE, V.42, 965-1020 (1954) 500T.

INSTITUTE OF RADIO ENGINEERS. STANDARDS ON GRAPHICAL SYMBOLS FOR SEMICONDUCTOR DEVICES. (57 IRE 21.S3) PROC. IRE V.45, 1612-7 (1957) 100T.

INSTITUTE OF RADIO ENGINEERS. STANDARDS ON INDUSTRIAL ELECTRONICS, DEFINITIONS... (55 IRE 10.S1) PROC. IRE, V.43, 1069-72 (1955) 70T.

INSTITUTE OF RADIO ENGINEERS. STANDARDS ON LETTER SYMBOLS AND MATHEMATICAL SIGNS. (REPRINTED, 57 IRE 21.S1) PROC. IRE V.45, 1140-7 (1957) 400T.

INSTITUTE OF RADIO ENGINEERS. STANDARDS ON LETTER SYMBOLS FOR SEMICONDUCTOR DEVICES. (56 IRE 28.S1) PROC. IRE. V.44, 934-7 (1956) 70T.

INSTITUTE OF RADIO ENGINEERS. STANDARDS ON MAGNETRONS, DEFINITIONS OF TERMS. (52 IRE 7.S1) PROC. IRE, V.40, 562-3 (1952) 10T.

INSTITUTE OF RADIO ENGINEERS. STANDARDS ON PULSES. DEFINITIONS OF TERMS-PT.2. (52 IRE 20.S1) PROC. IRE, V. 40, 552-4 (1952) 50T.

INSTITUTE OF RADIO ENGINEERS. STANDARDS ON REFERENCE DESIGNATIONS FOR ELECTRICAL AND ELECTRONIC EQUIPMENT (57 IRE 21.S2) PROC. IRE, V.45, 1493-1501 (1957) 200T.

INSTITUTE OF RADIO ENGINEERS. STANDARDS ON SOLID-STATE DEVICES, DEFINITIONS OF SEMICONDUCTOR TERMS. (60 IRE 28.S1) PROC. IRE, V.48, 1772-5 (1960) 90T.

ENGLISH

INSTITUTE OF RADIO ENGINEERS. STANDARDS ON SOLID-STATE DEVICES, DEFINITIONS OF SUPERCONDUCTIVE ELECTRONICS TERMS. (62 IRE 28.S1) PROC. IRE, V.50, 451-2 (1962) 10T.

INSTITUTE OF RADIO ENGINEERS. STANDARDS ON SOLID-STATE DEVICES, DEFINITIONS OF TERMS FOR NONLINEAR CAPACITORS. (61 IRE 28.S1) PROC. IRE, V.49, 1279-80 (1961) 20T.

INSTITUTE OF RADIO ENGINEERS. STANDARDS ON STATIC MAGNETIC STORAGE, DEFINITIONS OF TERMS. (59 IRE 8.S1) PROC. IRE, V.47, 427-30 (1959) 60T.

INSTITUTE OF RADIO ENGINEERS. STANDARDS ON TERMINOLOGY FOR FEEDBACK CONTROL SYSTEMS. (55 IRE26.52) PROC. IRE, V.44, 107-9 (1956) 40T.

JACOBOWITZ, H. ELECTRICITY AND MAGNETISM POCKET CRAMMER. GARDEN CITY,N.Y. DOUBLEDAY, 1963. 159P. 63-5117.

JUPE, J.H. A DICTIONARY OF TRONS. BRIT. COMMUN. ELECTRON. V. 9, 194-01 (1962) 600T.

MCDOUGAL, W.L. ET AL. FUNDAMENTALS OF ELECTRICITY. ED4. CHICAGO, AM. TECH. SOC, 1960. 342P. 60-6659.

MANLY, H.P. AND GORDER, L.O. DRAKE,S CYCLOPEDIA OF RADIO AND ELECTRONICS... ED14. CHICAGO, DRAKE, 1958. 1V. (UNPAGED) 58-4817. 3000T.

MANLY, H.P. DRAKE,S RADIO-TELEVISION ELECTRONIC DICTIONARY. CHICAGO, DRAKE, 1960. 1V. (UNPAGED) 60-4753. 3000T.

MECHANICAL RECTIFIER DEFINITIONS. TRANS. AM. INST. ELEC. ENGRS. PT.2,APPL/IND, V.79, 26-32 (1960) 100T.

MINNEAPOLIS-HONEYWELL REGULATOR CO. AUTOMATION DICTIONARY. PHILADELPHIA,(N.D) 19P. 100T.

MORGAN, R.E. ET AL. DEFINITIONS OF MAGNETIC AMPLIFIERS. TRANS. AM. INST. ELEC. ENG, V.77, PT.1, 429-52 (1958) 40T.

MOSES, G.L. GLOSSARY OF INSULATION ENGINEERING TERMS. INSULATION (LIBERTYVILLE) V. 8, NO. 6, 15-8(1962) 200T.

NATIONAL ELECTRIC MANUFACTURES ASSOC. DEFINITIONS FOR INDUSTRIAL AUTOMATIC SYSTEMS. (AS 1-1961) NEW YORK, 1961. 10P. 90T.

NATIONAL ELECTRICAL MANUFACTURERS ASSOCIATION. EIA-NEMA STANDARDS ON LETTER SYMBOLS AND ABBREVIATIONS FOR SEMICONDUCTOR DATA SHEETS AND SPECIFICATIONS. (RS-245/NEMA SK-53) NEW YORK, 1961. 8P. 150T.

NATIONAL RADIO INSTITUTE. RADIO-TELEVISION-ELECTRONICS DICTIONARY. NEW YORK, RIDER, 1962. 190P. 62-21929.

OCECODE. NAVIGATION ELECTRONICS (LAND, SEA, AIR, SPACE) HILVERSUM, 1962. 282P.

OLDFIELD, R.L. THE PRACTICAL DICTIONARY OF ELECTRICITY AND ELECTRONICS. CHICAGO, AM. TECH. SOC, 1959. 216P. 58-59540. 6000T.

PRECISION POTENTIOMETER MANUFACTURERS ASSOCIATION. PRECISION POTENTIOMETER TERMS AND DEFINITIONS. CHICAGO 1962. 22P. 80T.

RCA SERVICE CO. DIGEST OF MILITARY ELECTRONICS. CAMDEN, N.J, 1961. 205P. 61-1603. 800T.

RACKER, J. TECHNICAL WRITING TECHNIQUES FOR ENGINEERS. (GL, PP.129-234, 1130T) ENGLEWOOD CLIFFS, N.J, PRENTICE-HALL, 1960. 234P. 60-16623.

REYNER, J.H. ET AL. THE ENCYCLOPAEDIA OF RADIO AND TELEVISION... ED2. NEW YORK, PHIL. LIBR, 1958. 736P. 58-1326. 4500T.

RIDER, J.F. AND USLAN, S.D. ENCYCLOPEDIA ON CATHODE-RAY OSCILLOSCOPES AND THEIR USES. ED2. NEW YORK, RIDER, 1959. VAR.P. 59-15917.

RYERSON, C.M. GLOSSARY AND DICTIONARY OF TERMS AND DEFINITIONS RELATING SPECIFICALLY TO RELIABILITY. PP. 59-84. 300T. PROC. NATL. SYMP/RELIABILITY/QUALITY CONTROL IN ELECTRONICS, 3D. WASHINGTON, 1957.

SARBACHER, R.I. ENCYCLOPEDIC DICTIONARY OF ELECTRONICS AND NUCLEAR ENGINEERING. ENGLEWOOD CLIFFS, N.J, PRENTICE-HALL, 1959. 1417P. 59-11990. 16000T.

SAY, M.G. NEWNES CONCISE ENCYCLOPAEDIA OF ELECTRICAL ENGINEERING. LONDON, NEWNES, 1962. 918P.

SCIENTIFIC APPARATUS MAKERS ASSOCIATION. ACCURACY AND SENSITIVITY TERMINOLOGY AS APPLIED TO INDUSTRIAL INSTRUMENTS. (RC3-12-1955) NEW YORK, P.

SUSSKIND, C. THE ENCYCLOPEDIA OF ELECTRONICS. NEW YORK, REINHOLD, 1962. 974P. 62-13258. 500T.

TABLES, FORMULAS, ABBREVIATIONS AND SYMBOLS USEFUL TO THE INSULATION ENGINEER. INSULATION (LIBERTYVILLE) V.8, NO.6, 4-14 (1962) 300T.

U.S. ADVISORY GROUP ON ELECTRONIC PARTS. GLOSSARY OF TECHNICAL TERMS IN THE AGEP AREA OF INTEREST. PHILADELPHIA, UNIV. PENNSYLVANIA, 1960. IV. (VAR.P) 60-62451. 500T.

U.S. DEPT. OF DEFENSE. MILITARY STANDARD, ELECTRICAL AND ELECTRONIC SYMBOLS. (MIL-STD, 15A) WASHINGTON, 1954-- 70P. 54-61684.

ENGLISH

U.S. DEPT. OF DEFENSE. MILITARY STANDARD, PRINTED CIRCUIT TERMS AND DEFINITIONS. (MIL-STD-429) WASHINGTON, 1957. 4P. 58-62178.

U.S. DEPT. OF THE AIR FORCE. COMMUNICATIONS-ELECTRONICS TERMINOLOGY, USAF COMMUNICATIONS- ELECTRONICS DOCTRINE. (AFM100-39) WASHINGTON, 1959-- . 1V. LL. 61-60249.

U.S. JOINT CHIEFS OF STAFF. JCEC. STANDARD ABBREVIATIONS. (JANAP 169) WASHINGTON, 1953. 1V. LL.54-61379.

VAN NOSTRAND,S SCIENTIFIC ENCYCLOPEDIA... ED3. PRINCETON, N.J, VAN NOSTRAND,.1958. 1839P. 58-7085. 15000T.

WHAT,S THE RIGHT WORD. A DICTIONARY OF COMMON AND UNCOMMON TERMS IN RADIO, TELEVISION, ELECTRONICS. NEW YORK, R.C.A. INST. 1955. 50P. 55-3357. 500T.

WHITE, W.C. THE TRON FAMILY. (LIST OF WORDS WITH TRON SUFFIX) ELECTRONICS, V. 23, 112-4 (1950) 200T.

WITTY, M.B. ET AL. DICTIONARY OF COMMUNICATIONS ABBREVIATIONS, SIGNS, SYMBOLS AND TABLES. NEW YORK, SETI, 1963. 384P.

WITTY, M.B. ET AL. DICTIONARY OF ELECTRICAL ABBREVIATIONS, SIGNS AND SYMBOLS. NEW YORK, SETI,1963. 320P.

WITTY, M.B. ET AL. DICTIONARY OF ELECTRONICS ABBREVIATIONS, SIGNS, SYMBOLS AND TABLES. NEW YORK, SETI, 1963. 416P.

YOUNG, V.J. AND JONES, M.W. PICTORIAL MICROWAVE DICTIONARY. NEW YORK, RIDER, 1956. 110P. 56-11738. 350T.

FRENCH

BOITARD, A. DICTIONNAIRE TECHNIQUE ANGLAIS-FRANCAIS DE LA RADIO... (EN*FR RADIO D) PARIS, CHIRON, 1954. 84P. 4000T.

BROSSET,R. DICTIONNAIRE·MEMENTO D,ELECTRONIQUE. (ELECTRON. D, FR DEFS) PARIS, DUNOD, 1961. 402P.

COMITE ELECTROTECHNIQUE FRANCAIS. VOCABULAIRE ELECTROTECHNIQUE. ELECTROACOUSTIQUE. (ELEC.ENG. D, ELECTROACOUST, FR DEFS) PARIS, 1957. 45P.

CUSSET, F. VOCABULAIRE TECHNIQUE, ÉLECTRICITE, MECANIQUE, MINES, SCIENCES... (*FR*EN TECH. D) . ED4. PARIS, BERGER-LEVRAULT, 1954. 663P. 54-35644. 3000T.

DESARCES, H. ENCYCLOPEDIE PRATIQUE DE MECANIQUE ET D,ELECTRICITE.... (PRACT.ENCYCL.OF MECH/ELEC.ENG, FR DEFS) PARIS, QUILLET, 1961. 3V. 62-28854.

ENCYCLOPEDIE PRATIQUE DE MECANIQUE ET D, ELECTRICITE... (MECH/ELEC, FR DEFS) 3V. PARIS, LIBR. QUILLET, 1954. 3990P.

FROIDEVAUX, J. DOCUMENTATION FRANCO-ANGLAISE DE L,ENERGIE ELECTRIQUE.... (EN*FR D. OF ELEC. POWER) PARIS, DUNOD, 1955. 179P.

KING, G.G. DICTIONNAIRE ANGLAIS-FRANCAIS, ÉLECTRONIQUE, PHYSIQUE NUCLEAIRE, ET SCIENCES CONNEXES. EN*FR D. OF ELECTRON, NUCL. PHYS/RELATED SCI) PARIS, DUNOD, 1959. 311P. 60-20839. 21000T.

KING, G.G. DICTIONNARIE FRANCAIS-ANGLAIS, ELECTRONIQUE, PHYSIQUE NUCLEAIRE ET SCIENCES CONNEXES. (FR*EN D. OF ELECTRON, NUCL. PHYS/RELATED SCI) PARIS, DUNOD, 1961. 395P. 61-4361. 24000T.

MALGORN, G.M. LEXIQUE TECHNIQUE ANGLAIS-FRANCAIS...(EN*FR TECH.D) ED4. PARIS, GAUTHIER-VILLARS, 1956. 493P. 57-155. 9500T.

MALGORN, G.M. LEXIQUE TECHNIQUE FRANCAIS-ANGLAIS... (FR*EN TECH.D) PARIS, GAUTHIER-VILLARS, 1956. 475P. 57-156. 9500T.

MAREC,E. DICTIONNAIRE DE L,ELECTRICIEN PRACTICIEN... (ELECTRICIANS D, FR DEFS) PARIS, BAILLIERE, 1955. ·330P. 57-16202.

PIRAUX, H. DICTIONNARIE ANGLAIS-FRANCAIS DES. TERMES RELATIFS A L,ELECTROTECHNIQUE, L,ELECTRONIQUE ET AUX APPLICATIONS CONNEXES... (EN*ER D. OF ELEC. ENG, ELECTRON/RELATED SCI) ED4.. PARIS, EYROLLES, 1958. 308P. 59-26753. 20000T.

PIRAUX, H. DICTIONNARIE FRANCAIS-ANGLAIS DES TERMES RELATIFS A L,ELECTROTECHNIQUE, L,ELECTRONIQUE ET AUX APPLICATIONS CONNEXES... (FR*EN D. OF ELEC. ENG, ELECTRON,.RELATED SCI) PARIS, EYROLLES, 1956. 168P. 58-30505. 13000T.

PROULX, G. CANALISATION ET AMENAGEMENT HYDROELECTRIQUE. GLOSSAIRE ANGLAIS-FRANCAIS, BT-44. (WATERWAYS/ HYDROELEC.POWER, EN*FR GLI OTTAWA, DEPT.SECY.STATE, 1956. 90P. 2700T.

PROULX, G. ELECTROCHIMIE ET ELECTROMETALLURGIE, GLOSSAIRE ANGLAIS-FRANCIS, BT-48. (ELECTROCHEM/ ELECTROMET, EN*ER GLI OTTAWA, DEPT. SECY. STATE, 1956. 21P. 500T.

PROULX,G.J. DICTIONNAIRE ANGLAIS-FRANCAIS. ELECTRONIQUE ET TELECOMMUNICATIONS. (EN*FR ELECTRON/ TELECOMMUN. D) OTTAWA, 1959. 582P. SUPPL.1, 1960. 30000T.

PROULX, G.J. L,ELECTRONIQUE, GLOSSAIRE ANGLAIS-FRANCAIS. BT-36. (ELECTRON, EN*FR GL) OTTAWA, DEPT. SECY. STATE, 1955. ·39P. 800T.

GERMAN

AUCHAMP, K.G. GERMAN SEMICONDUCTOR TERMS FOUND IN TECHNICAL LITERATURE. ELEC. DESIGN NEWS, V.4, 60-3 959)

RKENHOFF,G. ENERGIE VON A BIS Z (ENERGY FROM A-Z, GE DEFS) MUNICH, OLDENBOURG, 1954. 192P. A55-1209.

UEGGE, S. ET AL. HANDBUCH DER PHYSIK. (ENCYCL. OF PHYS) V.17, DIELEKTRIKA. (DIELECTRICS, *GE*EN GL, ,392-406, 400T) BERLIN, SPRINGER, 1956. 406P. A56-2942.

UEGGE, S. ET AL. HANDBUCH DER PHYSIK. (ENCYCL. OF PHYS) V.16, ELEKTRISCHE FELDER UND WELLEN. (ELEC. ELD/WAVES, *GE*EN GL, PP.726-53, 900T) BERLIN, SPRINGER. 1958. 753P. A56-2942.

UEGGE, S. ET AL. HANDBUCH DER PHYSIK. (ENCYCL. OF PHYS) V.19, ELEKTRISCHE LEITUNGSPHAENOMENE 1, LEC. CONDUCTIVITY 1, *GE*EN GL, PP.396-411, 450T) BERLIN, SPRINGER,1956. 411P. A56-2942.

UEGGE, S. ET AL. HANDBUCH DER PHYSIK. (ENCYCL. OF PHYS) V.20, ELEKTRISCHE LEITUNGSPHAENOMENE 2. LEC. CONDUCTIVITY 2, *GE*EN GL, PP.480-9, 250T) BERLIN, SPRINGER, 1957. 491P. A56-2942.

UEGGE, S. ET AL. HANDBUCH DER PHYSIK. (ENCYCL. OF PHYS) V.21, ELEKTRON-EMISSION GASENTLADUNGEN 1. LEC-EMISSION GAS DISCHARGES 1, *GE*EN GL, PP.664-83, 650T) BERLIN, SPRINGER, 1956. 683P. A56-2942.

UEGGE, S. ET AL. HANDBUCH DER PHYSIK. (ENCYCL. OF PHYS) V.22, GASENTLADUNGEN 2. (GAS DISCHARGES 2, E*EN GL, PP.629-52, 750T) BERLIN, SPRINGER, 1956. 652P. A56-2942.

UEGGE, S. ET AL. HANDBUCH DER PHYSIK. (ENCYCL. OF PHYS) V.4, PRINZIPIEN DER ELEKTRODYNAMIK UND LATIVITAETSTHEORIE. (PRINCIPLES OF ELECTRODYN/RELATIVITY,*GE*EN GL, PP.273-90, 500T) BERLIN, SPRINGER, 62. 290P. A56-2942.

EEMAN, H.G. ELEKTROTECHNISCHES ENGLISCH. (*GE*EN D. OF ELEC. ENG) ED5. ESSEN, GIRARDET, 1956. 491P. 6-6601. 8000T.

TRIEBETECHNISCHE GRUNDLAGEN, BEGRIFFSBESTIMMUNGEN DER GETRIEBE. (POWER TRANSMISSION ENG, D, GE DEFS) ESSELDORF, VDI, 1962. 30P.

EDECKE, W. DIE TRON-GRUPPE, TECHNISCHE BEGRIFFE MIT DER ENDUNG TRON UND IHRE BEDEUTUNG. (TRON FAMILY, CH. T. WITH TRON SUFFIX, GE DEFS) RADIO UND FERNSEHEN, NO.21, 22. P.644,680 (1958) 250T.

MAN, C.J. AND IDLIN, R. DICTIONARY OF PHYSICS AND ALLIED SCIENCES. WOERTERBUCH DER PHYSIK UND RWANDTER WISSENSCHAFTEN. (V.1, GE*EN, 675P. V.2, EN*GE, 680P) NEW YORK, UNGAR, 1958-62. 62-9683. 000T.

NK, G. VERGLEICHENDE BEGRIFFSBESTIMMUNG VON DEUTSCHEN, ENGLISCHEN UND AMERIKANISCHEN FACHAUSDRUECKEN F DEM GEBIETE DER FEUERFLUESSIGEN UND ELEKTROLYTISCHEN KUPFERRAFFINATION. (COPPER REFINING GL, GE*EN) AUSTHAL-ZELLERFELD, GES. DEUT. METALLHUETTEN/BERGLEUTE, 1952. 89P.

KULIK, S. BILDWORT ENGLISCH TECHNISCHE SPRACHHEFTE, HEFT 2. (TECH.EN, ELEC) BERLIN, VDI, 1952. 32P.

TZ, W. AND HURST, R. ET AL. LUEGERS LEXIKON DER TECHNIK. .(ENCYCL. OF TECH) V.2 GRUNDLAGEN R ELEKTROTECHNIK UND KERNTECHNIK. (ELEC/NUCL. ENG, GE DEFS) ED4. STUTTGART, DEUTSCHE VERLAGS-ANSTALT, 60. 624P. A61-2000.

HWENKHAGEN, H.F. DICTIONARY OF ELECTRICAL ENGINEERING, GERMAN-ENGLISH, ENGLISH-GERMAN. NEW YORK, LEY, 1962. 1058P. 63-5266. 20000T.

S. PATENT OFFICE. GLOSSARY OF GERMAN WORDS USED IN PATENT LITERATURE RELATING TO COMMUNICATIONS, ECTRICITY AND ELECTRONICS. WASHINGTON, 1961. 21P. 900T.

GREEK

DRIKOPOULOS, M.C. ENCYCLOPEDIE ANGLO-HELLENIQUE DE TERMES D,ELECTRONIQUE, D,ELECTRICITE... PIRAEUS, UNTOURI, 1961. 720P.

HUNGARIAN

LLER, RAYMOND AND BROWN. ENGLISH-HUNGARIAN GLOSSARY OF ELECTRONIC TERMS. UNIVERSITY PARK, IV. PENNSYLVANIA, 195 . 48P. 1000T.

JAPANESE

MPA KOHO YOGO JITEN. (ELEC. NAVIGATION D, *EN*JA) TOKYO, KAIUNDO, 1959. J60-124. 2400T.

PAN. MINISTRY OF EDUCATION. DRAFT VOCABULARY FOR ELECTRICAL TERMS--WIRES AND CABLES. (EN*JA) TOKYO, 52. 116P.

PAN. MINISTRY OF EDUCATION. GLOSSARY OF ELECTRIC ENGINEERING, TELEPHONY AND TELEGRAPHY. (EN*JA) TOKYO, 52. 116P.

PAN. MINISTRY OF EDUCATION. JAPANESE SCIENTIFIC TERMS, ELECTRICAL ENGINEERING. (*JA*EN) TOKYO, INST. EC. ENG. JAPAN, 1957. 685P. 10000T.

PAN. MINISTRY OF EDUCATION. VOCABULARY ON ELECTRICITY... (EN*JA) TOKYO, 1952. 28P. 940T.

ODERA, H. WA-EI TAISHO DENKI YOGO JITEN. (ELEC.D,JA*EN) TOKYO, KEIBUNSHA, 1959. 1013P. J60-231. 9000T.

KEDA, K. TECHNICAL DICTIONARY OF ELECTRICAL TERMS. (*JA*EN) TOKYO, KEIBUNSHA, 1953. 383P.

ELECTRICAL AND ELECTRONIC ENGINEERING

JAPANESE

UCHIDA, T. DENKI JUTSUGO JITEN. (ELEC. ENG. D, JA*EN) TOKYO, OMU, 1955. 497+66P. J61-466. 4800T.

UCHIDA, T. DENKI JUTSUGO JITEN. (ELEC. ENG. D, JA*EN) TOKYO, OMU, 1960. 521P. J61-581. 45000T.

YONEZAWA, S. EREKUTORONIKUSU DAIJITEN. (ELECTRON.D, *EN*JA) TOKYO, CHIJIN, 1961. 699+132P. J62-515. 5000T.

POLISH

ZIMNICKI, H. ET AL. SLOWNIK ELEKTRYCZNY ANGIELSKO-POLSKI. (EN*PL D.OF ELEC. ENG) WARSAW, PANSTW. WYDAW. TECH, 1961. 639P. 62-25722. 24000T.

ZIMNICKI, H. SLOWNIK ELEKTRYCZNY POLSKO-ANGIELSKI. (PL*EN ELEC. ENG. D) WARSAW, WYDAW. NAUK-TECH, 1962. 372P. 62-46681. 24000T.

POLYGLOT

AKADEMIIA NAUK SSSR. KOM.TEKH.TERM. DIELEKTRIKI. (D.OF DIELECTRICS, RU*EN*FR*GE) (SB. REK. TERM, NO.53) MOSCOW, 1960. 21P. 60-37143. 210T.

AKADEMIIA NAUK SSSR. KOM. TEKH. TERM. ELEKTROTEKHNIKA I ELEKTRONIKA, TERMINOLOGIIA. (ELEC.ENG/ELECTRON.T, RU*EN*FR*GE) (SB.REK.TERM.NO.59) MOSCOW, 1962. 232P. 63-58902.

AKADEMII NAUK SSSR.KOM.TEKH.TERM. TERMINOLOGICHESKIE RABOTY V SSSR V OBLASTI TEORETICHESKOI ELEKTROTEKHNIKI. (THEOR.ELEC.ENG.) GR-05,OSNOVNYE OPREDELENIIA IEC 50-GR-05. (FUNDAMENTAL DEFS, RU*EN*FR) MOSCOW 1957. 94P. 60-29039. 550T.

AKADEMIIA NAUK SSSR. KOM.TEKH.TERM. TERMINOLOGIIA RELE. (D. OF RELAYS, RU*EN*FR*GE) (SB.REK.TERM. NO.49) MOSCOW 1958. 42P. 59-45194. 180T.

AKADEMIIA NAUK SSSR. KOM.TEKH.TERM. TERMINOLOGIIA SVETOTEKHNIKI. (ILLUM. ENG. D, *RU*EN*FR*GE) (SB. REK. TERM. NO.48) MOSCOW, 1957. 61P. 59-45328. 210T.

BABANI, B.B. INTERNATIONAL RADIO TUBE ENCYCLOPEDIA. (*CZ*DA*DU*EN*FR*GE*HE*IT*NO*PL*PR*RU*SP*SW*TU) ED3. LONDON, BERNARDS, 1958. VAR.P. 59-3704.

BARGIN, B.G. AND BUCHINSKII, A.S. SEMIIAZYCHNYI SLOVAR PO ELEKTRONIKE I VOLNOVODAM. (D. OF ELECTRON/ WAVEGUIDES, *RU*EN*DU*FR*GE*IT*SP) MOSCOW. FIZMATGIZ, 1961. 263P. 62-65717. 2000T.

BOUSEK, J. PRIRUCNI TECHNICKY SLOVNIK V (5) JAZ ... PRO OBOR PRUMYSLOVEHO MERENI A AUTOMATICKE REGULACE. (D. OF IND. METROL/AUTOM. CONTROL, CZ EN FR GE RU) PRAGUE, MATICE HORNICKO-HUTNICKA, 1955. 210P.

BRITISH ELECTRICAL AND ALLIED MANUFACTURERS ASSOCIATION. THE BEAMA CATALOGUE. (EN*FR*GE) LONDON, ILIFFE, 195 . VAR. P. 55-58858.

CHIANG, TS,UNG-CHI. O HUA YING TIEN KUNG TZ,U HUI. (RU CH EN ELEC. ENG. D) SHANGHAI, SCI/TECH, 1957. 437P. C60-422.

CLASON, W.E. DICTIONARY OF ELECTRICAL ENGINEERING. (*EN/AM*DU*FR*GE*IT*SP) NEW YORK, ELSEVIER. (IN PREP)

CLASON, W.E. ELSEVIER,S DICTIONARY OF AUTOMATIC CONTROL, *EN/AM*FR*GE*RU. NEW YORK, ELSEVIER, 1963. 211P. 63-16075. 2600T.

CLASON, W.E. ELSEVIER,S DICTIONARY OF ELECTRONICS AND WAVEGUIDES. (*EN/AM*DU*FR*GE*IT*SP) NEW YORK, ELSEVIER, 1957. 628P. 57-11038. 2000T.

CLASON, W.E. SUPPLEMENT TO THE ELSEVIER DICTIONARIES OF ELECTRONICS, NUCLEONICS AND TELECOMMUNICATION. (*EN/AM*DU*FR*GE*IT*SP) NEW YORK, ELSEVIER, 1963. 633P. 63-11369. 2500T.

CONTROL GEAR GLOSSARY. (*EN*FR*GE*IT*SW) ELEC. TIMES, LONDON, V.137, NO.3, 97-8 (1960) 100T.

DENKI YOGO JITEN HENSHU IINKAI. DENKI YOGO JITEN. (ELEC.D,*JA*EN*GE) TOKYO, KORONA, 1960. 1016P. J61-497. 4800T.

DORIAN, A.F. SIX-LANGUAGE DICTIONARY OF AUTOMATION, ELECTRONICS AND SCIENTIFIC INSTRUMENTS...(*EN*FR*GE* *IT*RU*SP) ENGLEWOOD CLIFFS, N.J. PRENTICE HALL, 1962. 732P. 63-5414. 5500T.

DORIAN, A.F. SIX-LANGUAGE DICTIONARY OF ELECTRONICS, AUTOMATION, AND SCIENTIFIC INSTRUMENTS. (EN*FR*GE*IT*RU*SP) ENGLEWOOD CLIFFS, N.J, PRENTICE-HALL, 1963. 732P. 63-510. 5500T.

DUSCHINSKY, W.J. ET AL. ELECTRONIC DICTIONARY...(EN FR GE SP) NEW YORK, CALDWELL-CLEMENTS, 1956. 64P. 56-27775.

EUROPEAN MINIATURE ELECTRONIC COMPONENTS DATA ANNUAL. (6-LANG. GL) NEW YORK, PERGAMON, 1963/64- .

FOSSATI, F. DIZIONARIO PLURILINGUE DI TECNICA ELETTRO-RADIOLOGICA. (ELEC/RADIOLOGY D, *IT*EN*FR*GE*SP) MILAN, WASSERMAN. 1952. 489P. 3500T.

FRIGYES, A. ET AL. IRANYITASTECHNIKA. (AUTOM. D, *HU*EN*GE*RU) (MUSZ. ERT. SZ, NO.19) BUDAPEST, TERRA, 1962. 135P. 1100T.

POLYGLOT

GOEDECKE, W. AMERIKANISCHE, DEUTSCHE, ENGLISCHE UND FRANZOESISCHE KURZWOERTER UND ABKUERZUNGEN VON FACHAUSDRUECKEN, MASSEINHEITEN UND FACHORGANISATIONEN DES NACHRICHTENWESENS UND VERWANDTER GEBIETE. (TELECOMMUN/ABBR, *GE*AM/EN*FR) BERLIN, TECHNIK, 1958. 116P. 61-45256. 3300T.

GOEDECKE, W. TECHNISCHE ABKUERZUNGEN, DEUTSCH-ENGLISCH-FRANZOESISCH... FUNKTECHNIK, FERNSEHEN... KERNTECHNIK... ELEKTROTECHNIK... (TECH. ABBRS, *GE*EN*FR, TELECOMMUN, NUCL/ELEC. ENG) WIESBADEN, BRANDSTETTER, 1961. 288P. 63-29594. 5000T.

INTERNATIONAL COMMISSION ON ILLUMINATION. VOCABULAIRE INTERNATIONAL DE L,ECLAIRAGE. (INTL. LIGHTING VOC. V.1, TERMS/DEFS *FR*EN*GE. 136P. V.2, INDEX. *FR*EN*DA*DU*GE*IT*PL*RU*SP*SW. 127P) ED2. PARIS, 1957/9. 60-39148. 550T.

INTERNATIONAL ELECTRONIC TUBE HANDBOOK. (EN*DU*FR*GE*IN*IT*PR*SP*SW) ED3. BUSSUM, NETHERLANDS, DE MUIDERKRING, 1955. 334P. 100T.

INTERNATIONAL ELECTROTECHNICAL COMMISSION. GENERAL CLASSIFICATION OF FERROMAGNETIC OXIDE MATERIALS AND DEFINITIONS OF TERMS. (IEC-125) GENEVA, 1961. P.

INTERNATIONAL ELECTROTECHNICAL COMMISSION. INTERNATIONAL ELECTROTECHNICAL VOCABULARY. *FR*EN*DU*GE*IT*PL*SP*SW. (IEC-50) ED2. GENEVA, 1955-- . (IN PROG)

GR-05 FUNDAMENTAL DEFINITIONS. 1956. 102P. 550T.
GR-07 ELECTRONICS. 1956. P. 700T.
GR-08 ELECTRO-ACOUSTICS. 1960. 67P.
GR-10 MACHINES AND TRANSFORMERS. 1956. 92P. 400T.
GR-11 STATIC CONVERTERS. 1956. 36P. 120T.
GR-12 TRANSDUCTORS. 1955. 15P. 40T.
GR-15 SWITCHBOARDS AND APPARATUS FOR CONNECTION AND REGULATION. 1957. 75P. 250T.
GR-16 PROTECTIVE RELAYS. 1956. 56P. 200T.
GR-20 SCIENTIFIC AND INDUSTRIAL MEASURING INSTRUMENTS. 1958. 88P. 350T.
GR-26 NUCLEAR POWER PLANTS FOR ELECTRIC ENERGY GENERATION. (IN PREP)
GR-30 ELECTRIC TRACTION. 1957. 94P. 400T.
GR-31 SIGNALLING AND SECURITY APPARATUS FOR RAILWAYS. 1959. 46P.
GR-35 ELECTROMECHANICAL APPLICATIONS. (IN PREP)
GR-40 ELECTRO-HEATING APPLICATIONS 1960. 40P.
GR-45 LIGHTING. 1958. 83P.
GR-50 ELECTROCHEMISTRY AND ELECTROMETALLURGY. (IN PREP)
GR-62 WAVEGUIDES. P. 150T. (IN PREP)
GR-66 DETECTION AND MEASUREMENT OF NUCLEAR RADIATIONS BY ELECTRICAL MEANS. (IN PREP)
GR-70 ELECTROBIOLOGY. 1959. 32P.

INTERNATIONAL ELECTROTECHNICAL COMMISSION. MEZHDUNARODNYI ELEKTROTEKHNICHESKII SLOVAR. (INTL. ELECTROTECH. VOC) (IEC 50-GR-07) ELEKTRONIKA. (ELECTRON, *RU*EN*DU*FR*GE*IT*PL*SP*SW) ED2. MOSCOW, FIZMATGIZ 1959. 335P. 700T.

INTERNATIONAL ELECTROTECHNICAL COMMISSION. MEZHDUNARODNYI ELEKTROTEKHNICHESKII SLOVAR. (INTL. ELECTROTECH. VOC) (IEC 50-GR-10) MASHINY I TRANSFORMATORY. (MACH/TRANSFORMERS, *RU*EN*FR*GE*IT*SP*SW) ED2. MOSCOW, FIZMATGIZ, 1958. 212P. 59-36649. 400T.

INTERNATIONAL ELECTROTECHNICAL COMMISSION. MEZHDUNARODNYI ELEKTROTEKHNICHESKII SLOVAR. (INTL. ELECTROTECH. VOC) (IEC 50-GR-16) RELEINAIIA ZASHCHITA. (PROTECTIVE RELAYS,*RU*EN*DU*FR*GE*IT*PL*SP*SW) ED2. MOSCOW, FIZMATGIZ, 1960. 115P. 200T.

INTERNATIONAL ELECTROTECHNICAL COMMISSION. MEZHDUNARODNYI ELEKTROTEKHNICHESKII SLOVAR. (INTL. ELECTROTECH. VOC) (IEC 50-GR-20) SCIENTIFIC AND INDUSTRIAL MEASURING INSTRUMENTS. ED2. (*RU*EN*FR*GE *SP*IT*DU*PL*SW) MOSCOW, 1962. 225P.

INTERNATIONAL ELECTROTECHNICAL COMMISSION. SCHWEIZERISCHES ELEKTROTECHNISCHES KOMITEE...ENZYKLOPAEDIE DER ELEKTRISCHEN ISOLIERSTOFFE... (ENCYCL. OF INSULATORS, GE EN FR IT PL SP SW) ZURICH, 1960. 83P. 61-28675.

INTERNATIONAL ELECTROTECHNICAL COMMISSION. SLOVENSKI ELEKTROTEHNISKI SLOVAR. (SV VERSION OF IEC 50-GR-07) ELEKTRONIKA. (ELECTRON, SV*FR*EN*GE*IT) ED2. LJUBLJANA, ELEKTROTEHN. DRUSTVA SLOVEN, 1959. 171P. 61-26371. 700T.

INTERNATIONAL ELECTROTECHNICAL COMMISSION. SYMBOLES LITTERAUX INTERNATIONAUX UTILISES EN ELECTRICITE. (INTL. LETTER SYMBOLS IN ELEC, FR EN SP) ED3. GENEVA, 1953. 15P. 54-43816.

INTERNATIONALE ABKUERZUNGEN AUF DEM GEBIETE DER ELEKTROTECHNIK. (INTL. ELEC. ENG. ABBR) BUL. ASSOC. SUISSE ELEC, V.46,1037 (1955) 60T.

KAWECKI, J. PODRECZNY SLOWNICZEK AUTOMATYKA. (AUTOM.D, PL*EN*FR*GE*RU) PRZEGLAD TECH. V.82, I-XIV (1961) 650T.

KERKHOF, H. AND GRAS, M. FACHWOERTERBUCH DER FERNMELDETECHNIK UND ELEKTRONIK. (TELECOMMUN/ELECTRON D) V.1. LEXIKON ENGLISH-AMERIKANISCHER ABKUERZUNGEN. (GL. OF EN/AM ABBRS, *EN*GE*FR) HAMM, WESTE. GROTE, 1956. 264P. 57-23532. 7500T.

KERKHOF, H. AND GRAS, M. FACHWOERTERBUCH DER FERNMELDETECHNIK UND ELEKTRONIK. (TELECOMMUN/ELECTRON.D) V.1,ABBR. V.2, EN*GE*FR. V.3, GE*FR*EN. V.4, FR*EN*GE. HAMM, WESTF.GROTE, 1956-- . 57-23532.

ELECTRICAL AND ELECTRONIC ENGINEERING

POLYGLOT

KHRAMOI, A.V. RUSSKO-ANGLO-NEMETSKO-FRANTSUZKII SLOVAR TERMINOV PO AVTOMATICHESKOMU UPRAVLENIIU. (*RU*EN *FR*GE D. OF AUTOM. CONTROL) MOSCOW, AKAD. NAUK. SSSR, 1963. 205P. 3100T.

KOVACS, K.P. ET AL. ALTALANOS ELEKTROTECHNIKA. (D. OF ELEC. ENG, *HU*EN*GE*RU) (MUSZ. ERT. SZ, NO.2) BUDAPEST, TERRA, 1958. 236P. 59-20477. 1300T.

KOVACS, K.P. ET AL. VILLAMOS GEPEK. (D. OF ELEC. MACH, *HU*EN*GE*RU)(MUSZ. ERT. SZ. NO.5) BUDAPEST, TERRA, 1959. 164P. 63-28491. 1100T.

LEIPZIG. INSTITUT FUER ENERGETIK. EINHEITLICHE BEGRIFFE DER ENERGIEWIRTSCHAFT. DDR. (D. OF STD. ELEC. ENG. T. AL BU CZ GE HU PL RO RU) LEIPZIG, GRUNDSTOFFIND, 1961-- . 62-44979.

LEXIQUE DES TERMES EMPLOYES DANS LA TECHNIQUE DU CONTACTEUR. (D. OF CONTACTOR ENG,*FR*EN*DU*GE*IT*RU*SP) NANTERRE, SODINA, 1961. 250P. 61-42968. 1200T.

MICHELS, W.C. ET AL. THE INTERNATIONAL DICTIONARY OF PHYSICS AND ELECTRONICS. ED2. (*EN*FR*GE*RU*SP) PRINCETON, VAN NOSTRAND, 1961. 1355P. 61-2485. 13500T.

MOSONYI, E. ET AL. VIZEROMUVEK ES VIZIUTAK. (D. OF HYDR. POWER PLANTS/HYDRO-TECH. STRUCT, *HU*EN*GE*RU) (MUSZ.ERT.SZ.NO.6) BUDAPEST, TERRA, 1960. 204P. 1200T.

NORWAY. RADET FOR TEKNISK TERMINOLOGI. ELECTRONIC VALVES AND TAPE RECORDERS. (RTT-9) (*EN*GE*NO) OSLO, 1962. 37P.

NORWAY. RADET FOR TEKNISK TERMINOLOGI. OSCILLATORY CIRCUITS AND WAVE GUIDES. (RTT-5) (*EN*GE*NO) OSLO, 1960. 20P.

RINT, C. LEXIKON DER HOCHFREQUENZ- , NACHRICHTEN- UND ELEKTROTECHNIK. (HIGH-FREQUENCY, TELECOMMUN/ELEC. ENG.D, GE*EN*FR*RU) 4V. BERLIN, TECHNIK, 1957-1961. 58-3142. 20000T.

SCHLOMANN, A. ET AL. ILLUSTRIERTE TECHNISCHE WOERTERBUECHER. V.2. ELEKTROTECHNIK UND ELEKTROCHEMIE. (ELEC. ENG/ELECTROCHEM, *GE*EN*FR*IT*RU*SP) ED2. BERLIN, OLDENBOURG, 1957. 1304P. 10700T.

SCIENTIFIC INSTRUMENTS MANUFACTURES ASSOCIATION (ENGLAND) BRITISH INSTRUMENTS DIRECTORY AND BUYERS GUIDE. (*FR*EN*GE*RU*SP GL, PP.194-256) ED3. LONDON, 1962. 667P.

SOVARY, E. ET AL. EROMUVEK. (ELEC. POWER PLANTS D, *HU*EN*GE*RU) (MUSZ. ERT. SZ, NO.21) BUDAPEST, TERRA, 1963. 172P. 1200T.

SZENDY, K. ET AL. VILLAMOS MUVEK. (D. OF ELEC. POWER/DISTR, *HU*EN*GE*RU) (MUSZ. ERT. SZ. NO.9) BUDAPEST, TERRA, 1960. 235P. 1300T.

THALI, H. TECHNICAL DICTIONARY OF TERMS USED IN ELECTRICAL ENGINEERING, RADIO, TELEVISION, TELECOMMUNICATION. (V.1 EN*GE*FR, ED6. 280P. 15000T. V.2 GE*EN*FR, ED4. 311P. 24000T. V.3 FR*EN*GE*, IN PREP) LUCERNE, THALI, 1960-- . 62-822.

TIAGUNOV, G.A. POLUPROVODNIKOVYE PRIBORY. (SEMICONDUCTOR DEVICES) PT.1, FUNDAMENTAL CONCEPTS. TERMINOLOGY. (*RU*EN*FR*GE) MOSCOW, 1962. 23P.

UNION INTERNATIONALE DES PRODUCTEURS ET DISTRIBUTEURS D.ENERGIE ELECTRIQUE. TERMINOLOGIE UTILISEE DANS LES STATISTIQUES DE L.ECONOMIE ELECTRIQUE. (STAT.T.IN ELEC. POWER SUPPLY, *FR*EN*GE*IT) PARIS, 1957. 120P. 70T.

UNION POUR LA COORDINATION DE LA PRODUCTION ET DU TRANSPORT DE L,ELECTRICITE. UCPTE-TERMINOLOGIE. (ELEC. ENG.T, FR DU GE IT) HEIDELBERG, 1958.

VOCABULAIRE TRILINGUE DE LA REGULATION AUTOMATIQUE. (GE EN FR AUTOM. GL) MESURES/CONTROLE IND, V.22, 137-8 (1957)

UNITED NATIONS. LIST OF TERMS CONCERNING NEW SOURCES OF ENERGY. (TERMINOLOGY BULL. NO.176) NEW YORK, 1961.

RUSSIAN

AKADEMIIA NAUK SSSR. KOM.TEKH.TERM. ELEKTRICHESKIE MASHINY. (D. OF ELEC.MACH, RU DEFS) (SB.REK.TERM, NO. 52) MOSCOW, 1960. 26P. 60-32946. 200T.

AKADEMIIA NAUK SSSR. KOM.TEKH.TERM. ELEKTROVAKUUMNYE PRIBORY... (D. OF ELECTRON-TUBE DEVICES, RU DEFS) (SB.REK.TERM,NO.54) MOSCOW, 1960. 20P. 62-32953.

AKADEMIIA NAUK SSSR. KOM. TEKH. TERM. TEORIIA NADEZHNOSTI V OBLASTI RADIOELEKTRONIKI... TERMINOLOGIIA. (THEORY OF RELIABILITY IN RADIO/ELECTRON, RU DEFS) (SB. REK. TERM. NO.60) MOSCOW, 1962. 46P. 63-33233.

AKADEMIIA NAUK SSSR. KOM.TEKH.TERM. TERMINOLOGIIA ELEKTRICHESKIKH IAVLENII V GAZAKH. (D. OF ELEC. PHENOMENA IN GASES, RU DEFS) (SB.REK.TERM.NO.13) MOSCOW, 1952. 29P. 54-32122. 110T.

AKADEMIIA NAUK SSSR. KOM.TEKH.TERM. TERMINOLOGIIA ELEKTRICHESKOI TIAGI MAGISTRALNYKH ZHELEZNYKH DOROG I METROPOLITENOV, ELEKTROTIAGOVAIA SET. (POWER NETWORKS FOR ELEC. R.R/SUBWAYS, RU DEFS) (SB.REK.TERM, NO.31) MOSCOW, 1954. 34P. 55-35585. 160T.

AKADEMIIA NAUK SSSR. KOM.TEKH.TERM. TERMINOLOGIIA ELEKTRICHESKOI TIAGI MAGISTRALNYKH ZHELEZNYKH DOROG I METROPOLITENOV, TIAGOVYE PODSTANTSII. (POWER SUBSTATIONS FOR ELEC. R.R/SUBWAYS, RU DEFS) (SB.REK.TERM, NO.32) MOSCOW, 1954. 17P. 56-46941. 80T.

58

ELECTRICAL AND ELECTRONIC ENGINEERING

RUSSIAN

AKADEMIIA NAUK SSSR. KOM.TEKH.TERM. TERMINOLOGIIA ELEKTROOBORUDOVANIIA SAMOLETOV. (AIRPLANE ELEC. EQUIP. RU DEFS) (SB.REK.TERM. NO.25) MOSCOW. 1954. 35P. 55-15035. 170T.

AKADEMIIA NAUK SSSR. KOM.TEKH.TERM. TERMINOLOGIIA ELEKTROTIAGI. (ELEC.R.R. D. RU DEFS) (BIUL. NO. 60) MOSCOW. 1952. 52P. 380T.

AKADEMIIA NAUK SSSR. KOM.TEKH.TERM. TERMINOLOGIIA ELEKTROVAKUUMNYKH PRIBOROV. (D. OF ELECTRON-TUBE DEVICES. RU DEFS) (SB.REK.TERM.NO.39) MOSCOW. 1956. 47P.56-42962. 180T.

AKADEMIIA NAUK SSSR. KOM. TEKH. TERM. TERMINOLOGIIA OSNOVNYKH PONIATII AVTOMATIKI. (BASIC CONCEPTS IN AUTOM. RU DEFS) (SB. REK. TERM. NO.35) MOSCOW.1954. 22P. 55-35588. 40T.

AKADEMIIA NAUK SSSR. KOM.TEKH.TERM. TERMINOLOGIIA PO STRUKTURNOMU ANALIZU I SINTEZU RELEINO-KONTAKTNYKH SKHEM. (D. OF STRUCT.ANAL/SYNTH.OF RELAY-CONTACT SYSTEMS. RU DEFS) (SB.REK.TERM. NO.8) MOSCOW. 1953. 22P. 54-27905. 50T.

AKADEMIIA NAUK SSSR. KOM.TEKH.TERM. TERMINOLOGIIA TEORETICHESKOI ELEKTROTEKHNIKI. (D. OF THEOR. ELEC. ENG. RU DEFS) (BIUL.NO.64) MOSCOW. 1952. 43P. 200T.

AKADEMIIA NAUK SSSR. KOM.TEKH.TERM. TERMINOLOGIIA TEORETICHESKOI ELEKTROTEKHNIKI. (D. OF THEOR. ELEC. ENG. RU DEFS) (SB.REK.TERM.NO.46) MOSCOW. 1958. 46P. 59-45329. 210T.

AKADEMIIA NAUK SSSR. KOM.TEKH.TERM. TERMINOLOGIIA ZHELEZNODOROZHNOI SIGNALIZATSII. TSENTRALIZATSII STRELOK. SIGNALOV I BLOKIROVKI. (R.R. SIGNALING. CENTRALIZATION OF SWITCHING. RU DEFS) (SB.REK.TERM.NO. 10) MOSCOW. 1952. 54P. 55-37885. 290T.

BERG. A.I. AND TRAPEZNIKOV. V.A. AVTOMATIZATSIIA PROIZVODSTVA I PROMYSHLENNAIA ELEKTRONIKA... (IND. AUTOM/ELECTRON. ENCYCL. RU DEFS) MOSCOW. SOV. ENTSIKL. 1962- . 63-32131.

CLASON. W.E. ELSEVIER.S DICTIONARY OF AMPLIFICATION. MODULATION. RECEPTION AND TRANSMISSION. RUSSIAN SUPPL. NEW YORK. ELSEVIER. 1961. 87P. 2900T.

CLASON. W.E. ELSEVIER.S DICTIONARY OF ELECTRONICS AND WAVEGUIDES. RUSSIAN SUPPL. NEW YORK. ELSEVIER. 1961. 57P. 2000T.

DOZOROV. N.I. ANGLO-RUSSKII SLOVAR PO RADIOELEKTRONIKE. (EN*RU RADIO/ELECTRON. D) MOSCOW. VOENIZDAT. 1959. 535P. 60-19763. 20000T.

DOZOROV. N.I. DOPOLNENIE K ANGLO-RUSSKOMU SLOVARIU PO RADIOELEKTRONIKE I SVIAZI. (SUPPL. TO EN*RU RADIO/ELECTRON D) MOSCOW. ATOMIZDAT. 1959. 115P. 3300T.

DOZOROV. N.I. DOPOLNENIE (VTOROE) K ANGLO-RUSSKOMU SLOVARIU PO RADIOELEKTRONIKE I SVIAZI. (SUPPL. 2 TO EN*RU RADIO/ELECTRON. D) MOSCOW. ATOMIZDAT. 1960. 68P.

GEILER. L.B. AND DOZOROV. N.I. ANGLO-RUSSKII ELEKTROTEKHNICHESKII SLOVAR. (EN*RU ELECTROTECH. D) ED3. MOSCOW. FIZMATGIZ. 1961. 711P. 62-5196. 37000T.

GERMAN-PROZOROVA. L.P. ET AL. ANGLO-RUSSKII RADIOTEKHNICHESKII SLOVAR. (EN*RU RADIO ENG. D) MOSCOW. FIZMATGIZ. 1960. 524P. 60-40798. 25000T.

IZAKOVA. O.N. ANGLO-RUSSKII SLOVAR TERMINOV PO POLUPROVODNIKOVOI ELEKTRONIKE. (EN*RU D. OF SEMICONDUCTOR ELECTRON) MOSCOW. GOS. KOM. AVTOMAT/MASHINOSTR. 1959. 48P. 400T.

KHRAMOI. A.V. AND ZHURKINA. E.G. RUSSKO-ANGLIISKII I ANGLO-RUSSKII SLOVAR PO AVTOMATICHESKOMU REGULIROVANIIU I UPRAVLENIIU. (*RU*EN D. OF AUTOM. CONTROL-IFAC) MOSCOW. AKAD. NAUK. SSSR. 1960. 91P. MIC 61-7392. 1600T.

PTASHNYI. L.K. ANGLO-RUSSKII SLOVAR PO AVTOMATIKE I KONTROLNO-IZMERITELNYM PRIBORAM. (EN*RU D. OF AUTOM/INSTR) MOSCOW. GITTL. 1957. 379P. 58-30223. 12000T.

ROBESON. P. JR. RUSSIAN-ENGLISH GLOSSARY OF ELECTRONICS AND PHYSICS. NEW YORK. CONSULTANTS BUR. 1957. 343P. 58-341. 20000T.

RUSSIAN-ENGLISH GLOSSARY OF ELECTRICITY AND MAGNETISM. NEW YORK. CONSULTANTS BUR. (IN PREP)

SAPOZHNIKOVA. M.K. SLOVAR TERMINOV PO NADEZHNOSTI. (D. OF RELIABILITY. RU TRANSL. OF RYERSON. C.M. D. OF RELIABILITY/QUALITY CONTROL IN ELECTRON) MOSCOW. GOS. KOM. RADIOELEKTRON. 1959. 112P. 300T.

SCHULTZ. G.F. RUSSIAN CONDENSER TERMINOLOGY. PROC. IRE. V.44. 1066 (1956) 100T.

SCHULTZ. G.F. RUSSIAN RESISTANCE AND RESISTOR TERMINOLOGY. PROC. IRE. V.44. 1622-3 (1956) 100T.

SCHULTZ. G.F. RUSSIAN VACUUM-TUBE TERMINOLOGY. PROC. IRE. V.44. 112 (1956) 30T.

U.S. DEPT. OF THE ARMY. ANGLO-RUSSKII SLOVAR PO RADIOELEKTRONIKE I SVIAZI. (REPR. OF *EN*RU ELECTRON.D. U.S.ARMY. 1956) MOSCOW. ATOMIZDAT. 1959. 548P. 59-52764. 25000T.

U.S. DEPT. OF THE ARMY. ENGLISH-RUSSIAN. RUSSIAN-ENGLISH ELECTRONICS DICTIONARY. (TM30-545) WASHINGTON. 1956. 944P. 58-3291. 25000T.

WITTY. M.B. POLON. D.D. ET AL. THE RUSSIAN ELECTRONICS DICTIONARY OF TERMS. ABBREVIATIONS AND TABLES. *RU*EN (IN PREP) 20000T.

ELECTRICAL AND ELECTRONIC ENGINEERING

SPANISH

ARTIGAS, J.A. VERSION ESPANOLA DEL VOCABULARIO ELECTROTECNICO INTERNACIONAL. (SP VERSION OF INTL. ELECTROTECH.D) MADRID, COM. NACL. ELECTROTEC. (IEC) 1959. 301P.

CARTER,H. DICCIONARIO DE ELECTRONICA. (ELECTRON.D, SP*EN) BUENOS AIRES, LERU, 1962. 419P. 3000T.

LAGUERUELA, F.J. DICCIONARIO DE ELECTRONICA INGLES-ESPANOL (EN*SP ELECTRON. D) MIAMI, FLA, OMEGA, 1963. 347P. 63-19789. 6000T.

RAMIREZ-VILLARREAL, H. DICCIONARIO ILUSTRADO DE ELECTRONICA, ESPANOL-INGLES E INGLES-ESPANOL. (ILLUS. *SP*EN D. OF ELECTRON) MEXICO, D.F, DIANA, 1961. 182P. 63-28223.

SELL,L.L. ENGLISH-SPANISH COMPREHENSIVE TECHNICAL DICTIONARY OF AIRCRAFT, AUTOMOBILE, ELECTRICITY, RADI TELEVISION, PETROLEUM,STEEL PRODUCTS... NEW YORK, MCGRAW-HILL, 1960. 1079P. 61-3462. 525000T.

SELL,L.L. ESPANOL-INGLES DICCIONARIO TECNICO COMPLETISIMO DE AERONAUTICA, AUTOMOVILES,FERROCARRILES, CARRETERAS, ELECTRICIDAD, ELECTRONICA, RADIO, TELEVISION...(SP*EN TECH. D) NEW YORK, MCGRAW-HILL, 1949. 1706P. 61-4329. 700000T.

SWEDISH

CLASON, W.E. ELSEVIER,S DICTIONARY OF ELECTRONICS AND WAVEGUIDES. SWEDISH SUPPL. NEW YORK, ELSEVIER, 1960. 43P. 2000T.

FOOD CHEMISTRY, RESEARCH, AND TECHNOLOGY

CHINESE

HUANG, CHEN-HSUN. K,O HSUEH CHI SHU MING TZ,U CHIEH SHIH. (SCI/TECH T... RELATING TO SUGAR, TOBACCO/WINE) PEKING, POPULAR SCI, 1958. 85P. C59-1206.

CZECH

KOCOUREK, R. AGRICULTURAL DICTIONARY. PRAGUE, SPN. (IN PREP) 15000T.

ENGLISH

BENDER, A.E. DICTIONARY OF NUTRITION AND FOOD TECHNOLOGY. NEW YORK, ACAD. PRESS, 1960. 143P. 60-15032 2200T.

DAVIS, J.G. A DICTIONARY OF DAIRYING. ED2. NEW YORK, INTERSCIENCE, 1955. 1132P. 56-58117.

FRANDSEN, J.H. ET AL. DAIRY HANDBOOK AND DICTIONARY. AMHERST, MASS, 1958. 843P. 58-59996.

JAMES, W. WINE, A BRIEF ENCYCLOPEDIA. NEW YORK, KNOPF, 1960. 208P. 60-50601.

LEON, S.I. ENCYCLOPEDIA OF CANDY AND ICE-CREAM MAKING. NEW YORK, CHEMICAL, 1959. 454P. 59-1340.

THORPE, J.F. ET AL. DICTIONARY OF APPLIED CHEMISTRY. ED4. NEW YORK, LONGMANS, GREEN, 1937-56. 12V. 37-28650.

U.S. DEPARTMENT OF AGRICULTURE. CHEESE VARIETIES. (U.S.D.A. HANDBOOK NO.54) WASHINGTON,1953. 151P. 800T.

WINBURNE,J. A DICTIONARY OF AGRICULTURAL AND ALLIED TERMINOLOGY. EAST LANSING, MICH. STATE UNIV.PRESS, 1962. 905P. 62-9169. 30000T.

FRENCH

LANCELOT, E. AND BERARD, H. FRENCH AND ENGLISH GLOSSARY OF DAIRY AND RELATED TERMS. WASHINGTON, INTL. DAIRY IND. SOC, 1954. 64P. 55-17206.

MENSIER,P.H. DICTIONNAIRE DES HUILES VEGETALES. (VEGETABLE OILS D, FR DEFS) PARIS, LECHEVALIER, 1957. 763P.

SEIGNEURIE, A. DICTIONNAIRE ENCYCLOPEDIQUE DE L,EPICERIE ET DES INDUSTRIES DE L,ALIMENTATION. (ENCYCL.D OF FOOD/SPICE IND, FR DEFS) PARIS, DUNOD, 1956. 964P.

GERMAN

BIRKHOFF,C. SEEFISCHEREI IN GEGENWART UND ZUKUNFT...(*GE*EN COM. SEA FISHING D) BREMERHAVEN, DITZEN, 1957. 153P. A59-2740.

DICTIONARY OF AGRICULTURAL TERMS, ENGLISH-GERMAN,GERMAN-ENGLISH. LONDON, NATL.FED.YOUNG FARMERS CLUBS, 1952. 40P.

DYCKERHOFF, H. WOERTERBUCH DER PHYSIOLOGISCHEN CHEMIE FUER MEDIZINER. (PHYSIOL. CHEM. FOR PHYSICIANS, G DEFS) BERLIN, DE GRUYTER, 1955. 175P. A55-3360.

FISCHER, W. ET AL. FACHWOERTERBUCH FUER BRAUEREI UND MAELZEREI. (*GE*EN*D. FOR BREWING IND) (V.1, GE*E 174P. V2, EN*GE, 159P) ED2. NUERNBERG, CARL, 1955. 56-16292. 5000T.

OETKER NAEHRMITTELFABRIK G.M.B.H. WARENKUNDE. (FOOD GL, GE DEFS) ED7. BIELEFELD, CERES-VERLAG, 1961. 818P. 62-42206. 8000T.

GERMAN

ULZ,M.E. MOLKEREI-LEXIKON. MILCHWIRTSCHAFT VON A-Z. (DAIRY D, GE DEFS) ED3. KEMPTEN, DEUT. MOLKEREI-, 1952. 820P.

EL, G. MUELLEREITECHNISCHES FACHWOERTERBUCH...(FLOUR MILLING D,*GE*EN) BRAUNSCHWEIG, VIEWEG, 1955. P. 57-19084. 1200T.

HINDI·

SHAL, S.C. FERMENTATION TECHNOLOGY, ENGLISH-HINDI DICTIONARY. ALLAHABAD, HINDI SAHITYA SAMMELAN, 0. 600T.

ITALIAN

NINGER, G. ITALIAN SUPPLEMENT TO HAENSCH, G. AND HABERKAMP, G. DICTIONARY OF AGRICULTURE. MUNICH, BLV, 3. 200P.

JAPANESE

AN. MINISTRY OF EDUCATION. DRAFT VOCABULARY FOR FISHERIES. (JA*EN) TOKYO, 1952. 10P.

URAI, Y. SOGO SHOKUHIN JITEN. (FOOD D. JA*EN) TOKYO, DOBUN SHOIN, 1960. 628+79+41P. J61-512.

POLISH

ONOWICZ, L. ENGLISH-POLISH AND POLISH-ENGLISH AGRICULTURAL DICTIONARY. LONDON, POLISH FARMERS ASSOC. GR. BRIT, 1959. 267P. 60-40658. 8000T.

POLYGLOT

SALSKI, E. TERMINOLOGIE DER LANDARBEITSWISSENSCHAFT. (AGR. D, GE EN FR) ED3. BAD KREUZNACH, MAX NCK INST, 1958. 71P.

ALIS, J. ET AL. MILCHWIRTSCHAFTLICHES WOERTERBUCH, ENGLISCH-FRANZOESISCH-DEUTSCH. (DAIRY D, EN FR GE) RNBERG, CARL, 1963. 700P.

D AND AGRICULTURE ORGANIZATION. (U.N.) RICE TRADE GLOSSARY. (DU EN FR GE IT SP) ROME, 1957. 111P. 4595. 70T.

D AND AGRICULTURE ORGANIZATION. (U.N.) TRILINGUAL DICTIONARY OF FISHERIES TECHNOLOGICAL TERMS--CURING. EN SP) ROME, 1960. 85P. 61-673. 550T.

HOT, H. DICTIONNAIRE TECHNIQUE DE L,INDUSTRIE DES JUS DE FRUITS. (FRUIT JUICE IND. D, EN FR GE) ZUG, WEIZ. OBSTVERBAND, 1957. 75P.

NSCH, G. AND HABERKAMP, G. WOERTERBUCH DER LANDWIRTSCHAFT. (AGR. D, *GE*EN*FR*SP) ED2. NEW YORK, EVIER, 1963. 720P. 10500T.

KO KOGYO YOGO JITEN HENSHU IINKAI. HAKKO YOGO JITEN. (FERMENTATION D, *JA*EN*GE) TOKYO, GIHODO, 0. 4+372P. J61-629.

TONG, B.D. ET AL. ELSEVIER,S DICTIONARY OF BARLEY, MALTING, AND BREWING... (*GE*EN/AM*DA*FR*IT*SP) YORK, ELSEVIER, 1961. 669P. 60-12356. 3900T.

TEREN, G.L. FISHERIES. (*EN/AM*FR*GE*IT*SP D) NEW YORK, ELSEVIER. (IN PREP)

TBRUKSLEXIKON...(AGR. D,*SW*EN*FR*GE) STOCKHOLM, LTS, 1960. 202P. 60-41312. 3000T.

I, L. MAATALOUDEN SANAKIRJA. (AGR. D, FI*EN*GE*SW) HELSINKI, OTAVA, 1958. 177P. 60-37751. 35000T.

ANIZATION FOR EUROPEAN ECONOMIC COOPERATION.E.P.A. MEAT CUTS IN O.E.E.C. MEMBER COUNTRIES. (NO.7/II-IB) IS,1961. 34P.

LAND, J. INDUSTRIE DES BOISSONS. (BEVERAGE IND, FR EN GE) PARIS, GELBARD, 1960. 61P.

CHL, G. ET AL. IL BIRRAIO IN 9 LINGUE. (BREWERY D, IT EN CZ DU FR GE PR SP SW) NUERNBERG, CARL, 1960. P. A60-5384. 2100T.

RUSSIAN

INOVA, N.V. AND USOVSKII, B.N. ANGLO-RUSSKII SELSKOKHOZIAISTVENNYI SLOVAR. (EN*RU AGR. D) ED3. COW, GITTL, 1956. 532P. 56-45936. 30000T.

HCHIN, . RUSSIAN SUPPLEMENT TO HAENSCH, G. AND HABERKAMP, G. DICTIONARY OF AGRICULTURE. MUNICH, BLV, 3. 200P.

OMAREV, N.A. ANGLO-RUSSKII SLOVAR TEKHNICHESKIKH TERMINOV PO MUKOMOLNOMU, KRUPIANOMU, I KOMBIKORMOVOMU IZVODSTVU I ELEVATORNOMU KHOZIAISTVU. (EN*RU D. OF FLOUR MILLING) MOSCOW, ZAGOTIZDAT, 1953. 107P. 26653.

VSKII, B.N. ET AL. RUSSKO-ANGLIISKII SELSKOKHOZIAISTVENNYI SLOVAR. (RU*EN AGR. D) MOSCOW, FIZMATGIZ, 0. 504P. 61-28060.

CH, T.M. ET AL. ANGLO-RUSSKII SLOVAR TERMINOV PO TEKHNOLOGII MIASA I MIASOPRODUKTOV. (EN*RU D. OF T PROCESS) MOSCOW, VNIIMP, 1960. 44P. 1800T.

FUELS (SOLID, LIQUID, AND GAS)

ENGLISH

ACHARD, F.H. AND HAMILTON, E.R. GLOSSARY OF TERMS COMMONLY USED IN THE MANUFACTURED AND MIXED GAS INDUSTRIES. BOSTON, DRAHCA PERS/TRAINING SERV, 1952. 48P.

AMERICAN SOCIETY FOR TESTING/MATERIALS. STANDARD DEFINITIONS FOR COMMERCIAL VARIETIES OF BITUMINOUS AND SUBBITUMINOUS COALS. (D493-39) ASTM STDS, PT. 8, 1347. PHILADELPHIA, 1961. 4T.

AMERICAN SOCIETY FOR TESTING/MATERIALS. STANDARD DEFINITIONS OF TERMS RELATING TO COAL AND COKE.(D121-30) ASTM STDS, PT. 8, 1345-6. PHILADELPHIA, 1961. 10T.

BRITISH STANDARDS INSTITUTION. GLOSSARY OF COAL TERMS. (B.S.3323) LONDON, 1960. 20P. 90T.

BRITISH STANDARDS INSTITUTION. GLOSSARY OF TERMS USED FOR SOLID FUEL BURNING AND ALLIED APPLIANCES. (B.S. 1846) LONDON, 1959. 26P. 200T.

BRITISH STANDARDS INSTITUTION. GLOSSARY OF TERMS USED IN COAL PREPARATION. (B.S. 3552) LONDON, 1962. 44P. 450T.

BRITISH STANDARDS INSTITUTION. GLOSSARY OF TERMS USED IN THE GAS INDUSTRY. (B.S.1179) LONDON, 1961. 80P. 700T.

PETROLEUM EDUCATIONAL INSTITUTE. ILLUSTRATED PETROLEUM DICTIONARY AND PRODUCTS MANUAL. LOS ANGELES, 1962. 754P. 62-18323. 10000T.

TOMKEIEFF, S.I. COALS AND BITUMENS AND RELATED FOSSIL CARBONACEOUS SUBSTANCES, NOMENCLATURE AND CLASSIFICATION. LONDON, PERGAMON, 1954. 122P. 55-671. 1300T.

FRENCH

DICTIONNAIRE DU PETROLE ET DES MINES. (*EN*FR PETROL/MINING D) PARIS, PARIS-MONDE, 1963. 700P.

RUELLE, P. LE VOCABULAIRE PROFESSIONEL DU HOUILLEUR BORAIN... (OCCUP.VOC. OF COAL MIN, FR DEFS) BRUSSELS, PALAIS/ACAD. 1953. 198P. A55-3614.

GERMAN

BERKENHOFF,G. ENERGIE VON A BIS Z (ENERGY FROM A-Z, GE DEFS) MUNICH, OLDENBOURG, 1954. 192P. A55-1209.

DIDIER-KOGAG-HINSELMANN, GMBH. WOERTERBUCH DER KOKEREITECHNIK. (COKE-OVEN PRACTICE D, *GE*EN) ESSEN, VULKAN, 1954. 329P. A55-5688. 6000T.

GUMZ, W. AND REGUL, R. DIE KOHLE. (COAL) KLEINES FACHLEXIKON DER KOHLENTECHNIK UND KOHLENWIRTSCHAFT. (COAL MIN. GL, GE DEFS, PP.381-427, 500T) ESSEN, GLUECKAUF, 1954. 427P. 54-39218.

JAPANESE

ISHIBASHI, K. SEKIYU KAGAKU JITEN. (PETROL.CHEM.D,*JA*EN) TOKYO, NIKKAN KOGYO SHIMBUNSHA, 1958. 245+46P. J62-1537. 3000T.

POLYGLOT

GLOSSARY OF STRATA CONTROL TERMS IN ENGLISH, FRENCH, AND GERMAN. LONDON, NATL. COAL BOARD, 1958. 40P. 59-54715. 600T.

INTERNATIONAL GAS UNION. ELSEVIER,S DICTIONARY OF THE GAS INDUSTRY.... (*EN/AM*DU*FR*GE*IT*PR*SP) NEW YORK, ELSEVIER, 1961. 628P. 61-19741. 2900T.

MALI, L. PEAT LAND TERMINOLOGY,*FI*EN*GE*SW. HELSINKI,1956. 14P.

NENRYO KYOKAI. KOKUSU BUKAI. KOKUSU KOGYO YOGO-SHU. (COKE IND. D, JA*EN*GE) TOKYO, SHIGEN SHIMPO, 1958. 148P. J62-971. 2000T. 300ABBR.

SPECTOR, J. COAL DICTIONARY. FR EN DU GE IT PL. NEW YORK, ELSEVIER. (IN PREP)

UNITED NATIONS. LIST OF TERMS CONCERNING NEW SOURCES OF ENERGY. (TERMINOLOGY BULL. NO.176) NEW YORK, 1961.

RUSSIAN

AKADEMIIA NAUK SSSR. KOM. TEKH. TERM. TERMINOLOGIIA GAZOVOI TEKHNIKI. (GAS TECH, RU DEFS) (SB. REK. TERM, NO.41) MOSCOW, 1957. 24P. 58-33553. 100T.

AKADEMIIA NAUK SSSR. KOM. TEKH. TERM. TERMINOLOGIIA TOPLIVA DLIA DVIGATELEI VNUTRENNEGO SGORANIIA (FUELS FOR INTERNAL COMBUSTION ENG, RU DEFS)(SB. REK. TERM, NO.44) MOSCOW, 1957. 28P. 57-45392. 100T.

BELODVORSKII, IU. M. KRATKII SLOVAR GAZOVIKA. (D. OF GAS TECH, RU DEFS) MOSCOW, MIN. KOMMUNAL. KHOZ, RSFSR, 1955. 187P. 56-37054. 500T.

CHOCHIA, A.P. ANGLO-RUSSKII SLOVAR PO TOPLIVAM I MASLAM. (EN*RU D. OF FUEL/OIL) MOSCOW, GITTL, 1956. 545P. 57-16901. 20000T.

PAPOK, K.K. AND RAGOZIN, N.A. TEKHNICHESKII SLOVAR-SPRAVOCHNIK PO TOPLIVU I MASLAM. (FUEL/OIL D, RU DEFS) ED3. MOSCOW, GOSTOPTEKHIZDAT, 1963. 767P. 63-41756. 1200T.

CHINESE

Y, J.E.S. AND BARNES, A.C. CHINESE-ENGLISH GLOSSARY OF MINERAL NAMES. NEW YORK, CONSULTANTS BUR, 120P. 63-20001.

KUO K,O HSUEH YUAN. PIEN I CHU. (ACAD. SINICA. BUR. OF COMPILATIONS/TRANSL) TI CHIH HSUEH MING (GEOL. T, CH EN) PEKING, 1954.

KUO K,O HSUEH YUAN. PIEN I CH,U PAN WEI YUAN HUI. (ACAD. SINICA. COMM. OF PUBL/TRANSL) TSUNG HO TI ING TZ,U. (GEOL. T, CH EN) PEKING, SCIENCE, 1957. 244P. C58-5277.

CZECH

A, J.F. ET AL. NAUCNY GEOLOGICKY SLOVNIK. (D. OF GEOL, CZ DEFS) PRAGUE, NAKL. CESKOSLOV, AKAD. 960-61. 2V. 60-36133. 20000T.

O. AND BENES, K. ENGLISH-CZECH GEOLOGICAL DICTIONARY... PRAGUE, NAKL. CESK. AKAD. VED, 1963. 63-24485.

ENGLISH

A SOCIETY OF PETROLEUM GEOLOGISTS. LEXICON OF GEOLOGIC NAMES IN THE WESTERN CANADA SEDIMENTARY AND ARCTIC ARCHIPELAGO. CALGARY, 1960. 380P. 62-44283.

AN GEOLOGICAL INSTITUTE. DICTIONARY OF GEOLOGICAL TERMS. GARDEN CITY, N.Y, DOLPHIN, 1962. 545P. 7. 7500T.

, W. AND TOMKEIEFF, S.I. ENGLISH ROCK TERMS, CHIEFLY AS USED BY MINERS AND QUARRY-MEN. NEW YORK, UNIV.PRESS, 1953. 139P. 53-4237.

, L. ET AL. LAROUSSE ENCYCLOPEDIA OF THE EARTH. LONDON, HAMLYN, 1961. 419P. 61-66629.

NOR, J. A DICTIONARY OF GEOLOGY. NEW YORK, OXFORD UNIV. PRESS,1962. 235P. 63-890. 1500T.

G.W. A DICTIONARY OF GEOLOGY. HARMONDSWORTH, MIDDLESEX, PENGUIN, 1954. 153P. 55-2576. 1500T.

, J.V. ET AL. GLOSSARY OF GEOLOGY AND RELATED SCIENCES...ED2. WASHINGTON, AM. GEOL. INST. 1960. SUPPL. 72P. 60-60083. 14500T.

H.L. AND LOCHMAN-BALK, C. LEXICON OF NEW MEXICO GEOLOGIC NAMES, PRECAMBRIAN THROUGH PALEOZOIC. O, N.M. INST. MIN/TECH, 1958. 137P. GS58-226. 350T.

AN, J.H. GLOSSARY OF PEDOLOGIC (SOILS) AND LANDFORM TERMINOLOGY FOR SOIL ENGINEERS. (HIGHWAY CH BOARD. SPEC. REPT. NO.25) WASHINGTON, 1957. 32P. 57-61134.

CIENCE SOCIETY OF AMERICA. SOIL DEFINITIONS. MADISON, WIS, 195 .

C.M. DICTIONARY OF GEOLOGICAL TERMS...ANN ARBOR, MICH, EDWARDS,1957. 465P. 59-22370. 19000T.

, W.L. AND VARNES, D.J. GLOSSARY OF SELECTED GEOLOGIC TERMS...(USED) IN ENGINEERING. DENVER, COLO. OC, 1955. 165P. A57-2059. 3300T.

EFF, S.I. COALS AND BITUMENS AND RELATED FOSSIL CARBONACEOUS SUBSTANCES, NOMENCLATURE AND FICATION. LONDON, PERGAMON, 1954. 122P. 55-671. 1300T.

OIL CONSERVATION SERVICE. NATIONAL CATALOG OF PRACTICES AND MEASURES USED IN SOIL AND WATER VATION. WASHINGTON, 1959. 11P. 59-64226. 130T.

M.B. ET AL. DICTIONARY OF GEOLOGY AND MINERALOGY ABBREVIATIONS, SIGNS AND SYMBOLS. NEW YORK, 196 . 192P.

FRENCH

, G.M. A FRENCH-ENGLISH VOCABULARY IN GEOLOGY AND PHYSICAL GEOGRAPHY. LONDON, MANN, 1960. 140P.

J. PETIT DICTIONNAIRE DE PEDOLOGIE. (D. OF SOIL SCI, EN*FR) BRUSSELS, MIN. COLONIES, 1954. 169P. 77.

NCE, G. AND GAILLEUX, A. DICTIONNAIRE DES SOLS. (D. OF SOILS, FR DEFS) PARIS, MAISON RUSTIQUÉ, 604P. 62-25442. 15000T.

GERMAN

ER, C.C. AND MURAWSKI, H. GEOLOGISCHES WOERTERBUCH... (GEOL.D, GE DEFS) ED5. STUTTGART, ENKE, 241P. 2200T.

KI, H. GEOLOGISCHES WOERTERBUCH. (GEOL. D, GE DEFS) ED5. STUTTGART, ENKE, 1963. 243P. 2000T.

, F. DEUTSCH-ENGLISCHES FACHWOERTERBUCH DER TIEFBOHRTECHNIK. (*GE*EN D. OF OIL-WELL DRILLING) , SCHMIDT, 1953. 147P. 56-29010. 4000T.

ERGER, F.A. TASCHENLEXIKON DER GEOGRAPHIE. (POCKET D. OF GEOG, GE DEFS) FRANKFURT/MAIN, HUMBOLDT, 192P. 56-57255.

GEOLOGY

ITALIAN

ZAVATTI, S. DIZIONARIO GEOGRAFICO, INGLESE-ITALIANO. (GEOG. D, EN*IT) CATANIA, CAMENE, 1952. 169P. 54-23939.

POLISH

GISMAN, S. ET AL. SLOWNIK GEOLOGICZNO-GORNICZY ANGIELSKO-POLSKI. (EN*PL D. FOR MIN/GEOL) WARSAW, PANSTW. WYDAW. TECH. 1956. 794P. 57-41449. 35000T.

KLECZKOWSKI, A. AND DZIEWANSKI, J. SLOWNIK GEOLOGICZNY. (GEOL.D, PL DEFS) WARSAW, ARS POLONA, 1959. 150P. 1500T.

POLYGLOT

BAULIG, H. VOCABULAIRE FRANCO-ANGLO-ALLEMAND DE GEOMORPHOLOGIE. (*FR*EN*GE GL. OF GEOMORPH) PARIS, BELLES LETTRES, 1956. 229P. 56-59002.

COOPER, S.A. CONCISE INTERNATIONAL DICTIONARY OF MECHANICS AND GEOLOGY, EN*FR*GE*SP) NEW YORK, PHIL.LIBR, 1958. 400P. 58-3594. 5500T.

DEVON AND COURTENAY CLAY CO. DEVON CLAY. (EN,FR,GE GL) ED4. KINGSTEIGHTON, NEWTON ABBOT, 1952.

DOLITSKII, A.V. AND KOLCHANOV, V.P. TEKTONICHESKII SLOVAR. (TECTONIC D, *EN*FR*GE*RU) MOSCOW, MEZHDUNAR.GEOL.KONGR, 1959. 43P. 90T.

GLOSSARY OF STRATA CONTROL TERMS IN ENGLISH, FRENCH, AND GERMAN. LONDON, NATL. COAL BOARD, 1958. 40P. 59-54715. 600T.

INTERNATIONAL GEOLOGICAL CONGRESS. LEXIQUE STRATIGRAPHIQUE INTERNATIONAL. (INTL. STRATIGR. GL, FR EN GE) PARIS, CENTRE NATL.RECH.SCI, 1950- . 2V. 60-37888. (IN PROGR)

INTERNATIONAL SOCIETY OF SOIL MECHANICS AND FOUNDATION ENGINEERING. TECHNICAL TERMS...USED IN SOIL MECHANICS AND FOUNDATION ENGINEERING. (*EN*FR*GE*PR*SP*SW) ED2. ZURICH, 1954. 103P. 54-4683. 1200T.

JACKS, G.V. ET AL. MULTILINGUAL VOCABULARY OF SOIL SCIENCE.(*FR*EN*DU*GE*IT*PR*SP*SW) ED2. ROME, FAO (UN) 1960. 428P. 60-50105. 340T.

KANT, E. POLYGLOT GLOSSARY OF GEOGRAPHICAL SCIENCES. (IN PREP)

LEINZ, V. AND MENDES, J.C. VOCABULARIO GEOLOGICO, COM A TERMINOLOGIA CORRESPONDENTE EM INGLES E ALEMAO. (GEOL. VOC, *PR*EN*GE) ED2. SAO PAULO, NACL, 1959. 180P. 61-59731. 1000T.

LEXIQUE DES TERMES RELATIFS AUX PRESSIONS DE TERRAIN. (MINE-PRESSURE D, FR GE EN) LONDON, NATL. COAL BOARD, 1958. 32P.

MACHATSCHEK, F. TERMINOLOGIA GEOMORFOLOGICA. (GEOMORPH.GL, SP*EN*FR*GE) TUCUMAN, ARGENTINA, UNIV. NACL, 1953. 204P. 55-27367. 1000T.

NOVITSKY, A. DICCIONARIO MINERO-METALURGICO-GEOLOGICO-MINERALOGICO-PETROGRAFICO Y DE PETROLEO. (D. OF MIN, MET, GEOL, MINERAL, PETROGR/PETROL, *SP*EN*FR*GE*RU) BUENOS AIRES, 1958. 2V. 217P. 18000T.

PIPA, V. AND SEDA, Z. CESKO-RUSKO-NEMECKO-ANGLICKY SLOVNIK Z OBORU HLUBINNEHO VRTANI A TEZBY NAFTY... (CZ*EN*GE*RU D. OF DEEP DRILLING/PETROL. ENG) PRAGUE, CSAV, 1958. 379P. 6000T.

PLAISANCE, G. LEXIQUE PEDOLOGIQUE TRILINGUE. (SOILS GL, FR EN GE) PARIS, S.E.D.E.S.1958. 357P. A59-1516.

SCHIEFERDECKER, A.A.G. GEOLOGICAL NOMENCLATURE. (EN DU FR GE) GORINCHEM, NOORDUIJN, 1959. 523P. A60-3024.

WATANABE, G. CHIKAG.U JITEN. (EARTH SCI.T.*JA*EN*FR*GE) TOKYO, 1955. 2027P. 2500T.

RUSSIAN

AKADEMIIA NAUK SSSR. TOLKOVYI SLOVAR PO POCHVOVEDENIIU. FIZIKA, MELIORATSIIA I MINERALOGIIA POCHV. (D. OF SOIL PHYS, IMPROVEMENT/MINERAL, RU DEFS) MOSCOW, 1960. 144P. 800T.

ANGLO-RUSSKII TERMINOLOGICHESKII SLOVAR PO GEOLOGOPOISKOVOMU BURENIIU. (EN*RU GEOPHYS. PROSPECTING D) LENINGRAD, 1963. 317P.

BURGUNKER, M.E. RUSSIAN-ENGLISH DICTIONARY OF EARTH SCIENCES. NEW YORK, TELBERG, 1961. 94P. 61-9081. 2500T.

ECKER, L. A GLOSSARY OF RUSSIAN TERMS PERTAINING TO GEOLOGY, BOTANY, GEOGRAPHY, ZOOLOGY, ICHTHYOLOGY AND ORNITHOLOGY. WASHINGTON, U.S. ARMY, 1957. 337P. 60-39318.

GRIGOREV,A.A. KRATKAIA GEOGRAFICHESKAIA ENTSIKLOPEDIA. (SHORT GEOG.ENCYCL, RU DEFS) 4V. MOSCOW, SOV.ENTSIKL, 1960- . 16000T.

KRISHTOFOVICH, A.N. ET AL. GEOLOGICHESKII SLOVAR. (GEOL. D, RU DEFS) MOSCOW, GOSGEOLTEKHIZDAT, 1960. 2V 61-32531. 13000T.

LIKHAREV, B.K. ET AL. STRATIGRAFICHESKII SLOVAR SSR. (STRATIGRAPHIC D. OF THE USSR, RU DEFS) MOSCOW, GOSGEOLTEKHIZDAT, 1956. 1282P. 57-33840. 4000T.

64

<u>GEOLOGY</u>

RUSSIAN

MAKKAVEEV, A.A. ET AL. SLOVAR PO GIDROGEOLOGII I INZHENERNOI GEOLOGII. (D. OF HYDROGEOL/ENG. GEOL, RU DEFS) MOSCOW, GOSTOPTEKHIZDAT, 1961. 186P. 61-48756. 10000T.

MIRCHINK, C.F. ET AL. SLOVAR PO GEOLOGII NEFTI. (PETROL. GEOL. D, RU DEFS) ED2. LENINGRAD, GOSTOPTEKHIZDAT, 1958. 776P. 59-23302.

MITCHELL, G.S. A RUSSIAN-ENGLISH DICTIONARY-GLOSSARY IN GEOMORPHOLOGY AND RELATED SCIENCES. (UNPUBL. MASTER,S ESSAY) OHIO STATE UNIV, 1957. 211P.

ROTAY, A.P. STRATIGRAFICHESKAIA KLASSIFIKATSIIA I TERMINOLOGIIA. (STRATIGRAPHIC T. USSR, RU DEFS) ED2. MOSCOW, GNTILGON, 1960. 57P. 62-29657.

SOFIANO, T.A. ET AL. ANGLO-RUSSKII GEOLOGICHESKII SLOVAR. (EN*RU GEOL. D) ED2. MOSCOW, FIZMATGIZ, 1961. 528P. 30000T.

SOFIANO, T.A. ET AL. RUSSKO-ANGLIISKII GEOLOGICHESKII SLOVAR. (RU*EN GEOL. D) MOSCOW, FIZMATGIZ, 1960. 559P. 61-34568. 35000T.

TELBERG, V.G. AMERICAN SUPPLEMENT TO SOFIANO,S RUSSIAN-ENGLISH GEOLOGICAL DICTIONARY. NEW YORK, TELBERG, 1961. 49P. 62-4342. 800T.

TELBERG, V.G. RUSSIAN-ENGLISH DICTIONARY OF GEOLOGICAL TERMS. NEW YORK, 1964. 149P. 64-13007.

SPANISH

DE NOVO, P. AND CHICARRO, F. DICCIONARIO DE GEOLOGIA Y CIENCIAS AFINES. (D. OF GEOL/ RELATED SCI, SP DEFS) BARCELONA, LABOR, 1957. 2V. 1685P. 57-45178. 14000T.

GUERRA, A.T. DICCIONARIO GEOLOGICO-GEOMORFOLOGICO. (D. OF GEOL/GEOMORPH, SP DEFS) RIO DE JANEIRO, INST. PAN-AM GEOG/HIST, 1954. 250P. 56-1377. 2500T.

VULETIN, A. GEOMORFONIMIA ARGENTINA. (ARGENTINE GEOMORPH, SP DEFS) SANTIAGO DEL ESTERO, UNIV. NACL, TUCUMAN, 1959. 82P. 60-25446. 300T.

<u>GEOPHYSICS AND PHYSICAL GEOGRAPHY</u>

CHINESE

CHUNG-KUO K,O HSUEH YUAN. PIEN I CH,U PAN WEI YUAN HUI. (ACAD. SINICA. COMM. OF PUBL/TRANSL) TZU JAN TI LI MING TZ,U. TI HSING CHIH PU. (PHYS. GEOG. T. TOPOGRAPHY SECT, CH EN) PEKING, SCIENCE, 1958. 61P. C59-1274.

U.S. ARMY LANGUAGE SCHOOL. CHINESE-MANDARIN EIGHTEEN MONTHS COURSE.... CHINESE GEOGRAPHY VOCABULARY. PRESIDIO OF MONTEREY, 1958. 36P. 58-62333.

DUTCH

PENKALA, E. AND PRAAG, H. ENCYCLOPEDIE VAN HET HEELAL. (ENCYCL. OF THE UNIVERSE, DU DEFS) ZEIST, HOLLAND, HAAN, 1960. 251P. 61-33463.

ENGLISH

ARMSTRONG, T.E. AND ROBERTS, B. ILLUSTRATED ICE GLOSSARY. CAMBRIDGE,ENG, SCOTT POLAR RES.INST, 1956. 12P. 57-18290.

BERTIN, L. ET AL. LAROUSSE ENCYCLOPEDIA OF THE EARTH. LONDON, HAMLYN, 1961. 419P. 61-66629.

BRITISH ASSOCIATION FOR THE ADVANCEMENT OF SCIENCE. A GLOSSARY OF GEOGRAPHICAL TERMS. LONDON, LONGMANS, 1962. 569P.

FLANDERS, P.L. AND SAUER, F.M. A GLOSSARY OF GEOPLOSICS. THE SYSTEMATIC STUDY OF EXPLOSION EFFECTS IN THE EARTH. MENLO PARK, CALIF, STANFORD RES. INST. 1960. 34P.

HOWELL, J.V. ET AL. GLOSSARY OF GEOLOGY AND RELATED SCIENCES...ED2. WASHINGTON, AM. GEOL. INST, 1960. 325P. SUPPL. 72P. 60-60083. 14500T.

HUXLEY, A. STANDARD ENCYCLOPEDIA OF THE WORLD,S MOUNTAINS. NEW YORK, PUTNAM, 1962. 383P.

HUXLEY, A. STANDARD ENCYCLOPEDIA OF THE WORLD,S OCEANS AND ISLANDS. NEW YORK, PUTNAM, 1962. 383P.

INTERNATIONAL ASSOCIATION OF HYDROLOGY. INTERNATIONAL CLASSIFICATION FOR SNOW. (TECH.MEMO NO.31) ONTARIO, NATL.RES.COUNCIL, 195 .

MOORE, W.G. A DICTIONARY OF GEOGRAPHY... DEFINITIONS IN PHYSICAL GEOGRAPHY. BALTIMORE, PENGUIN, 1959. 191P. 60-2688. 1800T.

SWAYNE, J.C. A CONCISE GLOSSARY OF GEOGRAPHICAL TERMS. LONDON, PHILIP, 1956. 164P. 57-3942.

U.S. ARCTIC, DESERT AND TROPIC INFORMATION CENTER. GLOSSARY OF ARCTIC AND SUBARCTIC TERMS. (ADTIC PUBL, A-105) MAXWELL AFB, ALA. 1955. 90P. 56-60228.

U.S. DEPT. OF THE ARMY. GLOSSARY OF NATURAL TERRAIN FEATURES. (I.G.NO.13) WASHINGTON, 195 .

GEOPHYSICS AND PHYSICAL GEOGRAPHY

ENGLISH

U.S. HYDROGRAPHIC OFFICE. A FUNCTIONAL GLOSSARY OF ICE TERMINOLOGY. (H.O.NO.609) WASHINGTON, 1952. 88P. 52-60807.

WIEGEL, R.L. WAVES, TIDES, CURRENTS, AND BEACHES, GLOSSARY OF TERMS AND LIST OF STANDARD SYMBOLS. COUNCIL ON WAVE RES. ENG. FOUND, 1953. 113P. A55-3914.

WORLD METEOROLOGICAL ORGANIZATION. INTERNATIONAL ICE NOMENCLATURE. LONDON, 1952.

FRENCH

DAVIES, G.M. A FRENCH-ENGLISH VOCABULARY IN GEOLOGY AND PHYSICAL GEOGRAPHY. LONDON, MANN, 1960. 140P.

NOMENCLATURE DES FORMES PROFONDES DU TERRAIN OCEANIQUE. (FR EN NOMENCL. OF OCEAN FLOOR T, PP.221-31) IN/FRANCE. CNRS. LA TOPOGRAPHIE ET LA GEOLOGIE DES PROFONDEURS OCEANIQUES. PARIS, 1959. 313P. 60-24516.

STEVENS, J.A.P. ENCYCLOPEDIE PRISMA DU MONDE SOUS-MARIN. (ENCYCL. OF OCEANOG, FR DEFS) PARIS, PRISMA, 1957. 558P. 57-43030.

GERMAN

FLUEGGE, S. ET AL. HANDBUCH DER PHYSIK. (ENCYCL. OF PHYS) V.47, GEOPHYSIK 1. (GEOPHYS.1, *GE*EN GL, PP.640-57, 1200T) BERLIN, SPRINGER, 1956. 659P. A56-2942.

FLUEGGE, S. ET AL. HANDBUCH DER PHYSIK. (ENCYCL. OF PHYS) V.48, GEOPHYSIK 2. (GEOPHYS.2, *GE*EN GL, PP.1012-44, 1800T) BERLIN, SPRINGER, 1957. 1046P. A56-2942.

NEEF, E. ET AL. DAS GESICHT DER ERDE, BROCKHAUS TASCHENBUCH DER PHYSISCHEN GEOGRAPHIE. (THE EARTH, BROCKHAUS POCKET BOOK OF PHYS.GEOG, GE DEFS) LEIPZIG, BROCKHAUS, 1956. 980P. 56-43303.

ROSENBERGER, F.A. TASCHENLEXIKON DER GEOGRAPHIE. (POCKET D. OF GEOG, GE DEFS) FRANKFURT/MAIN, HUMBOLDT, 1955. 192P. 56-57255.

TUCHEL, G. WOERTERBUCH DER ANGEWANDTEN GEOPHYSIK... (*GE*EN D. OF APPL.GEOPHYS) HANNOVER, SEISMOS, 1958. (2 PTS.IN 1V) 59-23520.

ITALIAN

MOORE, W.G. DIZIONARIO GEOGRAFICO... (D. OF PHYS. GEOG, IT DEFS) MILAN, MARTELLO, 1956. 250P.

ZAVATTI, S. DIZIONARIO GEOGRAFICO, INGLESE-ITALIANO. (GEOG. D, EN*IT) CATANIA, CAMENE, 1952. 169P. 54-23939.

JAPANESE

ROYAL GEOGRAPHICAL SOCIETY. NAMES FOR BRITISH OFFICIAL USE... (JA*EN) LONDON, 1954. 193P.

WADACHI, K. KAIYO NO JITEN. (ENCYCL.OF OCEANS, JA*EN) TOKYO, TOKYODO, 1960. 6+671P. J60-1043.

POLISH

STASZEWSKI, J. SLOWNIK GEOGRAFICZNY... (GEOG.D, PL DEFS) ED2. WARSAW, WIEDZA POWSZECHNA,1959. 351P. 60-32595.

POLYGLOT

AMERLINCK, T. DICCIONARIO POLIGLOTO DE NOMBRES GEOGRAFICOS. (PO D. OF GEOG. NAMES) MEXICO, UNIV. NACL, 1961. 111P. 62-32707.

BAULIG, H. VOCABULAIRE FRANCO-ANGLO-ALLEMAND DE GEOMORPHOLOGIE. (*FR*EN*GE GL. OF GEOMORPH) PARIS, BELLES LETTRES, 1956. 229P. 56-59002.

KANT, E. POLYGLOT GLOSSARY OF GEOGRAPHICAL SCIENCES. (IN PREP)

MACHATSCHEK, F. TERMINOLOGIA GEOMORFOLOGICA. (GEOMORPH.GL, SP*EN*FR*GE) TUCUMAN, ARGENTINA, UNIV. NACL, 1953. 204P. 55-27367. 1000T.

PERMANENT INTERNATIONAL ASSOCIATION OF NAVIGATION CONGRESSES. DICTIONNAIRE TECHNIQUE ILLUSTRE... (ILLUS. TECH. D, *FR*EN*DU*GE*IT*SP) V.1, LA MER. (THE SEA) BRUSSELS, 1957. 272P. 58-19041. 3000T.

RATAJSKI, L. ET AL. POLSKIE NAZEWNICTWO GEOGRAFICZNE SWIATA. (PO D. OF GEOG. NAMES) WARSAW, PANSTW. WYDAW. NAUK, 1959. 857P. 60-24517.

WATANABE, G. CHIKAG*U JITEN. (EARTH SCI.T,*JA*EN*FR*GE) TOKYO, 1955. 2027P. 2500T.

RUSSIAN

AKADEMIIA NAUK SSSR. TOLKOVYI SLOVAR PO POCHVOVEDENIIU. FIZIKA, MELIORATSIIA I MINERALOGIIA POCHV. (D. OF SOIL PHYS, IMPROVEMENT/MINERAL, RU DEFS) MOSCOW, 1960. 144P. 800T.

BARKOV, A.S. SLOVAR SPRAVOCHNIK PO FIZICHESKOI GEOGRAFII... (D. OF PHYS. GEOG, RU DEFS) MOSCOW, GOS. UCHEB. PED. IZD, 1958. 329P. 59-38897. 2400T.

GEOPHYSICS AND PHYSICAL GEOGRAPHY

RUSSIAN

BODNARSKII, M.S. SLOVAR GEOGRAFICHESKIKH NAZVANII. (D. OF GEOG, RU DEFS) ED2. MOSCOW, MIN.PROSV. RSFSR. 1958. 391P. 55-35488. 1800T.

BURGUNKER, M.E. RUSSIAN-ENGLISH DICTIONARY OF EARTH SCIENCES. NEW YORK, TELBERG, 1961. 94P. 61-9081. 2500T.

GORSKII, N.N. AND GORSKAIA, V.I. ANGLO-RUSSKII OKEANOGRAFICHESKII SLOVAR. (EN*RU D. OF OCEANOG) MOSCOW, GITTL, 1957. 292P. 58-30249. 8000T.

GRIGOREV,A.A. KRATKAIA GEOGRAFICHESKAIA ENTSIKLOPEDIA. (SHORT GEOG.ENCYCL, RU DEFS) 4V. MOSCOW, SOV.ENTSIKL, 1960- . 16000T.

MANDROVSKII, B.N. RUSSIAN-ENGLISH GLOSSARY AND SOVIET CLASSIFICATION OF ICE FOUND AT SEA. WASHINGTON, U.S. LIBR.CONGR, 1959. 30P. 59-60067. 300T.

MEZHDUNARODNAIA LEDOVAIA NOMENKLATURA. (INTL.ICE NOMENCL) (*RU*EN GL, PP.5-15, 110T) LENINGRAD, GIDROMETEOIZDAT, 1956. 300P.

MILKOV, F.N. SLOVAR-SPRAVOCHNIK PO FIZICHESKOI GEOGRAFII. (D. OF PHYS.GEOG, RU DEFS) MOSCOW, GOS.IZD. GEOG.LIT, 1960. 269P. 61-29567. 1000T.

MITCHELL, G.S. A RUSSIAN-ENGLISH DICTIONARY-GLOSSARY IN GEOMORPHOLOGY AND RELATED SCIENCES. (UNPUBL. MASTER*S ESSAY) OHIO STATE UNIV. 1957. 211P.

SARNA, A. RUSSIAN-ENGLISH DICTIONARY OF GEOGRAPHICAL TERMS. NEW YORK, TELBERG, 1962-- 2V. 62-14075.

TRIFONOVA, N.F. ET AL. ANGLO-RUSSKII ASTROGEOFIZICHESKII SLOVAR. (EN*RU ASTRON/GEOPHYS.D) MOSCOW, FIZMATGIZ, 1962. 512P. 63-40099. 16000T.

VOLOSTNOVA, M.B. SLOVAR RUSSKOI TRANSKRIPTSII GEOGRAFICHESKIKH NAZVANII,PT.1. GEOGRAFICHESKIE NAZVANIIA NA TERRITORII SSSR. (D.OF RU GEOG.NAMES) TRANSL.BY T.DERUGUINE. NEW YORK, TELBERG, 1958. 82P. 60-40175.

SPANISH

COSTA, L. DICCIONARIO DE GEOCOSMOGRAFIA. (GEOCOSMOGRAPHY, SP DEFS) LIMA, 1961. 539P. 62-1172.

GUERRA, A.T. DICCIONARIO GEOLOGICO-GEOMORFOLOGICO. (D. OF GEOL/GEOMORPH, SP DEFS) RIO DE JANEIRO, INST. PAN-AM GEOG/HIST, 1954. 250P. 56-1377. 2500T.

VULETIN, A. GEOMORFONIMIA ARGENTINA. (ARGENTINE GEOMORPH, SP DEFS) SANTIAGO DEL ESTERO, UNIV. NACL, TUCUMAN, 1959. 82P. 60-25446. 300T.

HYDRAULIC ENGINEERING

CHINESE

KUO LI PIEN KUAN. (NATL. INST. OF TRANSL) SHUI LI KUNG CH,ENG MING TZ,U. (WATER CONSERVATION ENG. T, *CH*EN) TAIPEI, 1960. 83P. C62-253.

ENGLISH

AMERICAN STANDARDS ASSOCIATION. LETTER SYMBOLS FOR HYDRAULICS. (Y10.2) NEW YORK, 1958.

GULHATI, N.D. IRRIGATION IN THE WORLD. (GL, PP. 119-23) NEW DELHI, INTL. COMM. IRRIG/DRAINAGE, 1955. 130P. 57-58587. 60T.

LANGBEIN, W.B. AND I.SERI, K.T. _GENERAL INTRODUCTION AND HYDROLOGIC DEFINITIONS. MANUAL OF HYDROLOGY, PT.1. (G.S. WATER SUPPLY PAPER NO.154)) WASHINGTON, U.S. GEOL. SURV, 1960. 29P. 300T.

U.S. SOIL CONSERVATION SERVICE. NATIONAL CATALOG OF PRACTICES AND MEASURES USED IN SOIL AND WATER CONSERVATION. WASHINGTON, 1959. 11P. 59-64226. 130T.

FRENCH

PROULX, G. CANALISATION ET AMENAGEMENT HYDROELECTRIQUE. GLOSSAIRE ANGLAIS-FRANCAIS, BT-44. (WATERWAYS/ HYDROELEC.POWER, FN*FR GL) OTTAWA, DEPT.SECY.STATE, 1956. 90P. 2700T.

ROWE, R.S. FRENCH-ENGLISH TRANSLATION GUIDE FOR RIVER AND HARBOR ENGINEERING. PRINCETON, N.J, PRINCETON UNIV, 1954. 90P. 54-6521. 2000T.

GERMAN

ROWE, R.S. GERMAN-ENGLISH TRANSLATION GUIDE FOR RIVER AND HARBOR ENGINEERING. PRINCETON, N.J, PRINCETON UNIV, 1953. 96P. 52-12056.

POLYGLOT

INTERNATIONAL COMMISSION ON IRRIGATION AND DRAINAGE. MULTILINGUAL DICTIONARY ON IRRIGATION AND DRAINAGE. (*EN*FR*GE) NEW DELHI, 1960- . (IN PROC) 800P. 10000T.

HYDRAULIC ENGINEERING

POLYGLOT

INTERNATIONAL COMMISSION ON LARGE DAMS. DICTIONNAIRE TECHNIQUE DES BARRAGES. (D. OF DAMS, *FR*EN*GE*IT*PF *SP) ED2. PARIS, 1960. 380P. 61-805. 5800T.

INTERNATIONAL COMMISSION ON LARGE DAMS. TEKHNICHESKII SLOVAR PO PLOTINAM NA 11 IAZYKAKH. (DAM BLDG. IN 11 LANG, RU EN BU SP IT GE PL PR RO CZ FR) MOSCOW, 1962. 379P.

INTERNATIONAL HYDROGRAPHIC BUREAU. HYDROGRAPHIC DICTIONARY. (*EN*FR*DA*DU*PR*SP*IT*NO*SW*GE) ED2. MONACO, 1951. 89+89P. 52-65869.

MOSONYI, E. ET AL. HIDRAULIKA ES MUSZAKI HIDROLOGIA. (D.OF HYDR. ENG. *HU*EN*GE*RU) (MUSZ. ERT. SZ, NO.3) BUDAPEST, TERRA, 1959. 156P. 59-41601. 1100T.

MOSONYI, E. ET AL. VIZEROMUVEK ES VIZIUTAK. (D. OF HYDR. POWER PLANTS/HYDRO-TECH. STRUCT. *HU*EN*GE*RU) (MUSZ.ERT.SZ,NO.6) BUDAPEST, TERRA, 1960. 204P. 1200T.

PERMANENT INTERNATIONAL ASSOCIATION OF NAVIGATION CONGRESSES. DICTIONNAIRE TECHNIQUE ILLUSTRE...(IILUS. TECH. D, *FR*EN*DU*GE*IT*SP) CH. 5. MATERIAUX. (MATER) BRUSSELS, 1951.204P.

PERMANENT INTERNATIONAL ASSOCIATION OF NAVIGATION CONGRESSES. DICTIONNAIRE TECHNIQUE ILLUSTRE... (ILLUS. TECH. D, *FR*EN*DU*GE*IT*SP) CH. 6. CONSTR. PLANT/METHODS. BRUSSELS, 1959. 237P. 58-16041. 3000T.

SPENGLER, U.A. AND E.N. GIDROLOGICHESKII SLOVAR NA INOSTRANNYKH IAZYKAKH. (D.OF HYDROL, *RU*EN*FR*GE) LENINGRAD, GIDROMETEOIZDAT, 1959. 214P. 60-33508. 2400T.

U.S. CORPS OF ENGINEERS. GLOSSARY OF TERMS PERTINENT TO MILITARY HYDROLOGY... (EN FR GE IT SP) WASHINGTON, 1957.

VAAD HA-LASHON HA-IVRIT BE-ERETS-YISRAEL. RESHIMAT MUNAHE HIDRAVLIKAH. (HYDR. ENG. D, HE EN FR GE) JERUSALEM, 1951. 56-55600.

RUSSIAN

AKADEMIIA NAUK SSSR. KOM.TEKH.TERM. GIDROMEKHANIKA, VOLNOVOE DVIZHENIE ZHIDKOSTI, STROITELNAIA MEKHANIKA, TERMINOLOGIIA (FLUID MECH, WAVE MOTION OF FLUIDS/STRUCT. MECH, RU DEFS) (SB. REK. TERM. NO.58. MOSCOW, 1962. 85P. 63-40826.

AKADEMIIA NAUK SSSR. KOM.TEKH.TERM. TERMINOLOGIIA GIDROTEKHNIKI. (HYDR.ENG, RU DEFS) (SB.REK.TERM,NO.27) MOSCOW, 1955. 70P. 56-21889. 440T.

AKADEMIIA NAUK SSSR. KOM.TEKH.TERM. TERMINOLOGIIA GIDROTURBIN. (HYDR.TURBINES, RU DEFS) (SB.REK.TERM, NO. 21) MOSCOW, 1953. 37P. 54-29072.

ROWE, R.S. RUSSIAN-ENGLISH TRANSLATION GUIDE FOR RIVER AND HARBOR ENGINEERING. PRINCETON, N.J, PRINCETON UNIV., 1954. 96P. 53-12066.

SITKOVSKII, P.A. ET AL. SLOVAR-SPRAVOCHNIK GIDROTEKHNIKA-MELIORATORA. (D/MANUAL FOR HYDR/AGR. ENG, RU DEFS) MOSCOW, SELKOLKHOZGIZ, 1955. 500P. 56-29904. 5000T.

SLOVAK

SLOVENSKA AKADEMIA VIED. TERMINOLOGIA VODNEHO HOSPODARSTVA. (D. OF HYDROL/HYDR.ENG, SL DEFS) BRATISLAVA 1953-54. 2V.IN 1. 56-42574. 1700T.

INDUSTRIAL ENGINEERING AND MANAGEMENT

DUTCH

POLAK, M.V. WOORDENBOEK. NEDERLANDS-ENGELS, ENGELS-NEDERLANDS. OCTROOI EN MERK.(*DU*EN PAT/TRADE MARK D HILVERSUM, OCECO, 1949. 104P. 58-45395.

ENGLISH

AMERICAN SOCIETY FOR TESTING/MATERIALS. STANDARD DEFINITIONS OF TERMS RELATING TO METHODS OF MECHANICAL TESTING. (E6-62) ASTM STDS,PT.3 SUPPL, 40-50. PHILADELPHIA, 1962. 70T.

AMERICAN SOCIETY OF MECHANICAL ENGINEERS. INDUSTRIAL ENGINEERING TERMINOLOGY. (ASME STD.NO.106) NEW YORK 1955. 48P. 56-1775.

BECKER, E.R. DICTIONARY OF PERSONNEL AND INDUSTRIAL RELATIONS. NEW YORK, PHIL. LIBR, 1958. 366P. 58-59649.

BENN, A.E. THE MANAGEMENT DICTIONARY.. NEW YORK, EXPOSITION PRESS, 1952. 381P. 4000T.

BRITISH STANDARDS INSTITUTION. GLOSSARY OF TERMS IN WORK STUDY (B.S. 3138) LONDON, 1959. 40P. 200T.

CLAUSER, H.R. ET AL. THE ENCYCLOPEDIA OF ENGINEERING MATERIALS AND PROCESSES. NEW YORK, REINHOLD, 1963. 787P. 63-13448.

DICTIONARY OF INDUSTRIAL ENGINEERING, WORDS, TERMS, AND PHRASES. CHICAGO, IND. ENG. COLL, 1959. 1V. (UNPAGED) 59-4333.

ENGLISH

DOHERTY, R.E. INDUSTRIAL AND LABOR RELATIONS TERMS... ITHACA,N.Y, STATE SCHOOL IND/LABOR RFL, CORNELL UNIV. 1962. 32P. 62-63050.

EASTMAN KODAK CO. SYMBOLS, DEFINITIONS AND TABLES FOR INDUSTRIAL STATISTICS AND QUALITY CONTROL. (DEFS/SYMBOLS,PP.1-61) ROCHESTER,N.Y, INST.TECH,1958. 202P.

HEYEL, C. THE ENCYCLOPEDIA OF MANAGEMENT. NEW YORK, REINHOLD, 1963. 1084P.

INFORMATION FOR INDUSTRY, INC. PRINCIPAL CHEMICAL AND CHEMICALLY RELATED TERMS USED IN U.S. PATENTS... WASHINGTON, SPARTAN, 1962. 80P. 62-2233P.

INFORMATION FOR INDUSTRY, INC. VOCABULARY OF PRINCIPAL MAJOR TERMS USED IN THE UNITERM INDEX TO CHEMICAL PATENTS. WASHINGTON, 1962. UNPAGFD. 62-52469.

MARTING, E. AMA ENCYCLOPEDIA OF SUPERVISORY TRAINING... NEW YORK, AM. MANAGEMENT ASSOC, 1961. 448P. 61-8594.

MICHEL, A.J. AND KELMAN, K. DICTIONARY OF INTELLECTUAL PROPERTY... NEW YORK, RES. PAT/TRADEMARKS, 1954. 352P. 54-3614.

MILFK, J.T. STANDARDS AND SPECIFICATIONS, DOCUMENTATION SYMBOLS AND ABBREVIATIONS. LOS ANGELES, STANDARDS, 1961- 1V, LL. 61-3463.

PRENTICE-HALL, INC. DIRECTORS AND OFFICERS ENCYCLOPEDIC MANUAL. NEW YORK, 1955. 641P, 55-5874.

ROBERTS, H.S. DICTIONARY OF LABOR-MANAGEMENT RELATIONS. HONOLULU, UNIV.HAWAII, 1957-- . V. 57-63600.

SOCIETY FOR THE ADVANCEMENT OF MANAGEMENT. GLOSSARY OF TIME AND MOTION STUDY. NEW YORK, 1953. P.

U.S. DEPT. OF LABOR. OCCUPATIONS IN ELECTRONIC DATA-PROCESSING SYSTEMS. WASHINGTON, 1959. 44P, 100T.

U.S. EMPLOYMENT SERVICE. DICTIONARY OF OCCUPATIONAL TITLES... ED2. WASHINGTON, 1949-- . 2V. SUPPL. NO.1, 1955. S S 49-12.

WITTY, M.B. ET AL. DICTIONARY OF ENVIRONMENTAL ENGINEERING ABBREVIATIONS, SIGNS, SYMBOLS AND TABLES. NEW YORK, SETI, 196 . 320P.

WITTY, M.B. ET AL. DICTIONARY OF HUMAN ENGINEERING ABBREVIATIONS. NEW YORK, SETI, 196 .

WITTY, M.B. ET AL. DICTIONARY OF INDUSTRIAL ENGINEERING ABBREVIATIONS, SIGNS AND SYMBOLS. NEW YORK, SETI, 1963. 224P.

WITTY, M.B. ET AL. DICTIONARY OF MANAGEMENT AND ENGINEERING ECONOMICS ABBREVIATIONS, SIGNS, SYMBOLS AND TABLES. NEW YORK, SETI, 196 . 192P.

FRENCH

BOUJU , A.L. LEXIQUE DE LA PROPRIETE INDUSTRIELLE, BREVETS D,INVENTION, DESSINS ET MODELES, MARQUES DE FABRIQUE. (GL.OF PAT/TRADE MARKS, FR DEFS) PARIS, DUNOD. 1955. 250P. 55-4017.

FRANCE. AMBASSADE. U.S. ORGANISATION INDUSTRIELLE, AMERICAIN-FRANCAIS. (EN*FR GL. OF IND. MANAGEMENT) ED2. WASHINGTON, 1953. 125P. 2500T.

FRANCE. BUREAU DES TEMPS ELEMENTAIRFS. LEXIQUE DES TERMES UTILISES DANS L,ANALYSE ET LE MESURE DU TRAVAIL. (GL OF WORK-STUDY T) PARIS. 1953.

TERMINOLOGIE DES SERVICES NATIONAUX DE L,EMPLOI EN GRANDE-BRETAGNE. GLOSSAIRE ANGLAIS-FRANCAIS,BT-64. (TERMS USED IN BRIT.NATL.EMPL.SERV, EN*FR GL) OTTAWA, DEPT.SECY.STATE,1958. 26P. 500T.

THIBAULT, W. BREVETS D,INVENTION, GLOSSAIRE ANGLAIS-FRANCAIS PROVISOIRE, BT-104. (PAT, EN*FR PROV. GL) OTTAWA, DEPT. SECY. STATE, 1962. 14P. 250T.

VINCELETTE, M.H. TERMINOLOGIE DE LA PRODUCTIVITE, GLOSSAIRE ANGLAIS-FRANCAIS, BT-26. (IND.PROD,EN*FR GL) OTTAWA, DEPT.SECY.STATF. 1955. 6P. 110T.

GERMAN

BREMBERGER, M. KONSTRUKTION UND FERTIGUNG. (DESIGN/PROD, *GE*EN D) MUNICH, OLDENBOURG, 1960. 276P. A61-4698. 7000T.

DAEBRITZ, E. BETRIEBSWIRTSCHAFTLICHES LITERATURLEXIKON. (IND. MANAGEMENT D, GE DEFS) WIESBADEN, GABLER, 1959. 300P.

DANIELS, H.A. WARENZEICHENVERWECHSELBARKEIT... (EXCHANGEABILITY OF TRADE MARKS, GE DEFS) MUNICH, HEYMANN, 1956. 56P. 59-26783.

ERNST, R. WOERTERBUCH DER INDUSTRIELLEN TECHNIK...(IND/TECH. D) (V.1, GE*EN, ED7. 805P. V.2, EN*GE, ED12. 890P) WIESBADEN, BRANDSTETTER, 1962. 60-3617. 45000T.

FORSCHUNGSINSTITUT FUER RATIONALISIERUNG. SCHLAGWORTREGISTER ZUR RATIONALISIERUNG. (IND. MANAGEMENT D, GE DEFS) (REPT. NO.353) AACHEN, 1957. 376P.

INDUSTRIAL ENGINEERING AND MANAGEMENT

GERMAN

GERMANY (DEMOCRATIC REPUBLIC, 1949-   ) AMT FUER ERFINDUNGS- UND PATENTWESEN. STICHWOERTER-VERZEICHNIS...
PATENTKLASSEN, GRUPPEN- UND UNTERGRUPPEN. (KEYWORDS FOR CLASSES/GROUPS OF PATENTS, GE DEFS) BERLIN, 1953.
398P. 54-24105.

GUTENBERG, E. GRUNDLAGEN DER BETRIEBSWIRTSCHAFTSLEHRE. ED7. (IND. MGT, GE DEFS) BERLIN, SPRINGER,
1962-   . 62-51758.

KLAFTEN, B. AND ALLISON, F.C. WOERTERBUCH DER PATENTFACHSPRACHE. (*GE*EN D.OF PAT.T) ED2. MUNICH,
WILA, 1959. 248, 312P. 60-36397. 8000T.

KRUEGER, K. DIE AMERIKANISCHEN BEGRIFFE DES ARBEITS- UND ZEITSTUDIUMS MIT DEFINITIONEN UND DEREN
DEUTSCHER UEBERSETZUNG. (TIME/MOTION STUDY T+EN*GE GL) BERLIN, BEUTH-VERTRIEB, 1958. 104P. 60-20153.

MIOSGA, W. VERWECHSLUNGSGEFAHR... KENNZEICHNUNGSRECHT. (TRADEMARK D, GE DEFS) MUNICH, WILA, 1958.
126P. 60-42408.

MOLLE, F. WOERTERBUCH DER BERUFSBEZEICHNUNG. (OCCUPATIONS D, GE DEFS) WOLFENBUETTEL, GRENZLAND/ROCK,
1952. 240P.

QUAK, K. DIN-BEGRIFFSLEXIKON... (DIN STDS, GE DEFS) BERLIN, BEUTH-VERTRIEB, 1961. 530P.

SOMMER, W. AND SCHOENFELD, H.M. FACHWOERTERBUCH FUER BETRIEBSWIRTSCHAFT, WIRTSCHAFTS-UND STEUERRECHT UND
LOCHKARTENWESEN. (MANAGEMENT D, EN*GE) ED2. BERLIN, DE GRUYTER, 1962. 229P. 10000T.

SOMMER, W. AND SCHOENFELD, H.M. FACHWOERTERBUCH FUER BETRIEBSWIRTSCHAFT... (MANAGEMENT D, GE*EN) BERLIN,
DE GRUYTER, 1960. 176P. A62-1297. 10000T.

STRELLER, J. WOERTERBUCH DER BERUFE. (OCCUPATIONS D, GE DEFS) STUTTGART, KROENER, 1953. 366P. A54-6532.
1000T.

U.S. PATENT OFFICE. GLOSSARY OF GERMAN WORDS USED IN PATENT LITERATURE RELATING TO COMMUNICATIONS,
ELECTRICITY AND ELECTRONICS. WASHINGTON, 1961. 21P. 900T.

VEREIN SCHWEIZERISCHER MASCHINEN-INDUSTRIELLER. FACHAUSDRUECKE UND ERLAEUTERUNGEN AUS DEM GEBIETE DER
BEARBEITUNGSTECHNIK UND DER ARBEITSVERFAHREN. (FABR/PROD.TECH, GE DEFS) ZURICH, 1954. 88P, A55-6517.

WEFELMEYER, R. AND H. LEXIKON DER BERUFSAUSBILDUNG UND BERUFSERZIEHUNG. (VOCATIONAL EDUC/TRAINING, GE
DEFS) WIESBADEN, STEINER, 1959. 554P. 59-40526.

WELLINGER, K. ET AL. LUEGER,S LEXIKON DER TECHNIK. (ENCYCL. OF TECH) V.3. WERKSTOFFE UND
WERKSTOFF-PRUEFUNG. (IND. MATER/MATER. TESTING, GE DEFS) ED4. STUTTGART, DEUT. VERLAGS-ANSTALT, 1961.
816P. 6200T.

NORWEGIAN

KOMITEEN FOR ARBEIDSSTUDIETEKNISK TERMINOLOGI. ARBEIDSSTUDIETEKNISK TERMINOLOGI. (GL. OF WORK STUDY T,
NO DEFS) OSLO, PROD/TEK.FORSKNINGSINST, 1952. 16P. 58-41238.

POLYGLOT

BENISLAWSKI, J. 5 JEZYCZNY PODRECZNY SLOWNIK EKONOMIKI PRZEMYSLU. (5-LANG. D. OF IND. ECON, PL*EN*FR*GE
*RU) WARSAW, POLSK. WYDAW. GOSP, 1959. 212P. 59-53166.

INSPECCAO GERAL DES PRODUTOS AGRICOLAS E INDUSTRIAIS. TERMINOLOGIA DAS TOLERANCIAS. (TOLERANCES T, PR EN
FR GE IT SP) LISBON, 1952. 7P.

MEDEIROS, M.F. DICIONARIO TECNICO POLIGLOTA, PORTUGUES-ESPANHOL-FRANCES-ITALIANO-INGLES-ALEMAO. (TECH. D,
PR*EN*FR*GE*IT*SP) LISBON, GOMES/RODRIGUES, 1949-54. 52-67939. 131000T.

NORWAY. RADET FOR TEKNISK TERMINOLOGI. STATISTICAL QUALITY CONTROL. (RTT-7) (*EN*GE*NO*SW) OSLO,
1960. 41P.

ORGANIZATION FOR EUROPEAN ECONOMIC COOPERATION. EPA. GLOSSARY OF WORK STUDY TERMS. (EN*FR*GE) PARIS,
1958. 124P. 58-2934. 700T.

ORGANIZATION FOR EUROPEAN ECONOMIC COOPERATION. EPA. TRILINGUAL (*FR*EN*GE) GLOSSARY OF THE TECHNICAL
TERMS USED IN THE ANALYSIS AND MEASURFMENT OF WORK. (EPA PROJECT 271) PARIS, 1955. 147P.

TEKNISKA NOMENKLATURCENTRALEN. ARBETSKUNSKAPS TERMINOLOGI JAEMTE FYRSPRAKIG ORDLISTA FOER ARBETSSTUDIER,
ARBETS- OCH MERITVAERDERING. (WORK STUDY T, EN FR GE SW) STOCKHOLM, 1960. 132P.

TOFET, K.F. ARBETSMARKNADSTERMINOLOGI... (LABOR MARKET T, SW EN FR GE) STOCKHOLM, SVENSKA
ARBETSGIVARFFOER. BIBLIOTEK, 1957. 12P. 250T.

RUSSIAN

AKADEMIIA NAUK SSSR. KOM.TEKH.TERM. OPREDELENIE PONIATII. NAUCHNOE OTKRYTIE, IZOBRETENIE I
RATSIONALIZATORSKOE PREDLOZHENIE. (SCI.DISCOVERY, INVENTION/EFFIC.SUGG, RU DEFS) (BIUL.NO.66) MOSCOW,
1955. 8P.

ALFAVITNYI SLOVAR ZANIATII. (OCCUP. TITLES, RU DEFS) MOSCOW, GOSSTATIZDAT, 1957. 246P. 20000T.

70

SPANISH

INOLOGIA DE ORGANIZACION CIENTIFICA DEL TRABAJO. (IND. MANAGEMENT, SP DEFS) MADRID, INST. NACL. ONAL. TRABAJO, 1962. 93P. 250T.

INOLOGIA INGLES-ESPANOL DE ORGANIZACION CIENTIFICA DEL TRABAJO. (EN*SP IND. MANAGEMENT T) MADRID, . NACL. RACIONAL. TRABAJO, 1958. 31P. 500T.

INSTRUMENTATION AND METROLOGY

ENGLISH

ICAN INSTITUTE OF ELECTRICAL ENGINEERS. DEFINITIONS OF ELECTRICAL TERMS. ELECTRON DEVICES. (GR-70, C42.70) NEW YORK, 1957. 29P. 300T.

ICAN INSTITUTE OF ELECTRICAL ENGINEERS. DEFINITIONS OF ELECTRICAL TERMS. INSTRUMENTS, METERS AND R TESTING. IGR-30, ASA C42.30) NEW YORK, 1957. 39P. 400T.

ICAN SOCIETY FOR TESTING/MATERIALS. TENTATIVE DEFINITIONS OF TERMS AND SYMBOLS RELATING TO ABSORPTION TROSCOPY. (E131-62T) ASTM STDS, SUPPL, PT.7, 280-2. PHILADELPHIA, 1962. 50T.

ICAN SOCIETY FOR TESTING/MATERIALS. TENTATIVE DEFINITIONS OF TERMS AND SYMBOLS RELATING TO EMISSION TROSCOPY. (E135-60T) ASTM STDS. PT.7, 1597-1600. PHILADELPHIA, 1961. 70T.

ICAN SOCIETY FOR TESTING/MATERIALS. TENTATIVE DEFINITIONS OF TERMS RELATING TO DENSITY AND SPECIFIC ITY OF SOLIDS, LIQUIDS, AND GASES. (F12-61T) ASTM STDS, PT.4, 1627-30. PHILADELPHIA, 1961. IOT.

ICAN SOCIETY FOR TESTING/MATERIALS. TENTATIVE DEFINITIONS OF TERMS RELATING TO DOSIMETRY. (E170-60T) STDS, PT.3, 330-2. PHILADELPHIA, 1961. 30T.

ICAN SOCIETY FOR TESTING/MATERIALS. TENTATIVE DEFINITIONS OF TERMS RELATING TO MICROSCOPY. (E175-61T) STDS, PT.3, 849-52. PHILADELPHIA, 1961. 70T.

ICAN STANDARDS ASSOCIATION. AMERICAN STANDARD TERMINOLOGY AND DEFINITIONS FOR BALL AND ROLLER INGS AND PARTS. (ASA-B3.7) NEW YORK, 1960. 31P. 700T.

ICAN STANDARDS ASSOCIATION. AUTOMATIC NULL-BALANCING ELECTRICAL MEASURING INSTRUMENTS. (C39.4-1956) YORK, 1956. P.

ICAN STANDARDS ASSOCIATION. DIRECT ACTING ELECTRICAL RECORDING INSTRUMENTS. (C39.2-1953) NEW YORK, . P.

ICAN STANDARDS ASSOCIATION. ELECTRICAL INDICATING INSTRUMENTS. (G39.1-1951) NEW YORK, 1951. P.

ICAN STANDARDS ASSOCIATION. NOMENCLATURE AND DEFINITIONS IN THE FIELD OF COLORIMETRY. (Z58.1.2) YORK, 1952. 11P. 30T.

ICAN STANDARDS ASSOCIATION. QUANTITIES AND UNITS USED IN ELECTRICITY. (C61.1-1961) NEW YORK, 1961.

ICAN VACUUM SOCIETY. GLOSSARY OF TERMS USED IN VACUUM TECHNOLOGY. NEW YORK, PERGAMON, 1958. 63P. 278. 430T.

EY, E.W. AND LINFORD, A. INSTRUMENT ENCYCLOPEDIA. (GL, PP.1-28) LONDON, HERBERT, 1958. 292P. 4430. 1340T.

ETT, A.H. GLOSSARY OF TERMS FREQUENTLY USED IN OPTICS AND SPECTROSCOPY. NEW YORK, AM. INST. PHYS, . 29P. 200T.

ERO, R.J. DICTIONARY OF AUTOMATIC CONTROL. NEW YORK, REINHOLD, 1960. 282P. 60-14156. 560T.

ISH STANDARDS INSTITUTION. DRAWING INSTRUMENTS FOR DRAWING OFFICE·USE. (B.S.1709) LONDON, 1958. 16P.

ISH STANDARDS INSTITUTION. GLOSSARY OF TERMS RELATING TO THE PERFORMANCE OF MEASURING INSTRUMENTS. .2643) LONDON, 1955. 20P. 50T.

ISH STANDARDS INSTITUTION. GLOSSARY OF TERMS USED IN HIGH VACUUM TECHNOLOGY. (B.S. 2951) LONDON, . 32P. 170T.

ISH STANDARDS INSTITUTION. GLOSSARY OF TERMS USED IN ILLUMINATION AND PHOTOMETRY. (B.S. 233) LONDON, .·20P. 110T.

ISH STANDARDS INSTITUTION. MEASUREMENT OF SPECTACLES, METHOD AND GLOSSARY (B.S. 3199) LONDON, 1960. 70T.

TEN, F.J. OLD CLOCKS AND WATCHES. (GL.OF TECH.T, APPENDIX 1) ED7. NEW YORK, DUTTON, 1956. 518P.

TEN, F.J. WATCH AND CLOCK MAKERS, HANDBOOK, DICTIONARY AND GUIDE. ED15. LONDON, SPON, 1955. 598P. 052.

ON, E. DICTIONARY OF CLOCKS AND WATCHES. NEW YORK, ARCHER, 1963. 201P. 63-14437.

INSTRUMENTATION AND METROLOGY

ENGLISH

CHILDS, F.P. GLOSSARY OF LOG AND TIMBER MEASURES. LONDON, BENN, 1955. 242P.

CLARK, G.L.ET AL. THE ENCYCLOPEDIA OF MICROSCOPY. NEW YORK, REINHOLD, 1961. 693P. 61-9698.

CLARK, G.L. ET AL. THE ENCYCLOPEDIA OF SPECTROSCOPY. NEW YORK, REINHOLD. 1960. 787P. 60-53028.

CLARK, G.L. THE ENCYCLOPEDIA OF X-RAYS AND GAMMA RAYS. NEW YORK, REINHOLD, 1963. 1149P. 63-13449. 900T.

ENCYCLOPEDIA OF INSTRUMENTATION FOR INDUSTRIAL HYGIENE... ANN ARBOR, UNIV. MICHIGAN, 1956.

INSTITUTE OF RADIO ENGINEERS. IRE DICTIONARY OF ELECTRONICS TERMS AND SYMBOLS... NEW YORK. 1961. 225P. 61-1732. 3700T.

INSTITUTE OF RADIO ENGINEERS. INDEX TO IRE STANDARDS ON DEFINITIONS OF TERMS. 1942-57. (58 IRE 20.S1) PROC. IRE, V.46, 449-76 (1958) 4000T.

INSTITUTE OF RADIO ENGINEERS. STANDARDS ON ELECTRON DEVICES, DEFINITIONS OF TERMS RELATED TO MICROWAVE TUBES (KLYSTRONS, MAGNETRONS/TRAVELING WAVE TUBES) (56 IRE 7.S1) PROC. IRE, V.44. 346-50 (1956) 80T.

INSTITUTE OF RADIO ENGINEERS. STANDARDS ON ELECTRON DEVICES, DEFINITIONS OF TERMS RELATED TO PHOTOTUBES. (54 IRE 7.S1) PROC.IRE, V.42, 1276-7 (1954) 10T.

INSTITUTE OF RADIO ENGINEERS. STANDARDS ON ELECTROSTATOGRAPHIC DEVICES. (60 IRE 28.S2) PROC. IRE, V.49, 619-21 (1961) 20T.

INSTITUTE OF RADIO ENGINEERS. STANDARDS ON INDUSTRIAL ELECTRONICS, DEFINITIONS... (55 IRE 10.S1) PROC. IRE, V.43, 1069-72 (1955) 70T.

INSTITUTE OF RADIO ENGINEERS. STANDARDS ON MAGNETRONS, DEFINITIONS OF TERMS. (52 IRE 7.S1) PROC. IRE, V.40, 562-3 (1952) 10T.

INSTITUTE OF RADIO ENGINEERS. STANDARDS ON NUCLEAR TECHNIQUES, DEFINITIONS FOR THE SCINTILLATION COUNTER FIELD. PROC. IRE, V.48, 1449-53 (1960) 80T.

INSTITUTE OF RADIO ENGINEERS. STANDARDS ON REFERENCE DESIGNATIONS FOR ELECTRICAL AND ELECTRONIC EQUIPMENT (57 IRE 21.S2) PROC. IRE, V.45, 1493-1501 (1957) 200T. ·

INSTITUTE OF RADIO ENGINEERS. STANDARDS ON TELEVISION, DEFINITIONS OF TELEVISION SIGNAL MEASUREMENT TERMS. (55 IRE 23.S1) PROC. IRE, V.43, 619-22 (1955) 50T.

INSTRUMENT SOCIETY OF AMERICA. GLOSSARY OF TERMS FOR FLIGHT TESTING INSTRUMENTATION. (BASED ON AIA-ARTC REPT.16) (IN PREP)

INTERNATIONAL ORGANIZATION FOR STANDARDIZATION. EXPRESSIONS OF THE PHYSICAL AND SUBJECTIVE MAGNITUDES OF SOUND OR NOISE. (ISO-R131, AGREES WITH AM. STD. S1.1-1960) GENEVA, 1959. 62P. 700T.

JERRARD, H.G. AND MCNEILL, D.B. A DICTIONARY OF SCIENTIFIC UNITS. LONDON, CHAPMAN/ HALL, 1963. 200P.

JONES, S.V. WEIGHTS AND MEASURES... WASHINGTON, PUBL. AFFAIRS PRESS, 1963. 141P. 63-19813. 800T.

PRECISION POTENTIOMETER MANUFACTURERS ASSOCIATION. PRECISION POTENTIOMETER TERMS AND DEFINITIONS. CHICAGO 1962. 22P. 80T.

RIDER, J.F. AND USLAN, S.D. ENCYCLOPEDIA ON CATHODE-RAY.OSCILLOSCOPES AND THEIR USES. ED2. NEW YORK, RIDER, 1959. VAR.P. 59-15917.

SCHAPERO, M. ET AL. DICTIONARY OF VISUAL SCIENCE. PHILADELPHIA, CHILTON, 1960. 785P. 60-5892. 14000T.

SCIENTIFIC APPARATUS MAKERS ASSOCIATION. ACCURACY AND SENSITIVITY TERMINOLOGY AS APPLIED TO INDUSTRIAL INSTRUMENTS. (RC3-12-1955) NEW YORK, P.

SOCIETY OF DYERS AND COLOURISTS. COLOUR INDEX. ED2. LOWELL, MASS. AM. ASSOC. TEXTILE/CHEM COLORISTS, 1956-1960. 4V. 57-908.

STILTZ, H.L. AEROSPACE TELEMETRY. (GL,PP. -) ENGLEWOOD CLIFFS, N.J, PRENTICE-HALL, 1961. 505P. 61-15664.

U.S. WHITE SANDS MISSILE RANGE. TELEMETRY STANDARDS [IRIG-106-60] (GL, 16P) NEW MEXICO, 1960.

ZIMMERMAN, O.T. CONVERSION FACTORS AND TABLES. ED3. DOVER, N.H, IND. RES. SERV, 1961.

FRENCH

GILLAM, D.J. A CONCISE DICTIONARY OF HOROLOGICAL TERMS. (*EN*FR) LA CHAUX-DE-FONDS, ECOLE SUPER.COM. 1956. 46P. 58-44162. 2300T.

GUYOT, E. DICTIONNAIRE DES TERMES UTILISES DANS LA MESURE DU TEMPS. (TIME MEAS. T, FR DEFS) LA CHAUX-DE-FONDS, CHAMBRE SUISSE HORLOG, 1953. 123P. A53-5630.

INTERNATIONAL ORGANIZATION FOR STANDARDIZATION. ISO TERMINOLOGY OF MICROSCOPY APPARATUS. (ISO-TC 46) GENEVA, 1961. 1P. 5T.

GERMAN

FLUEGGE, S. ET AL. HANDBUCH DER PHYSIK. (ENCYCL. OF PHYS) INSTRUMENTE HILFSMITTEL DER KERNPHYSIK. (NUCL. INSTR, *GE*EN GL, V.44, PP.450-73, 850T. V.45, PP.518-44, 1000T) BERLIN, SPRINGER, 1958-59. A56-2942.

GRUBER, A. ET AL. DAS ABC DES UHRMACHERS. (WATCHMAKERS ABC, GE DEFS) ULM, 1955.

HADERT, H. PRUEF-, MESS-, UND KONTROLL-GERAETE LEXIKON. (TESTING, MEAS/CONTROL INSTR. D, GE DEFS) ED3 BERLIN, HADERT, 1954-60. 1070P.

MARCHGRABER, R. TASCHENLEXIKON FUER DIE MESSPRAKTIK. (METROL. D, GE DEFS) LINZ, TECH. VERLAG, 1951. 461P. A51-8812.

MUETZE, K. ET AL. BROCKHAUS ABC DER OPTIK. (ABC OF OPTICS, GE DEFS) LEIPZIG, BROCKHAUS, 1961. 963P. 62-28707. 10000T.

NEUMANN-LEZIUS, H.H. HANDBUCH DER FEINMECHANISCHEN TECHNIK. (PREC. TOOL ENCYCL, GE DEFS) WIESBADEN, STEINER, 1952. 488P. A53-1907.

SACKLOWSKI, A. PHYSIKALISCHE GROESSEN UND EINHEITEN... (PHYS. MAGNITUDES/UNITS) STUTTGART, DEVA, 1960. 218P. 61-3130.

WERKMEISTER, W. LEXIKON DER VERMESSUNGSKUNDE. (METROL D, GE DEFS) BERLIN, WICHMANN, 195 . 504P.

GREEK

ANDRIKOPOULOS, M.C. ENCYCLOPEDIE ANGLO-HELLENIQUE DE TERMES D,ELECTRONIQUE, D,ELECTRICITE... PIRAEUS, KOUNTOURI, 1961. 720P.

ITALIAN

FERRARO, A. PICCOLO DIZIONARIO DI METROLOGIA GENERALE... (D.OF GEN. METROL, IT DEFS) BOLOGNA, ZANICHELLI, 1959. 292P. 60-35436. 1000T.

JAPANESE

JAPAN. MINISTRY OF EDUCATION. INDUSTRIAL STANDARD VOCABULARY OF CHRONOMETRY. (EN*JA) TOKYO, 1951. 18P.

SEIMITSU KOGYO SHIMBUN SHA. TOKEI JITSEN. (HOROLOGICAL D, JA EN) FUJISAWA, 1960. 5+341P. J61-1769.

POLYGLOT

BARANY,N. FINOMMECHANIKA, OPTIKA. (D. OF PREC. MECH/OPT, *HU*EN*GE*RU) (MUSZ. ERT. SZ, NO.16) BUDAPEST, TERRA, 1961. 214P. 61-48214. 1200T.

BOUSEK, J. PRIRUCNI TECHNICKY SLOVNIK V (5) JAZ ... PRO OBOR PRUMYSLOVEHO MERENI A AUTOMATICKE REGULACE. (D. OF IND. METROL/AUTOM. CONTROL, CZ EN FR GE RU) PRAGUE, MATICE HORNICKO-HUTNICKA, 1955. 210P.

BRITISH INSTRUMENTS DIRECTORY AND BUYER,S GUIDE. (SECT.6, 5 LANG. GL...FR*GE*RU*SP*EN, PP.194-256) LONDON, SCI. INSTR. MANUF. ASSOC, 1962. 376+291P.

CLASON, W.E. DICTIONARY OF SCIENTIFIC APPARATUS. (*EN/AM*DU*FR*GE*IT*SP) NEW YORK, ELSEVIER. (IN PREP)

CLASON, W.E. ELSEVIER,S DICTIONARY OF AUTOMATIC CONTROL, *EN/AM*FR*GE*RU. NEW YORK, ELSEVIER, 1963. 211P. 63-16075. 2600T.

CLASON, W.E. ELSEVIER,S DICTIONARY OF AUTOMATION, COMPUTERS, CONTROL AND MEASURING, *EN/AM*DU*FR*GE*IT *SP. NEW YORK, ELSEVIER, 1961. 848P. 60-53482. 3400T.

CLASON, W.E. ELSEVIER,S LEXICON OF INTERNATIONAL AND NATIONAL UNITS. (*EN/AM*GE*SP*FR*IT*JA*DU*PR*PL*SW RU) NEW YORK, ELSEVIFR, 1964. 75P. 63-11366. 900T.

CUSSET, F. TABLES COMPLETES DE CONVERSION DES MESURES AMERICAINES, BRITANNIQUES ET METRIQUES. (CONVERSION TABLES, AM/EN/METRIC MEASURES,*EN*FR*GE) PARIS, BLONDEL LA ROUGERY, 1959. 232P. 59-44412.

DORIAN, A.F. SIX-LANGUAGE DICTIONARY OF AUTOMATION, ELECTRONICS AND SCIENTIFIC INSTRUMENTS...(*EN*FR*GE* *IT*RU*SP) ENGLEWOOD CLIFFS, N.J. PRENTICE HALL, 1962. 732P. 63-5414. 5500T.

DORIAN, A.F. SIX-LANGUAGE DICTIONARY OF ELECTRONICS, AUTOMATION, AND SCIENTIFIC INSTRUMENTS. (EN*FR*GE*IT*RU*SP) ENGLEWOOD CLIFFS, N.J, PRENTICE-HALL, 1963. 732P. 63-510. 5500T.

EBAUCHES, S.A. DICTIONNAIRE TECHNOLOGIQUE DES PARTIES DE LA MONTRE. (D.OF WATCH PARTS,*GE*EN*FR*IT*SP) NEUCHATEL, 1953. 225P. A54-4990. 1000T.

FRIGYES, A. ET AL. IRANYITASTECHNIKA. (AUTOM. D, *HU*EN*GF*RU) (MUSZ. ERT. SZ, NO.19) BUDAPEST, TERRA, 1962. 135P. 1100T.

INA ROULEMENTS, S.A. CAGES A AIGUILLES ET ROULEMENTS A AIGUILLES-EXEMPLES DE MONTAGES. (WATCH MECHANISMS, FR*EN*GE) PARIS, 195 . 48P.

INSPECCAO GERAL DES PRODUTOS AGRICOLAS E INDUSTRIALS. TERMINOLOGIA DAS TOLERANCIAS. (TOLERANCES T, PR EN FR GE IT SP) LISBON, 1952. 7P.

INTERNATIONAL ELECTROTECHNICAL COMMISSION. INTERNATIONAL ELECTROTECHNICAL VOCABULARY. FUNDAMENTAL DEFINITIONS, *FR*EN*DU*GE*IT*PL*SP*SW. (IEC-50-GR-05) ED2. GENEVA, 1956. 102P. 550T.

POLYGLOT

INTERNATIONAL ELECTROTECHNICAL COMMISSION. INTERNATIONAL ELECTROTECHNICAL VOCABULARY. LIGHTING. (*FR*EN*DU*GE*IT*PL*SP*SW) (IEC-50-GR-45) ED2. GENEVA, 1959. 83P.

INTERNATIONAL ELECTROTECHNICAL COMMISSION. INTERNATIONAL ELECTROTECHNICAL VOCABULARY. SCIENTIFIC AND INDUSTRIAL MEASURING INSTRUMENTS. (IEC-50-GR-20) (*FR*EN*DU*GE*IT*PL*SP*SW) ED2. GENEVA, 1958. 88P. 350T.

INTERNATIONAL ELECTROTECHNICAL COMMISSION. MEZHDUNARODNYI ELEKTROTEKHNICHESKII SLOVAR. (INTL. ELECTROTECH. VOC) (IEC 50-GR-20) SCIENTIFIC AND INDUSTRIAL MEASURING INSTRUMENTS. ED2. (*RU*EN*FR*GE *SP*IT*DU*PL*SW) MOSCOW, 1962. 225P.

INTERNATIONAL ORGANIZATION FOR STANDARDIZATION. FUNDAMENTAL QUANTITIES AND UNITS OF THE MKSA SYSTEM AND QUANTITIES AND UNITS OF SPACE AND TIME. (R31-PT1) GENEVA, 1957.

INTERNATIONAL ORGANIZATION FOR STANDARDIZATION. QUANTITIES AND UNITS OF HEAT. (SIMILAR TO ASA Y10.4) (R31-PT6) GENEVA, 1960.

INTERNATIONAL ORGANIZATION FOR STANDARDIZATION. QUANTITIES AND UNITS OF MECHANICS. (SIMILAR TO ASA Z10.3) IR31-PT3) GENEVA, 1960.

INTERNATIONAL ORGANIZATION FOR STANDARDIZATION. QUANTITIES AND UNITS OF PERIODIC AND RELATED PHENOMENA (R31-PT2) GENEVA, 1958.

INTERNATIONAL ORGANIZATION FOR STANDARDIZATION. QUANTITIES, UNITS, SYMBOLS, CONVERSION FACTORS AND CONVERSION TABLES. QUANTITIES AND UNITS OF RADIATION AND LIGHT. (ISO/TC12) ED2. GENEVA, 1961. 11P. 70T.

KHRAMOI, A.V. RUSSKO-ANGLO-NEMETSKO-FRANTSUZKII SLOVAR TERMINOV PO AVTOMATICHESKOMU UPRAVLENIIU. (*RU*EN *FR*GE D. OF AUTOM. CONTROL) MOSCOW, AKAD. NAUK, SSSR, 1963. 205P. 3100T.

RACK, H. DIE UHRTEILE IN FREMDER SPRACHE. (WATCH PARTS IN FOREIGN LANG,*GE*EN*FR) ULM (DONAU), NEUE UHRMACHER-Z.1957. 52P, 59-48183.

SCHULZ, E. WOERTERBUCH DER OPTIK UND FEINMECHANIK. (OPT/PREC. MECH. D) V.1, GE*EN*FR, 111P. V.2, EN*FR *GE, 124P. V.3, FR*GE*EN, 109P. WIESBADEN, BRANDSTETTER, 1960-61. A61-3700. 2500T.

SCIENTIFIC INSTRUMENTS MANUFACTURES ASSOCIATION (ENGLAND) BRITISH INSTRUMENTS DIRECTORY AND BUYERS GUIDE. (*FR*EN*GE*RU*SP GL, PP.194-256) ED3. LONDON, 1962. 667P.

SWITZERLAND. OFFICE FOR INDUSTRIAL INFORMATION. DICTIONARY (AND BUYERS GUIDE FOR SWITZERLAND) OF THE WATCH INDUSTRY, JEWELLERY AND ALLIED INDUSTRY. (FR*EN*GE*SP GL) GENEVA(1952. 1124P.

SWITZERLAND. OFFICE FOR INDUSTRIAL INFORMATION. DICTIONARY (AND DIRECTORY FOR SWITZERLAND) OF MACHINES, APPARATUS AND TOOLS. (*FR*EN*GE*IT*SP GL) ED22. GENEVA, 1955. 1351P.

SYNDICAT GENERAL D.OPTIQUE. ANNUAIRE. ALPHABETICAL LIST OF PRODUCTS (*GE*EN*FR*SP GL) PARIS, 1958. 203P.

TWYMAN, F. OPTICAL GLASSWORKING. (FR*EN*GE GL, PP.262-70, 200T) LONDON, HILGER/WATTS, 1955. 275P. 55-4221.

UNITED NATIONS. ECONOMIC COMMISSION FOR ASIA AND THE FAR EAST. GLOSSARY OF COMMODITY TERMS INCLUDING CURRENCIES, WEIGHTS AND MEASURES USED IN CERTAIN COUNTRIES OF ASIA. BANGKOK,1955. 121P. 56-14584.

VOCABULAIRE TRILINGUE DE LA REGULATION AUTOMATIQUE. (GE EN FR AUTOM. GL) MESURES/CONTROLE IND, V.22, 137-8 (1957)

RUSSIAN

AKADEMIIA NAUK SSSR. KOM.TEKH.TERM. ELEKTROVAKUUMNYE PRIBORY... (D. OF ELECTRON-TUBE DEVICES, RU DEFS) (SB.REK.TERM.NO.54) MOSCOW, 1960. 20P. 62-32953.

AKADEMIIA NAUK SSSR. KOM.TEKH.TERM. TERMINOLOGIIA ELEKTROVAKUUMNYKH PRIBOROV. (D. OF ELECTRON-TUBE DEVICES, RU DEFS) (SB.REK.TERM.NO.39) MOSCOW, 1956. 47P.56-42962. 180T

AKADEMIIA NAUK SSSR. KOM. TEKH. TERM. TERMINOLOGIIA OSNOVNYKH PONIATII AVTOMATIKI. (BASIC CONCEPTS IN AUTOM, RU DEFS) (SB. REK. TERM. NO.35) MOSCOW,1954. 22P. 55-35588. 40T.

AKADEMIIA NAUK SSSR. KOM.TEKH,TERM. TERMINOLOGIIA VYCHISLITELNYKH MASHIN I PRIBOROV. (COMP/INSTR,RU DEFS) (SB,REK.TERM.NO.42) MOSCOW,1957. 15P. 58-33626.

AKADEMIIA NAUK SSSR. KOM.TEKW.TERM. TERMINOLOGY OF COMPUTER MACHINES AND INSTRUMENTS. (JPRS/NY-328) (TRANSL.OF ABOVE ENTRY) NEW YORK, U.S. JPRS, 1958. 16P. 58-61620.

BERG, A.I. AND TRAPEZNIKOV, V.A. AVTOMATIZATSIIA PROIZVODSTVA I PROMYSHLENNAIA ELEKTRONIKA... (IND. AUTOM/ELECTRON. ENCYCL. RU DEFS) MOSCOW, SOV. ENTSIKL, 1962. 63-32131.

CLASON, W.E. ELSEVIER,S DICTIONARY OF AUTOMATION, COMPUTERS, CONTROL AND MEASURING. RUSSIAN SUPPL, NEW YORK, ELSEVIER, 1962. 90P. 3400T.

KHRAMOI, A.V. AND ZHURKINA, E.G. RUSSKO-ANGLIISKII I ANGLO-RUSSKII SLOVAR PO AVTOMATICHESKOMU REGULIROVANIIU I UPRAVLENIIU. (*RU*EN D. OF AUTOM. CONTROL-IFAC) MOSCOW, AKAD. NAUK, SSSR, 1960. 91P. MIC 61-7392. 1600T.

INSTRUMENTATION AND METROLOGY

RUSSIAN

PTASHNYI, L.K. ANGLO-RUSSKII SLOVAR PO AVTOMATIKE I KONTROLNO-IZMERITELNYM PRIBORAM. (EN*RU D. OF AUTOM/INSTR) MOSCOW, GITTL, 1957. 379P. 58-30223. 12000T.

SOKOLOV, V.A. AND KRASAVIN, L.M. SPRAVOCHNIK MER. (METROL. MANUAL, RU DEFS) (GL, PP.149-240) ED2. MOSCOW, VNESHTORGIZDAT, 1960. 248P.

U.S. LIBRARY OF CONGRESS. GLOSSARY OF UNITS AND MEASURES, ENGLISH-RUSSIAN, RUSSIAN-ENGLISH. (OTS-61-31103) WASHINGTON, 1961. 531P. 2600T.

MACHINERY AND TOOLS

ARABIC

FLOOD, W.E. TRADES, MACHINES AND ENGINES. (GL, 171-83, EN*AR, 300T) NEW YORK, LONGMANS, GREEN, 1955. 183P. 56-1023.

CHINESE

FAN, FENG-YUAN. TU CHIEH CHI HSIEH TUNG TAO TZ,U TIEN. (MACH. D, CH EN) SHANGHAI,'SCIENCE, 1951. 246P. C61-1282.

CZECH

BARES, K. ANGLICKE ODBORNE TEXTY PRO STROJNI INZENYRSTVI. (CZ*EN MECH. ENG. D) PRAGUE, SNTL, 1957. 143P.

KOCOUREK, R. AGRICULTURAL DICTIONARY. PRAGUE, SPN. (IN PREP) 15000T.

VORACEK, Z. TEXTY ANGLICTINY PRO FAKULTU STROJNIHO INZENYRSTVI. (CZ*EN MECH. ENG. D) PRAGUE, SNTL, 1958. 2V. 350P.

ENGLISH

AEROSPACE INDUSTRIES ASSOCIATION. STANDARD GYRO TERMINOLOGY. (REPT. EETC-5) WASHINGTON, 1960. 10P. 80T.

AMERICAN FOUNDRYMEN,S SOCIETY. A.F.S. GLOSSARY OF FOUNDRY TERMS. CHICAGO, 1953. 77P. 58-35922.

AMERICAN INSTITUTE OF ELECTRICAL ENGINEERS. DEFINITIONS OF ELECTRICAL TERMS. ELECTROMECHANICAL DEVICES. (GR-45, ASA C42.45) NEW YORK, 1959. 15P. 150T.

AMERICAN INSTITUTE OF ELECTRICAL ENGINEERS. DEFINITIONS OF ELECTRICAL TERMS. ROTATING MACHINERY. (GR-10, ASA C42.10) NEW YORK, 1957. 34P. 320T.

AMERICAN INSTITUTE OF ELECTRICAL ENGINEERS. SPECIFICATION STANDARDS FOR ELECTROHYDRAULIC FLOW CONTROL SERVOVALVES. (AIEE 59-357) NEW YORK, 1959. 30P. 100T.

AMERICAN SOCIETY OF MECHANICAL ENGINEERS. DIAPHRAGM-ACTUATED.CONTROL VALVE TERMINOLOGY. (ASME STD. NO.112) NEW YORK, 1961. 14P. 62-1921.

AMERICAN STANDARDS ASSOCIATION. AMERICAN STANDARD TERMINOLOGY AND. DEFINITIONS FOR BALL AND ROLLER BEARINGS AND PARTS. (ASA-B3.7) NEW YORK, 1960. 31P. 700T.

AMERICAN STANDARDS ASSOCIATION. CONVEYOR TERMS AND DEFINITIONS. (ASA-MH4.1) NEW YORK, 1958. 78P. 1500T.

AMERICAN STANDARDS ASSOCIATION. GEAR NOMENCLATURE. (ASA B6.10') NEW YORK, AM. GEAR MANUF. ASSOC, 1955. 23P. 180T.

AMERICAN STANDARDS ASSOCIATION. MILLING CUTTERS. (ASA-B5.3) NEW YORK,AM. SOC. MECH. ENG, 1960. 73P. 70T.

AMERICAN STANDARDS ASSOCIATION. NOMENCLATURE OF GEAR TOOTH WEAR/FAILURE. (ASA-B6.12) NEW YORK, AM. SOC. MECH, ENG. 1954. 10P. 30T.

AMERICAN STANDARDS ASSOCIATION. SINGLE POINT AND TOOL POSTS. (ASA-B5.22, B5.36, B5.29) NEW YORK, AM. SOC. MECH. ENG, 1959. 31P. 80T.

BRITISH COMPRESSED AIR SOCIETY. TECHNICAL REFERENCE BOOK OF COMPRESSED AIR TERMS AND STANDARDS. LONDON, 1956. 108P. 57-18512.

BRITISH STANDARDS INSTITUTION. DESCRIPTIONS AND METHODS OF MEASURING SIZES AND OUTPUTS OF CRUSHING MACHINERY. (B.S. 2595, AMEND, PD 3682, 1960) LONDON, 1955. I2P.

BRITISH STANDARDS INSTITUTION. GLOSSARY FOR VALVES AND VALVE PARTS (FOR FLUIDS) (B.S. 2591) PT.·1, 48P. PT.2, 20P. PT.3, 20P. LONDON, 1955-56. 130T.

BRITISH STANDARDS INSTITUTION. GLOSSARY OF TERMS AND NOTATION FOR TOOTHED GEARING. (B.S. 2519, AMEND, PD2403, 1956) LONDON, 1956. 42P. 180T.

BRITISH STANDARDS INSTITUTION. GLOSSARY OF TERMS RELATING TO AGRICULTURAL MACHINERY AND IMPLEMENTS. (B.S. 2468) LONDON, 1963. 94P. 950T.

BRITISH STANDARDS INSTITUTION. TERMS AND DEFINITIONS FOR SINGLE-POINT CUTTING TOOLS FOR LATHES, BORING-MILLS, PLANING, SHAPING AND SIMILAR .MACHINES. (B.S. 1886) LONDON, 1952. 40P.

ENGLISH

BRITISH STANDARDS INSTITUTION. TYPES OF ENCLOSURE OF ELECTRICAL APPARATUS. (B.S. 2817. PT.1,GL) LONDON, 1957. 12P. 40T.

BRITTEN, F.J. OLD CLOCKS AND WATCHES. (GL.OF TECH.T, APPENDIX 1) ED7. NEW YORK, DUTTON, 1956. 518P.

BRUTON, E. DICTIONARY OF CLOCKS AND WATCHES. NEW YORK, ARCHER, 1963. 201P. 63-14437.

COLVIN, F.H. THE MACHINIST DICTIONARY.. NEW YORK, SIMMONS-BOARDMAN, 1956. 496P. 55-10428. 5000T.

FLUID CONTROLS INSTITUTE. STANDARD CLASSIFICATION AND TERMINOLOGY FOR POWER ACTUATED VALVES. DECATUR, ILL, 1955. 11P. 40T.

HINE, H.J. DICTIONARY OF AGRICULTURAL ENGINEERING... CAMBRIDGE, ENG, HEFFER, 1961. 252P. 62-1206.

HITCHOCK,S ASSEMBLY AND FASTENER DICTIONARY. V.1- . WHEATON, ILL. HITCHOCK, 1962- . 61-45423.

JONES, F.D. AND SCHUBERT, P.B. ENGINEERING ENCYCLOPEDIA... ED3. NEW YORK, IND. PRESS, 1963. 1431P. 63-10415.

NEWELL, F.B. DIAPHRAGM CHARACTERISTICS, DESIGN AND TERMINOLOGY. NEW YORK, AM. SOC. MECH. ENG, 1958. 74P 59-3706.

PALESTRANT, S.S. PRACTICAL PICTORIAL GUIDE TO MECHANISMS AND MACHINES. NEW YORK, UNIV. BOOKS, 1956. 265P 56-13016.

WINFIELD, H. A GLOSSARY OF METALWORKING TERMS. LONDON, BLACKIE, 1960.80P. 60-51881. 800T.

FRENCH

BUCKSCH, H. DICTIONNAIRE POUR LES TRAVAUX PUBLICS, LE BATIMENT ET L,EQUIPEMENT DES CHANTIERS DE CONSTRUCTION, ANGLAIS-FRANCAIS. (D. OF CIVIL ENG, CONSTR. MACH/ EQUIP,*EN*FR) PARIS, EYROLLES, 1960-62. 2V. 62-6556.

GILLAM, D.J. A CONCISE DICTIONARY OF HOROLOGICAL TERMS. (*EN*FR) LA CHAUX-DE-FONDS, ECOLE SUPER.COM. 1956. 46P. 58-44162. 2300T.

INTERNATIONAL ORGANIZATION FOR STANDARDIZATION. DEFINITIONS OF ROLLER BEARINGS, INTERNAL CLEARANCE IN UNLOADED BEARINGS,FR*EN GL. (R200) GENEVA, 1961. 31P. 300T.

MALGORN, G.M. LEXIQUE TECHNIQUE ANGLAIS-FRANCAIS...(EN*FR TECH.D) ED4. PARIS, GAUTHIER-VILLARS, 1956. 493P. 57-155. 9500T.

MALGORN, G.M. LEXIQUE TECHNIQUE FRANCAIS-ANGLAIS... (FR*EN TECH.D) PARIS, GAUTHIER-VILLARS, 1956. 475P. 57-156. 9500T.

NICHIL, P. LEXIQUE FRANCAIS-ANGLAIS ET ANGLAIS-FRANCAIS DES TERMES D,USAGE COURANT EN MACHINES-OUTILS ET MACHINES SIMILAIRES... (*FR*EN GL. OF MACH/TOOL T) PARIS, DUNOD, 1961. 56P.

PROULX, G. MATERIEL ET ENGINS DE CHANTIERS, GLOSSAIRE ANGLAIS-FRANCAIS, BT-41. (FIELD MATER/EQUIP, EN*F GL) OTTAWA, DEPT. SECY. STATE, 1956. 89P. 1300T.

VOCABULAIRE DES SCIERIES, GLOSSAIRE ANGLAIS-FRANCAIS, BT-56. (SAW-MILL T, EN*ER GL) OTTAWA, DEPT.SECY. STATE, 1957. 14P. 300T.

WUESTER, E. INTERLINGUAL DICTIONARY OF MACHINE TOOL TERMS... (*EN*FR) LONDON, TECH. PRESS, 1959-60. 60 1400T. (IN PREP)

GERMAN

AUSSCHUSS FUER WIRTSCHAFTLICHE FERTIGUNG. BEGRIFFSBESTIMMUNGEN. HEFT 1, EBENE KURBELGETRIEBE. (DEFS, PT.1, PLANE CRANK-GEARS, GE*EN) BERLIN, 1952. 12P.

BOSNJAKOVIC, F. ET AL. LUEGERS LEXIKON DER TECHNIK. (ENCYCL. OF TECH) V.1, GRUNDLAGEN DES MASCHINENBAUES. (MACH. DESIGN, GE DEFS) ED4. STUTTGART, DEUT. VERLAGS-ANSTALT, 1960. 696P. A61-2000.

BOWER, W.W. LUBRICATION GLOSSARY. WOERTERVERZEICHNIS DER SCHMIERTECHNIK. STAMFORD, CONN, 1958. 27P. 58-23903. 500T.

BUCKSCH, H. WOERTERBUCH.FUER INGENIEURBAU UND BAUMASCHINEN...(*GE*EN D. OF CIVIL ENG/CONSTR. MACH) (V.1 GE*EN, 512P. V.2, EN*GE, 436P) ED2. WIESBADEN, BAUVERLAG, 1958. 59-31910. 18000T.

DICTIONARY OF AGRICULTURAL TERMS, ENGLISH-GERMAN,GERMAN-ENGLISH. LONDON, NATL.FED.YOUNG FARMERS CLUBS, 1952. 40P.

DLUHY, R. SCHIFFSTECHNISCHES WOERTERBUCH, SCHIFFBAU, SCHIFFAHRT UND SCHIFFSMASCHINENBAU. (*GE*EN SHIPBLDG. D) ED2. (V.1, GE*EN, 879P. V.2, EN*GE, 945P) BREMEN, DORN, 1956. A57-583. 40000T.

FREEMAN, H.G. SPEZIAL-WOERTERBUCH FUER DAS MASCHINENWESEN... (*GE*EN D.OF MACH) ED7. ESSEN, GIRARDET, 1958. 207P. 58-48150. 3500T.

FREEMAN, H.G. WOERTERBUCH WERKZEUGE, DEUTSCH-ENGLISCH, ENGLISCH-DEUTSCH. (*GE*EN D. OF MACH. TOOLS) ED2 ESSEN, GIRARDET, 1960. 658P. 61-1734. 17500T.

GERMAN

KLEINSCHMIDT, R. WOERTERBUCH DER SCHLEIF-UND POLIERTECHNIK. DEUTSCH-ENGLISCH, ENGLISCH-DEUTSCH. (*GE*EN GRINDING/POLISHING D) BERLIN, CRAM, 1952. 96P. 57-25313. 2400T.

NEUMANN-LEZIUS, H.H. HANDBUCH DER FEINMECHANISCHEN TECHNIK. (PREC. TOOL ENCYCL. GE DEFS) WIESBADEN, STEINER, 1952. 488P. A53-1907.

SCHULENBURG, A. ET AL. GIESSEREI-LEXIKON... (FOUNDRY D, GE DEFS) ED3. BERLIN, SCHIELE/SCHOEN, 1962. 1082P. 63-38519. 7000T.

SPEER, G. WOERTERBUCH DER GIESSEREIKUNDE. (FOUNDRY D, GE DEFS) BERLIN, TECHNIK, 1953. 165P. 56-15361.

VEREIN DEUTSCHER MASCHINENBAUANSTALT. OELHYDRAULIK- UND PNEUMATIK-KATALOG 1962 (OIL HYDRAULICS/PNEUMATICS CATALOG, GE DEFS) WIESBADEN, KRAUSSKOPF,1962. 130P.

WALTHER, R. TECHNISCHES ENGLISCH. ZERSPANENDE WERKZEUGMASCHINEN, HOBELN, RAEUMEN, FRAESEN. (*EN*GE D. OF MACH/TOOLS, PLANING, BROACHING, MILLING) BERLIN, TECHNIK, 1959. 371P. 60-19094.

WALTHER, R. TERMINOLOGIE UND SPRACHGEBRAUCH DER FESTIGKEITSLEHRE... (*EN/AM*GE STRENGTH OF MATER. T) WISS. Z. HOCHSCH. 'MASCHINENBAU. KARL-MARX STADT, V.2, PP.163-99 (1960)

JAPANESE

JAPAN. MINISTRY OF EDUCATION. VOCABULARY COVERING GAS TURBINES. (EN*JA) TOKYO, 1952. 20P. 600T.

TANAKA, A. EI-WA WA-EI NOGYO KIKAI YOGO JITEN. (*JA*EN FARM MACH. D) TOKYO, SHINNORINSHA, 1962. 266P. J63-143.

POLYGLOT

ANTONY, FRANCE. CENTRE NATIONAL D.ETUDES ET D.EXPERIMENTATION DE MACHINISME AGRICOLE. DICTIONNAIRE TECHNIQUE DU MACHINISME AGRICOLE. (TECH.D.OF AGR.MACH.*FR*EN*GE) PARIS,IMPR. NATL,1959. 277P. 60-26599. 2000T.

ARBEITSGEMEINSCHAFT WERKZEUGE UND PRAEZISION WERKZEUGE. GESAMTKATALOG DER DEUTSCHEN WERKZEUGINDUSTRIE. (CAT. OF GE TOOL IND, GE EN FR PR SP GL) (V.1, 313P. V.2, 382P. V.3 IN PREP) ESSEN, GIRARDET, 1952-56.

BIESALSKI, E. TERMINOLOGIE DER LANDARBEITSWISSENSCHAFT. (AGR. D, GE EN FR) ED3. BAD KREUZNACH, MAX PLANCK INST, 1958. 71P.

BORASIO, L. AND GARIBOLDI, F. ILLUSTRATED GLOSSARY OF RICE PROCESSING MACHINES. (EN FR SP) ROME, FAO, 1957. 49P.

BRABEC, J. AND HELLMANN, B. SLEVARENSKY SLOVNIK RUSKO-CESKY A ANGLICKO-CESKY. (FOUNDRY D, *CZ EN RU) PRAGUE, SNTL,1953. 155P. 54-39200. 5000T.

CHUNG-KUO K.O HSUEH YUAN. PIEN I CH.U PAN WEI YUAN HUI. (ACAD. SINICA. COMM. OF PUBL/TRANSL) CHAN HSING CH.I CH.E P.EI CHIEN T.UNG I MING CH.ENG. (AUTO PARTS D, CH RU EN) 3V. PEKING, 1957. C58-5180.

CONTROL GEAR GLOSSARY. (*EN*FR*GE*IT*SW) ELEC. TIMES, LONDON, V.137, NO.3, 97-8 (1960) 100T.

DICTIONARY OF INDUSTRIAL AGRICULTURE... (*DU*EN-AM*FR*GE*IT*SP) NEW YORK, ELSEVIER (IN PREP)

EBAUCHES, S.A. DICTIONNAIRE TECHNOLOGIQUE DES PARTIES DE LA MONTRE. (D.OF WATCH PARTS,*GE*EN*FR*IT*SP) NEUCHATEL, 1953. 225P. A54-4990. 1000T.

FEDERATION EUROPEENNE DE LA MANUTENTION. ILLUSTRIERTE TERMINOLOGIEN. WOERTERBUCH FUER FACHAUSDRUECKE DER FOERDER-UND HEBETECHNIK IN 6 SPRACHEN.(ILLUS.D.OF MATER. HANDLING, GE EN FR IT SP SW) WIESBADEN, KRAUSSKOPF, 1961-- . V.1-7. (IN PROGR)

GIERDZIEJEWSKI, K. ET AL. SLOWNIK TERMINOLOGII ODLEWNICTWA... (FOUNDRY D, *PL*EN*CZ*FR*GE*RU) WARSAW, PANSTW.WYDAW.TECH, 1961. 391P. 61-28721. 1200T.

HEILER, T. TECHNISCHES BILDWOERTERBUCH FUER SPANNENDE WERKZEUGE ZUR METALLBEARBEITUNG. (PICTURE GL. OF METAL-EXTRUSION MACH, *GE*EN*FR*IT*SP) MUNICH, HANSER, 1963. 460P.

HERSCU, G. ET. AL. DICTIONARY OF ROLLING MILL TERMS. EN FR GE SP. NEW YORK, ELSEVIER. 500P. 5400T. (IN PREP)

ILUSTRIRANI TEHNICKI RJECNIK, HRVATSKI, NJEMACKI, ENGLESKI, FRANCUSKI,TALIANSKI, SPANJOLSKI, RUSKI. ELEMENTI STROJEVA. (D. OF MACH. PARTS, *CR*EN*FR*GE*IT*RU*SP) ZAGREB, TEH. KNJIGA, 1952. 534P. 55-16341.

INTERNATIONAL DIRECTORY OF MACHINES, APPARATUS AND TOOLS FOR PRECISION ENGINEERING. (FR EN GE IT RU SP) LONDON, BAILEY, 1957. 1064P.

INTERNATIONAL ELECTROTECHNICAL COMMISSION. INTERNATIONAL ELECTROTECHNICAL VOCABULARY. MACHINES AND TRANSFORMERS. *FR*EN*DU*GE*IT*PL*SP*SW. (IEC-50-GR-10) ED2. GENEVA, 1956. 92P. 400T.

INTERNATIONAL ELECTROTECHNICAL COMMISSION. MEZHDUNARODNYI ELEKTROTEKHNICHESKII SLOVAR. (INTL. ELECTROTECH., VOC) (IEC 50-GR-10) MASHINY I TRANSFORMATORY. (MACH/TRANSFORMERS, *RU*EN*FR*GE*IT*SP*SW) ED2. MOSCOW, FIZMATGIZ, 1958. 212P. 59-36649. 400T.

POLYGLOT

INTERNATIONAL FOUNDRY DICTIONARY COMMITTEE. DICTIONNAIRE INTERNATIONAL DE FONDERIE. (INTL. FOUNDRY D, *FR*GE*EN*SP*IT*DU*NO*SW) PARIS, DUNOD, 1962. 482P. 63-40325. 1900T.

INTERNATIONAL INSTITUTION FOR PRODUCTION ENGINEERING RESEARCH. WOERTERBUCH DER FERTIGUNGSTECHNIK. (PROD. ENG.D, GE.EN FR) V.1, SCHMIEDEN, FREIFORMSCHMIEDEN UND GESENKSCHMIEDEN. (FORGING, HAMMER FORGING/DROP FORGING).V.2, SCHLEIFEN UND TECHNISCHE OBERFLAECHEN. (GRINDING/SURFACE FINISHING, IN PREP) V.3, BLECHBEARBEITUNG. (SHEETMETAL PROCESS, IN PREP) ESSEN, GIRARDET, 1962- .

INTERNATIONAL WROUGHT NON-FERROUS METALS COUNCIL. GLOSSARY OF TERMS APPLICABLE TO WROUGHT PRODUCTS IN COPPER,ZINC, BRASS AND OTHER COPPER ALLOYS. (*GE*EN*FR) BIRMINGHAM, ENG, 1956. 87P. 130T.

KAUFFMANN, F. DICTIONNAIRE TECHNIQUE DES MATERIELS AGRICOLES ET DE TRAVAUX PUBLICS. (MACH. IN AGRIC/ PUBL. WORKS, FR*EN*GE*SP D) PARIS, G.E.P, 1953. 446P.

KOLPAKOV, B.T. ET AL. EKSPORTNO-IMPORTNYI SLOVAR. (EXPORT/IMPORT D, RU*EN*AL*BU*CZ*FI*FR*GE*HU*IT*PL*SP) MOSCOW, VNESHTORGIZDAT, 1952-54. 3V. 2392P. 3000T.

KOVACS, K.P. ET AL. VILLAMOS GEREK. (D. OF ELEC. MACH, *HU*EN*GE*RU)(MUSZ. ERT. SZ. NO.5) BUDAPEST, TERRA, 1959. 164P. 63-28491. 1100T.

LANGE, K. GESENKSCHMIEDEN, DREISPRACHIGES TASCHENWOERTERBUCH. (DROP FORGING, *GE*EN*FR D) HANNOVER, WITTKOPF, 1956. 45P. 800T.

LEMPICKI, J. ET AL. SZESCIOJEZYCZNY SLOWNIK MASZYN I URZADZEN ODLEWNIEZYCH. (6-LANG. D. OF FOUNDRY EQUIP, *PL*EN*CZ*FR*GE*RU) CRACOW, NAKL. STOWARZ. TECH. ODLEWN. POLSK, 1958. 127P. 61-24758.

MACHINERY PUBLISHING CO. MACHINERY, ANNUAL BUYERS, GUIDE. (EN*FR*GE*RU*SP GL) BRIGHTON, 1961-1190P.

MECHANICAL HANDLING ENGINEERS ASSOCIATION. INTERNATIONAL ILLUSTRATED DICTIONARY. (EN FR GE IT SC SP) ED6. LONDON, 1960. 42P. 160T.

NORWAY. RADET FOR TEKNISK TERMINOLOGI. MACHINE ELEMENTS 1. (RTT-6) (*EN*FR*GE*NO) OSLO, 1960. 43P.

RACK, H. DIE UHRTEILE IN FREMDER SPRACHE. (WATCH PARTS IN FOREIGN LANG,*GE*EN*FR) ULM (DONAU), NEUE UHRMACHER-Z.1957. 52P. 59-48183.

SCHLOMANN-OLDENBOURG. ILLUSTRIERTE TECHNISCHE WOERTERBUECHER. (ILLUS.TECH.D) V.1, DIE MASCHINEN-ELEMENTE UND DIE GEBRAEUCHLICHSTEN WERKZEUGE. (MACH.PARTS/TOOLS,*GE*EN*FR*IT*RU*SP) MUNICH, OLDENBOURG, 1958 (REPR) 438P. 5000T.

SCHOPPER, K. DAS FACHWORT IM MASCHINENBAU... ILLUSTRIERTES TECHNISCHES WOERTERBUCH IN 3 SPRACHEN-ENGLISCH DEUTSCH, FRANZOESISCH. (ILLUS.D.OF MACH.DESIGN,*EN*GE*FR) V.1, WERKZEUGMASCHINEN. (MACH.TOOLS) 383P. V.2 (IN PREP) STUTTGART, INDUSTRIEBLATT, 1955- . A56-2727.

SCHUURMANS-STEKHOVEN, G. DICTIONARY OF METAL-CUTTING TOOLS... (*EN/AM*FR*SP*IT*GE) NEW YORK, ELSEVIER (IN PREP)

STEINMETZ, H. LANDMASCHINEN UND GERAETE, MEHRSPRACHIGES BILDWOERTERBUCH. (FARM IMPLEMENTS/MACH, GE*EN*DU *FR*IT*SP) BETZDORF/SIEG, GERMANY, 1960. 168P. 900T.

SWEDISH EXPORT DIRECTORY. (*SW*EN*FR*GE*RU*SP) ED4. STOCKHOLM, GEN. EXPORT ASSOC, 1952. 810P.

SWITZERLAND. OFFICE FOR INDUSTRIAL INFORMATION. DICTIONARY (AND DIRECTORY FOR SWITZERLAND) OF MACHINES, APPARATUS AND TOOLS. (*FR*EN*GE*IT*SP GL) ED22. GENEVA, 1955. 1351P.

SYNDICAT DES CONSTRUCTEURS FRANCAIS DE MACHINES-OUTILS. MACHINES-OUTILS FRANCAISES. (FR MACH. TOOLS, FR EN GE SP GL) NEUILLY/SEINE, 1961. 273P. 62-65392.

TECH-TERM, ILLUSTRATED INTERNATIONAL TECHNICAL DICTIONARY. (V.1, HAND TOOLS FOR ALL TRADES, *GE*EN*DU*FR) AMSTERDAM, ELSEVIER, 1958. 124P. 62-51192. 1800T.

TEKNISK ORDLISTA SVENSK-TYSK-ENGELSK-FRANSK-SPANSK-PORTUGISISK-RYSK OEVER FACKUTTRYCK INOM VERKTYGS-OCH VERKTYGSMASKINBRANSHEN. (GL.OF TOOLS/MACH.TOOLS, SW*EN*FR*GE*PR*RU*SP) ED4. STOCKHOLM, MASKIN. KARLEBO, 1953. 129P. 1200T.

VARGA, J. ET AL. VIZGEPEK, BELSO EGESU MOTOROK. (D. OF HYDR/INTERN. COMB. ENGS, *HU*EN*GE*RU) (MUSZ. ERT. SZ. NO.20) BUDAPEST, TERRA, 1962. 138P. 62-66313. 1100T.

RUSSIAN

AKADEMIIA NAUK SSSR. KOM.TEKH.TERM. ELEKTRICHESKIE MASHINY. (D. OF ELEC.MACH, RU DEFS) (SB.REK.TERM. NO. 52) MOSCOW, 1960. 26P. 60-32946. 200T.

AKADEMIIA NAUK SSSR. KOM. TEKH. TERM. KLASSIFIKATSIIA I TERMINOLOGIIA GORNYKH MASHIN. (CLASSIF/T. OF MIN. MACH, RU DEFS) (SB. REK. TERM, NO.1) MOSCOW, 1952. 26P. 54-32054.

AKADEMIIA NAUK SSSR. KOM.TEKH.TERM. LOPASTNYE NASOSY. TSENTROBEZHNYE I OSEVYE. TERMINOLOGIIA I BUKVENNYE OBOZNACHENIIA. (WING-PUMPS, CENTRIFUGAL/AXIAL, RU DEFS/SYMBOLS) (SB.REK. TERM. NO.56) MOSCOW, 1961.

AKADEMIIA NAUK SSSR. KOM.TEKH.TERM. OBRABOTKA METALLOV DAVLENIEM... (METAL-WORKING BY PRESSURE, RU DEFS) (SB. REK. TERM. NO.55) MOSCOW, 1961. 25P. 62-29464.

MACHINERY AND TOOLS

RUSSIAN

AKADEMIIA NAUK SSSR. KOM.TEKH.TERM. PORSHNEVYE DVIGATELI VNUTRENNEGO SGORANIIA... (INTERNAL COMBUSTION PISTON ENG, RU DEFS) (SB.REK.TERM, NO.50) MOSCOW, 1959. 13P. 60-21844. 60T.

AKADEMIIA NAUK SSSR. KOM.TEKH.TERM. TERMINOLOGIIA DETALEI MACHIN, MUFTI. (MACH. PARTS, SLEEVES, RU DEFS) (SB. REK. TERM, NO.45) MOSCOW, 1958. 24P. 58-45652. 70T.

AKADEMIIA NAUK SSSR. KOM.TEKH.TERM. TERMINOLOGIIA DETALEI MASHIN, RAZEMNYE SOEDINENIIA. (MACH.PARTS, DETACHABLE JOINTS, RU DEFS) (SB.REK.TERM, NO.11) MOSCOW, 1953. 46P. 54-27904. 120T.

AKADEMIIA NAUK SSSR. KOM.TEKH.TERM. TERMINOLOGIIA GIDROTURBIN. (HYDR.TURBINES, RU DEFS) (SB.REK.TERM, NO. 21) MOSCOW, 1953. 37P. 54-29072.

AKADEMIIA NAUK SSSR. KOM.TEKH.TERM. TERMINOLOGIIA PORSHNEVYKH DVIGATELEI VNUTRENNEGO SGORANIIA. (INTERNAL COMBUSTION PISTON ENG, RU DEFS)(SB.REK.TERM, NO.34) MOSCOW, 1954. 58P.55-36951. 160T.

AKADEMIIA NAUK SSSR. KOM.TEKH.TERM. TERMINOLOGIIA VODOPODGOTOVKI DLIA PAROVYKH KOTLOV. (WATER PROCESS. FOR STEAM BOILERS, RU DEFS) (SB. REK. TERM. NO.38) MOSCOW, 1956. 38P. 56-46923. 250T.

AKADEMIIA NAUK SSSR. KOM.TEKH.TERM. ZUBCHATYE KOLESA, ZATSEPLENIIA I PEREDACHI S POSTOIANNYM PEREDATOCHNYM OTNOSHENIEM, TERMINOLOGIIA. (GEARING, TRANSMISSION... RU DEFS) (SB. REK. TERM. NO.57) MOSCOW, 1962. 67P.

BELKIND, L.D. ANGLO-RUSSKII SLOVAR PO DETALIAM MASHIN, S PRILOZHENIEM ALFAVITNOGO UKAZATELIA RUSSKIKH TERMINOV. (*EN*RU D. OF MACH.PARTS) MOSCOW, FIZMATGIZ, 1959. 309P. 60-19671. 10000T.

CARPOVICH, E.A. RUSSIAN-ENGLISH METALS AND MACHINES DICTIONARY. NEW YORK, TECH.DICT, 1960. 112P. 60-12013. 9000T.

HOWERTON, P.W. AND AKHONIN, A. RUSSIAN-ENGLISH GLOSSARY OF METALLURGICAL AND METAL-WORKING TERMS. CAMBRIDGE, MASS. INST. TECH, 1955. 175P. 55-4386. 3500T.

KRECHETNIKOV, S.I. ANGLO-RUSSKII SLOVAR PO MASHINOSTROENIIU I METALLOOBRABOTKE. (EN*RU D.OF MACH.DESIGN/ METAL-WORKING) ED2. MOSCOW, FIZMATGIZ, 1961. 678P. 61-44360. 30000T.

NARTOV, I.M. ANGLO-RUSSKII SLOVAR PO GAZOTURBINNYM USTANOVKAM. (*EN*RU D. OF GAS TURBINES) LENINGRAD, SUDOSTROIIZDAT, 1962. 214P. 63-31811.

SLOVAK

SLOVENSKA AKADEMIA VIED. TERMINOLOGIA CASTI STROJOV. (MACH.PARTS, SL DEFS) BRATISLAVA, 1952. 89P. 59-23657.

SLOVENSKA AKADEMIA VIED. TERMINOLOGIA OBRABANIA KOVOV. (METAL-WORKING, SL DEFS) BRATISLAVA, 1952. 95P. 59-23559.

SPANISH

KOGOS INTERNATIONAL CORP. DICCIONARIO DE TERMINOS TECNICOS... MAQUINAS DE COSER... (EN SP TECH. T. FOR SEWING MACH) GREAT NECK, N.Y, 1963. 81P. 62-9166.

MATERIALS TESTING AND INDUSTRIAL PRODUCTS

CHINESE

LIU, CHUNG-CH.IEN. CHUNG YING WEN TUI CHAO WU P,IN MING MU HUI PIEN. (CATALOG OF COMMODITIES/PRODUCTS, CH EN) HONG KONG, 1955. 479P. C58-5390.

ENGLISH

AMERICAN FOUNDRYMEN,S SOCIETY. A.F.S. GLOSSARY OF FOUNDRY TERMS. CHICAGO, 1953. 77P. 58-35922.

AMERICAN SOCIETY FOR TESTING/MATERIALS. GLOSSARY·OF TERMS RELATING TO RUBBER AND RUBBER-LIKE MATERIALS. PHILADELPHIA, 1956. 121P. 56-14327. 2000T.

AMERICAN SOCIETY FOR TESTING/MATERIALS. STANDARD DEFINITIONS OF TERMS RELATING TO ADHESIVES. (D907-60) ASTM STDS,PT.6, 504-12. PHILADELPHIA 1961. 180T.

AMERICAN SOCIETY FOR TESTING/MATERIALS. STANDARD DEFINITIONS OF TERMS RELATING TO CERAMIC WHITEWARES AND RELATED PRODUCTS. (C242-60) ASTM STDS, PT.5, 556-8. PHILADELPHIA, 1961. 60T.

AMERICAN SOCIETY FOR TESTING/MATERIALS. STANDARD DEFINITIONS OF TERMS RELATING TO GLASS AND GLASS PRODUCTS. (C162-56) ASTM STDS, PT.5, 730-44. PHILADELPHIA, 1961. 380T.

AMERICAN SOCIETY FOR TESTING/MATERIALS. STANDARD DEFINITIONS OF TERMS RELATING TO GYPSUM. (C11-60) ASTM STDS, PT.4, 350-1. PHILADELPHIA, 1961. 20T.

AMERICAN SOCIETY FOR TESTING/MATERIALS. STANDARD DEFINITIONS OF TERMS RELATING TO LIME.(C51-47)ASTM STDS, PT.4, 282-3. PHILADELPHIA, 1961. 20T.

AMERICAN SOCIETY FOR TESTING/MATERIALS. STANDARD DEFINITIONS OF TERMS RELATING TO METHODS OF MECHANICAL TESTING. (E6-62) ASTM STDS,PT.3 SUPPL, 40-50. PHILADELPHIA, 1962. 70T.

AMERICAN SOCIETY FOR TESTING/MATERIALS. STANDARD DEFINITIONS OF TERMS RELATING TO NAVAL STORES AND PRODUCTS. (D804-57) ASTM STDS, PT.8, 1220-4. PHILADELPHIA, 1961. 60T.

AMERICAN SOCIETY FOR TESTING/MATERIALS. STANDARD DEFINITIONS OF TERMS RELATING TO PETROLEUM. (D288-61) ASTM STDS, PT.7, 153-5. PHILADELPHIA, 1961. 30T.

AMERICAN SOCIETY FOR TESTING/MATERIALS. STANDARD DEFINITIONS OF TERMS RELATING TO REFRACTORIES. (C71-62) ASTM STDS, PT.5, SUPPL, 78-80. PHILADELPHIA, 1962. 60T.

AMERICAN SOCIETY FOR TESTING/MATERIALS. STANDARD DEFINITIONS OF TERMS RELATING TO TEXTILE MATERIALS... (D123-62) ASTM STDS, PT.10, SUPPL, 4-56. PHILADELPHIA, 1962. 1200T.

AMERICAN SOCIETY FOR TESTING/MATERIALS. STANDARD DEFINITIONS OF TERMS RELATING TO TIMBER. (D9-30) ASTM STDS,PT.6, 868-70. PHILADELPHIA, 1961. 60T.

AMERICAN SOCIETY FOR TESTING/MATERIALS. STANDARD DEFINITIONS OF TERMS RELATING TO TIMBER PRESERVATIVES. (D324-41) ASTM STDS, PT.6, 1058. PHILADELPHIA, 1961. 10T.

AMERICAN SOCIETY FOR TESTING/MATERIALS. STANDARD DEFINITIONS OF TERMS RELATING TO VENEER AND PLYWOOD. (D1038-52) ASTM STDS, PT.6, 873-8. PHILADELPHIA, 1961. 120T.

AMERICAN SOCIETY FOR TESTING/ MATERIALS. STANDARD DEFINITIONS OF TERMS USED IN POWDER METALLURGY. (B243-61) ASTM STDS, PT.2, 1028-32. PHILADELPHIA, 1961. 120T.

AMERICAN SOCIETY FOR TESTING/MATERIALS. TENTATIVE DEFINITIONS OF TERMS RELATING TO CERAMIC WHITEWARES AND RELATED PRODUCTS. (C242-60T) ASTM STDS, PT.5, 559-62. PHILADELPHIA, 1961. 110T.

AMERICAN SOCIETY FOR TESTING/MATERIALS. TENTATIVE DEFINITIONS OF TERMS RELATING TO FATIGUE TESTING AND TH STATISTICAL ANALYSIS OF FATIGUE DATA. (E206-62T) ASTM STDS, PT.3, SUPPL, 34-9. PHILADELPHIA, 1962. 60T.

AMERICAN SOCIETY FOR TESTING/MATERIALS. TENTATIVE DEFINITIONS OF TERMS RELATING TO HEAT TREATMENT OF METALS (E44-50T) ASTM STDS, PT. 2, 1650-5. PHILADELPHIA, 1961. 100T.

AMERICAN SOCIETY FOR TESTING/MATERIALS. TENTATIVE DEFINITIONS OF TERMS RELATING TO LEATHER. (D1517-60)AST STDS, PT.6, 1234-47. PHILADELPHIA, 1961. 300T.

AMERICAN SOCIETY FOR TESTING/MATERIALS. TENTATIVE DEFINITIONS OF TERMS RELATING TO METALLOGRAPHY. (E7-55T ASTM STDS, PT.3, 808-48. PHILADELPHIA, 1961. 700T.

AMERICAN SOCIETY FOR TESTING/MATERIALS. TENTATIVE DEFINITIONS OF TERMS RELATING TO PORCELAIN ENAMEL. (C286-61T) ASTM STDS, PT.5, 635-42. PHILADELPHIA, 1961. 260T.

AMERICAN SOCIETY FOR TESTING/MATERIALS. TENTATIVE DEFINITIONS OF TERMS RELATING TO RHEOLOGICAL PROPERTIE OF MATTER. (E24-58T) ASTM STDS, PT.4, 1644. PHILADELPHIA, 1961. 10T.

AMERICAN SOCIETY FOR TESTING/MATERIALS. TENTATIVE DEFINITIONS OF TERMS RELATING TO RUBBER AND RUBBER-LIKE MATERIALS. (D1566-60T) ASTM STDS, PT.11, 717-8. PHILADELPHIA, 1961. 10T.

AMERICAN SOCIETY FOR TESTING/MATERIALS. TENTATIVE DEFINITIONS OF TERMS RELATING TO SHIPPING CONTAINERS. (D 996-59T) ASTM STDS, PT.6, 415-24, PHILADELPHIA, 1961. 200T.

AMERICAN SOCIETY FOR TESTING/MATERIALS. TENTATIVE DEFINITIONS OF TERMS RELATING TO WOOD-BASE FIBER AND PARTICLE PANEL MATERIALS. (D1554-60T) ASTM STDS, PT.6, 879-82. PHILADELPHIA, 1961. 50T.

AMERICAN SOCIETY FOR TESTING/MATERIALS. TENTATIVE DEFINITIONS OF TERMS RELATING TO WROUGHT IRON. (A81-60 ASTM STDS, PT.1, 1429. PHILADELPHIA, 1961. 10T.

AMERICAN SOCIETY FOR TESTING/MATERIALS. TENTATIVE DEFINITIONS OF TERMS, SYMBOLS AND CONVERSION FACTORS RELATING TO MAGNETIC TESTING. (A340-61T) ASTM STDS, PT.3, 463-78. PHILADELPHIA, 1961. 140T.

AMERICAN SOCIETY FOR TESTING/MATERIALS. TENTATIVE INDUSTRIAL RADIOGRAPHIC TERMINOLOGY FOR USE IN RADIOGRAPHIC INSPECTION OF CASTINGS AND WELDMENTS. (E52-49T) ASTM STDS, PT.3, 961-2. PHILADELPHIA, 1961. 20T.

AMERICAN STANDARDS ASSOCIATION. ACOUSTICAL TERMINOLOGY, INCL.MECH. SHOCK/VIBRATIONS. (S1.1-1960) NEW YORK, 1960. 62P. 700T.

AMERICAN STANDARDS ASSOCIATION. NOMENCLATURE OF GEAR TOOTH WEAR/FAILURE. (ASA-B6.12) NEW YORK, AM. SOC. MECH, ENG. 1954. 10P. 30T.

AMERICAN WELDING SOCIETY. NONDESTRUCTIVE TESTING SYMBOLS. NEW YORK, 1958. 10P. 58-30488.

AUSTRALIAN INSTITUTE OF METALS. DEFINITIONS OF TERMS USED IN THE HEAT TREATMENT AND TESTING OF METALS. ED2. MELBOURNE, 1957. 88P. 58-42063.

BRITISH IRON AND STEEL RESEARCH ASSOCIATION. SURFACE DEFECTS IN INGOTS AND THEIR PRODUCTS. (RECOMMENDED DEFS)... ED2. LONDON, 1958. 58P. A59-4707.

BRITISH STANDARDS INSTITUTION. GLASS FOR GLAZING. (B.S. 952. AMEND. PD-2899; 3267. 3316; 3350, 3584) LONDON, 1957-59. 36P. 20T.

BRITISH STANDARDS INSTITUTION. GLOSSARY OF LEATHER TERMS. (B.S. 2780) LONDON, 1956. 24P. 160T.

MATERIALS TESTING AND INDUSTRIAL PRODUCTS

ENGLISH

BRITISH STANDARDS INSTITUTION. GLOSSARY OF TERMS APPLICABLE TO CORK AND CORK PRODUCTS. (B.S. 3519) LONDON, 1962. 10P. 70T.

BRITISH STANDARDS INSTITUTION. GLOSSARY OF TERMS APPLICABLE TO FILLINGS AND STUFFINGS FOR BEDDING, UPHOLSTERY, TOYS AND OTHER DOMESTIC ARTICLES. (B.S. 2005. AMEND. PD 2109, 2334-1955) LONDON, 1953-55. 16P. 90T.

BRITISH STANDARDS INSTITUTION. GLOSSARY OF TERMS RELATING TO IRON AND STEEL. (B.S.2094) PTS.1-8. LONDON, 1954-56. 1400T.

BRITISH STANDARDS INSTITUTION. GLOSSARY OF TERMS RELATING TO THE MANUFACTURE AND USE OF REFRACTORY MATERIALS. (B.S.3446) LONDON, 1962. 87P. 600T.

BRITISH STANDARDS INSTITUTION. GLOSSARY OF TERMS RELATING TO POWDERS. (B.S.2955) LONDON, 1958. 16P. 100T.

BRITISH STANDARDS INSTITUTION. GLOSSARY OF TERMS USED IN THE RUBBER INDUSTRY. (B.S. 3558) LONDON, 1962. 27P. 200T.

BRITISH STANDARDS INSTITUTION. GLOSSARY OF TERMS USED IN VIBRATION AND SHOCK TESTING. (B.S.3015) LONDON, 1958. 20P. 70T.

CAMPELL, J.B. MECHANICAL PROPERTIES AND TESTS. MATER/METHODS, V.40, 109-32 (1954) 160T.

CLAUSER, H.R. ET AL. THE ENCYCLOPEDIA OF ENGINEERING MATERIALS AND PROCESSES. NEW YORK, REINHOLD, 1963. 787P. 63-13448.

A COMPLETE DIRECTORY OF CERAMIC MATERIALS...CERAM. IND. V.74, 111-70 (1960) (REPR. BY INTL. COOP. ADMIN, WASHINGTON) 1960. 43P. 60-61806. 500T.

DICTIONARY OF INDUSTRIAL ENGINEERING, WORDS, TERMS, AND PHRASES. CHICAGO, IND. ENG. COLL, 1959. 1V. (UNPAGED) 59-4333.

GLOSSARY OF TERMS USED BY THE MECHANICAL RUBBER GOODS INDUSTRY. RUBBER AGE, V.74, 915-35 (1954) 1000T.

HORNBOSTEL, C. MATERIALS FOR ARCHITECTURE, AN ENCYCLOPEDIC GUIDE. NEW YORK, RHEINHOLD, 1961. 610P. 61-13206.

GUNDERSEN, J.L. RELIABILITY GLOSSARY. ED2. DOWNEY, CALIF, AUTONETICS, 1962. 73P. 63-916.

THE IRON AGE. HANDBOOK OF TERMS COMMONLY USED IN THE STEEL INDUSTRY. NEW YORK, 1953. 30P. 59-47587.

MANKOWITZ, W. AND HAGGAR, R.G. THE CONCISE ENCYCLOPEDIA OF ENGLISH POTTERY AND PORCELAIN. NEW YORK, HAWTHORN, 1957. 312P. 57-6366.

MERRIMAN, A.D. A DICTIONARY OF METALLURGY. LONDON, MACDONALD/EVANS, 1958. 401P. 59-480. 4000T.

OSBORNE, A.K. AN ENCYCLOPAEDIA OF THE IRON AND STEEL INDUSTRY. NEW YORK, PHIL. LIBR, 1956. 558P. 56-14371.

PRODUCT DESIGN AND DEVELOPMENT. PRODUCT ENCYCLOPEDIA... COMPONENT PARTS, R/D EQUIP... PHILADELPHIA, 1961. 253P. 61-59873. 2400T.

ROLFE, R.T. A DICTIONARY OF METALLOGRAPHY. NEW YORK, CHEMICAL, 1955. 287P. A 57-5037. 1000T.

SOCIETY OF AUTOMOTIVE ENGINEERS. DEFINITIONS OF HEAT-TREATING TERMS,PP.79-81. SAE HANDBOOK, NEW YORK,1961. 914P. 120T.

VAN SCHOICKE, E. CERAMIC GLOSSARY. COLUMBUS, AM. CERAMIC SOC, 1963. 31P. 1800T.

WITTY, M.B. ET AL. DICTIONARY OF MATERIALS ABBREVIATIONS. NEW YORK, SETI, 196 .

WITTY, M.B. ET AL. DICTIONARY OF PLASTICS AND CERAMICS, SIGNS, SYMBOLS AND TABLES. NEW YORK, SETI, 196 . 192P.

ZIMMERMAN, O.T. AND LAVINE, I. HANDBOOK OF MATERIAL TRADE NAMES. DOVER, N.H, IND. RES. SERV, 1953. 794P. SUPPL.1,1956. 383P. SUPPL.2, 1957. 356P. SUPPL.3, 1960. 400P. 53-1074.

FRENCH

BRITISH CAST IRON RESEARCH ASSOCIATION. A GLOSSARY OF FRENCH-ENGLISH, ENGLISH-FRENCH FOUNDRY AND METALLURGICAL TERMS. BIRMINGHAM, ENG, 1959. 28P. 2000T.

BRITISH IRON AND STEEL FEDERATION. CONCISE IRON AND STEEL DICTIONARY, FRENCH-ENGLISH, ENGLISH-FRENCH. (NEW SER. NO.1) LONDON, 1957. 38P.

CENTRE TECHNIQUE DES INDUSTRIES DE LA FONDERIE. VOCABULAIRE DE FONDERIE... ANGLAIS-FRANCAIS. (EN*FR FOUNDRY GL) PARIS, 1953. 77P. 54-27387. 1200T.

GENIN, G. ET AL. ENCYCLOPEDIE TECHNOLOGIQUE DE L,INDUSTRIE DU CAOUTCHOUC. (ENCYCL.OF RUBBER IND, FR DEFS) PARIS, DUNOD, 1956-60. 4V. A56-5968.

GERMAN

AYRENSCHMALZ, L. WOERTERBUCH ZUR FESTIGKEITSLEHRE, FORMAENDERUNG UND TRAGFAEHIGKEIT FESTER KOERPER. (STUDY OF STRENGTH, DEFORM/LOAD CAP.OF SOLIDS, GE DEFS) MUNICH, HANSER, 1958. 179P. A59-5633.

BRITISH IRON AND STEEL FEDERATION. CONCISE IRON AND STEEL DICTIONARY, GERMAN-ENGLISH, ENGLISH-GERMAN. (NEW SER, NO.2) LONDON, 1957. 57P.

ELMER, T.H. GERMAN-ENGLISH DICTIONARY OF GLASS, CERAMICS, AND ALLIED SCIENCES. NEW YORK, INTERSCIENCE, 1963. 304P. 63-17477. 21000T.

FLUEGGE, S. ET AL. HANDBUCH DER PHYSIK. (ENCYCL. OF PHYS) V.6. ELASTIZITAET UND PLASTIZITAET. (ELASTICITY/PLASTICITY, *GE*EN GL, PP.614-42, 1000T) BERLIN, SPRINGER,1958. 642P. A56-2942.

GOULDEN, W.O. ET AL. LEDERTECHNISCHES WOERTERBUCH. (*GE*EN D.OF LEATHER TECH) COLOGNE, STAUFEN, 1956. 172P. A57-1193. 7500T.

HELLMICH, K. ABC DER STOFFKUNDE. (MATER. ABC, GE DEFS) ED4. DUESSELDORF, 1957.

HOFFMANN, E. FACHWOERTERBUCH FUER DIE GLASINDUSTRIE. DEUTSCH-ENGLISCH, ENGLISCH-DEUTSCH. (*GE*EN GLASS IND. D) BERLIN, SPRINGER, 1963. 160P. 62-21033.

JAHRBUCH DER SCHWEIZERISCHEN LEDERWIRTSCHAFT. DEUTSCH-ENGLISCHES FACHWOERTER-VOKABULARIUM. (SWISS LEATHER YEARBOOK, GE*EN GL) ZURICH, WIRTSCHAFTSLIT, 196 .

JEBSEN-MARWEDEL, H. TAFELGLAS IN STICHWORTEN. (SHEET GLASS D, GE DEFS) ED2. ESSEN, GIRARDET, 1960. 100P. A61-3486. 500T.

KOEHLER, E.L. AND LEGAT, A. ENGLISCH-DEUTSCHES UND DEUTSCH-ENGLISCHES WOERTERBUCH FUER DIE EISEN- UND STAHLINDUSTRIE. T*GE*EN D. FOR IRON/STEEL' IND) VIENNA, SPRINGER, 1955. 168+162P. A55-6643. 8500T.

LVOFF, M. BILDWORT ENGLISCH TECHNISCHE SPRACHHEFTE, HEFT 5. (TECH. EN, ENG. MATER) BERLIN, VDI, 1952. 33P.

RIEDEL, M. AND MOSER, H. LEDER-ABC. (LEATHER ABC, GE DEFS) ED3. LEIPZIG, FACHBUCHVERLAG, 1960. 130P. A60-5167.

SCHNAUCK, W. ET AL. GLASLEXIKON, EIN HANDBUCH FUER HANDWERK, HANDEL UND INDUSTRIE. (GLASS D, HANDBOOK FOR MANUF.COM/IND, GE DEFS) MUNICH, CALLWEY, 1959. 267P. A60-4378. 1300T.

STEGMAIER, W. KERAMISCHES FACHWOERTERBUCH... (CERAMIC GL, V.1, EN*GE 292P. V.2, GE*EN, P) BONN, DEUT. KERAM. GES, 1954-- . 56-36503. 3000T.

WALTHER, R. TERMINOLOGIE UND SPRACHGEBRAUCH DER FESTIGKEITSLEHRE... (*EN/AM*GE STRENGTH OF MATER. T) WISS. Z. HOCHSCH. MASCHINENBAU, KARL-MARX STADT, V.2, PP.163-99 (1960)

WELLINGER, K. ET AL. LUEGER,S LEXIKON DER TECHNIK. (ENCYCL. OF TECH) V.3. WERKSTOFFE UND WERKSTOFF-PRUEFUNG. (IND. MATER/MATER. TESTING, GE DEFS) ED4. STUTTGART, DEUT. VERLAGS-ANSTALT, 1961. 816P. 6200T.

HINDI

RAMCHARAN, . AND KAUSHAL, S.C. GLASS TECHNOLOGY, ENGLISH-HINDI DICTIONARY. ALLAHABAD, HINDI SAHITYA SAMMELAN, 1950. 2000T.

ITALIAN

CARBONI, P. NUOVISSIMA ENCICLOPEDIA DI CHIMICA E MERCEOLOGIA... (ENCYCL.OF CHEM/CHEM.PROD, IT DEFS) MILAN, GOERLICH, 1959. 1072P. 60-42521. 2000T.

JAPANESE

JAPAN. MINISTRY OF EDUCATION. INDUSTRIAL STANDARD VOCABULARY OF RUBBER PRODUCTS. (EN*JA) TOKYO, 1950. 12P. 300T.

JAPAN. MINISTRY OF EDUCATION. VOCABULARY OF MECHANICAL VIBRATION. (EN*JA) TOKYO, 195 . 8P.

POLYGLOT

BRANDT, J. ET AL. EMAILS. EIN WOERTERBUCH IN VIER SPRACHEN. (GE EN FR IT D. OF ENAMELS) LEVERKUSEN, FARBENFABRIKEN BAYER, 1960. 181P. 62-39114.

CANADIAN MANUFACTURERS ASSOCIATION. CANADIAN TRADE INDEX. (FR*EN*PR* SP GL) TORONTO, 1954. 1127P.

CATALOGUS VOOR DE METAAL-INDUSTRIE. (MET.INO. CATALOG, DU*EN*FR*GE*SP GL, PP.273-884) ED2. HAARLEM BOOM-RUYGROK, 1952-3. 922P. 52-28570.

DANSK EXPORTKALENDER. (EXPORT DIREC. OF DENMARK, *DA*EN*FR*GE*SP) COPENHAGEN, KRAKSLEGAT, 1955. 350P. 27-7552. 1400T.

EISEN UND STAHL. DREISPRACHIGES FACHWOERTERBUCH... (IRON/STEEL D, GE EN FR) FRANKFURT/MAIN, MONTAN-/ WIRTSCHAFTSVERLAG, 1960. 196P. 60-28854.

POLYGLOT

ACHAUSDRUECKE AUF DEM GEBIET DES TEXTILEN PRUEFWESENS FUER CHEMIEFASERN. (TEST.T.FOR CHEM.TEXTILE FIBERS, E EN FR) RAYON ZELLWOLLE, V.7(1957) FF.

EDERATION INTERNATIONALE DE LA PRECONTRAINTE. 7-LANGUAGE DICTIONARY OF REINFORCED CONCRETE. (*FR*EN*GE SP*IT*RU*DU) AMSTERDAM, STUVO, 1962. UNPAGED.

INNISH FOREIGN TRADE DIRECTORY. (*FI*EN*FR*GE*RU*SP*SW) HELSINKI, FI,FED.FOR.TRADE, 1957. 528P. 53-34818.

ILLEMOT, L. ET AL. MECHANIKAI TECHNOLOGIA. PT.1, ANYAGSZERKEZETTAN ES ANYAGVIZSGALAT. (D. OF MECH. NG, TESTING/STRUCTURE OF MATER, *HU*EN*GE*RU) (MUSZ. ERT. SZ, NO.11) BUDAPEST, TERRA, 1960. 167P. 3-28979. 1100T.

ILLEMOT, L. ET AL. MECHANIKAI TECHNOLOGIA. PT.2, TECHNOLOGIAI MUVELETEK. (D. OF MECH. ENG. TECH. ALCULATIONS, *HU*EN*GE*RU) (MUSZ. ERT. SZ, NO.12) BUDAPEST, TERRA, 1961. 212P. 63-28979. 1200T.

ANDBOK OEVER SVERIGES INDUSTRI OCH NAERINGSLIV. (SW/FOR/DOMESTIC TRADE DIREC,*SW*EN*FR*GE*SP) STOCKHOLM, OMPASS, 1957. 1700P. 15000T.

HANDBUCH DER INTERNATIONALEN KAUTSCHUKINDUSTRIE. (INTL.RUBBER HANDBOOK, GE EN FR) ZURICH, INTL. WIRTSCHAFTSLIT.1953-- 61-49220. 3000T.

HARADA, S. NEW DICTIONARY OF ENGINEERING TECHNICAL TERMS, ENGLISH-JAPANESE, GERMAN-JAPANESE. TOKYO, KEIBUNSHA, 1955. 352P.

IMPERIAL CHEMICAL INDUSTRIES. A VOCABULARY OF TECHNICAL TERMS USED IN THE RUBBER INDUSTRY. (FR*EN*GE*SP) MANCHESTER,ENG. 1955. 127P. 55-31243. 900T.

INTERNATIONAL ELECTROTECHNICAL COMMISSION. SCHWEIZERISCHES ELEKTROTECHNISCHES KOMITEE...ENZYKLOPAEDIE DER ELEKTRISCHEN ISOLIERSTOFFE... (ENCYCL. OF INSULATORS, GE EN FR IT PL SP SW) ZURICH, 1960. 83P. 61-28675.

INTERNATIONAL INSTITUTE OF WELDING. NOMENCLATURE DES TERMES UTILISES DANS LE CONTROLE PAR ULTRASONS... (ULTRASONIC TESTING T, GE EN FR) PARIS, SOUDURE AUTOGENE, 1959. 27P. 63-28234.

KLEINES AUSSENHANDELSWOERTERBUCH IN ACHT SPRACHEN. (FOR.TRADE D.IN 8 LANG) BERLIN, WIRTSCHAFT, 1960. 280P.

KOLPAKOV, B.T. ET AL. EKSPORTNO-IMPORTNYI SLOVAR. (EXPORT/IMPORT D, RU*EN*AL*BU*CZ*FI*FR*GE*HU*IT*PL*SP) MOSCOW, VNESHTORGIZDAT. 1952-54. 3V. 2392P. 3000T.

KOLPAKOV, B.T. KRATKII VNESHNETORGOVYI SLOVAR. (FOR.TRADE D, RU*AL*BU*CZ*EN*FI*FR*GE*HU*PL*RO*SP) MOSCOW, VNESHTORGIZDAT, 1954. 545P. 55-44311. 1000T.

NEUBERG, H.A. EXPORT-WOERTERBUCH IN 4 SPRACHEN... (EXPORT D. IN 4 LANG, *GE*EN*FR*SP) BERLIN, SCHMIDT, 1960. 289P. A62-290.

NORDISK GLASTEKNISK FORENINGS INTERNATIONALE ORDBOG. (NORWEGIAN GLASS TECH. SOC. INTL.D, DU EN FI FR GE NO SW) VAXJO GLASINSTITUTET,1955.

NORWEGIAN EXPORT DIRECTORY. (*NO*EN*FR*GE*SP) OSLO,NO/EXPORT COUNCIL, 1956. 400P. 57-35292.

PALOTAS, L. ET AL. EPITOANYAGOK. (D. OF BLDG. MATER, HU*EN*GE*RU) (MUSZ. ERT. SZ, NO.1) BUDAPEST, TERRA, 1958. 174P. 59-20131. 1100T.

PERMANENT INTERNATIONAL ASSOCIATION OF NAVIGATION CONGRESSES. DICTIONNAIRE TECHNIQUE ILLUSTRE...(IILUS. TECH. D, *FR*EN*DU*GE*IT*SP) CH. 5. MATERIAUX. (MATER) BRUSSELS, 1951.204P.

PFOHL, E. WARENWOERTERBUCH FUER ALLE INDUSTRIE- ; HANDELS UND GEWERBEZWEIGE. (D.OF MATER/PROD,*GE*EN*FR* RU) ED2. LEIPZIG, BROCKHAUS, 1952. 455P. A54-1878.

RUBBER STICHTING, DELFT. ELSEVIER*S RUBBER DICTIONARY... (*DU*EN*FR*GE*IT*JA*MA*PR*SP*SW) NEW YORK, ELSEVIER, 1959. 1537P. 58-9206. 8000T.

STOECKHERT, K. KUNSTSTOFF-LEXIKON. (PLAST. D, GE*EN*FR*IT*SP) ED3. MUNICH, HANSER, 1961. 408P. 62-58103.

SWEDISH EXPORT DIRECTORY. (*SW*EN*FR*GE*RU*SP) ED4. STOCKHOLM, GEN. EXPORT ASSOC, 1952. 810P.

TEKNISKA NOMENKLATURCENTRALEN. STANDARDISERADE TERMER OCH DEFINITIONER FOER VAERMEBEHANDLING AV METALLISKA MATERIAL. (STD. T/DEFS. FOR HEAT-TREATMENT OF METALS, SW EN/AM FR GE) (PUBL. NO.19S) STOCKHOLM, SEELIG, 1959. 64P. 62-28011.

TIDESTROEM, S.H. ENCYKLOPEDI OEVER RAVAROR OCH MATERIAL... (RAW MATER/PROD.ENCYCL, SW*EN*FR*GE)STOCKHOLM, NORDISK ROTOGRAVYR. 1957. 1912P. 58-33018.

U.S. BUSINESS AND DEFENSE SERVICES ADMINISTRATION. SELECTED U.S. MARKETING TERMS AND DEFINITIONS. (40-43MM-C41.93) (V.,1 EN*FR,V.2 EN*GE, V.3 EN*IT, V.4 EN*SP, V.5 EN*SW) WASHINGTON, 1960. 60-60918. 90T.

WEBSTER, R. DICTIONARY OF MARKETING TERMS, U.S. USAGE. (GE*EN*FR) BASEL, RECHT/GESELLSCHAFT, 1952. 102P. 52-1408.

ZLATOVSKI, G.M. DICTIONNAIRE TRILINGUE DES ESSAIS DES MATERIAUX DE CONSTRUCTION. (D.OF MATER. TESTING,*FR *EN*GE) ED4. PARIS, RILEM, 1956. 451P. 3000T.

RUSSIAN

AKADEMIIA NAUK SSSR. KOM.TEKH.TERM. TERMINOLOGIIA TEORII UPRUGOSTI, ISPYTANII I MEKHANICHESKIKH SVOISTV
MATERIALOV I STROITELNOI MEKHANIKI. (THEORY OF ELASTICITY, TESTING/ MECH. PROP. OF MATER/STRUCT. MECH, R
DEFS) (SB.REK.TERM,NO.14) MOSCOW, 1952. 78P. 54-35126.

ANGLO-RUSSKII SLOVAR PO KAUCHUKU, REZINE I KHIMICHESKIM VOLOKNAM. (EN*RU D. OF RUBBER/SYN. FIBERS)
MOSCOW, FIZMATGIZ, 1962. 260P.

CARPOVICH, E.A. RUSSIAN-ENGLISH METALS AND MACHINES DICTIONARY. NEW YORK, TECH.DICT, 1960. 112P.
60-12013. 9000T.

DERUGUINE, T. RUSSIAN-ENGLISH DICTIONARY OF METALLURGY AND ALLIED SCIENCES. NEW YORK, UNGAR, 1962. 470P.
61-13632. 12000T.

FLEGON, A. ENGLISH-RUSSIAN DICTIONARY, LEATHER AND ALLIED INDUSTRIES. LONDON, 196 .

HOWERTON, P.W. AND AKHONIN, A. RUSSIAN-ENGLISH GLOSSARY OF METALLURGICAL AND METAL-WORKING TERMS.
CAMBRIDGE, MASS. INST. TECH, 1955. 175P. 55-4386. 3500T.

KORNEEV, L.A. KRATKII ANGLO-RUSSKII SLOVAR STEKOLNYKH TERMINOV. (EN*RU GLASS D) MOSCOW, NIIST, 1958.
112P. 2500T.

MACANDREW, A.R. GLOSSARY OF RUSSIAN TECHNICAL TERMS USED IN METALLURGY. NEW YORK, VARANGIAN, 1953.
127P. 53-2032. 6000T.

MIKHAILOV, A.N. ANGLO-RUSSKII KOZHEVENNO-OBUVNOI SLOVAR. (*EN*RU LEATHER/SHOE D) MOSCOW, FIZMATGIZ,
1963. 402P. 15000T.

PUGACHEV, I.A. TOVARNYI SLOVAR. (IND. PRODS. ENCYCL, RU DEFS) MOSCOW, GOSTORGIZDAT, 1956--61. 10V.
57-41279.

ROBESON P. JR. RUSSIAN-ENGLISH GLOSSARY OF ACOUSTICS AND ULTRASONICS. NEW YORK, CONSULTANTS BUR, 1958.
170P. 58-1685. 10000T.

SPANISH

BRITISH IRON AND STEEL FEDERATION. CONCISE IRON AND STEEL DICTIONARY, SPANISH-ENGLISH, ENGLISH-SPANISH.
(NEW SER, NO.4) LONDON, 1957. 82P.

SWEDISH

BRITISH IRON AND STEEL FEDERATION. CONCISE IRON AND STEEL DICTIONARY, ENGLISH-SWEDISH, SWEDISH-ENGLISH.
(NEW SER, NO.3) LONDON, 1954. 44P.

MATHEMATICS (PURE AND APPLIED)

CHINESE

CHUNG-KUO K,O HSUEH YUAN. PIEN I CH,U PAN WEI YUAN HUI. (ACAD. SINICA. COMM. OF PUBL/TRANSL) SHU HSUEN
MING TZ,U. (MATH. T, EN CH) PEKING, SCIENCE, 1956. 117P. C58-5314.

WANG, CHU-HSI ET AL. SHU HSUEH MING TZ,U HUI PIEN. (EN*CH MATH. D) HONG KONG, PRACTICAL SCI, 1961.
117P. C62-4303.

YEH, CH,UNG-CHEN. CHIEN MING SHU HSUEH TZ,U TIEN. (MATH. D. *CH*EN) HONG KONG, HUAN-LI BOOKS, 1962. 306P
C63-23.

CZECH

JEDNOTA CESKOSLOVENSKYCH MATEMATIKU A FYSIKU V PRAZE. NAZVY A ZNACKY SKOLSKE MATEMATIKY. (DEFS/NOTATIONS
IN SCHOOL MATH, CZ DEFS) PRAGUE, STATNI PED. NAKL, 1959. 74P. 61-45056.

ENGLISH

BAKER, C.C.T. DICTIONARY OF MATHEMATICS. LONDON, NEWNES, 1961. 338P.

BALLENTYNE, D.W.G. AND WALKER, L.E.Q. A DICTIONARY OF NAMED EFFECTS AND LAWS IN CHEMISTRY, PHYSICS, AND
MATHEMATICS. ED2. NEW YORK, MACMILLAN, 1961. 234P. 61-1620. 1200T.

GAYNOR, F. CONCISE DICTIONARY OF SCIENCE, PHYSICS, MATHEMATICS, NUCLEONICS, ASTRONOMY, CHEMISTRY. NEW
YORK, PHIL. LIBR, 1959. 546P. 59-16292. 5500T.

INSTITUTE OF RADIO ENGINEERS. STANDARDS ON INFORMATION THEORY, DEFINITIONS OF TERMS. (58 IRE 11.S1)
PROC. IRE V.46, 1646-8 (1958) 30T.

INSTITUTE OF RADIO ENGINEERS. STANDARDS ON LETTER SYMBOLS AND MATHEMATICAL SIGNS. (REPRINTED, 57 IRE
21.S1) PROC. IRE V.4S, 1140-7 (1957) 400T.

KARUSH,W. AND TARCOV, O. THE CRESCENT DICTIONARY OF MATHEMATICS. NEW YORK, MACMILLAN, 1962. 313P.
61-17163. 2500T.

KOBER, H. DICTIONARY OF CONFORMAL REPRESENTATIONS. NEW YORK, DOVER, 1952. 208P. 52-12554.

84

ENGLISH

CDOWELL, C.H. A DICTIONARY OF MATHEMATICS. LONDON, CASSELL, 1961. 136P.

CDOWELL, C.H. A SHORT DICTIONARY OF MATHEMATICS. PATERSON, N.J, LITTTLEFIELD, ADAMS, 1962. 103P. 1500T.

ACKAY, D.M. THE NOMENCLATURE OF INFORMATION THEORY. IRE TRANS. INFORM. THEORY, PP. 9-21 (FEB. 1953) 70T.

ITTY, M.B. ET AL. DICTIONARY OF PHYSICS AND MATHEMATICS ABBREVIATIONS, SIGNS, SYMBOLS AND TABLES. NEW ORK, SETI, 1963. 288P.

FRENCH

ICTIONNAIRE DES SCIENCES MATHEMATIQUES, ASTRONOMIE, PHYSIQUE, CHIMIE. (D. OF MATH, ASTRON, PHYS, CHEM, R DEFS) PARIS, SEGHERS, 1962. 336P.

OLY, A. DICTIONNAIRE DE MATHEMATIQUES. (D. OF MATH, FR DEFS) PARIS, HACHETTE, 1956. 252P. 56-33423. 200T.

UGLER, C. DICTIONNAIRE HISTORIQUE DE LA TERMINOLOGIE GEOMETRIQUE DES GRECS. (HIST. D. OF GR GEOM, FR EFS) PARIS, KLINCKSIECK, 1958-- .

GERMAN

LEKSANDROV, P.S. ET AL. ENZYKLOPAEDIE DER ELEMENTARMATHEMATIK. (ENCYCL. OF ELEM. MATH, GE DEFS) BERLIN, EB, 1954-- . 55-33361.

FLUEGGE, S. ET AL. HANDBUCH DER PHYSIK. (ENCYCL. OF PHYS) V.41, PT.1, KERNREAKTIONEN 2, THEORIE. (NUCL. REACTIONS 2, THEOR,*GE*EN GL,PP.561-80, 650T) BERLIN, SPRINGER 1959. 580P. A56-2942.

FLUEGGE, S. ET AL. HANDBUCH DER PHYSIK. (ENCYCL. OF PHYS) MATHEMATISCHE METHODEN. (MATH. METHODS, GE*EN GL, V.1, PP.353-64, 700T. V.2, PP.499-520, 700T) BERLIN, SPRINGER, 1955-56. A56-2942.

FLUEGGE, S. ET AL. HANDBUCH DER PHYSIK. (ENCYCL. OF PHYS) V.4, PRINZIPIEN DER ELEKTRODYNAMIK UND RELATIVITAETSTHEORIE. (PRINCIPLES OF ELECTRODYN/RELATIVITY,*GE*EN GL, PP.273-90, 500T) BERLIN, SPRINGER, 1962. 290P. A56-2942.

FLUEGGE, S. ET AL. HANDBUCH DER PHYSIK. (ENCYCL. OF PHYS) V.5/1, PRINZIPIEN DER QUANTENTHEORIE I. (PRINCIPLES OF QUANTUM THEORY, *GE*EN GL, PP.365-76, 700T) BERLIN, SPRINGER, 1958. 376P. A56-2942.

HERLAND, L.J. WOERTERBUCH DER MATHEMATISCHEN WISSENSCHAFTEN. (D. OF MATH. SCI, V.1, GE*EN 235P. V.2, EN*GE 336P) NEW YORK, UNGAR, 1951-54. 51-13545. 7000T.

HYMAN, C.J. GERMAN-ENGLISH MATHEMATICS DICTIONARY. NEW YORK, INTERLANG. DICT, 1960. 131P. 59-15818. 6000T.

KLAFTEN, B. MATHEMATISCHES VOKABULAR ENGLISCH-DEUTSCH, DEUTSCH-ENGLISCH. (*GE*EN* D. OF MATH) MUNICH, WILA, 1961. 186P. A61-5180. 2000T.

MACINTYRE, S. AND WITTE, E. GERMAN-ENGLISH MATHEMATICAL VOCABULARY. NEW YORK, INTERSCIENCE, 1956. 95P. 56-58097. 2500T.

MEYERS GROSSER RECHENDUDEN... (MATH. D, GE DEFS) MANNHEIM, DUDENVERLAG, 1962. 1002P. 63-2485.

NAAS, J. AND SCHMID, H.L. MATHEMATISCHES WOERTERBUCH. MIT EINBEZIEHUNG DER THEORETISCHEN PHYSIK. (D. OF MATH, THEOR, PHYS, GE DEFS) ED2. BERLIN, AKADEMIE, 1962. 2V. 1043+952P. 62-2409. 12000T.

TRAPP, V. STATISTISCHES WOERTERBUCH, ENGLISCH-DEUTCH. (EN*GE* STAT. D) ED2. MUNICH, DEUT. STAT. GES, 1956. 130P.

ITALIAN

BERZOLARI, L. ENCICLOPEDIA DELLE MATEMATICHE ELEMENTARI... (ENCYCL. OF ELEM. MATH, IT DEFS) MILAN, HDEPLI, 1930-54. 3V. 34-35033.

JAPANESE

IYANAGA, S. AND YOKOCHI, K. SUGAKU KYOIKU JITEN. (MATH. D, JA DEFS) TOKYO, MEIJI, 1961. 15+638P. J61-1541.

JAPAN. MINISTRY OF EDUCATION. JAPANESE SCIENTIFIC TERMS, MATHEMATICS. (*JA*EN) TOKYO, DAINIPPON TOSHO, 1957. 146P. 1500 MATH. T. 600 MATH. STAT. T.

JAPAN. MINISTRY OF EDUCATION. VOCABULARIES OF STATISTICS, RELATED MATHEMATICS, SAMPLING SURVEYS. (*JA*EN) TOKYO, 1950-51. VAR. PP. 750T.

POLYGLOT

BOLL, L. ET AL. MATHEMATISCHES WOERTERBUCH. (MATH. D, RU EN GE) BERLIN, VEB, 1959. 244P. 59-4101. 7000T.

FREIBERGER, W.F. ET AL. THE INTERNATIONAL DICTIONARY OF APPLIED MATHEMATICS (EN DEFS,*FR*GE*RU*SP) PRINCETON, N.J, VAN NOSTRAND, 1960. 1173P. 60-16931. 8300T.

JAMES, G. ET AL. MATHEMATICS DICTIONARY. MULTILINGUAL ED. (EN DEFS,*FR*GE*RU*SP) PRINCETON, N.J, VAN NOSTRAND, 1959. 546P. 59-8656. 4000T.

MATHEMATICS (PURE AND APPLIED)

POLYGLOT

KENDALL,M.G. AND BUCKLAND, W.R. DICCIONARIO DE TERMINOS ESTADISTICOS. (STAT.T, *SP*EN*FR*GE*IT) ROSARIO ARGENTINA, INST. INTERAM. ESTADISTICA, 1959. 482P. 1700T.

KENDALL, M.G. AND BUCKLAND, W.R. A DICTIONARY OF STATISTICAL TERMS... (EN DEFS, *FR*GE*IT*SP GL) ED2. NEW YORK, HAFNER, 1960. 575P. 61-1171.

KENDALL, M.G. AND BUCKLAND, W.R. DICTIONARY OF STATISTICAL TERMS. (EN*FR*GE*IT*SP) SUPPL. TO ED2. NEW YORK, HAFNER, 1960. 83P.

MATHEMATICAL SOCIETY OF JAPAN. IWANAMI SUGAKU JITEN. (MATH. D, JA*EN*FR*GE) TOKYO, IWANAMI, 1954. 591+98+89P. 2000T.

POLSKA AKADEMIIA NAUK. INSTYTUT MATEMATYCZNY SLOWNIK POLSKO-ROSYJSKO-ANGIELSKI STATYSTYKI MATEMATYCZNEJ I STATYSTYCZNEJ KONTROLI JAKOSCI PRODUKCJI. (PL*EN*RU D. OF MATH. STAT/IND. STAT. CONTROL) WARSAW, PANSTW. WYDAW.NAUK, 1958. 48P. 59-34620. 540T.

SPAIN. INSTITUTO NACIONAL DE ESTADISTICA. VOCABULARIO ESTADISTICO PLURILINGUE. (*SP*EN*EO*FR*GE*HU*IT *NO*PR*RU*SW STAT. GLI MADRID, I.N.E.ARTES GRAFICAS, 1959. 189P. 400T.

WARSAW. PANSTWOWY INSTYTUT MATEMATYCZNY. SLOWNIK ROSYJSKO-POLSKI I ANGIELSKO-POLSKI TERMINOW STATYSTYKI MATEMATYCZNEJ. (RU EN*PL D. OF MATH.STAT) WARSAW, NAKL.POLSK.TOW.MAT, 1952. 20P. 55-28826.

PORTUGUESE

SILVA RODRIGUES, M.C. VOCABULARIO BRASILERIO DE ESTATISTICA, SEGUIDO DE UM VOCABULARIO INGLES-PORTUGUES. (EN*PR GL. OF STAT) SAO PAULO, UNIV, 1956. 304P. 61-26731.

RUSSIAN

AKADEMIIA NAUK SSSR. ANGLO-RUSSKII SLOVAR MATEMATICHESKIKH TERMINOV. (EN*RU D. OF MATH) MOSCOW, IZD. INOSTR. LIT. 1962. 369P. 63-30041. 12000T.

AMERICAN MATHEMATICAL SOCIETY. RUSSIAN-ENGLISH VOCABULARY WITH A GRAMMATICAL SKETCH... NEW YORK, 1950. 66P. 51-600. 2800T.

BURLAK, J. AND BROOKE, K. RUSSIAN-ENGLISH MATHEMATICAL VOCABULARY. EDINBURGH, OLIVER/BOYD, 1963. 256P.

EMIN, I. ET AL. RUSSIAN-ENGLISH GLOSSARY OF NAMED EFFECTS, LAWS, AND REACTIONS AND MISCELLANEOUS TERMS I PHYSICS, MATHEMATICS AND ASTRONOMY. NEW YORK, INTERLANG. DICT, 1962. 22P. 62-51916. 2000T.

GUBIN, P.A. DICTIONARY OF MATHEMATICAL SCIENCES. (RU EN) NEW YORK, UNGAR. (IN PREP)

KRAMER, A.A. RUSSKO-ANGLIISKII MATEMATICHESKII SLOVAR. (RU*EN MATH. D) TRENTON, 1961. 123P. 61-27972. 5000T.

LOHWATER, A.J. AND GOULD, S.H. RUSSIAN-ENGLISH DICTIONARY OF MATHEMATICAL SCIENCES. PROVIDENCE, AM.MAT SOC, 1961. 267P. 61-15685. 12000T.

MILNE-THOMSON, L.M. RUSSIAN-ENGLISH MATHEMATICAL DICTIONARY... MADISON, UNIV. WISC. PRESS, 1962. 191P. 62-7217. 10000T.

SLOVAK

SLOVENSKA AKADEMIA VIED. TERMINOLOGIA ELEMENTARNEJ MATEMATIKY. (ELEM.MATH, SL DEFS) BRATISLAVA, 1957. 99P. 57-45744.

SPANISH

VERA, F. MATEMATICA, LEXICON KAPELUSZ. (D. OF MATH, SP DEFS) BUENOS AIRES, KAPELUSZ, 1960. 734P. 60-38757.

MECHANICAL ENGINEERING

CHINESE

CHUNG-KUO K,O HSUEH YUAN. PIEN I CHU. (ACAD. SINICA. BUR. OF COMPILATIONS/TRANSL) CHIEH KOU KUNG CH.ENG MING T,ZU. (STRUCT. ENG. T, CH EN) PEKING, 1954.

FAN, FENG-YUAN. TU CHIEH CHI HSIEH TUNG TAO TZ,U TIEN. (MACH. D, CH EN) SHANGHAI, SCIENCE, 1951. 246P. C61-1282.

LIU, HSIEN-CHOU. CHI HSIEH KUNG CHENG MING TZ,U. (MECH. ENG. T, EN*CHI HONG KONG, COMMERCIAL PRESS, 1961. 228P. C63-357.

CZECH

BARES, K. ANGLICKE ODBORNE TEXTY PRO STROJNI INZENYRSTVI. (CZ*EN MECH. ENG. D) PRAGUE, SNTL, 1957. 143P.

VORACEK, Z. TEXTY ANGLICTINY PRO FAKULTU STROJNIHO INZENYRSTVI. (CZ*EN MECH. ENG. D) PRAGUE, SNTL, 195 2V. 350P.

RUSSIAN

AKADEMIIA NAUK SSSR. KOM.TEKH.TERM. TERMINOLOGIIA TEORII UPRUGOSTI, ISPYTANII I MEKHANICHESKIKH SVOISTV MATERIALOV I STROITELNOI MEKHANIKI. (THEORY OF ELASTICITY, TESTING/ MECH. PROP. OF MATER/STRUCT. MECH, RU DEFS) (SB.REK.TERM,NO.14) MOSCOW, 1952. 78P. 54-35126.

AKADEMIIA NAUK SSSR. KOM.TEKH.TERM. ZUBCHATYE KOLESA, ZATSEPLENIIA I PEREDACHI S POSTOIANNYM PEREDATOCHNYM OTNOSHENIEM, TERMINOLOGIIA. (GEARING, TRANSMISSION... RU DEFS) (SB. REK. TERM. NO.57) MOSCOW, 1962. 67P.

BELKIND, L.D. ANGLO-RUSSKII SLOVAR PO DETALIAM MASHIN, S PRILOZHENIEM ALFAVITNOGO UKAZATELIA RUSSKIKH TERMINOV. (*EN*RU D. OF MACH.PARTS) MOSCOW, FIZMATGIZ, 1959. 309P. 60-19671. 10000T.

KRECHETNIKOV, S.I. ANGLO-RUSSKII SLOVAR PO MASHINOSTROENIIU I METALLOOBRABOTKE. (EN*RU D.OF MACH.DESIGN/ METAL-WORKING) ED2. MOSCOW, FIZMATGIZ, 1961. 678P. 61-44360. 30000T.

NARTOV, I.M. ANGLO-RUSSKII SLOVAR PO GAZOTURBINNYM USTANOVKAM. (*EN*RU D. OF GAS TURBINES) LENINGRAD, SUDOSTROIIZDAT, 1962. 214P. 63-31811.

SLOVAK

SLOVENSKA AKADEMIA VIED. TERMINOLOGIA CASTI STROJOV. (MACH.PARTS, SL DEFS) BRATISLAVA, 1952. 89P. 59-23657.

SPANISH

GUINLE, R.L. MODERN SPANISH-ENGLISH, ENGLISH-SPANISH TECHNICAL AND ENGINEERING DICTIONARY...NEW YORK, DUTTON, 1959. 311P. 15000T.

ROBB, L.A. ENGINEERS DICTIONARY, SPANISH-ENGLISH AND ENGLISH-SPANISH. ED2. NEW YORK, WILEY, 1956. 664P. 56-4369. 30000T.

METALLURGY AND METALLOGRAPHY

CZECH

FURCH, J. SEZNAM ANGLICKO-CESKYCH HORNICKYCH VYRAZU. (EN*CZ MIN. GL) PRAGUE, MAT. HORN-HUTN, 1952. 430P.

ENGLISH

AMERICAN FOUNDRYMEN,S SOCIETY. A.F.S. GLOSSARY OF FOUNDRY TERMS. CHICAGO, 1953. 77P. 58-35922.

AMERICAN INSTITUTE OF ELECTRICAL ENGINEERS. DEFINITIONS OF ELECTRICAL TERMS. ELECTROCHEMISTRY AND ELECTROMETALLURGY. (GR-60, ASA C42.60) NEW YORK, 1956.30P. 300T.

AMERICAN SOCIETY FOR TESTING/MATERIALS. STANDARD DEFINITIONS OF TERMS RELATING TO REFRACTORIES. (C71-62) ASTM STDS, PT.5, SUPPL, 78-80. PHILADELPHIA, 1962. 60T.

AMERICAN SOCIETY FOR TESTING/MATERIALS. TENTATIVE DEFINITIONS OF TERMS RELATING TO ELECTROPLATING. (B374-62T) ASTM STDS, PT.2, SUPPL.203-12. PHILADELPHIA, 1962. 250T.

AMERICAN SOCIETY FOR TESTING/ MATERIALS. STANDARD DEFINITIONS OF TERMS USED IN POWDER METALLURGY. (B243-61) ASTM STDS, PT.2, 1028-32. PHILADELPHIA, 1961. 120T.

AMERICAN SOCIETY FOR TESTING/MATERIALS. TENTATIVE DEFINITIONS OF TERMS RELATING TO HEAT TREATMENT OF METALS (E44-50T) ASTM STDS, PT. 2, 1650-5. PHILADELPHIA, 1961. 100T.

AMERICAN SOCIETY FOR TESTING/MATERIALS. TENTATIVE DEFINITIONS OF TERMS RELATING TO METALLOGRAPHY. (E7-55T) ASTM STDS, PT.3, 808-48. PHILADELPHIA, 1961. 700T.

AMERICAN SOCIETY FOR TESTING/MATERIALS. TENTATIVE DEFINITIONS OF TERMS RELATING TO WROUGHT IRON. (A81-60T) ASTM STDS, PT.1, 1429. PHILADELPHIA, 1961. 10T.

AMERICAN SOCIETY FOR TESTING/MATERIALS. TENTATIVE INDUSTRIAL RADIOGRAPHIC TERMINOLOGY FOR USE IN RADIOGRAPHIC INSPECTION OF CASTINGS AND WELDMENTS. (E52-49T) ASTM STDS, PT.3, 961-2. PHILADELPHIA, 1961. 20T.

AUSTRALIAN INSTITUTE OF METALS. DEFINITIONS OF TERMS USED IN THE HEAT TREATMENT AND TESTING OF METALS. ED2. MELBOURNE, 1957. 88P. 58-42063.

BRIGGS, C.W. STEEL CASTINGS HANDBOOK. (GL, PP.624-48, 300T) ED3. CLEVELAND, STEEL FOUNDERS SOC. AM, 1960. 670P. 60-52114.

BRITISH IRON AND STEEL RESEARCH ASSOCIATION. SURFACE DEFECTS IN INGOTS AND THEIR PRODUCTS. (RECOMMENDED DEFS)... ED2. LONDON, 1958. 58P. A59-4707.

BRITISH STANDARDS INSTITUTION. GLOSSARY OF TERMS RELATING TO IRON AND STEEL. (B.S.2094) PTS.1-8, LONDON, 1954-56. 1400T.

BRITISH STANDARDS INSTITUTION. GLOSSARY OF TERMS RELATING TO THE MANUFACTURE AND USE OF REFRACTORY MATERIALS. (B.S.3446) LONDON, 1962. 87P. 600T.

BRITISH STANDARDS INSTITUTION. GLOSSARY OF TERMS USED IN THE WROUGHT ALUMINIUM INDUSTRY. (B.S. 3660) LONDON, 1963. 40P. 450T.

ENGLISH

GLOSSARY OF TERMS USED IN METAL CLEANING AND FINISHING. IRON AGE, V.174, F49-65 (1954) 110T.

HENDERSON, J.G. AND BATES, J.M. METALLURGICAL DICTIONARY. NEW YORK, REINHOLD, 1953. 396P. 53-12371.4000T.

THE IRON AGE. HANDBOOK OF TERMS COMMONLY USED IN THE STEEL INDUSTRY. NEW YORK, 1953. 30P. 59-47587.

MERRIMAN, A.D. A DICTIONARY OF METALLURGY. LONDON, MACDONALD/EVANS, 1958. 401P. 59-480. 4000T.

MILLER, W. GLOSSARY OF TERMS FREQUENTLY USED IN SOLID STATE PHYSICS. NEW YORK, AM. INST.PHY6. 1959. 26P. 200T.

OSBORNE, A.K. AN ENCYCLOPAEDIA OF THE IRON AND STEEL INDUSTRY. NEW YORK, PHIL. LIBR, 1956. 558P. 56-14371.

PRYOR, E.J. DICTIONARY OF MINERAL TECHNOLOGY. LONDON, MINING PUBL, 1963. 437P.

ROLFE, R.T. A DICTIONARY OF METALLOGRAPHY. NEW YORK, CHEMICAL, 1955. 287P. A 57-5037. 1000T.

SOCIETY OF AUTOMOTIVE ENGINEERS. DEFINITIONS OF HEAT-TREATING TERMS,PP.79-81. SAE HANDBOOK, NEW YORK,1961. 914P. 120T.

WINFIELD, H. A GLOSSARY OF METALWORKING TERMS. LONDON, BLACKIE, 1960.80P. 60-51881. 800T.

WITTY, M.B. ET AL. DICTIONARY OF METALLURGICAL ABBREVIATIONS. NEW YORK, SETI, 196 .

WOLDMAN, N.E. ENGINEERING ALLOYS. ED4. NEW YORK, REINHOLD, 1962. 62-19661. 35000T.

ZIMMERMAN, O.T. AND LAVINE, I. HANDBOOK OF MATERIAL TRADE NAMES. DOVER, N.H, IND. RES. SERV, 1953. 794P. SUPPL.1,1956. 383P. SUPPL.2, 1957. 356P. SUPPL.3, 1960. 400P. 53-1074.

FRENCH

BADER, O. AND THERET, M.   DICTIONNAIRE DE METALLURGIE. (MET.D, *EN*FR) PARIS. EYROLLES, 1961. 701P. A62-812. 1400T.

BRITISH CAST IRON RESEARCH ASSOCIATION. A GLOSSARY OF FRENCH-ENGLISH, ENGLISH-FRENCH FOUNDRY AND METALLURGICAL TERMS. BIRMINGHAM, ENG, 1959. 28P. 2000T.

BRITISH IRON AND STEEL FEDERATION. CONCISE IRON AND STEEL DICTIONARY, FRENCH-ENGLISH, ENGLISH-FRENCH. (NEW SER, NO.1) LONDON, 1957. 38P.

CENTRE TECHNIQUE DES INDUSTRIES DE LA FONDERIE. VOCABULAIRE DE FONDERIE... ANGLAIS-FRANCAIS. (EN*FR FOUNDRY GL) PARIS, 1953. 77P. 54-27387. 1200T.

CHARLES, V. VOCABULAIRE DU METALLURGISTE... (MET. GL, FR DEFS) PARIS, GAUTHIER-VILLARS, 1956. 166P. 57-22265. 1700T.

FRANCE. AMBASSADE. U.S GLOSSAIRE DE L.INDUSTRIE SIDERURGIQUE.   (EN*FR MET. GL) WASHINGTON, (IN PREP)

PROULX, G. ELECTROCHIMIE ET ELECTROMETALLURGIE, GLOSSAIRE ANGLAIS-FRANCIS, BT-48. (ELECTROCHEM/ ELECTROMET, EN*FR GL) OTTAWA, DEPT. SECY. STATE, 1956. 21P. 500T.

GERMAN

BLASBERG-LEXIKON FUER KORROSIONSSCHUTZ UND MODERNE GALVANOTECHNIK. (ANTI-CORROSION/METAL-PLATING D, GE DEFS) ED3. SAULGAU, WUERTTEMBERG, LEUZE, 1960. 366P. 500T.

BRITISH IRON AND STEEL FEDERATION. CONCISE IRON AND STEEL DICTIONARY, GERMAN-ENGLISH, ENGLISH-GERMAN. (NEW SER, NO.2) LONDON, 1957. 57P.

CAPITO UND KLEIN, A.G. NIROSTA BLECHE, WERKSTOFF UND VERARBEITUNG VON A-Z. (NIROSTA STAINLESS-STEEL SHEETS, GE DEFS) ED2. DUESSELDORF-BENRATH, 1960. 238P. 63-26793.

DETTNER, H.W. FACHWOERTERBUCH FUER DIE METALLOBERFLAECHENVEREDELUNG... (*GE*EN D. OF MET. FINISHING) BERLIN, SIEMENS, 1960. 391P. A60-5542. 8500T.

KOEHLER, E.L. AND .LEGAT, A. ENGLISCH-DEUTSCHES UND DEUTSCH-ENGLISCHES WOERTERBUCH FUER DIE EISEN- UND STAHLINDUSTRIE. (*GE*EN D. FOR IRON/STEEL IND) VIENNA, SPRINGER, 1955. 168+162P. A55-6643. 8500T.

LENK, G. VERGLEICHENDE BEGRIFFSBESTIMMUNG VON DEUTSCHEN, ENGLISCHEN UND AMERIKANISCHEN FACHAUSDRUECKEN AUF DEM GEBIETE DER FEUERFLUESSIGEN UND ELEKTROLYTISCHEN KUPFERRAFFINATION. (COPPER REFINING GL, GE*EN) CLAUSTHAL-ZELLERFELD, GES. DEUT. METALLHUETTEN/BERGLEUTE, 1952. 89P.

LENK, G. AND BOERNER, H. TECHNISCHES FACHWOERTERBUCH DER GRUNDSTOFF-INDUSTRIEN... (TECH.D. FOR BASIC IND (V.1, EN*GE, 638P. 1958. V.2, GE*EN, 734P. 1962) ED2. GOETTINGEN, VANDENHOECK/RUPRECHT, 1958-62. A59-324. 45000T.

LUEGERS LEXIKON DER TECHNIK. (ENCYCL. OF TECH) V.5, LEXIKON DER HUETTENTECHNIK. (MET. ENG. D, GE DEFS) ED4. DUESSELDORF, STAHLEISEN, 1963. 720P. 3500T.

SCHULENBURG, A. ET AL. GIESSEREI-LEXIKON... (FOUNDRY D, GE DEFS) ED3. BERLIN, SCHIELE/SCHOEN, 1962. 1082P. 63-38519. 7000T.

GERMAN

SPEER, G. WOERTERBUCH DER GIESSEREIKUNDE. (FOUNDRY D, GE DEFS) BERLIN, TECHNIK, 1953. 165P. 56-15361.

VEREIN DEUTSCHER EISENHUETTENLEUTE. STAHLEISEN-WOERTERBUCH, DEUTSCH-ENGLISCH, ENGLISCH-DEUTSCH. (*GE*EN IRON/STEEL D) ED2. DUESSELDORF, STAHLEISEN, 1962. 338P. 63-34657.

JAPANESE

CASTING INSTITUTE OF JAPAN. DICTIONARY OF CASTING TERMS... (JA EN) TOKYO, NIKKAN KOGYO SHIMBUNSHA, 1957. 142P.

JAPAN. MINISTRY OF EDUCATION. JAPANESE SCIENTIFIC TERMS, MINING AND METALLURGY. (*JA*EN) TOKYO, MIN.INST. JAPAN, 1954. 263P. 3600T.

JAPAN. MINISTRY OF EDUCATION. STANDARD VOCABULARY FOR METALLURGICAL INDUSTRY. (EN*JA) TOKYO, 1952. 12P. 370T.

OWAKU, S. AND TERAZAWA, M. KINZOKU JUTSUGO JITEN. (MET. D, JA EN) TOKYO, AGUNE, 1960. 378+10+13P. J62-130.

NORWEGIAN

NORGES GULLSMEDFORBUND. ENGELSK ORDLISTE FOR GULLSMEDFAGET. (*NO*EN GOLDSMITHING T) OSLO, 1953. 11P. 56-31158. 400T.

POLYGLOT

BRABEC, J. AND HELLMANN, B. SLEVARENSKY SLOVNIK RUSKO-CESKY A ANGLICKO-CESKY. (FOUNDRY D, *CZ EN RU) PRAGUE, SNTL,1953. 155P. 54-39200. 5000T.

CATALOGUS VOOR DE METAAL-INDUSTRIE. (MET.IND. CATALOG, DU*EN*FR*GE*SP GL, PP.273-884) ED2. HAARLEM BOOM-RUYGROK. 1952-3. 922P. 52-28570.

CENTRE DE DOCUMENTATION SIDERURGIQUE. DICTIONNAIRE SIDERURGIQUE. (MET.D, CZ EN FR GE IT PR RU SP SW) PARIS, 1953.

CHUNG-KUO K,O HSUEH YUAN. PIEN I CHU. (ACAD. SINICA. BUR. OF COMPILATIONS/TRANSL) YEH CHIN HSUEH MING TZ,U. (MET. T, EN RU CH) PEKING, 1955. 524P. C58-5151.

CLASON, W.E. ELSEVIER,S DICTIONARY OF METALLURGY,*DU*EN*FR*GE*IT*SP) NEW YORK, ELSEVIER. 102P. (IN PREP)

EISEN UND STAHL. DREISPRACHIGES FACHWOERTERBUCH... (IRON/STEEL D, GE EN FR) FRANKFURT/MAIN, MONTAN-/ WIRTSCHAFTSVERLAG, 1960. 196P. 60-28854.

GIERDZIEJEWSKI, K. ET AL. SLOWNIK TERMINOLOGII ODLEWNICTWA... (FOUNDRY D, *PL*EN*CZ*FR*GE*RU) WARSAW, PANSTW.WYDAW.TECH, 1961. 391P. 61-28721. 1200T.

GIERDZIEJEWSKI, K. ET AL. VOCABULARY OF FOUNDRY PRACTICE, IN 6 LANGUAGES... (*PL*EN*CZ*FR*GE*RU) NEW YORK, PERGAMON, 1963. 306P. 62-15654. 1200T.

HEILER, T. TECHNISCHES BILDWOERTERBUCH FUER SPANNENDE WERKZEUGE ZUR METALLBEARBEITUNG. (PICTURE GL. OF METAL-EXTRUSION MACH, *GE*EN*FR*IT*SP) MUNICH, HANSER, 1963. 460P.

HERSCU, G. ET. AL. DICTIONARY OF ROLLING MILL TERMS, EN FR GE SP. NEW YORK, ELSEVIER. 500P. 5400T. (IN PREP)

HRUSA, J. PRIRUCNI TECHNICKY SLOVNIK PRO HUTNICTVI A KOVOPRUMYSL. (MET/STEEL IND. D, CZ*EN*FR*GE*IT*SP) PRAGUE, 195 . 107P. 1000T.

HUTNICKE NAZVOSLOVI. SUROVE ZELEZO A JEHO VYROBA. (MET. T, IRON ORE PROCESS, *CZ*RU*GE*EN) PRAGUE, 1959. 340P.

ILVA, ALTI FORNI E ACCIAIERIE D,ITALIA, S.P.A. DIZIONARIO TECNICO. (TECH. D, IT EN FR GE SP) GENOA, 1956. 55P. 60-21394. 850T.

INTERNATIONAL ELECTROTECHNICAL COMMISSION. INTERNATIONAL ELECTROTECHNICAL VOCABULARY. ELECTROCHEMISTRY AND ELECTROMETALLURGY, *FR*EN*DU*GE*IT*PL*PR*SP*SW. (IEC-50-GR-50) ED2. GENEVA, (IN PREP)

INTERNATIONAL FOUNDRY DICTIONARY COMMITTEE. DICTIONNAIRE INTERNATIONAL DE FONDERIE. (INTL. FOUNDRY D, *FR*GE*EN*SP*IT*DU*NO*SW) PARIS, DUNOD, 1962. 482P. 63-40325. 1900T.

INTERNATIONAL WROUGHT NON-FERROUS METALS COUNCIL. GLOSSARY OF TERMS APPLICABLE TO WROUGHT PRODUCTS IN COPPER,ZINC, BRASS AND OTHER COPPER ALLOYS. (*GE*EN*FR) BIRMINGHAM, ENG, 1956. 87P. 130T.

KANEKO, K. DICTIONARY OF METAL INDUSTRY... (JA EN GE) TOKYO, TEKKO SHIMBUNSHA, 1955. 675P.

LEMPICKI, J. ET AL. SZESCIOJEZYCZNY SLOWNIK MASZYN I URZADZEN ODLEWNIEZYCH. (6-LANG. D. OF FOUNDRY EQUIP, *PL*EN*CZ*FR*GE*RU) CRACOW, NAKL. STOWARZ. TECH. ODLEWN. POLSK, 1958. 127P. 61-24758.

NORWAY. RADET FOR TEKNISK TERMINOLOGI. METALLURGY. (RTT-10) (*EN*GE*NO) OSLO, 1962. 127P.

POLYGLOT

NOVITSKY, A. DICCIONARIO MINERO-METALURGICO-GEOLOGICO-MINERALOGICO-PETROGRAFICO Y DE PETROLEO. (D. OF MIN, MET, GEOL, MINERAL, PETROGR/PETROL, *SP*EN*FR*GE*RU) BUENOS AIRES, 1958. 2V. 217P. 18000T.

SIMANDL, D. SEDMIJAZYCNY SLOVNICEK PRO PRACOVNIKY HRUDKOVEN. (7-LANG.STEEL MILL GL, MNISEK/BRDY, 1960. 69P. 62-36510.

TEKNISKA NOMENKLATURCENTRALEN. (CORROSION D,SW DEFS, *EN*GE GL) STOCKHOLM,INGENIOERSVETENSKAPSAKADEMIEN, 1957. 72P. 140T.

TEKNISKA NOMENKLATURCENTRALEN. PULVERMETALLURGISK ORDLISTA. (POWDER METAL. GL, SW EN FR GE) STOCKHOLM, 1961. 48P.

TEKNISKA NOMENKLATURCENTRALEN. STANDARDISERADE TERMER OCH DEFINITIONER FOER VAERMEBEHANDLING AV METALLISH MATERIAL. (STD. T/DEFS. FOR HEAT-TREATMENT OF METALS, SW EN/AM FR GE) (PUBL. NO.19S) STOCKHOLM, SEELIG 1959. 64P. 62-28011.

UNITED STATES STEEL CORPORATION. CONCISE ENGLISH-JAPANESE DICTIONARY OF TERMS IN IRON AND STEEL INDUSTR (EN*JA, APPENDIX, EN FR GE JA) TOKYO, IRON/STEEL UNION, JAPAN, 1954. 115P.

VIERSPRACHIGE NOMENKLATUR FUER GIESS-SYSTEME. (GE EN FR SW FOUNDRY T) GIESSEREI, V.40, 617-9 (1953) 60T

RUSSIAN

AKADEMIIA NAUK SSSR. KOM.TEKH.TERM. OBRABOTKA METALLOV DAVLENIEM... (METAL-WORKING BY PRESSURE, RU DEFS) (SB. REK. TERM. NO.55) MOSCOW, 1961. 25P. 62-29464.

AKADEMIIA NAUK SSSR. KOM. TEKH. TERM. OBRABOTKA METALLOV DAVLENIEM, VOLOCHENIE, TERMINOLOGIIA. (METAL WORKING BY DRAWING/PRESSURE, RU DEFS) (SB. REK. TERM, NO.61) MOSCOW, 1962. 15P. 63-42867.

AKADEMIIA NAUK SSSR. KOM. TEKH. TERM. TERMINOLOGIIA PO KORROZII I ZASHCHITE METALLOV. (CORR/ANTI-CORR. OF MET, RU DEFS) (SB. REK. TERM. NO.4) MOSCOW, 1951. 42P. 54-35127.

BRITISH IRON AND STEEL FEDERATION. CONCISE IRON AND STEEL DICTIONARY, ENGLISH-RUSSIAN, RUSSIAN-ENGLISH. (NEW SER, NO.5) LONDON, 1959. 110P.

CARPOVICH, E.A. RUSSIAN-ENGLISH METALS AND MACHINES DICTIONARY. NEW YORK, TECH.DICT, 1960. 112P. 60-12013. 9000T.

DERUGUINE, T. RUSSIAN-ENGLISH DICTIONARY OF METALLURGY AND ALLIED SCIENCES. NEW YORK, UNGAR, 1962. 470P 61-13632. 12000T.

DERUGUINE, T. STEEL DICTIONARY, RUSSIAN-ENGLISH. NEW YORK, UNGAR, 196 . 248P. (IN PREP)

EMIN,I. RUSSIAN-ENGLISH GLOSSARY OF SOLID STATE PHYSICS. NEW YORK, CONSULTANTS BUR, 1958. 90P. 58-909. 40000T.

HOWERTON, P.W. AND AKHONIN, A. RUSSIAN-ENGLISH GLOSSARY OF METALLURGICAL AND METAL-WORKING TERMS. CAMBRIDGE, MASS. INST. TECH, 1955. 175P. 55-4386. 3500T.

MACANDREW, A.R. GLOSSARY OF RUSSIAN TECHNICAL TERMS USED IN METALLURGY. NEW YORK, VARANGIAN, 1953. 127P. 53-2032. 6000T.

MIKHAILOV, V.V. AND MELNIKOVA, M.M. ANGLO-RUSSKII SLOVAR PO ELEKTROKHIMII I KORROZII. (EN*RU ELECTROCHE CORR. D) MOSCOW, VINITI, 1963. 234P. 63-59367. 20000T. 450 ABBR.

SLOVAK

SLOVENSKA AKADEMIA VIED. TERMINOLOGIA OBRABANIA KOVOV. (METAL-WORKING, SL DEFS) BRATISLAVA, 1952. 95P. 59-23559.

SPANISH

BRITISH IRON AND STEEL FEDERATION. CONCISE IRON AND STEEL DICTIONARY, SPANISH-ENGLISH, ENGLISH-SPANISH. (NEW SER, NO.4) LONDON, 1957. 82P.

SWEDISH

BECKIUS, K. ENGELSK-SVENSK OCH SVENSK-ENGELSK ORDLISTA,UPPTAGANDE FACKTERMER INOM BERGSHANTERINGEN OCH ANGRAENSANDE OMRAEDEN. (*SW*EN D. OF MIN. ENG/ALLIED FIELDS) ED2. STOCKHOLM, SV. BERGSING. FOER, 1957. 68P. 5000T.

BRITISH IRON AND STEEL FEDERATION. CONCISE IRON AND STEEL DICTIONARY, ENGLISH-SWEDISH, SWEDISH-ENGLISH. (NEW SER, NO.3) LONDON, 1954. 44P.

METEOROLOGY

ENGLISH

AMERICAN SOCIETY FOR TESTING/MATERIALS. DEFINITIONS OF TERMS RELATING TO ATMOSPHERIC SAMPLING AND
ANALYSIS. (D1356-60) ASTM STDS, PT. 10, 1681-6. PHILADELPHIA, 1961. 100T.

AMERICAN STANDARDS ASSOCIATION. LETTER SYMBOLS FOR METEOROLOGY. (Y10.10) NEW YORK, 1953.

HECHTLINGER, A. MODERN SCIENCE DICTIONARY... PALISADE, N.J, FRANKLIN, 1959. 784P. 59-2320. 14500T.

HUSCHKE, R.E. GLOSSARY OF METEOROLOGY. BOSTON, AM. METEOROL. SOC, 1959. 638P. 59-65380. 10000T.

INTERNATIONAL ASSOCIATION OF HYDROLOGY. INTERNATIONAL CLASSIFICATION FOR SNOW. (TECH.MEMO NO.31)
ONTARIO, NATL.RES.COUNCIL, 195 .

LANGBEIN, W.B. AND ISERI, K.T. GENERAL INTRODUCTION AND HYDROLOGIC DEFINITIONS. MANUAL OF HYDROLOGY,
PT.1. (G.S. WATER SUPPLY PAPER NO.1541) WASHINGTON, U.S. GEOL. SURV. 1960. 29P. 300T.

WITTY,M.B. ET AL. DICTIONARY OF METEOROLOGY, ASTRONOMY AND OCEANOGRAPHY ABBREVIATIONS, SIGNS, SYMBOLS,
AND TABLES. NEW YORK, SETI, 196 . 256P.

WORLD METEOROLOGICAL ORGANIZATION. INTERNATIONAL ICE NOMENCLATURE. LONDON, 1952.

FRENCH

LA METEOROLOGIE, GLOSSAIRE ANGLAIS-FRANCAIS, BT-90. (METEOROL, EN*FR GL.I OTTAWA, DEPT.SECY.STATE, 1960.
44P. 900T.

VOCABULAIRE ANGLAIS-FRANCAIS, TERMES RELATIFS A LA METEOROLOGIE. (EN*FR METEOROL.D) J. MARINE, LE YACHT,
V.80, 7 (1957)

GERMAN

SCHINDLER, G. METEOROLOGISCHES WOERTERBUCH. (METEOROL.D, GE DEFS) WELS, OBEROESTERREICH,LEITNER, 1953.
131P. 56-30525.

HUNGARIAN

THURONYI, G.T. COLLECTION OF HUNGARIAN AND ENGLISH METEOROLOGICAL TERMS AND GRAMMATICAL ENDINGS. (*HU*EN)
(PROV. DRAFT) BOSTON, AM. METEOROL. SOC, 1953. 116P. 1700T.

ICELANDIC

CROTTY, P.G. ICELANDIC-ENGLISH GLOSSARY OF METEOROLOGICAL AND RELATED TERMS. WASHINGTON, U.S.DEPT.AIR
FORCE, AWS, 1952. 9P. 300T.

JAPANESE

CYCLOPEDIA OF WEATHER AND CLIMATE... (JA*EN) TOKYO, TENNENSHA, 1957. 393+24+60P. 2400T.

JAPAN. MINISTRY OF EDUCATION. GLOSSARY OF AGRICULTURAL METEOROLOGY. (EN*JA) TOKYO, 1952. 14P. 400T.

WADACHI, K. AND KAWABATA, Y. KISHO NO JITEN. (METEOROL. D, JA*EN) TOKYO, TOKYODO, 1954. 572P. J59-172.
2000T.

POLYGLOT

BELLISARIO, A. TERMINOLOGIA METEOROLOGICA. (IT*EN*FR*SP) N.P. 1951.17P. 700T.

BERGERON, T. SECHSSPRACHIGES METEOROLOGISCHES WOERTERBUCH. (*GE*EN*FR*IT*RU*SP) IN/LINKES.
METEOROLOGISCHES TASCHENBUCH. V.1, PP.142-265. LEIPZIG, GEEST/PORTIG,1951. 52-41222. 2500T.

CHUNG-KUO K*O HSUEH YUAN. PIEN I CH*U PAN WEI YUAN HUI. (ACAD. SINICA. COMM. OF PUBL/TRANSL) CH,I
HSIANG HSUEH MING TZ*U. (METEOROL. T, RU EN CH) PEKING, 1958. 408P. C59-540.

GT.BRIT. METEOROLOGICAL OFFICE. THE METEOROLOGICAL GLOSSARY, EN*DA*DU*FR*GE*IT*NO*PR*SP*SW. ED3. NEW YORK,
CHEMICAL, 1953. 253P. 900T.

SAKURABA, S. NICHI EI FUTSU RO KISHOGAKU YOGO JITEN. (METEOROL. D, *JA*EN*FR*RU) TOKYO, IZUMI SHOBO,
1960. 3+166+29P. J61-143. 2000T.

SPENGLER, O.A. AND E.N. GIDROLOGICHESKII SLOVAR NA INOSTRANNYKH IAZYKAKH. (D.OF HYDROL, *RU*EN*FR*GE)
LENINGRAD, GIDROMETEOIZDAT, 1959. 214P. 60-33508. 2400T.

UNITED NATIONS. LIST OF METEOROLOGICAL TERMS. (TERMINOLOGY BULL. NO.169) NEW YORK, 1960.

WORLD METEOROLOGICAL ORGANIZATION. INTERNATIONAL METEOROLOGICAL VOCABULARY... (*EN*FR*RU*SP) PROV.ED.
GENEVA, 1959. 521P. 61-21455. 1000T.

RUSSIAN

AINBINDER, M. ANGLO-RUSSKII METEOROLOGICHESKII SLOVAR. (EN*RU METEOROL. D) MOSCOW, FIZMATGIZ, 1959. 244P.
59-51073. 7000T.

95

METEOROLOGY

RUSSIAN

BAUM, W.A. RUSSIAN-ENGLISH DICTIONARY OF METEOROLOGICAL TERMS AND EXPRESSIONS. WASHINGTON, HOBART, 1949. 126P. 52-18696. 6000T.

KHROMOV, S.P. AND MAMONTOVA, L.I. METEOROLOGICHESKII SLOVAR. (METEOROL. D, RU DEFS) LENINGRAD, GIDROMETEOIZDAT. 1955. 454P. 56-30040. 4000T.

MAMONTOVA, L.I. AND KHROMOV, S.P. ANGLO-RUSSKII METEOROLOGICHESKII SLOVAR. (EN*RU METEOROL. D) LENINGRAD GIDROMETEOIZDAT, 1959, 172P. 59-38863. 6000T.

NOVECK, S. AND EMIN, I. RUSSIAN-ENGLISH GLOSSARY OF PHYSICS OF FLUIDS AND METEOROLOGY. NEW YORK, INTERLANG. DICT. 1959. 93P. 59-4252. 4000T.

SWEET, J.S. AMERICAN-RUSSIAN, RUSSIAN-AMERICAN HYDROLOGIC VOCABULARY. WASHINGTON, U.S. WEATHER BUR, 1958 24P. 58-62255. 300T.

U.S. CENTRAL AIR DOCUMENTS OFFICE. LIST OF RUSSIAN-ENGLISH METEOROLOGICAL TERMS. DAYTON, OHIO, WRIGHT-PATTERSON AFB, 1948. 56P. 58-46380.

SPANISH

BRAZOL, D. DICCIONARIO DE TERMINOS METEOROLOGICOS Y AFINES. (D. OF METEOROL/RELATED T.*EN*SP) BUENOS AIRES, HACHETTE, 1955. 2 PTS.IN 1 V. 557P. 57-38283. 8000T.

HERNANDEZ, H. DICCIONARIO DE METEOROLOGIA. (METEOROL.D, SP DEFS) MONTEVIDEO, CASA/ESTUD,1953. 328P.3000T

SWEET, J.S. AMERICAN-SPANISH, SPANISH-AMERICAN HYDROLOGIC VOCABULARY. WASHINGTON, U.S. WEATHER BUR, 1958 26P. 59-60614. 350T.

TURKISH

CROTTY, P.G. TURKISH-ENGLISH GLOSSARY OF METEOROLOGICAL TERMS. WASHINGTON, U.S. DEPT. AIR FORCE, AWS, 1951. 10P. 300T.

MILITARY SCIENCE AND ENGINEERING

AFRIKAANS

SOUTH AFRICA. DEFENCE TERMINOLOGY BOARD. WEERMAGSWOORDEBOEK ENGELS-AFRIKAANS... (EN*AF MIL. D) PRETORIA STAATSDRUKKER, 1954. 533P. 54-43796. 33000T.

ARABIC

IRAQ. MINISTRY OF DEFENSE. ENGLISH-ARABIC MILITARY DICTIONARY. 195-. 537P.

U.S. ARMY LANGUAGE SCHOOL. MILITARY TERMINOLOGY, ARABIC. (*EN*AR) PRESIDIO OF MONTEREY, 1953. 87P. 54-61043.

BURMESE

U.S. ARMY LANGUAGE SCHOOL. BURMESE, MILITARY RANKS, TERMINOLOGY, CONVENTIONAL SIGNS AND SYMBOLS HANDBOOK PRESIDIO OF MONTEREY, 1962. 42P. 63-61513.

CHINESE

LI, PAO-CHUN. A TEXT OF CHINESE MILITARY TERMS. NEW HAVEN, YALE UNIV, 1959. 390P. 60-2071.

MO, SHU-CH,IN. HAN YING CHUN YU TZ,U HUI. (CH EN MIL. D) TAIPEI, CHUN-SHIH I TS,UI CH,U PAN SHE, 1952. 281P.

U.S. ARMY. 500TH MILITARY INTELLIGENCE GROUP. A CHINESE-ENGLISH DICTIONARY OF TERMS. 1954. 709P. 55-63371.

U.S. ARMY LANGUAGE SCHOOL. CHINESE-CANTONESE. DICTIONARY OF UNITED STATES ARMY TERMS (EN*CH) PRESIDI OF MONTEREY, 1963- . 2V. 63-62172.

U.S. ARMY LANGUAGE SCHOOL. CHINESE-MANDARIN, MILITARY TERMINOLOGY DICTIONARY, ENGLISH-CHINESE. PRESID OF MONTEREY, 1959. 232P. 60-60377. 2300T.

U.S. ARMY LANGUAGE SCHOOL. A GLOSSARY OF CHINESE MILITARY TERMS. MONTEREY, CALIF, PRESIDIO OF MONTEREY 1951. 126P. 52-61700.

WU, KUANG-CHIEH. YING HAN CHUN YU TZU TIEN. (EN CH MIL. D) TAIPEI, WEN-HUA BOOKS, 1953. 356P. C62-41

CZECH

CANADA. DIRECTORATE OF MILITARY INTELLIGENCE. CZECH-ENGLISH GLOSSARY OF MILITARY TERMS USED IN THE CZECHOSLOVAK ARMED FORCES. OTTAWA, 1959. 90P. 63-38780.

U.S. ARMY LANGUAGE SCHOOL. CZECH MILITARY TERMINOLOGY. (CZ*EN) PRESIDIO OF MONTEREY, 1951. 29P. 52-61751.

CZECH

U.S. ARMY LANGUAGE SCHOOL. CZECH, VOCABULARY TO MILITARY TERMINOLOGY OF THE CZECHOSLOVAK ARMED FORCES. (CZ*EN) PRESIDIO OF MONTEREY, 1958. 89P. 58-62103. 3200T.

DANISH

DENMARK. CIVILFORSVARSSTYRELSEN. ENGELSK-DANSK CIVILFORSVARS-ORDBOG. (EN*DA D. OF CIVIL DEFENSE) COPENHAGEN, 1957.42P. 58-40151. 4200T.

U.S. ARMY LANGUAGE SCHOOL. DANISH MILITARY TERMINOLOGY. PRESIDIO OF MONTEREY, 1951. 115P. 52-61719.

ENGLISH

ADAMS, F.D. AERONAUTICAL DICTIONARY. WASHINGTON, U.S. NATL. AERON/SPACE ADMIN, 1959. 199P. 60-60459. 4000T.

ALLEN, W.H. DICTIONARY OF SPACE TERMS. WASHINGTON, U.S. NATL. AERON/SPACE ADMIN. (IN PRESS)

ALLEN, W.H. AND MULCAHY, B.A. SHORT GLOSSARY OF SPACE TERMS. WASHINGTON, U.S. NATL. AERON/SPACE ADMIN, 1962. 57P. 62-61784. 440T.

AMERICAN ROCKET SOCIETY. MISSILE GLOSSARY. NEW YORK, 1958.

ASTROLOG, CURRENT STATUS OF U.S. MISSILE AND SPACE PROGRAMS PLUS ALL ORBITING SATELLITES. MISSILES/ ROCKETS, V.12, NO.1, 25-32 (1963) 150T.

BROWNELL, F.R. ET AL. ENCYCLOPEDIA OF MODERN FIREARMS, PARTS AND ASSEMBLY. MONTEZUMA, IOWA, 1959-- V. 60-20044.

DODSON, B.E. A GLOSSARY OF JAMMING TERMINOLOGY. (MEWD REPT.NO.R-101-125) WHITE SANDS M.R, N.M, 1959. 27P.

FEDOROFF, B.T. ET AL. ENCYCLOPEDIA OF EXPLOSIVES AND RELATED ITEMS. DOVER, N.J. PICATINNY ARSENAL, 1960-   . V.1. 61-61759.

GENTLE, E.J. AND CHAPEL, C.E. AVIATION AND SPACE DICTIONARY. ED4. LOS ANGELES, AERO, 1961. 444P. 61-15652. 8000T.

GOLDSWORTHY, H.E. GLOSSARY OF OBSERVER TERMS. (NO.APG/SAR/497-A) EGLIN AFB, FLA. 1955. 7P.

GUIDED MISSILE ENCYCLOPEDIA, 1ST ANNUAL. MISSILES/ROCKETS, V.2, NO.2, 123-64. (1957) 30T.

HEFLIN, W.A. AEROSPACE GLOSSARY. MAXWELL AFB, ALA, AIR UNIV. 1959. 115P. 60-60268.

HEFLIN, W.A. INTERIM GLOSSARY, AEROSPACE TERMS. MAXWELL AFB, ALA, AIR UNIV. 1958. 35P. 58-61455. 500T.

HEFLIN, W.A. ET AL. THE UNITED STATES AIR FORCE DICTIONARY. MAXWELL AFB, AIR UNIV, 1956. 578P. 56-61737. 16500T.

HERRICK, J.W. AND BURGESS, E. ROCKET ENCYCLOPEDIA, ILLUSTRATED. LOS ANGELES, AERO, 1959. 607P. 59-8488.

JACOBS, H. AND WHITNEY, E.E. MISSILE AND SPACE PROJECTS GUIDE. NEW YORK, PLENUM, 1962. 235P. 62-13473.

MCLAUGHLIN, C. SPACE AGE DICTIONARY. PRINCETON, N.J, VAN NOSTRAND, 1959. 128P. 59-14613. 600T.

MERRILL, G. ET AL. DICTIONARY OF GUIDED MISSILES AND SPACE FLIGHT. PRINCETON, N.J, VAN NOSTRAND, 1959. 688P. 59-10112. 8400T.

MILITARY ASTRONAUTICS GLOSSARY. AIR FORCE MAG, V.41,157-67 (1958) 200T.

MISSILE AND SPACE GLOSSARY. AIR FORCE SPACE DIG, V.43, 148-52 (1960) AND V.44, 164-6 (1961)

NEW YORK (STATE) CIVIL DEFENSE MANPOWER SERVICE. NEW YORK STATE DICTIONARY OF CIVIL DEFENSE OCCUPATIONAL TITLES AND CODES... NEW YORK, 1957. 2V. A57-9199.

NEWELL, H.E. GUIDE TO ROCKETS, MISSILES, AND SATELLITES. ED2. NEW YORK, WHITTLESEY, 1961. 95P. 61-17343.

NORTHROP AIRCRAFT, INC. DEFINITIONS OF OPERATIONAL RANGE AND ALTITUDE PERFORMANCE FOR THE SM-62A. (REPT. NO. NAI-55-1007) HAWTHORNE, CALIF, 1955. 3P.

RCA SERVICE CO. DIGEST OF MILITARY ELECTRONICS. CAMDEN, N.J, 1961. 205P. 61-1603. 800T.

SCOTT, H.L. AND RYWELL, M. CIVIL WAR MILITARY DICTIONARY... HARRIMAN,TENN, PIONEER, 1956. IV. 56-9499.

SELL,S BRITISH AVIATION. LONDON, BUSINESS DICT, 1961-   . (ANNUAL) VAR. PP. 57-22102. 600T.

SMITH, W.H.B. THE BOOK OF PISTOLS AND REVOLVERS, AN ENCYCLOPEDIC REFERENCE WORK. ED4. HARRISBURG, PA, STACKPOLE, 1960. 744P 62-3948.

STRAUBEL, J.H. ET AL. SPACE WEAPONS, A HANDBOOK OF MILITARY ASTRONAUTICS. (GL. PP.205-26) NEW YORK, PRAEGER, 1959. 245P. 59-7882.

U.S. AIR FORCE. ARDC. VOCABULARY FOR CURRENT ARDC TECHNICAL EFFORTS. WASHINGTON, 1960. 159P. 60-64594. 5000T.

U.S. AIR FORCE MISSILE TEST CENTER. MISSILE GLOSSARY. PATRICK AFB, FLA, 1958.

U.S. AIR FORCE SYSTEMS COMMAND. GLOSSARY OF MANAGEMENT SYSTEMS TERMS (WITH ACRONYMS) WASHINGTON, D.C. 1962. 21P. 80T.

U.S. AIR FORCE TERMINOLOGY CONTROL AND TRANSLATION BRANCH. INTERIM GLOSSARY OF MILITARY TERMS AND DEFINITIONS, JCS-NATO. WASHINGTON, 1957. 79P. 58-61709. 500T.

U.S. ARMY. ORDNANCE CORPS. ORDNANCE ENGINEERING DESIGN HANDBOOK. AMMUNITION SERIES. (ORDP 20-210) FUZES, GENERAL AND MECHANICAL. (GL, PP.140-4. 110T) WASHINGTON, 1960. 146P.

U.S. ARMY. ORDNANCE CORPS. ORDNANCE ENGINEERING DESIGN HANDBOOK. ARTILLERY AMMUNITION SERIES. (ORDP 20-244, SECT. 1) (GL,PP. G1-G19. 300T) WASHINGTON, 1957. 72P. 57-60865.

U.S. ARMY. ORDNANCE SCHOOL. ORDNANCE TECHNICAL TERMINOLOGY. (ST 9-152) ABERDEEN PROVING GROUND, MD, 1962. 355P. 10500T.

U.S. ARMY LANGUAGE SCHOOL. ILLUSTRATED MILITARY SITUATIONS. PRESIDIO OF MONTEREY, 1956. 57P. 56-63766.

U.S. COMMAND AND GENERAL STAFF COLLEGE. U.S. ARMY ENGLISH FOR ALLIED STUDENTS. (ST21-150-2) FORT LEAVENWORTH, KAN, 1956. 162P. 56-62038.

U.S. COMMAND AND GENERAL STAFF COLLEGE. GLOSSARY OF TERMS AND MILITARY SLANG. (ST21-150-2 SUPPL) FORT LEAVENWORTH, KAN. 1956. 167P. 56-62038.

U.S. DEPT. OF DEFENSE. ENVIRONMENTAL TERMINOLOGY INCLUDING ELECTROMAGNETIC RADIATION HAZARDS COMMON TO PERSONNEL, FUEL AND EQUIPMENT. WASHINGTON, 1961.

U.S. DEPT. OF DEFENSE. MILITARY STANDARD, ELECTRICAL AND ELECTRONIC SYMBOLS. (MIL-STD. 15A) WASHINGTON, 1954-- 70P. 54-61684.

U.S. DEPT. OF DEFENSE. MILITARY STANDARD, PRINTED CIRCUIT TERMS AND DEFINITIONS. (MIL-STD-429) WASHINGTON, 1957. 4P. 58-62178.

U.S. DEPT. OF HEALTH, EDUCATION AND WELFARE. GLOSSARY OF CIVIL DEFENSE TERMS. WASHINGTON, 1955. 13P.

U.S. DEPT. OF THE AIR FORCE. GLOSSARY OF OBSERVER TERMS. (AF MANUAL 50-26) WASHINGTON, 1956. 83P. 56-62003.

U.S. DEPT. OF THE AIR FORCE. GLOSSARY OF STANDARDIZED TERMS. ADMINISTRATIVE PRACTICES. (MANUAL AFM 11-1) WASHINGTON, 1959- 1 V. LL. 59-60487.

U.S. DEPT. OF THE AIR FORCE. INTERIM AEROSPACE TERMINOLOGY REFERENCE, ADMINISTRATIVE PRACTICES. (AF PAMPHLET 11-1-4) WASHINGTON, 1959, 75P. 60-60256. 700T.

U.S. DEPT. OF THE ARMY. GLOSSARY OF NATURAL TERRAIN FEATURES. (I.G.NO.13) WASHINGTON, 195 .

U.S. DEPT. OF THE ARMY. MILITARY TERMS, ABBREVIATIONS AND SYMBOLS, DICTIONARY OF U.S. ARMY TERMS. WASHINGTON, 1961.

U.S. FEDERAL CIVIL DEFENSE ADMINISTRATION. CIVIL DEFENSE GLOSSARY. HANDBOOK. WASHINGTON, 1956. 72P. 56-62495.

U.S. JOINT CHIEFS OF STAFF. DICTIONARY OF U.S. MILITARY TERMS FOR JOINT USAGE. (JCS PUBL. NO.1) WASHINGTON, 1959. 161P. 59-62410. 1600T.

U.S. JOINT CHIEFS OF STAFF. A DICTIONARY OF U.S. MILITARY TERMS... WASHINGTON, PUBL. AFFAIRS, 1963. 316P. 63-942.

U.S. OFFICE OF ORDNANCE RESEARCH. GLOSSARY OF ORDNANCE TERMS. PRELIM. ED. DURHAM, N.C, DUKE UNIV, 1959 323P. 9000T.

WALLACE, C. DICTIONARY OF CIVIL DEFENSE. NEW YORK, PHIL. LIBR, 1952. 165P.

WITTY, M.B. ET AL. DICTIONARY OF AERONAUTICS, MISSILES AND ROCKETS ABBREVIATIONS, SIGNS, SYMBOLS AND TABLES. NEW YORK, SETI, 1963. 352P.

WITTY, M.B. ET AL. DICTIONARY OF MILITARY SCIENCE ABBREVIATIONS, SIGNS AND SYMBOLS. NEW YORK, SETI, 196 .

WITTY, M.B. POLON, D.D. ET AL. THE AMERICAN DICTIONARY OF AERONAUTICS, MISSILES, ROCKETS, AND SPACE TERMS. NEW YORK, SETI. 416P. (IN PREP)

WORLD MISSILE/SPACE ENCYCLOPEDIA, 6TH ANNUAL. MISSILES/ROCKETS, V.11, NO.5, 41-112 (1962) 250T.

WORLD MISSILE/SPACE ENCYCLOPEDIA, 7TH ANNUAL. MISSILES/ROCKETS, V.13, NO.5, 36-153 (1963) 400T.

MILITARY SCIENCE AND ENGINEERING

ESPERANTO

.S. DEPT. OF THE ARMY. AGGRESSOR, THE MANEUVER ENEMY, ESPERANTO... WASHINGTON, 1959, 95P. 60-64701.

.S. DEPT. OF THE ARMY. ESPERANTO THE AGGRESSOR LANGUAGE. WASHINGTON, 1962. 233P. 62-61164.

FINNISH

OROILA, E.E. ENGLANTILAIS-SUOMALAINEN, SUOMALAIS-ENGLANTILAINEN SOTILASLYHENNESANASTO. (*FI*EN GL. OF IL. ABBR) HELSINKI, 1954. 133P. 63-331.

FRENCH

ARDI, P.F. A DICTIONARY FOR THE FORCES, ENGLISH-FRENCH AND FRENCH-ENGLISH. LONDON, FREDERICK, 1955. 54P. 55-1305. 5500T.

HALMETTE, M. ENGLISH-FRENCH VOCABULARY OF AERONAUTICAL TERMS. LONDON, AIRCRAFT ENG, 1952. 36P. 2-41476.

JBOIS, R.J. AND PREUX, L. LEXIQUE MILITAIRE FRANCAIS-ANGLAIS... (FR*EN MIL. INTERPRETER) PARIS, HARLES-LAVAUZELLE, 1957. 191P. 62-51245.

ENRY, L. DICTIONNAIRE AERO-TECHNIQUE ANGLAIS-FRANCAIS.... (EN*FR AERON. D) PARIS, PETIT, 1963. 584P.

JMBERT,S. AVIATION ENGLISH... (V.1 FR*EN, 257P. V.2 EN*FR, 223P) PARIS, DUNOD, 1955. 56-28848.

GAELIC

RELAND (EIRE) ARMY. FOCLOIR BEARLA-GAEILGE DE THEARMAI MILEATA AGUS DE THEARMAI GAOLMHARA. (EN*GA MIL.) DUBLIN, GOVT. PRINT. OFFICE, 1953. 151P. 59-47299.

GERMAN

ESCOTTI, R. LUFTFAHRT-DEFINITIONEN, ENGLISCH-DEUTSCH, DEUTSCH-ENGLISCH. (GL. OF AERON. DEFS,*EN*GE) JNICH, REICH, 1956. 270P. 57-2237. 2500T.

ESCOTTI, R. LUFTFAHRT-WOERTERBUCH, DEUTSCH-ENGLISCH, ENGLISCH-DEUTSCH. (AVIATION D, *GE*EN) ED2. JNICH, REICH, 1957. 448P. 60-24363. 5500T.

ARCY, H.L. ET AL. AIR TECHNICAL DICTIONARY, GERMAN-ENGLISH. NEW YORK, DUELL, SLOAN/PEARCE, 1960. 12P. 60-16109. 30000T.

ARCY, H.L. ET AL. LUFTFAHRTTECHNISCHES WOERTERBUCH... (AIR TECH. D, V.2, EN*GE, IN PREP) BERLIN, DE RUYTER, 1962. 62-33521. 30000T.

ITZEN, K.H. GERMAN-ENGLISH, ENGLISH-GERMAN MILITARY DICTIONARY... 2000 ABBR... ED4. NEW YORK, PRAEGER, 957. 549P. 56-13090. 10000T.

NGELMANN, W. AND GOLDHAGEN, C. ENGLISH FUER DIE BUNDESWEHR. (EN FOR GE FED. ARMED FORCES) MUNICH, JEBER, 1957. 96+115P.

EDOROFF, B.T. ET AL. DICTIONARY OF EXPLOSIVES, AMMUNITION AND WEAPONS, GERMAN SECTION. DOVER, N.J. ICATINNY ARSENAL, 1958. 345P. 9000T.

JCHS, K.H. MILITAERISCHES TASCHENLEXIKON... (MIL. GL, GE DEFS) BONN, ATHENAEUM, 1958. 360P.)-22770. 3000T.

ROLLMANN, F. LANGENSCHEIDTS FACHWOERTERBUCH WEHRWESEN, ENGLISCH-DEUTSCH, DEUTSCH-ENGLISCH. (*GE*EN MIL.) BERLIN, LANGENSCHEIDT, 1960. 792P. 40000T.

EIDECKER,K.F. GERMAN-ENGLISH TECHNICAL DICTIONARY OF AERONAUTICS, ROCKETRY, SPACE NAVIGATION... 'W YORK,VANNI, 1950-51. 2V. 968P. 50-14702.
ELSEVIER. 800P. 6500T. (IN PREP)

.S. ARMY LANGUAGE SCHOOL. GERMAN, MILITARY TERMINOLOGY WORD LIST. (*EN*GE) PRESIDIO OF MONTEREY, 1957,)P. 57-61174. 900T.

GREEK

SPINES, C. ENGLISH-GREEK DICTIONARY OF THE MILITARY TECHNICAL AND TACTICAL TERMS. ATHENS, 1954. 118P. -22827. 2500T.

S. ARMY LANGUAGE SCHOOL. GREEK-ENGLISH MILITARY TERMINOLOGY DICTIONARY. PRESIDIO OF MONTEREY, 1951. '4P.

S. ARMY LANGUAGE SCHOOL. A MILITARY TERMINOLOGY WORKBOOK. PRESIDIO OF MONTEREY, 1952. 105P. 53-60637.

HEBREW

AVIA, A. AND GOLDBERG, S.R. DICTIONARY OF MILITARY TERMS, ENGLISH-HEBREW. HAIFA, 1951.

HUNGARIAN

S. ARMY LANGUAGE SCHOOL. HUNGARIAN MILITARY DICTIONARY. (HU*EN) PRESIDIO OF MONTEREY, 1955. 56-60229.

99

MILITARY SCIENCE AND ENGINEERING

INDONESIAN

U.S. ARMY LANGUAGE SCHOOL. INDONESIAN, MILITARY TERMINOLOGY WORD LIST. PRESIDIO OF MONTEREY, 1956. 23P. 56-60341. 600T.

ITALIAN

HELDER, M.P. AND POLIMENI, A. DIZIONARIO PER LE FORZE ARMATE, ITALIANO-INGLESE, INGLESE-ITALIANO. (*IT*E MIL. D) ED2. TURIN, 1959. 250P.

U.S. ARMY LANGUAGE SCHOOL. ITALIAN, ILLUSTRATED MILITARY SITUATIONS. PRESIDIO OF MONTEREY, 1958. 57P. 59-61522.

U.S. ARMY LANGUAGE SCHOOL. ITALIAN, MILITARY TERMINOLOGY WORD LIST. (*IT*EN) PRESIDIO OF MONTEREY, 1957. 50P. 57-61557. 650T.

JAPANESE

MORISAWA, K. ANGLO-AMERICAN-JAPANESE DICTIONARY OF MILITARY TERMS AND RELATING NEW WORDS. TOKYO, KOYOSHA, 1953. 348P. 55-23685 REV.

U.S. ARMY LANGUAGE SCHOOL. JAPANESE MILITARY TERMS. PRESIDIO OF MONTEREY, 1955. 92P. 55-60627.

KOREAN

U.S. ARMY LANGUAGE SCHOOL. KOREAN MILITARY WORD LIST. PRESIDIO OF MONTEREY, 1956. 49P. 56-61439.

U.S. ARMY LANGUAGE SCHOOL. MILITARY TERMINOLOGY... (*KO*EN) PRESIDIO OF MONTEREY, 1953-54. 413+113+95P. 53-61602.

U.S. ARMY LANGUAGE SCHOOL. A TEXT FOR MILITARY TERMINOLOGY. (KO*EN) PRESIDIO OF MONTEREY, 1951. 106P. 52-61663.

LITHUANIAN

U.S. ARMY LANGUAGE SCHOOL. LITHUANIAN, BASIC COURSE MILITARY WORD LIST. (EN*LI) PRESIDIO OF MONTEREY, 1956. 56-60421. 30P. 450T.

NORWEGIAN

MARM, I. ENGELSK-AMERIKANSK-NORSK MILITAER ORDBOK. (EN-AM-NO MIL.D) OSLO, FABRITIUS, 1955. 183P. 56-43103. 5400T.

U.S. ARMY LANGUAGE SCHOOL. NORWEGIAN MILITARY TERMINOLOGY. (NO*EN) PRESIDIO OF MONTEREY, 1952. 158P. 52-61593.

POLISH

ELSZTEIN, P. ET AL. TYSIAC SLOW O LOTNICTWIE...(1000 AERON. WORDS, PL DEFS) WARSAW, MIN. OBRONY NAR, 1958. 406P. 58-32660. 1000T.

MALINOWSKI, W. ET AL. SLOWNIK WOJSKOWY, ANGIELSKO-POLSKI (EN*PL MIL.D) WARSAW, WYDAW. MIN. OBRONY NAR, 1961. 512P. 62-33500. 6000T.

POLAND. MINISTERSTWO OBRONY NARODOWEJ. SLOWNIK TERMINOW WOJSKOWYCH. (MIL. D, PL DEFS) WARSAW, 1958. 325P. 58-43241. 3000T.

U.S. ARMY LANGUAGE SCHOOL. ESSENTIAL MILITARY VOCABULARY, ENGLISH-POLISH. PRESIDIO OF MONTEREY, 1955. 15P. 55-60220. 750T.

U.S. ARMY LANGUAGE SCHOOL. POLISH, BASIC COURSE, MILITARY WORD LIST. PRESIDIO OF MONTEREY, 1955. 23P. 55-63642. 700T.

POLYGLOT

DO THIEU LIET, D. FRENCH-ENGLISH-VIETNAMESE MILITARY DICTIONARY. SAIGON, 1957. 527P.

DORIAN, A.F. DICTIONARY OF AERONAUTICS. *EN*FR*GE*IT*PR*SP. NEW YORK, ELSEVIER. 800P. 6500T. (IN PREP)

FRENOT, G.H. ET AL. NATO-AGARD AERONAUTICAL MULTILINGUAL DICTIONARY.*EN*DU*FR*GE*IT*RU*SP*TU. NEW YORK, PERGAMON, 1960. 1000P. 58-9477. 3000T.

HOLLOWAY, A.H. AGARD AERONAUTICAL MULTILINGUAL DICTIONARY. SUPPL. 1. (*EN*FR*GE*SP*GR*IT*DU*RU*TU) NEW YORK, PERGAMON, 1963. 334P. 58-9477. 1300T.

PARTEL, G. DIZIONARIO DI TECNICA DEI RAZZI E D.ASTRONAUTICA. (D. OF ROCKETS/ASTRONAUTICS *IT*EN*FR *GE) ROME, IST. POLIGR. STATO, 1955. 107P. A57-3506. 1400T.

U.S. CORPS OF ENGINEERS. GLOSSARY OF TERMS PERTINENT TO MILITARY HYDROLOGY... (EN FR GE IT SP) WASHINGTON, 1957.

PORTUGUESE

U.S. ARMY LANGUAGE SCHOOL. AERONAUTICAL VOCABULARY. (PR*EN) PRESIDIO OF MONTEREY, 1953. 12P. 53-61214.

U.S. ARMY LANGUAGE SCHOOL. PORTUGUESE. MILITARY TERMINOLOGY WORD LIST. (*PR*EN) PRESIDIO OF MONTEREY, 1957. 55P. 57-61249. 550T.

ROMANIAN

U.S. ARMY LANGUAGE SCHOOL. ROMANIAN MILITARY TERMINOLOGY. PRESIDIO OF MONTEREY, 1955. 160P. 56-60444. 2000T.

U.S. ARMY LANGUAGE SCHOOL. ROMANIAN. MILITARY TERMINOLOGY WORD LIST.(*EN*RO) PRESIDIO OF MONTEREY, 1957. 46P. 57-61556. 500T.

RUSSIAN

BAKANOV, R.A. KRATKII ANGLO-RUSSKII I RUSSKO-ANGLIISKII VOENNYI SLOVAR. (*RU*EN MIL. D) MOSCOW, VOENIZDAT, 1963. 560P. 63-44395. 28000T.

BLUVSHTEIN, V.O. AND STOLBOV, V.S. KRATKII RUSSKO-ANGLIISKII VOENNYI SLOVAR. (RU*EN MIL. GL) GOS. IZD. INOSTR/NATS. SLOV, 1955. 336P.

BORISOV, V.V. ET AL. SLOVAR INOSTRANNYKH VOENNYKH SOKRASHCHENII. (D.OF FOR. MIL. ABBRS, RU DEFS) MOSCOW, VOENIZDAT, 1961. 895P. 62-38360.

BURIAKOV, IU. ET AL. ANGLO-RUSSKII AVIATSIONNYI SLOVAR. (EN*RU AVIATION D) MOSCOW, VOENIZDAT, 1963. 544P. 63-58318.

BUZINOV, V.M. ET AL. ANGLO-RUSSKII ARTILLERIISKII SLOVAR. (EN*RU ARTILLERY D) MOSCOW, VOENIZDAT, 1959. 415P. 60-19662. 17000T.

CHIROKOV, K.V. AND SUPRUN, . ANGLO-RUSSKII AEROKOSMICHESKII SLOVAR. (EN*RU AEROSPACE D) MOSCOW, VOENIZDAT, 1963.

CHOCHIA, A.P. AND SHCHEGLOV, A.S. ANGLO-RUSSKII AVTOBRONETANKOVYI SLOVAR. (EN*RU D. OF ARMORED WEAPONS) MOSCOW, VOENIZDAT, 1961. 783P. 62-28563. 30000T.

DREMICHEV, I.D. AND GRECHKIN, V.P. ANGLO-RUSSKII SLOVAR PO REAKTIVNOMU ORUZHIIU. (*EN*RU D. OF ROCKET WEAPONS) MOSCOW, VOENIZDAT, 1960. 383P. 61-29176. 7500T.

ELIANOV, D.I. AND MOROZOVSKII, N.G. ANGLO-RUSSKII I RUSSKO-ANGLIISKII SLOVAR VOENNO-MORSKIKH KOMAND. (*EN *RU NAVAL COMMAND D) MOSCOW, VOENIZDAT, 1960. 190P. 60-41744.

FAVOROV, P.A. ET AL. ANGLO-RUSSKII SLOVAR PO PODVODNYM LODKAM I PROTIVOLODOCHNOI OBORONE. (EN*RU D. OF SUBMARINE/ANTI-SUBMARINE DEFENSE) MOSCOW, VOENIZDAT, 1963. 260P. 63-43903. 7000T.

FEDOROFF, B.T. ET AL. DICTIONARY OF RUSSIAN AMMUNITION AND WEAPONS. DOVER, N.J, PICATINNY ARSENAL, 1955. 47P.

GLOSSARY OF RUSSIAN TERMS ASSOCIATED WITH GUIDED MISSILES, EARTH SATELLITE, SPACE VECHICLE AND OTHER RELATED SUBJECTS... WASHINGTON, 1958. 61-40335.

GORELIK, IA.M. ET AL. KRATKII SLOVAR NEKOTORYKH TERMINOV I OPREDELENII PO ATOMNOI ENERGII, ATOMNOMU ORUZHIIU I PROTIVOATOMNOI ZASHCHITE. (GL. OF AT. ENERGY, WEAPONS/ANTI-NUCL. DEFENSE, RU DEFS) MOSCOW, VOSAAF, 1958. 64P. 58-36797. 300T.

KONARSKI, M.M. HANDBOOK FOR AIR FORCE AND CIVIL AVIATION INTERPRETERS (RUSSIAN) V.1, ELEMENTARY. NEW YORK, PERGAMON, 1963. 150P.

KONARSKI, M.M. RUSSIAN-ENGLISH DICTIONARY OF MODERN TERMS IN AERONAUTICS AND ROCKETRY. NEW YORK, PERGAMON, 1962. 515P. 62-16918. 14500T.

KRAMER, A.A. RUSSKO-ANGLIISKI SLOVAR PO RAKETNOI TEKHNIKE I BALLISTICHESKIM SNARIADAM. (RU*EN ROCKET/ BALLISTIC MISSILE D) TRENTON, N.J, 1960. 240P. 61-23952. 10000T.

MARCHENKO, V.G. AND MOROZOVSKII, N.G. ANGLO-RUSSKII VOENNO-MORSKOI SLOVAR. (EN*RU MIL/NAVAL D) MOSCOW, VOENIZDAT, 1962. 851P. 63-35236. 40000T.

MOSCOW. VOENNAIA AKADEMIIA IMENI M.V. FRUNZE. KRATKII SLOVAR OPERATIVNO-TAKTICHESKIKH I OBSHCHEVOENNYKH SLOV. MOSCOW, VOENIZDAT,1958. 323P. 59-24708. (FOR EN TRANS, SEE BELOW/ U.S. DEPT. OF THE ARMY)

MURASHKEVICH, A.M. ANGLO-RUSSKII SLOVAR PO RAKETNOI TEKHNIKE. (EN*RU ROCKET D) MOSCOW, FIZMATGIZ, 1958. 731P. 59-18428. 5000T.

NIKITIN, S.M. AND KHRUSHCHEV, IU.1. ANGLO-RUSSKII SLOVAR PO AVIATSIONNYM I RAKETNYM BAZAM. (EN*RU D. OF AIR/ROCKET BASES) MOSCOW, VOENIZDAT, 1962. 335P. 62-65970. 8000T.

OSENBERG, A. RUSSIAN-ENGLISH GLOSSARY OF GUIDED MISSILE, ROCKET, AND SATELLITE TERMS. WASHINGTON, U.S. LIBR. CONGR, 1958. 352P. 58-60055. 4500T.

PAZHEV, IU.A. KURS VOENNOGO PEREVODA, ANGLIISKII IAZYK. (EN RU MIL. TRANSL. GUIDE) MOSCOW, VOENIZDAT, 1962-- 62-42769.

MILITARY SCIENCE AND ENGINEERING

RUSSIAN

SUDZILOVSKII, G.A. ET AL. ANGLO-RUSSKII SLOVAR PO PROTIVOVOZDUSHNOI I PROTIVORAKETNOI OBORONE. (EN*RU D. OF ANTI-AIRCRAFT/ANTI-MISSILE DEFENSE) MOSCOW, VOENIZDAT,1961. 720P. 62-34518. 27000T.

SUDZILOVSKII, G.A. ET AL. ANGLO-RUSSKII VOENNYI SLOVAR. (EN*RU MIL. D) MOSCOW, VOENIZDAT, 1960. 965P. 61-24492. 50000T.

SUDZILOVSKII, G.A. ANGLO-RUSSKII VOENNYI SLOVAR TERMINOV PO TYLU I SNABZHENIIU. (EN*RU MIL. D. OF LOGISTICS/SUPPLY) MOSCOW, VOENIZDAT, 1958. 449P. 59-17449. 25000T.

U.S. AIR TECHNICAL INTELLIGENCE CENTER. GLOSSARY OF RUSSIAN-ENGLISH MILITARY AND TECHNICAL TERMS. WRIGHT-PATTERSON AFB,OHIO, 1955. 246P. 55-61309.

U.S. ARMY LANGUAGE SCHOOL. KURS VOENNOI TERMINOLOGII. (COURSE IN MIL. T, RU*EN) PRESIDIO OF MONTEREY, 195 . 52P. 52-24631.

U.S. ARMY LANGUAGE SCHOOL. RUSSIAN BASIC MILITARY TERMINOLOGY EXERCISES. PRESIDIO OF MONTEREY, 1955. 42P. 56-60221.

U.S. ARMY LANGUAGE SCHOOL. RUSSIAN MILITARY TERMINOLOGY WORD LIST. (EN*RU) PRESIDIO OF MONTEREY, 1960. 53P. 60-62012. 600T.

U.S. ARMY ORDNANCE CORPS. RUSSIAN-ENGLISH SMALL ARMS DICTIONARY. (ORDI 7-106) WASHINGTON, 1956. 91P. 60-33821.

U.S. DEPT. OF THE ARMY. GLOSSARY OF SOVIET MILITARY AND RELATED ABBREVIATIONS. (TM30-546) WASHINGTON, 1957. 178P. 58-61484. 5400T.

U.S. DEPT. OF THE ARMY. GLOSSARY OF SOVIET MILITARY TERMINOLOGY, ENGLISH-RUSSIAN, RUSSIAN-ENGLISH. (TM30-544) WASHINGTON, 1955. 802P. 55-61853. 22000T.

U.S. DEPT. OF THE ARMY. RUSSIAN-ENGLISH DICTIONARY OF OPERATIONAL, TACTICAL AND GENERAL MILITARY TERMS. (TRANSL. OF MOSCOW. VOEN. AKAD... SEE ABOVE) WASHINGTON, OTS, 1960. 359P. 60-64579. 1000T.

U.S. DEPT. OF THE ARMY. SOVIET MILITARY SYMBOLS. (TM30-547) WASHINGTON, 1958. 217P. 59-62261.

VOLODIN, N.V. ANGLO-RUSSKII VOENNO-INZHENERNYI SLOVAR. (EN*RU MIL. ENG. D) MOSCOW, VOENIZDAT, 1962. 783P. 63-56315. 33000T.

SPANISH

INTER-AMERICAN DEFENSE BOARD. DICCIONARIO DE TERMINOS MILITARES PARA LAS FUERZAS ARMADAS, INGLES-ESPANOL. (EN*SP MIL.D) ED2. WASHINGTON, 1957. 245P. 58-20616.

LIZARRAGA, F. DICCIONARIO TECNICO, INGLES-ESPANOL Y ESPANOL-INGLES, PARA USO DE LOS EJERCITOS DE TIERRA, MAR Y AIRE. (*SP*EN MIL.D, LAND,SEA/AIR) MADRID, BIBLIOG. ESP, 1953. 706P. 54-33732.

MANGOLD, W. TERMINOLOGIA MILITAR-NAVAL-AEREA. (POCKET MANUAL OF MIL.T... LAND, SEA/AIR,*SP*EN) MADRID, MANGOLD, 1955. 191P. 55-1306. 3000T.

MERINO, J. DICCIONARIO MILITAR-TECNICO, ESPANOL-INGLES, INGLES-ESPANOL. (*SP*EN MIL.D) MADRID, 1953. 463P. A54-4002.

SPAIN. SERVICIO HISTORICO MILITAR. NOMENCLATOR HISTORICO-MILITAR. (D. OF MIL. HIST, SP DEFS) MADRID, 1954. 372P. 59-39294. 6000T.

U.S. AIR COMMAND AND STAFF COLLEGE. GLOSSARY OF U.S. AIR FORCE TERMS, ENGLISH-SPANISH. MAXWELL AFB, ALA, 1955. 27P. 55-12650.

U.S. AIR FORCE SCHOOL FOR LATIN AMERICA. DICCIONARIO AERONAUTICO. (AERON.D, EN*SP) (HSLAUSAF 129) ALBROOK AFB, CANAL ZONE, 1961. 437P. 62-64446.

U.S. ARMY LANGUAGE SCHOOL. SPANISH MILITARY WORD LIST. (*SP*EN) PRESIDIO OF MONTEREY, 1957. 79P. 57-61354. 700T.

SWEDISH

BROBERG, B. AND AHLBERG, A. AMERIKANSK/ENGELSK-SVENSK MILITAERORDBOK. (AM/EN*SW MIL. D) STOCKHOLM, SVENSKA BOK, 1957. 172P. 58-33767. 6500T.

U.S. ARMY LANGUAGE SCHOOL. SWEDISH MILITARY TERMINOLOGY. (SW EN) PRESIDIO OF MONTEREY, 1952. 75P. 52-61699.

THAI

U.S. ARMY LANGUAGE SCHOOL. THAI, MILITARY TERMINOLOGY WORD LIST. PRESIDIO OF MONTEREY, 1956. 34P. 56-60340 500T.

TURKISH

TURKEY. ERKANIHARBIYEI UMUMIYE RIYASETI. INGILIZCE-TURKCE ASKERI TERIMLER SOZLUGU. (EN*TU MIL. D) ANKARA, BASIMEVI, 1956. 487P. 59-54181.

TURKISH

IRKEY. ERKANSHARBIYEI UMUMIYE RIYASETI. RESMI AMERIKAN ASKERI KISALTMALARI VE TURKCE MUKABILLERI. (AM
L. ABBR. TU DEFS) ANKARA, BASIMEVI, 1955. 49P. 59-47624. 1500T.

.S. ARMY LANGUAGE SCHOOL. MILITARY DICTIONARY, ENGLISH-TURKISH. PRESIDIO OF MONTEREY,1951. 105P.
!-61701. 1500T.

.S. ARMY LANGUAGE SCHOOL. MILITARY TERMINOLOGY. (TU*EN) PRESIDIO OF MONTEREY, 1953. 65P. 54-61143.

.S. ARMY LANGUAGE SCHOOL. TURKISH, MILITARY SITUATIONS. PRESIDIO OF MONTEREY, 1959. 217P. 59-62251.

UKRAINIAN

.S. ARMY LANGUAGE SCHOOL. UKRAINIAN MILITARY DICTIONARY. (UK EN) PRESIDIO OF MONTEREY, 1958. 216P.

VIETNAMESE

.S. ARMY LANGUAGE SCHOOL. VIETNAMESE, MILITARY TERMINOLOGY WORD LIST. PRESIDIO OF MONTEREY, 1957. 29P.
'-60390. 500T.

MINING ENGINEERING

AFRIKAANS

)UTH AFRICA. DIVISON OF THE GOVERNMENT MINING ENGINEER. VOORLOPIGE LYS MYNBOU- EN VERWANTE TERME.
'RELIM. LIST OF MIN/RELATED T, AF*EN) PRETORIA, 1958. 147P. 59-19502.

CZECH

IRCH, J. SEZNAM ANGLICKO-CESKYCH HORNICKYCH VYRAZU. (EN*CZ MIN. GL) PRAGUE, MAT. HORN-HUTN, 1952. 430P.

ENGLISH

IERICAN INSTITUTE OF ELECTRICAL ENGINEERS. DEFINITIONS OF ELECTRICAL TERMS. MINING. (GR-85,ASA C42.85)
IW YORK, 1956. 12P. 90T.

!KELL, W. AND TOMKEIEFF, S.I. ·ENGLISH ROCK TERMS, CHIEFLY AS USED BY MINERS AND QUARRY-MEN. NEW YORK,
:FORD UNIV.PRESS, 1953. 139P. 53-4237.

!ITISH STANDARDS INSTITUTION. GLOSSARY OF TERMS USED IN COAL PREPARATION. (B.S. 3552) LONDON, 1962. 44P.
iOT.

:DOROFF, B.T. ET AL. ENCYCLOPEDIA OF EXPLOSIVES AND RELATED ITEMS. DOVER, N.J. PICATINNY ARSENAL,
'60-   . V.1. 61-61759.

.ANDERS, P.L. AND SAUER, F.M. A GLOSSARY OF GEOPLOSICS. THE SYSTEMATIC STUDY OF EXPLOSION EFFECTS
I THE EARTH. MENLO PARK, CALIF, STANFORD RES. INST. 1960. 34P.

)NG, A.E. A GLOSSARY OF THE DIAMOND-DRILLING INDUSTRY. (BUL.NO.583) WASHINGTON, U.S. BUR. MINES, 1960.
IP. 60-61567.

!YOR, E.J. DICTIONARY OF MINERAL TECHNOLOGY. LONDON, MINING PUBL, 1963. 437P.

'OKES, W.L. AND VARNES, D.J. GLOSSARY OF SELECTED GEOLOGIC TERMS...(USED) IN ENGINEERING. DENVER, COLO.
'I. SOC, 1955. 165P. A57-2059. 3300T.

FRENCH

CYIONNAIRE DU PETROLE ET DES MINES. (*EN*FR PETROL/MINING D) PARIS, RARIS-MONDE, 1963. 700P.

ANCE. AMBASSADE. U.S. INDUSTRIES MINIERES, AMERICAIN-FRANCAIS. (EN*FR GL. OF MIN. IND) WASHINGTON,
53. 133P. 59-31396. 1800T.

ELLE, P. LE VOCABULAIRE PROFESSIONEL DU HOUILLEUR BORAIN... (OCCUP.VOC. OF COAL MIN, FR DEFS) BRUSSELS,
LAIS-/ACAD. 1953. 198P.. A55-3614.

GERMAN

CHWOERTERBUCH, BETRIEBSWIRTSCHAFTLICHES... BERGBAU (GE EN MIN. ENG. D) ESSEN, GLUECKAUF, 1959. 187P.

DOROFF, B.T. ET AL. DICTIONARY OF EXPLOSIVES, AMMUNITION AND WEAPONS, GERMAN SECTION. DOVER, N.J.
CATINNY ARSENAL, 1958. 345P. 9000T.

OTHE, H. ET AL, LUEGERS LEXIKON DER TECHNIK. (ENCYCL. OF TECH) WOERTERBUCH DES BERGBAUES.
IN. D, GE DEFS) ED4. STUTTGART, DEUT. VERLAGS-ANSTALT, 1962. 727P. 5800T.

MZ, W. AND REGUL, R. DIE KOHLE. (COAL) KLEINES FACHLEXIKON DER KOHLENTECHNIK UND KOHLENWIRTSCHAFT.
OAL MIN. GL, GE DEFS, PP.381-427, 500T) ESSEN, GLUECKAUF, 1954. 427P. 54-39218.

NK, G. AND BOERNER, H. TECHNISCHES FACHWOERTERBUCH DER GRUNDSTOFF-INDUSTRIEN... (TECH.D. FOR BASIC IND)
.1, EN*GE, 638P. 1958. V.2, GE*EN, 734P. 1962) ED2. GOETTINGEN, VANDENHOECK/RUPRECHT, 1958-62.
9-324. 45000T.

EBACH, H.J. FACHWOERTERBUCH FUER BERGBAUTECHNIK UND BERGBAUWIRTSCHAFT. (*GE*EN D. FOR MIN. ENG/ECON)
SEN, GIRARDET, 1954. 311P.

MINING ENGINEERING

GERMAN

TUCHEL, G. WOERTERBUCH DER ANGEWANDTEN GEOPHYSIK... (*GE*EN D. OF APPL.GEOPHYS) HANNOVER, SEISMOS, 1958.
(2 PTS.IN 1V) 59-23520.

JAPANESE

JAPAN. MINISTRY OF EDUCATION. JAPANESE SCIENTIFIC TERMS, MINING AND METALLURGY. (*JA*EN) TOKYO, MIN.INST.
JAPAN. 1954. 263P. 3600T.

KOGYO KYOIKU KENKYUKAI. ZUKAI KOGYO YOGO JITEN. (ILLUS. MIN.D, *JA*EN) TOKYO, 1961. 446P. J62-1110.
45000T. 330 ABBR.

POLISH

GISMAN, S. ET AL. SLOWNIK GEOLOGICZNO-GORNICZY ANGIELSKO-POLSKI. (EN*PL D. FOR MIN/GEOL) WARSAW, PANSTW.
WYDAW. TECH. 1956. 794P. 57-41449. 35000T.

POLYGLOT

INSTITUT NATIONAL DE L,INDUSTRIE CHARBONNIERE. DICTIONNAIRE TECHNIQUE MINIER... (MIN. ENG. D, FR EN GE)
BRUSSELS, LOUIS, 1957.

LEXIQUE DES TERMES RELATIFS AUX PRESSIONS DE TERRAIN. (MINE-PRESSURE D, FR GE EN) LONDON, NATL. COAL
BOARD. 1958. 32P.

LUOSSAVAARA-KIIRUNAVAARA AB. GRUVTEKNISK ORDLISTA. (MIN. ENG. D, SW*EN*FR*GE) STOCKHOLM, 1960. 300P.

MIJNBOUW KUNDIGE NOMENCLATOR EN AARDOLIETECHNIK. (MIN/PETROL. ENG. GL, *DU*EN*FR*GE*SP) SOONINGEN, 1953.
148P.

NOVITSKY, A. DICCIONARIO MINERO-METALURGICO-GEOLOGICO-MINERALOGICO-PETROGRAFICO Y DE PETROLEO. (D. OF
MIN, MET, GEOL, MINERAL, PETROGR/PETROL, *SP*EN*FR*GE*RU) BUENOS AIRES. 1958. 2V. 217P. 18000T.

RUSSIAN

AKADEMIIA NAUK SSSR. KOM. TEKH. TERM. KLASSIFIKATSIIA I TERMINOLOGIIA GORNYKH MASHIN. (CLASSIF/T. OF MIN.
MACH, RU DEFS) (SB. REK. TERM. NO.1) MOSCOW, 1952. 26P. 54-32054.

AKADEMIIA NAUK SSSR. KOM. TEKH. TERM. TERMINOLOGIIA GORNOGO DAVLENIIA. (MINE PRESSURE, RU DEFS) (SB.
REK. TERM, NO.40) MOSCOW, 1956. 11P. 58-17312. 50T.

AKADEMIIA NAUK SSSR. KOM. TEKH. TERM. TERMINOLOGIIA GORNOGO DELA, GORNYE KREPI. (MINE TIMBERING, RU DEFS)
(SB.REK. TERM,NO.9) MOSCOW, 1952. 54-33032. 60T.

AKADEMIIA NAUK SSSR. KOM. TEKH. TERM. TERMINOLOGIIA GORNOGO DELA, GORNYE RABOTY I ELEMENTY SISTEM
RAZRABOTKI TVERDYKH POLEZNYKH ISKOPAEMYKH. (MIN. WORKING SYST,RU DEFS)(SB. REK. TERM, NO.5) MOSCOW, 1952.
20P. 54-32053. 60T.

AKADEMIIA NAUK SSSR. KOM. TEKH. TERM. TERMINOLOGIIA GORNOGO DELA, GORNYE RABOTY I GORNYE VYRABOTKI. (MIN.
SYST/WORKINGS, RU DEFS) (SB. REK. TERM, NO.36) MOSCOW,1954. 27P. 55-36937. 140T.

AKADEMIIA NAUK SSSR. KOM. TEKH. TERM. TERMINOLOGIIA SISTEM RAZRABOTKI MESTOROZHDENII TVERDYKH POLEZNYKH
ISKOPAEMYKH PODZEMNYM SPOSOBOM. (WORKING SYST. FOR UNDERGROUND MIN, RU DEFS) (SB. REK.TERM. NO.51)
MOSCOW, 1959. 13P. 60-30443. 90T.

AKADEMIIA NAUK SSSR. KOM. TEKH. TERM. TERMINOLOGIIA VZRYVNYKH RABOT. (BLASTING OPERATIONS, RU DEFS)
(SB. REK. TERM. NO.22) MOSCOW, 1953. 19P. 54-27906. 90T.

BARON, L.I. AND ERSHOV, N.N. ANGLO-RUSSKII GORNYI SLOVAR. (EN*RU MIN.D) MOSCOW, FIZMATGIZ, 1958. 992P.
59-38855. 40000T.

GLAGOLEV, V.A. TERMINOLOGIIA PO OSNOVNYM VOPROSAM GORNOGO DELA. (MIN.T, RU DEFS) MOSCOW, MIN. VYSSH.
OBRAZ.SSSR, 1958. 40P. 500T.

KOSMINSKII, B.M. ET AL. ANGLO-RUSSKII GORNOTEKHNICHESKII SLOVAR. (EN*RU MIN. ENG. D) MOSCOW,
UGLETEKHIZDAT, 1958. 478P. 59-29373. 30000T.

MAKKAVEEV, A.A. ET AL. SLOVAR PO GIDROGEOLOGII I INZHENERNOI GEOLOGII. (D. OF HYDROGEOL/ENG. GEOL,
RU DEFS) MOSCOW, GOSTOPTEKHIZDAT, 1961. 186P. 61-48756. 10000T.

TERPIGOREV, A.M. ET AL. GORNOE DELO, ENTSIKLOPEDICHESKII SPRAVOCHNIK. (MIN, ENCYCL. HANDBOOK, RU DEFS)
MOSCOW, UGLETEKHIZDAT, 1957-- 58-20669.

SLOVAK

SLOVENSKA AKADEMIA VIED. BANICKY TERMINOLOGICKY SLOVNIK. (MINERAL IND. D, SL DEFS) BRATISLAVA, S.A.V,
1955. 167P. 57-20723.

SWEDISH

BECKIUS, K. ENGELSK-SVENSK OCH SVENSK-ENGELSK ORDLISTA,UPPTAGANDE FACKTERMER INOM BERGSHANTERINGEN OCH
ANGRAENSANDE OMRAEDEN. (*SW*EN D. OF MIN. ENG/ALLIED FIELDS) ED2. STOCKHOLM, SV. BERGSING. FOER, 1957.
68P. 5000T.

NAVAL SCIENCE AND ENGINEERING

DUTCH

FITZ-VERPLOEGH, A. DUTCH-ENGLISH AND ENGLISH-DUTCH TECHNICAL TERMS FOR SHIPBUILDING, MECHANICS, METAL-
WORKERS. AMSTERDAM, 1955. 100P.

SCHOENMAKER, P.W. ENGLISH FOR SHIPS, OFFICERS, DU*EN. ED3. AMSTERDAM, DUWAER, 1958. 236P. 4200T.

ENGLISH

AMERICAN SOCIETY FOR TESTING/MATERIALS. STANDARD DEFINITIONS OF TERMS RELATING TO NAVAL STORES AND
PRODUCTS. (D804-57) ASTM STDS, PT.8, 1220-4. PHILADELPHIA, 1961. 60T.

BURGESS, F.H. A DICTIONARY OF SAILING. BALTIMORE, PENGUIN, 1961. 237P. 61-19223.

COURSE, A.G. A DICTIONARY OF NAUTICAL TERMS. LONDON, ARCO, 1962. 216P. 62-6885. 1500T.

INSTITUTE OF RADIO ENGINEERS. STANDARDS ON NAVIGATION AIDS, DIRECTION FINDER MEASUREMENTS. (ABBRS/DEFS,PP.
1350-2) (59 IRE 12.S1) PROC. IRE, V.47, 1349-71 (1959) 30T.

INSTITUTE OF RADIO ENGINEERS. STANDARDS ON RADIO AIDS TO NAVIGATION, DEFINITIONS OF TERMS. (54 IRE 12.S1)
PROC. IRE. V.43, 189-209 (1955) 600T.

LAYTON, C.W.T. DICTIONARY OF NAUTICAL WORDS AND TERMS. GLASGOW, BROWN/FERGUSON, 1955. 413P.
55-4773. 8000T.

LOVETTE, L.P. NAVAL CUSTOMS, TRADITIONS AND USAGE. ED4. ANNAPOLIS, U.S. NAVAL INST. 1959.358P. 59-11628.

MCEWEN, W.A. AND LEWIS, A.H. ENCYCLOPEDIA OF NAUTICAL KNOWLEDGE. CAMBRIDGE, MD, CORNELL MARITIME, 1953.
618P. 53-9685.

NOEL, J.V. NAVAL TERMS DICTIONARY. NEW YORK, VAN NOSTRAND, 1952. 247P. 52-10480. 5000T.

OCECODE. NAVIGATION ELECTRONICS (LAND, SEA, AIR, SPACE) HILVERSUM, 1962. 282P.

TALBOT-BOOTH, E.C. MERCHANT SHIPS 1963. LONDON, JOSEPH, 1963.   P. 10000T.

TAYLOR, J.M. A PRACTICAL DICTIONARY OF UNDERWATER ACOUSTIC DEVICES. ORLANDO, FLA, U.S. NAVY UNDERWATER
SOUND REF. LAB. 1953. 39P.

THOMPSON, JOHN I. AND CO. THE DEVELOPMENT OF A STANDARD GLOSSARY OF TORPEDO RUN TERMS. WASHINGTON. 1955.

U.S. DIVISION OF NAVAL HISTORY. DICTIONARY OF AMERICAN NAVAL FIGHTING SHIPS. WASHINGTON, 1959-- .
60-60198.

U.S. NAVY. HYDROGRAPHIC OFFICE. NAVIGATION DICTIONARY. WASHINGTON,1956. 253P. 56-60471. 8000T.

WITTY, M.B. EL AL. DICTIONARY OF MARINE ENGINEERING AND NAVAL ARCHITECTURE ABBREVIATIONS, SIGNS AND
SYMBOLS. NEW YORK, SETI, 196 . 256P.

WITTY, M.B. ET AL. DICTIONARY OF NAVIGATION ABBREVIATIONS, SIGNS AND SYMBOLS. NEW YORK, SETI, 196 .

FRENCH

FREMINVILLE, R.M. DICTIONNARIE DE LA MER... (MARINE D. FR DEFS) PARIS, LAFFONT, 1958. 643P.
59-40566. 3200T.

HAZARD, J. DICTIONNARIE ANGLAIS-FRANCAIS ET FRANCAIS-ANGLAIS DES TERMES DE MARINE. (*FR*EN MARINE D) ED2.
PARIS, MARIT/COLONIALES, 1956. 197P. 57-40837. 7500T.

HUDON, C. PILOTAGE ET HYDROGRAPHIE,GLOSSAIRE ANGLAIS-FRANCAIS,BT-105. (PILOTING/HYDR, EN*FR GL) OTTAWA,
DEPT. SECY.STATE, 1962. 48P. 1200T.

LE CLERE, J. GLOSSAIRE DES TERMES DE MARINE. (NAVAL GL, FR DEFS) PARIS, DUNOD, 1961. 426P.

LE FRANCOIS, G. LE VOCABULAIRE DU NAVIRE, ANGLAIS-FRANCAIS... (EN*FR D. OF MARINE ENG) PARIS, SOC. ED.
GEOGT MARIT/COLONIALES, 1953. 202P. 57-45276. 10000T.

GERMAN

ANDRIANO, . DEUTSCH-ENGLISCHES SCHIFFSWOERTERBUCH. (GE*EN NAVAL D) BERLIN, BERNARD/GRAEFE, 1952.

BREDT, A. WEYERS FLOTTENTASCHENBUCH. (WEYERS LIST OF SHIPS, GE DEFS) MUNICH, LEHMANN, 1963. 404P.

DIETEL,W. SEEFAHRTS-WOERTERBUCH, DEUTSCH-ENGLISCH,ENGLISCH-DEUTSCH. (SEAFARING D,*GE*EN) MUNICH, LEHMANN,
1954. 288P. 55-27563.

DLUHY, R. SCHIFFSTECHNISCHES WOERTERBUCH, SCHIFFBAU, SCHIFFAHRT UND SCHIFFSMACHINENBAU. (*GE*EN
SHIPBLDG. D) ED2. (V.1, GE*EN, 879P. V.2, EN*GE, 945P) BREMEN, DORN, 1956. A57-583. 40000T.

GREEK

VASILIADI, H. MODERN PRACTICAL ENGLISH-GREEK POCKET DICTIONARY FOR GREEK MERCANTILE MARINE, 1953.
262+233P.

105

ITALIAN

ARIOTTI, P.L. DIZIONARIO INGLESE-ITALIANO E ITALIANO-INGLESE DEI TERMINI NAVALI. (*IT*EN NAVAL D) ALASSIO, SIES, 1957. 130P. A57-7394.

CASTAGNA, L. DIZIONARIO MARINARO. (NAVAL D, IT DEFS) ROME, 1955. 483P. 55-30306.

ITALY. MINISTERO DELLA DIFESA. MARINA (DEPT) DIZIONARIO DI TERMINOLOGIA TECNICA NAVALE, ITALIANO-INGLESE E INGLESE-ITALIANO. (NAVAL T, *IT*EN) ROME, IST. POLIGR. STATO, 1952. 212P. 53-31694.

TISCIONE, N. MANUALE DI STUDIO DELLA TERMINOLOGIA TECNICA E NAVALE, ITALIANO-INGLESE, INGLESE-ITALIANO. (*IT*EN TECH/NAVAL D) NAPLES, TINES, 1957. 195P.

JAPANESE

DEMPA KOHO YOGO JITEN. (ELEC. NAVIGATION D, *EN*JA) TOKYO, KAIUNDO, 1959. J60-124. 2400T.

JAPAN. MINISTRY OF EDUCATION. JAPANESE SCIENTIFIC TERMS, NAVAL ARCHITECTURE AND MARINE ENGINEERING. I*JA *EN) TOKYO, SOC. NAVAL ARCHIT. JAPAN, 1955. 526P. 7000T.

JAPAN. MINISTRY OF EDUCATION. REVISED VOCABULARY OF SHIPBUILDING TERMS... (EN*JA) TOKYO, 1951. 22P. 670T.

JAPAN. MINISTRY OF EDUCATION. SHIPBUILDING TERMS. NEW WORDS REPLACING PRE-WAR TERMS. (JA*EN) TOKYO, 1952. 36P. 1600T.

KURATA, O. JAPANESE-ENGLISH VOCABULARY OF SHIPBUILDING. (*JA*EN) KOBE, KAIBUNDO, 1957. 240P.

MASUDA, M. EI-WA, WA-EI HAKUYO KIKAN YOGO SHU. (EN-JA, JA-EN NAVAL ENG. D) TOKYO, SEIBUNDO, 1960. 215P. J60-691. 6000T.

OZEKI, T. ENGLISH-JAPANESE TECHNICAL TERMS IN SHIPPING, SHIPBUILDING AND FOREIGN TRADE. KOBE, KAIBUNDO, 1955. 224P.

TAMURA, M. SAISHIN SEMPAKU KIKAN YOGO SHU. (MARINE ENG. D, EN*JA) TOKYO, KAIBUNDO, 1961. 370P. J62-888. 4800T.

YAMAGUCHI, M. ZOSEN YOGO JITEN. (SHIPBLDG. D, *JA*EN) KOBE, KAIBUNDO, 1960. 391P. 61-4906. 3000T.

NORWEGIAN

ASKIM, P. ENGELSK-NORSK MARITIM TEKNISK ORDBOK. (EN*NO MARINE ENG.D) ED3. OSLO, GROENDAHL, 1953. 219P.

ASKIM, P. NORSK-ENGELSK MARITIM TEKNISK ORDBOK. (NO*EN MARINE ENG.D) ED6. OSLO, GROENDAHL, 1958. 219P.

POLISH

GRABOWSKI, Z. AND WOJCICKI, J. TYSIAC SLOW O MORZU I OKRECIE. (1000 NAVAL T, PL DEFS) WARSAW, MIN. OBRONY NAR, 1955. 236P. 56-57358. 1000T.

MILEWSKI, S. ENGLISH-POLISH MARITIME DICTIONARY. WARSAW, 1963.

ZABROCKI, L. PRACE I MATERIALY Z ZAKRESU POLSKIEGO SLOWNICTWA MORSKIEGO. (POLISH NAVAL T, PL DEFS) DANZIG, ZAKLAD OSSOLINSKI WE WROCLAWIU, 1955-- . 56-34484.

POLYGLOT

AMICH, B.J. DICCIONARIO MARITIMO. (NAVAL D, *SP*EN*FR) BARCELONA, JUVENTUD, 1956. 455P. 56-46821.

GRADISNIK, J. ET AL. POMORSKA SLOVENSCINA. (NAVAL D, SV SC EN GE) LJUBLJANA, MLAD. KNJ, 1961. 281P. 62-58556. 2300T.

INTERNATIONAL HYDROGRAPHIC BUREAU. GLOSSARY OF CARTOGRAPHIC TERMS AND MANUAL OF SYMBOLS AND ABBREVIATIONS USED ON THE LATEST NAVIGATION CHARTS... (*EN*FR+21 LANG) ED3. MONACO, 1951. 188P.

KERCHOVE, R. DE. INTERNATIONAL MARITIME DICTIONARY... EN*FR*GE. ED2. PRINCETON, N.J. VAN NOSTRAND, 1961. 1018P, 61-16272. 13000T.

LLOYD,S CORP. GLOSSARY OF MARITIME AND COMMERCIAL TERMS IN LLOYD,S CALENDAR,*EN*FR*GE*IT*NO*SP. LONDON, 196 . 300T.

PAASCH, ET AL. DE LA OUILLE A LA POMME DU MAT. (FROM KEEL TO TRUCK, *FR*EN*GE*IT*SP D) REV.ED. PARIS,SOC. ED. GEOG, MARIT/COLONIALES, 1960. 1127P.

PERMANENT INTERNATIONAL ASSOCIATION OF NAVIGATION CONGRESSES. DICTIONNAIRE TECHNIQUE ILLUSTRE... (ILLUS. TECH. D *FR*EN*DU*GE*IT*SP) BRUSSELS, 1934-- . (IN PROGR) CH.1, LA MER (THE SEA) 1957. 272P. CH.2, FLEUVES, RIVIERES, CANAUX (STREAMS, RIVERS, CANALS) 1939. 122P. CH.3, (IN PREP) CH.4, (IN PREP) CH.5, MATERIAUX (MATER) 1951. ZO4R. CH.6, (CONSTRUCTION, PLANT/METHODS) 1959. 237P. CH.7, LES PORTS (PORTS) 1938. 58P. CH.8, ECLUSES ET CALES SECHES (LOCKS/DRY DOCKS) 1936. 86P. CH.9, (IN PREP) CH.10, BARRAGES EN RIVIERES (RIVER WEIRS) 1934. 88P. CH.11, (IN PREP) CH.12, SIGNALISATION MARITIME. (NAVAL TELECOMMUN) 1937. 143P. CH.13, EQUIPMENT (IN PREP) CH.14, (STAFF, ADMINISTRATION, EXPLOITATION (IN PREP) CH.15, FOUNDATIONS (IN PREP)

POPOVIC, P. TERMINOLOGIE DES TRANSPORTS PAR VOIES NAVIGABLES. (INLAND NAVIG. T, FR EN GE) GENEVA, 195 . 135P.

POLYGLOT

ROAD AND INLAND WATER TRANSPORT, 5 LANGUAGES. AMSTERDAM, ELSEVIER. (IN PREP)

SEGDITSAS, P.E. ET. AL. NAUTICAL DICTIONARY (*EN*FR*GE*IT*SP) (V.1, SHIPS/EQUIP, 400P. 4300T. V.2, MARINE ENG, 550P. 6000T. V.3, MARITIME T. 400P. 4470T) NEW YORK, ELSEVIER, 1963- . (IN PREP)

U.S. NAVAL ACADEMY. NAVAL PHRASEOLOGY IN ENGLISH, FRENCH, SPANISH, ITALIAN, GERMAN. REV. ED. ANNAPOLIS, 1953. 326P. 53-8844.

VASARHELYI, B. ET AL. KOZLEKEDESUGY.PT.2, HAJOZAS, REPULES, POSTA ES CSOVEZETEKES SZALLITAS. (D. OF NAVIGATION, AVIATION, MAIL/PNEUMATIC TRANSP,*HU*EN*GE*RU) (MUSZ. ERT. SZ, NO.8) BUDAPEST, TERRA, 1960. 174P. 60-34451. 1300T.

YSITA. E. GLOSSARY OF INTER-AMERICAN MARITIME TERMINOLOGY, ENGLISH-SPANISH-PORTUGUESE-FRENCH. WASHINGTON, PAN AM. UNION, 1959. 128P. PA59-38.

YUGOSLAVIA. REGISTAR BRODOVA. BRODSKA NOMENKLATURA, SRPSKO-HRVATSKI, ENGLESKI I TALIJANSKI. (NAVAL T, SC EN IT) RIJEKA, POMORSTVO, 1951. 254P. 56-29762.

PORTUGUESE

ESPARTEIRO, A.M. DICIONARIO ILUSTRADO DE MARINHA. (ILLUS. NAVAL D, PR DEFS) LISBON, LIVRARIA CLASSICA, 1962. 594P. 63-48619.

PENTEADO, F. COMO SE FALA A BORDO. (HOW TO SPEAK ON SHIPBOARD, PR DEFS) SAO PAULO, UNIV, 1952. 55P. 61-28135.

RUSSIAN

BELKINA, S.S. ANGLO-RUSSKII SLOVAR PO SUDOSTROENIIU I SUDOVOMU MASHINOSTROENIIU. (EN*RU SHIPBLDG/MARINE ENG.D) LENINGRAD, SUDPROMGIZ, 1958. 578P. 58-47290. 25000T.

CHERNOV, M.I. ET AL. SLOVAR MORSKIKH I RECHNYKH TERMINOV. (NAVAL/RIVER D, RU DEFS) MOSCOW, RECH. TRANSP, 1955-56. 2V. 56-36904. 8000T.

ELIANOV, D.I. AND MOROZOVSKII, N.G. ANGLO-RUSSKII I RUSSKO-ANGLIISKII SLOVAR VOENNO-MORSKIKH KOMAND. (*EN *RU NAVAL COMMAND D) MOSCOW, VOENIZDAT, 1960. 190P. 60-41744.

FADEEV, V.G. KRATKII MORSKOI SLOVAR. (NAVAL GL, RU DEFS) MOSCOW, VOENIZDAT, 1955. 119P. 56-39944. 90T.

FAVOROV, P.A. ET AL. ANGLO-RUSSKII SLOVAR PO PODVODNYM LODKAM I PROTIVOLODOCHNOI OBORONE. (EN*RU D. OF SUBMARINE/ANTI-SUBMARINE DEFENSE) MOSCOW, VOENIZDAT, 1963. 260P. 63-43903. 7000T.

GERNGROSS, V.M. AND FADEEV, V.G. ET AL. MORSKOI SLOVAR. (NAVAL RU*EN D) MOSCOW, VOENIZDAT, 1959. 2V. 59-51658. 12000T.

GOTSKII, M.V. ANGLIISKIE MORSKIE POSOBIIA I KARTY. (EN*RU D. OF NAVAL MANUALS/MAPS, PP. 195-230, 4000T) MOSCOW, MORSK. TRANSP, 1958. 258P. 59-42465.

MARCHENKO, V.G. AND MOROZOVSKII, N.G. ANGLO-RUSSKII VOENNO-MORSKOI SLOVAR. (EN*RU MIL/NAVAL D) MOSCOW, VOENIZDAT, 1962. 851P. 63-35236. 40000T.

RUTKOVSKAIA, T.L. AND SHANDABYLOV, V.D. ANGLO-RUSSKII SHTURMANSKII SLOVAR. (*EN*RU NAVIG.D) LENINGRAD, WMF, 312P.

TAUBE, A.M. AND SHMID, V.A. ANGLO-RUSSKII MORSKOI SLOVAR. (EN*RU NAVAL D) ED2. MOSCOW, GOS.IZD.INOSTR/ NATS. SLOVAR, 1951. 648P. 30000T.

TELBERG, V.G. AND SARNA, A. RUSSIAN-ENGLISH DICTIONARY OF NAUTICAL TERMS. ED2. NEW YORK, TELBERG, 1964. 72P. 64-13005.

U.S. NAVAL ACADEMY. NAVAL PHRASEOLOGY. RUSSIAN SUPPL. ED2. ANNAPOLIS, 1954. 140P. 53-8844.

SERBO-CROATIAN

POMORSKA ENCIKLOPEDIJA. (NAVAL ENCYCL, SC DEFS) ZAGREB, LEKSIKOGR. FNRJ, 1954-- V. 55-23893.

SPANISH

DICCIONARIO TECNICO-MARITIMO, INGLES-ESPANOL Y ESPANOL-INGLES. (*EN*SP NAVAL D) HAVANA, MARINA/GUERRA, 1955. 236+227P. 57-45961.

GARCIA CALERO, A. DICCIONARIO GENERAL DE MARINA. (NAVAL D, SP DEFS) MEXICO, GARCIA CALERO, 1954. 256+39P. 56-40310.

INTER-AMERICAN DEFENSE BOARD. DICCIONARIO DE TERMINOS MILITARES PARA LAS FUERZAS ARMADAS, INGLES-ESPANOL. (EN*SP MIL.D) ED2. WASHINGTON, 1957. 245P. 58-20616.

LIZARRAGA, F. DICCIONARIO TECNICO, INGLES-ESPANOL Y ESPANOL-INGLES, PARA USO DE LOS EJERCITOS DE TIERRA, MAR Y AIRE. (*SP*EN MIL.D, LAND,SEA/AIR) MADRID, BIBLIOG. ESP, 1953. 706P. 54-33732.

MANGOLD, W. TERMINOLOGIA MILITAR-NAVAL-AEREA. (POCKET MANUAL OF MIL.T... LAND, SEA/AIR,*SP*EN) MADRID, MANGOLD, 1955. 191P. 55-1306. 3000T.

MARTINEZ-HIDALGO, T.J.M. ENCICLOPEDIA GENERAL DEL MAR. (NAVAL ENCYCL, SP DEFS) MADRID, GARRIGA, 1957-- . 58-19475.

NAVAL SCIENCE AND ENGINEERING

SPANISH

NAVARRO DAGNINO, J. VOCABULARIO MARITIMO... INGLES-ESPANOL Y ESPANOL-INGLES. (*SP*EN NAVAL D) ED3.
BARCELONA, GILI, 1957. 151P. 62-53648.

ORTIZ DUENAS, T. VOCABULARIO ORTOGRAFICO MARITIMO. (NAVAL ORTHOGR.D,SP DEFS) LIMA, ESCUELA NAVAL/PERU,
1960. 80P. 61-41521.

PANDO Y VILLARROYA, J.L. DICCIONARIO MARITIMO. (NAVAL D, SP DEFS) MADRID, DOSSAT, 1956. 235P.
56-33059.

SWEDISH

GJOERES, A. ET AL. SOHLMANS SJOELEXIKON. (SOHLMAN,S NAVAL D,*SW*EN) STOCKHOLM, 1955. 1220P. 55-56560.

TURKISH

KAHANE, H.R. ET AL. THE LINGUA FRANCA IN THE LEVANT, TURKISH NAUTICAL TERMS OF ITALIAN AND GREEK ORIGIN
URBANA, UNIV. ILLINOIS, 1958. 752P. 58-6996.

UKRAINIAN

STEPANOWSKY, W.P. AMERICAN-UKRAINIAN NAUTICAL DICTIONARY. NEW YORK,1953. 236P.

NUCLEAR PHYSICS AND ENGINEERING

CHINESE

UNITED NATIONS. PROVISIONAL GLOSSARY ON ATOMIC ENERGY. ADDENDUM 1, ENGLISH-CHINESE. NEW YORK, 1956.
132P. 1400T.

CZECH

NEMEC, J. TERMINOLOGIE V JADERNE ENERGETICE, CESKO-ANGLICKY. (CZ*EN NUCL. ENG. GL) PRAGUE, ENERG. USTAV
1957. 37P.

PRAGUE. VYZKUMNY USTAV TEPELNE TECHNIKY. VYKLADOVY SLOVNICEK 101 ANGLICKYCH VYRAZU Z OBORU ATOMOVE A
JADERNE ENERGIE. PRAGUE, 1956. (101 EN T. IN ATOM/NUCL. ENERGY, CZ DEFS) 10P. 59-31651.

REZANKA, I. ANGLICKO-CESKY SLOVNICEK Z JADERNE FYSIKY A TECHNOLOGIE. (EN*CZ NUCL. PHYS/ENG GL) PRAGUE,
SNTL, 1957. 53P. 58-15847. 2200T.

ENGLISH

AMERICAN INSTITUTE OF ELECTRICAL ENGINEERS. DEFINITIONS OF ELECTRICAL TERMS. RADIOLOGY. IGR-75, ASA
C42.75) NEW YORK (IN PREP)

AMERICAN SOCIETY FOR TESTING/MATERIALS. TENTATIVE DEFINITIONS OF TERMS RELATING TO DOSIMETRY. (E170-60T
ASTM STDS, PT.3, 330-2. PHILADELPHIA, 1961. 30T.

BARNES, D.E. ET AL. CONCISE ENCYCLOPAEDIA OF NUCLEAR ENERGY. NEW YORK, INTERSCIENCE, 1962. 886P.
63-1048.

BRITISH STANDARDS INSTITUTION. GLOSSARY OF TERMS USED IN NUCLEAR SCIENCE. (B.S. 3455) LONDON, 1962. 12
2000T.

BRITISH STANDARDS INSTITUTION. GLOSSARY OF TERMS USED IN RADIOLOGY. (B.S. 2597) LONDON, 1955. 84P. 750

BRITISH STANDARDS INSTITUTION. LETTER SYMBOLS, SIGNS AND ABBREVIATIONS. PT.2 CHEMICAL ENGINEERING,
NUCLEAR SCIENCE AND APPLIED CHEMISTRY. (B.S. 1991) LONDON, 1961. 48P. 550T.

CLARK, G.L. THE ENCYCLOPEDIA OF X-RAYS AND GAMMA RAYS. NEW YORK, REINHOLD, 1963. 1149P. 63-13449.
900T.

COOKE, N.M. AND MARKUS, J. ELECTRONICS AND NUCLEONICS DICTIONARY... NEW YORK, MCGRAW-HILL, 1960. 543P.
60-10605. 13000T.

CROSBY, J.W. A DESCRIPTIVE GLOSSARY OF RADIOACTIVE MINERALS. PULLMAN, WASHINGTON STATE COLL, 1955. 14
400T.

EDISON ELECTRIC INSTITUTE. GLOSSARY OF ELECTRIC UTILITY TERMS, FINANCIAL AND TECHNICAL. NUCLEAR SUPPL
(PUB. NO.61-49) NEW YORK, 1961. 13P.

ESSO RESEARCH AND ENGINEERING CO. 101 ATOMIC TERMS AND WHAT THEY MEAN. NEW YORK, 1959. 20P. 100T.

ETTER, L.E. GLOSSARY OF WORDS AND PHRASES USED IN RADIOLOGY AND NUCLEAR MEDICINE. SPRINGFIELD, ILL,
THOMAS, 1960. 203P. 59-14918.

GREAT BRITAIN. CENTRAL ELECTRICITY GENERATING BOARD. A GLOSSARY OF NUCLEAR POWER TERMS. LONDON, 1963.
44P.

HIX, C.F. AND ALLEY, R.P. PHYSICAL LAWS AND EFFECTS. NEW YORK, WILEY, 1958. 291P. 58-13461.

HOGERTON, J.F. ET AL. THE ATOMIC ENERGY DESKBOOK. NEW YORK, REINHOLD, 1963. 673P. 63-13445. 1000T.

NUCLEAR PHYSICS AND ENGINEERING

ENGLISH

INSTITUTE OF RADIO ENGINEERS. STANDARDS ON NUCLEAR TECHNIQUES, DEFINITIONS FOR THE SCINTILLATION COUNTER FIELD. PROC. IRE. V.48, 1449-53 (1960)   80T.

NATIONAL RESEARCH COUNCIL CONFERENCE ON GLOSSARY OF TERMS IN NUCLEAR SCIENCE AND TECHNOLOGY. A GLOSSARY OF TERMS IN NUCLEAR SCIENCE AND TECHNOLOGY. (SAME AS ASA N.1.1) NEW YORK, AM.SOC.MECH.ENG, 1957. 188P. 59-40. 1800T.

SACHS, A.M. AND SCHWARTZ, M. GLOSSARY OF TERMS FREQUENTLY USED IN HIGH ENERGY PHYSICS. NEW YORK, AM.INST. PHYS, 1961. 21P. 100T.

SARBACHER, R.I. ENCYCLOPEDIC DICTIONARY OF ELECTRONICS AND NUCLEAR ENGINEERING. ENGLEWOOD CLIFFS, N.J, PRENTICE-HALL, 1959. 1417P. 59-11990. 16000T.

STEARNS, R.L. GLOSSARY OF TERMS FREQUENTLY USED IN NUCLEAR PHYSICS. NEW YORK, AM. INST. PHYS, 1962. 37P. 200T.

UNITED KINGDOM ATOMIC ENERGY AUTHORITY. GLOSSSARY OF ATOMIC TERMS... ED4. LONDON, 1962. 62P. 63-40326. 500T.

U.S. ATOMIC ENERGY COMMISSION. AEC-GREGG SHORTHAND DICTIONARY... WASHINGTON, 1957. 124P. 57-61288.

WHITEHOUSE, D.R. GLOSSARY OF TERMS FREQUENTLY USED IN PLASMA PHYSICS. NEW YORK, AM.INST. PHYS,1960. 30P. 180T.

WITTY, M.B. ET AL. DICTIONARY OF NUCLEAR ABBREVIATIONS, SIGNS, SYMBOLS AND TABLES. NEW YORK, SETI, 1963. 192P.

FRENCH

CHAVANNE, A. DICTIONNAIRE, AGENDA, ANNUAIRE ATOMIQUE. (AT. D, AGENDA, ANNUAL, FR DEFS) PARIS, IND. AT 1961. 356P. 62-46365.

COMBE, J. DICTIONNAIRE NUCLEAIRE. (NUCL.D, FR DEFS) GENEVA, KISTER, 1961.

ENCYCLOPEDIE FRANCAISE. V.2, LA PHYSIQUE. (PHYS, FR DEFS) PARIS, LAROUSSE, 1956. 508P.

KING, G.G. DICTIONNAIRE ANGLAIS-FRANCAIS, ELECTRONIQUE, PHYSIQUE NUCLEAIRE, ET SCIENCES CONNEXES. EN*FR D. OF ELECTRON, NUCL. PHYS/RELATED SCI) PARIS, DUNOD, 1959. 311P. 60-20839. 21000T.

KING, G.G. DICTIONNARIE FRANCAIS-ANGLAIS, ELECTRONIQUE, PHYSIQUE NUCLEAIRE ET SCIENCES CONNEXES. (FR*EN D. OF ELECTRON, NUCL. PHYS/RELATED SCI) PARIS, DUNOD, 1961. 395P. 61-4361. 24000T.

OSTOYA, P. VOCABULAIRE DE L,ENERGIE NUCLEAIRE. (NUCL. ENERG. D, FR DEFS) PARIS, INST. PED. NATL, 1959.

PIRAUX, H. PETIT LEXIQUE DE L,ENERGIE ATOMIQUE. (AT.ENERGY GL, FR DEFS) PARIS, EYROLLES, 1958. 139P. 59-20687. 450T.

GERMAN

ERZEUGNISSE UND DIENSTLEISTUNGEN DER DEUTSCHEN INDUSTRIE FUER VERSCHIEDENE KERNTECHNISCHE ARBEITSGEBIETE. (GE*EN GL. OF AT.ENERGY) ATOMIND. DEUT, NO.4, 159-   (1960)

FLUEGGE, S. ET AL. HANDBUCH DER PHYSIK. (ENCYCL. OF PHYS) V.38, PT.1, AEUSSERE EIGENSCHAFTEN DER ATOMKERNE. (EXTERNAL PROPERTIES OF ATOMIC NUCLEI, *GE*EN GL, PP.454-71, 650T) BERLIN, SPRINGER, 1958. 471P. A56-2942.

FLUEGGE, S. ET AL. HANDBUCH DER PHYSIK. (ENCYCL. OF PHYS) V.35, ATOME 1. (ATOMS 1, *GE*EN GL, PP.437-54, 630T) BERLIN, SPRINGER, 1957. 454P. A56-2942.

FLUEGGE, S. ET AL. HANDBUCH DER PHYSIK. (ENCYCL. OF PHYS) V.36, ATOME 2. (ATOMS 2, *GE*EN GL, PP.409-24, 500T) BERLIN, SPRINGER, 1956. 424P. A56-2942.

FLUEGGE, S. ET AL. HANDBUCH DER PHYSIK. (ENCYCL. OF PHYS) V.37, PT.1, ATOME 3-MOLEKUELE 1. (ATOMS 3-MOLECULES 1, *GE*EN GL, PP.416-39, 840T) BERLIN, SPRINGER, 1959. 439P. A56-2942.

FLUEGGE, S. ET AL. HANDBUCH DER PHYSIK. (ENCYCL. OF PHYS) V.39, BAU DER ATOMKERNE. (STRUCT. OF AT. NUCLEI, *GE*EN GL, PP.551-66, 560T) BERLIN, SPRINGER, 1957. 566P. A56-2942.

FLUEGGE, S. ET AL. HANDBUCH DER PHYSIK. (ENCYCL. OF PHYS) V.41/2, BETAZERFALL. (BETA DECAY, *GE*EN GL, PP.106-17, 600T) BERLIN, SPRINGER, 1962. 117P. A56-2942.

FLUEGGE, S. ET AL. HANDBUCH DER PHYSIK. (ENCYCL. OF PHYS) INSTRUMENTE HILFSMITTEL DER KERNPHYSIK. (NUCL. INSTR, *GE*EN GL, V.44, PP.450-73, 850T. V.45, PP.518-44, 1000T) BERLIN, SPRINGER, 1958-59. A56-2942.

FLUEGGE, S. ET AL. HANDBUCH DER PHYSIK. (ENCYCL. OF PHYS) V.40, KERNREAKTIONEN 1. (NUCL. REACTIONS 1, *GE*EN GL, PP.538-53, 500T) BERLIN, SPRINGER, 1957. 553P. A56-2942.

FLUEGGE, S. ET AL. HANDBUCH DER PHYSIK. (ENCYCL. OF PHYS) V.41, PT.1, KERNREAKTIONEN 2, THEORIE. (NUCL. REACTIONS 2, THEOR,*GE*EN GL,PP.561-80, 650T) BERLIN, SPRINGER 1959. 580P. A56-2942.

FLUEGGE, S. ET AL. HANDBUCH DER PHYSIK. (ENCYCL. OF PHYS) V.42, KERNREAKTIONEN 3. (NUCL. REACTIONS 3, *GE*EN GL, PP.611-26, 450T) BERLIN, SPRINGER, 1957. 626P. A56-2942.

NUCLEAR PHYSICS AND ENGINEERING

GERMAN

FLUEGGE, S. ET AL. HANDBUCH DER PHYSIK. (ENCYCL. OF PHYS) V.34, KORPUSKELN UND STRAHLUNG IM MATERIE 2. (CORPUSCLES/RADIATION IN MATTER 2. *GE*EN GL, PP.298-316, 630T) BERLIN, SPRINGER, 1958. 316P. A56-2942

FLUEGGE, S. ET AL. HANDBUCH DER PHYSIK. (ENCYCL. OF PHYS) V.46, KOSMISCHE STRAHLUNG 1. (COSMIC RAYS 1 *GE*EN GL, PP.316-33, 550T) BERLIN, SPRINGER, 1961. 333P. A56-2942.

FLUEGGE, S. ET AL. HANDBUCH DER PHYSIK. (ENCYCL. OF PHYS) V.38, PT.2, NEUTRONEN UND VERWANDTE GAMMASTRAHLPROBLEME. (NEUTRONS/RELATED GAMMA RAY PROBLEMS, *GE*EN GL, PP.818-68, 1800T) BERLIN, SPRINGER 1959. 868P. A56-2942.

FLUEGGE, S. ET AL. HANDBUCH DER PHYSIK. (ENCYCL. OF PHYS) V.30, ROENGENSTRAHLEN. (X-RAYS, *GE*EN GL, PP.371-84, 500T) BERLIN, SPRINGER, 1957. 384P. A56-2942.

FRANKE, H. ET AL. LEXIKON DER PHYSIK. (PHYS. ENCYCL, GE DEFS) STUTTGART, FRANCKH, 1959. 2V. 1687P. 59-34885.

FRANZEN, L.F. ET AL. WOERTERBUCH DER KERNENERGIE, ENGLISCH-DEUTSCH. (EN*GE NUCL.PHYS.D) DUESSELDORF, VDI 1957. 240P. 58-39335. 6000T.

GAYNOR, F. POCKET ENCYCLOPEDIA OF ATOMIC ENERGY. (EN*GE) NEW YORK, PHIL.LIBR, 1957. 204P. 57-4605.

GOERHE, L. ET AL. KLEINES ABC DER KERNPHYSIK UND KERNTECHNIK. (NUCL. PHYS/ENG. ABC, GE DEFS) LEIPZIG, DEUT. VERLAG/GRUNDSTOFFIND, 1961. 121P.

HYMAN, C.J. AND IDLIN, R. DICTIONARY OF PHYSICS AND ALLIED SCIENCES. WOERTERBUCH DER PHYSIK UND VERWANDTER WISSENSCHAFTEN. (V.1, GE*EN 675P. V.2, EN*GE, 680P) NEW YORK, UNGAR, 1958-62. 62-9683. 20000T.

MUELLER, W.D. ATOM ABC. (AT.ABC, GE DEFS) DUESSELDORF, ECON, 1959. 322P. A60-4028.

PUTZ, W. AND HURST, R. ET AL. LUEGERS LEXIKON DER TECHNIK. (ENCYCL. OF TECH) V.2 GRUNDLAGEN DER ELEKTROTECHNIK UND KERNTECHNIK. (ELEC/NUCL. ENG, GE DEFS) ED4. STUTTGART, DEUTSCHE VERLAGS-ANSTALT, 1960. 624P. A61-2000.

RAU, H. WOERTERBUCH DER KERNPHYSIK, DEUTSCH-ENGLISCH/AMERIKANISCH, ENGLISCH/AMERIKANISCH-DEUTSCH.(*GE*EN NUCL. PHYS. D) WIESBADEN, BRANDSTETTER, 1957. 247P. A59-5023. 5000T.

REDDING, A.Z. NUCLEAR ENERGY TERMS. A BILINGUAL GLOSSARY, ENGLISH-GERMAN, GERMAN-ENGLISH. NEW YORK, NUCL. TRANSL. SERV, 1960. 121P. 62-2153. 1200T.

SCHWENKHAGEN, H.F. ATOMKERN-ENERGIE IN STICHWORTEN... (AT.ENERGY T, GE DEFS) KARLSRUHE, VERSICHERUNGSWIRTSCHAFT, 1956. 51P. A57-4155.

JAPANESE

JAPAN ATOMIC INDUSTRY FORUM. DICTIONARY OF ATOMIC ENERGY. (*JA*EN) TOKYO, OMU-SHA, 1957. 258P. 1000T.

TAKIUCHI, M. ET AL. RADIOLOGICAL DICTIONARY... (JA EN) KYOTO, KIMPODO, 1954. 474+78+47P.

VOCABULARY OF ATOMIC ENERGY. (EN*JA) TOKYO, ASAHI SHIMBUNSHA, 1957. 205P.

POLYGLOT

BENE, G.J. ATOMIC AND MOLECULAR PHYSICS. (EN/AM*FR*GE*IT*RU*SP) NEW YORK, ELSEVIER. (IN PREP)

BENE, G.J. ET AL. NUCLEAR PHYSICS AND ATOMIC ENERGY... *EN*FR*GE*RU. NEW YORK, ELSEVIER, 1960. Z14P. 59-12583. 2100T.

CHARLES, V. DICTIONNARIE ATOMIQUE. (AT. ENERGY D, FR DEFS, *EN*GE*RU) PARIS, HACHETTE, 1960. 317P. A61-1772. 1500T.

CLASON, W.E. ELSEVIER,S DICTIONARY OF NUCLEAR SCIENCE AND TECHNOLOGY....*EN/AM*DU*FK*GE*IT*SP. NEW YORK ELSEVIER, 1958. 914P. 58-12242. 4000T.

CLASON, W.E. SUPPLEMENT TO THE ELSEVIER DICTIONARIES OF ELECTRONICS, NUCLEONICS AND TELECOMMUNICATION. (*EN/AM*DU*FR*GE*IT*SP) NEW YORK, ELSEVIER, 1963. 633P. 63-11369. 2500T.

DEUTSCHER MEDIZINISCHER SPRACHENDIENST. TERMINI RADIOLOGICI, DEUTSCH,ENGLISCH,FRANCAIS,ESPANOL (RADIOLO T, GE EN FR SP) MUNICH, URBAN/SCHWARZENBERG, 1959. 78P. 60-41407.

DUNWORTH, J.V. ET AL. GLOSSARY OF NUCLEAR TERMS... GE EN FR JA RU SP.LONDON, PERGAMON. (IN PREP)

ESPE, W. AND KUHN, A. ELEMENTARE GRUNDLAGEN DER KERNPHYSIK... (FUNDAMENTALS OF NUCL. PHYS, GE EN FR RU) ED2. LEIPZIG, GEEST/PORTIG, 1958. 263P. 58-37346. 300T.

FOSSATI, F. DIZIONARIO TECNICO DI RADIOLOGIA... (RADIOLOGY D, IT EN FR GE SP) MILAN, 1952. 490P.

FUKSA, J. AND VELART, W. PETIJAZYCNY SLOVNIK Z OBORU JADERNE ENERGIE A TECHNIKY. (5-LANG. NUCL. PHYS/EN D, CZ*EN*FR*GE*RU) PRAGUE, SNTL, 1959-60.

HOECKER, K.H. AND WEIMER, K. LEXIKON DER KERN-UND REAKTORTECHNIK. (NUCL. PHYS/REACTOR ENG. ENCYCL, GE*E *FR) STUTTGART, FRANCKH, 1959. 2V. 1685P. 59-2376. 3000T.

NUCLEAR PHYSICS AND ENGINEERING

POLYGLOT

NTERNATIONAL ELECTROTECHNICAL COMMISSION. INTERNATIONAL ELECTROTECHNICAL VOCABULARY. DETECTION AND
EASUREMENT OF NUCLEAR RADIATIONS BY ELECTRICAL MEANS. (*FR*EN*DU*GE*IT*PL*SP*SW) (IEC-50-GR-66) ED2.
ENEVA. (IN PREP)

NTERNATIONAL ELECTROTECHNICAL COMMISSION. INTERNATIONAL ELECTROTECHNICAL VOCABULARY. NUCLEAR POWER
LANTS FOR ELECTRIC ENERGY GENERATION *FR*EN*DU*GE*IT*PL*SP*SW) (IEC-50-GR-26) ED2. GENEVA. (IN PREP)

ETTENMEYER, L. ATOMTERMINOLOGIE... (AT. T, *EN*GE*FR*IT) NEW YORK, PHIL. LIBR, 1959. 298P. 59-65415.
800T.

JBE, R. DICTIONARY OF NUCLEAR PHYSICS AND TECHNOLOGY. (EN*GE*FR*RU) NEW YORK, PERGAMON, 1961. 1606P.
1-18857. 15000T.

JBE, R. NUCLEAR PHYSICS AND ENGINEERING. HUNGARIAN SUPPLEMENT. (*HU*EN*FR*GE*RU) BUDAPEST, 1962.
790P. 15000T.

JGIMOTO, A. AND HASHIGUCHI, R. GLOSSARY OF ATOMIC TERMS IN JAPANESE, ENGLISH, FRENCH,AND RUSSIAN. TOKYO,
INOKUNIYA, 1956. 330P.

EKNISKA NOMENKLATURCENTRALEN. KAERNTEKNISK ORDLISTA... (NUCL. SCI/ENG. GL, *SW*EN*FR) (TNC PUBL. NO.36)
TOCKHOLM, SEELIG, 1962. 109P. 63-32836. 1000T.

HEWLIS, J. ET AL. ENCYCLOPAEDIC DICTIONARY OF PHYSICS, GENERAL, NUCLEAR, SOLID STATE,MOLECULAR,CHEMICAL,
ETAL AND VACUUM PHYSICS, ASTRONOMY, GEOPHYSICS, BIOPHYSICS AND RELATED SUBJECTS, EN DEFS. MULTILINGUAL
_, *CH*FR*GE*JA*SP. NEW YORK, PERGAMON, 1961-63. 9V. 60-7069. 15000T.

NITED NATIONS. ATOMIC ENERGY, GLOSSARY OF TECHNICAL TERMS, *EN*FR*RU*SP. ED4. NEW YORK, 1958. 215P.
8-4232. 5500T.

NITED NATIONS. LIST OF TERMS CONCERNING NEW SOURCES OF ENERGY. (TERMINOLOGY BULL. NO.176) NEW YORK,
961.

NITED NATIONS. PROVISIONAL GLOSSARY OF TERMS RELATING TO THE BIOLOGICAL EFFECTS OF ATOMIC RADIATIONS, AND
DDENDUM (EN FR RU SP) (TERM. BULL. NO. 139/REV.1) NEW YORK, 1959-60. 2V.

DSKOBOINIK, D.I. SEMIIAZYCHNYI IADERNYI SLOVAR. (7-LANG. NUCL. D, RU*EN*FR*GE*IT*DU*SP) MOSCOW,
IZMATGIZ, 1961. 462P. 62-26811. 4000T.

RUSSIAN

KADEMIIA NAUK SSSR. INST. NAUCH. INFORM. ANGLO-RUSSKII SLOVAR PO IADERNOI FIZIKE I TEKHNIKE. (EN*RU NUCL.
HYS/ENG.D) MOSCOW, 1955. 288P. 56-18269. 15000T.

KADEMIIA NAUK SSSR. INST. NAUCH. INFORM. RUSSKO-ANGLIISKII SLOVAR PO IADERNOI FIZIKE I TEKHNIKE. (RU*EN
UCL. PHYS/ENG.D) MOSCOW,1955. 349P. 56-18270. 15000T.

ARPOVICH, E.A. RUSSIAN-ENGLISH ATOMIC DICTIONARY. ED2. NEW YORK, TECH. DICT, 1959. 317P. 59-2755.
3000T.

LASON, W.E. DICTIONARY OF NUCLEAR SCIENCE AND TECHNOLOGY... RUSSIAN SUPPL. NEW YORK, ELSEVIER, 1961.
3P. 4000T.

ONSULTANTS BUREAU. RUSSIAN-ENGLISH GLOSSARY OF NUCLEAR PHYSICS AND ENGINEERING. NEW YORK,1957. 195P.
7-3050. 10000T.

MELIANOV, V.S. KRATKAIA ENTSIKLOPEDIIA, ATOMNAIA ENERGIIA. (CONCISE AT. ENERGY ENCYCL, RU DEFS)
DSCOW, BOLSH. SOV. ENTSIKL, 1958. 612P. 59-32217. 3000T.

MIN, I. RUSSIAN-ENGLISH PHYSICS DICTIONARY. NEW YORK, WILEY, 1963. 554P. 63-8056. 40000T.

DRELIK, IA.M. ET AL. KRATKII SLOVAR NEKOTORYKH TERMINOV I OPREDELENII PO ATOMNOI ENERGII, ATOMNOMU
RUZHIIU I PROTIVOATOMNOI ZASHCHITE. (GL. OF AT. ENERGY, WEAPONS/ANTI-NUCL. DEFENSE, RU DEFS) MOSCOW,
DSAAF, 1958. 64P. 58-36797. 300T.

DZAK, A.S. AND SMITH, C.H. STUDIES IN MACHINE TRANSLATION. PT.12, GLOSSARY OF RUSSIAN PHYSICS, SANTA
DNICA, CAL, RAND, 1960. (AD-252-609) 297P. 63-4338.

.S. ATOMIC ENERGY COMMISSION. GLOSSARY OF RUSSIAN TERMS IN NUCLEAR TECHNOLOGY. (PT.1, RU*EN. PT.2,
#*RU) OAK, RIDGE, TENN, 1952. 50P. 1000T.

DSKOBOINIK, D.I. AND TSIMMERMAN, M.G. ANGLO-RUSSKII IADERNYI SLOVAR.(EN*RU NUCL.D) MOSCOW, FIZMATGIZ,
)60. 400P. 61-24483. 20000T.

DSKOBOINIK, D.I. AND TSIMMERMAN, M.G. RUSSKO-ANGLIISKII IADERNYI SLOVAR. (RU*EN NUCL.D) MOSCOW,
IZMATGIZ, 1960. 334P. 61-29520. 20000T.

VEDENSKII, B.A. ET AL. FIZICHESKII ENTSIKLOPEDICHESKII SLOVAR. (ENCYCL. D. OF PHYS, RU DEFS) MOSCOW,
DV. ENTSIKL, 1960- . 4V. 61-29525.

SERBO-CROATIAN

ELIMIROVIC, M. ET AL. MALA ATOMSKA ENCIKLOPEDIJA. (AT. ENERGY D, SC DEFS) ZAGREB, EPOHA, 1962. 659P.
)-38440.

NUCLEAR PHYSICS AND ENGINEERING

SERBO-CROATIAN

VELIMIROVIC, M. RECNIK OSNOVNIH POJMOVA O ATOMSKOJ ENERGIJI. (BASIC AT. ENERGY T, SC DEFS) ED2. BELGRADE, TEH.KNJ,1960. 88P. 61-33460.

OCEANOGRAPHY AND HYDROLOGY

ENGLISH

ARMSTRONG, T.E. AND ROBERTS, B. ILLUSTRATED ICE GLOSSARY. CAMBRIDGE,ENG, SCOTT POLAR RES.INST, 1956. 12P. 57-18290.

BECKMANN, W. AND YASSO, W.E. GLOSSARY OF TERMS FREQUENTLY USED IN PHYSICS OF OCEANOGRAPHY. NEW YORK, AM. INST. PHYS. 1962. 23P. 200T.

HUXLEY, A. STANDARD ENCYCLOPEDIA OF THE WORLD,S OCEANS AND ISLANDS. NEW YORK, PUTNAM, 1962. 383P.

LANGBEIN, W.B. AND ISERI, K.T. GENERAL INTRODUCTION AND HYDROLOGIC DEFINITIONS. MANUAL OF HYDROLOGY, PT.1. (G.S. WATER SUPPLY PAPER NO.1541) WASHINGTON, O.S. GEOL. SURV, 1960. 29P. 300T.

TAYLOR, J.M. A PRACTICAL DICTIONARY OF UNDERWATER ACOUSTIC DEVICES. ORLANDO, FLA, U.S. NAVY UNDERWATER SOUND REF. LAB, 1953. 39P.

U.S. ARCTIC, DESERT AND TROPIC INFORMATION CENTER. GLOSSARY OF ARCTIC AND SUBARCTIC TERMS. (ADTIC PUBL, A-105) MAXWELL AFB, ALA. 1955. 90P. 56-60228.

U.S. HYDROGRAPHIC OFFICE. A FUNCTIONAL GLOSSARY OF ICE TERMINOLOGY. (H.O.NO.609) WASHINGTON, 1952. 88P. 52-60807.

U.S. HYDROGRAPHIC OFFICE. GLOSSARY OF OCEANOGRAPHIC TERMS. (SPEC. PUBL. NO. 35) WASHINGTON, 1960. 12P. 60-61612. 300T.

WIEGEL, R.L. WAVES, TIDES, CURRENTS, AND BEACHES, GLOSSARY OF TERMS AND LIST OF STANDARD SYMBOLS. COUNCIL ON WAVE RES, ENG. FOUND, 1953. 113P. A55-3914.

WITTY,M.B. ET AL. DICTIONARY OF METEOROLOGY, ASTRONOMY AND OCEANOGRAPHY ABBREVIATIONS, SIGNS, SYMBOLS, AND TABLES. NEW YORK, SETI, 196 . 256P.

WORLD METEOROLOGICAL ORGANIZATION. INTERNATIONAL ICE NOMENCLATURE. LONDON, 1952.

FRENCH

FREMINVILLE, R.M. DICTIONNARIE DE LA MER... (MARINE D, FR DEFS) PARIS, LAFFONT, 1958. 643P. 59-40566. 3200T.

HAZARD, J. DICTIONNARIE ANGLAIS-FRANCAIS ET FRANCAIS-ANGLAIS DES TERMES DE MARINE. (*FR*EN MARINE D) ED2, PARIS, MARIT/COLONIALES, 1956. 197P. 57-40837. 7500T.

HUDON, C. PILOTAGE ET HYDROGRAPHIE,GLOSSAIRE ANGLAIS-FRANCAIS,BT-105. (PILOTING/HYDR, EN*FR GL) OTTAWA, DEPT. SECY.STATE, 1962. 48P. 1200T.

NOMENCLATURE DES FORMES PROFONDES DU TERRAIN OCEANIQUE. (FR EN NOMENCL. OF OCEAN FLOOR T, PP.221-31) IN/FRANCE. CNRS. LA TOPOGRAPHIE ET LA GEOLOGIE DES PROFONDEURS OCEANIQUES. PARIS, 1959. 313P. 60-24516.

STEVENS, J.A.P. ENCYCLOPEDIE PRISMA DU MONDE SOUS-MARIN. (ENCYCL. OF OCEANOG, FR DEFS) PARIS, PRISMA, 1957. 558P. 57-43030.

UNITED NATIONS. LIST OF TERMS CONCERNING OCEANOGRAPHY. (*FR*EN) (TERMINOLOGY BULL. NO.158) NEW YORK, 1959.

JAPANESE

WADACHI, K. KAIYO NO JITEN. (ENCYCL.OF OCEANS, JA*EN) TOKYO, TOKYODO, 1960. 6+671P. J60-1043.

POLYGLOT

PERMANENT INTERNATIONAL ASSOCIATION OF NAVIGATION CONGRESSES. DICTIONNAIRE TECHNIQUE ILLUSTRE... (ILLUS. TECH. D, *FR*EN*DU*GE*IT*SP) V.1, LA MER. (THE SEA) BRUSSELS, 1957. 272P. 58-19041. 3000T.

SPENGLER, O.A. AND E.N. GIDROLOGICHESKII SLOVAR NA INOSTRANNYKH IAZYKAKH. (D.OF HYDROL, *RU*EN*FR*GE) LENINGRAD, GIDROMETEOIZDAT, 1959. 214P. 60-33508. 2400T.

RUSSIAN

GORSKII, N.N. AND GORSKAIA, V.I. ANGLO-RUSSKII OKEANOGRAFICHESKII SLOVAR. (EN*RU D. OF OCEANOG) MOSCOW, GITTL, 1957. 292P. 58-30249. 8000T.

MANDROVSKII, B.N. RUSSIAN-ENGLISH GLOSSARY AND SOVIET CLASSIFICATION OF ICE FOUND AT SEA. WASHINGTON, U.S. LIBR.CONGR, 1959. 30P. 59-60067. 300T.

MEZHDUNARODNAIA LEDOVAIA NOMENKLATURA. (INTL.ICE NOMENCL) (*RU*EN GL, PP.5-15, 110T) LENINGRAD, GIDROMETEOIZDAT. 1956. 300P.

NOVECK, S. AND SINCLAIR, F.L. RUSSIAN-ENGLISH GLOSSARY OF HYDROBIOLOGY. NEW YORK, INTERLANG. DICT, 1958. 113P. 59-305. 3500T.

OCEANOGRAPHY AND HYDROLOGY

RUSSIAN

SMIRNOV, N.N. ANGLO-RUSSKII GIDROBIOLOGICHESKII SLOVAR. (EN*RU HYDROBIOL. D) MOSCOW, GITTL, 1955. 168P. 57-29043. 4000T.

SWEET, J.S. AMERICAN-RUSSIAN, RUSSIAN-AMERICAN HYDROLOGIC VOCABULARY. WASHINGTON, U.S. WEATHER BUR, 1958. 24P. 58-62255. 300T.

SPANISH

BRAZOL, D. DICCIONARIO DE TERMINOS METEOROLOGICOS Y AFINES. (D. OF METEOROL/RELATED T.*EN*SP) BUENOS AIRES, HACHETTE, 1955. 2 PTS.IN 1 V. 557P. 57-38283. 8000T.

MARTINEZ-HIDALGO, T.J.M. ENCICLOPEDIA GENERAL DEL MAR. (NAVAL ENCYCL, SP DEFS) MADRID, GARRIGA, 1957-- . 58-19475.

SWEET, J.S. AMERICAN-SPANISH, SPANISH-AMERICAN HYDROLOGIC VOCABULARY. WASHINGTON, U.S. WEATHER BUR, 1958. 26P. 59-60614. 350T.

OPTICS AND SPECTROSCOPY

ENGLISH

AMERICAN INSTITUTE OF ELECTRICAL ENGINEERS. DEFINITIONS OF ELECTRICAL TERMS. ILLUMINATING ENGINEERING. (GR-55, ASA C42.55) NEW YORK, 1956. 14P. 120T.

AMERICAN SOCIETY FOR TESTING/MATERIALS. TENTATIVE DEFINITIONS OF TERMS AND SYMBOLS RELATING TO ABSORPTION SPECTROSCOPY. (E131-62T) ASTM STDS, SUPPL. PT.7, 280-2. PHILADELPHIA, 1962. 50T.

AMERICAN SOCIETY FOR TESTING/MATERIALS. TENTATIVE DEFINITIONS OF TERMS AND SYMBOLS RELATING TO EMISSION SPECTROSCOPY. (E135-60T) ASTM STDS, PT.7, 1597-1600. PHILADELPHIA, 1961. 70T.

AMERICAN SOCIETY FOR TESTING/MATERIALS. TENTATIVE DEFINITIONS OF TERMS RELATING TO MICROSCOPY. (E175-61T) ASTM STDS, PT.3, 849-52. PHILADELPHIA, 1961. 70T.

AMERICAN STANDARDS ASSOCIATION. NOMENCLATURE AND DEFINITIONS IN THE FIELD OF COLORIMETRY. (Z58.1.2) NEW YORK, 1952. 11P. 30T.

BENNETT, A.H. GLOSSARY OF TERMS FREQUENTLY USED IN OPTICS AND SPECTROSCOPY. NEW YORK, AM. INST. PHYS, 1961. 29P. 200T.

BRITISH STANDARDS INSTITUTION. GLOSSARY OF TERMS USED IN ILLUMINATION AND PHOTOMETRY. (B.S. 233) LONDON, 1953. 20P. 110T.

BRITISH STANDARDS INSTITUTION. GLOSSARY OF TERMS RELATING TO OPHTHALMIC LENSES AND SPECTACLE FRAMES. (B.S. 3521) LONDON, 1962. 81P. 650T.

BRITISH STANDARDS INSTITUTION. GLOSSARY OF COLOUR TERMS USED IN SCIENCE AND INDUSTRY. (B.S. 1611) LONDON, 1953. 20P. 110T.

BRITISH STANDARDS INSTITUTION. MEASUREMENT OF SPECTACLES, METHOD AND GLOSSARY (B.S. 3199) LONDON, 1960. 20P. 70T.

CLARK, G.L.ET AL. THE ENCYCLOPEDIA OF MICROSCOPY. NEW YORK, REINHOLD, 1961. 693P. 61-9698.

CLARK, G.L. ET AL. THE ENCYCLOPEDIA OF SPECTROSCOPY. NEW YORK, REINHOLD, 1960. 787P. 60-53028.

DERIBERE, M. ENCYCLOPEDIA OF COLOUR PHOTOGRAPHY. LONDON, FOUNTAIN, 1962. 177P. 63-3054. (TRANSL. OF DERIBERE,S ENCYCLOPEDIE DE LA COULEUR. PHOTO-CINEMA)

ILLUMINATING ENGINEERING SOCIETY. IES LIGHTING HANDBOOK. (NOMENCLATURE, CH.3, PP.3-21) ED3. NEW YORK, 1959. 250T.

KELLY, K.L. AND JUDD, D.B. THE ISCC-NBS METHOD OF DESIGNATING COLORS AND A DICTIONARY OF COLOR NAMES. (CIRC. 553) WASHINGTON, U.S. NATL. BUR. STDS, 1955. 158P. 55-63637. 12000T.

MAERZ, A.J. AND PAUL, M.R. A DICTIONARY OF COLOR. (EN DEFS, FR GE IT LA SP GL, PP.18-9) ED2. NEW YORK, MCGRAW-HILL, 1950. 208P. 50-11444. 7000T.

SCHAPERO, M. ET AL. DICTIONARY OF VISUAL SCIENCE. PHILADELPHIA, CHILTON, 1960. 785P. 60-5892. 14000T.

SOCIETY OF DYERS AND COLOURISTS. COLOUR INDEX. ED2. LOWELL, MASS, AM. ASSOC. TEXTILE/CHEM COLORISTS, 1956-1960. 4V. 57-908.

FRENCH

DERIBERE, M. AND CALLAUD, L. ENCYCLOPEDIE DE LA COULEUR. PHOTO-CINEMA. (COLOR ENCYCL. PHOTOG/CINEMATOG, FR DEFS) PARIS, DUNOD, 1961. 250P.

INTERNATIONAL ORGANIZATION FOR STANDARDIZATION. ISO TERMINOLOGY OF MICROSCOPY APPARATUS. (ISO-TC 46) GENEVA, 1961. 1P. 5T.

OPTICS AND SPECTROSCOPY

GERMAN

FLUEGGE, S. ET AL. HANDBUCH DER PHYSIK. (ENCYCL. OF PHYS) V.24, GRUNDLAGEN DER OPTIK. (FUNDAMENTALS OF OPTICS, *GE*EN GL, PP.646-53, 200T) BERLIN, SPRINGER, 1956. 656P. A52-2942.

FLUEGGE, S. ET AL. HANDBUCH DER PHYSIK. (ENCYCL. OF PHYS) V.25/1, KRISTALLOPTIK, BEUGUNG, (CRYSTAL OPTICS, DIFFRACTION, *GE*EN GL, PP.574-92, 500T) BERLIN, SPRINGER, 1961. 592P. A56-2942.

FLUEGGE, S. ET AL. HANDBUCH DER PHYSIK. (ENCYCL. OF PHYS) V.26, LICHT UND MATERIE 2. (LIGHT/MATTER 2, *GE*EN GL, PP.938-55, 600T) BERLIN, SPRINGER, 1958. 965P. A56-2942.

FLUEGGE, S. ET AL. HANDBUCH DER PHYSIK. (ENCYCL. OF PHYS) SPEKTROSKOPIE. (SPECTROSCOPY) V.27, PT.1, APPROX. 496P. IN PRESS. V.28, PT.2, 448P. 1957. *GE*EN GL, PP.433-46, 360T. BERLIN, SPRINGER, 1957-6 A56-2942.

FLUEGGE, S. ET AL. HANDBUCH DER PHYSIK. (ENCYCL. OF PHYS) V.33, KORPUSKULAROPTIK. (OPTICS OF CORPUSCLES, *GE*EN GL, PP.684-702, 600T) BERLIN, SPRINGER, 1956. 702P. A56-2942.

MUETZE, K. ET AL. BROCKHAUS ABC DER OPTIK. (ABC OF OPTICS, GE DEFS) LEIPZIG, BROCKHAUS, 1961. 963P. 62-28207. 10000T.

ITALIAN

FIORENTINI, A. VOCABOLARIO DELL OTTICO. (OPTICS D, IT DEFS) ED2. BOLOGNA, ZANICHELLI, 1958. 170P. A59-3086.

POLYGLOT

AKADEMIIA NAUK SSSR. KOM.TEKH.TERM. TERMINOLOGIIA SVETOTEKHNIKI. (ILLUM. ENG. D, *RU*EN*FR*GE) (SB. REK. TERM. NO.48) MOSCOW, 1957. 61P. 59-45328. 210T.

ALVARO, M.E. ET AL. LEXICON OPHTHALMOLOGICUM. (PO OPHTHALM.D, LA*EN*FR*GE*IT*SP) PHILADELPHIA, LIPPINCOTT, 1959. 217P. 59-13468. 2200T.

BARANY,N. FINOMMECHANIKA, OPTIKA. (D. OF PREC. MECH/OPT, *HU*EN*GE*RU) (MUSZ. ERT. SZ, NO.16) BUDAPEST TERRA, 1961. 214P. 61-48214. 1200T.

CAGNET, M. ET AL. ATLAS OF OPTICAL PHENOMENA. (GE*EN*FR) BERLIN, SPRINGER, 1962. 45P. 62-15420.

CLEVELAND, F.F. ET AL. DICTIONARIO MULTILINGUAL PRO LE SPECTROSCOPIA. (PO SPECTRY. D, IA*EN*GE*IT*PR*RU *SP) NEW YORK, STORM. (IN PREP) 1500T.

INTERNATIONAL COMMISSION ON ILLUMINATION. VOCABULAIRE INTERNATIONAL DE L.ECLAIRAGE. (INTL. LIGHTING VOC. V.1, TERMS/DEFS *FR*EN*GE. 136P. V.2, INDEX. *FR*EN*DA*DU*GE*IT*PL*RU*SP*SW. 127P) ED2. PARIS, 1957/9. 60-39148. 550T.

INTERNATIONAL ELECTROTECHNICAL COMMISSION. INTERNATIONAL ELECTROTECHNICAL VOCABULARY. LIGHTING. (*FR*EN*DU*GE*IT*PL*SP*SW) (IEC-50-GR-45) ED2. GENEVA, 1959. 83P.

INTERNATIONAL ORGANIZATION FOR STANDARDIZATION. QUANTITIES, UNITS, SYMBOLS, CONVERSION FACTORS AND CONVERSION TABLES. QUANTITIES AND UNITS OF RADIATION AND LIGHT. (ISO/TC12) ED2. GENEVA, 1961. 11P. 70T.

MAERZ, A.J. AND PAUL, M.R. A DICTIONARY OF COLOR. (EN DEFS, FR GE IT LA SP GL, PP.18-9) ED2. NEW YORK, MCGRAW-HILL, 1950. 208P. 50-11444. 7000T.

SCHULZ, E. WOERTERBUCH DER OPTIK UND FEINMECHANIK. (OPT/PREC. MECH. D) V.1, GE*EN*FR, 111P. V.2, EN*F *GE, 124P. V.3, FR*GE*EN, 109P. WIESBADEN, BRANDSTETTER, 1960-61. A61-3700. 2500T.

SYNDICAT GENERALE D,OPTIQUE. ANNUAIRE. ALPHABETICAL LIST OF PRODUCTS (*GE*EN*FR*SP GL) PARIS, 1958. 203P.

TWYMAN, F. OPTICAL GLASSWORKING. (FR*EN*GE GL, PP.262-70, 200T) LONDON, HILGER/WATTS, 1955. 275P. 55-4221.

RUSSIAN

NOVECK, S. AND EMIN, I. RUSSIAN-ENGLISH GLOSSARY OF OPTICS AND SPECTROSCOPY... NEW YORK, INTERLANG. DICT, 1959. 78P. 59-1224. 4000T.

RABKIN, E.B. ATLAS TSVETOV. (COLOR ATLAS) MOSCOW, MEDGIZ, 1956. 52P. 58-23276.

PAINTS, DYES, AND PROTECTIVE COATINGS

ENGLISH

AMERICAN SOCIETY FOR TESTING/MATERIALS. STANDARD DEFINITIONS OF TERMS RELATING TO PAINT, VARNISH, LACQUE AND RELATED PRODUCTS (D16-59) ASTM STDS, PT.8, 1133-8. PHILADELPHIA, 1961. 120T.

AMERICAN SOCIETY FOR TESTING/MATERIALS. TENTATIVE DEFINITIONS OF TERMS RELATING TO PORCELAIN ENAMEL. (C286-61T) ASTM STDS, PT.5, 635-42. PHILADELPHIA, 1961. 260T.

BRITISH STANDARDS INSTITUTION. GLASS FOR GLAZING. (B.S. 952. AMEND. PD-2899, 3267, 3316, 3350, 3584) LONDON, 1957-59. 36P. 20T.

PAINTS, DYES, AND PROTECTIVE COATINGS

ENGLISH

RITISH STANDARDS INSTITUTION. GLOSSARY OF PAINT TERMS. (B.S.2015) LONDON, 1953. 44P. 300T.

OODIER, J.H. DICTIONARY OF PAINTING AND DECORATING TRADE TERMS. SOUTHPORT, LANCS, SUTHERLAND, 1961.
07P. 62-5477. 1500T.

ARTIN, J.H. AND MORGANS, W.M. GUIDE TO PIGMENTS AND TO VARNISH AND LACQUER CONSTITUENTS. NEW YORK,
HEMICAL, 1959. 111P. 54-42002. 1500T.

ADI, L.J. GLOSSARY FOR THE PROTECTIVE COATINGS AND PLASTIC INDUSTRY. ED4. HAWTHORNE, N.J,
NTERCHEMICAL, 1959. 158P.

FRENCH

E PEINTRE EN BATIMENT... GLOSSAIRE FRANCAIS-ANGLAIS ET ANGLAIS-FRANCAIS, BT-15. (HOUSE-PAINTER, *FR*EN
L) OTTAWA, DEPT. SECY. STATE, 1954. 14P. 180T.

GERMAN

ABEL, E. ET AL. ABC DER ANSTRICHSTOFFE UND ANSTRICHTECHNIK. (ABC OF PAINT TECH,GE DEFS) ED3. LEIPZIG,
ACHBUCHVERLAG, 1960. 394P.

ITTEL, H. FARBEN- LACK-, UND KUNSTSTOFF-LEXIKON... (PAINT, LACQUER, PLAST. D, GE DEFS) STUTTGART, WISS.
ERLAGSGES, 1952. 858P. 52-38532.

ERZ, O.A. DEUTSCH-ENGLISCHES UND ENGLISCH-DEUTSCHES FACHWOERTERBUCH FUER FACHAUSDRUECKE AUS DEM LACK-
ND FARBENGEBIET. (*GE*EN D.`OF LACQUER/PAINT) ED2. STUTTGART, WISSENSCHAFTLICHE-VERLAG,1954. 351P.
5-22330. 4400T.

UELLER AND BATTI. FACHWOERTERBUCH FUER DIE LACK-FARBEN-UND VERWANDTEN INDUSTRIEN. (PAINT/LACQUER IND. T,
E DEFS) STUTTGART, DEUT. FARBEN. Z, 195 . 100P.

EUFERT, G. FARBNAMENLEXIKON VON A-Z. (D. OF PAINT NAMES, A-Z, GE DEFS) GOETTINGEN, MUSTERSCHMIDT, 1955.
05P. 56-29374. 3000T.

ENZEL, F. MALERFIBEL. (PAINT PRIMER, GE DEFS) DUESSELDORF, WERNER, 1961. 287P. 61-49187. 1800T.

HINDI

AUSHAL, S.C. PAINT TECHNOLOGY. ENGLISH-HINDI DICTIONARY. ALLAHABAD, HINDI SAHITYA SAMMELAN, 1950. 250T.

POLYGLOT

RANDT, J. ET AL. EMAILS. EIN WOERTERBUCH IN VIER SPRACHEN. (GE EN FR IT D. OF ENAMELS) LEVERKUSEN,
ARBENFABRIKEN BAYER, 1960. 181P. 62-39114.

AAFF, J.J. INDEX VOCABULORUM QUADRILINGUIS, VERE EN VERNIS... (PAINT/VARNISH D, DU EN FR GE) THE HAGUE,
ER.VERNIS/VERFFABRIKANTEN, 1958. 898P. 59-27978. 2300T.

ANTHOLZER, R. AND KORINSKY, J.   PETIJAZYCNY SLOVNIK, BARVY, LAKY, POVRCHOVA, UPRAVA, KOROSE. (PAINT,
ACQUER/VARNISH CORR D, CZ*EN*FR*GE*RU) ED2. PRAGUE, SNTL, 1956. 436P. 60-37933. 2900T.

EKNISKA NOMENKLATURCENTRALEN. PAINTS AND VARNISHES GLOSSARY. (SW*EN*GE) (TNC PUBL. NO.14) STOCKHOLM,
96 . (REV. ED. IN PREP)

RUSSIAN

IBSON, A.J. AN ENGLISH-RUSSIAN, RUSSIAN-ENGLISH GLOSSARY OF TERMS USED IN THE PAINT INDUSTRY. REPR,
AINT, OIL/COLOUR J. (1958) 16P.

PAPER CHEMISTRY AND TECHNOLOGY

CZECH

ILIP, J. AND RUBES, V. PAPIRENSKY SLOVNIK. (PAPER D, CZ DEFS) PRAGUE, PRUMYSLOVE VYDAV, 1952. 368P.
4-29283.

ENGLISH

MERICAN SOCIETY FOR TESTING/MATERIALS. TENTATIVE DEFINITIONS OF TERMS RELATING TO CELLULOSE AND
ELLULOSE DERIVATIVES. (D1695-60T) ASTM STDS, PT.6, 1182-7. PHILADELPHIA, 1961. 150T.

RITISH STANDARDS INSTITUTION. GLOSSARY OF PAPER, STATIONERY AND ALLIED TERMS. (B.S. 3203) LONDON, 1960.
02P. 140T.

AY, F.T. AN A.B.C. INDEX OF PAPERS (TRADE TERMS...) LONDON, TRADE, 1959. 161P. 59-52609.

LAISTER, G.A. AN ENCYCLOPEDIA OF THE BOOK TERMS USED IN PAPER-MAKING, PRINTING, BOOKBINDING...
LEVELAND, WORLD, 1960. 484P. 61-2811.

OCKET ENCYCLOPEDIA OF PAPER AND GRAPHIC ARTS TERMS. KAUKAUNA, WIS, THOMAS, 1960. 94P. 60-4619.

115

PAPER CHEMISTRY AND TECHNOLOGY

ENGLISH

WEST, C.J. DICTIONARY OF PAPER. ED2. NEW YORK, AM. PULP/PAPER ASSOC, 1953. 393P.

WHEELWRIGHT, W.B. PAPER TRADE TERMS... BOSTON, SILTON, 1958. 48P.

FRENCH

LAFONTAINE, G.H. DICTIONARY OF TERMS USED IN THE PAPER, PRINTING, AND ALLIED INDUSTRIES, ENGLISH-FRENCH, FRENCH-ENGLISH. ED2. MONTREAL, SMITH, 1957. 192P.

GERMAN

GARTE, H. FACHWOERTERBUCH DES GRAPHISCHEN GEWERBES UND DER PAPIERINDUSTRIE. (*GE*EN PRINTING/PAPER IND) V.1 EN*GE,1954. 113P. V.2 GE*EN (IN PREP) ED2. BRAUNSCHWEIG, GARTE, 1954—

HADERT, H. HADERT DRUCK-LEXIKON... (PRINTING D, GE DEFS) BERLIN, HADERT, 1956. 182P. 58-49146.

HANDBUCH DER PAPIER-UND PAPPENFABRIKATION, PAPIERLEXIKON. (PAPER/PAPERBOARD D, GE DEFS) WIESBADEN, SAENDIG, 1961. 80P.

HOYER, F) ET AL. HANDBUCH DER PAPIER-UND PAPPENFABRIKATION, PAPIER LEXIKON. (PAPER/PAPERBOARD D, GE DEFS) 2V. WIESBADEN, SAENDIG, 1953. 2064P.

MATERIALLEXIKON FUER DIE GRAPHISCHE INDUSTRIE. (ENCYCL. OF PRINTING MATER, GE DEFS) LEIPZIG, BIBLIOG. INST, 1955. 388P. 56-44308.

MOHRBERG, W. TECHNISCHES WOERTERBUCH, ZELLSTOFF UND PAPIER... (CELLULOSE/PAPER D) V.1 EN*GE, 223P. V.2 GE*EN, 226P. DARMSTADT, ROETHER, 1955-6. A55-10642.

POLYGLOT

GIANNI, E. CARTE, CARTONCINI, CARTONI-FABBRICAZIONE, CARATTERISTICHE, USI. CON DIZIONARI..., ITALIANA, FRANCESE, INGLESE, TEDESCA E SPAGNOLA... (CARTONS/BOXES, IT EN FR GE SP D) ED2. MILAN, HOEPLI, 1959. 809P A59-6674.

INSTITUTUL DE DOCUMENTARE TEHNICA. DICTIONAR TEHNIC PENTRU SECTORUL LEMNHIRTIE. (ROMINA, RUSA, UNGARA, GERMANA, FRANCEZA, ITALIANA, SI ENGLEZA) (WOOD/PAPER D, RO*EN*FR*GE*IT*HU*RU) BUCHAREST, 1954.

INTERNATIONAL ORGANIZATION FOR STANDARDIZATION. PAPER VOCABULARY, *EN*FR*RU. (ISO R-66, 1ST SER) GENEVA, 1958.

INTERNATIONAL ORGANIZATION FOR STANDARDIZATION. PAPER VOCABULARY,*EN*FR*RU. (ISO R-135, 2D SER) GENEVA, 1959.

INTERNATIONAL ORGANIZATION FOR STANDARDIZATION. PAPER VOCABULARY, *EN*FR*RU. (ISO R-231, 3D SER) GENEVA 1961. 19P. 40T.

KOTTE, H. ET AL. WELCHES PAPIER IST DAS (PAPER D, GE EN FR...) STUTTGART, FRANCKH, 1959. 462P. A60-4741.

LABARRE, E.J. DICTIONARY AND ENCYCLOPAEDIA OF PAPER AND PAPER-MAKING, GE*EN*DU*FR*IT*SP*SW. ED2. LONDO OXFORD UNIV. PRESS. 1952. 488P. 53-29414.

PHILLIP,S PAPER TRADE DIRECTORY OF THE WORLD. (TRADE T, GL, EN FR GE SP SW, PP.10-29) LONDON, PHILLIPS. 1954. 806P.

RUSSIAN

ELIASHBERG, A.IA. ET AL. ANGLO-RUSSKII SLOVAR PO TSELLIULOZNO-BUMAZHNOMU PROIZVODSTVU. (EN*RU D. OF PAPER-MAKING) MOSCOW, FIZMATGIZ, 1958. 263P. 59-41045. 10000T.

SWEDISH

SVENSKA PAPPERS- OCH CELLULOSAINGENIOERSFOERENINGEN. ORDLISTA. TERMER OCH DEFINITIONER INOM MASSA-PAPPERS-OCH FIBERSKIVEINDUSTRIN. (PULP, PAPER/FIBER IND, SW DEFS) STOCKHOLM, 1958. 93P. 62-37886.

PETROLEUM CHEMISTRY, ENGINEERING, AND GEOLOGY

ENGLISH

ALBERTA SOCIETY OF PETROLEUM GEOLOGISTS. LEXICON OF GEOLOGIC NAMES IN THE WESTERN CANADA SEDIMENTARY BASIN AND ARCTIC ARCHIPELAGO. CALGARY, 1960. 380P. 62-44283.

AMERICAN PETROLEUM INSTITUTE. GLOSSARY OF TERMS USED IN PETROLEUM REFINING. ED2. NEW YORK, 1962.

AMERICAN SOCIETY FOR TESTING/MATERIALS. STANDARD DEFINITIONS OF TERMS RELATING TO PETROLEUM. (D288-61) ASTM STDS, PT.7, 153-5. PHILADELPHIA, 1961. 30T.

AMERICAN STANDARDS ASSOCIATION. LETTER SYMBOLS FOF PETROLEUM RESERVOIR ENGINEERING AND ELECTRIC LOGGING. (Y10.15) NEW YORK, 1958.

ATLANTIC REFINING CO. DICTIONARY OF ABBREVIATIONS PECULIAR TO THE OIL INDUSTRY. DALLAS, 1963. 62P. 63-5675. 2000T.

BOONE, L.P. THE PETROLEUM DICTIONARY. NORMAN, OKLA, UNIV. OKLAHOMA PRESS, 1952. 332P.

ENGLISH

ETROLEUM EDUCATIONAL INSTITUTE. ILLUSTRATED PETROLEUM DICTIONARY AND PRODUCTS MANUAL. LOS ANGELES, 1962. 54P. 62-18323. 10000T.

OBERTSON, J. OIL SLANGUAGE. EVANSVILLE, IND, PETROL, 1954. 181P. 54-14807.

ELL, G. A GLOSSARY OF PETROLEUM TERMS. ED3. LONDON, INST, PETROL, 1961. 39P. 62-43419.

FRENCH

NTERNATIONAL LABOR ORGANIZATION. VOCABULAIRE DES TERMES EMPLOYES DANS L,INDUSTRIE DU PETROLE... (*EN*ER ETROL.IND.GL) GENEVA, 1952. 300T. 43P. 900T.

ICTIONNAIRE DU PETROLE ET DES MINES. (*EN*FR PETROL/MINING D) PARIS, PARIS-MONDE, 1963. 700P.

OUREAU, M. AND ROUGE, J. DICTIONNAIRE TECHNIQUE DES TERMES UTILISES DANS L,INDUSTRIE DU PETROLE. *EN*FR PETROL. IND. D) PARIS, INST. FRANCAIS DE PETROLE (TECHNIQUE) 1963. 875P.

UERE, H. AND BENAMOU, M. VOCABULAIRE TECHNIQUE ANGLAIS-FRANCAIS DE LA CHIMIE DU PETROLE. (EN*FR D. OF ETROL. CHEM) PARIS, DUNOD, 1957. 122P. 58-2855. 300T.

GERMAN

OWER, W.W. LUBRICATION GLOSSARY. WOERTERVERZEICHNIS DER SCHMIERTECHNIK. STAMFORD, CONN, 1958. 27P. 8-23903. 500T.

EHMANN, G.H. ERDOEL LEXIKON... (PETROL. GL, *GE*EN) ED4. MAINZ, HUETHIG/DREYER, 1963.

ERSCH, F. DEUTSCH-ENGLISCHES FACHWOERTERBUCH DER TIEFBOHRTECHNIK. (*GE*EN D. OF OIL-WELL DRILLING) ERLIN, SCHMIDT, 1953. 147P. 56-29010. 4000T.

ERSCH, F. ENGLISH-GERMAN OIL DICTIONARY. BERLIN,SCHMIDT, 1955. 412P. 56-35030. 10700T.

JAPANESE

HIYODA KAKO KENSETSU GIJUTSUBU. SEKIYU KAGAKU YOGO JITEN. (PETROL. CHEM. D, EN*JA) TOKYO, SEKYU KOGYO IHYO, 1960. 106P. 1200T.

SHIBASHI, K. SEKIYU KAGAKU JITEN. (PETROL.CHEM.D,*JA*EN) TOKYO, NIKKAN KOGYO SHIMBUNSHA, 1958. 245+46P. 62-1537. 3000T.

POLYGLOT

ULIEV, S.M. AND MDIVANI, A.A. ANGLO-AZERBAIDZHANSKO-RUSSKII SLOVAR PO NEFTEPROMYSLOVOMU DELU. (EN*AZ* U PETROL. IND. D) BAKU, AZNEFTEIZDAT, 1958. 575P. 58-44721. 12000T.

IJNBOUW KUNDIGE NOMENCLATOR EN AARDOLIETECHNIK. (MIN/PETROL. ENG. GL, *DU*EN*FR*GE*SP) SOONINGEN, 1953. 48P.

APA, V. AND SEDA, Z. CESKO-RUSKO-NEMECKO-ANGLICKY SLOVNIK Z OBORU HLUBINNEHO VRTANI A TEZBY NAFTY... CZ*EN*GE*RU D. OF DEEP DRILLING/PETROL. ENG) PRAGUE, CSAV, 1958. 379P. 6000T.

RUSSIAN

AKADEMIIA NAUK SSSR. KOM. TEKH. TERM. TERMINOLOGIIA TOPLIVA DLIA DVIGATELEI VNUTRENNEGO SGORANIIA FUELS FOR INTERNAL COMBUSTION ENG, RU DEFS)(SB. REK. TERM, NO.44) MOSCOW, 1957. 28P. 57-45392. 100T.

NGLO-RUSSKII TERMINOLOGICHESKII SLOVAR PO GEOLOGOPOISKOVOMU BURENIIU. (EN*RU GEOPHYS. PROSPECTING D) LENINGRAD, 1963. 317P.

HOCHIA, A.P. ANGLO-RUSSKII SLOVAR PO TOPLIVÁM I MASLAM. (EN*RU D. OF FUEL/OIL) MOSCOW, GITTL, 1956. 545P. 57-16901. 20000T.

ZRAILEVA, E.IU. AND TAUMIN, I.M. ANGLO-RUSSKII SLOVAR PO NEFTEPROMYSLOVOMU DELU. ED2. (EN*RU PETROL. ND. D) MOSCOW, GOSTOPTEKHIZDAT, 1963. 391P. 63-58994. 15000T.

KEDRINSKII, V.V. ANGLO-RUSSKII SLOVAR PO KHIMII I PERERABOTKE NEFTI. (EN*RU D.OF PETROL. CHEM/REFINING) LENINGRAD, GOSTOPTEKHIZDAT, 1962. 910P. 62-49596. 35000T.

MAKKAVEEV, A.A. ET AL. SLOVAR PO GIDROGEOLOGII I INZHENERNOI GEOLOGII. (D. OF HYDROGEOL/ENG. GEOL, RU DEFS) MOSCOW, GOSTOPTEKHIZDAT, 1961. 186P. 61-48756. 10000T.

MIRCHINK, C.F. ET AL. SLOVAR PO GEOLOGII NEFTI. (PETROL. GEOL. D, RU DEFS) ED2. LENINGRAD, GOSTOPTEKHIZDAT, 1958. 776P. 59-23302.

PAPOK, K.K. AND RAGOZIN, N.A. TEKHNICHESKII SLOVAR-SPRAVOCHNIK PO TOPLIVU I MASLAM. (FUEL/OIL D, RU DEFS) ED3. MOSCOW, GOSTOPTEKHIZDAT, 1963. 767P. 63-41756. 1200T.

SPANISH

INSTITUTO SUDAMERICANO DEL PETROLEO. GLOSARIO TECNICO DE LA INDUSTRIA DEL PETROLEO, ESPANOL-INGLES, INGLES-ESPANOL. (*SP*EN GL. OF PETROL. IND) BUENOS AIRES, 1960. 619P.

KOLSTER, T.A. TECHNICAL DICTIONARY... OF THE PETROLEUM INDUSTRY, ENGLISH-SPANISH, SPANISH-ENGLISH. CARACAS, CREOLE PETROL, 1950. 493P. 25000T.

PHOTOGRAPHY AND CINEMATOGRAPHY

CZECH

JIRACEK, M. ET AL. FOTOGRAFICKY SLOVNIK. (PHOT. D, CZ DEFS) PRAGUE, ORBIS, 1955. 143P. 56-40522. 1000T.

DUTCH

DUIJN, C. FOTOGRAFISCHE CHEMICALIEN... (PHOT. CHEM, DU DEFS) ED2. DOETINCHEM, MISSET, 1955. 208P. 59-49361.

HEYSE, P. AND CRAEYBECKX, A.S.H. ENCYCLOPEDIE VOOR FOTOGRAFIE EN CINEMATOGRAFIE. (PHOT/CINEMATOG. ENCYCL, DU DEFS) AMSTERDAM, ELSEVIER, 1958. 896P. A59-5699.

ENGLISH

AMERICAN STANDARDS ASSOCIATION. NOMENCLATURE FOR MOTION-PICTURE FILM USED IN STUDIOS AND PROCESSING LABORATORIES. (ASA-PH22.56) NEW YORK, 1961. 7P. 90T.

AVEDON, D.M. GLOSSARY OF TERMS FOR MICROPHOTOGRAPHY AND FOR REPRODUCTION MADE FROM MICRO-IMAGES. ANNAPOLIS, NAT.L. MICROFILM ASSOC, 1962. 50P.

BARRET, W.J. GLOSSARY OF PHOTOCOPYING TERMS. LONDON, HALL-HARDING, 1961. 45P. 63-33428. 250T.

CAMERON, J.R. AND CIFRE, J.S. CAMERON,S ENCYCLOPEDIA OF SOUND MOTION PICTURES. ED6. CORAL GABLES, FLA, CAMERON, 1959. 1V. (UNPAGED) 59-27346.

CARROLL, J.S. AND LESTER, H.M. PHOTO-LAB-INDEX. (SECT.23, PHOTO WORDS) ED21. NEW YORK, MORGAN, 1961. LL, 1400P.

DERIBERE, M. ENCYCLOPEDIA OF COLOUR PHOTOGRAPHY. LONDON, FOUNTAIN, 1962. 177P. 63-3054. (TRANSL. OF DERIBERE,S ENCYCLOPEDIE DE LA COULEUR. PHOTO-CINEMA)

EASTMAN KODAK CO. GLOSSARY OF TERMS FOR THE MINICARD SYSTEM. ROCHESTER, N.Y, 195 .

HASELGROVE, M.L. PHOTOGRAPHERS DICTIONARY. NEW YORK, ARCHER, 1963. 202P. 63-14427.

LATHAM, S. FILTER GUIDE. PHILADELPHIA, CHILTON BOOKS, 1962. 96P. 62-20133.

MORGAN, W.D. ET AL. THE ENCYCLOPEDIA OF PHOTOGRAPHY... NEW YORK, GREYSTONE, 1963- . 63-5178.

MORGAN, W.D. AND B. PHOTO DICTIONARY AND QUICK REFERENCE GUIDE... NEW YORK, MORGAN, 1957. 128P. 57-11892. 2000T.

NATIONAL ASSOCIATION OF BLUEPRINT AND DIAZOTYPE COATERS. GLOSSARY...WASHINGTON, 1956. 22P. A57-5215.

PURVES, F. ET AL. THE FOCAL ENCYCLOPEDIA OF PHOTOGRAPHY. NEW YORK, MACMILLAN, 1960. 1298P. 60-51826.

RECORDAK CORP. A GLOSSARY OF TERMS FOR MICROPHOTOGRAPHY. NEW YORK, 1959. 28P. 600T.

ROSE, J.J. AMERICAN CINEMATOGRAPHER HANDBOOK AND REFERENCE GUIDE. ED9. HOLLYWOOD, CALIF. AM. SOC. CINEMATOG, 1956. 319P. 56-2589.

SHARPS, W.S. DICTIONARY OF CINEMATOGRAPHY AND SOUND. RECORDING. LONDON, FOUNTAIN, 1959. 144P. 60-39267. 500T.

SHENKLE, W. GLOSSARY OF PHOTOGRAPHIC AND RECONNAISSANCE.TERMS. (WADC TECH. NOTE NO.56-510) WRIGHT-PATTERSON AFB, OHIO, 1956. 61P.

SKILBECK, O. ABC OF FILM AND TV WORKING TERMS. NEW YORK, FOCAL, 1960. 157P. 60-4032. 1400T.

SOWERBY, A.L.M. DICTIONARY OF PHOTOGRAPHY... ED19. LONDON, ILIFFE, 1961. 715P. 62-68245.

TENEYCK, H. GLOSSARY OF TERMS USED IN MICROREPRODUCTION. HINGHAM,MASS, NATL. MICROFILM ASSOC, 1955. 88

U.S. DEPT. OF DEFENSE. GLOSSARY OF PHOTOGRAPHIC TERMS, INCLUDING DOCUMENT REPRODUCTION. (TM11-411) WASHINGTON, 1961. 128P. 62-60293. 2500T.

FRENCH

DELAYE, R. AND HEMARDINQUER, P. TERMINOLOGIE DE LA PHOTOGRAPHIE ET DU CINEMA, GLOSSAIRE ANGLAIS-FRANCAI BT-57. (PHOT/CINEMATOG, EN*FR GL) OTTAWA, DEPT.SECY.STATE, 1957. 22P. 270T.

DERIBERE, M. AND CALLAUD, L. ENCYCLOPEDIE DE LA COULEUR. PHOTO-CINEMA. (COLOR ENCYCL. PHOTOG/CINEMATOG. FR DEFS) PARIS, DUNOD, 1961. 250P.

ENCYCLOPEDIE PRISMA DE LA COULEUR PHOTO CINEMA. (ENCYCL. OF COLOR PHOT, FR DEFS) PARIS, PRISMA, 1957. 250P. 57-41413.

GIBBS, C.R. DICTIONNAIRE TECHNIQUE DU CINEMA (MOTION-PICTURE TECH. D, *EN*FR) PARIS, FILM/TECH, 1959. 106+117P. 60-23435. 4000T.

VORONTZOFF, A.N. VOCABULAIRE FRANCAIS-ANGLAIS ET ANGLAIS-FRANCAIS DU CINEMA. (*FR*EN MOTION-PICTURE GL) PARIS, GUILHAMOU, 1953. 190+232P. 57-16338. 3600T.

GERMAN

DE, A.W.   DAS KLEINE FILM-LEXIKON... (MOTION-PICTURE GL, GE DEFS)   FRANKFURT, HUMBOLDT, 1954.   158P.
-26636.   600T.

DY, O.   BILD-LEHRBUCH DER FOTOGRAFIE... MIT EINEM FOTO-LEXIKON ZUM NACHSCHLAGEN. (PICTURE TEXTBOOK OF
OT... GL, GE DEFS)   HALLE (SAALE) KNAPP, 1955.   220P.   55-38354.

NG, M.K.   PHOTO-FACHWOERTERBUCH.   (PHOT.D,*GE*EN)   DUESSELDORF, BACH, 1961.   450P.   12000T.

HNERT, H.   FILM-LICHT-FARBE,EIN HANDBUCH FUER KAMERALEUTE. (FILM, LIGHT, COLOR,-HANDBOOK FOR MOTION-
CTURE CAMERAMEN, GE GL)   HALLE (SAALE)   FOTOKINOVERLAG HALLE, 1958.   252P.   59-36943.   70T.   EN*GE
00 GE T.

HULZE, A.R.   LEXIKON DER KINOTECHNIK... (MOTION-PICTURE TECH. D, GE DEFS)   HALLE (SAALE)   KNAPP, 1956.
8P.   57-18188.   6000T.

ITALIAN

VEY, G.H.   DIZIONARIO DEI TERMINI CINEMATOGRAFICI. (*IT*EN CINEMATOG. T)   ROME, MEDITERRANEA, 1952.
+95P. A52-8990. 2000T.

CICLOPEDIA DELLO SPETTACOLO. (THEATER/MOTION-PICTURE ENCYCL, IT DEFS)   ROME, MASCHERE, 1954-   .
5-2513.

POLYGLOT

ASON, W.E.   ELSEVIER,S DICTIONARY OF CINEMA, SOUND, AND MUSIC. *EN-AM,*FR*DU*GE*IT*SP.   NEW YORK,
SEVIER, 1956. 948P. 56-13141. 3200T.

AEYBECKX, A.S.H.   DICTIONARY OF PHOTOGRAPHY. (EN*FR*GE)   NEW YORK, ELSEVIER.   850P.   14000T. (IN PREP)

AU, W.   WOERTERBUCH DER PHOTO-, FILM- UND KINOTECHNIK MIT RANDGEBIETEN. (PHOTO/MOTION-PICTURE D) (V.1,
*GE*FR)   BERLIN-BORSIGWALDE, RADIO-FOTO KINOTECHNIK, 1958-   .   663P.   A59-5693.   16000T.

TERNATIONAL SOCIETY FOR PHOTOGRAMMETRY. MULTI-LINGUAL DICTIONARY FOR PHOTOGRAMMETRY... (*EN*FR*GE*IT*PL
P*SW)   7V.   AMSTERDAM, ARGUS, 1961.

XIQUE DES TERMES CINEMATOGRAPHIQUES.   (CINEMATOG. GL, FR 16P. EN 27P. DU 28P. SP 50P)   LONDON,
  EUROPEAN UNION, 1959.   1900T.

STERREICHISCHE GESELLSCHAFT FUER PHOTOGRAMMETRIE. PHOTOGRAMMETRISCHES WOERTERBUCH. (PHOTOGRAMMETRIC D,
E*EN*FR*IT*PL*SP*SW)   VIENNA.   100P.   5000T.   (IN PREP)

LTER, F.W. AND MAURER, S.   FOTOKINO WOERTERBUCH... (PHOTO/CINEMATOG.D, *GE*EN*FR*RU)   HALLE (SAALE)
TOKINOVERLAG HALLE, 1960. 4V.   61-33069.   17000T.

RUSSIAN

ADEMIIA NAUK SSSR. KOM.TEKH.TERM.   TERMINOLOGIIA PO VOZDUSHNOMU FOTOGRAFIROVANIIU. (AERIAL PHOT, RU
FS)   (SB. REK. TERM. NO.29)   MOSCOW, 1954.   29P.   59-53689.   120T.

PAURI, A.A. AND SHEBERSTOV, V.I.   KRATKII FOTOGRAFICHESKII SLOVAR. (PHOT.GL, RU DEFS)   MOSCOW, ISKUSSTVO,
56, 385P.   57-33786.   1100T.

KHAROV, A.A. AND GOLDOVSKII, E.M.   ANGLO-RUSSKII SLOVAR PO FOTOGRAFII I KINEMATOGRAFII. (EN*RU PHOT/
NEMATOG. D)   MOSCOW, FIZMATGIZ, 1960.   395P.   60-42019.   10000T.

LBERG, V.   RUSSIAN-ENGLISH DICTIONARY OF SCIENCE, TECHNOLOGY AND ART OF CINEMATOGRAPHY. NEW YORK,
LBERG, 1961. 103P. 61-14392. 2600T.

SLOVAK

OVENSKA AKADEMIA VIED.   FOTOGRAFICKA TERMINOLOGIA. (PHOT.T, SL DEFS)   BRATISLAVA, 1958.   50P.   59-39477.

SWEDISH

GLUND, H.   ENGELSK-SVENSKT FOTOGRAFISKT LEXIKON. (EN*SW PHOT. D)   STOCKHOLM, NORDISK ROTOGRAVYR, 1955.
6P. A56-5260. 6000T.

PHYSICS

ARABIC

ITED ARAB REPUBLIC.   SCIENTIFIC TERMS.   SER. 1. EN*AR. CAIRO, SCI. COUNCIL, 1961. 435P. NE 62-1569.

CHINESE

UNG-KUO K,O HSUEH YUAN.   PIEN I CH,U PAN WEI YUAN HUI.   (ACAD. SINICA. COMM. OF PUBL/TRANSL) SHENG
UEH SHU YU.   (ACOUSTICS T, CH EN) PEKING, 1958.   205P.   C59-2509.

UNG-KUO K,O HSUEH YUAN.   PIEN I CH,U PAN WEI YUAN HUI.   (ACAD. SINICA. COMM. OF PUBL/TRANSL) WU LI HSUEH
NG TZ,U.   (PHYS. T, CH EN) PEKING, SCIENCE, 1956.   358P.   C58-5315.

CHINESE

WANG, CHU-HSI ET AL. WU LI HSUEH MING TZ,U HUI PIEN. (*EN*CH PHYS. D) HONG KONG, SCIENCE, 1961. 218P.
C62-2611.

ENGLISH

AMERICAN INSTITUTE OF ELECTRICAL ENGINEERS. DEFINITIONS OF ELECTRICAL TERMS. ELECTROBIOLOGY, INCLUDING
ELECTROTHERAPEUTICS (GR-80,ASA C42.80) NEW YORK, 1957. 13P. 120T.

AMERICAN INSTITUTE OF ELECTRICAL ENGINEERS. DEFINITIONS OF ELECTRICAL TERMS. GENERAL... (FUNDAMENTAL/
DERIVED) TERMS. (GR-05, ASA C42.05) NEW YORK. (IN PREP)

AMERICAN INSTITUTE OF ELECTRICAL ENGINEERS. DEFINITIONS OF ELECTRICAL TERMS. RADIOLOGY. ·IGR-75, ASA
C42.75) NEW YORK (IN PREP)

AMERICAN SOCIETY FOR TESTING/MATERIALS. TENTATIVE DEFINITIONS OF TERMS RELATING TO DENSITY AND SPECIFIC
GRAVITY OF SOLIDS, LIQUIDS, AND GASES. (E12-61T) ASTM STDS, PT.4, 1627-30. PHILADELPHIA, 1961. 10T.

AMERICAN SOCIETY FOR TESTING/MATERIALS. TENTATIVE DEFINITIONS OF TERMS RELATING TO DOSIMETRY. (EI70-60T)
ASTM STDS, PT.3, 330-2. PHILADELPHIA, 1961. 30T.

AMERICAN STANDARDS ASSOCIATION. ACOUSTICAL TERMINOLOGY, INCL.MECH. SHOCK/VIBRATIONS. (S1.1-1960)
NEW YORK, 1960. 62P. 700T.

AMERICAN STANDARDS ASSOCIATION. LETTER SYMBOLS FOR ACOUSTICS. (Y10.11) NEW YORK, 1959.

AMERICAN STANDARDS ASSOCIATION. LETTER SYMBOLS FOR HEAT AND THERMODYNAMICS. (Y10.4) NEW YORK, 1957.

AMERICAN STANDARDS ASSOCIATION. QUANTITIES AND UNITS USED IN ELECTRICITY. (C61.1-1961) NEW YORK, 1961.
2P.

AMERICAN VACUUM SOCIETY. GLOSSARY OF TERMS USED IN VACUUM TECHNOLOGY. NEW YORK, PERGAMON, 1958. 63P.
59-8278. 430T.

BALLENTYNE, D.W.G. AND WALKER, L.E.Q. A DICTIONARY OF NAMED EFFECTS AND LAWS IN CHEMISTRY, PHYSICS, AND
MATHEMATICS. ED2. NEW YORK, MACMILLAN, 1961. 234P. 61-1620. 1200T.

BATTEY, E.W. AND LINFORD, A. INSTRUMENT ENCYCLOPEDIA. (GL, PP.1-28) LONDON, HERBERT, 1958. 292P.
58-44430. 1340T.

BECKMANN, W. AND YASSO, W.E. GLOSSARY OF TERMS FREQUENTLY USED IN PHYSICS OF OCEANOGRAPHY. NEW YORK, AM.
INST. PHYS. 1962. 23P. 200T.

BRIGGS, G.A. A TO Z IN AUDIO. NEW YORK, GERNSBACK LIBR, 1961. 224P. 61-12273.

BRITISH STANDARDS INSTITUTION. GLOSSARY OF ACOUSTICAL TERMS. (B.S. 661) LONDON, 1955. 44P. 300T.

BRITISH STANDARDS INSTITUTION. GLOSSARY OF TERMS RELATING TO THE PERFORMANCE OF MEASURING INSTRUMENTS.
(B.S.2643) LONDON, 1955. 20P. 50T.

BRITISH STANDARDS INSTITUTION. GLOSSARY OF TERMS USED IN HIGH VACUUM TECHNOLOGY. (B.S. 2951) LONDON,
1958. 32P. 170T.

BRITISH STANDARDS INSTITUTION. GLOSSARY OF TERMS USED IN RADIOLOGY. (B.S. 2597) LONDON, 1955. 84P. 750T.

BRITISH STANDARDS INSTITUTION. LETTER SYMBOLS, SIGNS AND ABBREVIATIONS. PT.3. FLUID MECHANICS. (B.S.
1991) LONDON, 1961. 36P. 400T.

BRITISH STANDARDS INSTITUTION. LETTER SYMBOLS, SIGNS AND ABBREVIATIONS. PT.5. APPLIED THERMODYNAMICS.
(B.S. 1991) LONDON, 1961. 32P. 320T.

CLARK, G.L. THE ENCYCLOPEDIA OF X-RAYS AND GAMMA RAYS. NEW YORK, REINHOLD, 1963. 1149P. 63-13449.
900T.

ETTER, L.E. GLOSSARY OF WORDS AND PHRASES USED IN RADIOLOGY AND NUCLEAR MEDICINE. SPRINGFIELD, ILL,
THOMAS, 1960. 203P. 59-14918.

FOX, P. GLOSSARY OF TERMS FREQUENTLY USED IN PHYSICS AND COMPUTERS. NEW YORK, AM.INST. PHYS, 1962. 24P.
180T.

GAYNOR, F. CONCISE DICTIONARY OF SCIENCE, PHYSICS, MATHEMATICS, NUCLEONICS, ASTRONOMY, CHEMISTRY. NEW
YORK, PHIL. LIBR, 1959. 546P. 59-16292. 5500T.

GRAHAM. F.D. AUDELS NEW ELECTRIC SCIENCE DICTIONARY... NEW YORK, AUDEL, 1963. 555P. 64-590. 9000T.

GRAY, H.J. ET AL. DICTIONARY OF PHYSICS... NEW YORK, LONGMANS, GREEN, 1958. 544P. 58-3300. 5400T.

HIX, C.F. AND ALLEY, R.P. PHYSICAL LAWS AND EFFECTS. NEW YORK, WILEY, 1958. 291P. 58-13461.

HOGERTON, J.F. ET AL. THE ATOMIC ENERGY DESKBOOK. NEW YORK, REINHOLD, 1963. 673P. 63-13445. 1000T.

HOUGH, J.N. SCIENTIFIC TERMINOLOGY. NEW YORK, RINEHART, 1953. 231P. 52-13874.

ENGLISH

STITUTE OF RADIO ENGINEERS. STANDARDS ON AMERICAN RECOMMENDED PRACTICE FOR VOLUME MEASUREMENTS OF ECTRICAL SPEECH AND PROGRAM WAVES. (53 IRE 3.S2) PROC.IRE, V.42, 815-7 (1954) 20T.

STITUTE OF RADIO ENGINEERS. STANDARDS ON ANTENNAS AND WAVEGUIDES, DEFINITIONS FOR WAVEGUIDE COMPONENTS. 5 IRE 2.S1) PROC.IRE, V. 43, 1073-4 (1955) 40T.

STITUTE OF RADIO ENGINEERS. STANDARDS ON ANTENNAS AND WAVEGUIDES... (59 IRE 2.S1) PROC. IRE, V.47, 8-82 (1959) 20T.

STITUTE OF RADIO ENGINEERS. STANDARDS ON AUDIO TECHNIQUES, DEFINITIONS OF TERMS. (58 IRE 3.S1) PROC.IRE, 46, 1928-34 (1958) 180T.

STITUTE OF RADIO ENGINEERS. STANDARDS ON SOLID-STATE DEVICES, DEFINITIONS OF SUPERCONDUCTIVE LECTRONICS TERMS. (62 IRE 28.S1) PROC. IRE, V.50, 451-2 (1962) 10T.

NTERNATIONAL ORGANIZATION FOR STANDARDIZATION. EXPRESSIONS OF THE PHYSICAL AND SUBJECTIVE MAGNITUDES OF OUND OR NOISE. (ISO-R131, AGREES WITH AM. STD, S1.1-1960) GENEVA, 1959. 62P. 700T.

RWIN, S. DICTIONARY OF PIPE ORGAN STOPS... NEW YORK, SCHIRMER, 1962. 264P. 62-52299. 600T.

ERRARD, H.G. AND MCNEILL, D.B. A DICTIONARY OF SCIENTIFIC UNITS. LONDON, CHAPMAN/ HALL, 1963. 200P.

OW, M.J.D. PHYSICS POCKET CRAMMER. GARDEN CITY, N.Y, DOUBLEDAY, 1963. 160P. 63-5118.

CDOUGAL, W.L. ET AL. FUNDAMENTALS OF ELECTRICITY. ED4. CHICAGO, AM. TECH. SOC, 1960. 342P. 60-6659.

AURO, A. GLOSSARY OF TERMS FREQUENTLY USED IN BIOPHYSICS. NEW YORK, AM. INST. PHYS, 1963. 20P. 120T.

ILLER, W. GLOSSARY OF TERMS FREQUENTLY USED IN SOLID STATE PHYSICS. NEW YORK, AM. INST.PHYS, 1959. 26P. 00T.

ACHS, A.M. AND SCHWARTZ, M. GLOSSARY OF TERMS FREQUENTLY USED IN HIGH ENERGY PHYSICS. NEW YORK, AM.INST. HYS, 1961. 21P. 100T.

HARPS, W.S. DICTIONARY OF CINEMATOGRAPHY AND SOUND RECORDING. LONDON, FOUNTAIN, 1959. 144P. 60-39267. 00T.

TEARNS, R.L. GLOSSARY OF TERMS FREQUENTLY USED IN NUCLEAR PHYSICS. NEW YORK, AM. INST. PHYS, 1962. 7P. 200T.

TRUVE, O. AND ZEBERGS, V. ASTRONOMY OF THE 20TH CENTURY. (GL, PP.515-25, 150T) NEW YORK, MACMILLAN, 962. 544P. 62-21206.

AYLOR, J.M. A PRACTICAL DICTIONARY OF UNDERWATER ACOUSTIC DEVICES. ORLANDO, FLA, U.S. NAVY UNDERWATER OUND REF. LAB, 1953. 39P.

HADDEUS, P. GLOSSARY OF TERMS FREQUENTLY USED IN SPACE PHYSICS. NEW YORK, AM. INST. PHYS, 1963. 18P. 110T.

REMAINE, H.M. THE AUDIO CYCLOPEDIA. INDIANAPOLIS, SAMS, 1959. 1269P. 58-14290.

RENT, H.M. AND ANDERSON, B. GLOSSARY OF TERMS FREQUENTLY USED IN ACOUSTICS. NEW YORK, AM. INST. PHYS, 960. 44P. 200T.

UVAROV, E.B. AND CHAPMAN, D.R. A DICTIONARY OF SCIENCE... BALTIMORE, PENGUIN, 1959. 239P. 60-2541. 3500T

WHITEHOUSE, D.R. GLOSSARY OF TERMS FREQUENTLY USED IN PLASMA PHYSICS. NEW YORK, AM.INST. PHYS,1960. 30P. 180T.

WITTY, M.B. ET AL. DICTIONARY OF ASTRO-PHYSICS ABBREVIATIONS. NEW YORK, SETI, 196 .

WITTY, M.B. ET AL. DICTIONARY OF BIO-PHYSICS ABBREVIATIONS. NEW YORK, SETI, 196 .

WITTY, M.B. ET AL. DICTIONARY OF PHYSICS AND MATHEMATICS ABBREVIATIONS, SIGNS, SYMBOLS AND TABLES. NEW YORK, SETI, 1963. 288P.

WITTY, M.B. ET AL. DICTIONARY OF THERMODYNAMICS ABBREVIATIONS. NEW YORK, SETI, 196 .

ZIMMERMAN, O.T. CONVERSION FACTORS AND TABLES. ED3. DOVER, N.H, IND. RES. SERV, 1961.

FRENCH

COMITE ELECTROTECHNIQUE FRANCAIS. VOCABULAIRE ELECTROTECHNIQUE. ELECTROACOUSTIQUE. (ELEC.ENG. D, ELECTROACOUST, FR DEFS) PARIS, 1957. 45P.

DE VRIES, L. FRENCH-ENGLISH SCIENCE DICTIONARY... ED3. NEW YORK, MCGRAW-HILL, 1962. 655P. 61-17943. 53000T.

DICTIONNAIRE DES SCIENCES MATHEMATIQUES, ASTRONOMIE, PHYSIQUE, CHIMIE. (D. OF MATH, ASTRON, PHYS, CHEM, FR DEFS) PARIS, SEGHERS, 1962. 336P.

ENCYCLOPEDIE FRANCAISE. V.2, LA PHYSIQUE. (PHYS, FR DEFS) PARIS, LAROUSSE, 1956. 508P.

FRENCH

GILLAM, D.J. A CONCISE DICTIONARY OF HOROLOGICAL TERMS. (*EN*FR) LA CHAUX-DE-FONDS, ECOLE SUPER.COM. 1956. 46P. 58-44162. 2300T.

GUYOT, E. DICTIONNAIRE DES TERMES UTILISES DANS LA MESURE DU TEMPS. (TIME MEAS. T. FR DEFS) LA CHAUX-DE-FONDS, CHAMBRE SUISSE HORLOG, 1953. 123P. A53-5630.

GERMAN

DEVRIES, L. AND CLASON, W.E. DICTIONARY OF PURE AND APPLIED PHYSICS. V.1, GE*EN, 367P. V.2, EN*GE, 360P. NEW YORK, ELSEVIER, 1963. 63-14278. 31000T.

ERZEUGNISSE UND DIENSTLEISTUNGEN DER DEUTSCHEN INDUSTRIE FUER VERSCHIEDENE KERNTECHNISCHE ARBEITSGEBIETE (GE*EN GL. OF AT.ENERGY) ATOMIND. DEUT. NO.4, 159-   (1960)

FLUEGGE, S. ET AL. HANDBUCH DER PHYSIK. (ENCYCL. OF PHYS) AKUSTIK. (ACOUST, *GE*EN GL, V.11/1, PP.418-43, 1000T. V.11/2, PP.288-307, 800T) BERLIN, SPRINGER, 1961. A56-2942.

FLUEGGE, S. ET AL. HANDBUCH DER PHYSIK. (ENCYCL. OF PHYS) V.35, ATOME 1. (ATOMS 1, *GE*EN GL, PP.437-54, 630T) BERLIN, SPRINGER, 1957. 454P. A56-2942.

FLUEGGE, S. ET AL. HANDBUCH DER PHYSIK. (ENCYCL. OF PHYS) V.36, ATOME 2. (ATOMS 2, *GE*EN GL, PP.409-24, 500T) BERLIN, SPRINGER, 1956. 424P. A56-2942.

FLUEGGE, S. ET AL. HANDBUCH DER PHYSIK. (ENCYCL. OF PHYS) V.37, PT.1, ATOME 3-MOLEKUELE 1. (ATOMS 3-MOLECULES 1, *GE*EN GL, PP.416-39, 840T) BERLIN, SPRINGER, 1959. 439P. A56-2942.

FLUEGGE, S. ET AL. HANDBUCH DER PHYSIK. (ENCYCL. OF PHYS) V.16, ELEKTRISCHE FELDER UND WELLEN. (ELEC FIELD/WAVES, *GE*EN GL, PP.726-53, 900T) BERLIN, SPRINGER, 1958. 753P. A56-2942.

FLUEGGE, S. ET AL. HANDBUCH DER PHYSIK. (ENCYCL. OF PHYS) V.19, ELEKTRISCHE LEITUNGSPHAENOMENE 1. (ELEC. CONDUCTIVITY 1, *GE*EN GL, PP.396-411, 450T) BERLIN, SPRINGER,1956. 411P. A56-2942.

FLUEGGE, S. ET AL. HANDBUCH DER PHYSIK. (ENCYCL. OF PHYS) V.20, ELEKTRISCHE LEITUNGSPHAENOMENE 2. (ELEC. CONDUCTIVITY 2, *GE*EN GL, PP.480-9, 250T) BERLIN, SPRINGER, 1957. 491P. A56-2942.

FLUEGGE, S. ET AL. HANDBUCH DER PHYSIK. (ENCYCL. OF PHYS) V.21, ELEKTRON-EMISSION GASENTLADUNGEN 1. (ELEC-EMISSION GAS DISCHARGES 1, *GE*EN GL, PP.664-83, 650T) BERLIN, SPRINGER, 1956. 683P. A56-2942.

FLUEGGE, S. ET AL. HANDBUCH DER PHYSIK. (ENCYCL. OF PHYS) V.22, GASENTLADUNGEN 2. (GAS DISCHARGES 2, *GE*EN GL, PP.629-52, 750T) BERLIN, SPRINGER, 1956. 652P. A56-2942.

FLUEGGE, S. ET AL. HANDBUCH DER PHYSIK. (ENCYCL. OF PHYS) V.14, KAELTEPHYSIK 1. (LOW TEMP. PHYS. 1, *GE*EN GL, PP. 338-49, 420T) BERLIN, SPRINGER, 1956. 349P. A56-2942.

FLUEGGE, S ET AL. HANDBUCH DER PHYSIK. (ENCYCL. OF PHYS) V.15, KAELTEPHYSIK 2. (LOW TEMP. PHYS. 2, *GE*EN GL, PP.462-77, 500T) BERLIN, SPRINGER, 1956. 477P. A56-2942.

FLUEGGE, S. ET AL. HANDBUCH DER PHYSIK. (ENCYCL. OF PHYS) V.34, KORPUSKELN UND STRAHLUNG IM MATERIE 2. (CORPUSCLES/RADIATION IN MATTER 2, *GE*EN GL, PP.298-316, 630T) BERLIN, SPRINGER, 1958. 316P. A56-2942.

FLUEGGE, S. ET AL. HANDBUCH DER PHYSIK. (ENCYCL. OF PHYS) V.7, PT.1, KRISTALLPHYSIK 1. (CRYSTAL PHYS 1, *GE*EN GL, PP.666-87, 750T) BERLIN, SPRINGER, 1955. 687P. A56-2942.

FLUEGGE, S. ET AL. HANDBUCH DER PHYSIK. (ENCYCL. OF PHYS) V.7, PT.2, KRISTALLPHYSIK 2. (CRYSTAL PHYS 2, *GE*EN GL, PP.254-73, 650T) BERLIN, SPRINGER, 1958. 273P. A56-2942.

FLUEGGE, S. ET AL. HANDBUCH DER PHYSIK. (ENCYCL. OF PHYS) V.37, PT.2, MOLEKUELE 2. (MOLECULES 2, *GE*EN GL, PP.282-303, 770T) BERLIN, SPRINGER, 1961. 303P. A56-2942.

FLUEGGE, S. ET AL. HANDBUCH DER PHYSIK. (ENCYCL. OF PHYS) V.4, PRINZIPIEN DER ELEKTRODYNAMIK UND RELATIVITAETSTHEORIE. (PRINCIPLES OF ELECTRODYN/RELATIVITY,*GE*EN GL, PP.273-90, 500T) BERLIN, SPRINGER, 1962. 290P. A56-2942.

FLUEGGE, S. ET AL. HANDBUCH DER PHYSIK. (ENCYCL. OF PHYS) V.3, PT.1, PRINZIPIEN DER KLASSISCHEN MECHANIK UND FELDTHEORIE. (PRINC. OF CLASSICAL MECH/FIELD THEORY, *GE*EN GL, PP.859-902, 1500T) BERLIN, SPRINGER, 1960. 902P. A56-2942.

FLUEGGE, S. ET AL. HANDBUCH DER PHYSIK. (ENCYCL. OF PHYS) V.3, PT.2, PRINZIPIEN DER THERMODYNAMIK UND STATISTIK. (PRINC. OF THERMODYNAMICS/STAT, *GE*EN GL, PP.652-78, 900T) BERLIN, SPRINGER, 1959. 678P. A56-2942.

FLUEGGE, S. ET AL. HANDBUCH DER PHYSIK. (ENCYCL. OF PHYS) STROEMUNGSMECHANIK. (FLUID DYNAMICS, *GE*EN GL, V.8/1, PP.451-71, 700T. V.8/2, PP.663-96, 1000T. V.9, PP.779-814, 12000T) BERLIN, SPRINGER, 1959-63. A56-2942.

FLUEGGE, S. ET AL. HANDBUCH DER PHYSIK. (ENCYCL. OF PHYS) V.10, STRUKTUR DER FLUESSIGKEITEN. (STRUCT. OF LIQUIDS, *GE*EN GL, PP.305-320, 500T) BERLIN, SPRINGER, 1960. 320P. A56-2942.

FLUEGGE, S. ET AL. HANDBUCH DER PHYSIK. (ENCYCL. OF PHYS) V.13, THERMODYNAMIK DER FLUESSIGKEITEN UND FESTKOERPER. (THERMODYNAMICS OF LIQUIDS/SOLIDS, *GE*EN GL, PP.646-78, 900T) BERLIN, SPRINGER, 1962. 678P. A56-2942.

FLUEGGE, S. ET AL. HANDBUCH DER PHYSIK. (ENCYCL. OF PHYS) V.12, THERMODYNAMIK DER GASE. (THERMODYNAMIC OF GASES, *GE*EN GL, PP.664-86, 900T) BERLIN, SPRINGER, 1958. 686P. A56-2942.

GERMAN

, H. ET AL. LEXIKON DER PHYSIK. (PHYS. ENCYCL, GE DEFS) STUTTGART, FRANCKH, 1959. 2V. 1687P. 85.

, L. ET AL. KLEINES ABC DER KERNPHYSIK UND KERNTECHNIK. (NUCL. PHYS/ENG. ABC, GE DEFS) LEIPZIG, VERLAG/GRUNDSTOFFIND, 1961. 121P.

, H. PRUEF-, MESS-, UND KONTROLL-GERAETE LEXIKON. (TESTING, MEAS/CONTROL INSTR. D, GE DEFS) ED3 , HADERT, 1954-60. 1070P.

BERG, R.S. AND GOODMAN, T.P. KINEMATICS, A GERMAN-ENGLISH GLOSSARY. MECH. ENG, V.82, 49-53 600T.

C.J. AND IDLIN, R. DICTIONARY OF PHYSICS AND ALLIED SCIENCES. WOERTERBUCH DER PHYSIK UND DTER WISSENSCHAFTEN. (V.1, GE*EN, 675P. V.2, EN*GE, 680P) NEW YORK, UNGAR, 1958-62. 62-9683. .

ER, O.W. AND LEIBIGER, I.S. GERMAN-ENGLISH AND ENGLISH-GERMAN DICTIONARY FOR SCIENTISTS. ANN MICH, EDWARDS, 1959. (REPR) 741P.

RABER, R. TASCHENLEXIKON FUER DIE MESSPRAKTIK. (METROL. D, GE DEFS) LINZ, TECH. VERLAG, 1951. A51-8812.

J. AND SCHMID, H.L. MATHEMATISCHES WOERTERBUCH, MIT EINBEZIEHUNG DER THEORETISCHEN PHYSIK. (D. OF THEOR, PHYS, GE DEFS) ED2. BERLIN, AKADEMIE, 1962. 2V. 1043+952P. 62-2409. 12000T.

WSKI, A. PHYSIKALISCHE GROESSEN UND EINHEITEN... (PHYS. MAGNITUDES/UNITS) STUTTGART, DEVA, 1960. 61-3130.

ISTER, W. LEXIKON DER VERMESSUNGSKUNDE. (METROL D, GE DEFS) BERLIN, WICHMANN, 195 . 504P.

AL, W.H. PHYSIKALISCHES WOERTERBUCH. (PHYS. D, GE DEFS) BERLIN, SPRINGER, 1952. 1618P. 52-31600. .

ITALIAN

ARI, L. ENCICLOPEDIA DELLE MATEMATICHE ELEMENTARI... (ENCYCL. OF ELEM. MATH, IT DEFS) MILAN, , 1930-54. 3V. 34-35033.

O, A. PICCOLO DIZIONARIO DI METROLOGIA GENERALE... (D.OF GEN. METROL, IT DEFS) BOLOGNA, ZANICHELLI, 292P. 60-35436. 1000T.

, E.B. ET AL. DIZIONARIO DELLE SCIENZE. (SCI. D, IT DEFS) MILAN, 1957.

JAPANESE

T. ET AL. IWANAMI,S DICTIONARY OF PHYSICS AND CHEMISTRY. (*JA*EN) TOKYO, IWANAMI,1953. 6+121P.

Y. KAGAKU, RIKAGAKU, KOGYOKAGAKU, NETSU, NENSHO KANKEI EI-WA JUKUGO JITEN. (SCI, PHYS, CHEM, IND. ECH.D, EN*JA) OSAKA, NENRYO OYOBl NENRYOSHA, 1958. 464P. J62-27. 35000T.

MINISTRY OF EDUCATION. INDUSTRIAL STANDARD VOCABULARY OF CHRONOMETRY. (EN*JA) TOKYO, 1951. 18P.

MINISTRY OF EDUCATION. JAPANESE SCIENTIFIC TERMS, PHYSICS. (*JA*EN) TOKYO, DAINIPPON TOSHO, 1954. 24+221P. 3000T.

MINISTRY OF EDUCATION. VOCABULARY ON ELECTRICITY... (EN*JA) TOKYO, 1952. 2BP. 940T.

KU JITEN. (JA*EN D. OF PHYS/CHEM) TOKYO, FUZAMBO, 1959. 938P.

HI, M. ET AL. RADIOLOGICAL DICTIONARY... (JA EN) KYOTO, KIMPODO, 1954. 474+78+47P.

LITHUANIAN

OS TSR MOKSLU AKADEMIJA. FIZIKOS TERMINU ZODYNAS. (PHYS. D, LI DEFS) VILNIUS, VALSTYBINE POLITINES/ NES LIT. LEIDYKLA, 1958. 122P. 60-33128.

POLISH

, S. AND SKRZYNSKA, M. SKROCONY SLOWNIK MECHANICZNY POLSKO-ANGIELSKI. ED2. (PL*EN D. OF MECH. ENG) ; PANSTW. WYDAW. NAUK. TECH, 1962. 185P. 63-28073.

, S. SLOWNIK MECHANICZNY ANGIELSKO-POLSKI. (EN*PL D.OF MECH.ENG) WARSAW, PANSTW.WYDAW.TECH. 1960. 60-43037.

POLYGLOT

IIA NAUK SSSR. KOM. TEKH. TERM. MINOLOGICHESKIE RABOTY V SSSR V OBLASTI TEORETICHESKOI OTEKHNIKI. (THEOR.ELEC.ENG.) GR-05,OSNOVNYE OPREDELENIIA IEC 50-GR-05. (FUNDAMENTAL DEFS, RU*EN*FR) , 1957. 94P. 60-29039. 550T.

PHYSICS

POLYGLOT

BARANY,N. FINOMMECHANIKA, OPTIKA. (D. OF PREC. MECH/OPT, *HU*EN*GE*RU) (MUSZ. ERT. SZ, NO.16) BUDAPE
TERRA, 1961. 214P. 61-48214. 1200T.

BENE, G.J. ATOMIC AND MOLECULAR PHYSICS. (EN/AM*FR*GE*IT*RU*SP) NEW YORK, ELSEVIER. (IN PREP)

CLASON, W.E. DICTIONARY OF SCIENTIFIC APPARATUS. (*EN/AM*DU*FR*GE*IT*SP) NEW YORK, ELSEVIER. (IN PREP

CLASON, W.E. ELSEVIER,S DICTIONARY OF AMPLIFICATION, MODULATION, RECEPTION, AND TRANSMISSION IN 6
LANGUAGES. *EN/AM*DU*FR*GE*IT*SP. NEW YORK, ELSEVIER. 1960. 804P. 60-7173. 2900T.

CLASON, W.E. ELSEVIER,S DICTIONARY OF CINEMA, SOUND, AND MUSIC, *EN-AM,*FR*DU*GE*IT*SP. NEW YORK,
ELSEVIER, 1956. 948P. 56-13141. 3200T.

CLASON, W.E. ELSEVIER,S DICTIONARY OF GENERAL PHYSICS, *EN/AM*DU*FR*GE*IT*SP. NEW YORK, ELSEVIER, 196
859P. 62-13015. 3400T.

CLASON, W.E. ELSEVIER,S LEXICON OF INTERNATIONAL AND NATIONAL UNITS. (*EN/AM*GE*SP*FR*IT*JA*DU*PR*PL*
RU) NEW YORK, ELSEVIER, 1964. 75P. 63-11366. 900T.

CUSSET, F. TABLES COMPLETES DE CONVERSION DES MESURES AMERICAINES, BRITANNIQUES ET METRIQUES. (CONVERS
TABLES, AM/EN/METRIC MEASURES,*EN*FR*GE) PARIS, BLONDEL LA ROUGERY, 1959. 232P. 59-44412.

DEUTSCHER MEDIZINISCHER SPRACHENDIENST. TERMINI RADIOLOGICI, DEUTSCH,ENGLISCH,FRANCAIS,ESPANOL (RADIOL
T, GE EN FR SP) MUNICH, URBAN/SCHWARZENBERG, 1959. 78P. 60-41407.

FLUEGGE, S. ET AL. HANDBUCH DER PHYSIK. (ENCYCL. OF PHYS, GE EN FR) BERLIN, SPRINGER, 1955- .
A56-2942. (IN PROGR)

FOSSATI, F. DIZIONARIO PLURILINGUE DI TECNICA ELETTRO-RADIOLOGICA. (ELEC/RADIOLOGY D, *IT*EN*FR*GE*S
MILAN, WASSERMAN, 1952. 489P. 3500T.

FREIBERGER, W.F. ET AL. THE INTERNATIONAL DICTIONARY OF APPLIED MATHEMATICS (EN DEFS,*FR*GE*RU*SP)
PRINCETON, N.J, VAN NOSTRAND, 1960. 1173P. 60-16931. 8300T.

INOUE, T. ET AL. IWANAMI RIKAGAKU JITEN. (PHYS/CHEM. D, *JA*EN*FR*GE) ED2. TOKYO, IWANAMI, 1958.
1744P.

INTERNATIONAL ELECTROTECHNICAL COMMISSION. INTERNATIONAL ELECTROTECHNICAL VOCABULARY. ELECTRO-ACOUSTIC
*FR*EN*DU*GE*IT*PL*SP*SW. (IEC-50-GR-08) ED2. GENEVA, 1960. 67P.

INTERNATIONAL ELECTROTECHNICAL COMMISSION. INTERNATIONAL ELECTROTECHNICAL VOCABULARY. ELECTROBIOLOGY.
*FR*EN*DU*GE*IT*PL*SP*SW. (IEC-50-GR-70) ED2. GENEVA, 1959. 32P.

INTERNATIONAL ELECTROTECHNICAL COMMISSION. INTERNATIONAL ELECTROTECHNICAL VOCABULARY. FUNDAMENTAL
DEFINITIONS. *FR*EN*DU*GE*IT*PL*SP*SW. (IEC-50-GR-05) ED2. GENEVA, 1956. 102P. 550T.

INTERNATIONAL ELECTROTECHNICAL COMMISSION. INTERNATIONAL ELECTROTECHNICAL VOCABULARY. SCIENTIFIC AND
INDUSTRIAL MEASURING INSTRUMENTS. (IEC-50-GR-20) (*FR*EN*DU*GE*IT*PL*SP*SW) ED2. GENEVA, 1958. 88P. 35

INTERNATIONAL ELECTROTECHNICAL COMMISSION. MEZHDUNARODNYI ELEKTROTEKHNICHESKII SLOVAR. (INTL.
ELECTROTECH. VOC) (IEC 50-GR-20) SCIENTIFIC AND INDUSTRIAL MEASURING INSTRUMENTS. ED2. (*RU*EN*FR*G
*SP*IT*DU*PL*SW) MOSCOW, 1962. 225P.

INTERNATIONAL ORGANIZATION FOR STANDARDIZATION. FUNDAMENTAL QUANTITIES AND UNITS OF THE MKSA SYSTEM AN
QUANTITIES AND UNITS OF SPACE AND TIME. (R31-PT1) GENEVA, 1957.

INTERNATIONAL ORGANIZATION FOR STANDARDIZATION. QUANTITIES AND UNITS OF HEAT. (SIMILAR TO ASA Y10.4)
(R31-PT6) GENEVA, 1960.

INTERNATIONAL ORGANIZATION FOR STANDARDIZATION. QUANTITIES AND UNITS OF MECHANICS. (SIMILAR TO
ASA Z10.3) (R31-PT3) GENEVA, 1960.

INTERNATIONAL ORGANIZATION FOR STANDARDIZATION. QUANTITIES AND UNITS OF PERIODIC AND RELATED PHENOMENA
(R31-PT2) GENEVA, 1958.

INTERNATIONAL ORGANIZATION FOR STANDARDIZATION. QUANTITIES, UNITS, SYMBOLS, CONVERSION FACTORS AND
CONVERSION TABLES. QUANTITIES AND UNITS OF RADIATION AND LIGHT. (ISO/TC12) ED2. GENEVA, 1961. 11P.
70T.

MICHELS, W.C. ET AL. THE INTERNATIONAL DICTIONARY OF PHYSICS AND ELECTRONICS. ED2. (*EN*FR*GE*RU*SP)
PRINCETON, VAN NOSTRAND, 1961. 1355P. 61-2485. 13500T.

PALOTAS, L. ET AL. MUSZAKI MECHANIKA. (ENG. MECH. D, *HU*EN*GE*RU) (MUSZ. ERT. SZ, NO.4) BUDAPEST,
TERRA, 1959. 167P. 59-40060. 1200T.

POLAND. POLSKI KOMITET NORMALIZACYJNY. VOCABULARY OF MECHANICS... EN*GE*FR*PL*RU. NEW YORK, PERGAMON,
1962. 189P. 62-11559. 1500T.

SCHULZ, E. WOERTERBUCH DER OPTIK UND FEINMECHANIK. (OPT/PREC. MECH. D) V.1, GE*EN*FR, 111P. V.2, EN
*GE, 124P. V.3, FR*GE*EN, 109P. WIESBADEN, BRANDSTETTER, 1960-61. A61-3700. 2500T.

124

PHYSICS

POLYGLOT

CIENTIFIC INSTRUMENTS MANUFACTURES ASSOCIATION (ENGLAND) BRITISH INSTRUMENTS DIRECTORY AND BUYERS GUIDE. (FR*EN*GE*RU*SP GL, PP.194-256) ED3. LONDON, 1962. 667P.

LIBICKI, W. ET AL. SLOWNIK TERMINOW FIZYCHNYCH, POLSKO-ANGIELSKO-FRANCUSKO-NIEMIECKO-ROSYJK. (PHYS. D, L*EN*FR*GE*RU) WARSAW, PANSTW. WYDAW. NAUK, 1961. 776P. 62-25891. 7700T.

WITKOWSKI, J. SLOWNIK TERMINOLOGII MECHANIKI KLASYCZNE... POLSKI,NIEMIECKI, ANGIELSKI, FRANCUSKI, ROSYJSKI. (CLASSICAL MECH, GL PL*GE*EN*FR*RU) WARSAW, WYDAW.TECHN,1959- .

SYNDICAT GENERALE D,OPTIQUE. ANNUAIRE. ALPHABETICAL LIST OF PRODUCTS (*GE*EN*FR*SP GL) PARIS, 1958. D3P.

THALI, H. TECHNICAL DICTIONARY OF TERMS USED IN ELECTRICAL ENGINEERING, RADIO, TELEVISION, TELECOMMUNICATION. (V.1 EN*GE*FR, ED6. 280P, 15000T. V.2 GE*EN*FR, ED4. 311P. 24000T. V.3 FR*EN*GE*, IN PREP) LUCERNE, THALI, 1960-- . 62-822.

THEWLIS, J. ET AL. ENCYCLOPAEDIC DICTIONARY OF PHYSICS, GENERAL, NUCLEAR, SOLID STATE,MOLECULAR,CHEMICAL, METAL AND VACUUM PHYSICS, ASTRONOMY, GEOPHYSICS, BIOPHYSICS AND RELATED SUBJECTS. EN DEFS. MULTILINGUAL GL, *CH*FR*GE*JA*SP. NEW YORK, PERGAMON, 1961-63. 9V. 60-7069. 15000T.

RUSSIAN

AKADEMIIA NAUK SSSR. KOM.TEKH.TERM. GIDROMEKHANIKA, VOLNOVOE DVIZHENIE ZHIDKOSTI, STROITELNAIA MEKHANIKA, TERMINOLOGIIA (FLUID MECH, WAVE MOTION OF FLUIDS/STRUCT. MECH, RU DEFS) (SB. REK. TERM. NO.58. MOSCOW, 1962. 85P. 63-40826.

AKADEMIIA NAUK SSSR. KOM.TEKH.TERM. TERMINOLOGIIA AERODINAMICHESKOGO RASCHETA SAMOLETA. (AERODYN. FOR AIRPLANE DESIGN, RU DEFS) (SB.REK.TERM, NO.17) MOSCOW, 1954. 20P. 55-36936. 60T.

AKADEMIIA NAUK SSSR. KOM.TEKH.TERM. TERMINOLOGIIA ELEKTRICHESKIKH IAVLENII V GAZAKH. (D. OF ELEC. PHENOMENA IN GASES, RU DEFS) (BIUL.NO.59) MOSCOW, 1952. 32P. 110T.

AKADEMIIA NAUK SSSR. KOM.TEKH.TERM. TERMINOLOGIIA ELEKTRICHESKIKH IAVLENII V GAZAKH. (D. OF ELEC. PHENOMENA IN GASES, RU DEFS) (SB.REK.TERM.NO.13) MOSCOW, 1952. 29P. 54-32122. 110T.

AKADEMIIA NAUK SSSR. KOM.TEKH.TERM. TERMINOLOGIIA MEKHANIKI ZHIDKOSTI. (FLUID MECH, RU DEFS) (SB.REK. TERM. NO.12) MOSCOW, 1952. 40P. 140T.

AKADEMIIA NAUK SSSR. KOM. TEKH. TERM. TERMINOLOGIIA OBSHCHEI MEKHANIKI. (GEN. MECH, RU DEFS) (SB. REK. TERM. NO.33) MOSCOW, 1955. 57-15814. 42P. 200T.

AKADEMIIA NAUK SSSR. KOM.TEKH.TERM. TERMINOLOGIIA TEORETICHESKOI ELEKTROTEKHNIKI. (D. OF THEOR. ELEC. ENG. RU DEFS) (BIUL.NO.64) MOSCOW, 1952. 43P. 200T.

AKADEMIIA NAUK SSSR. KOM.TEKH.TERM. TERMINOLOGIIA TEORETICHESKOI ELEKTROTEKHNIKI. (D. OF THEOR. ELEC. ENG. RU DEFS) (SB.REK.TERM.NO.46) MOSCOW, 1958. 46P. 59-45329. 210T.

AKADEMIIA NAUK SSSR. KOM. TEKH. TERM. TERMINOLOGIIA TERMODINAMIKI. (THERMODYN, RU DEFS) (SB. REK. TERM, NO. 7) MOSCOW, 1952. 54P. 54-32121. 180T.

AKADEMIIA NAUK SSSR. KOM. TEKH. TERM. TERMINOLOGIIA VOLNOVYKH DVIZHENII ZHIDKOSTI. (WAVE MOTION IN FLUIDS, RU DEFS) (SB. REK. TERM, NO.30) MOSCOW, 1954. 14P. 50T.

CLASON, W.E. ELSEVIER,S DICTIONARY.OF AMPLIFICATION, MODULATION, RECEPTION AND TRANSMISSION. RUSSIAN SUPPL. NEW YORK, ELSEVIER, 1961. 87P. 2900T.

EMIN, I. ET AL. RUSSIAN-ENGLISH GLOSSARY OF NAMED EFFECTS, LAWS, AND REACTIONS AND MISCELLANEOUS TERMS IN PHYSICS, MATHEMATICS AND ASTRONOMY. NEW YORK, INTERLANG. DICT, 1962. 22P. 62-51916. 2000T.

EMIN,I. RUSSIAN-ENGLISH GLOSSARY OF SOLID STATE PHYSICS. NEW YORK, CONSULTANTS BUR, 1958. 90P. 58-909. 40000T.

EMIN, I. RUSSIAN-ENGLISH PHYSICS DICTIONARY. NEW YORK, WILEY, 1963. 554P. 63-8056. 40000T.

KOTIK, M.G. ANGLO-RUSSKII SLOVAR PO AEROGIDRODINAMIKE. (EN*RU D. AEROHYDRODYN. D) MOSCOW, FIZMATGIZ, 1960. 457P. 61-30949. 13000T.

KOZAK, A.S. AND SMITH, C.H. STUDIES IN MACHINE TRANSLATION. PT.12, GLOSSARY OF RUSSIAN PHYSICS. SANTA MONICA, CAL. RAND, 1960. (AD-252-609) 297P. 63-4338.

NOVECK, S. AND EMIN, I. RUSSIAN-ENGLISH GLOSSARY OF PHYSICS OF FLUIDS AND METEOROLOGY. NEW YORK, INTERLANG. DICT, 1959. 93P. 59-4252. 4000T.

ROBESON P. JR. RUSSIAN-ENGLISH GLOSSARY OF ACOUSTICS AND ULTRASONICS. NEW YORK, CONSULTANTS BUR, 1958. 170P. 58-1685. 10000T.

ROBESON, P. JR. RUSSIAN-ENGLISH GLOSSARY OF ELECTRONICS AND PHYSICS. NEW YORK, CONSULTANTS BUR, 1957. 343P. 58-341. 20000T.

RUSSIAN-ENGLISH GLOSSARY OF ABBREVIATIONS OCCURRING IN PHYSICS LITERATURE...NEW YORK, INTERLANGUAGE DICT, 1960. 64P. 60-3086. 1500T.

RUSSIAN

SOKOLOV, V.A. AND KRASAVIN, L.M. SPRAVOCHNIK MER. (METROL. MANUAL, RU DEFS) (GL, PP.149-240) ED2. MOSCO, VNESHTORGIZDAT, 1960. 248P.

U.S. LIBRARY OF CONGRESS. GLOSSARY OF UNITS AND MEASURES, ENGLISH-RUSSIAN, RUSSIAN-ENGLISH. (OTS-61-31103) WASHINGTON, 1961. 531P. 2600T.

VVEDENSKII, B.A. ET AL. FIZICHESKII ENTSIKLOPEDICHESKII SLOVAR. (ENCYCL. D. OF PHYS, RU DEFS) MOSCOW, SOV. ENTSIKL, 1960-   . 4V. 61-29525.

SPANISH

FERNANDEZ FERRER, J. ENCICLOPEDIA DE LA FISICA. (PHYS.ENCYCL, SP DEFS) BARCELONA, DE GASSO, 1960. 370, 62-65062.

UVAROV, E.B. ET AL. DICCIONARIO DE CIENCIAS... (SCI. D, SP DEFS) MADRID, DOSSAT, 196 .

PLASTICS AND POLYMERS

CHINESE

CHUNG-KUO K,O HSUEH YUAN. PIEN I CHU. (ACAD. SINICA BUR. COMPIL/TRANSL) KAO FEN TZU HUA HSUEH HUA KUNG SHU YU. (HIGH POLYMER CHEM/CHEM. ENG. T, EN CH) PEKING, SCIENCE, 1957. 35P. C59-706.

CHUNG-KUO K,O HSUEH YUAN. PIEN I CH,U PAN WEI YUAN HUI. (ACAD. SINICA. COMM. OF PUBL/TRANSL) KAO FEN T, HUA HSUEH MING TZ,U. (HIGH POLYMER CHEM, CH EN) PEKING, 1956.

ENGLISH

AMERICAN SOCIETY FOR TESTING/MATERIALS. GLOSSARY OF TERMS RELATING TO RUBBER AND RUBBER-LIKE MATERIALS. PHILADELPHIA, 1956. 121P. 56-14327. 2000T.

AMERICAN SOCIETY FOR TESTING/MATERIALS. TENTATIVE ABBREVIATIONS OF TERMS RELATING TO PLASTICS. (D1600-61T) ASTM STDS, PT.9. 791-3. PHILADELPHIA, 1961. 60T.

AMERICAN SOCIETY FOR TESTING/MATERIALS. TENTATIVE NOMENCLATURE RELATING TO PLASTICS. (D 883-61T) ASTM STDS, PT.9. 796-810. PHILADELPHIA,1961. 220T.

BRITISH STANDARDS INSTITUTION. GLOSSARY OF TERMS USED IN THE PLASTICS INDUSTRY. (B.S. 1755, AMENDS PD 1594-1953, PD 3825-1960) LONDON, 1951-60. 60P. 450T.

BRITISH STANDARDS INSTITUTION. GLOSSARY OF TERMS USED IN THE RUBBER INDUSTRY. (B.S. 3558) LONDON, 1962. 27P. 200T.

BRITISH STANDARDS INSTITUTION. LIST OF COMMON NAMES AND ABBREVIATIONS FOR PLASTICS. (B.S.3502) LONDON, 1962. 7P.

GLOSSARY OF TERMS USED BY THE MECHANICAL RUBBER GOODS INDUSTRY. RUBBER AGE, V.74, 915-35 (1954) 1000T.

LENNOX-KERR, P. INDEX TO MAN-MADE FIBRES OF THE WORLD. MANCHESTER, ENG, MAN-MADE TEXTILES, 1961. 117P. 62-51652.

MARK, H.F. AND GAYLORD, N.G. ENCYCLOPEDIA OF POLYMER SCIENCE AND TECHNOLOGY. NEW YORK, INTERSCIENCE. (IN PREP)

MODERN PLASTICS ENCYCLOPEDIA ISSUE FOR 1963. (GL,PP. 16-36, 500T) NEW YORK, MODERN PLASTICS, 1962. 1195P.

PRESS, J.J. MAN-MADE TEXTILE ENCYCLOPEDIA. NEW YORK, TEXTILE BOOK, 1959, 913P. 59-15700.

RADI, L.J. GLOSSARY FOR THE PROTECTIVE COATINGS AND PLASTIC INDUSTRY. ED4. HAWTHORNE, N.J, INTERCHEMICAL, 1959. 158P.

WITTY, M.B. ET AL. DICTIONARY OF PLASTICS AND CERAMICS, SIGNS, SYMBOLS AND TABLES. NEW YORK, SETI, 196 192P.

FRENCH

COMMISSION FRANCAISE DE NORMALISATION INTERNATIONALE DES MATIERES PLASTIQUES. NOMENCLATURE ET TERMES EQUIVALENTS. PARIS, CENTRE MAT. PLAST. (IN PREP)

ENCYCLOPEDIE FRANCAISE DES MATIERES PLASTIQUES. (PLAST. ENCYCL, FR DEFS) PARIS, IND. PLAST. MOD, 1959. 575P. 60-50542.

GENIN, G. ET AL. ENCYCLOPEDIE TECHNOLOGIQUE DE L,INDUSTRIE DU CAOUTCHOUC. (ENCYCL.OF RUBBER IND, FR DEFS) PARIS, DUNOD, 1956-60. 4V. A56-5968.

GERMAN

BAUER, R. CHEMIEFASER-LEXIKON. (SYNTHETIC FIBERS D, GE DEFS) ED3. FRANKFURT/MAIN, DEUT. FACHVERLAG, 1963. 126P.

KITTEL, H. FARBEN- LACK-, UND KUNSTSTOFF-LEXIKON... (PAINT, LACQUER, PLAST. D, GE DEFS) STUTTGART, WISS. VERLAGSGES, 1952. 858P. 52-38532.

LEUCHS, O. DIE HOCHPOLYMEREN WERKSTOFFE. (PLASTICS, GE DEFS) KUNSTSTOFFE (MUNICH) V.45, 323-34 (1955)

PLASTICS AND POLYMERS

GERMAN

/ITTFOHT, A. KUNSTSTOFFTECHNISCHES WOERTERBUCH. (PLAST/D, *GE*EN) ED3. NEW YORK, INTERSCIENCE, 1959-61.
'V. 61-65177. 22000T.

HINDI

;ADGOPAL, . AND KAUSHAL, S.C. TEXTILE TECHNOLOGY AND PLASTICS, ENGLISH-HINDI DICTIONARY. ALLAHABAD,
HINDI SAHITYA SAMMELAN. 195-.

JAPANESE

JAPAN. MINISTRY OF EDUCATION. INDUSTRIAL STANDARD VOCABULARY OF PLASTICS. (EN*JA) TOKYO, 1951. 90P.
!900T.

JAPAN. MINISTRY OF EDUCATION. INDUSTRIAL STANDARD VOCABULARY OF RUBBER PRODUCTS. (EN*JA) TOKYO,
.950. 12P. 300T.

;INKI CHEMICAL ENGINEERING SOCIETY. PLASTICS DICTIONARY. (EN*JA) KYOTO, KOBUNSHI KAGAKU KANKOKAI, 1953.
.43P.

POLYGLOT

)ELORME, J. DICTIONNAIRE DES MATIERES PLASTIQUES ET LEURS APPLICATIONS. (D. OF PLAST/APPL, FR GE EN)
'ARIS, 1959. 400+112P. A59-3166.

'ACHAUSDRUECKE AUF DEM GEBIET DES TEXTILEN PRUEFWESENS FUER CHEMIEFASERN. (TEST.T.FOR CHEM.TEXTILE FIBERS,
;E EN FR) RAYON ZELLWOLLE, V.7(1957) FF.

IANDBUCH DER INTERNATIONALEN KAUTSCHUKINDUSTRIE. (INTL.RUBBER HANDBOOK, GE EN FR) ZURICH, INTL.
/IRTSCHAFTSLIT.1953-- 61-49220. 3000T.

MPERIAL CHEMICAL INDUSTRIES. A VOCABULARY OF TECHNICAL TERMS USED IN THE RUBBER INDUSTRY. (FR*EN*GE*SP)
IANCHESTER,ENG. 1955. 127P. 55-31243. 900T.

NTERNATIONAL ORGANIZATION FOR STANDARDIZATION. LIST OF EQUIVALENT TERMS FOR PLASTICS. (EN*FR*RU)
ISO/R194) GENEVA, 1962. 800T.

1UOVISANASTO. PLASTICS VOCABULARY, FI*EN*FR*GE*SW. HELSINKI, KUSTANTAJA MUOVIVIESTI, 1960. 120P.
.1-25531.

'URASUCHIKKUSU YOGO JITEN. (PLAST. D, EN*JA*GE) TOKYO, KOGYO CHOSA KAI, 1959. 756+70+530+25P. 6500T.
.200 EN*JA ABBR.

IUBBER STICHTING, DELFT. ELSEVIER,S RUBBER DICTIONARY... (*DU*EN*FR*GE*IT*JA*MA*PR*SP*SW) NEW YORK,
'LSEVIER, 1959. 1537P. 58-9206. 8000T.

;TOECKHERT, K. KUNSTSTOFF-LEXIKON. (PLAST. D, GE*EN*FR*IT*SP) ED3. MUNICH, HANSER, 1961. 408P.
.2-58103.

'EKNISKA NOMENKLATURCENTRALEN. PLASTICS TECHNICAL VOCABULARY. (*EN*FR*GE*SW) STOCKHOLM, 1958. 173P.
'000T.

'EREIN SCHWEIZERISCHER MASCHINEN-INDUSTRIELLER. NORMALIENBURO. KUNSTSTOFFE. (PLAST. D, *GE*EN*FR*IT)
URICH, 1963. 70+18+17+18P. 1200T.

!ITTFOHT, A.M. PLASTICS LEXICON, PROCESSING AND MACHINERY, IN GERMAN, ENGLISH, FRENCH, ITALIAN, SPANISH
IND DUTCH. NEW YORK, ELSEVIER,-1963. 216P. 1200T.

RUSSIAN

.NGLO-RUSSKII SLOVAR PO KAUCHUKU, REZINE I KHIMICHESKIM VOLOKNAM. (EN*RU D. OF RUBBER/SYN. FIBERS)
IOSCOW, FIZMATGIZ, 1962. 260P.

IURARII, M. AND IOFFE, S. ANGLO-RUSSKII SLOVAR PO PLASTMASSAM. (EN*RU PLAST. D) MOSCOW, 1963. 144P.

PRINTING TECHNOLOGY AND INDUSTRY

ENGLISH

.LLEN, E.M. HARPER,S DICTIONARY OF THE GRAPHIC ARTS. NEW YORK, HARPER/ROW, 1963. 295P. 63-16540.
'500T.

.VIS, F.C. THE BOOKMAN,S CONCISE DICTIONARY. NEW YORK, PHIL.LIBR, 1956. 318P. 57-678. 9000T.

ERRY, W.T. ET AL. ENCYCLOPAEDIA OF TYPE FACES. ED3. NEW YORK, PITMAN, 1962. 420P. 62-21098.

RITISH STANDARDS INSTITUTION. TYPEFACE NOMENCLATURE. (B.S.2961) LONDON, 1958. 12P. 20T.

'OLLINS, F.H. ET AL. AUTHORS, AND PRINTERS DICTIONARY... ED10. LONDON, OXFORD UNIV. PRESS, 1962. 442P.

:LAISTER, G.A. AN ENCYCLOPEDIA OF THE BOOK TERMS USED IN PAPER-MAKING, PRINTING, BOOKBINDING...
'LEVELAND, WORLD, 1960. 484P. 61-2811.

IARROD, L.M. THE LIBRARIANS GLOSSARY... ED2. LONDON, GRAFTON, 1959. 332P. 59-2822.

ENGLISH

POCKET ENCYCLOPEDIA OF PAPER AND GRAPHIC ARTS TERMS. KAUKAUNA, WIS, THOMAS, 1960. 94P. 60-4619.

SHERA, J.H. ET AL. ENCYCLOPEDIA OF LIBRARY SCIENCE AND DOCUMENTATION. NEW YORK, INTERSCIENCE. (IN PREP)

FRENCH

ARCHAMBEAUD, P. DICTIONNAIRE ANGLAIS-FRANCAIS, FRANCAIS-ANGLAIS DES INDUSTRIES GRAPHIQUES. (*FR*EN D. OF PRINTING) PARIS, CO. FRANCAISE D.EDITIONS, 1952. 199P.

LAFONTAINE, G.H. DICTIONARY OF TERMS USED IN THE PAPER, PRINTING, AND ALLIED INDUSTRIES, ENGLISH-FRENCH, FRENCH-ENGLISH. ED2. MONTREAL, SMITH, 1957. 192P.

GERMAN

BORN, E. LEXIKON FUER DAS GRAPHISCHE GEWERBE. (PRINTING ENCYCL, GE DEFS) FRANKFURT/MAIN, POLYGRAPH, 1958. 526P. 59-49792.

GARTE, H. FACHWOERTERBUCH DES GRAPHISCHEN GEWERBES UND DER PAPIERINDUSTRIE. (*GE*EN PRINTING/PAPER IND) V.1 EN*GE,1954. 113P. V.2 GE*EN (IN PREP) ED2. BRAUNSCHWEIG, GARTE, 1954--

GROSS, O. FACHAUSDRUCKE DES BIBLIOTHEKSWESENS UND SEINER NACHBARGEBIETE. (*GE*EN D.OF LIBR.T) ED2. HAMBURG, EBERHARD STICHNOTE, 1952. 163P. 53-15675.

HADERT, H. HADERT DRUCK-LEXIKON... (PRINTING D, GE DEFS) BERLIN, HADERT, 1956. 182P. 58-49146.

HILLER, H. WOERTERBUCH DES BUCHES. (PRINTING D, GE DEFS) ED2. FRANKFURT/MAIN, KLOSTERMANN, 1958. 332P.

KIRCHNER, J. ET AL. LEXIKON DES BUCHWESENS. (ENCYCL. OF BOOKS/PRINTING, GE DEFS) STUTTGART, HIERSEMANN, 1952-56. 4V. 53-17416.

LEXIKON DER GRAPHISCHEN TECHNIK. (PRINTING D, GE DEFS) LEIPZIG, VEB, 1962. 472P. 63-33198.

MARTIN, W. KLEINES FREMDWOERTERBUCH DES BUCH-UND SCHRIFTWESENS. (FOR. T. IN BOOK/PRINTING IND, GE DEFS) LEIPZIG, HARRASSOWITZ, 1959. 169P. 59-30052.

MATERIALLEXIKON FUER DIE GRAPHISCHE INDUSTRIE. (ENCYCL. OF PRINTING MATER, GE DEFS) LEIPZIG, BIBLIOG. INST. 1955. 388P. 56-44308.

SAEUBERLICH, O. OBRAL WOERTERBUCH, BUCHGEWERBLICH-GRAPHISCHES TASCHEN-LEXIKON. (BOOK/PRINTING IND. GL, GE DEFS) ED2. WIESBADEN, BRANDSTETTER, 1957, 292P.

TRONDT, L. POLYGRAPH DICTIONARY, FACHAUSDRUECKE DER GRAPHISCHEN INDUSTRIE. V.1, GE*EN 391P. V.2, EN*GE 374P. FRANKFURT/MAIN, POLYGRAPH, 1959. 60-22021.

ITALIAN

GAMBIGLIANI-ZOCCOLI, B. DIZIONARIO DI TERMINOLOGIA BIBLIOGRAFICA... (*IT*EN D. OF BIBL) PT.1, EN*IT /LA RICERCA SCIENTIFICA,V.26, 655-63 (1956) MONTHLY THROUGH V.27, 2610-5 (1957). PT.2 IT*EN/V.27, 2907-12 THROUGH V.27, 3761-5 (1957) (INCOMPL)

POLISH

KAFEL, M. MALY ILUSTROWANY SLOWNIK TECHNIKI WYDAWNICZEJ. (ILLUS. PRINTING GL, PL DEFS) WARSAW, PANSTW. WYDAW.TECH.1953. 112P. 55-15169.

PRZYBYLSKI, E.S. A DICTIONARY OF SELECTED BIBLIOGRAPHICAL TERMS, BOOKTRADE TERMS, AND PLACE NAMES IN POLISH. LEXINGTON, UNIV. KENTUCKY LIBRS, 1955. 36P. 55-62450.

POLYGLOT

DANMARKS BIBLIOTEKSSKOLE. BIBLIOTEKSGLOSER, DANSK-ENGELSK-FRANSK-TYSK.(LIBR.GL, DA*EN*FR*GE) COPENHAGEN, DANSK BIBL.KONTOR, 1962. 29P. 300T.

HOSTETTLER, R. TECHNICAL TERMS OF THE PRINTING INDUSTRY.*FR*EN*DU*GE*IT. ED4. ST. GALLEN, SWITZERLAND, 1963. 195P.

KHAVKINA, L.B. ET AL. SLOVARI BIBLIOTECHNO-BIBLIOGRAFICHESKIKH TERMINOV... (D. OF LIBR. T, *EN*RU*GE*FR) MOSCOW, VSESOIUZ.KNIZHN.PALATA, 1952. 234P. 53-25638.

LOVASZ, K. NYOMDAIPAR. (PRINTING IND. D, *HU*EN*GE*RU) (MUSZ. ERT. SZ. NO.15) BUDAPEST, TERRA, 1961. 232P. 1200T.

MAMIYA, F. A COMPLETE DICTIONARY OF LIBRARY TERMS... *EN*GE*FR*CH*JA. TOKYO, JAPAN LIBR. BUR, 1952. 645P. 10000T.

MORAVEK, E. AND BERNATH-BODNAR, E. VERZEICHNIS UNGARISCHER FACHAUSDRUECKE UND ABKUERZUNGEN AUS DEM BUCH-UND BIBLIOTHEKSWESEN... (BOOK/LIBR.T/ABBR, HU*EN*FR*GE) VIENNA, OESTERR.NATL.-BIBL. 1958. 61P. 59-52242.

NADVORNIK, M. ET AL. SLOVNIK KNIHOVNICKYCH TERMINU V SESTI JAZYCICH... (D. OF LIBR. T, CZ RU PL GE EN FR) PRAGUE, (OLOMOUC) STATNI PED NAKL, 1958. 632P. 59-30054. 2500T.

POLYGLOT

IHON INSATSU GAKKAI. INSATSU JITEN. (PRINTING D, JA*EN*GE). TOKYO, SEIFU KANKOBUTSU SABIS SENTA, 1961.
77+50+55P. J62-450. 3500T.

CHLEMMINGER, J. FACHWOERTERBUCH DES BUCHWESENS, DEUTSCH, ENGLISCH, FRANZOESISCH... (D. OF BOOK T, *GE*EN
FR) ED2. DARMSTADT, STOYTSCHEFF, 1954. 367P. A56-2927. 6000T.

URNER, M.C. THE BOOKMAN,S GLOSSARY. (FOREIGN BOOK TRADE T, *DA*FR*GE*IT*RU*SP, PP.181-203) ED4. NEW
ORK, BOWKER, 1961. 212P. 61-13239. 1100T.

ON OSTERMANN, G.F. MANUAL OF FOREIGN LANGUAGES... (130 LANG) ED4. NEW YORK, CENTRAL BOOK, 1952. 414P.
2-2409.

IECKOWSKA, H. AND PLISZCZYNSKA, H. PODRECZNY SLOWNIK BIBLIOTEKARZA. (LIBR. GL, *PL*EN*FR*GE*RU) WARSAW,
ANSTW. WYDAW. NAUK, 1955. 309P. 55-39069. 3000T.

RUSSIAN

IURIN, A.A. AND BOROZINA, A.M. ANGLO-RUSSKII POLIGRAFICHESKII SLOVAR. (EN*RU PRINTING D) MOSCOW,
IZMATGIZ, 1962. 450P. 62-65794. 17000T.

SPANISH

EPPER, W.M. DICTIONARY OF NEWSPAPER AND PRINTING TERMS, ENGLISH-SPANISH, SPANISH-ENGLISH. NEW YORK,
OLUMBIA UNIV. PRESS, 1959. 344P. 59-16345. 2500T.

ODRIGUEZ, C. DICCIONARIO BILINGUE DES ARTES GRAFICAS, INGLES-ESPANOL...(EN*SP PRINTING D) NEW YORK. NATL.
APER/TYPE, 1956. 177P. 56-30823. 5000T.

SWEDISH

ERSSON, O. GRAFISK UPPSLAGSBOK. (PRINTING MANUAL, SW DEFS) ED2. STOCKHOLM, SVER.LITOGR. TRYCKERIER,1956.
072P. 57-32735.

RAILROAD ENGINEERING

CHINESE

HUNG-K,O HSUEH YUAN. PIEN I CH,U PAN WEI YUAN HUI. (ACAD. SINICA. COMM. OF PUBL/TRANSL) T,IEH TAO
U KUNG LU KUNG CH,ENG MING TZ,U. (R.R./HIGHWAY ENG. T, CH EN) PEKING, SCIENCE, 1956. 218P. C58-5143.

ENGLISH

MERICAN INSTITUTE OF ELECTRICAL ENGINEERS. DEFINITIONS OF ELECTRICAL TERMS. TRANSPORTATION. (GR-40,
ENERAL,ASA C42.40/GR-41, AIR, ASA C42.41/ GR-42, LAND, ASA C42.42/ GR-43, MARINE, ASA C4Z.43) NEW YORK,
956. 42P. 420T.

ARTER, E.F. THE MODEL RAILWAY ENCYCLOPEDIA. ED5. LONDON, STARKE, 1963. 468P.

ANSOME-WALLIS, P.L.J.C. ET AL. THE CONCISE ENCYCLOPAEDIA OF WORLD RAILWAY LOCOMOTIVES. NEW YORK,
IAWTHORNE, 1959. 512P. 59-9600.

GERMAN

IUEBENER, E. TASCHENLEXIKON FUER DEN STELLWERKSDIENST. (SIGNALING D, GE DEFS) LEIPZIG, FACHBUCHVERLAG,
955. 115P. 57-16242.

CHMITZ,W. ENGLISCHES WOERTERBUCH FUER EISENBAHNSIGNALWESEN UND FERNMELDETECHNIK. (*GE*EN D. OF R.R.
IGNALING/TELECOMMUN) V.1 EN*GE,246P. V.2 GE*EN,201P. ED.2 FRANKFURT/MAIN, TETZLAFF, 1954. 54-34312.
000T.

TUMPF, B. EISENBAHN-LEXIKON...(R.R. D,GE DEFS) MAINZ, HUETHIG/DREYER, 1960. 298P. 61-46631. 4000T.

JAPANESE

IAPANESE STANDARDS ASSOCIATION. ROLLING STOCK TERMINOLOGY...(*JA*EN) TOKYO, 1953. 145P.

IAPANESE STANDARDS ASSOCIATION. VOCABULARY OF TERMS CONNECTED WITH RAILWAY TRACKS AND STATIONS... (*JA
EN) TOKYO, 1953. 102P.

POLYGLOT

NTERNATIONAL ELECTROTECHNICAL COMMISSION. INTERNATIONAL ELECTROTECHNICAL VOCABULARY. ELECTRIC TRACTION.
*FR*EN*DU*GE*IT*PL*SP*SW. (IEC-50-GR-30) ED2. GENEVA, 1957. 94P. 400T.

NTERNATIONAL ELECTROTECHNICAL COMMISSION. INTERNATIONAL ELECTROTECHNICAL VOCABULARY. SIGNALING AND
ECURITY APPARATUS FOR RAILWAYS. *FR*EN*DU*GE*IT*PL*SP*SW. (IEC-50-GR-31) ED2. GENEVA, 1959. 46P.

NTERNATIONAL RAILWAY DOCUMENTATION BUREAU. CHEMINS DE FER, GLOSSAIRE DES TERMES FERROVIAIRES... (R.R.
I, *FR*EN*GE*IT*SP*SW) AMSTERDAM, ELSEVIER, 1960. 414P. 60-7857. 2000T.

NTERNATIONAL RAILWAY UNION. LEXIQUE GENERAL DES TERMES FERROVIAIRES. (D. OF R.R, FR*EN*GE*IT*SP) BERN,
IENTELI, 1957. 829P. 58-30935. 50000T.

RAILROAD ENGINEERING

POLYGLOT

INTERNATIONAL RAILWAY UNION. RECUEIL DES TERMES CONCERNANT L.EMPLOI ET L.ECHANGE DU MATERIEL ROULANT...
(ROLLING STOCK D. *FR*EN*GE*IT*PL*RU) V.1, 629P. WARSAW, MIN. COMMUNIC. POLAND, 1958-- . 59-29905.

JAPANESE NATIONAL RAILWAYS. RAILWAY DICTIONARY. (*JA*CH*EN*FR*GE*RU) TOKYO, INAGAKI, 1952. 870P.

PAN AMERICAN RAILWAY CONGRESS. BOLETIN. (JUNE-AUGUST 1963-) (*FR*EN*SP*IT*GE) BUENOS AIRES, 1963

VASARHELYI, B. ET AL. KOZLEKEDESUGY. PT.1, KENYSZERPALYAS ES KOZUTI KOZLEKEDES. (RAIL/ROAD TRANSP. D.
*HU*EN*GE*RU) (MUSZ. ERT. SZ, NO.7) BUDAPEST, TERRA. 1960. 207P. 60-34451. 1200T.

RUSSIAN

AKADEMIIA NAUK SSSR. KOM.TEKH.TERM. TERMINOLOGIIA ELEKTRICHESKOI TIAGI MAGISTRALNYKH ZHELEZNYKH DOROG
METROPOLITENOV. ELEKTROTIAGOVAIA SET. (POWER NETWORKS FOR ELEC. R.R/SUBWAYS, RU DEFS) (SB.REK.TERM,
NO.31) MOSCOW, 1954. 34P. 55-35585. 160T.

AKADEMIIA NAUK SSSR. KOM.TEKH.TERM. TERMINOLOGIIA ELEKTRICHESKOI TIAGI MAGISTRALNYKH ZHELEZNYKH DOROG
METROPOLITENOV, TIAGOVYE PODSTANTSII. (POWER SUBSTATIONS FOR ELEC. R.R/SUBWAYS, RU DEFS) (SB.REK.TERM
NO.32) MOSCOW, 1954. 17P. 56-46941. 80T.

AKADEMIIA NAUK SSSR. KOM. TEKH. TERM. TERMINOLOGIIA KHIMICHESKOI TEKHNOLOGII VODY, IDUSHCHEI NA PITANI
PAROVOZNYKH KOTLOV. (CHEM PREP. OF WATER FOR LOCOMOTIVES, RU DEFS) (BIUL, NO.62) MOSCOW, 1952. 240T.

AKADEMIIA NAUK SSSR. KOM.TEKH.TERM. TERMINOLOGIIA ZHELEZNODOROZHNOI SIGNALIZATSII, TSENTRALIZATSII
STRELOK, SIGNALOV I BLOKIROVKI. (R.R. SIGNALING, CENTRALIZATION OF SWITCHING, RU DEFS) (SB.REK.TERM,NO
10) MOSCOW, 1952. 54P. 55-37885. 290T.

AKADEMIIA NAUK SSSR. KOM.TEKH.TERM. TERMINOLOGIIA ELEKTROTIAGI. (ELEC.R.R. D, RU DEFS) (BIUL. NO. 60
MOSCOW, 1952. 52P. 380T.

AKADEMIIA NAUK SSSR. KOM.TEKH.TERM. TERMINOLOGIIA PODVIZHNOGO SOSTAVA ZHELEZNYKH DOROG. (R.R. ROLLING
STOCK, RU DEFS) (BIUL. NO.61) MOSCOW, 1952. 40P. 170T.

CHERNUKHIN, A.E. ET AL. ANGLO-RUSSKII ZHELEZNODOROZHNYI SLOVAR. (EN*RU R.R. D) MOSCOW,
TRANSZHELDORIZDAT, 1958. 662P. 59-33897. 45000T.

GLUZMAN, I.S. ANGLO-RUSSKII SLOVAR PO ZHELEZNODOROZHNOI AVTOMATIKE, TELEMEKHANIKE I SVIAZI. (EN*RU D.
R.R. SIGNALING/COMMUN) MOSCOW, FIZMATGIZ, 1958. 427P. 59-33853. 16000T.

SMITH, R.E.F. RAILWAY TRANSPORT TERMS, RUSSIAN-ENGLISH. BIRMINGHAM, ENG. UNIV, 1958. 11P.

ZHELEZNODOROZHNAIA ENTSIKLOPEDIIA. (ABBR.TRANSL.OF AM.R.R.CARS, RU DEFS) MOSCOW, TRANSZHELDORIZDAT,
1961. 484P.

SPANISH

PAN AMERICAN RAILWAY CONGRESS ASSOCIATION. 8TH CONGRESS. TERMINOLOGIA FERROVIARIA AMERICANA.(SP*EN R.R.
WASHINGTON, D.C., 1953. 46P. 53-4498. 900T.

PAN AMERICAN RAILWAY CONGRESS ASSOCIATION. 9TH CONGRESS. TERMINOLOGIA FERROVIARIA AMERICANA.(SP*EN R.R.
BUENOS AIRES, 1957. 169P.

REFRIGERATION, CRYOGENICS, HEATING, AND AIR CONDITIONING

ENGLISH

AMERICAN SOCIETY FOR TESTING/MATERIALS. TENTATIVE DEFINITIONS OF TERMS RELATING TO CONDITIONING. (E41
60T) ASTM STDS., PT.4, 1624-6. PHILADELPHIA, 1961. 40T.

AMERICAN SOCIETY OF HEATING, REFRIGERATING AND AIR-CONDITIONING ENGINEERS. ASHRAE GUIDE AND DATA BOOK.
(GL.OE PHYS/HEAT/VENT/REFRIG/AIR COND. T.IN TEXT,PP.845-54, 400T) NEW YORK, 1961. V.1. 880P. 62-1033.

AMERICAN STANDARDS ASSOCIATION. REFRIGERATION TERMS AND DEFINITIONS. (ASA B53.1, SAME AS ASRE 12-58)
NEW YORK. AM.SOC.REFRIG.ENG, 1958. 33P. 750T.

BRITISH STANDARDS INSTITUTION. GLOSSARY OF TERMS RELATING TO THERMAL INSULATION. (B.S. 3533) LONDON,
1962. 24P. 130T.

MOSES, G.L. GLOSSARY OF INSULATION ENGINEERING TERMS. INSULATION (LIBERTYVILLE) V. 8, NO. 6, 15-8(196
200T.

TABLES, FORMULAS, ABBREVIATIONS AND SYMBOLS USEFUL TO THE INSULATION ENGINEER. INSULATION (LIBERTYVILL
V.8, NO.6, 4-14 (1962) 300T.

FRENCH

DUSNICKIS, I. AND CHAUMELLE, P. DICTIONNAIRE TECHNIQUE ANGLAIS-FRANCAIS, CHAUFFAGE INDUSTRIEL. (*EN*FR
IND. HEATING D) PARIS, DUNOD, 1954. 143P. A54-4039. 6000T.

GERMAN

DANNIES, J.H. LEXIKON DER KAELTETECHNIK. (REFRIG. D, GE DEFS) ED2. DISSEN, BEUCKE, 1959. 572P.

REFRIGERATION, CRYOGENICS, HEATING, AND AIR CONDITIONING

GERMAN

FLUEGGE, S. ET AL. HANDBUCH DER PHYSIK. (ENCYCL. OF PHYS) V.14, KAELTEPHYSIK 1. (LOW TEMP, PHYS. 1, *GE*EN GL, PP. 338-49, 420T) BERLIN, SPRINGER, 1956. 349P. A56-2942.

FLUEGGE, S ET AL. HANDBUCH DER PHYSIK. (ENCYCL. OF PHYS) V.15, KAELTEPHYSIK 2. (LOW TEMP. PHYS. 2, *GE*EN GL, PP.462-77, 500T) BERLIN, SPRINGER, 1956. 477P. A56-2942.

JAPANESE

JAPANESE STANDARDS ASSOCIATION. JAPANESE ENGINEERING TERMS, PLUMBING, HEATING, AND VENTILATION...(*JA*EN) TOKYO, 1955. 176P.

POLYGLOT

CHUNG-KUO K,O HSUEH YUAN. PIEN I CH,U PAN WEI YUAN HUI. (ACAD. SINICA. COMM. OF PUBL/TRANSL) CHI SHUI P,AI SHUI KUNG NUAN T,UNG FENG KUNG CH,ENG MING TZ,U. (DRAINAGE, HEATING/VENTILATION ENG. T, RU EN CH) PEKING, SCIENCE, 1957. 154P. C58-5311.

EMBLIK, E. FUENF SPRACHEN KAELTE-WOERTERBUCH. (5-LANG. REFRIG. D, *GE*EN*FR*SP*SW) HANNOVER-BRUECKE, SCHMERSOW, 1954. 192P. A54-5448. 1200T.

INTERNATIONAL INSTITUTE OF REFRIGERATION. INTERNATIONAL DICTIONARY OF REFRIGERATION (EN*FR*GE*RU*SP*IT) NEW YORK, PERGAMON, 1962. 278P. 62-22208. 1600T.

LANG, O. ET AL. FUENF SPRACHEN WOERTERBUCH FUER DIE KAELTE- UND KLIMATECHNIK, HEIZUNG UND LUEFTUNG. (5-LANG.D. OF REFRIG, AIR COND, HEAT/VENT, GE*EN*FR*IT*SP) HAMBURG, LINDOW, 1959. 588P. A60-1971.

RUSSIAN

KOBULASHVILI, SH.N. KHOLODILNAIA TEKHNIKA, ENTSIKLOPEDICHESKII SPRAVOCHNIK. (REFRIG. ENCYCL, RU DEFS) 2V. LENINGRAD, GOSTORGIZDAT, 1960-61. 992P. 61-27512.

VOLPOVA, M.V. ANGLO-RUSSKII SLOVAR-MINIMUM PO KHOLODILNOI TEKHNIKE. (EN*RU D. OF REFRIG. TECH) ODESSA, TEKH. INST. PISHCH/KHOLODIL. PROM, 1960. 27P. 61-42236. 1000T.

SANITARY ENGINEERING

ENGLISH

AMERICAN SOCIETY FOR TESTING/MATERIALS. GLOSSARY OF TERMS ON INDUSTRIAL WATER. (STP NO.148 D) NEW YORK, 1960.

AMERICAN SOCIETY FOR TESTING/MATERIALS. STANDARD DEFINITIONS OF TERMS RELATING TO INDUSTRIAL WATER AND INDUSTRIAL WASTE WATER (D 1129-61) ASTM STDS, PT.10, SUPPL, 316-23 PHILADELPHIA, 1962. 100T.

BERRY, E. AN ILLUSTRATED DICTIONARY OF PLUMBING TERMS. LONDON, TECH.PRESS, 1960. 244P. 61-3609.

GECKLER, J.R. ET AL. GLOSSARY OF...WATER AND WASTE WATER CONTROL. CINCINNATI, U.S. HEW, 1963. 22P. 63-65430.

ISAAC, P.S.G. A GLOSSARY OF SANITARY ENGINEERING TERMS. NEWCASTLE-UPON-TYNE, UNIV. DURHAM, 1955. 72P.

WITTY, M.B. ET AL. DICTIONARY OF SANITARY ENGINEERING ABBREVIATIONS, SIGNS, SYMBOLS AND TABLES. NEW YORK SETI, 196 . 192P.

FRENCH

COLAS, R. AND GASSER, . LEXIQUE DE L,EAU, ANGLAIS-FRANCAIS ET FRANCAIS-ANGLAIS. (*EN*ER GL. OF WATER) LONDON, INTL. WATER SUPPLY ASSOC, 1955. 60P. 750T.

TERMINOLOGIE DE LA PREVENTION ET DE LA SUPPRESSION DES POUSSIÈRES DANS LES USINES, GALERIES ET CARRIERES, GLOSSAIRE ANGLAIS-FRANCAIS. BT-61. (IND. DUST CONTROL, EN*FR GL) OTTAWA, DEPT. SECY. STATE, 1957. 10P. 130T.

WORLD HEALTH ORGANIZATION. A GLOSSARY OF WATER AND SEWAGE TERMS USED IN SANITARY ENGINEERING. (*EN*FR) (WORKING PAPER) GENEVA, 1956. 74+92P. 1100T.

GERMAN

WEBER, P. FACHWOERTERBUCH DER ABWASSER TECHNIK. (*GE*EN D. OF SEWAGE/DISPOSAL) ESSEN, GIRARDET,195 . 63P.

POLYGLOT

ASOCIACION INTERAMERICANA DE INGENIERIA SANITARIA. LA TERMINOLOGIA TECNICA DE LA INGENIERIA SANITARIA. (SANIT. ENG. T, *SP EN FR*PR) INGENIERIA SANIT, MEXICO. V.10, 305-29. (1957)

CHUNG-KUO K,O HSUEH YUAN. PIEN I CH,U PAN WEI YUAN HUI. (ACAD. SINICA. COMM. OF PUBL/TRANSL) CHI SHUI P,AI SHUI KUNG NUAN T,UNG FENG KUNG CH,ENG MING TZ,U. (DRAINAGE, HEATING/VENTILATION ENG. T, RU EN CH) PEKING, SCIENCE, 1957. 154P. C58-5311.

MEINCK, F. AND MOEHLE, H. WOERTERBUCH FUER DAS WASSER- UND ABWASSERFACH IN DEUTSCH, ENGLISCH, FRANZOESISCH, ITALIENISCH. (D. OF WATER/SEWAGE ENG, GE EN FR IT) NEW YORK, ELSEVIER, 1963. 480P. 6000T.

SANITARY ENGINEERING

POLYGLOT

MEYER, A.F. ET AL. TRINKWASSER UND ABWASSER IN STICHWOERTERN. (DRINKING WATER/SEWERAGE D, GE*EN*FR*IT) ED2. WIESBADEN, BRANDSTETTER, 1955. 1058P.

WEI SHENG PU. (MIN. PUBL. HEALTH. COMM/COMPIL) KUNG KUNG WEI SHENG HSUEH MING TZ,U. (PUBLIC HEALTH T, RU CH EN) PEKING, PEOPLE,S HEALTH PRESS, 1956. 95P. C59-2822.

SPANISH

MOYA, V.J. NOMENCLATURA DE INGENIERIA SANITARIA. (SANIT. ENG. NOMENCL, EN*SP) MEXICO, ROLLAND, 1952. 153P. 62-30394. 3000T.

SCIENCE AND RESEARCH

ARABIC

UNITED ARAB REPUBLIC. SCIENTIFIC TERMS. SER. 1, EN*AR. CAIRO, SCI. COUNCIL, 1961. 435P. NE 62-1569.

CHINESE

KUO LI PIEN I KUAN. (NATL. INST OF TRANSL) K,O HSUEH MING TZ,U HUI PIEN. (SCI. T, EN CH) 7V. TAIPEI, CHENG-CHUNG BOOKS 1959. C59-2928.

WANG, YU-MING, ET AL. TZU JAN K,O HSUEH TZ,U TIEN. (NATURAL SCI. D, CH EN) HONG KONG, WORLD, 1959. 169P. C59-2803.

CZECH

DOBROVOLNY, B. ET AL. MALY TECHNICKY NAUCNY SLOVNIK...(TECH/SCI. D, CZ DEFS) ED2. PRAGUE, SNTL, 1959. 1010P. 60-37130. 8000T.

KORBAR, T. AND STRANSKY, A. TECHNICKY NAUCNY SLOVNIK. (SCI/TECH. D, CZ DEFS) PRAGUE, SNTL, 1962-- . 62-41602.

ENGLISH

AMERICAN INSTITUTE OF ELECTRICAL ENGINEERS. DEFINITIONS OF ELECTRICAL TERMS. ELECTROBIOLOGY, INCLUDING ELECTROTHERAPEUTICS IGR-80,ASA C42.80) NEW YORK, 1957. 13P. 120T.

ASIMOV, I. WORDS OF SCIENCE, AND THEIR HISTORY. BOSTON, HOUGHTON MIFFLIN. 1959. 266P. 59-5198. 250T.

BRITISH STANDARDS INSTITUTION. GLOSSARY OF COLOUR TERMS USED IN SCIENCE AND INDUSTRY. (B.S. 1611) LONDON 1953. 20P. 110T.

BROWN, R.W. COMPOSITION OF SCIENTIFIC WORDS... REV. ED. WASHINGTON, 1956. 882P. 56-56233.

BUTTRESS, F.A. WORLD LIST OF ABBREVIATIONS OF SCIENTIFIC, TECHNOLOGICAL AND COMMERCIAL ORGANIZATIONS. ED2. NEW YORK, HAFNER, 1960. 300P. 60-2449. 2500T.

CARAKER, G.E. JUNIOR SCIENCE DICTIONARY. WASHINGTON, BUTTERWORTHS, 1963. 99P. 63-13715. 2000T.

CLARK, G.L.ET AL. THE ENCYCLOPEDIA OF MICROSCOPY. NEW YORK, REINHOLD, 1961. 693P. 61-9698.

ENCYCLOPEDIA OF POPULAR SCIENCE FOR YOUNG PEOPLE. NEW YORK, LITTLE/IVES, 1963- V. 62-21834.

ENGEL, L. STERLING JUNIOR PICTORIAL ENCYCLOPEDIA OF SCIENCE. NEW YORK, STERLING, 1962. 256P. 62-18633.

EVANS, R. OUR NEW AGE, ILLUSTRATED SCIENCE DICTIONARY. NEW YORK, MCKAY, 1962.

FLOOD,W.E. AND WEST,M. AN ELEMENTARY SCIENTIFIC AND TECHNICAL DICTIONARY. ED3. LONDON, LONGMANS, 1962. 413P. 63-892. 12000T.

FLOOD, W.E. SCIENTIFIC WORDS, THEIR STRUCTURE AND MEANING. NEW YORK, DUELL, SLOAN/PEARCE. 1960. 220P. 60-12827. 2000T.

GAYNOR, F. CONCISE DICTIONARY OF SCIENCE, PHYSICS, MATHEMATICS, NUCLEONICS, ASTRONOMY, CHEMISTRY. NEW YORK, PHIL. LIBR; 1959. 546P. 59-16292. 5500T.

GIDLEY, W.F. AND MORENO, J.R. PREFIXES AND SUFFIXES OF SCIENTIFIC NOMENCLATURE. ED4. AUSTIN, TEX, HEMPHILL, 1958. 172P. 1800T.

HECHTLINGER, A. MODERN SCIENCE DICTIONARY... PALISADE, N.J, FRANKLIN, 1959. 784P. 59-2320. 14500T.

HOUGH, J.N. SCIENTIFIC TERMINOLOGY. NEW YORK, RINEHART, 1953. 231P. 52-13874.

THE ILLUSTRATED ENCYCLOPEDIA OF MODERN SCIENCE. NEW YORK, STUTTMAN, 1958. 1528P. 59-26938.

MCGRAW-HILL ENCYCLOPEDIA OF SCIENCE AND TECHNOLOGY... NEW YORK, MCGRAW-HILL, 1960. 15V. YEARBOOKS, 1961-63. 60-11000.

NEWMAN, J.R. ET AL. THE HARPER ENCYCLOPEDIA OF SCIENCE. NEW YORK, HARPER, 1962. 4V. 62-14541. 4000T.

NYBAKKEN, O.E. GREEK AND LATIN IN SCIENTIFIC TERMINOLOGY. AMES, IOWA STATE COLLEGE, 1959. 321P. 59-5992. 1600T.

SCIENCE AND RESEARCH

ENGLISH

, J. SCIENCE VOCABULARY BUILDER. BOSTON, HUMAN ENG. LAB, 1956. (UNPAGED) 57-20230.

SCIENCE ENCYCLOPEDIA OF THE SCIENCES. GARDEN CITY, N.J., DOUBLEDAY, 1963. 762P. 63-8070. 4500T.

.E. ET AL. CONCISE SCIENCE ENCYCLOPEDIA. NEW YORK, CROWELL, 1955. 255P. 55-6879.

.E. ET AL. JUNIOR PICTORIAL ENCYCLOPAEDIA OF SCIENCE. LONDON, WARD/LOCK. 1961. 256P.

R.S. GLOSSARY OF TERMS FREQUENTLY USED IN SCIENTIFIC DOCUMENTATION. NEW YORK, AM. INST. PHYS, P. 100T.

F. DICTIONARY OF BUSINESS AND SCIENTIFIC TERMS. HOUSTON, TEX, GULF, 1961. 330P. 61-13963. 6500T.

E.B. AND CHAPMAN, D.R. A DICTIONARY OF SCIENCE... BALTIMORE, PENGUIN, 1959. 239P. 60-2541. 3500T

RAND,S SCIENTIFIC ENCYCLOPEDIA... ED3. PRINCETON, N.J, VAN NOSTRAND, 1958. 1839P. 58-7085.

FRENCH

F. VOCABULAIRE TECHNIQUE, ELECTRICITE, MECANIQUE, MINES, SCIENCES... (*FR*EN TECH. D) ED4. ERGER-LEVRAULT. 1954. 663P. 54-35644. 3000T.

, L. FRENCH-ENGLISH SCIENCE DICTIONARY... ED3. NEW YORK, MCGRAW-HILL, 1962. 655P. 61-17943.

ES DU COMITE D, ETUDE DES TERMES TECHNIQUES FRANCAIS.(BT-76(1959) 40P,40T. BT-81(1960)56P, 100T. 60) 40P,40T. BT-91(1960) 40P,40T. BT-99(1961)33P,30T,BT-106(1963)43P,40T.(TECH.T.DEF.BY STUDY *FR) OTTAWA, DEPT.SECY. STATE,1959--

E, J.O. FRENCH-ENGLISH AND ENGLISH-FRENCH DICTIONARY OF TECHNICAL TERMS AND PHRASES. ED4. V.1, 41P. V.2, EN*ER, 544P. LONDON, ROUTLEDGE, KEGAN, PAUL, 1955.

E.B. ET AL. DICTIONNAIRE DES SCIENCES... (SCI.D, FR DEFS) PARIS, PRESSES UNIV. FRANCE, 1956. -2097. 3500T.

GERMAN

S ABC DER NATURWISSENSCHAFT UND TECHNIK... (ABC OF SCI/TECH, GE DEFS) ED8. LEIPZIG, BROCKHAUS, 05P. 10000T.

S DER NATURWISSENSCHAFTEN UND DER TECHNIK. (D.OF SCI/TECH, GE DEFS) ED5. WIESBADEN, BROCKHAUS, 0P. 61-28882.

L. ENGLISH-GERMAN TECHNICAL AND ENGINEERING DICTIONARY. NEW YORK, MCGRAW-HILL, 1954. 997P. . 130000T. SUPPL. 1962. 285P.

, L. ET AL. GERMAN-ENGLISH SCIENCE DICTIONARY... ED3. NEW YORK, MCGRAW-HILL, 1959. 592P. 59-9412.

L. GERMAN-ENGLISH TECHNICAL AND ENGINEERING DICTIONARY. NEW YORK, MCGRAW-HILL, 1950. 928P. . 125000T.

L. GERMAN-ENGLISH TECHNICAL AND ENGINEERING DICTIONARY. SUPPL. WIESBADEN, BRANDSTETTER, 1959. -12204. 50000T.

ENGLISCHES WOERTERBUCH... WISSENSCHAFT UND TECHNIK. (GE EN SCI/TECH D) LEIPZIG, ENZYKLOPAEDIE, 6P. 40000T.

NORMENAUSSCHUSS. (DNA) ABKUERZUNGEN TECHNISCH-WISSENSCHAFTLICHER ORGANISATIONEN DES AUSLANDES UND ROEFFENTLICHUNGEN. (ABBR. OF TECH/SCI. ORG. IN FOR. COUNTRIES... GE DEFS) BERLIN,1961. 14P.

LEXIKON A-Z, NATURWISSENSCHAFTEN, TECHNIK, WIRTSCHAFT. (SCI-TECH D, GE DEFS) LEIPZIG, AEDIE, 1959. 1108P. 30000T.

, O.W. AND LEIBIGER, I.S. GERMAN-ENGLISH AND ENGLISH-GERMAN DICTIONARY FOR SCIENTISTS. ANN ICH, EDWARDS, 1959. (REPR) 741P.

FER, J. LEXIKON DER GESCHICHTE' DER NATURWISSENSCHAFTEN. (ENCYCL. OF NATURAL SCI. HIST, GE DEFS) HOLLINEK, (IN PROGR)

W.F. ET AL. KOSMOS-LEXIKON DER NATURWISSENSCHAFTEN... (SCI. ENCYCL, GE DEFS) STUTTGART, 1953-55. 2V. 53-31162.

. A GERMAN-ENGLISH DICTIONARY OF TECHNICAL, SCIENTIFIC, AND GENERAL TERMS... NEW YORK. DUTTON, 9P. 53-3264. 80000T.

HINDI

RACHARINI SABHA, BENARES. THE HINDI SCIENTIFIC GLOSSARY. ALLAHABAD, INDIAN PRESS, 195-. A60-4290.

RA. ELEMENTARY ENGLISH-INDIAN DICTIONARY OF SCIENTIFIC TERMS. NAGPUR, 1950. 110P.

HINDI

RAGHU VIRA. ET AL. AN EXHAUSTIVE ENGLISH-HINDI DICTIONARY... SCIENCE, INDUSTRY, ART, LITERATURE. NAGPUR, INTL. ACAD. IND. CULT, 1954- . 10000P. (IN PROGR)

HUNGARIAN

RANKI, A. TERMESZETTUDOMANYI ES MUSZAKI ROVIDITESEK, JELEK, JELOLESEK. (SCI-TECH. ABBRS, SYMBOLS/NOTATIONS, HU DEFS) ED2. BUDAPEST, TANKONYVKIADO, 1959. 126P. 60-37679.

ITALIAN

LEONARDI, R. DIZIONARIO ILLUSTRATO DELLE SCIENZE PURE E APPLICATE. (ILLUS.D.OF PURE/APPL.SCI, IT DEFS) ED2. MILAN, HOEPLI, 1950-53. 2V. 3090P.

RICERCA E SCIENZA. (ENCICLOPEDIA MONOGRAFICA DELL,INFORMAZIONE) (RES/SCI, IT DEFS) BOLOGNA, ZANICHELL 1959. 622P. 60-25044.

UVAROV, E.B. ET AL. DIZIONARIO DELLE SCIENZE. (SCI. D, IT DEFS) MILAN, 1957.

JAPANESE

ISHII, Y. KAGAKU, RIKAGAKU, KOGYOKAGAKU, NETSU, NENSHO KANKEI EI-WA JUKUGO JITEN. (SCI, PHYS, CHEM, IN CHEM.TECH.D, EN*JA) OSAKA, NENRYO OYOBI NENRYOSHA, 1958. 464P. J62-27. 35000T.

UEDA, R. AND SATO J. ET AL. ENGLISH-JAPANESE SCIENCE DICTIONARY. (*EN*JA) TOKYO, KYORITSU,1958. 455+124

POLISH

BRAMSON, M. ET AL. ENGLISH-POLISH DICTIONARY OF SCIENCE AND TECHNOLOGY. NEW YORK, GORDON/BREACH. (IN PREP) 270,000T.

BRAMSON, M. ET AL. POLISH-ENGLISH DICTIONARY OF SCIENĆE AND TECHNOLOGY. NEW YORK, GORDON/BREACH. (IN PREP) 270,000T.

MASLANKIEWICZ,K. MALA ENCYKLOPEDIA PRZYRODNICZA. (SCI. ENCYCL. PL DEFS) ED2. WARSAW, PANSTW WYDAW. NAUK 1962. 849P. 62-67913.

POLYGLOT

CAILLEUX, A. AND KOMORN, J. DICTIONNAIRE DES RACINES SCIENTIFIQUES. (D. OF POLYGLOT ROOTS USED IN SCI) PARIS, SOC. ED. D,ENSEIGNEMENT SUP, 1961. 246P. 63-32067.

KWAHAK SAJON PYONCHANHOE. HYONDAE KWAHAK TAESAJON. (NATURAL SCI. ENCYCL, KO*EN*FR*GE) SEOUL, 1962. 1500+180+94P. K62-807.

UNION OF INTERNATIONAL ASSOCIATIONS. INTERNATIONAL INITIALESE, INDEX TO INTERNATIONAL ABBREVIATIONS IN CURRENT USE. ED2. BRUSSELS, 1963. 50P.

PORTUGUESE

VALLANDRO, L. DICIONARIO INGLES-PORTUGUES... TERMOS TECNICOS E CIENTIFICOS... ABREVIATURAS... (EN*PR TECH/SCI. D/ABBR) RIO DE JANEIRO, GLOBO, 1954. 1135P. 54-44677.

RUSSIAN

AKADEMIIA NAUK SSSR. INDEX OF ABBREVIATED AND FULL TITLES OF SCIENTIFIC AND TECHNICAL PERIODICAL LITERATURE. (UKRAZATEL SOKR. I POLN. NAZV. NAUCH/TEKH. LIT) TRANSL. BY WRIGHT-PATTERSON AFB, OHIO, 1960. 247P. 60-60261. 1800T.

AKADEMIIA NAUK SSSR. KOM.TEKH.TERM. RUKOVODSTVO PO RAZRABOTKE I UPORIADOCHENIIU NAUCHNO-TEKHNICHESKOI TERMINOGOLII. (MANUAL FOR DEVELOP.STDS IN SCI/TECH,RU DEFS) MOSCOW, 1952. 54P.

CALLAHAM L.I. AND UVAROV, E.V. RUSSIAN-ENGLISH CHEMICAL AND POLYTECHNICAL DICTIONARY. ED2. NEW YORK, WILEY, 1962. 892P. 62-18989. 70000T.

FISHER, E.L. ABBREVIATIONS OF RUSSIAN SCIENTIFIC SERIAL PUBLICATIONS. AM. DOC, V.10, 192-208 (1959) 20

FISHER, E.L. SOKRASHCHENIIA, RUSSIAN ABBREVIATIONS FOR BIBLIOGRAPHIC SEARCH. SPEC. LIBR, V.49, 365-70 (1958) 240T.

KRAMER, A. AND E. ABBREVIATIONS AND SYMBOLS IN SOVIET SCIENTIFIC AND TECHNICAL LITERATURE. TRENTON, N. 1960. 12P. 60-9262. 500T.

LOTTE,D.S. OSNOVY POSTROENIIA NAUCHNO-TEKHNICHESKOI TERMINOLOGII... (COMPOSITION OF SCI/TECH. T, RU DEFS) MOSCOW, AKAD. NAUK, SSSR, 1961. 156P, 61-41148.

U.S. LIBRARY OF CONGRESS. SOVIET-RUSSIAN SCIENTIFIC AND TECHNICAL TERMS, A SELECTIVE LIST. WASHINGTON, 1962. 668P. 60-60977. 26000T.

SLOVAK

DOBROVOLNY, B. AND HORECKY, J. SLOVNICEK NOVEJ TECHNIKY...(SCI/TECH D, SL DEFS) BRATISLAVA, ROH, 1961. 149P. 62-32103.

SCIENCE AND RESEARCH

SPANISH

BROCKHAUS DICCIONARIO POPULAR DE LAS CIENCIAS Y DE LAS TECNICAS. (POPULAR SCI/TECH D,SP DEFS) BARCELONA, GILI, 1961. 658P.

UVAROV, E.B. ET AL. DICCIONARIO DE CIENCIAS... (SCI. D, SP DEFS) MADRID, DOSSAT, 196 .

STATISTICS (MATHEMATICAL AND APPLIED)

AFRIKAANS

LOOR, B. DE. STATISTIEKWOORDEBOEK. (STAT. D, *EN*AF) PRETORIA, SUID-AFRIKAANSE AKAD. WETENSKAP EN KUNS, 1961. 104P. 63-1783.

ALBANIAN

ALBANIA. DREJTORIA E STATISTIKES. TRANSLATION AND GLOSSARY OF ALBANIAN STATISTICAL YEARBOOK, 1958. NEW YORK, U.S. JPRS, 1959. 90P. 59-64166. 1600T.

DUTCH

ROOSWINKEL, A.J.M. STATISTIEK VAN A-Z... (STAT. A-Z, DU DEFS) ZEIST, HAAN, 1958. 231P. 59-14692.

ENGLISH

EASTMAN KODAK CO. SYMBOLS, DEFINITIONS AND TABLES FOR INDUSTRIAL STATISTICS AND QUALITY CONTROL. (DEFS/ SYMBOLS,PP.1-61) ROCHESTER,N.Y, INST.TECH,1958. 202P.

FRENCH

BOUCHER, E. STATISTICAL VOCABULARY, EN*FR. PRELIM.ED. OTTAWA, CAN. BUR. STAT, 1950. 74P. 1500T.

GERMAN

FLUEGGE, S. ET AL. HANDBUCH DER PHYSIK. (ENCYCL. OF PHYS) V.3, PT.2, PRINZIPIEN DER THERMODYNAMIK UND STATISTIK. (PRINC. OF THERMODYNAMICS/STAT, *GE*EN GL, PP.652-78, 900T) BERLIN, SPRINGER, 1959. 678P. A56-2942.

TRAPP, V. STATISTISCHES WOERTERBUCH, ENGLISCH-DEUTCH. (EN*GE* STAT. D) ED2. MUNICH, DEUT. STAT. GES, 1956. 130P.

JAPANESE

JAPAN. MINISTRY OF EDUCATION. JAPANESE SCIENTIFIC TERMS, MATHEMATICS. (*JA*EN) TOKYO, DAINIPPON TOSHO, 1957. 146P. 1500 MATH. T. 600 MATH. STAT. T.

JAPAN. MINISTRY OF EDUCATION. VOCABULARIES OF STATISTICS, RELATED MATHEMATICS, SAMPLING SURVEYS. (*JA*EN) TOKYO, 1950-51. VAR. PP. 750T.

POLYGLOT

DENMARK. STATISTISKE DEPARTEMENT. BETAENKNING ANGAEDE NORDISK STATISTISK NOMENKLATUR. (SCAND.STAT. NOMENCL, DA*EN*FI*NO*SW) COPENHAGEN, 1954. 26P. 56-36079.

HUNGARY. KOZPONTI STATISZTIKAI HIVATAL. STATISZTIKAI SZOTAR. 1700 STATISZTIKAI KIFEJEZES HET NYELVEN. (7-LANG. STAT. D, HU*EN*BU*CZ*GE*PL*RU) ED2. BUDAPEST, STAT. KIADO, 1961. 171P. 61-41924. 1700T.

INTER-AMERICAN STATISTICAL INSTITUTE. STATISTICAL VOCABULARY. (*SP*EN*FR*PR) ED2. WASHINGTON, PAN AM. UNION, 1960. 83P. PA60-56.

INTERNATIONAL STATISTICAL INSTITUTE. LISTE (PROVISOIRE) DES TERMES UTILISES DANS LA STATISTIQUE OFFICIELLE. (PROV. GL. OF OFFIC. STAT, FR*EN*DU) THE HAGUE, 1961.

KENDALL, M.G. AND BUCKLAND, W.R. A DICTIONARY OF STATISTICAL TERMS... (EN DEFS, *FR*GE*IT*SP GL) ED2. NEW YORK, HAFNER, 1960. 575P. 61-1171.

KENDALL, M.G. AND BUCKLAND, W.R. DICTIONARY OF STATISTICAL TERMS. (EN*FR*GE*IT*SP) SUPPL. TO ED2. NEW YORK, HAFNER, 1960. 83P.

KENDALL,M.G. AND BUCKLAND, W.R. DICCIONARIO DE TERMINOS ESTADISTICOS. (STAT.T, *SP*EN*FR*GE*IT) ROSARIO, ARGENTINA, INST. INTERAM. ESTADISTICA, 1959. 482P. 1700T.

NORWAY. RADET FOR TEKNISK TERMINOLOGI. STATISTICAL QUALITY CONTROL. (RTT-7) (*EN*GE*NO*SW) OSLO, 1960. 41P.

NORWAY. STATISTISK SENTRALBYRA. FRAMLEGG TIL NORDISK STATISTISK TERMINOLOGI. (STAT. GL, NO*EN*DA*FI*SW) OSLO. 1954. 32P. A55-788.

POLSKA AKADEMIIA NAUK. INSTYTUT MATEMATYCZNY SLOWNIK POLSKO-ROSYJSKO-ANGIELSKI STATYSTYKI MATEMATYCZNEJ I STATYSTYCZNEJ KONTROLI JAKOSCI PRODUKCJI. (PL*EN*RU D. OF MATH. STAT/IND. STAT. CONTROL) WARSAW, PANSTW. WYDAW.NAUK, 1958. 48P. 59-34620. 540T.

SPAIN. INSTITUTO NACIONAL DE ESTADISTICA. VOCABULARIO ESTADISTICO PLURILINGUE. (*SP*EN*EO*FR*GE*HU*IT *NO*PR*RU*SW STAT. GL) MADRID, I.N.E.ARTES GRAFICAS, 1959. 189P. 400T.

UNION INTERNATIONALE DES PRODUCTEURS ET DISTRIBUTEURS D.ENERGIE ELECTRIQUE. TERMINOLOGIE UTILISEE DANS LES STATISTIQUES DE L.ECONOMIE ELECTRIQUE. (STAT.T.IN ELEC. POWER SUPPLY, *FR*EN*GE*IT) PARIS, 1957. 120P. 70T.

135

STATISTICS (MATHEMATICAL AND APPLIED)

POLYGLOT

UNITED NATIONS. TRILINGUAL LIST OF STATISTICAL TERMS. (TERMINOLOGY BULL. NO.134) NEW YORK, 1957.

UNITED NATIONS. DEPT. OF ECONOMIC AND SOCIAL AFFAIRS. MULTILINGUAL DEMOGRAPHY DICTIONARY. EN*FR*SP. (POPULATION STUDIES NO.29) NEW YORK, 1958/59.

WARSAW. PANSTWOWY INSTYTUT MATEMATYCZNY. SLOWNIK ROSYJSKO-POLSKI I ANGIELSKO-POLSKI TERMINOW STATYSTYKI MATEMATYCZNEJ. (RU EN*PL D. OF MATH.STAT) WARSAW, NAKL.POLSK.TOW.MAT, 1952, 20P. 55-28826.

PORTUGUESE

SILVA RODRIGUES, M.C. VOCABULARIO BRASILEIRO DE ESTATISTICA, SEGUIDO DE UM VOCABULARIO INGLES-PORTUGUES. (EN*PR GL. OF STAT) SAO PAULO, UNIV, 1956. 304P. 61-26731.

RUSSIAN

DERUGUINE, T. RUSSIAN-ENGLISH GLOSSARY OF STATISTICAL TERMS. NEW YORK, TELBERG, 1959. 39P. 59-1981.

TECHNOLOGY AND INDUSTRY

AFRIKAANS

TERBLANCHE, H.J. ENGELS-AFRIKAANSE TEGNIESE WOORDEBOEK. (*EN*AF TECH. D) KAAPSTAD, NASL. BOEKHANDL, 1953. 639P. 55-28935.

ARABIC

FLOOD, W.E. TRADES, MACHINES AND ENGINES. (GL, 171-83, EN*AR, 300T) NEW YORK, LONGMANS, GREEN, 1955. 183P. 56-1023.

THEODORY, C. A DICTIONARY OF MODERN TECHNICAL TERMS, ARABIC-ENGLISH. BEIRUT, DAR-AL-KUTUB, 1959.

BULGARIAN

FURNESS, K.Z. BULGARIAN ABBREVIATIONS, A SELECTIVE LIST. WASHINGTON, U.S. LIBR. CONGR, 1961. 326P. 61-60056. 3600T.

CHINESE

HUANG, CHEN-HSUN. K,O HSUEH CHI SHU MING TZ,U CHIEH SHIH. (SCI/TECH T... RELATING TO SUGAR, TOBACCO/WINE) PEKING, POPULAR SCI, 1958. 85P. C59-1206.

U.S. NATIONAL SCIENCE FOUNDATION. MODERN CHINESE-ENGLISH TECHNICAL AND GENERAL DICTIONARY. NEW YORK, MCGRAW-HILL, 1963. 3V. 3112P. 21000T.

CZECH

BECKMAN, P. TECHNICKA ANGLICTINA PRO CASTECNE POKROCILE. (EN*CZ TECH. GL) ED3. PRAGUE, SNTL, 1958. 290P.

CACEK, K. AND KRATKY, M. SLOVNIK ANGLO-AMERICKYCH TECHNICKYCH ZKRATEK. (D. OF EN/AM TECH. ABBRS, CZ DEFS) PRAGUE, SNTL, 1961. 191P. 61-46640. 3500T.

DOBROVOLNY, B. ET AL. MALY TECHNICKY NAUCNY SLOVNIK...(TECH/SCI. D, CZ DEFS) ED2. PRAGUE, SNTL, 1959. 1010P, 60-37130. 8000T.

HORECKY, P.L. CZECH AND SLOVAK ABBREVIATIONS, A SELECTIVE LIST. WASHINGTON, U.S. LIBR. CONGR, 1956. 164P. 56-60067. 3500T.

KORBAR, T. AND STRANSKY, A. TECHNICKY NAUCNY SLOVNIK. (SCI/TECH. D, CZ DEFS) PRAGUE, SNTL, 1962-. 62-41602.

NOVAK, J. KAPESNI ANGLICKO-CESKY A CESKO-ANGLICKY TECHNICKY SLOVNIK. (*EN*CZ TECH. D) ED2. PRAGUE, SNTL, 1959. 495P. 60-26578. 10500T.

PEKAREK, O. ET AL. VELKY ANGLICKO-CESKY TECHNICKY SLOVNIK. (LARGE EN*CZ TECH. D) PRAGUE, SNTL, 1957-60. 3V. 3000P. 58-17081. 120000T.

DANISH

WARRERN, A. DANSK-ENGELSK TEKNISK ORDBOG. (DA*EN TECH. D) ED2. COPENHAGEN, CLAUSEN, 1957. 333P. 58-22125. 18000T.

WARRERN, A. ENGELSK-DANSK TEKNISK ORDBOG. (EN*DA TECH. D) ED3. COPENHAGEN, CLAUSEN, 1960. 311P. 63-26788. 24000T.

DUTCH

GRAUS, J.M.A. TECHNISCH ENGELS WOORDENBOEK. (TECH. D) (V.1, EN*DU, 279P. 5500T. V.2, DU*EN, 224P. 4400T) HAARLEM, STAM, 1955-56. 59-36944.

FITZ-VERPLOEGH, A. DUTCH-ENGLISH AND ENGLISH-DUTCH TECHNICAL TERMS FOR SHIPBUILDING, MECHANICS, METAL-WORKERS, AMSTERDAM, 1955. 100P.

ENGLISH

ALEXANDER, R.S. ET AL. MARKETING DEFINITIONS... CHICAGO, AM. MARKETING ASSOC, 1960. 23P. 61-2002.

AMERICAN HOME ECONOMICS ASSOCIATION. HANDBOOK OF HOUSEHOLD EQUIPMENT TERMINOLOGY. WASHINGTON, 1959. 34P. 60-20228.

AMERICAN SOCIETY FOR TESTING/MATERIALS. GLOSSARY OF TERMS RELATING TO RUBBER AND RUBBER-LIKE MATERIALS. PHILADELPHIA, 1956. 121P. 56-14327. 2000T.

AMERICAN SOCIETY FOR TESTING/MATERIALS. STANDARD DEFINITIONS OF TERMS RELATING TO ADHESIVES. (D907-60) ASTM STDS,PT.6, 504-12. PHILADELPHIA 1961. 180T.

AMERICAN SOCIETY FOR TESTING/MATERIALS. STANDARD DEFINITIONS OF TERMS RELATING TO GLASS AND GLASS PRODUCTS. (C162-56) ASTM STDS, PT.5, 730-44. PHILADELPHIA, 1961. 380T.

AMERICAN SOCIETY FOR TESTING/MATERIALS. TENTATIVE DEFINITIONS OF TERMS RELATING TO LEATHER. (D1517-60)ASTM STDS, PT.6, 1234-47. PHILADELPHIA, 1961. 300T.

AMERICAN SOCIETY FOR TESTING/MATERIALS. TENTATIVE DEFINITIONS OF TERMS RELATING TO RUBBER AND RUBBER-LIKE MATERIALS. (D1566-60T) ASTM STDS, PT.11, 717-8. PHILADELPHIA, 1961. 10T.

AMERICAN SOCIETY FOR TESTING/MATERIALS. TENTATIVE DEFINITIONS OF TERMS RELATING TO SHIPPING CONTAINERS. (D 996-59T) ASTM STDS, PT.6, 415-24. PHILADELPHIA, 1961. 200T.

AMERICAN VOCATIONAL ASSOCIATION. DEFINITIONS OF TERMS IN VOCATIONAL AND PRACTICAL ARTS EDUCATION. WASHINGTON, 1954. 28P. A57-6452.

AUDELS DO-IT-YOURSELF ENCYCLOPEDIA... NEW YORK, AUDEL, 1959. 2V. 1012P. 60-338.

AUDELS NEW MECHANICAL DICTIONARY FOR TECHNICAL TRADES...NEW YORK, AUDEL, 1962. 740P. 62-51109. 11000T.

BENNETT, H. CONCISE CHEMICAL AND TECHNICAL DICTIONARY. ED2. NEW YORK, CHEMICAL, 1962. 1039P. 62-4271. 60000T.

BERRY, E. AN ILLUSTRATED DICTIONARY OF PLUMBING TERMS. LONDON, TECH.PRESS, 1960. 244P. 61-3609.

BRITISH COMPRESSED AIR SOCIETY. TECHNICAL REFERENCE BOOK OF COMPRESSED AIR TERMS AND STANDARDS. LONDON, 1956, 108P. 57-18512.

BRITISH STANDARDS INSTITUTION. GLOSSARY OF COLOUR TERMS USED IN SCIENCE AND INDUSTRY. (B.S. 1611) LONDON, 1953. 20P. 110T.

BRITISH STANDARDS INSTITUTION. GLOSSARY OF LEATHER TERMS. (B.S. 2780) LONDON, 1956. 24P. 160T.

BRITISH STANDARDS INSTITUTION. GLOSSARY OF PACKAGING TERMS. (B.S.3130) LONDON, 1959. 108P. 1200T.

BRITISH STANDARDS INSTITUTION. GLOSSARY OF TERMS APPLICABLE TO CORK AND CORK PRODUCTS. (B.S. 3519) LONDON, 1962. 10P. 70T.

BRITISH STANDARDS INSTITUTION. GLOSSARY OF TERMS APPLICABLE TO FILLINGS AND STUFFINGS FOR BEDDING, UPHOLSTERY, TOYS AND OTHER DOMESTIC ARTICLES. (B.S. 2005. AMEND. PD 2109, 2334-1955) LONDON, 1953-55. 16P. 90T.

BRITISH STANDARDS INSTITUTION. GLOSSARY OF TERMS RELATING TO POWDERS. (B.S.2955) LONDON, 1958. 16P. 100T.

BRITISH STANDARDS INSTITUTION. GLOSSARY OF TERMS RELATING TO THE MANUFACTURE AND USE OF REFRACTORY MATERIALS. (B.S.3446) LONDON, 1962. 87P. 600T.

BRITISH STANDARDS INSTITUTION. GLOSSARY OF TERMS USED FOR SOLID FUEL BURNING AND ALLIED APPLIANCES. (B.S. 1846) LONDON, 1959. 26P. 200T.

BRITISH STANDARDS INSTITUTION. GLOSSARY OF TERMS USED IN INDUSTRIAL HIGH-FREQUENCY INDUCTION AND DIELECTRIC HEATING. (B.S.2759) LONDON, 1956. 16P. 90T.

BRITISH STANDARDS INSTITUTION. GLOSSARY OF TERMS USED IN THE GAS INDUSTRY. (B.S.1179) LONDON, 1961. 80P. 700T.

BRITISH STANDARDS INSTITUTION. LETTER SYMBOLS, SIGNS AND ABBREVIATIONS. PT.1. GENERAL. (B.S. 1991, AMEND. PD 2241-1955, PD 2707-1957, PD 3920-1960) LONDON, 1954-60. 48P. 500T.

BUTTRESS, F.A. WORLD LIST OF ABBREVIATIONS OF SCIENTIFIC, TECHNOLOGICAL AND COMMERCIAL ORGANIZATIONS. ED2. NEW YORK, HAFNER, 1960. 300P. 60-2449. 2500T.

COLVIN, F.H. THE MACHINIST DICTIONARY.. NEW YORK, SIMMONS-BOARDMAN, 1956. 496P. 55-10428. 5000T.

CRISPIN, F.S. DICTIONARY OF TECHNICAL TERMS...ED9. MILWAUKEE, BRUCE, 1961. 454P. 61-15639. 9000T.

DE SOLA, R. ABBREVIATIONS DICTIONARY... NEW YORK, DUELL, SLOAN/PEARCE, 1958. 177P. 58-5564. 9600T.

DOSSETT, H.A. PACKAGING AND DISPLAY ENCYCLOPAEDIA. ED5. LONDON, NEWNES, 1959. 705P. 60-163.

FLOOD,W.E. AND WEST,M. AN ELEMENTARY SCIENTIFIC AND TECHNICAL DICTIONARY. ED3. LONDON, LONGMANS, 1962. 413P. 63-892. 12000T.

FLORINSKY, M.T. MCGRAW-HILL ENCYCLOPEDIA OF RUSSIA AND THE SOVIET UNION. NEW YORK, MCGRAW-HILL, 1961. 624P. 61-18169.

GALE RESEARCH CO. ACRONYMS DICTIONARY, A GUIDE TO ALPHABETIC DESIGNATIONS, CONTRACTIONS, AND INITIALISMS ...DETROIT, 1960. 211 P. 60-10869. 12000T.

GALE RESEARCH CO. CODE NAMES DICTIONARY. DETROIT, 1963. 460P. 7500T.

GRIGSON, G. ET AL. THINGS, A VOLUME OF OBJECTS DEVISED BY MAN,S GENIUS... NEW YORK, HAWTHORN, 1957. 466P. 56-10840.

HERKIMER, H. ENGINEER,S ILLUSTRATED THESAURUS. NEW YORK, CHEM, 1952. 590P. 52-647. 8000T.

HITCHCOCK,S ASSEMBLY AND FASTENER DICTIONARY. V.1- . WHEATON, ILL. HITCHCOCK, 1962- . 61-45423.

HORNER, J.G. AND ABBEY, S. DICTIONARY OF TERMS USED IN THE THEORY AND PRACTICE OF MECHANICAL ENGINEERING ED8. LONDON, TECH.PRESS, 1960. 121+417P. 60-4707. 8000T.

HUGHES, L.E.C. AND BREMNER, J.P. HUTCHINSON,S POCKET TECHNICAL ENCYCLOPAEDIA. NEW YORK, HUTCHINSON, 1952 182P. 52-3054.

INSTITUTION OF FIRE ENGINEERS. DICTIONARY OF FIRE TECHNOLOGY. REV.ED. LONDON, 1958. 111P. 1900T.

JAHN, R. TOBACCO DICTIONARY. NEW YORK, PHIL. LIBR, 1954. 199P. 54-11964.

JONES, F.D. AND SCHUBERT, P.B. ENGINEERING ENCYCLOPEDIA... ED3. NEW YORK, IND. PRESS, 1963. 1431P. 63-10415.

KIMBALL, W.Y. A SELECTION OF FIRE TERMINOLOGY. ED3. BOSTON, NATL. FIRE PROT. ASSOC, 1961. 62P. 62-65950. 900T.

LONG, A.E. A GLOSSARY OF THE DIAMOND-DRILLING INDUSTRY. (BUL.NO.583) WASHINGTON, U.S. BUR. MINES, 1960. 98P. 60-61567.

MCGRAW-HILL ENCYCLOPEDIA OF SCIENCE AND TECHNOLOGY... NEW YORK, MCGRAW-HILL, 1960. 15V. YEARBOOKS, 1961-63. 60-11000.

MAXWELL, R. INFORMATION U.S.S.R. (EN TRANSL. OF GREAT SOV. ENCYCL. V.50) NEW YORK, PERGAMON, 1962. 982P. 62-9879.

MAYBERRY, G. A CONCISE DICTIONARY OF ABBREVIATIONS. NEW YORK, TUDOR, 1961. 159P. 61-9227.

MECHANIX ILLUSTRATED. HOW-TO-DO-IT ENCYCLOPEDIA. NEW YORK, GOLDEN, 1961-- 17V. 61-65947.

MILEK, J.T. STANDARDS AND SPECIFICATIONS, DOCUMENTATION SYMBOLS AND ABBREVIATIONS. LOS ANGELES, STANDARDS, 1961- 1V. LL. 61-3463.

MODERN PACKAGING, ENCYCLOPEDIA ISSUE FOR 1963. MODERN PACKAGING, V.36, NO.3A (1962) 896P. 28-29834.

NATIONAL ASSOCIATION OF BLUEPRINT AND DIAZOTYPE COATERS. GLOSSARY...WASHINGTON, 1956. 22P. A57-5215.

NEW YORK (STATE) CIVIL DEFENSE MANPOWER SERVICE. NEW YORK STATE DICTIONARY OF CIVIL DEFENSE OCCUPATIONAL TITLES AND CODES... NEW YORK, 1957. 2V. A57-9199.

NEWMAN, J.R. ET AL. THE HARPER ENCYCLOPEDIA OF SCIENCE. NEW YORK, HARPER, 1962. 4V. 62-14541. 4000T.

PACKAGING INSTITUTE. GLOSSARY OF PACKAGING TERMS... NEW YORK, 1955. 323P. 49-48271. 3500T.

RACKER, J. TECHNICAL WRITING TECHNIQUES FOR ENGINEERS. (GL, PP.129-234, 1130T) ENGLEWOOD CLIFFS, N.J, PRENTICE-HALL, 1960. 234P. 60-16623.

REDMAN, H.F. AND GODFREY, L.E. DICTIONARY OF REPORT SERIES CODES. NEW YORK, SPEC.LIBR.ASSOC, 1962. 656P 12500T.

SCHWARTZ, R.J. THE COMPLETE DICTIONARY OF ABBREVIATIONS. NEW YORK, CROWELL, 1955. 211P. 55-5843. 25000T.

SCHWARTZ, R.J. THE DICTIONARY OF BUSINESS AND INDUSTRY. NEW YORK, FORBES, 1954. 561P. 54-3133. 25000T.

STOUTENBURGH, J.L. DICTIONARY OF ARTS AND CRAFTS. NEW YORK, PHIL. LIBR, 1956. 259P. 56-13756. 2500T.

TVER, D.F. DICTIONARY OF BUSINESS AND SCIENTIFIC TERMS. HOUSTON, TEX, GULF, 1961. 330P. 61-13963. 6500T

TWENEY, C.F. AND HUGHES, L.E.C. CHAMBERS,S TECHNICAL DICTIONARY. ED3. NEW YORK, MACMILLAN, 1958. 1028P. 59-16000. 60000T. SUPPL. 1962.

U.S. AIR FORCE. ARDC. VOCABULARY FOR CURRENT ARDC TECHNICAL EFFORTS. WASHINGTON, 1960. 159P. 60-64594. 5000T.

U.S. DEPT. OF AGRICULTURE. GLOSSARY OF TERMS USED IN FOREST FIRE CONTROL. ED3. WASHINGTON, 1956. 24P. AGR. 56-321.

TECHNOLOGY AND INDUSTRY

ENGLISH

U.S. DEPT. OF DEFENSE. ENVIRONMENTAL TERMINOLOGY INCLUDING ELECTROMAGNETIC RADIATION HAZARDS COMMON TO PERSONNEL, FUEL AND EQUIPMENT. WASHINGTON, 1961.

U.S. DEPT. OF LABOR. OCCUPATIONS IN ELECTRONIC DATA-PROCESSING SYSTEMS. WASHINGTON, 1959. 44P. 100T.

U.S. EMPLOYMENT SERVICE. DICTIONARY OF OCCUPATIONAL TITLES... ED2. WASHINGTON, 1949-- . 2V. SUPPL. NO.1, 1955. S S 49-12.

VAN NOSTRAND,S SCIENTIFIC ENCYCLOPEDIA... ED3. PRINCETON, N.J, VAN NOSTRAND, 1958. 1839P. 58-7085. 15000T.

WITTY, M.B. ET AL. DICTIONARY OF ENGINEERING SIGNS AND SYMBOLS. NEW YORK, SETI. 1963. 352P.

WITTY, M.B. ET AL. DICTIONARY OF ENVIRONMENTAL ENGINEERING ABBREVIATIONS, SIGNS, SYMBOLS AND TABLES. NEW YORK, SETI, 196 . 320P.

WOODLEY, D.R. THE ENCYCLOPEDIA OF MATERIALS HANDLING. NEW YORK, MACMILLAN, 1000P. (IN PREP)

WOOLAM, W.G. SHIPPING TERMS AND ABBREVIATIONS, MARITIME, INSURANCE, INTERNATIONAL TRADE. CAMBRIDGE, MD. CORNELL MARITIME, 1963. 144P. 62-22181. 2200T.

WRIGLEY, W. AND HOVORKA, J. ENCYCLOPEDIA OF FIRE CONTROL. V.1. CAMBRIDGE, MASS, M.I.T, 1957. 74P.

ZIMMERMAN, O.T. AND LAVINE, I. HANDBOOK OF MATERIAL TRADE NAMES. DOVER, N.H, IND. RES. SERV, 1953. 794P. SUPPL.1,1956. 383P. SUPPL.2, 1957. 356P. SUPPL.3, 1960. 400P. 53-1074.

FINNISH

TALVITIE, Y. ENGLANTILAIS-SUOMALAINEN TEKNIIKAN JA KAUPAN SANAKIRJA. (EN*FI TECH/COM. D) ED2. HELSINKI, TIETOTEOS, 1960. 1507P. 61-40925.

FRENCH

BAUDRY, H. NOUVEAU DICTIONNAIRE D,ABREVIATIONS D.A. FRANCAISES ET ETRANGERES...(D. OF ABBRS, FR. DEFS) LA CHAPELLE-MONTLIGEON (ORNE), 1956. 418P. A56-5893. 10000T.

CUSSET, F. VOCABULAIRE TECHNIQUE, ELECTRICITE, MECANIQUE, MINES, SCIENCES... (*FR*EN TECH. D) ED4. PARIS, BERGER-LEVRAULT, 1954. 663P. 54-35644. 3000T.

DUSNICKIS, I. AND CHAUMELLE, P. DICTIONNAIRE TECHNIQUE ANGLAIS-FRANCAIS, CHAUFFAGE INDUSTRIEL. (*EN*FR IND. HEATING D) PARIS, DUNOD, 1954. 143P. A54-4039. 6000T.

LES FICHES DU COMITE D, ETUDE DES TERMES TECHNIQUES FRANCAIS.(BT-76(1959) 40P,40T. BT-81(1960)56P, 100T. BT-82(1960) 40P,40T. BT-91(1960) 40P,40T. BT-99(1961)33P,30T,BT-106(1963)43P,40T.(TECH.T.DEF.BY STUDY GROUP,EN*FR) OTTAWA, DEPT.SECY. STATE,1959--

FRANCE. AMBASSADE. U.S. INDUSTRIES MECANIQUES, AMERICAIN-FRANCAIS. (AM*FR IND/ENG.GL) ED2. WASHINGTON, 1955. 173P. 3800T.

FRANCE. AMBASSADE. U.S. INDUSTRIES MECANIQUES, FRANCAIS-AMERICAIN. (FR*AM IND/ENG. GL) WASHINGTON. 1955. 187P. 59-31415. 3800T.

FRANCE. AMBASSADE. U.S. INDUSTRIES MINIERES, AMERICAIN-FRANCAIS. (EN*FR GL. OF MIN. IND) WASHINGTON, 1953. 133P. 59-31396. 1800T.

FRANCE. INSTITUT NATIONAL DE LA STATISTIQUE ET DES ETUDES ECONOMIQUES.DICTIONNAIRE DES METIERS ET DES APPELLATIONS D,EMPLOI... (OCCUP.TITLES, FR DEFS) PARIS, PRESSES UNIV. FRANCE, 1955. 271P. A56-4076.

KETTRIDGE, J.O. FRENCH-ENGLISH AND ENGLISH-FRENCH DICTIONARY OF TECHNICAL TERMS AND PHRASES. ED4. V.1, FR*EN, 541P. V.2, EN*FR, 544P. LONDON, ROUTLEDGE, KEGAN, PAUL, 1955.

MACQUINGHEN, R. DICTIONNARIE DES TERMES COMMERCIAUX ET TECHNIQUES RELATIF AUX AFFAIRES EN GENERAL. (COM/ TECH. T, *FR*EN) PARIS, DUNOD, 1954. 203P. 54-624. 19000T.

MALGORN, G.M. LEXIQUE TECHNIQUE ANGLAIS-FRANCAIS...(EN*FR TECH.D) ED4. PARIS, GAUTHIER-VILLARS, 1956. 493P. 57-155. 9500T.

MALGORN, G.M. LEXIQUE TECHNIQUE FRANCAIS-ANGLAIS... (FR*EN TECH.D) PARIS, GAUTHIER-VILLARS, 1956. 475P. 57-156. 9500T.

LE MENUISIER DE BATIMENT... GLOSSAIRE FRANCAIS-ANGLAIS ET ANGLAIS-FRANCAIS, BT-14. (BLDG. CARPENTER, *FR*EN GLI OTTAWA, DEPT. SECY. STATE, 1954. 18P. 200T.

MICHIL, P. LEXIQUE FRANCAIS-ANGLAIS ET ANGLAIS-FRANCAIS DES TERMES D,,USAGE COURANT EN MACHINES-OUTILS ET MACHINES SIMILAIRES... (*FR*EN GL. OF MACH/TOOL T) PARIS, DUNOD, 1961. 56P.

NORMANDEAU, L. LEXIQUE DE MECANIQUE D,AJUSTAGE. (EN*FR MECH. T) MONTREAL, REV. TECH, 1957. 255P.

ORGANIZATION FOR EUROPEAN ECONOMIC COOPERATION. GLOSSAIRE DE SYMBOLES ET D,ABREVIATIONS. (GL. OF SYMBOLS/ABBRS, *FR*EN) ED2. PARIS, 1956. 238P. 4500T.

TECHNOLOGY AND INDUSTRY

FRENCH

TERMES DIVERS, GLOSSAIRE ANGLAIS-FRANCAIS. BT-93, LISTS NOS.1-6. (MISC. T, EN*ER GL) OTTAWA, DEPT. SECY. STATE, 1961-63. 97P. 380T.

TERMINOLOGIE DE LA LUTTE CONTRE LES INCENDIES DE FORETS, GLOSSAIRE ANGLAIS-FRANCAIS,BT-45. (FOREST FIRE T, EN*ER) OTTAWA, DEPT.SECY.STATE, 1956. 11P. 300T.

TERMINOLOGIE DE LA PREVENTION ET DE LA SUPPRESSION DES POUSSIERES DANS LES USINES, GALERIES ET CARRIERES, GLOSSAIRE ANGLAIS-FRANCAIS. BT-61. (IND. DUST CONTROL, EN*FR GL) OTTAWA, DEPT. SECY. STATE, 1957. 10P. 130T.

TERMINOLOGIE DES SERVICES NATIONAUX DE L.EMPLOI EN GRANDE-BRETAGNE, GLOSSAIRE ANGLAIS-FRANCAIS,BT-64. (TERMS USED IN BRIT.NATL.EMPL.SERV, EN*FR GL) OTTAWA, DEPT.SECY.STATE,1958. 26P. 500T.

VINCELETTE, M.H. TERMINOLOGIE DE LA PRODUCTIVITE, GLOSSAIRE ANGLAIS-FRANCAIS, BT-26. (IND.PROD,EN*FR GL) OTTAWA, DEPT.SECY.STATE, 1955. 6P. 110T.

GERMAN

BEER, B. ET AL. TECHNIK. (TECH. D, GE DEFS) ED2. LEIPZIG, ENZYKLOPAEDIE, 1961. 947P. 62-34566.

BLACK, K. SPECIALISTS GERMAN VOCABULARIES, PROFESSIONAL, TECHNICAL, COMMERCIAL... (EN*GE) LONDON, PITMAN, 1955. 189P. 55-4490. 6000T.

BOSCH, R. FACHWOERTERBUCH DEUTSCH-ENGLISCH. (GE*EN TECH. D) STUTTGART, BOSCH, 1957. 167P. 11000T.

BOSCH, R. TECHNOLOGICAL DICTIONARY, ENGLISH-GERMAN. STUTTGART, BOSCH, 1955. 149P. 11000T.

BOWER, W.W. LUBRICATION GLOSSARY. WOERTERVERZEICHNIS DER SCHMIERTECHNIK. STAMFORD, CONN, 1958. 27P. 58-23903. 500T.

BROCKHAUS ABC DER NATURWISSENSCHAFT UND TECHNIK... (ABC OF SCI/TECH, GE DEFS) ED8. LEIPZIG, BROCKHAUS, 1962. 1005P. 10000T.

BROCKHAUS-BILDWOERTERBUCH, ENGLISH-DEUTSCH. (PICTURE D, EN*GE) WIESBADEN, BROCKHAUS, 1953. 728P.

BROCKHAUS DER NATURWISSENSCHAFTEN UND DER TECHNIK. (D.OF SCI/TECH, GE DEFS) ED5. WIESBADEN, BROCKHAUS, 1960. 640P. 61-28882.

CAPITO UND KLEIN, A.G. NIROSTA BLECHE, WERKSTOFF UND VERARBEITUNG VON A-Z. (NIROSTA STAINLESS-STEEL SHEETS, GE DEFS) ED2. DUESSELDORF-BENRATH, 1960. 238P. 63-26793.

DEUTSCH-ENGLISCHES WOERTERBUCH... WISSENSCHAFT UND TECHNIK. (GE EN SCI/TECH D) LEIPZIG, ENZYKLOPAEDIE, 1958. 706P. 40000T.

DEUTSCHE NORMENAUSSCHUSS. (DNA) ABKUERZUNGEN TECHNISCH-WISSENSCHAFTLICHER ORGANISATIONEN DES AUSLANDES UND IHRER VEROEFFENTLICHUNGEN. (ABBR. OF TECH/SCI. ORG. IN FOR. COUNTRIES... GE DEFS) BERLIN,1961. 14P.

DEVRIES, L. ENGLISH-GERMAN TECHNICAL AND ENGINEERING DICTIONARY. NEW YORK, MCGRAW-HILL, 1954. 997P. 54-14586. 130000T. SUPPL. 1962. 285P.

DEVRIES, L. ENGLISH-GERMAN TECHNICAL AND ENGINEERING DICTIONARY. SUPPL. WIESBADEN, 1962. 285P.

DEVRIES, L. GERMAN-ENGLISH TECHNICAL AND ENGINEERING DICTIONARY. NEW YORK, MCGRAW-HILL, 1950. 928P. 50-12204. 125000T.

DEVRIES, L. GERMAN-ENGLISH TECHNICAL AND ENGINEERING DICTIONARY. SUPPL. WIESBADEN, BRANDSTETTER, 1959. 386P. 50-12204. 50000T.

DIDIER-KOGAG-HINSELMANN, GMBH. WOERTERBUCH DER KOKEREITECHNIK. (COKE-OVEN PRACTICE D, *GE*EN). ESSEN, VULKAN, 1954. 329P. A55-5688. 6000T.

ENGLISH-DEUTSCHES WOERTERBUCH... TECHNIK UND WIRTSCHAFT. (EN*GE TECH/ECON. D) LEIPZIG, ENZYKLOPAEDIE, 195 . 784P.

EHRHARDT, A. AND FRANKE, H. LUEGERS LEXIKON DER TECHNIK. (LUEGER,S ENCYCL. OF TECH. GE DEFS. TO BE COMPLETE IN 17V) V.1. GRUNDLAGEN DES MACHINENBAUES. (PRINCIPLES OF MACH. DESIGN) V.2. GRUNDLAGEN DER ELEKTROTECHNIK UND KERNTECHNIK. (PRINCIPLES OF ELEC/NUCL.ENG) V.3. WERKSTOFFE UND WERKSTOFF-PRUEFUNG. (IND.MATER.TESTING) V4. BERGBAU. (MINING ENG) V5. HUETTENTECHNIK. (MET. ENG) STUTTGART, DEUTSCHE VERLAGS-ANSTALT, 1960-- . A61-2000.

ERNST, R. WOERTERBUCH DER INDUSTRIELLEN TECHNIK...(IND/TECH. D) (V.1 GE*EN, ED7. 805P. V.2, EN*GE, ED12, 890P) WIESBADEN, BRANDSTETTER, 1962. 60-3617. 45000T.

EULENSTEIN, R. LEXIKON DES OFENSETZERS. (FURNACE/OVEN BLDG.T, GE DEFS) HALLE (SAALE) MARHOLD, 1955. 280P. 60-37667.

FREEMAN, H.G. DAS ENGLISCHE FACHWORT. (*EN*GE TECH.T) ED7. ESSEN, GIRARDET, 1955. 498P.

FREEMAN, H.G. TECHNISCHES ENGLISCH... (TECH.EN, WITH *GE*EN D) ED6. ESSEN, GIRARDET, 1956. 475P. A57-4738.

GOEBEL, E.H. TECHNISCHES TASCHENWOERTERBUCH...(*GE*EN TECH. POCKET D)ED5. BERLIN, SIEMENS, 1963. 530P. 63-24499.

140

TECHNOLOGY AND INDUSTRY

GERMAN

GOULDEN, W.O. ET AL. LEDERTECHNISCHES WOERTERBUCH. (*GE*EN D.OF LEATHER TECH) COLOGNE, STAUFEN, 1956. 172P, A57-1193, 7500T.

DAS GROSSE BUCH DER TECHNIK. (TECH. ENCYCL, GE DEFS) GUETERSLOH, BERTELSMANN, 1961. 720P. 1000 ILLUS.

HELLMICH, K. ABC DER STOFFKUNDE. (MATER. ABC, GE DEFS) ED4. DUESSELDORF, 1957.

HOFFMANN, E. FACHWOERTERBUCH FUER DIE GLASINDUSTRIE. DEUTSCH-ENGLISCH, ENGLISCH-DEUTSCH. (*GE*EN GLASS IND. D) BERLIN, SPRINGER, 1963. 160P. 62-21033.

JANSEN, H. AND MACKENSEN, L. RECHTSCHREIBUNG DER TECHNISCHEN UND CHEMISCHEN FREMDWOERTER...(ORTHOGRAPHY OF TECH/CHEM.WORDS OF FOR. ORIGIN, GE DEFS) DUESSELDORF, VDI, 1959. 267P. 61-40164. 10000T.

JEBSEN-MARWEDEL, H. TAFELGLAS IN STICHWORTEN. (SHEET GLASS D, GE DEFS) ED2. ESSEN, GIRARDET, 1960. 100P. A61-3486. 500T.

KLEINE ENZYKLOPAEDIE, TECHNIK. (TECH. ENCYCL, GE DEFS) LEIPZIG, ENZYKLOPAEDIE, 195 . 941P.

KLEINES LEXIKON A-Z, NATURWISSENSCHAFTEN, TECHNIK, WIRTSCHAFT. (SCI-TECH D, GE DEFS) LEIPZIG, ENZYKLOPAEDIE, 1959. 1108P. 30000T.

KLEINSCHMIDT, B. WOERTERBUCH DER SCHLEIF-UND POLIERTECHNIK. DEUTSCH-ENGLISCH, ENGLISCH-DEUTSCH. (*GE*EN GRINDING/POLISHING D) BERLIN, CRAM, 1952. 96P. 57-25313. 2400T.

KOEPPER, G. FREMDWOERTERBUCH FUER HANDEL, GEWERBE UND INDUSTRIE. (FOR. T. IN COM, TRADE/IND) ED6. BADEN-BADEN, LUTZEYER, 1958. 522P, A59-5896.

KOLLMANN, F. AND F.G. DAS KLEINE LEXIKON DER TECHNIK... (TECH. GL, GE DEFS) ED9. STUTTGART, UNION, 1959. 397P. A58-4073.

LENK, G. AND BOERNER, H. TECHNISCHES FACHWOERTERBUCH DER GRUNDSTOFF-INDUSTRIEN... (TECH.D. FOR BASIC IND) (V.1 EN*GE. 638P. 1958. V.2, GE*EN, 734P. 1962) ED2. GOETTINGEN, VANDENHOECK/RUPRECHT, 1958-62. A59-324. 45000T.

LUBIG, E. SCHUH-LEXIKON. (SHOE T, GE DEFS) LEIPZIG, FACHBUCHVERLAG, 1956. 221P. A56-6680. 2000T.

LUEGERS LEXIKON DER TECHNIK. (ENCYCL. OF TECH) V.5, LEXIKON DER HUETTENTECHNIK. (MET. ENG. D, GE DEFS) ED4. DUESSELDORF, STAHLEISEN, 1963. 720P. 3500T.

MOLLE, F. WOERTERBUCH DER BERUFSBEZEICHNUNG. (OCCUPATIONS D, GE DEFS) WOLFENBUETTEL, GRENZLAND/ROCK, 1952. 240P.

QUAK, K. DIN-BEGRIFFSLEXIKON... (DIN STDS, GE DEFS) BERLIN, BEUTH-VERTRIEB, 1961. 530P.

RIEDEL, M. AND MOSER, H. LEDER-ABC. (LEATHER ABC, GE DEFS) ED3. LEIPZIG, FACHBUCHVERLAG, 1960. 130P. A60-5167.

SCHNAUCK, W. ET AL. GLASLEXIKON, EIN HANDBUCH FUER HANDWERK, HANDEL UND INDUSTRIE. (GLASS D, HANDBOOK FOR MANUF.COM/IND, GE DEFS) MUNICH, CALLWEY, 1959. 267P. A60-4378. 1300T.

SCHOEFFLER-WEIS, . TASCHENWOERTERBUCH DER ENGLISCHEN UND DEUTSCHEN SPRACHE... TECHNIK, WISSENSCHAFT... (EN*GE TECH. D) ED10. PT.1, EN*GE. STUTTGART, KLETT, 1961. 628P.

SCHOEFFLER-WEIS, . TASCHENWOERTERBUCH DER ENGLISCHEN UND DEUTSCHEN SPRACHE... TECHNIK, WISSENSCHAFT... (GE*EN TECH D) ED9. PT.2, GE*EN. STUTTGART, KLETT, 1961. 1176P.

STEGMAIER, W. KERAMISCHES FACHWOERTERBUCH... (CERAMIC GL, V.1, EN*GE 292P. V.2, GE*EN, P) BONN, DEUT. KERAM. GES, 1954-- . 56-36503. 3000T.

STRELLER, J. WOERTERBUCH DER BERUFE. (OCCUPATIONS D, GE DEFS) STUTTGART, KROENER, 1953. 366P. A54-6532. 1000T.

VEREIN SCHWEIZERISCHER MASCHINEN-INDUSTRIELLER. FACHAUSDRUECKE UND ERLAEUTERUNGEN AUS DEM GEBIETE DER BEARBEITUNGSTECHNIK UND DER ARBEITSVERFAHREN. (FABR/PROD.TECH, GE DEFS) ZURICH, 1954. 88P. A55-6517.

WEBEL, A. A GERMAN-ENGLISH DICTIONARY OF TECHNICAL, SCIENTIFIC, AND GENERAL TERMS... NEW YORK, DUTTON, 1953. 939P. 53-3264. 80000T.

WEFELMEYER, R. AND H. LEXIKON DER BERUFSAUSBILDUNG UND BERUFSERZIEHUNG. (VOCATIONAL EDUC/TRAINING, GE DEFS) WIESBADEN, STEINER, 1959. 554P. 59-40526.

WOERTERBUCH ENGLISH-DEUTSCH, DEUTSCH-ENGLISCH. TECHNIK, WIRTSCHAFT. (*GE*EN TECH D) GUETERSLOH, BERTELSMANN, 1959. 640P. 60000T.

GREEK

AEROPORIKA NEA. ENGLISH-GREEK DICTIONARY OF TECHNICAL AND AERONAUTICAL TERMS. ED2. ATHENS, 1950. 144P. 4800T.

CHARALAMPES, I.B. TECHNIKON ANGLOHELLENIKON LEXIKON. (EN*GR TECH. D) ATHENS, 1958. 486P.

GREEK

HIONIDES, H. AN ENGLISH-GREEK LEXICON OF TECHNICAL TERMS. NEW YORK, LONGMANS,GREEN, 1955. 273P. 56-2449. 14000T.

HINDI

BHANDARI, S. TWENTIETH CENTURY ENGLISH-HINDI DICTIONARY...ENGINEERING (ELECTRICAL, AUTOMOBILE, MECHANICAL AERONAUTICAL, RADIO)...BRAHMAPURI, AJMER, DICT. PUBL, 1931- 1952. 5V.

INDIA. MINISTRY OF EDUCATION, CENTRAL HINDI DIRECTORATE. CONSOLIDATED GLOSSARY OF TECHNICAL TERMS. (HI EN) NEW DELHI, 1962. 1370P.

RAGHU, V. HINDI-ENGLISH DICTIONARY OF TECHNICAL TERMS. NAGPUR, INTL. ACAD. IND. CULT, 1951. 439P.

RAMCHARAN, . AND KAUSHAL, S.C. GLASS TECHNOLOGY, ENGLISH-HINDI DICTIONARY. ALLAHABAD, HINDI SAHITYA SAMMELAN, 1950. 2000T.

VARMA, R. PRAMANIK HINDI KOSH. (EN*HI TECH D) 1951. 1250P.

HUNGARIAN

BAKO, E. HUNGARIAN ABBREVIATIONS, A SELECTIVE LIST. WASHINGTON, U.S. LIBR. CONGR, 1961. 146P. 61-60004. 2700T.

FONO, L. ET AL. ANGOL-MAGYAR MUSZAKI SZOTAR... (EN*HU TECH. D) BUDAPEST, AKAD. KIADO, 1951. 976P. 52-31346.

GRETSY, L. AND WACHA, I. A MUSZAKI NYELV MUVELESE. (HU TECH. T) BUDAPEST, AKAD. KIADO, 1961. 43P. 62-36939.

NAGY, E. ET AL. ANGOL-MAGYAR MUSZAKI SZOTAR. (EN*HU TECH. D) ED2. BUDAPEST, AKAD. KIADO, 1959. 791P. 60-39292. 120000T.

NAGY, E. ET AL. MAGYAR-ANGOL MUSZAKI SZOTAR. (HU*EN TECH.D) BUDAPEST,AKAD. KIADO, 1957. 752P. 57-49792. 120000T.

RANKI, A. TERMESZETTUDOMANYI ES MUSZAKI ROVIDITESEK, JELEK, JELOLESEK. (SCI-TECH. ABBRS, SYMBOLS/ NOTATIONS, HU DEFS) ED2. BUDAPEST, TANKONYVKIADO, 1959. 126P. 60-37679.

RAZSO, I. ET AL. ANGOL-MAGYAR MUSZAKI SZOTAR. (EN*HU TECH. D) BROOKLYN, SCHICK, 1957. 971P. 100000T.

INDONESIAN

ANWIR, B.S. ET AL. KAMUS ISTILAH TEHNIK, BAHASA INGGERIS-BAHASA INDONESIA. (EN*IN TECH. D) DJAKARTA, STAM, 1953. 358P. 55-39696.

ITALIAN

AGHINA, L. DIZIONARIO TECNICO ITALIANO-INGLESE CON PARTICOLARE RIFERIMENTO ALLA INDUSTRIA CHIMICA. (IT*EN TECH/CHEM.D) FLORENCE, VALLECCHI, 1961. 431P. A61-3420. 12000T.

DENTI, R. DIZIONARIO TECNICO ITALIANO-INGLESE, INGLESE-ITALIANO...(*IT*EN TECH.D) ED5. MILAN, HOEPLI, 1962. 1307P. 62-5402. 25000T.

GATTO, S. DIZIONARIO TECNICO SCIENTIFICO ILLUSTRATO ITALIANO-INGLESE,INGLESE-ITALIANO.(*IT*EN TECH/SCI.D) MILAN, CESCHINA, 1960. 1381P. A60-4377. 60000T.

LEONARDI, R. DIZIONARIO ILLUSTRATO DELLE SCIENZE PURE E APPLICATE. (ILLUS.D.OF PURE/APPL.SCI, IT DEFS) ED2. MILAN, HOEPLI, 1950-53. 2V. 3090P.

MAROLLI, G. DIZIONARIO TECNICO, INGLESE-ITALIANO, ITALIANO-INGLESE. (*IT*EN TECH. D) ED7. FLORENCE, LE MONNIER, 1961. 1524P. A61-4348. 90000T.

PERUCCA, E. DIZIONARIO D.INGEGNERIA. (ENG. D, IT DEFS) TURIN, UNIONE TIPOGR. ED, 1951-56. 52-37332.

STELLA, M. ET AL. ENCICLOPEDIA PRATICA DI MECCANICA... (PRACT.ENCYCL.OF MECH, IT DEFS) MILAN, CIANCIMINO, 1952. 2V. A53-2530.

TISCIONE, N. MANUALE DI STUDIO DELLA TERMINOLOGIA TECNICA E NAVALE. ITALIANO-INGLESE, INGLESE-ITALIANO. (*IT*EN TECH/NAVAL D) NAPLES, TINES, 1957. 195P.

TISCIONE, N. VOCABOLARIO TECNICO ILLUSTRATO, ITALIANO-INGLESE, INGLESE-ITALIANO...(*IT*EN TECH. D) NAPLES, TINES, 1958. 200P.

TRAMONTI, N. DIZIONARIO DELLE SIGLE E DELLE ABBREVIAZIONI. (D. OF ACRONYMS/ABBRS, IT DEFS) ED3. BUSTO ARSIZIO, 1957. 330P. A58-5061.

JAPANESE

JAPAN. MINISTRY OF EDUCATION. STANDARD VOCABULARY FOR MECHANICAL ENGINEERING INDUSTRY. (EN*JA) TOKYO, 1952. 56P.

TECHNOLOGY AND INDUSTRY

JAPANESE

APANESE STANDARDS ASSOCIATION. JAPANESE ENGINEERING TERMS, PLUMBING, HEATING, AND VENTILATION...(*JA*EN) OKYO, 1955. 176P.

IDZUNO,S CONCISE DICTIONARY OF TECHNICAL TERMS, ENGLISH-JAPANESE, JAPANESE-ENGLISH. TOKYO, 195 , 403P.)00T.

ITANDA, T. ILLUSTRATED DICTIONARY OF INDUSTRIAL TERMS... (*JA*EN) KYOTO, GAKUGEI, 1952. 359P.

JPREME COMMANDER FOR THE ALLIED POWERS. JAPANESE-ENGLISH DICTIONARY OF TECHNICAL TERMS. TOKYO, ASSOC. 'I. DOC. INFORM, 1954. 1041P.

LITHUANIAN

DVODVORSKIS, A. ANGLU-LIETUVIU KALBU POLITECHNINIS ZODYNAS. (EN*LI TECH. D) VILNIUS, VALSTYBINE POLIT. OKSLINES LIT. LEIDYKLA, 1958. 172P. 61-49203. 10000T.

MONGOLIAN

JCK, F.H. GLOSSARY OF MONGOLIAN TECHNICAL TERMS. NEW YORK, AM. COUNCIL LEARNED SOC, 1958. 79P. 8-59834. 4500T.

NORWEGIAN

NSTEINSSON, J. ENGELSK-NORSK TEKNISK ORDBOK. (EN*NO TECH. D) ED2. (REPR) TRONDHEIM, BRUN, 1958. 442P. 1-16772. 8800T.

NSTEINSSON, J. NORSK-ENGELSK TEKNISK ORDBOK. (NO*EN TECH. D) TRONDHEIM, BRUN, 1954. 327P. A'55-1958. 500T.

LEIBER, B.A. NORSK-ENGELSK, ENGELSK-NORSK TEKNISK-MERKANTIL ORDBOK. (NO*EN TECH/COM. D) ED2. OSLO, ASJONALFORLAGET, 1954. 568P. 58-39074. 7500T.

RGES GULLSMEDFORBUND. ENGELSK ORDLISTE FOR GULLSMEDFAGET. (*NO*EN GOLDSMITHING T) OSLO, 1953. 11P. -31158. 400T.

POLISH

AMSON, M. ET AL. ENGLISH-POLISH DICTIONARY OF SCIENCE AND TECHNOLOGY. NEW YORK, GORDON/BREACH. IN PREP) 270,000T.

RAMSON, M. ET AL. POLISH-ENGLISH DICTIONARY OF SCIENCE AND TECHNOLOGY. NEW YORK, GORDON/BREACH. IN PREP) 270,000T.

ZERNI, S. AND SKRZYNSKA, M. MALY SLOWNIK TECHNICZNY ANGIELSKO-POLSKI. (EN*PL SHORT TECH. D) WARSAW, YDAW. NAUK-TECH, 1963. 244P. 63-38521. 10000T.

ZERNI, S. AND SKRZYNSKA, M. MALY SLOWNIK TECHNICZNY POLSKO-ANGIELSKI. (PL*EN SHORT TECH. D) WARSAW, YDAW. NAUK-TECH, 1962. 174P. 63-38522. 10000T.

ZERNI,S. AND SKRZYNSKA, M. SLOWNIK TECHNICZNY. (TECH. D, V.1, EN*PL, 442P. 3400T. V.2, PL*EN, 372P. 100T) NEW YORK, PERGAMON, 1962. 62-8850.

AZUR, M. TERMINOLOGIA TECHNICZNA. (TECH. T, PL DEFS) WARSAW, WYDAW. NAUK. TECH, 1961. 251P. 62-57961.

KIBICKI, W. SLOWNIK TECHNICZNY ANGIELSKO-POLSKI. (EN*PL TECH. D) ED2. WARSAW, RANST. WYDAW. TECH, 952. 672P. 54-30735.

ROSKOLANSKI, A.T. MALA ENCYKLOPEDIA TECHNIKI. (CONCISE TECH. ENCYCL, PL DEFS) ED2. WARSAW, PANST. YDAW. NAUK, 1962. 1500P.

ARYWODA, A. ENCYKLOPEDIA TECHNICZNA. (TECH. ENCYCL, PL DEFS) CRACOW, ZESPOL PRAC. NAUK, 1957-- . V. 9-27942.

OJCICKA, J. POLISH ABBREVIATIONS, A SELECTIVE LIST. ED2. WASHINGTON, U.S. LIBR. CONGR, 1957. 164P. 7-60055. 2500T.

POLYGLOT

JRAS, V. ET AL. TEKNIKAN SANASTO, SAKSA, ENGLANTI, SUOMI, RUOTSI, VENAJA. (TECH. VOC, *GE*EN*FI*RU*SW) D2. HELSINKI, KUSTANNUSOSAKEYHTIO OTAVA, 1950-52. 2V. 52-33789. 60000T.

KADEMIIA NAUK SSSR. KOM. TEKH.TERM. SBORNIKI REKOMENDUEMYKH TERMINOV,NOS.1-(COLLECTION OF RECOMMENDED T, ER. OF RU/PO D) MOSCOW,1952-- 56-21869. (FOR GL IN THIS SERIES, SEE VAR. SUBJECTS)

NNUARIO POLITECNICO ITALIANO. GUIDA GENERALE DELLE INDUSTRIE NAZIONALI. (DIRECT. OF IT IND, *IT*EN*FR GE*SP) ED38. MILAN, 1961.

SOCIATIA STIINTIFICA A INGINERILOR SI TEHNICIENILOR DIN REPUBLICA POPULARA ROMANA. LEXICONUL TEHNIC OMAN. (RO TECH. ENCYCL, RO*EN*FR*GE*HU*RU) 7V. BUCHAREST, TEHNICA, 1949-55. 51-34211.

SOCIATIA STIINTIFICA A INGINERILOR SI TEHNICIENILOR DIN REPUBLICA POPULARA ROMANA. LEXICONUL TEHNIC OMAN. (RO TECH. D, RO*EN*FR*GE*HU*RU, TO BE COMPLETE IN 7V) ED2. BUCHAREST, TEHNICA, 1957-- . 8-22479.

POLYGLOT

BENISLAWSKI, J. 5 JEZYCZNY PODRECZNY SLOWNIK EKONOMIKI PRZEMYSLU. (5-LANG. D. OF IND. ECON, PL*EN*FR*GE *RU) WARSAW, POLSK. WYDAW. GOSP, 1959. 214P. 59-53166.

BOSCH, A. AND OBERG, E.L. VIERTALIG TECHNISCH WOORDENBOEK. (4-LANG. TECH. D) ED5. (V.1, DU*EN*FR*GE, 690P. V.2, EN*DU, 393P. V.3, GE*DU, 406P. V.4, FR*DU, 392P) DEVENTER, KLUWER, 1959-- . 61-94.

BUECKEN, F.J. VOCABULARIO TECNICO PORTUGUES-INGLES-FRANCES-ALEMAO... APENDICE DE TERMOS AUTOMOBILISTICOS. (TECH. D, PR*EN*GE, WITH APPENDIX OF AUTO. T) ED4. SAO PAULO, MELHORAMENTOS, 1961. 600P. 62-3680. 45000T.

CHALKIOPOULOS, G. PENTAGLOSSON LEXILOGION TECHNIKON HORON. (TECH. VOC. IN 5 LANG, *GR*EN*FR*GE*LA) ATHENS, 1960. 61-31355. 1030P. 34000T.

CANADIAN MANUFACTURERS ASSOCIATION. CANADIAN TRADE INDEX. (FR*EN*PR* SP GL) TORONTO, 1954. 1127P.

DANSK EXPORTKALENDER. (EXPORT DIREC. OF DENMARK, *DA*EN*FR*GE*SP) COPENHAGEN, KRAKSLEGAT, 1955. 350P. 27-7552. 1400T.

DICTIONAR TEHNIC POLIGLOT.... (TECH. D, RO RU EN GE FR HU) BUCHAREST, TEHNICA, 1963. 1235P. 63-40320.

DICTIONARY OF INDUSTRIAL AGRICULTURE... (*DU*EN-AM*FR*GE*IT*SP) NEW YORK, ELSEVIER (IN PREP)

DREISPRACHIGES VERZEICHNIS DER NORMEN FUER DIE VERPACKUNGSWIRTSCHAFT. (GE*EN*FR LIST OF PACKAGING IND. STDS) BERLIN, BEUTH-VERTRIEB, 1960.

ETTINGEN, S. MILON HA-TEKHNIKAH VEHA-MADAIM HA-MEDUYAKIM. (TECH. D. IN 5 LANG, *HE*EN*FR*GE*RU) TEL-AVIV, 1961- . 61-57327.

EUROPEAN GLASS MANUFACTURERS. EUROPEAN VOCABULARY OF GLASS-CONTAINER MANUFACTURING TERMS, DA EN DU FR GE IT NO SW. LONDON, 1958. 22P.

FINNISH FOREIGN TRADE DIRECTORY. (*FI*EN*FR*GE*RU*SP*SW) HELSINKI, FI,FED.FOR.TRADE, 1957. 528P. 53-34818.

FORSCHUNGSINSTITUT FUER AUFBEREITUNG. FACHWOERTERBUCH SIEBTECHNIK. (SIZING/SCREENING T, GE EN FR) BERLIN, AKADEMIE, 1961. 800T.

HAFERKORN, R. ET AL. SCIENCA KAJ TEKNIKA TERMINARO,DESTINATA POR KOMPLEMENTI LA PLENAN VORTARON. (SCI/ TECH. T, EO*EN*FR*GE) PARIS, SENNACIECA ASOCIO TUTMONDA, 1956. 248P. 6000T.

HANDBOK OEVER SVERIGES INDUSTRI OCH NAERINGSLIV. (SW/FOR/DOMESTIC TRADE DIREC,*SW*EN*FR*GE*SP) STOCKHOLM, KOMPASS, 1957. 1700P. 15000T.

HANDBUCH DER INTERNATIONALEN KAUTSCHUKINDUSTRIE. (INTL.RUBBER HANDBOOK, GE EN FR) ZURICH, INTL. WIRTSCHAFTSLIT.1953-- 61-49220. 3000T.

HARADA, S. NEW DICTIONARY OF ENGINEERING TECHNICAL TERMS, ENGLISH-JAPANESE, GERMAN-JAPANESE. TOKYO, KEIBUNSHA, 1955. 352P.

HERZKA, A. LEXICON OF PRESSURIZED PACKAGING (AEROSOLS) 20 LANG. AMSTERDAM, ELSEVIER. 150P. 260T.(IN PREP)

ILVA, ALTI FORNI E ACCIAIERIE D,ITALIA, S.P.A. DIZIONARIO TECNICO. (TECH. D, IT EN FR GE SP) GENOA, 1956. 55P. 60-21394. 850T.

INTERNATIONAL ELECTROTECHNICAL COMMISSION. INTERNATIONAL ELECTROTECHNICAL VOCABULARY. ELECTRO-HEATING APPLICATIONS.*FR*EN*DU*GE*IT*PL*SP*SW. (IEC-50-GR-40)ED2. GENEVA,1960.40P.

INTERNATIONAL GAS UNION. ELSEVIER,S DICTIONARY OF THE GAS INDUSTRY.... (*EN/AM*DU*FR*GE*IT*PR*SP) NEW YORK, ELSEVIER, 1961. 628P. 61-19741. 2900T.

INTERNATIONAL INSTITUTION FOR PRODUCTION ENGINEERING RESEARCH. WOERTERBUCH DER FERTIGUNGSTECHNIK. (PROD. ENG.O, GE EN FR) V.1, SCHMIEDEN, FREIFORMSCHMIEDEN UND GESENKSCHMIEDEN. (FORGING, HAMMER FORGING/DROP FORGING) V.2, SCHLEIFEN UND TECHNISCHE OBERFLAECHEN. (GRINDING/SURFACE FINISHING, IN PREP) V.3, BLECHBEARBEITUNG. (SHEETMETAL PROCESS, IN PREP) ESSEN, GIRARDET, 1962- .

JANDER, N. SKOTERMER PA FYRA SPRAK.(SHOE T,*SW*EN*FR*GE) STOCKHOLM, SKOIND. FORSKNINGSINST, 1956. 272P. 57-35496. 1000T.

KLEINES AUSSENHANDELSWOERTERBUCH IN ACHT SPRACHEN. (FOR.TRADE D.IN 8 LANG) BERLIN, WIRTSCHAFT, 1960. 280P.

KOLPAKOV, B.T. ET AL. EKSPORTNO-IMPORTNYI SLOVAR. (EXPORT/IMPORT D, RU*EN*AL*BU*CZ*FI*FR*GE*HU*IT*PL*SP) MOSCOW, VNESHTORGIZDAT, 1952-54. 3V. 2392P. 3000T.

KOLPAKOV, B.T. KRATKII VNESHNETORGOVYI SLOVAR. (FOR.TRADE D, RU*AL*BU*CZ*EN*FI*FR*GE*HU*PL*RO*SP) MOSCOW, VNESHTORGIZDAT, 1954. 545P. 55-44311. 1000T.

LANGE, K. GESENKSCHMIEDEN, DREISPRACHIGES TASCHENWOERTERBUCH. (DROP FORGING, *GE*EN*FR D) HANNOVER, WITTKOPF, 1956. 45P. 800T.

LANGFORD, R. AND AEBERHARD, R.W. TECHNICAL AND COMMERCIAL DICTIONARY. (*GE*EN*FR) ZURICH, ENGLISH INST. 1952. 1024P. 52-2054. 20000T.

MACHARLSKI, J. AND RAPACZYNSKI, E.M. HANDY TECHNICAL DICTIONARY ILLUSTRATED, IN 8 LANGUAGES, *FR*EN*GE*IT
*PL*PR*RU*SP. LONDON, K.L.R, 1952. 1088P. 53-35260. 8000T.

MALY EKONOMICKO-TECHNICKY SLOVNICEK. (ECON/TECH GL, EN FR GE HU RU SL)TECH. PRAC (PRAGUE) 556-61
(1958)·

MEDEIROS, M.F. DICIONARIO TECNICO POLIGLOTA, PORTUGUES-ESPANHOL-FRANCES-ITALIANO-INGLES-ALEMAO. (TECH. D,
PR*EN*FR*GE*IT*SP) LISBON, GOMES/RODRIGUES, 1949-54. 52-67939. 131000T.

MUSZAKI ERTELMEZO SZOTAR. (TECH. DEFINITIVE D, *HU*EN*GE*RU, NOS.1-21) BUDAPEST, TERRA, 1958   .
NO.1 PALOTAS,L. ET AL. EPITOANYAGOK. (BLDG. MATER) 1958. 174P. 59-20131. 1100T.
NO.2 KOVACS, K.P. ET AL. ALTALANOS ELEKTROTECHNIKA. (ELEC. ENG) 1958. 236P. 59-20477. 1300T.
NO.3 MOSONYI, E. ET AL. HIDRAULIKA ES MUSZAKI HIDROLOGIA. (HYDR. ENG) 1959. 156P. 59-41601. 1200T.
NO.4 PALOTAS, L. ET AL. MUSZAKI MECHANIKA. (MECH. ENG) 1959. 167P. 59-40060. 1200T.
NO.5 KOVACS, K.P. ET AL. VILLAMOS GEPEK. (ELEC. MACH) 1959. 164P. 63-28491. 1000T.
NO.6 MOSONYI, E. ET AL. VIZEROMUVEK ES VIZIUTAK. (HYDR.POWER PLANTS/WATERWAYS) 1960. 204P. 1200T.
NO.7/8 VASARHELYI, B. ET AL. KOZLEKEDESUGY I. KENYSZERPALYAS ES KOZUTI KOZLEKEDES. (TRANSPORT, PT.1,R.R.
-STREETCARS) 1960. 207P. 60-34451. 1200T.
NO.7/8 VASARHELYI, B. ET AL. KOZLEKEDESUGY II. HAJOZAS,REPULES,POSTA ES CSOVEZETEKES SZALLITAS.(PT.2,
NAVIGATION,AVIATION, MAIL/PNEUMATIC TRANSPORT) 1960. 174P.60-34451.1200T.
NO.9 SZENDY, K. ET AL. VILLAMOS MUVEK.(ELEC.POWER/DISTR) 1960. 235P. 1300T.
NO.10 SZECHY, K. AND KEZDI, A. ALAGUTAK,ALAPOZAS,FOLDMUVEK, TALAJMECHANIKA.(TUNNELS,SOIL ENG/MECH) 1960.
252P. 1400T.
NO.11 GILLEMOT, L. MECHANIKAI TECHNOLOGIA, I. ANYAGSZERKEZETTAN ES ANYAGVIZSGALAT.(MECH.ENG,PT.1
TESTING/STRUCT.MATER) 1960. 168P. 1200T.
NO.12 GILLEMOT, L. MECHANIKAI TECHNOLOGIA, II.TECHNOLOGIAI MUVELETEK.(MECH.ENG,PT.2.TECH.OPER)1961.
212P. 1300T.
NO.13 REDEY, I. ET AL. ALTALANOS GEODEZIA.(GEOD) 1961. 216P.61-31346.1200T.
NO.14 PALOTAS, L. ET AL. TARTOSZERKEZETEK.(SUPP.STRUCT)1961. 190P. 62-46390. 1100T.
NO.15 LOVASZ, K. NYOMDAIPAR. (PRINTING IND) 1961. 232P. 1200T.
NO.16 BARANY, N. ET AL. FINOMMECHANICA, OPTIKA.(PREC.MECH/OPTICS) 1961. 214P. 61-48214. 1200T.
NO.17/18 CSUROS, Z. KEMIA. (CHEM) 1961. 62-66364. 2500T.
NO.19 FRIGYES, A. IRANYITASTECHNIKA. (AUTOM) 1962. 135P. 1100T.
NO.20 VARGA,J. ET AL. VIZGEPEK, BELSO EGESU MOTOROK. (HYDR/INTERN.COMB.ENG) 1962. 138P. 1100T.
NO.21 SOVARY, E. VILLAMOS EROMUVEK. (ELEC. POWER PLANTS) 1963. 172P. 1200T.

NASLIN, P. VOCABULARIE TECHNIQUE TRILINGUE... (EN FR GE TECH. D) ED2. PARIS, ED. REV. OPT/THEOR.
INSTR, 1962. 420P. 63-25045.

NENRYO KYOKAI. KOKUSU BUKAI. KOKUSU KOGYO YOGO-SHU. (COKE IND. D, JA*EN*GE) TOKYO, SHIGEN SHIMPO,
1958. 148P. J62-971. 2000T. 300ABBR.

NEUBERG, H.A. EXPORT-WOERTERBUCH IN 4 SPRACHEN... (EXPORT D. IN 4 LANG, *GE*EN*FR*SP) BERLIN, SCHMIDT,
1960. 289P. A62-290.

NORWEGIAN EXPORT DIRECTORY. (*NO*EN*FR*GE*SP) OSLO,NO/EXPORT COUNCIL, 1956. 400P. 57-35292.

OPPEGAARD, S. TEKNISK ORDLISTE...(TECH.D, NO*EN*GE) ED3. TRONDHEIM, BRUN, 1954. 232P. A55-7256. 3700T.

PERMANENT INTERNATIONAL ASSOCIATION OF NAVIGATION CONGRESSES. DICTIONNAIRE TECHNIQUE ILLUSTRE... (ILLUS.
TECH. D *FR*EN*DU*GE*IT*SP) BRUSSELS, 1934-- . (IN PROGR) CH.1, LA MER (THE SEA) 1957. 272P. CH.2,
FLEUVES, RIVIERES, CANAUX (STREAMS, RIVERS, CANALS) 1939. 122P. CH.3, (IN PREP) CH.4, (IN PREP)
CH.5, MATERIAUX (MATER) 1951. 204P. CH.6, (CONSTRUCTION. PLANT/METHODS) 1959. 237P.
CH.7, LES PORTS (PORTS) 1938. 58P. CH.8, ECLUSES ET CALES SECHES (LOCKS/DRY DOCKS) 1936. 86P. CH.9,
(IN PREP) CH.10, BARRAGES EN RIVIERES (RIVER WEIRS) 1934. 88P. CH.11, (IN PREP) CH.12, SIGNALISATION
MARITIME. (NAVAL TELECOMMUN) 1937. 143P. CH.13, EQUIPMENT (IN PREP) CH.14, (STAFF, ADMINISTRATION,
EXPLOITATION (IN PREP) CH.15, FOUNDATIONS (IN PREP)

PFOHL, E. WARENWOERTERBUCH FUER ALLE INDUSTRIE- , HANDELS UND GEWERBEZWEIGE. (D.OF MATER/PROD,*GE*EN*FR*
RU) ED2. LEIPZIG, BROCKHAUS, 1952. 455P. A54-1878.

RISTIC, S. ET AL. WOERTERBUCH TECHNISCHER AUSDRUECKE. (TECH. D. V1, EN*FR*GE*SC. V.2, SC*EN*FR*GE)
BELGRADE, TEH. KNJ, 1961. 61-65041.

RUBBER STICHTING, DELFT. ELSEVIER,S RUBBER DICTIONARY... (*DU*EN*FR*GE*IT*JA*MA*PR*SP*SW) NEW YORK,
ELSEVIER, 1959. 1537P. 58-9206. 8000T.

SHUNG-MING, W. RUSSIAN-CHINESE-ENGLISH TECHNICAL AND CHEMICAL VOCABULARY. PEKING, ACAD. SINICA, 1961.
279P.

STEPANOV, I.A. ET AL. KRATKII POLITEKHNICHESKII SLOVAR. (POLYTECH. D, RU EN FR GE...) MOSCOW, GITTL,
1955. 1136P. 56-29909.

SWEDISH EXPORT DIRECTORY. (*SW*EN*FR*GE*RU*SP) ED4. STOCKHOLM, GEN. EXPORT ASSOC, 1952. 810P.

SYBRANDY, O. AND DE GROOT, B. DICTIONARY OF PACKAGING. (EN FR DU GE) NEW YORK, ELSEVIER. 7000T.
(IN PREP)

SYNDICAT DES CONSTRUCTEURS FRANCAIS DE MACHINES-OUTILS. MACHINES-OUTILS FRANCAISES. (FR MACH. TOOLS,
FR EN GE SP GL) NEUILLY/SEINE, 1961. 273P. 62-65392.

TECHNOLOGY AND INDUSTRY

POLYGLOT

TECH-TERM, ILLUSTRATED INTERNATIONAL TECHNICAL DICTIONARY. (V.1, HAND TOOLS FOR ALL TRADES, *GE*EN*DU*FR) AMSTERDAM, ELSEVIER, 1958. 124P. 62-51192. 1800T.

TEKNISKA NOMENKLATURCENTRALEN. ARBETSKUNSKAPS TERMINOLOGI JAEMTE FYRSPRAKIG ORDLISTA FOER ARBETSSTUDIER, ARBETS- OCH MERITVAERDERING. (WORK STUDY T, EN FR GE SW) STOCKHOLM, 1960. 132P.

TEKNISK ORDLISTA SVENSK-TYSK-ENGELSK-FRANSK-SPANSK-PORTUGISISK-RYSK OEVER FACKUTTRYCK INOM VERKTYGS-OCH VERKTYGSMASKINBRANSHEN. (GL.OF TOOLS/MACH.TOOLS, SW*EN*FR*GE*PR*RU*SP) ED4. STOCKHOLM, MASKIN. KARLEBO, 1953. 129P. 1200T.

TIDESTROEM, S.H. ENCYKLOPEDI OEVER RAVAROR OCH MATERIAL... (RAW MATER/PROD.ENCYCL, SW*EN*FR*GE)STOCKHOLM NORDISK ROTOGRAVYR, 1957. 1912P. 58-33018.

U.S. BUSINESS AND DEFENSE SERVICES ADMINISTRATION. SELECTED U.S. MARKETING TERMS AND DEFINITIONS. (40-43MM-C41.93) (V.1 EN*FR,V.2 EN*GE, V.3 EN*IT, V.4 EN*SP, V.5 EN*SW) WASHINGTON, 1960. 60-60918. 90T.

VOYE, A. VOOR INGENIEURS EN TECHNICA-- 500 DER BELANGRIJKSTE WOORDERN IN VIER TALEN. (ENG/TECH.GL,FR EN DU EN) LIEGE, PRESSES UNIV, 195 . 87P. 500T.

WEBER, H. ET AL. SCHUH WOERTERBUCH. (SHOE T, GE EN FR IT) FRANKFURT/MAIN, UMSCHAU, 1958. 326P. A59-3859 6000T.

WEBSTER, R. DICTIONARY OF MARKETING TERMS, U.S. USAGE. (GE*EN*FR) BASEL, RECHT/GESELLSCHAFT, 1952. 102P. 52-1408.

WRIGHT, H.M. THE SHOEMAN.S FOREIGN TERMS. ED3. LEICESTER, ENGLAND, HALFORD, 1962. 103P.

PORTUGUESE

BUZZONI, H.A. DICIONARIO DE TERMOS TECNICOS, INGLES-PORTUGUES. (EN*PR TECH. T) SAO PAULO, LEP, 1954. 300P.

ENCICLOPEDIA TECNICA UNIVERSAL. (TECH. ENCYCL, PR DEFS) PORTO ALEGRE, GLOBO, 1958-- . 3V. 59-30909.

FURSTENAU, E.E. DICIONARIO DE TERMOS TECNICOS, INGLES-PORTUGUES. (EN*PR TECH. T) ED4. RIO DE JANEIRO, GLOBO, 1961. 929P. 30000T.

QUEIROZ, H.J. FRASEARIO COMERCIAL E INDUSTRIAL DE PORTUGUES-INGLES. (PR*EN COM/IND D) LISBON, 1955. 2V. 1972P. 59-33305. 45000T.

SELL, L.L. ENGLISH-PORTUGUESE COMPREHENSIVE TECHNICAL DICTIONARY.. NEW YORK, MCGRAW-HILL, 1953. 1168P. 53-10660. 500000T.

SELL L.L. PORTUGUESE-ENGLISH COMPREHENSIVE TECHNICAL DICTIONARY. NEW YORK, MCGRAW-HILL. (IN PREP)

STERNBERG, B.L. DICIONARIO TECNICO.(*PR*EN TECH. D)(V.1,EN*PR,148P. 6000T. V.2,PR*EN,93P. 5500T) RIO DE JANEIRO, MIN. AERON, 1956. 61-38640.

TAYLOR, J.L. POLYTECHNICAL AMERICAN-BRAZILIAN DICTIONARY. PIEDMONT,CAL. TAYLOR, 1000P. 100000T.

VALLANDRO, L. DICIONARIO INGLES-PORTUGUES... TERMOS TECNICOS E CIENTIFICOS... ABREVIATURAS... (EN*PR TECH/SCI. D/ABBR) RIO DE JANEIRO, GLOBO, 1954. 1135P. 54-44677.

ROMANIAN

FLEGON, A. DICTIONAR TECHNIC ENGLES-ROMIN. (EN*RO TECH. D) LONDON, 1962. 160P.

KARNIOL,Z. ET AL. DICTIONAR POLITEHNIC. (TECH. D, RO DEFS) BUCHAREST,TEHNICA, 1957. 768P. 58-46245. 15000T.

RUSSIAN

AKADEMIIA NAUK SSSR. KOM.TEKH.TERM. OPREDELENIE PONIATII. NAUCHNOE OTKRYTIE, IZOBRETENIE I RATSIONALIZATORSKOE PREDLOZHENIE. (SCI.DISCOVERY, INVENTION/EFFIC.SUGG, RU DEFS) (BIUL.NO.66) MOSCOW, 1955. 8P.

AKADEMIIA NAUK SSSR. KOM.TEKH.TERM. RUKOVODSTVO PO RAZRABOTKE I UPORIADOCHENIIU NAUCHNO-TEKHNICHESKOI TERMINOGOLII. (MANUAL FOR DEVELOP.STDS IN SCI/TECH,RU DEFS) MOSCOW, 1952. 54P.

AKADEMIIA NAUK SSSR. KOM. TEKH. TERM. TERMINOLOGIIA GAZOVOI TEKHNIKI. (GAS TECH, RU DEFS) (SB. REK. TERM, NO.41) MOSCOW, 1957. 24P. 58-33553. 100T.

AKADEMIIA NAUK SSSR. KOM.TEKH.TERM. TERMINOLOGIIA VODOPODGOTOVKI DLIA PAROVYKH KOTLOV. (WATER PROCESS. FOR STEAM BOILERS, RU DEFS) (SB. REK. TERM. NO.38) MOSCOW, 1956. 38P. 56-46923. 250T.

ALFAVITNYI SLOVAR ZANIATII. (OCCUP. TITLES, RU DEFS) MOSCOW, GOSSTATIZDAT, 1957. 246P. 20000T.

ARBUZOV, G.A. ET AL. ANGLO-RUSSKII KOZHEVENNO-OBUVNOI SLOVAR. (*EN*RU LEATHER/SHOE D) MOSCOW, FIZMATGIZ, 1963. 402P. 63-58903.

BELODVORSKII, IU. M. KRATKII SLOVAR GAZOVIKA. (D. OF GAS TECH, RU DEFS) MOSCOW, MIN. KOMMUNAL. KHOZ, RSFSR, 1955. 187P. 56-37054. 500T.

TECHNOLOGY AND INDUSTRY

RUSSIAN

LUVSHTEIN, V.O. ET AL. SLOVAR ANGLIISKIKH I AMERIKANSKIKH SOKRASHCHENII. (D. OF EN/AM ABBRS, RU DEFS) D3. MOSCOW, GOS. IZD. INOSTR/NATS. SLOV, 1957. 767P. 57-36383. 31000T.

ALLAHAM, L.I. AND UVAROV, E.V. RUSSIAN-ENGLISH CHEMICAL AND POLYTECHNICAL DICTIONARY. ED2. EW YORK, WILEY, 1962. 892P. 62-18989. 70000T.

ARPOVICH, E.A. RUSSIAN-ENGLISH POLYTECHNIC DICTIONARY. NEW YORK, TECH. DICT. (IN PREP)

HERNUKHIN, A.E. ANGLO-RUSSKII POLITEKHNICHESKII SLOVAR... (EN*RU TECH. D) MOSCOW, FIZMATGIZ, 1962. 63P. 63-31248. 75000T.

OSEH, M. RUSSIAN-ENGLISH DICTIONARY OF CHEMICAL AND TECHNICAL TERMS(TENT.TITLE). NEW YORK, REINHOLD. IN PREP)

NSTITUT ZUR ERFORSCHUNG DER UDSSR. SPISOK RUSSKIKH SOKRASHCHENII, PRIMENIAEMYKH V SSSR. (LIST OF USSR BBRS) MUNICH, 1954. 304P. 54-41132. 8000T.

ONDRATOV, L.N. RUSSKO-ANGLIISKII POLITEKHNICHESKII SLOVAR. (RU*EN TECH. D) LONDON, FLEGON, 1962. 348P.

ORNEEV, L.A. KRATKII ANGLO-RUSSKII SLOVAR STEKOLNYKH TERMINOV. (EN*RU GLASS D) MOSCOW, NIIST, 1958. 12P. 2500T.

RAMER, A. AND E. ABBREVIATIONS AND SYMBOLS IN SOVIET SCIENTIFIC AND TECHNICAL LITERATURE. TRENTON, N.J, 960. 12P. 60-9262. 500T.

OTTE,D.S. OSNOVY POSTROENIIA NAUCHNO-TEKHNICHESKOI TERMINOLOGII... (COMPOSITION OF SCI/TECH. T, RU EFS) MOSCOW, AKAD. NAUK, SSSR, 1961. 156P. 61-41148.

IKHAILOV, A.N. ANGLO-RUSSKII KOZHEVENNO-OBUVNOI SLOVAR. (*EN*RU LEATHER/SHOE D) MOSCOW, FIZMATGIZ, 963. 402P. 15000T.

PUGACHEV, I.A. TOVARNYI SLOVAR. (IND. PRODS. ENCYCL, RU DEFS) MOSCOW, GOSTORGIZDAT, 1956--61. 10V. 57-41279.

ROSENBERG, A. RUSSIAN ABBREVIATIONS, A SELECTIVE LIST. ED2. WASHINGTON, U.S. LIBR. CONGR, 1957. 513P. 57-60063. 3000T.

U.S. AIR TECHNICAL INTELLIGENCE CENTER. GLOSSARY OF RUSSIAN-ENGLISH MILITARY AND TECHNICAL TERMS. WRIGHT-PATTERSON AFB,OHIO. 1955. 246P. 55-61309.

U.S. AIR TECHNICAL INTELLIGENCE CENTER. RUSSIAN-ENGLISH GLOSSARY,AERONAUTICAL AND MISCELLANEOUS TERMS. WRIGHT-PATTERSON AFB, OHIO, 1956. VAR. P. 57-61417. 30000T.

U.S. ARMY MAP SERVICE. RUSSIAN GLOSSARY.(AMS TECH.MANUAL, NO.12) ED2. WASHINGTON, 1951. 881P. 52-61255.

U.S. LIBRARY OF CONGRESS. SOVIET-RUSSIAN SCIENTIFIC AND TECHNICAL TERMS, A SELECTIVE LIST. WASHINGTON, 1962. 668P. 60-60977. 26000T.

SERBOCROATIAN

PLAMENATZ, I.P. YUGOSLAV ABBREVIATIONS, A SELECTIVE LIST. ED2. WASHINGTON, U.S. LIBR. CONGR, 1962. 198P. 62-60076. 3200T.

SLOVAK

DOBROVOLNY, B. AND HORECKY, J. SLOVNICEK NOVEJ TECHNIKY...(SCI/TECH D, SL DEFS) BRATISLAVA, ROH, 1961. 149P. 62-32103.

NOVAK, J. AND BINDER, R. VRECKOVY ANGLICKO-SLOVENSKY A SLOVENSKO-ANGLICKY TECHNICKY SLOVNIK. (*EN*SL TECH. D) BRATISLAVA, SLOV. VYDAV. TECH. LIT, 1961. 611P. 62-30396.

SLOVENSKA AKADEMIA VIED. BANICKY TERMINOLOGICKY SLOVNIK. (MINERAL IND. D, SL DEFS) BRATISLAVA, S.A.V, 1955. 167P. 57-20723.

SPANISH

OCKHAUS DICCIONARIO POPULAR DE LAS CIENCIAS Y DE LAS TECNICAS. (POPULAR SCI/TECH D,SP DEFS) BARCELONA, LI, 1961. 658P.

CASTILLA,S SPANISH AND ENGLISH TECHNICAL DICTIONARY.(V.1, EN*SP, 1611P, 150000T. V.2, SP*EN, 1137P. 120000T.) NEW YORK, PHIL. LIBR. 1958. 58-2320.

COSTA RICA. MINISTERIO DE RELACIONES EXTERIORES. SIGLAS INTERNACIONALES... (INTL ABBRS, SP DEFS) SAN JOSE, COSTA RICA, IMPR. NACL, 1954. 23P. 56-34855.

COULT, M. AND PERDOMO, J.E. DICTIONARY OF THE CUBAN TOBACCO INDUSTRY...(SP*EN) WASHINGTON, U.S. DEPT.AGR, 1952. 64P. 52-61000.

GUINLE, R.L. MODERN SPANISH-ENGLISH, ENGLISH-SPANISH TECHNICAL AND ENGINEERING DICTIONARY...NEW YORK, DUTTON, 1959. 311P. 15000T.

POPULAR MECHANICS MAGAZINE. VOCABULARIO TECNICO, INGLES-ESPANOL..(EN*SP TECH D) NEW ED. NEW YORK, HAWTHORN, 1961. 165P. 61-11445. 6000T.

147

SPANISH

ROBAYO, L.A. SPANISH-ENGLISH, ENGLISH-SPANISH TECHNICAL, LEGAL, AND COMMERCIAL DICTIONARY. MONTREAL, DICT. PUBL, 1952. 334P. 52-13398.

SALAZAR-PACHECO, S. TECHNICAL ENGLISH, CIVIL ENGINEERING AND AGRICULTURE. MEXICO, IMPR. ACOSTA, 1956. 225P.

SELL,L.L. ENGLISH-SPANISH COMPREHENSIVE TECHNICAL DICTIONARY OF AIRCRAFT, AUTOMOBILE, ELECTRICITY, RADI TELEVISION, PETROLEUM,STEEL PRODUCTS... NEW YORK, MCGRAW-HILL, 1960. 1079P. 61-3462. 525000T.

SELL,L.L. ESPANOL-INGLES DICCIONARIO TECNICO COMPLETISIMO DE AERONAUTICA, AUTOMOVILES,FERROCARRILES, CARRETERAS, ELECTRICIDAD, ELECTRONICA, RADIO, TELEVISION...(SP*EN TECH. D) NEW YORK, MCGRAW-HILL, 1949. 1706P. 61-4329. 700000T.

TODD, E.F.H. DICCIONARIO TECNICO-AGRICOLA...(EN*SP TECH/AGR. D) MEXICO, 1953. 99P. 53-35917. 3000T

TWENEY, C.F. ET AL. CHAMBERS DICCIONARIO TECNOLOGICO...(*SP*EN TECH.D) BARCELONA, OMEGA, 1952. 1227+289 60000T.

SWEDISH

ENGSTROEM, E. ENGELSK-SVENSK TEKNISK ORDBOK. (EN*SW TECH. D) ED8. STOCKHOLM, SVENSK TRAEVARU-TIDN, 1960. 541P. 61-32546. 70000T.

ENGSTROEM, E. SVENSK-ENGELSK TEKNISK ORDBOK. (SW*EN TECH. D) ED6. STOCKHOLM, SVENSK TRAEVARU-TIDN, 1961 543P. 61-49207. 70000T.

GULLBERG, I.E. A SWEDISH-ENGLISH BUSINESS DICTIONARY. (INCL. SCI/TECH. T) STOCKHOLM, NORSTEDT, 1963. 1350P. 130,000T.

TURKISH

ISTANBUL. TEKNIK UNIVERSITESI. TEKNIK TERIMLER. (TECH. T, TU DEFS) ANKARA, DOGUS MATBAASI, 1949- V. NE6Z-652.

TURNER, C.E. ENGLISH-TURKISH BASIC-TECHNICAL DICTIONARY. ANKARA, BASILDIGIYER, 1960. 124P. 61-3002. 1500T.

WELSH

WALES. UNIVERSITY. TERMAU TECHNEGOL. (EN*WE TECH. T) CAERDYDD, GWASG PRIFYSGOL CYMRU, 1950. 85P. 59-42893. 1600T.

TELECOMMUNICATION ENGINEERING

DUTCH

HOOFDCOMMISSIE VOOR DE NORMALISATIE IN NEDERLAND. TELECOMMUNICATIE. BENAMINGEN OP HET GEBIED VAN DE TELEVISIE. (DU*EN TV T) DELFT, WALTMAN, 1953. 42P.

STRABEL, A. ET AL. TECHNISCHE ENCYCLOPEDIE VOOR RADIO, TELEVISIE, RADAR, ELECTRONICA... (RADIO,TV,RADAR ELECTRON.D, DU DEFS) AMSTERDAM, STRENGHOLT, 1954. 320P. A55-1123.

ENGLISH

AMERICAN INSTITUTE OF ELECTRICAL ENGINEERS. DEFINITIONS OF ELECTRICAL TERMS. COMMUNICATION. (GR-65,ASA C42.65) NEW YORK, 1957. 128P. 1800T.

AMERICAN INSTITUTE OF ELECTRICAL ENGINEERS. DEFINITIONS OF ELECTRICAL TERMS. ELECTRON DEVICES. (GR-70 ASA C42.70) NEW YORK, 1957. 29P. 300T.

AMERICAN STANDARDS ASSOCIATION. LETTER SYMBOLS FOR RADIO. (Y10.9) NEW YORK, 1953.

AMERICAN VACUUM SOCIETY. GLOSSARY OF TERMS USED IN VACUUM TECHNOLOGY. NEW YORK, PERGAMON, 1958. 63P. 59-8278. 430T.

BEAM, R.E. A DICTIONARY OF ELECTRONIC TERMS. CONCISE DEFINITIONS OF WORDS USED IN RADIO, TELEVISION, AND ELECTRONICS. ED7. CHICAGO, ALLIED RADIO, 1963. 88P. 63-5264.

BRACKEN,J.A. GLOSSARY OF TELEPHONE ABBREVIATIONS. TELEPHONY, V.150, NO.17-18, FF, (1956) 1150T.

BRIGGS, G.A. A TO Z IN AUDIO. NEW YORK, GERNSBACK LIBR, 1961. 224P. 61-12273.

BRITISH STANDARDS INSTITUTION. GLOSSARY OF TERMS FOR ELECTRICAL CHARACTERISTICS OF RADIO RECEIVERS. (B.S. 2065) LONDON, 1954. 42P. 150T.

BRITISH STANDARDS INSTITUTION. GLOSSARY OF TERMS USED IN TELECOMMUNICATION (INCL.RADIO/ELECTRON) ED3. (B.S.204 AMEND. 1, PD4694, 30T) LONDON, 1960. 352P. 3500T.

CAIDIN, M. THE MAN-IN-SPACE DICTIONARY, A MODERN GLOSSARY. NEW YORK,DUTTON, 1963. 224P. 63-14274. 1900T.

148

\MM, F.J. PRACTICAL WIRELESS ENCYCLOPEDIA... ED13. LONDON, NEWNES, 1954. 371P. A56-5654.

\MM, F.J. TELEVISION PRINCIPLES AND PRACTICE. (TV T, PP.166-212) LONDON, NEWNES, 1952. 215P. 53-22561.

\RTER, H. DICTIONARY OF ELECTRONICS. NEW YORK, PITMAN, 1960. 377P. 62-51362. 3000T.

JDLIN, E.M. AND MOORE, C.K. LIST OF RECENTLY-COINED TERMS IN ELECTRONICS... LONDON, ASLIB, 1960. 14P.

JOKE, B.W. ET AL. COYNE TELEVISION SERVICING CYCLOPEDIA... CHICAGO, COYNE ELEC/TV SCHOOL, 1955. 868P.
5-2293.

JOKE, N.M. AND MARKUS, J. ELECTRONICS AND NUCLEONICS DICTIONARY... NEW YORK, MCGRAW-HILL, 1960. 543P.
0-10605. 13000T.

OPE, S.T. GLOSSARY OF ABBREVIATIONS FOR NAMES OF... ORGANISATIONS... (IN) THE TELECOMMUNICATIONS
NDUSTRY. ED2. GREAT BADDOW, ESSEX, MARCONI,S WIRELESS TELEGRAPH CO, 1957. 38P. 57-43854. 800T.

OYNE TECHNICAL DICTIONARY OF 4000 TERMS USED IN TELEVISION, RADIO, ELECTRICITY AND ELECTRONICS.. CHICAGO,
OYNE ELEC/TV SCHOOL, 1955. 152P. 55-14738. 4000T.

ODSON, B.E. A GLOSSARY OF JAMMING TERMINOLOGY. (MEWD REPT.NO.R-101-125) WHITE SANDS M.R, N.M, 1959, 27P.

RANKLIN, K.L. GLOSSARY OF TERMS FREQUENTLY USED IN RADIO ASTRONOMY. NEW YORK, AM, INST, PHYS, 1962. 28P.
30T.

RAF, R.F. HOWARD W. SAMS MODERN DICTIONARY OF ELECTRONICS... INDIANAPOLIS, SAMS,1962. 370P. 61-18659.
0000T.

RAHAM, F.D. AUDELS NEW ELECTRIC SCIENCE DICTIONARY... NEW YORK, AUDEL, 1963, 555P. 64-590. 9000T.

REEN, A.R. ELECTRONIC TERMINOLOGY...ABBREVIATIONS... HILVERSUM, OCECO, 1950. 64P. 53-37520. 1600T.

\ANDEL, S. A DICTIONARY OF ELECTRONICS. BALTIMORE, PENGUIN, 1962. 383P. 62-52677. 5000T.

ANNUM, D.E. GLOSSARY FOR DATA TRANSMISSION STUDY GROUP. DOWNEY, CALIF, NORTHROP AVIATION, 195 . 26P.
90T.

OLMES, J.F. COMMUNICATIONS DICTIONARY, A COMPILATION OF THE TERMS USED IN ELECTRONIC COMMUNICATIONS AND
ATA PROCESSING. NEW YORK. RIDER, 1962. 88P. 62-13397.

NSTITUTE OF RADIO ENGINEERS. INDEX TO IRE STANDARDS ON DEFINITIONS OF TERMS, 1942-57.   (58 IRE 20.S1)
ROC. IRE, V.46, 449-76 (1958) 4000T.

NSTITUTE OF RADIO ENGINEERS. IRE DICTIONARY OF ELECTRONICS TERMS AND SYMBOLS... NEW YORK, 1961. 225P.
1-1732. 3700T.

NSTITUTE OF RADIO ENGINEERS. STANDARDS ON ABBREVIATIONS OF RADIO-ELECTRONIC TERMS. (51 IRE 21.S1) PROC.
RE, V.39, 397-400 (1951) 180T.

NSTITUTE OF RADIO ENGINEERS. STANDARDS ON AMERICAN RECOMMENDED PRACTICE FOR VOLUME MEASUREMENTS OF
ELECTRICAL SPEECH AND PROGRAM WAVES. (53 IRE 3.S2) PROC.IRE, V.42, 815-7 (1954) 20T.

INSTITUTE OF RADIO ENGINEERS. STANDARDS ON ANTENNAS AND WAVEGUIDES, DEFINITIONS FOR WAVEGUIDE COMPONENTS.
55 IRE 2.S1) PROC.IRE, V. 43, 1073-4 (1955) 40T.

INSTITUTE OF RADIO ENGINEERS. STANDARDS ON ANTENNAS AND WAVEGUIDES... (59 IRE 2.S1) PROC. IRE, V.47,
368-82 (1959) 20T.

INSTITUTE OF RADIO ENGINEERS. STANDARDS ON AUDIO TECHNIQUES, DEFINITIONS OF TERMS. (58 IRE 3.S1) PROC.IRE,
V.46, 1928-34 (1958) 180T.

INSTITUTE OF RADIO ENGINEERS. STANDARDS ON CIRCUITS, DEFINITIONS OF TERMS FOR LINEAR PASSIVE RECIPROCAL
TIME INVARIANT NETWORKS. (60 IRE 4.S2) PROC. IRE, V.48, 1608-10 (1960)30T.

INSTITUTE OF RADIO ENGINEERS. STANDARDS ON CIRCUITS, DEFINITIONS OF TERMS FOR LINEAR SIGNAL FLOW GRAPHS.
(60 IRE 4.S1) PROC. IRE, V.48, 1611-2 (1960) 30T.

INSTITUTE OF RADIO ENGINEERS. STANDARDS ON CIRCUITS, DEFINITIONS OF TERMS IN THE FIELD OF LINEAR VARYING
PARAMETER AND NONLINEAR CIRCUITS. (53 IRE 4.S1) PROC. IRE. V.42,554-5 (1954) 20T.

INSTITUTE OF RADIO ENGINEERS. STANDARDS ON ELECTRON DEVICES, DEFINITIONS OF SEMICONDUCTOR TERMS.
(54-IRE 7.S2) PROC. IRE, V.42, 1505-8 (1954) 100T.

INSTITUTE OF RADIO ENGINEERS, STANDARDS ON ELECTRON DEVICES, DEFINITIONS OF TERMS RELATED TO MICROWAVE
TUBES (KLYSTRONS, MAGNETRONS/TRAVELING WAVE TUBES) (56 IRE 7.S1) PROC. IRE, V.44. 346-50 (1956) 80T.

INSTITUTE OF RADIO ENGINEERS, STANDARDS ON ELECTRON DEVICES, DEFINITIONS OF TERMS RELATED TO PHOTOTUBES.
(54 IRE 7.S1) PROC.IRE, V.42, 1276-7 (1954) 10T.

INSTITUTE OF RADIO ENGINEERS, STANDARDS ON ELECTRON DEVICES, DEFINITIONS OF TERMS RELATED TO STORAGE
TUBES. (56 IRE 7.S1) PROC.IRE, V.44, 521-2 (1956) 30T.

ENGLISH

INSTITUTE OF RADIO ENGINEERS. STANDARDS ON ELECTRON TUBES, DEFINITIONS OF TERMS. (57 IRE 7.S2) PROC. IRE, V.45, 983-1010 (1957) 800T.

INSTITUTE OF RADIO ENGINEERS. STANDARDS ON ELECTRON TUBES. TR AND ATR TUBE DEFINITIONS. (56 IRE 7.S3) PROC. IRE. V.44, 1037-9 (1956) 50T.

INSTITUTE OF RADIO ENGINEERS. STANDARDS ON ELECTROSTATOGRAPHIC DEVICES. (60 IRE 28.S2) PROC. IRE, V.49, 619-21 (1961) 20T.

INSTITUTE OF RADIO ENGINEERS. STANDARDS ON FACSIMILE, DEFINITIONS OF TERMS. (56 IRE 9.S1) PROC. IRE, V.44, 776-81 (1956) 110T.

INSTITUTE OF RADIO ENGINEERS. STANDARDS ON GRAPHICAL SYMBOLS FOR ELECTRICAL DIAGRAMS. (54 IRE 21.S1) PROC. IRE, V.42, 965-1020 (1954) 500T.

INSTITUTE OF RADIO ENGINEERS. STANDARDS ON GRAPHICAL SYMBOLS FOR SEMICONDUCTOR DEVICES. (57 IRE 21.S3) PROC. IRE V.45, 1612-7 (1957) 100T.

INSTITUTE OF RADIO ENGINEERS. STANDARDS ON MAGNETRONS, DEFINITIONS OF TERMS. (52 IRE 7.S1) PROC. IRE, V.40, 562-3 (1952) 10T.

INSTITUTE OF RADIO ENGINEERS. STANDARDS ON MODULATION SYSTEMS, DEFINITIONS OF TERMS. (53 IRE 11.S1) PROC. IRE, V.41, 612-5 (1953) 60T.

INSTITUTE OF RADIO ENGINEERS. STANDARDS ON NAVIGATION AIDS, DIRECTION FINDER MEASUREMENTS. (ABBRS/DEFS,PP. 1350-2) (59 IRE 12.S1) PROC. IRE, V.47, 1349-71 (1959) 30T.

INSTITUTE OF RADIO ENGINEERS. STANDARDS ON PULSES. DEFINITIONS OF TERMS-PT.2. (52 IRE 20.S1) PROC. IRE, V. 40, 552-4 (1952) 50T.

INSTITUTE OF RADIO ENGINEERS. STANDARDS ON RADIO AIDS TO NAVIGATION, DEFINITIONS OF TERMS. (54 IRE 12.S1) PROC. IRE. V.43, 189-209 (1955) 600T.

INSTITUTE OF RADIO ENGINEERS. STANDARDS ON RADIO TRANSMITTERS, DEFINITIONS OF TERMS. (61 IRE 15.S1) PROC. IRE, V.49, 486-7 (1961) 40T.

INSTITUTE OF RADIO ENGINEERS. STANDARDS ON RECEIVERS, DEFINITIONS OF TERMS. (52 IRE 17.S1) PROC. IRE,V.40, 1681-5 (1952) 100T.

INSTITUTE OF RADIO ENGINEERS. STANDARDS ON SOLID-STATE DEVICES, DEFINITIONS OF SEMICONDUCTOR TERMS. (60 IRE 28.S1) PROC. IRE, V.48, 1772-5 (1960) 90T.

INSTITUTE OF RADIO ENGINEERS. STANDARDS ON SOLID-STATE DEVICES, DEFINITIONS OF TERMS FOR NONLINEAR CAPACITORS. (61 IRE 28.S1) PROC. IRE, V.49, 1279-80 (1961) 20T.

INSTITUTE OF RADIO ENGINEERS. STANDARDS ON TELEVISION, DEFINITIONS OF COLOR TERMS. (55 IRE 22.S1) PROC. IRE, V.43, 742-8 (1955) 110T.

INSTITUTE OF RADIO ENGINEERS. STANDARDS ON TELEVISION, DEFINITIONS OF TELEVISION SIGNAL MEASUREMENT TERMS. (55 IRE 23.S1) PROC. IRE, V.43, 619-22 (1955) 50T.

INSTITUTE OF RADIO ENGINEERS. STANDARDS ON VIDEO TECHNIQUES, DEFINITIONS OF TERMS RELATING TO TELEVISION. (61 IRE 23.S1) PROC. IRE, V.49, 1193-5 (1961) 50T.

JOHNSON, J.R. COLOR TV DICTIONARY. NEW YORK, RIDER, 1954. 70P. 54-9286. 260T.

JUPE, J.H. A DICTIONARY OF TRONS. BRIT. COMMUN. ELECTRON. V. 9, 194-01 (1962) 600T.

MACLANACHAN, W. ET AL. TELEVISION AND RADAR ENCYCLOPAEDIA. ED2. NEW YORK, PITMAN, 1954. 216P. 55-935. 2000T.

MADRID, D.C. GLOSSARY OF ASTRONAUTICS TERMINOLOGY. IRE TRANS. S.E.T. V.5, 73-5 (1959)

MANLY, H.P. DRAKE,S RADIO-TELEVISION ELECTRONIC DICTIONARY. CHICAGO, DRAKE, 1960. 1V. (UNPAGED) 60-4753. 3000T.

MANLY, H.P. AND GORDER, L.O. DRAKE,S CYCLOPEDIA OF RADIO AND ELECTRONICS... ED14. CHICAGO, DRAKE, 1958. 1V. (UNPAGED) 58-4817. 3000T.

NATIONAL RADIO INSTITUTE. RADIO-TELEVISION-ELECTRONICS DICTIONARY. NEW YORK, RIDER, 1962. 190P. 62-21929.

OCECODE.- NAVIGATION ELECTRONICS (LAND, SEA, AIR, SPACE) HILVERSUM, 1962. 282P.

OLDFIELD, R.L. THE PRACTICAL DICTIONARY OF ELECTRICITY AND ELECTRONICS. CHICAGO, AM. TECH. SOC, 1959. 216P. 58-59540. 6000T.

REYNER, J.H. ET AL. THE ENCYCLOPAEDIA OF RADIO AND TELEVISION... ED2. NEW YORK, PHIL. LIBR, 1958. 736P. 58-1326. 4500T.

RYERSON, C.M. GLOSSARY AND DICTIONARY OF TERMS AND DEFINITIONS RELATING SPECIFICALLY TO RELIABILITY. PP. 59-84. 300T. PROC. NATL. SYMP/RELIABILITY/QUALITY CONTROL IN ELECTRONICS, 3D. WASHINGTON, 1957.

SAMS (HOWARD W) AND COMPANY, INC. DICTIONARY OF ELECTRONICS COMMUNICATIONS TERMS. INDIANAPOLIS, 1963. 157P. 63-17018.

ENGLISH

:ILBECK, O. ABC OF FILM AND TV WORKING TERMS. NEW YORK, FOCAL, 1960. 157P. 60-4032. 1400T.

IITH, E.C. GLOSSARY OF TELEPHONE WORDS AND TERMS. REV. ED. HONOLULU, 1954. 50P. 55-15191.

ISSKIND, C. THE ENCYCLOPEDIA OF ELECTRONICS. NEW YORK, REINHOLD, 1962. 974P. 62-13258. 500T.

:EMAINE, H.M. THE AUDIO CYCLOPEDIA.' INDIANAPOLIS, SAMS, 1959. 1269P. 58-14290.

.S. ADVISORY GROUP ON ELECTRONIC PARTS. GLOSSARY OF TECHNICAL TERMS IN THE AGEP AREA OF INTEREST.
IILADELPHIA, UNIV. PENNSYLVANIA, 1960. IV. (VAR.P) 60-62451. 500T.

.S. DEPT. OF DEFENSE. MILITARY STANDARD, ELECTRICAL AND ELECTRONIC SYMBOLS. (MIL-STD, 15A) WASHINGTON,
)54-- 70P. 54-61684.

.S. DEPT. OF DEFENSE. MILITARY STANDARD, PRINTED CIRCUIT TERMS AND DEFINITIONS. (MIL-STD-429)
ISHINGTON, 1957. 4P. 58-62178.

.S. DEPT. OF THE AIR FORCE. COMMUNICATIONS-ELECTRONICS TERMINOLOGY, USAF COMMUNICATIONS- ELECTRONICS
)CTRINE. (AFM100-39) WASHINGTON, 1959-- . 1V. LL. 61-60249.

.S. JOINT CHIEFS OF STAFF. JCEC. STANDARD ABBREVIATIONS. (JANAP 169) WASHINGTON, 1953. 1V. LL.54-61379.

IAT,S THE RIGHT WORD. A DICTIONARY OF COMMON AND UNCOMMON TERMS IN RADIO, TELEVISION, ELECTRONICS. NEW
)RK, R.C.A. INST. 1955. 50P. 55-3357. 500T.

IITE, W.C. THE TRON FAMILY. (LIST OF WORDS WITH TRON SUFFIX) ELECTRONICS, V. 23, 112-4 (1950) 200T.

ITTY, M.B. ET AL. DICTIONARY OF COMMUNICATIONS ABBREVIATIONS, SIGNS, SYMBOLS AND TABLES. NEW YORK,
'TI, 1963. 384P.

ITTY, M.B. ET AL. DICTIONARY OF ELECTRONICS ABBREVIATIONS, SIGNS, SYMBOLS AND TABLES. NEW YORK, SETI,
)63. 416P.

)UNG, V.J. AND JONES, M.W. PICTORIAL MICROWAVE DICTIONARY. NEW YORK, RIDER, 1956. 110P. 56-11738. 350T.

FRENCH

)ITARD, A. DICTIONNAIRE TECHNIQUE ANGLAIS-FRANCAIS DE LA RADIO... (EN*ER RADIO D) PARIS, CHIRON, 1954.
iP. 4000T.

ITERNATIONAL TELECOMMUNICATION UNION. REPERTOIRE DES DEFINITIONS DES TERMES ESSENTIELS UTILISES DANS LE
)MAINE DES TELECOMMUNICATIONS. (EN*FR TELECOMMUN.T) (PT.1. GEN,TEL,TELEG.T) GENEVA, 1957. 300P. 58-36477.
?00T.

ITERNATIONAL TELEPHONE CONSULTATIVE COMMITTEE. PROJET DE REPERTOIRE DES DEFINITIONS DES TERMES
SSENTIELS EN TELEPHONIE. (FR*EN TEL. T) FLORENCE, 1951. 291P. 56-43212.

ING, G.G. DICTIONNAIRE ANGLAIS-FRANCAIS, ELECTRONIQUE, PHYSIQUE NUCLEAIRE, ET SCIENCES CONNEXES. EN*FR
. OF ELECTRON, NUCL. PHYS/RELATED SCI) PARIS, DUNOD, 1959. 311P. 60-20839. 21000T.

ING, G.G. DICTIONNARIE FRANCAIS-ANGLAIS, ELECTRONIQUE, PHYSIQUE NUCLEAIRE ET SCIENCES CONNEXES. (FR*EN
. OF ELECTRON, NUCL. PHYS/RELATED SCI) PARIS, DUNOD, 1961. 395P. 61-4361. 24000T.

ROULX,G.J. DICTIONNAIRE ANGLAIS-FRANCAIS. ELECTRONIQUE ET TELECOMMUNICATIONS. (EN*FR ELECTRON/
:LECOMMUN. D) OTTAWA. 1959. 582P. SUPPL.1, 1960. 30000T.

ROULX, G.J. L.ELECTRONIQUE, GLOSSAIRE ANGLAIS-FRANCAIS. BT-36. (ELECTRON, EN*FR GL) OTTAWA, DEPT.
:CY. STATE, 1955. 39P. 800T.

GERMAN

RNOLDT, . FUNKTECHNISCHES WOERTERBUCH IN DEUTSCHER UND ENGLISCHER SPRACHE.(GE*EN RADIO D) 2V. STUTTGART,
JCHBINDER, 195 .

EAUCHAMP, K.G. GERMAN SEMICONDUCTOR TERMS FOUND IN TECHNICAL LITERATURE. ELEC. DESIGN NEWS, V.4, 60-3
1959)

ACHWOERTERBUCH FUER DAS FERNMELDEWESEN. (TELECOMMUN. D, PT.1, GE*EN, PP.1-293, PT.2, EN*GE, PP.294-307)
RAUNSCHWEIG, WESTERMANN, 1952, 307P.

)EDECKE, W. DIE TRON-GRUPPE, TECHNISCHE BEGRIFFE MIT DER ENDUNG TRON UND IHRE BEDEUTUNG. (TRON FAMILY,
ECH. T. WITH TRON SUFFIX, GE DEFS) RADIO UND FERNSEHEN, NO.21, 22. P.644,680 (1958) 250T.

ERMANY. BUNDESMINISTERIUM FUER DAS POST- UND FERNMELDEWESEN. DEUTSCH-ENGLISCHES UND ENGLISCH-DEUTSCHES
ACHWOERTERBUCH FUER DEN POST-BETRIEBS- UND -VERWALTUNGSDIENST. (*GE*EN D. FOR POSTAL SERV) V.1 GE*EN.
40P) BONN, 1952-- . 59-20557.

UEBENER, E. TASCHENLEXIKON FUER DEN STELLWERKSDIENST. (SIGNALING D, GE DEFS) LEIPZIG, FACHBUCHVERLAG,
955. 115P. 57-16242.

RETZER, K. AND DIEFENBACH, W. HANDBUCH FUER HOCHFREQUENZ- UND ELEKTRO-TECHNIKER. V.5. FACHWOERTERBUCH
IT DEFINITIONEN UND ABBILDUNGEN. (HANDBOOK OF HIGH FREQUENCY/ELEC. ENG. V.5, D. WITH DEFS/ILLUS) BERLIN,
ERLAG RADIO, FOTO, KINOTECHNIK, 1957.

GERMAN

MENGEL, M. KLEINES FERNSEHLEXIKON, ENGLISCH-DEUTSCH, DEUTSCH-ENGLISCH. (*GE*EN TV D) ED3. BERLIN, VEB, 1961. 112P.

MORGENROTH, O. LEXIKON FUER FUNK UND FERNSEHEN. (RADIO/TV D, GE DEFS) BERLIN, SPORT/TECHNIK, 1958. 190P. 59-41969.

RACKOW, H. HANDWOERTERBUCH DES POSTWESENS. (POSTAL SERV. HANDBOOK/SUPPL (1957) GE DEFS) ED2. FRANKFURT/ MAIN, 1953. 827P. 57-41773.

SCHMITZ,W. ENGLISCHES WOERTERBUCH FUER EISENBAHNSIGNALWESEN UND FERNMELDETECHNIK. (*GE*EN D. OF R.R. SIGNALING/TELECOMMUN) V.1 EN*GE,246P. V.2 GE*EN,201P. ED.2 FRANKFURT/MAIN, TETZLAFF, 1954. 54-34312. 6000T.

STELLRECHT, W. AND MIRAM, P. ENGLISCH FUER RADIO-PRAKTIKER. (GE*EN RADIO T) MUNICH, FRANZIS,1955.64P.

U.S. PATENT OFFICE. GLOSSARY OF GERMAN WORDS USED IN PATENT LITERATURE RELATING TO COMMUNICATIONS, ELECTRICITY AND ELECTRONICS. WASHINGTON, 1961. 21P. 900T.

GREEK

ANDRIKOPOULOS, M.C. ENCYCLOPEDIE ANGLO-HELLENIQUE DE TERMES D,ELECTRONIQUE, D,ELECTRICITE... PIRAEUS, KOUNTOURI, 1961. 720P.

MPATAIMES, D.I. LEXIKON TELEPIKOINONIAS. (TELECOMMUN. D, *GR*EN) ATHENS, 1952. 495P. 55-21483. 3250T.

ITALIAN

BIZZARRI, L. DIZIONARIO ITALIANO INGLESE-INGLESE ITALIANO DEI TERMINI DI RADIO E TELEVISIONE. (*IT*EN RADIO/TV T) ROME, 1958-59. 2V.IN 1. 222+16P. A58-5939.

FERRARO, A. ENCICLOPEDIA DELLA... RADIO-TECNICA-TELEVISIONE E ARGOMENTI CONNESSI. (RADIO ENG. TV ENCYCL. IT DEFS) 2V. FLORENCE, SANSONI, 1954. 818+839P. A55-5828.

JAPANESE

BROADCASTING CORPORATION OF JAPAN. DICTIONARY OF TERMS OF TELEVISION TECHNIQUE AND DIRECTION... (JA EN) TOKYO, TOKYO RADIO SERV. CENTER, 1955. 242P.

DEMPA KOHO YOGO JITEN. (ELEC. NAVIGATION D, *EN*JA) TOKYO, KAIUNDO, 1959. J60-124. 2400T.

IZUMI, H. ANNOTATED TERMINOLOGY OF RADIO AND TELEVISION. (*JA*EN) TOKYO, SEIBUNDO SHINKOSHA, 1953. 241P.

JAPAN. MINISTRY OF EDUCATION. GLOSSARY OF ELECTRIC ENGINEERING, TELEPHONY AND TELEGRAPHY. (EN*JA) TOKYO, 1952. 116P.

JAPAN. MINISTRY OF EDUCATION. RADIO COMMUNICATIONS VOCABULARY... (EN*JA) TOKYO, 1952. 42P. 410T.

MORITA, K. SAISHIN JITSUYO RAJIO, TEREBI YOGO JITEN. (NEW PRACT. RADIO/TV D, JA*EN) TOKYO, RAJIOKAGAKU, 1960. 744P. J61-822. 6500T.

RAJIO TOKYO. TEREBI RAJIO JITEN. (TV, RADIO D, JA*EN) TOKYO, ASAHI SHIMBUN, 1959. 46+310+33P. J62-184. 1200T.

TOKYO RADIO INSTITUTE. DICTIONARY OF RADIO, TELEVISION AND PHONOGRAPH. (*JA*EN) TOKYO, SANKYO, 1955. 347P.

POLYGLOT

ACADEMY OF THE HEBREW LANGUAGE, JERUSALEM. MILON LE-MUNAHE HA-TELEFONAUT. (TEL. D, HE EN FR GE) JERUSALEM, 1957. 318P. A59-7636.

BABANI, B.B. INTERNATIONAL RADIO TUBE ENCYCLOPAEDIA. (*CZ*DA*DU*EN*FR*GE*HE*IT*NO*PL*PR*RU*SP*SW*TU) ED3. LONDON, BERNARDS, 1958. VAR,P. 59-3704.

BARGIN, B.G. AND BUCHINSKII, A.S. SEMIIAZYCHNYI SLOVAR PO ELEKTRONIKE I VOLNOVODAM. (D. OF ELECTRON/ WAVEGUIDES, *RU*EN*DU*FR*GE*IT*SP) MOSCOW, FIZMATGIZ, 1961. 263P. 62-65717. 2000T.

BARGIN, B.G. AND BUCHINSKI, A.S. SEMIIAZYCHNYI SLOVAR PO TELEVIDENIIU, RADIOLOKATSII I ANTENNAM. (TV, RADAR/ANTENNAS D, *DU*EN*FR*GE*IT*RU*SP) MOSCOW, FIZMATGIZ, 1961. 244P. 62-65715. 2200T. (SEE CLASON BELOW)

BINCER, S. TYSIAC SLOW O TELEWIZJI. (1000 TV T, PL EN GE RU) WARSAW, ARS POLONA, 1961. 250P.

CENTRO INTERNAZIONALE RADIO MEDICO. MEDRAD. ISTRUZIONI PER LA COMPILAZIONE DEI MESSAGGI RADIO-MEDICI (IN LINGUA ITALIANA, INGLESE, FRANCESE)(INSTR.FOR COMP.RADIO-MEDICAL MESSAGES. IT EN FR) ROME, AERONAUTICA, STAB.FOTOMECCANICO, 1952. 220P. 59-27878.

CLASON, W.E. ELSEVIER,S DICTIONARY OF AMPLIFICATION, MODULATION, RECEPTION, AND TRANSMISSION IN 6 LANGUAGES. *EN/AM*DU*FR*GE*IT*SP. NEW YORK, ELSEVIER. 1960. 804P. 60-7173. 2900T.

CLASON, W.E. ELSEVIER,S DICTIONARY OF ELECTRONICS AND WAVEGUIDES. (*EN/AM*DU*FR*GE*IT*SP) NEW YORK, ELSEVIER, 1957. 628P. 57-11038. 2000T.

TELECOMMUNICATION ENGINEERING

POLYGLOT

ASON, W.E. ELSEVIER,S DICTIONARY OF TELEVISION, RADAR, AND ANTENNAS IN 6 LANGUAGES, *EN/AM*DU*FR*GE*IT P. NEW YORK, ELSEVIER, 1955. 760P. 55-6216. 2400T.

ASON, W.E. SUPPLEMENT TO THE ELSEVIER DICTIONARIES OF ELECTRONICS, NUCLEONICS AND TELECOMMUNICATION. EN/AM*DU*FR*GE*IT*SP) NEW YORK, ELSEVIER, 1963. 633P. 63-11369. 2500T.

NMARK. TEKNISKE BIBLIOTHEK. RADIOTEKNISK ORDLISTE. TERMINOLOGI VEDRORENDE RADIO OG FJERNSYN. (RADIO/ D,*DA*EN*FR*GE*SW) COPENHAGEN, 1954. 330P. 1500T.

)SCHINSKY, W.J. ET AL. ELECTRONIC DICTIONARY...(EN FR GE SP) NEW YORK, CALDWELL-CLEMENTS, 1956. 64P. -27775.

RMANY (FEDERAL REPUBLIC, 1949-) BUNDESMINISTERIUM FUER DAS POST- UND FERNMELDEWESEN. VERZEICHNIS DER DEWENDUNGEN IM ENTSTOERUNGS- UND MESSDIENST AN INTERNATIONALEN FERNSPRECH-, TELEGRAPHEN- UND LDLEITUNGEN. (IDIOMS IN INTERFERENCE/MEAS. SERV, INTL. TELECOMMUN, GE FR EN) BONN, 1955. 119P.

DEDECKE, W. AMERIKANISCHE, DEUTSCHE, ENGLISCHE UND FRANZOESISCHE KURZWOERTER UND ABKUERZUNGEN VON CHAUSDRUECKEN, MASSEINHEITEN UND FACHORGANISATIONEN DES NACHRICHTENWESENS UND VERWANDTER GEBIETE. TELECOMMUN/ABBR. *GE*AM/EN*FR) BERLIN, TECHNIK, 1958. 116P. 61-45256. 3300T.

DEDECKE, W. KURZWOERTER UND ABKUERZUNGEN DES NACHRICHTENWESENS... (TELECOMMUN. ABBR, *GE*EN*FE) BERLIN, EB, 1963. 116P.

DEDECKE, W. TECHNISCHE ABKUERZUNGEN, DEUTSCH-ENGLISCH-FRANZOESISCH... FUNKTECHNIK, FERNSEHEN... ERNTECHNIK... ELEKTROTECHNIK... (TECH. ABBRS, *GE*EN*FR, TELECOMMUN, NUCL/ELEC. ENG) WIESBADEN, RANDSTETTER, 1961. 288P. 63-29594. 5000T.

NTERNATIONAL ADVISORY COUNCIL FOR TELECOMMUNICATION. REDEWENDUNGEN IM INTERNATIONALEN FERNSPRECH-ETRIEBSDIENTS. (IDIOMS IN INTL. SERV, GE EN FR RU) GENEVA, 1952. 48P.

NTERNATIONAL ELECTRONIC TUBE HANDBOOK. (EN*DU*FR*GE*IN*IT*PR*SP*SW) ED3. BUSSUM, NETHERLANDS, DE UIDERKRING, 1955. 334P. 100T.

NTERNATIONAL ELECTROTECHNICAL COMMISSION. INTERNATIONAL ELECTROTECHNICAL VOCABULARY. SIGNALING AND ECURITY APPARATUS FOR RAILWAYS. *FR*EN*DU*GE*IT*PL*SP*SW. (IEC-50-GR-31) ED2. GENEVA, 1959. 46P.

NTERNATIONAL ELECTROTECHNICAL COMMISION. INTERNATIONAL ELECTROTECHNICAL VOCABULARY. WAVEGUIDES. *FR*EN DU*GE*IT*PL*SP*SW. (IEC-50-GR-62) ED2. GENEVA. (IN PREP) 150T.

NTERNATIONAL ELECTROTECHNICAL COMMISSION. MEZHDUNARODNYI ELEKTROTEKHNICHESKII SLOVAR. (INTL. LECTROTECH. VOC) (IEC 50-GR-07) ELEKTRONIKA. (ELECTRON. *RU*EN*DU*FR*GE*IT*PL*SP*SW) ED2. MOSCOW, IZMATGIZ, 1959. 335P. 700T.

NTERNATIONAL ELECTROTECHNICAL COMMISSION. SLOVENSKI ELEKTROTEHNISKI SLOVAR. (SV VERSION OF IEC 0-GR-07) ELEKTRONIKA. (ELECTRON, SV*FR*EN*GE*IT) ED2. LJUBLJANA, ELEKTROTEHN. DRUSTVA SLOVEN, 1959. 71P. 61-26371. 700T.

NTERNATIONAL TELECOMMUNICATION UNION. CODES ET ABREVIATIONS A L,USAGE DES SERVICES INTERNATIONAUX DE ELECOMMUNICATIONS. (CODES/ABBRS, INTL TELECOMMUN, FR EN SP) GENEVA, 1958. 312P.

INTERNATIONAL TELEPHONE AND TELEGRAPH CONSULTATIVE COMMITTEE. VOCABULARY OF BASIC TERMS USED IN LINE TRANSMISSION. (*EN*FR*GE*RU*SP*IT*DU*PL*PR*SW) GENEVA, 1959. 108P.

KERKHOF, H. AND GRAS, M. FACHWOERTERBUCH DER FERNMELDETECHNIK UND ELEKTRONIK. (TELECOMMUN/ELECTRON.D) V.1,ABBR. V.2, EN*GE*FR. V.3, GE*FR*EN. V.4, FR*EN*GE. HAMM, WESTF.GROTE, 1956-- . 57-23532.

KERKHOF, H. AND GRAS, M. FACHWOERTERBUCH DER FERNMELDETECHNIK UND ELEKTRONIK. (TELECOMMUN/ELECTRON D) V.1. LEXIKON ENGLISH-AMERIKANISCHER ABKUERZUNGEN. (GL. OF EN/AM ABBRS, *EN*GE*FR) HAMM, WESTF. GROTE, 1956. 264P. 57-23532. 7500T.

KHAIKIN, S.E. SLOVAR RADIOLIUBITELIA. (RADIO-AMATEUR D, RU DEFS,*EN*FR*GE INDEX) ED2. MOSCOW, GOSENERGIZDAT, 1960. 607P. 60-34171.

MIKOLAJCZYK, P. UNIVERSAL VADE-MECUM. (ELECTRON-TUBE D, PL*EN*FR*GE*IT*RU*SP) V.1,ELECTRON TUBES/ SEMICONDUCTOR ELEM. NEW YORK, PERGAMON, 1960- . 60-53074.

MONTU, E. TELEVISIONE. (TV GL, IT EN FR GE, PP.455-6) ED3. MILAN, RADIOGIORN, 1952. 456P. A52-6129.

NAZVOSLOVI SDELOVACI TECHNIKY. PRENOS VEDENIM. (TELECOMMUN. T, TRANSMISSION LINES, *CZ*RU*FR*EN*GE*SP) PRAGUE, CSN, 1954. 122P.

NORWAY. RADET FOR TEKNISK TERMINOLOGI. ELECTRONIC VALVES AND TAPE RECORDERS. (RTT-9) (*EN*GE*NO) OSLO, 1962. 37P.

NORWAY. RADET FOR TEKNISK TERMINOLOGI. OSCILLATORY CIRCUITS AND WAVE GUIDES. (RTT-5) (*EN*GE*NO) OSLO, 1960. 20P.

NORWAY. RADET FOR TEKNISK TERMINOLOGI. RADIO TRANSMITTERS AND RECEIVERS. (RTT-8) '(*EN*GE*NO) OSLO, 1961. 37P.

NORWAY. RADET FOR TEKNISK TERMINOLOGI. RADIO WAVES. (RTT-2) (*EN*GE*NO) OSLO, 1959. 16P.

NORWAY. RADET FOR TEKNISK TERMINOLOGI. TELEVISION. (RTT-3) (*EN*GE*NO) OSLO, 1959. 28P.

153

POLYGLOT

PLOEHN, H. FUNK- UND FERNMELDEANLAGEN. (RADIO/TELEG. D, EN FR GE RU. BERLIN, VEB, 1962. 1001P. 1200C

RINT, C. LEXIKON DER HOCHFREQUENZ- , NACHRICHTEN- UND ELEKTROTECHNIK. (HIGH-FREQUENCY, TELECOMMUN/ELEC ENG.D, GE*EN*FR*RU) 4V. BERLIN, TECHNIK, 1957-1961. 58-3142. 20000T.

SHORT GUIDE TO RADIO NAVIGATION AND AIR TRAFFIC CONTROL. (*EN*FR*GE*SP) INTERAVIA, V.13, 607-10 (1958) 70T.

TELEVISNI NAZVOSLOVI. (TV T,*CZ*SP*RU*EN*FR*GE) PRAGUE, CSN, 1954. 133P.

THALI, H. TECHNICAL DICTIONARY OF TERMS USED IN ELECTRICAL ENGINEERING, RADIO, TELEVISION, TELECOMMUNICATION. (V.1 EN*GE*FR, ED6. 280P. 15000T. V.2 GE*EN*FR, ED4. 311P. 24000T. V.3 FR*EN*GE*, IN PREP) LUCERNE, THALI, 1960-- . 62-822.

U.S.S.R. MINISTERSTVO SVIAZI. KRATKII ANGLO-FRANKO-RUSSKII SLOVAR TERMINOV PO TELEGRAFII I FOTOTELEGRAFII. (EN*FR*RU TELEG/PHOTOTELEG.GL) MOSCOW, 1958. 48P.

UNION POSTALE UNIVERSELLE. BUREAU INTERNATIONAL. VOCABULAIRE POLYGLOTTE DU SERVICE POSTAL INTERNATIONAL (PO POSTAL SERV. D, FR EN GE...) BERN, 1963.

VISSER, A. ELSEVIER.S TELECOMMUNICATION DICTIONARY IN 6 LANGUAGES,*EN/AM*DU*FR*GE*IT*SP. NEW YORK, ELSEVIER, 1960. 1011P. 58-10159. 9900T.

VISSER, A. ZESTALIG TECHNISCH WOORDENBOEK IN HOOFDZAAK BETREFFENDE DE VERREBERICHTGEVING. (6-LANG.D.OF TELECOMMUN.*DU*EN*FR*GE*IT*SP) THE HAGUE, PTT, 1955. 778P. 4LL. SUPPL. 1956-57. 56-27958. 8700T.

RUSSIAN

AKADEMIIA NAUK SSSR. KOM.TEKH.TERM. ELEKTROVAKUUMNYE PRIBORY... (D. OF ELECTRON-TUBE DEVICES, RU DEFS) (SB.REK.TERM*NO.54) MOSCOW, 1960. 20P. 62-32953.

AKADEMIIA NAUK SSSR. KOM. TEKH. TERM. TEORIIA NADEZHNOSTI V OBLASTI RADIOELEKTRONIKI... TERMINOLOGIIA. (THEORY OF RELIABILITY IN RADIO/ELECTRON, RU DEFS) (SB. REK. TERM. NO.60) MOSCOW, 1962. 46P. '63-3323

AKADEMIIA NAUK SSSR. KOM.TEKH.TERM. TERMINOLOGIIA ELEKTROVAKUUMNYKH PRIBOROV. (D. OF ELECTRON-TUBE DEVICES, RU DEFS) (SB.REK.TERM.NO.39) MOSCOW, 1956. 47P.56-42962. 180T.

AKADEMIIA NAUK SSSR. KOM.TEKH.TERM. TERMINOLOGIIA RASPROSTRANENIIA RADIOVOLN. (RADIO-WAVE PROPAGATION, RU DEFS) (SB. REK. TERM. NO.47) MOSCOW, 1957. 28P. 120T.

CLASON, W.E. ELSEVIER.S DICTIONARY OF AMPLIFICATION, MODULATION, RECEPTION AND TRANSMISSION. RUSSIAN SUPPL. NEW YORK, ELSEVIER, 1961. 87P. 2900T.

CLASON, W.E. ELSEVIER.S DICTIONARY OF ELECTRONICS AND WAVEGUIDES. RUSSIAN SUPPL. NEW YORK, ELSEVIER, 1961. 57P. 2000T.

DOZOROV, N.I. ANGLO-RUSSKII SLOVAR PO RADIOELEKTRONIKE. (EN*RU RADIO/ELECTRON. D) MOSCOW, VOENIZDAT, 1959. 535P. 60-19763. 20000T.

DOZOROV, N.I. DOPOLNENIE K ANGLO-RUSSKOMU SLOVARIU PO RADIOELEKTRONIKE I SVIAZI. (SUPPL. TO EN*RU RADIO/ELECTRON D) MOSCOW, ATOMIZDAT, 1959. 115P. 3300T.

DOZOROV, N.I. DOPOLNENIE (VTOROE) K ANGLO-RUSSKOMU SLOVARIU PO RADIOELEKTRONIKE I SVIAZI. (SUPPL. 2 EN*RU RADIO/ELECTRON. D) MOSCOW, ATOMIZDAT, 1960. 68P.

EIDELMAN, L. ANGLO-RUSSKII SLOVAR PO PROVODNOI SVIAZI. (EN*RU TEL/TELEG. T) MOSCOW, GITTL, 1957. 712P

GERMAN-PROZOROVA, L.P. ET AL. ANGLO-RUSSKII RADIOTEKHNICHESKII SLOVAR. (EN*RU RADIO ENG. D) MOSCOW, FIZMATGIZ, 1960. 524P. 60-40798. 25000T.

GERMAN-PROZOROVA, L.P. ET AL. ANGLO-RUSSKII SLOVAR PO TELEVIDENIIU. (EN*RU TV D) MOSCOW, FIZMATGIZ, 1960. 429P. 61-39428. 12000T.

GLUZMAN, I.S. ANGLO-RUSSKII SLOVAR PO ZHELEZNODOROZHNOI AVTOMATIKE, TELEMEKHANIKE I SVIAZI. (EN*RU D. C R.R. SIGNALING/COMMUN) MOSCOW, FIZMATGIZ, 1958. 427P. 59-33853. 16000T.

IZAKOVA, O.N. ANGLO-RUSSKII SLOVAR TERMINOV PO POLUPROVODNIKOVOI ELEKTRONIKE. (EN*RU D. OF SEMICONDUCTC ELECTRON) MOSCOW, GOS. KOM. AVTOMAT/MASHINOSTR, 1959. 48P. 400T.

SAPOZHNIKOVA, M.K. SLOVAR TERMINOV PO NADEZHNOSTI. (D. OF RELIABILITY, RU TRANSL. OF RYERSON, C.M, D. C RELIABILITY/QUALITY CONTROL IN ELECTRON) MOSCOW, GOS. KOM. RADIOELEKTRON, 1959. 112P. 300T.

SCHULTZ, G.F. RUSSIAN VACUUM-TUBE TERMINOLOGY. PROC. IRE, V.44, 112 (1956) 30T.

U.S. DEPT. OF THE ARMY. ANGLO-RUSSKII SLOVAR PO RADIOELEKTRONIKE I SVIAZI. (REPR. OF *EN*RU ELECTRON.D, U.S.ARMY, 1956) MOSCOW, ATOMIZDAT, 1959. 548P. 59-52764. 25000T.

U.S. DEPT. OF THE ARMY. ENGLISH-RUSSIAN, RUSSIAN-ENGLISH ELECTRONICS DICTIONARY. (TM30-545) WASHINGTON 1956. 944P. 58-3291. 25000T.

U.S.S.R. MINISTERSTVO SVIAZI. ANGLO-RUSSKII SLOVAR PO PROVODNOI I POCHTOVOI SVIAZI. (*EN*RU D. OF TEL, TELEG/ POSTAL COMMUN) MOSCOW, 1961. 474P. 14000T.

SLOVAK

LOVENSKA AKADEMIA VIED. TERMINOLOGIA TELEVIZIE. (TV T, SL DEFS) BRATISLAVA, 1956 52P. 61-49184.

ACLAVIK, J. ANGLICKE ODBORNE TEXTY PRO POSLUCHACE FAK- RADIOTECHNIKY. (EN*SL GL. FOR RADIO LISTENERS) RAGUE, SNTL, 1957. 199P.

SPANISH

RTIGAS, J.A. VERSION ESPANOLA DEL VOCABULARIO ELECTROTECNICO INTERNACIONAL. (SP VERSION OF INTL. LECTROTECH.D) MADRID, COM. NACL. ELECTROTEC. (IEC) 1959. 301P.

CARTER,H. DICCIONARIO DE ELECTRONICA. (ELECTRON.D, SP*EN) BUENOS AIRES, LERU, 1962. 419P. 3000T.

AMIREZ-VILLARREAL, H. DICCIONARIO ILUSTRADO DE ELECTRONICA, ESPANOL-INGLES E INGLES-ESPANOL. (ILLUS. SP*EN D. OF ELECTRON) MEXICO, D.F, DIANA, 1961. 182P. 63-28223.

ELL,L.L. ENGLISH-SPANISH COMPREHENSIVE TECHNICAL DICTIONARY OF AIRCRAFT, AUTOMOBILE, ELECTRICITY, RADIO, ELEVISION, PETROLEUM,STEEL PRODUCTS... NEW YORK, MCGRAW-HILL, 1960. 1079P. 61-3462. 525000T.

ERMINOLOGIA USUAL EN LA CIENCIA Y EN LA TECNICA DE LA TELECOMUNICACION. (TELECOMMUN. T, SP DEFS) MADRID, 1959. 135P.

SWEDISH

ANDO, B. AND SCHROEDER, J. ENGELSK-SVENSK RADIOTEKNISK ORDLISTA. (EN*SW RADIO ENG.D) STOCKHOLM, NORDISK ROTOGRAVYR, 1954. 62P. A55-1519.

CLASON, W.E. ELSEVIER,S DICTIONARY OF ELECTRONICS AND WAVEGUIDES. SWEDISH SUPPL. NEW YORK, ELSEVIER, 1960. 43P. 2000T.

ONNERMARK, A. SVENSK-ENGELSK OCH ENGELSK-SVENSK ORDBOK FOER TELETJAENSTEN. (*SW*EN TELECOMMUN. D) STOCKHOLM, 1960. 156P.

TEXTILE CHEMISTRY, ENGINEERING, AND RESEARCH

ENGLISH

AMERICAN FABRICS. ENCYCLOPEDIA OF TEXTILES. ENGLEWOOD CLIFFS, N.J, PRENTICE HALL, 1960. 702P. 59-8054.

AMERICAN SOCIETY FOR TESTING/MATERIALS. STANDARD DEFINITIONS OF TERMS RELATING TO TEXTILE MATERIALS... (D123-62) .ASTM STDS, PT.10, SUPPL, 4-56. PHILADELPHIA, 1962. 1200T.

BLACKSHAW, H. AND BRIGHTMAN, R. DICTIONARY OF DYEING AND TEXTILE PRINTING. NEW YORK, INTERSCIENCE, 1961. 221P. 61-65748. 2000T.

BRITISH STANDARDS INSTITUTION. GLOSSARY OF TERMS RELATING TO SILK. (B.S. 2804) LONDON, 1956. 8P. 10T.

BRITISH STANDARDS INSTITUTION. GLOSSARY OF TERMS USED BY THE LIGHT CLOTHING INDUSTRY. (B.S. 1903) LONDON, 1952. 12P. 30T.

BRITISH STANDARDS INSTITUTION. GLOSSARY OF TERMS. WOVEN APPAREL FABRICS CONTAINING WOOL. (B.S. 2020. AMEND. PD 3836, 1960) LONDON, 1953. 8P. 10T.

BRITISH STANDARDS INSTITUTION. PRINCIPLES AND TERMS FOR THE DESCRIPTION OF FABRICS... (B.S. 3257, AMEND. PD4131, 1961) LONDON, 1960. 20P. 80T.

DENNY, G.G. FABRICS. ED8. PHILADELPHIA, LIPPINCOTT, 1962. 163P. 63-7030.

LENNOX-KERR, P. INDEX TO MAN-MADE FIBRES OF THE WORLD. MANCHESTER, ENG, MAN-MADE TEXTILES, 1961. 117P. 62-51652.

LINTON, G.E. THE MODERN TEXTILE DICTIONARY. NEW YORK, DUELL,SLOAN/PEARCE, 1954. 772P. 54-8300. 14000T.

MARKS, S.S. FAIRCHILD,S DICTIONARY OF TEXTILES. NEW YORK, FAIRCHILD, 1959. 627P. 58-13421. 12000T.

POCKET TEXTILE DICTIONARY...NEW YORK, KOGOS, 1962. 60P. 62-9023.

PRESS, J.J. MAN-MADE TEXTILE ENCYCLOPEDIA. NEW YORK, TEXTILE BOOK, 1959. 913P. 59-15700.

PRITCHARD, M.E. A SHORT DICTIONARY OF WEAVING, INCLUDING SOME SPINNING, DYEING AND TEXTILE TERMS...NEW YORK, PHIL. LIBR, 1956. 196P. 56-13754.

SOCIETY OF DYERS AND COLOURISTS. COLOUR INDEX. ED2. LOWELL, MASS, AM. ASSOC. TEXTILE/CHEM COLORISTS, 1956-1960. 4V. 57-908.

TEXTILE INSTITUTE. TEXTILE TERMS AND DEFINITIONS. ED4. MANCHESTER, ENG, 1960. 167P. 62-701. 1600T

WITHERS, J.C. TEXTILE TERMS AND DEFINITIONS. ASLIB PROC, V.4, 25-100 (1952)

WOMEN,S WEAR DAILY. FABRIC FACTS. NEW YORK, FAIRCHILD, 1961. 98P. 61-65866. 700T.

ZIELINSKI, S.A. ENCYCLOPEDIA OF HANDWEAVING. NEW YORK,FUNK/WAGNALLS, 1959. 190P. 59-11308. 800T.

FRENCH

BERNUY,J. TERMINOLOGIE DES TEXTILES - GLOSSAIRE ANGLAIS-FRANCAIS. (BT-58) (TEXTILE T, EN*FR GL) OTTAWA, DEPT.SECY.STATE, 1957. 11P. 200T.

FRANCE.AMBASSADE. U.S. FILATURE ET TISSAGE DU COTON, AMERICAN-FRANCAIS. (EN*FR COTTON SPINNING/WEAVING GL) WASHINGTON, 1953. 79P. 1400T.

GERMAN

BAUER, R. CHEMIEFASER-LEXIKON. (SYNTHETIC FIBERS D, GE DEFS) ED3. FRANKFURT/MAIN, DEUT. FACHVERLAG, 1963. 126P.

BOLTON, H. GEWEBE-LEXIKON (TEXTILE D, GE DEFS) HERFORD, W. GERMANY, BUSSE. (IN PREP)

DE VRIES, L. WOERTERBUCH DER TEXTILINDUSTRIE. (TEXTILE IND. D) (V.1, GE*EN, 386P. V.2, EN*GE, 368P) WIESBADEN, BRANDSTETTER, 1959-1960. 59-42656. 15000T.

FISCHER-BOBSIEN, C.H. LEXIKON TEXTILVEREDLUNG UND GRENZGEBIETE (TEXTILE FINISHING D, GE DEFS) DUELMEN, GERMANY, LAUMANN, 1960. 2386P. A61-5015.

HELLMICH, K. DAMIT KLEIDET SICH DIE WELT, ABC DER TEXTIL-ROHSTOFFE. (HOW THE WORLD DRESSES, ABC OF TEXTILE-RAW MATER, GE DEFS) ED2. DUESSELDORF, ABC STOFFKUNDE, 1959. 135P. A61-287.

HOFER, A. ILLUSTRIERTES TEXTIL-LEXIKON. (ILLUS.TEXTILE D, GE DEFS) FRANKFURT/MAIN, DEUT. FACHVERLAG, 1961. 137P. A62-2686.

HUENLICH, R. TEXTIL-FACHWOERTERBUCH. (TEXTILE D, GE DEFS) BERLIN, SCHIELE/SCHOEN, 1958. 140P. 1500T.

KOCH, AND SATLOW, . LEXIKON DES GESAMTEN TEXTILWESENS.(TEXTILE D, GE DEFS) STUTTGART, DEUT. VERLAGS-ANSTALT. (IN PREP)

KRETSCHMER, R. TEXTILFAERBEREI UND ANGRENZENDE GEBIETE. ENGLISCH-DEUTSCH, DEUTSCH-ENGLISCH. (TEXTILE DYEING..., *GE*EN D) BERLIN, TECHNIK, 1961. 181P. 4600T.

LOHSE, R. WEBWAREN VON A BIS Z. (WOVEN FABRICS, A TO Z, GE DEFS) ED3. LEIPZIG, FACHBUCHVERLAG, 1956. 124P. 56-46581. 1200T.

MASCHEN ABC. KLEINES LEXIKON FUER WIRK- UND STRICKWAREN. (ABC OF WOVEN/KNIT GOODS, GE DEFS) BERLIN, MATTHESS, 1959. 40P. 1000T.

MEYER,E. APPRETURKUNDE. WIRK-UND STRICKWAREN. (TEXTILE FINISHING. KNIT/WOVEN FABRICS, GE DEFS) ED2. BERLIN, VOLK/WISSEN, 1952. 135P.

POLANYI, M. DICTIONARY OF TEXTILE TERMS. (*GE*EN) ED2. NEW YORK, PERGAMON, 1956. 328P. 56-58903. 10000T.

RUSCHA FACHWOERTERBUCH DER TEXTILKUNDE. (TEXTILE D, GE DEFS) ED2. CHUR, SWITZERLAND, SCHALTEGGER, 1956. 186P. A56-6420.

SCHAEFFER,A. ENCYCLOPAEDIE DER GESAMTEN TEXTILVEREDLUNG.(TEXTILE FINISHING ENCYCL, GE DEFS) WIESBADEN, SAENDIG, 1961. 80P.

SCHWANDT, W. KLEINES TEXTIL-LEXIKON... (TEXTILE D, GE DEFS) HAMBURG, HANSEAT, 1955. 115P. A55-6532. 200T.

TECHNOLOGICAL DICTIONARY FOR INDUSTRIES CONSUMING DYESTUFFS AND TEXTILE AUXILIARIES. PT.1, EN*GE, 627P. PT.2, GE*EN, 489P. FRANKFURT, FARBWERKE HOECHST, 1952.

UHLMANN, H. TERMINOLOGIE IN DER WIRKEREI UND STRICKEREI. (KNITTING/WEAVING T, GE DEFS) HEIDELBERG, MELLIAND, 1954. 46P. 59-38938.

UHLMANN, H. TERMINOLOGIE IN DER WIRKEREI UND STRICKEREI. (KNITTING//WEAVING T, EN*GE) MELLIAND-TEXTILBER, V.36-7, FF (1955-6) 500T.

WIEGEL,K. TEXTILTECHNISCHES ENGLISCH. (TEXTILE D, *GE*EN) ESSEN, GIRARDET, 1952.

HINDI

SADGOPAL, , AND KAUSHAL, S.C. TEXTILE TECHNOLOGY AND PLASTICS, ENGLISH-HINDI DICTIONARY. ALLAHABAD, HINDI SAHITYA SAMMELAN. 195-.

ITALIAN

DIZIONARIO TECNICO-COMMERCIALE,ITALIANO-INGLESE E INGLESE-ITALIANO PAR L,INDUSTRIA COTONIERA. (*IT*EN D. FOR COTTON IND) ROME, 1955. 137P.

DIZIONARIO TESSILE LANIERO, INGLESE-ITALIANO, ITALIANO-INGLESE. (*IT*EN WOOL D) VICENZA, LANEROSSI, 1958. 160P. 62-31333. 6400T.

JAPANESE

JAPAN. MINISTRY OF EDUCATION. VOCABULARY OF FIBRES (EN*JA) TOKYO, 1950. 171P.

JAPANESE

PON GAKUJUTSU SHINKOKAI. DAI 120 (SENSHOKU KAKO) IINKAI. SENI SENSHOKU KAKO JITEN. (TEXTILE
/FINISH. D, *JA*EN) TOKYO, NIKKAN KOGYO SHIMBUNSHA. 1962. 605+39P. J63-101. 3900T.

POLYGLOT

TANY, F. DICTIONARY OF TEXTILES. (SP EN FR) LONDON, BAILEY, 195 . 482P.

RY, J. VOCABULAIRE TEXTILE TRILINGUE. (TEXTILE D, *FR*EN*GE) TROYES, 1962. 2V.

IERKIEWICZ, W. PODRECZNY SLOWNIK WLOKIENNICZY W 5 JEZYKACH... (TEXTILE T,*PL*EN*FR*GE*RU) WARSAW,
STW. WYDAW. TECH, 1955. 305P. 55-38912. 4600T.

HAUSDRUECKE AUF DEM GEBIET DES TEXTILEN PRUEFWESENS FUER CHEMIEFASERN. (TEST.T.FOR CHEM.TEXTILE FIBERS,
EN FR) RAYON ZELLWOLLE, V.7(1957) FF.

EDERIKSEN, P.S. DANSK-SVENSK-ENGELSK OG SVENSK-DANSK-ENGELSK LOMMEORDBOG FOR HORERHVERVET. (*DA*SW*EN
CKET D. FLAX IND) KOLDING, TIDSSKR. LIN, 1956. 38P. 62-31339. 1500T.

NDBUCH DER SCHWEIZERISCHEN TEXTILINDUSTRIE. (SWISS TEXTILE IND. HANDBOOK...GE EN FR) ZURICH,
RTSCHAFTSLIT, 1954. 172P. 55-29576. 160T.

PERIAL CHEMICAL INDUSTRIES LTD. A VOCABULARY OF TECHNICAL TERMS USED IN THE TEXTILE AND RELATED
DUSTRIES. (*EN*FR*GE) MANCHESTER, 1958. 103P.

NK, P. DICCIONARIO LANERO. (WOOL D, EN SP FR GE) ED3. BUENOS AIRES, 1954, 199P. 59-2078. 800T.

NK, P. ENCICLOPEDIA TEXTIL. (TEXTILE ENCYCL, *SP*EN*FR*GE) ED2. BUENOS AIRES, 1956. 774P.

REPKA, A. TEXTILE DICTIONARY. (*EN/AM*FR*IT*SP*SW*GE) NEW YORK, ELSEVIER. (IN PREP)

PPINCK, P. AND PAOLO, E. PICCOLO DIZIONARIO TESSILE IN CINQUE LINGUE... (TEXTILE D..., IT*EN*FR*GE*SP)
ME, E.L.S.A, 1956. 226P. A56-5439.

HLOHMANN, A. ILLUSTRIERTES TECHNISCHES WOERTERBUCH. (ILLUS.TECH. D, GE*EN*FR*IT*RU*SP) V.14, FASERN
D ROHSTOFFE. (TEXTILE FIBERS/RAW MATER) V.15, SPINNEREI UND GESPINSTE. (SPINNING) V.16, WEBEREI UND
WEBE. (WEAVING) MUNICH, OLDENBOURG, 1956-1958. (REPR)

INNER,S COTTON TRADE DICTIONARY OF THE WORLD. (EN*FR*GE*IT*PR*SP) MANCHESTER, ENG, SKINNER, 1953.
48P.

INNER,S WOOL TRADE DIRECTORY OF THE WORLD. (EN*FR*GE*IT*PR*SP) BRADFORD, ENG, SKINNER, 1952,
-14741.

UOMEN TEKSTIILIMIESTEN LIITTO. TEKSTIILISANASTO. (TEXTILES D, FI*EN*GE*SW) TAMPERE, 1959. 202P.
-58537.

AS, J. VIERTALIG TEXTIEL-WOORDENBOEK VOOR DE HANDEL. (TEXTILE D,*DU*EN*FR*GE) DOETINCHEM, MISSET,
956. 269P.

ILHELMSEN, L.J. NORSK TEKSTILORDBOK, MED OVERSETTELSER TIL ENGELSK OG TYSK. (TEXTILE D,...,NO*EN*GE)
ERGEN, NORSK TEKSTIL TEKNISK FORBUND, 1954. 200P. A55-6776. 3900T.

RUSSIAN

NGLO-RUSSKII SLOVAR PO KAUCHUKU, REZINE I KHIMICHESKIM VOLOKNAM. (EN*RU D. OF RUBBER/SYN. FIBERS)
OSCOW, FIZMATGIZ, 1962. 260P.

ABINOVICH, Z.E. AND LUPANDIN, K.K. ANGLO-RUSSKII TEKSTILNYI SLOVAR. (EN*RU TEXTILE D) ED2. MOSCOW,
IZMATGIZ, 1961. 640P. 61-50652. 25000T.

SPANISH

NK, P. ENCICLOPEDIA TEXTIL. (TEXTILE ENCYCL, *SP*EN) ED3, BUENOS AIRES, 1954. 630P. 59-31911. 6300T.

TRAFFIC ENGINEERING AND TRANSPORTATION

ENGLISH

MERICAN INSTITUTE OF ELECTRICAL ENGINEERS. DEFINITIONS OF ELECTRICAL TERMS. TRANSPORTATION. (GR-40,
ENERAL,ASA C42.40/GR-41, AIR, ASA C42.41/ GR-42, LAND, ASA C42.42/ GR-43, MARINE, ASA C42.43) NEW YORK,
956. 42P. 420T.

AKER, J.S. ET AL. DICTIONARY OF HIGHWAY TRAFFIC. EVANSTON, ILL. NORTHWESTERN UNIV, 1960. 304P. 60-4093.

ES, J. CHARTERING AND SHIPPING TERMS... ED5. HILVERSUM, DE BOER, 1960. 410P. 61-2840.

URKE, J. ET AL. ENCYCLOPEDIA OF ROAD TRAFFIC LAW AND PRACTICE. LONDON, SWEET/MAXWELL, 1960. 1510P.
1-66374.

COURSE, A.G. AND OR'AM, R.B. GLOSSARY OF CARGO-HANDLING TERMS. GLASGOW, BROWN/FERGUSON, 1961. 88P.

XPORTERS ENCYCLOPAEDIA... NEW YORK, ASHWELL, 1956. ED51.

TRAFFIC ENGINEERING AND TRANSPORTATION

ENGLISH

IATA TRAFFIC GLOSSARY. AIR TRANSP, V.27, 42-3 (1955) 130T.

NATIONAL HIGHWAY USERS CONFERENCE. THE RIGHT WORD, A GLOSSARY OF HIGHWAY TERMS. WASHINGTON, 1958. 18P. 60T.

STEVENS, E.F. DICTIONARY OF SHIPPING TERMS AND PHRASES. LONDON, PITMAN, 1958. 59-28107.

STUFFLEBEAM, G.T. THE TRAFFIC DICTIONARY. ED4. NEW YORK, SIMMONS-BOARDMAN, 1950. 292P. 50-8273.

U.S. FEDERAL AVIATION AGENCY. GLOSSARY OF AIR TRAFFIC CONTROL TERMS. WASHINGTON, 1962. 13P. 80T.

WOODLEY, D.R. THE ENCYCLOPEDIA OF MATERIALS HANDLING. NEW YORK, MACMILLAN, 1000P. (IN PREP)

WOOLAM, W.G. SHIPPING TERMS AND ABBREVIATIONS. MARITIME, INSURANCE, INTERNATIONAL TRADE. CAMBRIDGE, MD, CORNELL MARITIME, 1963. 144P. 62-22181. 2200T.

FRENCH

LA CIRCULATION ROUTIERE, GLOSSAIRE ANGLAIS-FRANCAIS,BT-89. (TRAFFIC ENG, EN*FR GL) OTTAWA, DEPT.SECY. STATE, 1960. 52P. 1000T.

UNITED NATIONS. LISTE DE TERMES RELATIFS A LA CONSTRUCTION ET A LA CIRCULATION ROUTIERES. (ROAD BLDG/ TRAFFIC ENG,FR*EN GL)(BUL.NO.109) NEW YORK,195 .

GERMAN

BES, J. CHARTERING AND SHIPPING TERMS... GE DEFS. HAMBURG, ECKHART/MESSTORFF, 1956.

DLUHY, R. SCHIFFSTECHNISCHES WOERTERBUCH, SCHIFFBAU, SCHIFFAHRT UND SCHIFFSMACHINENBAU. (*GE*EN SHIPBLDG. D) ED2. (V.1, GE*EN, 879P. V.2, EN*GE, 945P) BREMEN, DORN, 1956. A57-583. 40000T.

FACHWOERTERBUCH FUER DIE ZIVILLUFTFAHRT. (EN*GE D. OF CIVIL AVIATION) ED2. FRANKFURT/MAIN, BUNDESANSTALT FLUGSICHERUNG, 1954. 200P.

GERMANY. BUNDESMINISTERIUM FUER DAS POST- UND FERNMELDEWESEN. DEUTSCH-ENGLISCHES UND ENGLISCH-DEUTSCHES FACHWOERTERBUCH FUER DEN POST-BETRIEBS- UND -VERWALTUNGSDIENST. (*GE*EN D. FOR POSTAL SERV) V.1 GE*EN. 240P) BONN, 1952-- . 59-20557.

HEINZE, S. AND ENGELEN-WEYBRIDGE, V. FACHWOERTERBUCH DES TRANSPORTWESENS. (TRANSP. D. V.1, GE*EN, 390P. V.2, EN*GE, IN PREP) WIESBADEN, BRANDSTETTER, 1961-62. 62-5007. 6000T.

LUETCKE,E. ABC DES LUFTVERKEHRS. (AIR TRAFFIC ABC, GE DEFS) HAMBURG, 1955.

RACKOW, H. HANDWOERTERBUCH DES POSTWESENS. (POSTAL SERV. HANDBOOK/SUPPL (1957) GE DEFS) ED2. FRANKFURT/ MAIN, 1953. 827P. 57-41773.

GREEK

VASILIADI, H. MODERN PRACTICAL ENGLISH-GREEK POCKET DICTIONARY FOR GREEK MERCANTILE MARINE, 1953. 262+233P.

JAPANESE

JAPAN. MINISTRY OF EDUCATION. DRAFT VOCABULARY FOR TRANSPORT OPERATION. (JA*EN) TOKYO, 1952. 33P. 520T.

POLISH

SKIBICKI, W. ANGIELSKO-POLSKA TERMINOLOGIA HANDLU MORSKIEGO. (EN*PL SHIPPING D) WARSAW. POLSK.WYDAW. GOSP, 1951. 267P. 53-34032.

POLYGLOT

THE AIR TRAFFIC LANGUAGE. FRENCH AND SPANISH TRANSLATIONS OF DEFINITIONS IN THE IATA TRAFFIC GLOSSARY. INTL. AIR TRAFFIC ASSOC. BULL, V.17, 55-64 (1953) 130T.

CURD, W.J. A DICTIONARY OF INSURANCE AND SHIPPING TERMS AND EXPRESSIONS IN ENGLISH, FRENCH, GERMAN, SPANISH, ITALIAN AND DANISH. LONDON, STONE/COX, 1956. 35P.

FEDERATION EUROPEENNE DE LA MANUTENTION. ILLUSTRIERTE TERMINOLOGIEN. WOERTERBUCH FUER FACHAUSDRUECKE DER FOERDER-UND HEBETECHNIK IN 6 SPRACHEN.(ILLUS.D.OF MATER. HANDLING, GE EN FR IT SP SW) WIESBADEN, KRAUSSKOPF, 1961-- . V.1-7. (IN PROGR)

GAROCHE,P. DICTIONARY OF COMMODITIES CARRIED BY SHIP. (EN FR SP...) CAMBRIDGE, MD, CORNELL MARITIME, 1952. 357P. 52-4689.

INTERNATIONAL CIVIL AVIATION ORGANIZATION. LEXICO DE TERMINOS USADOS EN AVIACION CIVIL INTERNACIONAL, ESPANOL-INGLES-FRANCES... (D. OF INTL. CIVIL AVIATION, SP EN FR) MONTREAL, 1953. 204P. 54-18476. 1500T.

INTERNATIONAL CIVIL AVIATION ORGANIZATION. LEXICON OF TERMS USED IN CONNEXION WITH INTERNATIONAL CIVIL AVIATION, EN FR SP. MONTREAL, 1952. 197P. 52-30278. 1500T.

INTERNATIONAL RAILWAY UNION, RECUEIL DES TERMES CONCERNANT L,EMPLOI ET L,ECHANGE DU MATERIEL ROULANT... (ROLLING STOCK D, *FR*EN*GE*IT*PL*RU) V.1, 629P. WARSAW, MIN. COMMUNIC, POLAND, 1958-- . 59-29905.

POLYGLOT

S CORP. GLOSSARY OF MARITIME AND COMMERCIAL TERMS IN LLOYD,S CALENDAR,*EN*FR*GE*IT*NO*SP. LONDON, 300T.

ICAL HANDLING ENGINEERS ASSOCIATION. INTERNATIONAL ILLUSTRATED DICTIONARY. (EN FR GE IT SC SP) ED6. , 1960. 42P. 160T.

ENT INTERNATIONAL ASSOCIATION OF ROAD CONGRESSES. DICTIONNAIRE TECHNIQUE ROUTIER EN 8 LANGUES. (D. D T. *FR*EN*DA*DU*GE*IT*RU*SP) ED3. PARIS. (IN PREP)

C, P. TERMINOLOGIE DES TRANSPORTS ROUTIERS INTERNATIONAUX. (INTL.HIGHWAY TRANSP.T, FR EN GE RU) ... 195 .

F. VISUTE LANOVE DRAHY. (WIRE-ROPE TRANSP, CZ EN FR GE RU) PRAGUE, SNTL, 1953. 317P.

ND INLAND WATER TRANSPORT, 5 LANGUAGES. AMSTERDAM, ELSEVIER. (IN PREP)

POSTALE UNIVERSELLE. BUREAU INTERNATIONAL. VOCABULAÎRE POLYGLOTTE DU SERVICE POSTAL INTERNATIONAL. STAL SERV. D, FR EN GE...) BERN, 1963.

ELYI, B. ET AL. KOZLEKEDESUGY. PT.1, KENYSZERPALYAS ES KOZUTI KOZLEKEDES. (RAIL/ROAD TRANSP. D, *GE*RU) (MUSZ. ERT. SZ, NO.7) BUDAPEST, TERRA, 1960. 207P. 60-34451. 1200T.

ELYI, B. ET AL. KOZLEKEDESUGY.PT.2, HAJOZAS, REPULES, POSTA ES CSOVEZETEKES SZALLITAS. (D. OF TION, AVIATION. MAIL/PNEUMATIC TRANSP,*HU*EN*GE*RU) (MUSZ, ERT. SZ, NO.8) BUDAPEST, TERRA, 1960. 60-34451. 1300T.

TOURING AND AUTOMOBILE ORGANISATION. INTERNATIONALES WOERTERBUCH FUER DIE STRASSENVERKEHRSTECHNIK. TRAFFIC ENG. VOC. *GE*EN*DU*FR*IT*SP) LONDON, 1957-- . LL. 58-4785.

RUSSIAN

RUSSKII SLOVAR PO TRANSPORTNOMU DELU. (EN*RU TRANSP. D) MOSCOW, 1957. 192P.

MORSKIE FRAKHTOVYE I TRANSPORTNYE TERMINY. (CHARTERING/SHIPPING T, RU DEFS) MOSCOW, 1961.189P.

N, IA.B. AND ORNATSKII, N.V. ANGLO-RUSSKII SLOVAR DOROZHNIKA. (EN*RU D. OF ROAD BLDG) MOSCOW, ANSIZDAT, 1956. 319P. 57-29754. 16000T.

R.E.F. RAILWAY TRANSPORT TERMS, RUSSIAN-ENGLISH. BIRMINGHAM, ENG. UNIV, 1958. 11P.

SPANISH

. AND URIARTE Y LARRAONDO, S. FLETAMENTOS Y TERMINOS DE EMBARQUE. (CHARTERING/SHIPPING T, *SP*EN) MADRID, OFIC. CENTRAL MARITIMA, 1959. 343P. 61-20927.

WELDING RESEARCH AND TECHNOLOGY

DUTCH

OMMISSIE VOOR DE NORMALISATIE IN NEDERLAND. BENAMINGEN LASTECHNIEK. NEDERLANDS-ENGELS (AMERIKAANS) WELDING T) DELFT, WALTMAN, 1952. 24P.

ENGLISH

AN INSTITUTE OF ELECTRICAL ENGINEERS. DEFINITIONS OF ELECTRICAL TERMS. ELECTRIC WELDING AND G. (GR-50, ASA C42.50) NEW YORK, 1958. 12P. 100T.

AN WELDING SOCIETY. AWS DEFINITIONS, WELDING AND CUTTING... NEW YORK, 1961. 59P. 61-2169. 500T.

AW, J. DESIGN AND PRODUCIBILITY CRITERIA FOR WELDED STRUCTURES. (ERR-SD-136) SAN DIEGO, CALIF, YNAMICS-CONVAIR, 1961. 24P.

H STANDARDS INSTITUTION. GLOSSARY OF TERMS (WITH SYMBOLS) RELATING TO THE WELDING AND CUTTING OF . (B.S.499 IN 8 SECT/SUPPL. AMENDS.PD-2220, 1955. PD-2972, 1958. PD-3282, 1959. PD-3496, 1959). , 1952-1959. 125P. 350T.

ZIE, L.B. AND JEFFERSON, T. WELDING ENCYCLOPEDIA. NEW YORK, MCGRAW-HILL, 1955. ED13.
POLYGLOT

Y OF THE HEBREW LANGUAGE. MILON LE-MUNHE HA-RATAKHUT. (D.OF WELDING, HE EN FR GE) JERUSALEM, 89P. A62-457.

AN WELDING SOCIETY. DICTIONARY OF WELDING TERMS. (EN FR GE RU SP) NEW YORK, 195 .

OLSKI, Z. SLOWNIK SPAWALNICZY POLSKO-ROSYJSKO-ANGIELSKO-FRANCUSKO-NIMIECKI. (WELDING D, PL*RU*EN* WARSAW, PANST.WYDAW.TECH, 1952. 112P. 54-19257. 500T.

ATIONAL INSTITUTE OF WELDING. MULTILINGUAL COLLECTION OF TERMS FOR WELDING AND ALLIED PROCESSES. RESISTANCE WELDING. BASEL, ASSOC. SUISSE TECH. SOUDAGE, 1961. 253P. (EN/17 LANG)

ATIONAL INSTITUTE OF WELDING. MULTILINGUAL COLLECTION OF TERMS FOR WELDING AND ALLIED PROCESSES. LDING, SUPPL. SC/SL T. BASEL, ASSOC.SUISSE TECH.SOUDAGE, 1958. 24P. 330T.

POLYGLOT

INTERNATIONAL INSTITUTE OF WELDING. MULTILINGUAL COLLECTION OF TERMS FOR WELDING AND ALLIED PROCESSES. PT.2 GENERAL TERMS.*EN*CR*CZ*DA*DU*FI*FR*GE*IT*NO*SP*SW. BASEL, SOC.SUISSE ACETYLENE, 1955. 132P. 59-25725. 1000T.

INTERNATIONAL INSTITUTE OF WELDING. MULTILINGUAL COLLECTION OF TERMS FOR WELDING AND ALLIED PROCESSES. PT.3, ARC WELDING.*EN*CR*CZ*DA*DU*FI*FR*GE*IT*NO*SP*SW) BASEL, ASSOC.SUISSE TECH.SOUDAGE, 1958. 140P. 59-25725. 940T.

INTERNATIONAL INSTITUTE OF WELDING. MULTILINGUAL COLLECTION OF TERMS FOR WELDING AND ALLIED PROCESSES. *CZ*PL*RU*SL*TU. SUPPL.TO PTS.2/3 ABOVE. BASEL, ASSOC.SUISSE TECH.SOUDAGE, 1961.

INTERNATIONAL INSTITUTE OF WELDING. MULTILINGUAL TERMINOLOGY FOR WELDING AND ALLIED PROCESSES. GAS WELDING.*EN*DA*DU*FI*FR*GE*IT*NO*SP*SW. BASEL, SOC. SUISSE ACETYLENE, 1953. 78P. 57-18870. 330T.

INTERNATIONAL INSTITUTE OF WELDING. NOMENCLATURE DES TERMES UTILISES DANS LE CONTROLE PAR ULTRASONS... (ULTRASONIC TESTING T, GE EN FR) PARIS, SOUDURE AUTOGENE, 1959. 27P. 63-28234.

RUSSIAN

ZOLOTYKH, V.T. ANGLO-RUSSKII SLOVAR PO SVAROCHNOMU PROIZVODSTVU. (EN*RU WELDING D) MOSCOW, FIZMATGIZ, 1961. 191P. 61-39461. 6000T.

WOOD RESEARCH AND TECHNOLOGY

CHINESE

CHUNG K,O HSUEH YUAN. PIEN I CH,U PAN WEI YUAN HUI. (ACAD. SINICA. COMM. OF PUBL/TRANSL) YING HAN LIN YEH TZ,U HUI. (EN CH FORESTRY GL) PEKING, 1959. 184P. C61-4330.

KUO LI PIEN KUAN. (NATL. INST. OF TRANSL) LIN HSUEH MING TZ,U. (FORESTRY T, EN CH) TAIPEI, 1954. 156P. C59-3085.

CZECH

AMBROS, J. NAZVOSLOVI ANGLICKO-CESKE PRO LESNICTVI A DREVARSTVI. (EN*CZ FORESTRY/LUMBER D) PRAGUE, MATICE HOR.-HUT, 1958. 523P.

ENGLISH

AMERICAN SOCIETY FOR TESTING/MATERIALS. STANDARD DEFINITIONS OF TERMS RELATING TO TIMBER. (D9-30) ASTM STDS.PT.6, 868-70. PHILADELPHIA, 1961. 60T.

AMERICAN SOCIETY FOR TESTING/MATERIALS. STANDARD DEFINITIONS OF TERMS RELATING TO TIMBER PRESERVATIVES. (D324-41) ASTM STDS, PT.6, 1058. PHILADELPHIA, 1961. 10T.

AMERICAN SOCIETY FOR TESTING/MATERIALS. STANDARD DEFINITIONS OF TERMS RELATING TO VENEER AND PLYWOOD. (D1038-52) ASTM STDS, PT.6, 873-8. PHILADELPHIA, 1961. 120T.

AMERICAN SOCIETY FOR TESTING/MATERIALS. STANDARD NOMENCLATURE OF DOMESTIC HARDWOODS AND SOFTWOODS. (D1165-52) ASTM STDS, PT.6, 863-7. PHILADELPHIA, 1961. 200T.

AMERICAN SOCIETY FOR TESTING/MATERIALS. TENTATIVE DEFINITIONS OF TERMS RELATING TO WOOD-BASE FIBER AND PARTICLE PANEL MATERIALS. (D1554-60T) ASTM STDS, PT.6, 879-82. PHILADELPHIA, 1961. 50T.

BRITISH STANDARDS INSTITUTION. GLOSSARY OF TERMS RELATING TO TIMBER AND WOODWORK. (B.S. 565) LONDON, 1963. 104P. 750T. 70 ABBR.

BRITISH STANDARDS INSTITUTION. NOMENCLATURE OF COMMERCIAL TIMBERS, INCLUDING SOURCES OF SUPPLY. (B.S. 881, 589) LONDON, 1955. 144P. 900T.

CHILDS, F.P. GLOSSARY OF LOG AND TIMBER MEASURES. LONDON, BENN, 1955. 242P.

EMPIRE FORESTRY ASSOCIATION. BRITISH COMMONWEALTH FOREST TERMINOLOGY. PT.1 SILVICULTURE, PROTECTION, MENSURATION, AND MANAGEMENT, 163P. PT.2, FOREST PRODUCTS RESEARCH, EXTRACTION. LONDON, 1953-57. 2V.

HOUGH, R.B. AND HARRAR, E.S. HOUGH,S ENCYCLOPEDIA OF AMERICAN WOODS. NEW YORK, SPELLER, 1957. 2V. 57-10592.

MCCULLOCH, W.F. WOODS WORDS. A COMPREHENSIVE DICTIONARY OF LOGGERS TERMS. PORTLAND, OREGON HIST.SOC, 1958. 219P. 58-63667. 4000T.

RODDIS PLYWOOD CORP. CHARACTERISTICS OF MODERN WOODS. ED5. MARSHFIELD, WIS. 1956. 64P. 56-34376.

SOCIETY OF AMERICAN FORESTERS. FORESTRY TERMINOLOGY, A GLOSSARY OF TECHNICAL TERMS... ED3. WASHINGTON, 1958. 97P. 58-9365. 3600T.

TITMUSS, F.H. A CONCISE ENCYCLOPEDIA OF WORLD TIMBERS. NEW YORK, PHIL.LIBR, 1959. 26P. 59-1965.

FRENCH

VOCABULAIRE DES SCIERIES, GLOSSAIRE ANGLAIS-FRANCAIS, BT-56. (SAW-MILL T, EN*FR GL) OTTAWA, DEPT.SECY. STATE, 1957. 14P. 300T.

WOOD RESEARCH AND TECHNOLOGY

GERMAN

K. HOLZ-ABC. (WOOD ABC, GE DEFS) LEIPZIG, FACHBUCHVERLAG, 1957. 199P. A58-2712. 2000T.

'UER DIE GESAMTE HOLZINDUSTRIE. HOLZLEXIKON. (WOOD IND. HANDBOOK/ENCYCL, GE DEFS) WIESBADEN, 59- . (IN PROC)

HOLZLEXIKON. (WOOD D, GE DEFS) STUTTGART, HOLZZENTRALBLATT, 1962. 950P. 8000T.

JAPANESE

, OKAMOTO, S. AND HAYASHI,S. ATLAS OF WOOD IN COLOUR. (*JA*LA*EN*GE) OSAKA, HOIKUSHA, 1962. T.

ERSITY. WOOD RESEARCH INSTITUTE. DICTIONARY OF WOOD... (EN*JA) OSAKA, SOGENSHA, 1956. 417P.

POLYGLOT

N TECHNIQUE INTERNATIONAL DES BOIS TROPICAUX. NOMENCLATURE DES BOIS TROPICAUX EN AMERIQUE DU AMERIQUE CENTRALE. (NOMENCL.OF TROP.TREES IN SOUTH/CENTRAL AM, FR DEFS, SP PR) NOGENT-SUR- 5. 140P.

EEKMAN, W. DICTIONARY OF WOOD AND TIMBER (*DU*EN*FR*GE*IT*SP*SW) NEW YORK, ELSEVIER. (IN

GRICULTURE ORGANIZATION OF THE UNITED NATIONS. PROVISIONAL ARAB FORESTRY TERMINOLOGY WITH WORDS IN ENGLISH AND FRENCH. (FAO-NERO-FO-490) ROME, 1955. 135+30P. 56-2241.

DE DOCUMENTARE TEHNICA. DICTIONAR TEHNIC PENTRU SECTORUL LEMNHIRTIE. (ROMINA, RUSA, UNGARA, RANCEZA, ITALIANA, SI ENGLEZA) (WOOD/PAPER D, RO*EN*FR*GE*IT*HU*RU) BUCHAREST, 1954.

.M. AND ALIASHBERG, A.I. LESOTEKHNICHESKII RUSSKO-ANGLO-NEMETSKO-FRANTSUZSKII SLOVAR. (*RU*EN D D) MOSCOW, GOSLESBUMIZDAT, 1963. 300P. 7000T.

-ROIUMITUSKUNTA. SUOMALAIS-RUOTSALAIS-SAKSALAIS-ENGLANTILAINEN METSASANAKIRJA.(FI*EN*GE*SW) HELSINKI, KUSTANNUSOSAKEYHTIO OTAVA, 1954.

.E. SKOGSLEXIKON. SVENSKA, ENGELSKA, TYSKA, FRANSKA. (FORESTRY D.*SW*EN*FR*GE*) ED2. SVENSKA SKOGSVARDS-FOREN, 1955. 284P. 58-38211. 6000T.

, D. RUSSKO-NEMECKO-FRANCOUZSKO-ANGLICKO-CESKY LESNICKY SLOVNIK. (RU*EN*CZ*FR*GE FORESTRY D) ATNI PED. NAKL, 1959-61. 2V. 60-40651.

G. VOCABOLARIO TECNICO E COMMERCIALE DEL LEGNO. (TECH/COM. GL. OF WOOD, IT EN FR GE) ROME, COM. LEGNO/SUGHERO, 1957. 593P. 59-35313.

RUSSIAN

G. ET AL. ANGLO-RUSSKII LESOTEKHNICHESKII SLOVAR. (EN*RU TIMBER D) GOSLESBUMIZDAT, 1960. 8990. 12000T.

.V. RUSSKO-ANGLIISKII SPRAVOCHNIK TERMINOV PO EKSPORTU LESNYKH TOVAROV. (RU*EN D. OF LUMBER OSCOW, VNESHTORGIZDAT, 1956. 114P. 58-32440.

IA, L.F. ET AL. ANGLO-RUSSKII LESOTEKHNICHESKII SLOVAR. (EN*RU TIMBER D) LENINGRAD, MIN. Z.SSSR, 1957. 100P.

SPANISH

UERA, C. GLOSARIO DE TERMINOLOGIA FORESTAL. (*SP*EN D. OF FORESTRY) SAN JUAN, DEPT. AGR/COM, . 56-62652. 250T.

3.1. ABBREVIATIONS USED FOR NAMES OF LANGUAGES

AF	AFRIKAANS	FR	FRENCH	MO	MONGOLIAN
AL	ALBANIAN	GA	GAELIC	NO	NORWEGIAN
AM	AMERICAN	GE	GERMAN	PL	POLISH
	ANNAMESE (SEE	GR	GREEK	PO	POLYGLOT
	VIETNAMESE)	HE	HEBREW	PR	PORTUGUESE
AR	ARABIC	HI	HINDI	RO	ROMANIAN
AZ	AZERBAIJANI	HU	HUNGARIAN	RU	RUSSIAN
BR	BURMESE	IC	ICELANDIC	SC	SERBOCROATIAN
BU	BULGARIAN	IN	INDONESIAN	SL	SLOVAK
CH	CHINESE	IA	INTERLINGUA	SV	SLOVENIAN
CR	CROATIAN		IRISH (SEE GAELIC)	SP	SPANISH
CZ	CZECH	IT	ITALIAN	SW	SWEDISH
DA	DANISH	JA	JAPANESE	TH	THAI
DU	DUTCH	KO	KOREAN	TU	TURKISH
EN	ENGLISH	LA	LATIN	UK	UKRAINIAN
EO	ESPERANTO	LI	LITHUANIAN	VI	VIETNAMESE
ES	ESTONIAN		MALAY (SEE	WE	WELSH
FI	FINNISH		INDONESIAN)	WR	WHITE RUSSIAN

3.2. ABBREVIATIONS USED IN TRANSLATIONS OF
FOREIGN-LANGUAGE TITLES AND SERIES

ABBR.(S)	ABBREVIATION(S)	CHEM.	CHEMI/STRY -CA -CAL	ELECTROTECH.	ELECTROTECHNICAL
ABSTR.	ABSTRACT	CHIM.	CHIMI/CA -E -QUE	ELEK.	ELEKTRI/SCH -CHESKII
ACAD.	ACADEM/Y -IA -ICA -IE	CINEMATOG.	CINEMATOGRAPHY	ELEKTRON.	ELEKTRONI/SCH -KA
ACOUST.	ACOUSTIC/S -AL	CLASSIF.	CLASSIFICATION	ELEM.	ELEMENT/ -ARY
ADMIN.	ADMINISTRAT/ION -IVE	CO.	COMPANY	EMPL.	EMPLOY/EE -MENT
ADP	AUTOMATIC DATA	COLL.	COLLEGE	ENCYCL.	ENCYCLOPEDI/A -E
	PROCESSING	COM.	COMMERC/E -IAL	ENERG.	ENERG/Y -ETICHESKII
AERODYN.	AERODYNAMIC/S -AL	COMB.	COMBUSTION	ENG.	ENGINE/ -ER -ING
AEROHYDRODYN.	AEROHYDRODYNAMIC/S	COMM.	COMMI/TTEE -SSION	ENTSIKL.	ENTSIKLOPEDIIA
	-AL	COMMUN.	COMMUNICATION	ENZYKL.	ENZYKLOPEDIE
AERON.	AERONAUTIC/S -AL	COMP.	COMPUT/ER -ATION	EQUIP.	EQUIPMENT
AF	AIR FORCE	COMPIL.	COMPILATION	EQUIV.	EQUIVALENT
AFB	AIR FORCE BASE	COMPOS.	COMPOSITION	ET AL.	ET ALII (AND OTHERS)
AGR.	AGRICULTUR/E -AL	COND.	CONDITION/ -ING	EXAM.	EXAMINATION
AKAD.	AKADEM/IA -IIA	CONF.	CONFERENCE		
AM.	AMERICA/ -N	CONGR.	CONGRESS	FABR.	FABRICA/NT -TION
AMEND.	AMENDMENT	CONSTR.	CONSTRUCTION	FED.	FEDERA/L -TION
ANAL.	ANALY/SIS -TIC	CORP.	CORPORATION	FF	FOLLOWING PAGES
ANN.	ANNUAL	CONV.	CONVENTION	FIZ.	FIZI/KA -CHESKII
APPL.	APPLI/CATION -ED	CORR.	CORROSION		(PHYSICS)
ARCHIT.	ARCHITECTUR/E -AL	CRYST.	CRYSTALLOGRAPHY	FOR.	FOREIGN
ASSOC.	ASSOCIA/TION -TED			FORM.	FORMULA
ASTRODYN.	ASTRODYNAMICS	D.	DICTIONARY	FOUND.	FOUNDATION
ASTRON.	ASTRONOM/Y -ICAL	DEF(S)	DEFINITION(S)		
ASTROPHYS.	ASTROPHYSI/CS -CAL	DEFORM.	DEFORMATION	GAZ.	GAZETTE
AT.	ATOM/IC -IQUE -NYI	DEPT.	DEPARTMENT	GEMOL.	GEMOLOGY
AUTO.	AUTOMOBILE	DERIV.	DERIVAT/ION -IVE	GEN.	GENERAL
AUTOM.	AUTOMAT/IC -ION	DEUT.	DEUTSCH	GEOCHEM.	GEOCHEMISTRY
BIBL.	BIBLIOTHE/K -QUE	DEVELOP.	DEVELOPMENT	GEOD.	GEODE/SY -TIC
	(LIBRARY)	DIG.	DIGITAL, DIGEST	GEOG.	GEOGRAPH/Y -IC
BIBLIOG.	BIBLIOGRAPH/Y -IC	DIREC.	DIREC/TION -TORY	GEOL.	GEOLOG/Y -ICAL
BIOCHEM.	BIOCHEMI/STRY -CAL	DIV.	DIVISION/ -AL	GEOM.	GEOMETRY
BIOPHYS.	BIOPHYSIC/S -AL	DISTR.	DISTRIBUTION	GEOMORPH.	GEOMORPHOLOGY
BIT.	BITUMEN/ -OUS	DOC.	DOCUMENT/ -ATION	GEOPHYS.	GEOPHYSIC/S -AL
BIUL.	BIULLETEN	DOK.	DOKUMENTATION	GES.	GESELLSCHAFT
BLDG.	BUILDING	DOKL.	DOKLADY (PROCEEDINGS)	GIDROLOG.	GIDROLOGI/CHESKII -IA
BRIT.	BRIT/AIN -ISH	DYN.	DYNAMICS	GL.	GLOSSARY
B.S.	BRITISH STANDARD			GOS.	GOSUDARSTVENNYI
BUKV.	BUKVENNYI (LETTER)	ECON.	ECONOM/Y -IC		(STATE, GOVERNMENT)
BUL.	BULLETIN	ED.	EDIT/ION -ED	GOVT.	GOVERNMENT
BUR.	BUREAU	EDUC.	EDUCATION/ -AL	GR.	GROUP
		EFFIC.	EFFICIENCY	GT.	GREAT
CAP.	CAPACITY	ELEC.	ELECTRIC/ -AL -ITY		
CARTOGR.	CARTOGRAPHY	ELECTROACOUST.	ELECTROACOUSTICS	HEAT.	HEATING
CESK.	CESKOSLOVENSKE	ELECTROCHEM.	ELECTROCHEMISTRY	HIST.	HISTORY
CH.	CHAPTER	ELECTROMET.	ELECTROMETALLURGY	HYDR.	HYDRAULIC(S)
CHAR.	CHARACTERISTIC/S	ELECTRON.	ELECTRONIC/S	HYDRODYN.	HYDRODYNAMICS

HYDROELECTRIC		
HYDROGEOLOGY		
HYDROGRAPHY -IC		
HYDROLOGY		
ILLUMINATI/ON -NG		
ILLUSTRAT/ION -ED		
IMPERIAL		
IMPRI/NT -MERIA		
-MERIE		
INCORPORATED		
INCLU/DING -SIVE		
INCOMPLETE		
INDUSTR/Y -IAL		
INFORMATION		
INORGANIC		
INOSTRANNYI (FOREIGN)		
INSTITUT/E -ION		
INSTRUMENT/ -ATION		
INTERNATIONAL		
ISSLEDOVA/NIE		
-TELSKII (RESEARCH)		
ISTITUTO (INSTITUTE)		
IZDATEL'STVO(PUBLISH-		
ER)		
IZDANIE (EDITION)		
JOURNAL		
KHIMI/IA -CHESKII		
(CHEMISTRY)		
KM. KOMITET TEKHNI-		
CHESKOI TERMINOLOGII		
(COMMITTEE ON TECH.		
TERMINOLOGY).		
KOMISS/IIA -ION		
KONFERENTSIIA		
KONGRES(S)		
KRISTALLICHESKII		
LABORATOR/Y -IES		
LANGUAGE		
LIBR/ARY -AIRIE		
LITERATUR/E -A		
LOOSE-LEAF		
LIMITED		
MACHINE/ -RY		
MAGAZINE		
MANUFACTUR/E -ING		
MATERIAL/ -S		
MATHEMATIC/S -AL		
MEASURE/ -MENT		
MECANIQUE		
MECHANIC/S -AL		
MEDIC/AL -INE		
MEMOIR		
METAL/ -LURGY		
-LURGICAL		
METALLOGRAPH/Y -IC		
METEOROLOG/Y -ICAL		
METROLOGY		
MEZHDUNARODNYI		
(INTERNATIONAL)		
MICROFILM		
MICROSCOPY		
MILITARY		
MINING		
MINERALOG/Y -ICAL		
MISCELLANEOUS		
MODERN		
MORSKOI (NAVAL,		
NAUTICAL)		
MISSILE RANGE		
MUSZAKI ERTELMEZO		
SZOTAR (DEFINING		
TECHNICAL DICTIONARY)		

NACL.	NACIONAL	
NAKL.	NAKLADATELSTVI(PUBLISHER)	
NAR.	NARODNYI (NATIONAL,	
	PEOPLE'S)	
NATL.	NATIONAL	
NATS.	NATSIONALNYI	
NAUCH(N).	NAUCHNYI (SCIENTIFIC)	
NAVIG.	NAVIGATION	
NAZ.	NAZIONAL	
NAZV.	NAZVANIE (NAME,TITLE)	
N.D.	NO DATE	
NEFT.	NEFTIANOI (PETROLEUM)	
NETH.	NETHERLANDS	
NO.	NUMBER	
NOMENCL.	NOMENCLATURE	
NUCL.	NUCLEAR	
OBOZN.	OBOZNACHENIE (DESIG-	
	NATION, MEANING)	
OBS.	OBSERVATORY	
OCCUP.	OCCUPATION/ -AL	
OCEANOG.	OCEANOGRAPHY	
OFFIC.	OFFICIAL	
OPT.	OPTIC/ -S	
ORG.	ORGANI/C -ZATION	
ORTHOGR.	ORTHOGRAPHY	
P(P).	PAGE(S)	
PAT.	PATENT(S)	
PED.	PEDAGOG/ICHESKII	
	(TEACHING)	
PER.	PERIODICAL(S)	
PETROGR.	PETROGRAPHY	
PETROL.	PETROL/EUM -OGY	
PHARM.	PHARMAC/Y -EUTICAL	
PHIL.	PHILOSOPHIC/AL	
PHOT.	PHOTOGRAPH/Y -IC	
PHOTOCHEM.	PHOTOCHEMI/STRY -CAL	
PHOTOTOPOGR.	PHOTOTOPOGRAPHY	
PHYS.	PHYSIC/S -A -AL	
PHYSICOCHEM.	PHYSICOCHEMICAL	
PHYSIOL.	PHYSIOLOGY	
PLAST.	PLASTICS	
POLIGR.	POLIGRAFI/CHESKII	
	-OO (PRINTING)	
POLN.	POLNYI (COMPLETE)	
POLYTECH.	POLYTECHNICAL	
PP.	PAGES	
PRACT.	PRACTIC/E -AL	
PREC.	PRECISION	
PRELIM.	PRELIMINARY	
PREP.	PREPARATION	
PRINT.	PRINTING	
PROC.	PROCEEDINGS	
PROCESS.	PROCESS/ING	
PROD.	PRODUCT/ -ION	
PROG.	PROGRAM/ -MING	
PROGR.	PROGRESS	
PROIZV.	PROIZVODSTVO (MANU-	
	FACTURE, PRODUCTION)	
PROM.	PROMYSHLENNOST'	
	(INDUSTRY)	
PROP.	PROPOSED, PROPERTY	
PROV.	PROVISIONAL	
PSEUD.	PSEUDONYM	
PT(S).	PART(S)	
PUBL.	PUBLI/C -CATION	
	-SHER -SHING	
QUART.	QUARTERLY	
R/D	RESEARCH AND	
	DEVELOPMENT	
RECH.	RECHERCHE (RESEARCH)	
REF.	REFER/ENCE -ATIVNYI	
	(ABSTRACT)	
REFRIG.	REFRIGERAT/ION -ING	

REPR.	REPR/INT -ODUCTION
REPT.	REPORT
RES.	RESEARCH
RETR.	RETRIEVAL
REV.	REV/IEW -ISION -ISED
RHEOL.	RHEOLOGY
R.R.	RAILROAD(S)
SANIT.	SANIT/ATION -ARY
SB.REK.TERM.	SBORNIKI REKOMENDUEMYKH
	TERMINOV (COLLECTION OF RECOMMENDED T)
SCI.	SCIEN/CE -TIFIC
SECT.	SECTION
SECY.	SECRETARY
SER.	SER/IAL -IES
SERV.	SERVICE
SHIPBLDG.	SHIPBUILDING
SLOV.	SLOVAR' (DICTIONARY)
SOC.	SOCIETY
SOKR.	SOKRASHCHEN/IE -NYI
	(ABBREVIAT/ION -ED)
SOV.	SOV/IET -ETSKII
SPEC.	SPECIAL
SPECTRY.	SPECTROSCOPY
STAT.	STATISTIC/S -AL
STD(S).	STANDARD(S)
STRUCT.	STRUCTUR/E -AL
SUPPL.	SUPPLEMENT -ARY
SUPT.	SUPERINTENDENT
SURV.	SURVEY/ -ING -OR
SYMP.	SYMPOSIUM
SYNTH.	SYNTHE/SIS -TIC
SYST.	SYSTEM
T.	TERM/S -INOLOGY
TEC.	TECNIC/A -O
TECH.	TECHN/OLOGY -ICAL
TEK.	TEKHNI/X -SK
TEKH.	TEKHN/ICHESKII -OLOGIIA
TEL.	TELEPHONE
TELECOMMUN.	TELECOMMUNICATION
TELEGR.	TELEGRAPH
TEMP.	TEMPERATURE
TENT.	TENTATIVE
TEOR.	TEOR/IIA -ETICHESKII
THEOR.	THEOR/Y -ETICAL
THERMODYN.	THERMODYNAMIC(S)
T.M.	TECHNICAL MANUAL
TOPOG.	TOPOGRAPH/Y -ER
TR.	TRUDY (PROCEEDINGS)
TRANS.	TRANSACTIONS
TRANSL.	TRANSLATION
TRANSP.	TRANSPORTATION
TV	TELEVISION
UCHEB.	UCHEBNYI (STUDY)
UNIV.	UNIVERSIT/Y -ET -E -ÄT
V.	VOLUME(S)
VAR.	VARIOUS
VENT.	VENTILATION
VER.	VEREIN
VOC.	VOCABULARY
VYDAV.	VYDAVATEL'STVO (PUBLISHER)
W.	WEST/ERN
WISS.	WISSENSCHAFT/LICH
WYDAW.	WYDAWNICTWO (PUBLISHER)
YR.	YEAR
Z.	ZEITSCHRIFT
ZTG.	ZEITUNG
ZH.	ZHURNAL (JOURNAL)

ACAD.PRESS	ACADEMIC PRESS, INC., NEW YORK.
ACAD.SINICA.BUR. COMPIL/TRANSL.	ACADEMIA SINICA. BUREAU OF COMPILATIONS AND TRANSLATIONS, PEKING.
ACAD.SINICA.COMM. PUBL/TRANSL.	ACADEMIA SINICA. COMMITTEE OF COMPILATIONS, PUBLICATIONS AND TRANSLATIONS, PEKING.
AGARD	ADVISORY GROUP FOR AERONAUTICAL RESEARCH AND DEVELOPMENT, PARIS.
AKAD. KIADO	AKADEMIAI KIADO, BUDAPEST.
AKAD.NAUK SSSR. INST.NAUCH.INFORM.	AKADEMIIA NAUK SSSR. INSTITUT NAUCHNOI INFORMATSII, MOSCOW.
AKAD.NAUK SSSR. KOM.TEKH.TERM.	AKADEMIIA NAUK SSSR. KOMITET TEKHNICHESKOI TERMINOLOGII, MOSCOW.
AM.CHEM.SOC.(ACS)	AMERICAN CHEMICAL SOCIETY, WASHINGTON.
AM.DOC.INST.(ADI)	AMERICAN DOCUMENTATION INSTITUTE,WASH.
AM.GEOL.INST. (AGI)	AMERICAN GEOLOGICAL INSTITUTE, WASHINGTON.
AM.INST.ELEC. ENG. (AIEE)	AMERICAN INSTITUTE OF ELECTRICAL ENGINEERS, NEW YORK.
AM.INST.PHYS.(AIP)	AMERICAN INSTITUTE OF PHYSICS,NEW YORK.
AM.MATH.SOC.(AMS)	AMERICAN MATHEMATICAL SOCIETY, PROVIDENCE, R.I.
AM.METEOR.SOC.	AMERICAN METEOROLIGICAL SOCIETY,BOSTON.
AM.SOC.CINEMATOG.	AMERICAN SOCIETY OF CINEMATOGRAPHERS, HOLLYWOOD.
AM.SOC.CIV.ENG. (ASCE)	AMERICAN SOCIETY OF CIVIL ENGINEERS, NEW YORK.
AM.SOC.HEAT. REFRIG.AIR COND. ENG. (ASHRAE)	AMERICAN SOCIETY OF HEATING,REFRIGERATING AND AIR-CONDITIONING ENGINEERS, NEW YORK.
AM.SOC.MECH. ENG. (ASME)	AMERICAN SOCIETY OF MECHANICAL ENGINEERS, NEW YORK.
AM.STD.ASSOC. (ASA)	AMERICAN STANDARDS ASSOCIATION, NEW YORK.
AM.TECH.SOC.	AMERICAN TECHNICAL SOCIETY, CHICAGO.
ASSOC.SPEC.LIBR. INFORM.BUR.(ASLIB)	ASSOCIATION OF SPECIAL LIBRARIES AND INFORMATION BUREAUX, LONDON.
ASSOC.SUISSE TECH.SOUDAGE	ASSOCIATION SUISSE POUR LA TECHNIQUE DU SOUDAGE, BASEL.
ASTM	AMERICAN SOCIETY FOR TESTING AND MATERIALS, PHILADELPHIA.
ATOMIZDAT	IZDATEL'STVO GLAVNOGO UPRAVLENIIA PO ISPOL'ZOVANIIU ATOMNOI ENERGII PRI SOVETE MINISTROV SSSR, MOSCOW.
AVTOTRANSIZDAT	NAUCHNO-TEKHNICHESKOE IZDATEL'STVO AVTO-TRANSPORTNOI LITERATURY, MOSCOW.
AZNEFTEIZDAT	AZERBAIDZHANSKOE NEFTIANOE IZDATEL'STVO, BAKU.
BIBLIOG.ESP.	COMPANIA BIBLIOGRAFICA ESPANOLA,MADRID.
BLV	BAYERISCHER LANDWIRTSCHAFTSVERLAG GMBH, MUNICH.

BRIT.STAND. INST.(BSI)	BRITISH STANDARDS INSTITUTION,LONDON.
CAN.BUR.STAT.	CANADIAN BUREAU OF STATISTICS, OTTAWA.
CEAC	EDICIONES CEAC, BARCELONA.
CELANESE CORP.AM.	CELANESE CORPORATION OF AMERICA, CLARKWOOD,TEXAS.
CENTRE MAT. PLAST.	CENTRE D'ÉTUDES DES MATIÈRES PLASTIQUES, PARIS.
CHEM.IND.	CHEMISCHE INDUSTRIE, AUGSBURG.
CNRS	CENTRE NATIONAL DE LA RECHERCHE SCIENTIFIQUE, PARIS.
COLO.SCI.SOC.	COLORADO SCIENTIFIC SOCIETY, DENVER.
CONSULTANTS BUR. (CB)	CONSULTANTS BUREAU ENTERPRISES, NEW YORK.
CSAV	NAKLADATELSTVI CESKOSLOVENSKE AKADEMIE VED, PRAGUE.
DEPT.SECY.STATE	DEPARTMENT OF SECRETARY OF STATE,OTTAWA.
DEUT.GES.DOK.	DEUTSCHE GESELLSCHAFT FUER DOKUMENTATION, FRANKFURT AM MAIN.
DEUT.KERAM.GES.	DEUTSCHE KERAMISCHE GESELLSCHAFT, BONN.
DEUT.STAT.GES.	DEUTSCHE STATISTISCHE GESELLSCHAFT,MUNICH.
DEUT.VERLAG WISS.	VEB DEUTSCHER VERLAG DER WISSENSCHAFTEN, BERLIN.
DEVA	DEVA FACHVERLAG IN DER DEUTSCHEN VERLAGS-ANSTALT, STUTTGART.
DOSAAF	VSESOIUZNOE DOBROVOL'NOE OBSHCHESTVO SODEISTVIIA ARMII,AVIATSII I FLOTY,MOSCOW
ENERG.USTAV.	ENERGETICKY USTAV, PRAGUE.
EPA	EUROPEAN PRODUCTIVITY AGENCY, PARIS.
FAO (UN)	FOOD AND AGRICULTURE ORGANIZATION OF THE UNITED NATIONS, ROME.
FED.INTL. GEOM.	INTERNATIONAL FEDERATION OF SURVEYORS, VIENNA.
FID	INTERNATIONAL FEDERATION FOR DOCUMENTATION, THE HAGUE.
FILM/TECH.	NOUVELLES ÉDITIONS, FILM ET TECHNIQUE, PARIS.
FIZMATGIZ	GOSUDARSTVENNOE IZDATEL'STVO FIZIKO-MATEMATICHESKOI LITERATURY, MOSCOW.
G.E.P.	ÉDITIONS G.E.P., PARIS.
GEMOL.INST. AM. (GIA)	GEMOLOGICAL INSTITUTE OF AMERICA, LOS ANGELES.
GIDROMETEOIZDAT	GIDROMETEOROLOGICHESKOE IZDATEL'STVO, LENINGRAD.
GITTL	SEE GOSTEKHIZDAT
GNTILGON	SEE GOSGEOLTEKHIZDAT
GOSENERGOIZDAT	GOSUDARSTVENNOE ENERGETICHESKOE IZDATEL'STVO, MOSCOW.

GOSGEOGIZDAT	GOSUDARSTVENNOE IZDATEL'STVO GEOGRAFICHES-KOI LITERATURY, MOSCOW.
GOSGEOLIZDAT	GOSUDARSTVENNOE IZDATEL'STVO GEOLOGICHES-KOI LITERATURY, MOSCOW.
GOSGEOLTEKHIZ-DAT	GOSUDARSTVENNOE NAUCHNO-TEKHNICHESKOE IZDATEL'STVO LITERATURY PO GEOLOGII I OKHRANE NEDR, MOSCOW.
GOS.IZD.INOSTR. NATS.SLOV.	GOSUDARSTVENNOE IZDATEL'STVO INOSTRANNYŇH I NATSIONAL'NIKH SLOVAREI, MOSCOW.
GOSKHIMIZDAT	GOSUDARSTVENNOE NAUCHNO-TEKHNICHESKOE IZDATEL'STVO KHIMICHESKOI LITERATURY,MOSCOW.
GOS.KOM.AVTOMAT. MASHINOSTR.	GOSUDARSTVENNYI KOMITET PO AVTOMATIZATSII I MASHINOSTROENIIU, MOSCOW.
GOS.KOM. RADIOELEK.	GOSUDARSTVENNYI KOMITET PO RADIOELEK-TRONIKE, MOSCOW.
GOSLESBUMIZDAT	GOSUDARSTVENNOE IZDATEL'STVO LESOTEKHNI-CHESKO-BUMAZHNOI LITERATURY, MOSCOW.
GOSMASHMETIZDAT	GOSUDARSTVENNOE NAUCHNO-TEKHNICHESKOE IZDATEL'STVO PO MASHINOSTROENIIU I METALLOOBRABOTKE, MOSCOW.
GOSSTATIZDAT	GOSUDARSTVENNOE STATISTICHESKOE IZDATEL'STVO, MOSCOW.
GOSSTROIIZDAT	GOSUDARSTVENNOE IZDATEL'STVO STROITELNOI LITERATURY, MOSCOW AND KIEV.
GOSTEKHIZDAT	GOSUDARSTVENNOE IZDATEL'STVO TEKHNIKO-TEORETICHESKOI LITERATURY, MOSCOW.
GOSTOPTEKHIZ-DAT	GOSUDARSTVENNOE NAUCHNO-TEKHNICHESKOE IZDATEL'STVO NEFTIANOI I GORNO-TOPLIVNOI PROMYSHLENNOSTI, MOSCOW.
GOSTORGIZDAT	GOSUDARSTVENNOE IZDATEL'STVO TORGOVOI LITERATURY, LENINGRAD.
GOS.UCHEB.PED.IZD.	SEE UCHGIZ
GOSVOENIZDAT	SEE VOENIZDAT
IATA	INTERNATIONAL AIR TRANSPORT ASSOCIATION, MONTREAL.
IBM	INTERNATIONAL BUSINESS MACHINES CORP., NEW YORK.
IEC	INTERNATIONAL ELECTROTECHNICAL COMMISSION, GENEVA.
IFAC	INTERNATIONAL FEDERATION OF AUTOMATIC CONTROL, DUESSELDORF.
IMP.CHEM.IND.	IMPERIAL CHEMICAL INDUSTRIES,WELLINGTON.
IMPR.NATL.	IMPRIMERIE NATIONALE, PARIS.
IND.AT.	INDUSTRIES ATOMIQUES, PARIS.
IND.ENG.COLL.	INDUSTRIAL ENGINEERING COLLEGE,CHICAGO.
IND.PLAST.MOD.	INDUSTRIE DES PLASTIQUES MODERNES,PARIS.
IND.PRESS	INDUSTRIAL PRESS, NEW YORK.
IND.RES.SERV.	INDUSTRIAL RESEARCH SERVICE, DOVER,N.H.
INST.BIBL.MEX.	INSTITUTO BIBLIOGRAFICO DE MEXICO, D.F.
INST.ELEC.ELECTRON. ENG. (IEEE)	INSTITUTE OF ELECTRICAL AND ELECTRONICS ENGINEERS, NEW YORK.

INST.GEOG.NATL.	INSTITUT GEOGRAPHIQUE NATIONAL,PARIS.
INST.NACL. RACIONAL.TRABAJO	INSTITUTO NACIONAL DE RACIONALIZACION DEL TRABAJO, MADRID.
INTERLANG.DICT.	INTERLANGUAGE DICTIONARIES PUBLISHING CORP., NEW YORK.
INTL.ACAD.IND. CULT.	INTERNATIONAL ACADEMY OF INDIAN CULTURE, NAGPUR.
IRE	INSTITUTE OF RADIO ENGINEERS,NEW YORK.
ISO	INTERNATIONAL ORGANIZATION FOR STANDARDIZATION, GENEVA.
IST.GEOG.MIL.	ISTITUTO GEOGRAFICO MILITARE,FLORENCE.
IST.POLIGR.STATO	ISTITUTO POLIGRAFICO DELLO STATO,ROME.
IZD.INOSTR.LIT.	IZDATEL'STVO INOSTRANNOI LITERATURY, MOSCOW.
KAZAKH.GOS.UCHEB. PED.IZD.	KAZAKHSKOE GOSUDARSTVENNOE UCHEBNO-PEDAGOGICHESKOE IZDATEL'STVO,ALMA-ATA.
K.L.R.	K.L.R. PUBLISHERS, LONDON.
LEKSIKOGR.ZAV.FNRJ.	LEKSIKOGRAFSKI ZAVOD FNRJ.,ZAGREB.
MARIT/COLONIALES	ÉDITIONS MARITIMES ET COLONIALES,PARIS.
MASS.INST.TECH. (MIT)	MASSACHUSETTS INSTITUTE OF TECHNOLOGY, CAMBRIDGE, MASS.
MAT.HORN.-HUTN.	MATICE HORNICKO-HUTNICKA, PRAGUE.
MEDGIZ	GOSUDARSTVENNOE IZDATEL'STVO MEDITSINSKOI LITERATURY, MOSCOW.
MIN.COLONIES	MINISTERE DES COLONIES, BRUSSELS.
MIN.KOMMUNAL. KHOZ.RSFSR.	MINISTERSTVO KOMMUNAL'NOGO KHOZIASTVA, RSFSR, MOSCOW.
MIN.OBRONY NAR.	WYDAWNICTWO MINISTERSTWA OBRONY NARODOWEJ, WARSAW.
MIN.PROSV.RSFSR	MINISTERSTVO PROSVESHCHENIIA RSFSR, MOSCOW.
MIN.VYSSH.OBRAZ. SSSR	MINISTERSTVO VYSSHEGO OBRAZOVANIIA SSSR, MOSCOW.
MLAD KNJ	MLADINSKA KNJIGA, LJUBLJANA.
MORSK.TRANSP.	MORSKOI TRANSPORT, MOSCOW.
NAKL.POLSK.TOW. MAT.WARSAW	NAKLAD POLSKIEGO TOWARZYSTWA MATEMATYCZNEGO, WARSAW.
NAKL.STOWARZ.TECH. ODLEWN.POLSK.	NAKLAD STOWARZYSZENIA TECHNICZNEGO ODLEWNIKOW POLSKICH, CRACOW.
NATL.INST.TRANSL.	NATIONAL INSTITUTE OF TRANSLATION, TAIPEI.
NATO	NORTH AMERICAN TREATY ORGANIZATION, PARIS.
NIIST	GOSUDARSTVENNYI NAUCHNO-ISSLEDO-VATELSKII INSTITUT STEKLA, MOSCOW.
OCECO	(OCEANIC EXCHANGE CO.) OCECO TECHNICAL PUBLISHERS, HILVERSUM.
OEEC	ORGANIZATION FOR EUROPEAN ECONOMIC COOPERATION, PARIS.

ORSZ.MUSZ.KONYVTAR	ORSZAGOS MUSZAKI KONYVTAR,BUDAPEST.
PAN.AM.UNION (PAU)	PAN AMERICAN UNION, WASHINGTON.
PANSTW.PRZED. WYDAW.KARTOGR.(PPWK)	PANSTWOWE PRZEDSIEBIORSTWO WYDAWNICTW KARTOGRAFICZNYCH, WARSAW.
PANSTW.WYDAW. NAUK-TECH.	PANSTWOWE WYDAWNICTWO NAUKOWO-TECHNICZNE, WARSAW.
PANSTW.WYDAW.TECH.	PANSTWOWE WYDAWNICTWO TECHNICZNE,WARSAW
PANSTW.ZAKLAD. WYDAW.LEK.	PANSTWOWY ZAKLAD WYDAWNICTW LEKARSKICH, WARSAW.
PHIL.LIBR.	PHILOSOPHICAL LIBRARY,INC.,NEW YORK
PIANC	PERMANENT INTERNATIONAL ASSOCIATION OF NAVIGATION CONGRESSES,BRUSSELS.
PIARC	PERMANENT INTERNATIONAL ASSOCIATION OF ROAD CONGRESSES, PARIS.
POLSK.WYDAW.GOSP.	POLSKIE WYDAWNICTWO GOSPODARCZE,WARSAW
PRESSES SCI.INTL.	PRESSES SCIENTIFIQUES INTERNATIONALES, PARIS.
PROV.INTL.COMP. CENTRE	PROVISIONAL INTERNATIONAL COMPUTATION CENTRE, ROME.
PTT	STAATSBEDRIJF DER POSTERIJEN, TELEGRAFIE EN TELEFONIE,THE HAGUE.
RCA	RADIO CORPORATION OF AMERICA,NEW YORK
RECH.TRANSP.	RECHNOI TRANSPORT, MOSCOW.
RILEM	INTERNATIONAL ASSOCIATION OF TESTING AND RESEARCH LABORATORIES FOR MATERIALS AND STRUCTURES, PARIS.
ROH	VYDAVATEL'STVO ROH, BRATISLAVA.
SAV	VYDAVATEL'STVO SLOVENSKEJ AKADEMIE VIED, BRATISLAVA.
SCI.INSTR. MANUF.ASSOC.	SCIENTIFIC INSTRUMENT MANUFACTURERS ASSOCIATION OF GREAT BRITAIN,LONDON.
S.E.D.E.S.	CENTRE DE DOCUMENTATION UNIVERSITAIRE ET S.E.D.E.S. REUNIS, PARIS.
SEL'KOLKHOZGIZ	GOSUDARSTVENNOE IZDATEL'STVO SEL'SKO-KHOZIAISTVENNOI I KOLKHOZNO-KOOPERATIVNOI LITERATURY,· MOSCOW.
SETI	SCIENTIST AND ENGINEER TECHNOLOGICAL INSTITUTE, NEW YORK.
SLOV.VYDAV.TECH. LIT.	SLOVENSKE VYDAVATEL'STVO TECHNICKEJ LITERATURY, BRATISLAVA.
SNTL	STATNI NAKLADATELSTVI TECHNICKE LITERATURY, PRAGUE.
SOC.AUTO.ENG. (SAE)	SOCIETY OF AUTOMOTIVE ENGINEERS, NEW YORK.
SOC.ED.GEOG. MARIT/COLONIALES	SOCIÉTÉ D'ÉDITIONS GÉOGRAPHIQUES, MARITIMES ET COLONIALES, PARIS.
SOV.ENTSIKL.	SOVETSKAIA ENTSIKLOPEDIIA,MOSCOW.
SPEC.LIBR.ASSOC. (SLA)	SPECIAL LIBRARIES ASSOCIATION, NEW YORK.
STANFORD RES. INST.	STANFORD RESEARCH INSTITUTE, MENLO PARK, CALIF.
STATNI PED. NAKL. (SPN)	STATNI PEDAGOGICKE NAKLADATELSTVI, PRAGUE.
STATNI ZDRAV. NAKL.	STATNI ZDRAVOTNICKE NAKLADATELSTVI, PRAGUE.
STEEL FOUNDERS SOC. AM. (SFSA)	STEEL FOUNDERS SOCIETY OF AMERICA, CLEVELAND.

SUDOSTROIZDAT (SUDPROMGIZ)	GOSUDARSTVENNOE SOIUZNOE IZDATEL'STVO SUDOSTROITEL'NOI PROMYSHLENNOSTI, LENINGRAD.
SV.BERGSING.FOER.	SVERIGES BERGSINGENIOERERS FOERENING, STOCKHOLM.
TECH.DICT.	TECHNICAL DICTIONARIES CO.,NEW YORK.
TECH.PRESS	TECHNICAL PRESS, LONDON.
TECH.VED.VYDAV.	TECHNICKO-VEDECKE VYDAVATELSTVI,PRAGUE.
TECH.VERLAG	TECHNISCHER VERLAG "DAS ELEKTRON," LINZ.
TEH.KNJ.	TEHNICKA KNJIGA,BELGRADE AND ZAGREB.
TEKH.INST.PISHCH/ KHOLODIL PROM.	TEKHNICHESKII INSTITUT PISHCHEVOI I KHOLODIL'NOI PROMYSHLENNOSTI, ODESSA.
TIP.OPERAI	TIPOGRAFIA OPERAI, VICENZA.
TNC	TEKNISKA NOMENKLATURCENTRALEN, STOCKHOLM.
TRANSZHELDORIZDAT	GOSUDARSTVENNOE TRANSPORTNOE ZHELEZNO-DOROZHNOE IZDATEL'STVO, MOSCOW.
UCHGIZ	GOSUDARSTVENNOE IZDATEL'STVO UCHEBNO-PEDAGOGICHESKOI LITERATURY, MOSCOW.
UGLETEKHIZDAT	GOSUDARSTVENNOE NAUCHNO-TEKHNICHESKOE IZDATEL'STVO LITERATURY PO UGOL'NOI PROMYSHLENNOSTI, MOSCOW.
UNESCO	UNITED NATIONS EDUCATIONAL,SCIENTIFIC, AND CULTURAL ORGANIZATION, PARIS.
UNION.DEUT. VERLAGSGES.	UNION DEUTSCHE VERLAGSGESELLSCHAFT, STUTTGART.
U.S.BUR.MINES	U.S. BUREAU OF MINES, WASHINGTON.
U.S.GEOL.SURV.	U.S. GEOLOGICAL SURVEY, WASHINGTON
U.S. JPRS	U.S. JOINT PUBLICATIONS RESEARCH SERVICE, WASHINGTON.
U.S.LIBR.CONGR.(LC)	U.S. LIBRARY OF CONGRESS, WASHINGTON.
U.S.NATL.AERON./ SPACE ADMIN.(NASA)	U.S.NATIONAL AERONAUTICAL AND SPACE ADMINISTRATION, WASHINGTON.
U.S.NAT.BUR.STDS. (NBS)	U.S. NATIONAL BUREAU OF STANDARDS, WASHINGTON.
U.S.OFFICE TECH. SERV. (OTS)	U.S.DEPARTMENT OF COMMERCE,OFFICE OF TECHNICAL SERVICES, WASHINGTON.
VDI	VEREIN DEUTSCHER INGENIEURE,BERLIN AND DUESSELDORF.
VEB	VOLKSEIGENER BUCHVERLAG,LEIPZIG & BERLIN.
VINITI	VSESOIUZNYI INSTITUT NAUCHNOI I TEKHNICHESKOI INFORMATSII, MOSCOW.
VMF	VOENNO-MORSKOI FLOT, LENINGRAD.
VNESHTORGIZDAT	IZDATEL'STVO VNESHNEI TORGOVLI, MOSCOW.
VNIIMP	VSESOIUZNYI NAUCHNO-ISSLEDOVATEL'SKII INSTITUT MIASNOI PROMYSHLENNOSTI, MOSCOW.
VOENIZDAT (VOENGIZ)	GOSUDARSTVENNOE VOENNOE IZDATEL'STVO, MOSCOW.
VSESOIUZ.KNIZHN. PALATA	VSESOIUZNAIA KNIZHNAIA PALATA, MOSCOW.
WILA	WILA VERLAG FUER WIRTSCHAFTSWERBUNG, MUNICH.
WISS.VERLAGSGES.	WISSENSCHAFTLICHE VERLAGSGESELLSCHAFT, STUTTGART.
WYDAW.NAUK TECH.	WYDAWNICTWO NAUKOWO-TECHNICZNE, WARSAW.
ZAGOTIZDAT	GOSUDARSTVENNOE IZDATEL'STVO TEKHNI-CHESKOI I EKONOMICHESKOI LITERATURY PO VOPROSAM ZAGOTOVKI, MOSCOW.

4. BIBLIOGRAPHIC REFERENCES

AMERICAN SOCIETY FOR TESTING AND MATERIALS. ASTM STANDARDS, 1961. 11V. SUPPL, 1962-63. PHILADELPHIA, 1961-63.

AMERICAN STANDARDS ASSOCIATION. 1964 CATALOG OF AMERICAN STANDARDS... NEW YORK, 1964. 74P.

ASSOCIATED TECHNICAL SERVICES, INC. DICTIONARIES AND BOOKS: SCIENCE, TECHNOLOGY, GENERAL. CATALOG NO.2.
    GLEN RIDGE, N.J., 1963.

BACHMANN, W. ENGLISCHE FACHWOERTERBUECHER. FREIBERG, BERGAKADEMIE FREIBERG, FERNSTUDIUM, 1959. 145P. 60-19107.

BAILEY'S CATALOGUE OF DICTIONARIES AND GRAMMARS IN THE EUROPEAN LANGUAGES... 1961. LONDON, BAILEY/SWINFEN, 1961. 44P.

BAILEY'S TECHNICAL DICTIONARIES. CATALOGUE 1958 AND SUPPL. LONDON, BAILEY/SWINFEN, 1958. 40P.

BESTERMAN, T. INDEX BIBLIOGRAPHICUS. V.1, SCIENCE AND TECHNOLOGY. ED3. PARIS, UNESCO, 1952. 52P. 52-3142.

BONI, A. PHOTOGRAPHIC LITERATURE, AN INTERNATIONAL BIBLIOGRAPHIC GUIDE TO GENERAL AND SPECIFIC LITERATURE ON PHOTOGRAPHIC
    PROCESSES. NEW YORK, MORGAN/MORGAN, 1962. 335P. 62-21351.

BOROV, T. ET AL. DIE BIBLIOGRAPHIE IN DEN EUROPAEISCHEN LAENDERN DER VOLKSDEMOKRATIE. LEIPZIG, VERLAG FUER BUCH UND
    BIBLIOTHEKSWESEN, 1960. 165P. 60-35569.

BOWER, W.W. INTERNATIONAL MANUAL OF LINGUISTS AND TRANSLATORS. NEW YORK, SCARECROW, 1959. 451P. SUPPL 1, 450P. 1961.
    59-6548.

BRITISH STANDARDS INSTITUTION. BRITISH STANDARDS YEARBOOK, 1963. LONDON, 1963. 711P.

BRNO. UNIVERSITA. KNIHOVNA. SOUPIS JAZYKOVYCH SLOVNIKU... 2V. BRNO, 1960-62. 61-48828.

CALCUTTA. NATIONAL LIBRARY. INDIAN SCIENTIFIC AND TECHNICAL PUBLICATIONS, EXHIBITION 1960; A BIBLIOGRAPHY. NEW DELHI,
    COUNCIL SCI/IND. RES, 1960. 198 + 195P. 60-50222.

COLLISON, R.L. DICTIONARIES OF FOREIGN LANGUAGES... NEW YORK, HAFNER, 1955. 210P. 55-3665.

CRANE, E.J., PATTERSON, A.M., AND MARR, E.B. A GUIDE TO THE LITERATURE OF CHEMISTRY. ED2. NEW YORK, WILEY, 1957. 397P.
    57-8881.

HAMBURG. WELT-WIRTSCHAFTS-ARCHIV. BIBLIOTHEK. WOERTERBUECHER, ALLGEMEIN UND FACHLICH. DEUTSCH-ENGLISCH, ENGLISCH-
    MEHRSPRACHIG... HAMBURG, 1951. 38P. 59-22405.

HAWKINS, R.R. SCIENTIFIC, MEDICAL, AND TECHNICAL BOOKS PUBLISHED IN THE U.S.A. ... ED2. WASHINGTON, 1958. 1491P. 58-62286

HOLLOWAY, O. FOREIGN LANGUAGE DICTIONARIES AND PHRASE BOOKS AVAILABLE IN THE TA&GMS LIBRARY. FORT SILL, OKLA, ARTILLERY &
    GUIDED MISSILE SCHOOL LIB, 1955. 18P. 56-60701.

HORECKY, P.L. ET AL. BASIC RUSSIAN PUBLICATIONS; AN ANNOTATED BIBLIOGRAPHY ON RUSSIA AND THE SOVIET UNION. CHICAGO,
    UNIVERSITY OF CHICAGO PRESS, 1962. 313P. 62-20022.

INSTITUTE OF RADIO ENGINEERS. PROCEEDINGS. 1952 - TO DATE.

INTERNATIONAL CIVIL AVIATION ORGANIZATION. A BIBLIOGRAPHY OF AVIATION DICTIONARIES. MONTREAL, 1957. 14P. 58-46482.

JUMPELT, R.W. MEHRSPRACHIGE SPEZIALWOERTERBUECHER. NACHR.DOK, V.5, PP. 111-14, 179-83 (1954), V.6, PP. 25-8, 49-52 (1955)

KAISER, F.E. TRANSLATORS AND TRANSLATIONS: SERVICES AND SOURCES. NEW YORK, SPEC.LIB.ASSOC., 1959. 60P. 59-7523.
    (NEW ED. IN PREP.)

KATALOG NOVINOK. (CATALOG OF NEW RUSSIAN BOOKS) WASHINGTON, KAMKIN, 1960 -- TO DATE.

KAUFMAN, I.M. RUSSKIE ENTSIKLOPEDII. MOSCOW, 1960 -- V. 61-29611.

KAUFMAN, I.M. TERMINOLOGICHESKIE SLOVARI; BIBLIOGRAFIIA. MOSCOW, SOVETSKAIA ROSSIIA, 1961. 419P. 62-36201.

LEWANSKI, R.C. A BIBLIOGRAPHY OF SLAVIC DICTIONARIES. NEW YORK, NEW YORK PUB.LIB., 1959-63. 3V. 62-18516.

LINDA HALL LIBRARY, KANSAS CITY, MO. SCIENTIFIC AND TECHNICAL DICTIONARIES, ENCYCLOPEDIAS AND HANDBOOKS. KANSAS CITY,
    1956. 51P. 57-38286.

MAICHEL, K. ET AL. GUIDE TO RUSSIAN REFERENCE BOOKS. STANFORD, CALIF., HOOVER INST., STANFORD UNIVERSITY, 1962 -- V.
    62-14067.

MALCLES, L. ET AL. LES SOURCES DU TRAVAIL BIBLIOGRAPHIQUE. VOL.3. BIBLIOGRAPHIES SPECIALISEES (SCIENCES EXACTES ET
    TECHNIQUES). PARIS, MINARD, 1958. 575P.

MAXWELL SCIENTIFIC INTERNATIONAL, INC. THE DOCUMENTATION AND PROCUREMENT CENTRE. SPECIAL SUBJECT BIBLIOGRAPHY, LIBRARY
    SCIENCES, BIBLIOGRAPHIES, REFERENCE WORKS. NEW YORK, 1963. 50P.

MELLON, M.G. CHEMICAL PUBLICATIONS. ED3. NEW YORK, MCGRAW-HILL, 1958. 327P. 57-12588.

MOORE, C.K. AND SPENCER, K.J. ELECTRONICS, A BIBLIOGRAPHICAL GUIDE. LONDON, MACDONALD, 1961. 411P. 62-32724.

MURPHEY, R.W. HOW AND WHERE TO LOOK IT UP. NEW YORK, MCGRAW-HILL, 1958. 721P. 58-6692.

NEISWENDER, R. GUIDE TO RUSSIAN REFERENCE AND LANGUAGE AIDS. NEW YORK, SPEC.LIBR.ASSOC., 1962. 92P. 62-21081.

OLIVA, P.F. INSTRUCTIONAL AIDS AND SOURCES FOR FOREIGN LANGUAGES. GAINESVILLE, UNIVERSITY OF FLORIDA, 1959. 40P. 59-63058

PARKE, N.G. GUIDE TO THE LITERATURE OF MATHEMATICS AND PHYSICS... ED2. NEW YORK, DOVER, 1958. 436P. 58-13365.

PARKER, S. ET AL. SCIENTIFIC TRANSLATIONS, A GUIDE TO SOURCES AND SERVICES. WASHINGTON, U.S. DEPT. HEALTH, EDUCATION/ WELFARE, 1959. 19P.

PEZHANSKYI, M. SPYSOK SLOVNYKIV U.A.N.; A LIST OF UKRAINIAN TERMINOLOGICAL DICTIONARIES AVAILABLE IN THE UNITED STATES AND CANADA. NEW YORK, 1955. 12P. 56-45770.

PIFFARD, G. A BIBLIOGRAPHY OF DICTIONARIES AND GRAMMARS. SAN DIEGO, CALIF., 1960. 26P. 61-34832.

PIFFARD, G. A BIBLIOGRAPHY OF DICTIONARIES AND GRAMMARS. SAN DIEGO, CALIF., 1961. 72P. 61-41526.

PRAGUE. STATNI TECHNICKA KNIHOVNA. ODBORNE JAZYKOVE SLOVNIKY VE STATNI TECHNICKE KNIHOVNE. PRAGUE, 1961. 93P. 63-26829.

PRAKKEN, S.L. ET AL. BOOKS IN PRINT. NEW YORK, BOWKER, 1963. 2454P.

PRAKKEN, S.L. ET AL. SUBJECT GUIDE TO BOOKS IN PRINT. NEW YORK, BOWKER, 1963. 1966P.

THE PUBLISHERS' TRADE LIST ANNUAL, 1963. NEW YORK, BOWKER, 1963. 3V.

REICHARDT, G. SOWJETISCHE LITERATUR ZUR NATURWISSENSCHAFT UND TECHNIK. ED2. WIESBADEN, STEINER, 1959. 306P. 60-29425.

RUSSIAN TECHNICAL LITERATURE. PARIS, OECD, 1959 -- TO DATE.

SCIENCE MUSEUM. LIST OF ACCESSIONS TO THE LIBRARY. LONDON, 1952-63.

SCIENCE MUSEUM. TECHNICAL GLOSSARIES AND DICTIONARIES. LONDON, SCIENCE LIBRARY, 1952. 82P.

SHUPPAN NYUSU SHA. JITEN JITEN SOGO MOKUROKU. LIST OF DICTIONARIES AND ENCYCLOPEDIIAS. TOKYO, 1961. 247P. J62-76.

SLOVARI-ENTSIKLOPEDII, KATALOG. WASHINGTON, KAMKIN, 1963. 12P.

TAPIA, E.W. GUIDE TO METALLURGICAL INFORMATION. (BIBL.NO.3) NEW YORK, SPEC.LIBR.ASSOC., 1961. 85P.

TECHNICAL TRANSLATING DICTIONARIES. MANCHESTER, ENG., MANCHESTER PUBLIC LIBRARIES, 1962. 33P.

THOMPSON, N.R. ET AL. CUMULATIVE BOOK INDEX. NEW YORK, WILSON, 1952-- TO DATE.

TOTOK, W. AND WEITZEL, R. HANDBUCH DER BIBLIOGRAPHISCHEN NACHSCHLAGEWERKE. ED2. FRANKFURT AM MAIN, KLOSTERMANN, 1959. 335P. 59-45784.

UNDERBRINK, R.L. ABOUT ENCYCLOPEDIAS, AN ANNOTATED BIBLIOGRAPHY. JACKSONVILLE, ILL., 1960. 11P. 60-51933.

UNESCO. BIBLIOGRAPHY OF INTERLINGUAL SCIENTIFIC AND TECHNICAL DICTIONARIES. ED4. PARIS, 1961. 236P.

UNESCO BULLETIN FOR LIBRARIES. PARIS, 1952 -- TO DATE.

UNESCO BULLETIN ON BIBLIOGRAPHY, DOCUMENTATION AND TERMINOLOGY. PARIS, 1960 -- TO DATE.

UNESCO LIBRARY. SELECTION OF WORKS RECEIVED. (UNESCO/CUA NOTES) PARIS, 1960 -- TO DATE.

UNESCO. SCIENTIFIC AND TECHNICAL TRANSLATING AND OTHER ASPECTS OF THE LANGUAGE PROBLEM. PARIS, 1957. 282P. 57-59014.

U.S. ARMY ARTILLERY AND MISSILE SCHOOL, FORT SILL, OKLA. LIBRARY. FOREIGN LANGUAGE DICTIONARIES AVAILABLE IN THE USAAMS LIBRARY. REV. FORT SILL, OKLA., 1961. 14P. 61-60717.

U.S. DEPARTMENT OF COMMERCE. PATENT OFFICE. SCIENTIFIC LIBRARY. LIST OF RECENT ACCESSIONS AND FOREIGN PATENT TRANSLATIONS. WASHINGTON, 1952 -- TO DATE.

U.S. DEPARTMENT OF THE ARMY. ARMY LIBRARY. GLOSSARIES; A PRELIMINARY SURVEY OF SELECTED TITLES OF TECHNICAL AND SCIENTIFIC, DOMESTIC AND FOREIGN TERMS AND DEFINITIONS EMPLOYED BY THE DEPARTMENT OF DEFENSE. WASHINGTON, 1956. 27P. 56-62385.

U.S. LIBRARY OF CONGRESS. AUTHOR CATALOG, 1948-52. PATERSON, N.J., PAGEANT, 1960. 24V.

U.S. LIBRARY OF CONGRESS. NATIONAL UNION CATALOG. AUTHOR LIST, 1953-7. PATERSON, N.J., ROWMAN/LITTLEFIELD, 1961. 28V.

U.S. LIBRARY OF CONGRESS. NATIONAL UNION CATALOG. AUTHOR LIST, 1958-62. NEW YORK, ROWMAN/LITTLEFIELD, 1963. 54V. 56-60041.

U.S. LIBRARY OF CONGRESS. NATIONAL UNION CATALOG, A CUMULATIVE AUTHOR LIST, 1963. NEW YORK, ROWMAN/LITTLEFIELD, 1964. 4V. (IN PREP.)

U.S. LIBRARY OF CONGRESS CATALOG. BOOKS: SUBJECTS, 1955-59. PATERSON, N.J., PAGEANT, 1960. 22V. 50-60682.

U.S. LIBRARY OF CONGRESS. LIBRARY OF CONGRESS CATALOG. BOOKS: SUBJECTS. WASHINGTON, 1960, 1961, 1962, 1963. 3V. EACH. 50-60682.

U.S. LIBRARY OF CONGRESS. GENERAL REFERENCE AND BIBLIOGRAPHY DIVISION. FOREIGN LANGUAGE-ENGLISH DICTIONARIES. V.1 SPECIAL SUBJECT DICTIONARIES WITH EMPHASIS ON SCIENCE AND TECHNOLOGY. 246P. V.2 GENERAL LANGUAGE DICTIONARIES. 239P. WASHINGTON, 1955. 55-60042.

4. BIBLIOGRAPHIC REFERENCES (CONTINUED)

U.S. NATIONAL LIBRARY OF MEDICINE. SCIENTIFIC TRANSLATIONS; A GUIDE TO SOURCES AND SERVICES. WASHINGTON, U.S. DEPT. OF HEALTH, EDUCATION, AND WELFARE, 1959. 19P. 59-60653.

VEDRAL, D. CZECH AND SLOVAK LEXICOGRAPHIC MATERIALS AND DICTIONARIES. WASHINGTON, U.S. DEPARTMENT OF THE ARMY, 1959. 80P.

WHITFORD, R.H. PHYSICS LITERATURE... WASHINGTON, SCARECROW, 1954. 228P. 54-10734.

WINCHELL, C.M. GUIDE TO REFERENCE BOOKS. ED7. CHICAGO, AM. LIBR. ASSOC., 1951. 645P. SUPPL.1, 1950-52. 117P. SUPPL.2, 1953-55. 134P. SUPPL.3, 1956-58. 145P. SUPPL.4, 1959-62. 160P. 51-11157.

THE WORLD'S LANGUAGES. GRAMMARS, DICTIONARIES (GENERAL, SPECIALIZED, SCIENTIFIC, TECHNICAL). ED13. NEW YORK, STECHERT-HAFNER, 1964. 172P.

WUESTER, E. BIBLIOGRAPHY OF MONOLINGUAL SCIENTIFIC AND TECHNICAL GLOSSARIES. V.1, NATIONAL STANDARDS. NEW YORK, UNESCO, 1955. 219P. 55-4638.

WUESTER, E. BIBLIOGRAPHY OF MONOLINGUAL SCIENTIFIC AND TECHNICAL GLOSSARIES. V.2, MISCELLANEOUS SOURCES. NEW YORK, UNESCO, 1959. 146P. 55-4638.

ZAUNMUELLER, W. BIBLIOGRAPHISCHES HANDBUCH DER SPRACHWOERTERBUECHER... NEW YORK, HAFNER, 1958. 496P. 59-732.

ZISCHKA, G.A. INDEX LEXICORUM, BIBLIOGRAPHIE DER LEXIKALISCHEN NACHSCHLAGEWERKE. VIENNA, HOLLINEK, 1959. 290P. 59-34653.

SELECTED FOREIGN NATIONAL BIBLIOGRAPHIES

ASSOCIAZIONE ITALIANA EDITORI. CATALOGO COLLETTIVO DELLA LIBRERIA ITALIANA, 1959. MILAN, S.A. PUBLICAZIONI BIBLIOGRAFICO-EDITORIALI, 1959. 3 V. 62-45507.

BIBLIOGRAFIA ESPANOLA. MADRID, MIN. EDUC. NACL., 1958 - TO DATE. 60-44645.

BIBLIOGRAPHIE DE LA FRANCE... PARIS, AU CERCLE DE LA LIBRAIRIE... 1952 - TO DATE. 6-1189.

BOLETIN DE INFORMACION DOCUMENTAL. SECCION DE CIENCIAS. MADRID, BIBLIOTECA GENERAL. CONSEJO SUPERIOR DE INVESTIGACIONES CIENTIFICAS, 1952 - TO DATE.

BRITISH MUSEUM. DEPT. OF PRINTED BOOKS. GENERAL CATALOGUE OF PRINTED BOOKS. LONDON, 1952 - TO DATE.

THE BRITISH NATIONAL BIBLIOGRAPHY. LONDON, COUNCIL OF THE BRITISH NATIONAL BIBLIOGRAPHY, 1952 - TO DATE. 51-6468.

THE BRITISH NATIONAL BIBLIOGRAPHY CUMULATED SUBJECT CATALOGUE. LONDON, COUNCIL OF THE BRITISH NATIONAL BIBLIOGRAPHY, 1952 - TO DATE. 59-246.

DEUTSCHE BIBLIOGRAPHIE; FÜNFJAHRES-VERZEICHNIS. BÜCHER UND KARTEN. FRANKFURT/MAIN, BUCHHÄNDLER-VEREINIGUNG, 1952 - TO DATE. 53-39084 REV.

FLORENCE. BIBLIOTECA NAZIONALE CENTRALE. BOLLETTINO DELLE PUBBLICAZIONI ITALIANE RICEVUTE PER DIRITTO DI STAMPA. FLORENCE, 1952 - TO DATE. 5-29458.

FRANKFURT AM MAIN. DEUTSCHE BIBLIOTHEK. DEUTSCHE BIBLIOGRAPHIE. FRANKFURT/MAIN, BUCHHÄNDLER-VEREINIGUNG, 1952 - TO DATE. 57-25074.

KNIZHNAIA LETOPIS. MOSCOW, VSESOIUZNAIA KNIZHNAIA PALATA, 1952 - TO DATE.

EL LIBRO ESPANOL. MADRID, INSTITUTO NACIONAL DEL LIBRO ESPANOL, 1958 - TO DATE. 59-48413.

PARIS. BIBLIOTHEQUE NATIONALE. CATALOGUE GÉNÉRAL DES LIVRES IMPRIMÉS: AUTEURS. PARIS, IMPRIMERIE NATIONALE, 1955 - TO DATE.

ABBEY, S.
  SEE HORNER, J.B. 88 (EN)
ACADEMY OF THE HEBREW LANGUAGE,
  JERUSALEM. 26, 152, 159 (PO).
ACHARD, F.H. 62 (EN).
ADAMS, F.D. 16 (EN)
AEBERHARD, R.W.
  SEE LANGFORD, R. 144 (PO)
AEROPORIKA NEA 18 (GR)
AEROSPACE INDUSTRIES ASSOCIATION
  23, 50.(EN)
AGHINA, L. 33 (IT)
AHLBERG, A.
  SEE BROBERG, B. 102 (SW)
AIKELE, E. 48 (PO)
AINBINDER, M. 95 (RU)
AIRAS, V. 143 (PO)

AKADEMIIA NAUK SSSR. 15, 19-20, 24,
  26, 36, 42, 45, 56, 58-9, 62, 68,
  70, 78-9, 86, 94, 104, 111, 114,
  119, 125, 130, 134, 143, 146, 154
  (RUSSIAN OR POLYGLOT)

AKAVIA, A. 99 (HE)
AKHONIN, A.
  SEE HOWERTON, P.W. 94 (RU)
ALBANIA. DREJTORIA STATISTIKES 135
  (AL)
ALBERTA SOCIETY OF PETROLEUM
  GEOLOGISTS 63 (EN)
ALEKSANDROV, P.S. 85 (GE)
ALEXANDER, R.S. 137 (EN)
ALIASHBERG, A.I.
  SEE MELCHER, G.M. 161 (PO)
ALLEN, E.M. 127 (EN)
ALLEN, W.H. 16 (EN)
ALLERDING, J.E. 14 (PO)
ALLEY, R.P.
  SEE HIX, C.F. 120 (EN)
ALLISON, F.C.
  SEE KLAFTEN, B. 70 (GE)
ALOKOV, D. 25 (BU)
ALVARO, M.E. 114 (PO)
ALVEY, G.H. 119 (IT)
AMBROS, J. 160 (OZ)
AMBURGER, P.G. 42 (RU)
AMERICAN FABRICS... 155 (EN)
AMERICAN FOUNDRYMEN'S SOCIETY 91(EN)
AMERICAN GEOLOGICAL INSTITUTE
  63 (EN)
AMERICAN HOME ECONOMICS
  ASSOCIATION 37 (EN)
AMERICAN INSTITUTE OF CHEMICAL
  ENGINEERS 29 (EN)
AMERICAN INSTITUTE OF ELECTRICAL
  ENGINEERS 23, 50 (EN)
AMERICAN MATHEMATICAL SOCIETY 86 (EN)
AMERICAN PETROLEUM INSTITUTE 116 (EN)
AMERICAN ROCKET SOCIETY 16 (EN)

AMERICAN SOCIETY FOR TESTING/MATERIALS
  11, 29, 37-8, 50-1, 62, 68, 71,
  79-80, 87, 91, 95, 113, 114, 116,
  120, 126, 130, 131, 137, 155, 160
  (EN)

AMERICAN SOCIETY OF CIVIL ENGINEERS
  27 (EN)
AMERICAN SOCIETY OF HEATING, REFRIGER-
  ATING... 11, 130 (EN)
AMERICAN SOCIETY OF MECHANICAL
  ENGINEERS 11, 23, 68 (EN)
AMERICAN STANDARDS ASSOCIATION 11,
  16, 23, 29, 43, 47, 51, 71, 75,
  87, 95, 116, 118, 120, 130, 148
  (EN)

AMERICAN VACUUM SOCIETY 120 (EN)
AMERICAN VOCATIONAL ASSOCIATION
  137 (EN)
AMERICAN WELDING SOCIETY 80
  159 (EN)
AMERLINCK, T. 66 (PO)
AMICH, B.J. 106 (PO)
ANDERSON, B.
  SEE TRENT, H.M. 121 (EN)
ANDERSON, E. 29.(EN)
ANDERSON, N.C.
  SEE RUDLER, G. 46 (FR)
ANDO, B. 155 (SW)
ANIRIANO, . 105 (GE)
ANSTEINSSON, J. 143 (NO)
ANTONY, FRANCE. CENTRE... 177 (PO)
ANWIR, B.S. 142 (IN)
ARAKI, T. 22 (PO)
ARBEITSGEMEINSCHAFT WERKZEUGE ...
  77 (PO)
ARBUZOV, G.A. 146 (RU)
ARCHAMBEAUD, P. 128 (FR)
ARIOTTI, P.L. 106 (IT)
ARKELL, W. 63 (EN)
ARMSTRONG, T.E. 65 (EN)
ARNOLDT, . 151 (GE)
ARRAMBIDE, J.
  SEE DURIEZ, M. 39 (FR)
ARTIGAS, J.A. 60 (SP)
ASHBROOK, J. 21 (EN)
ASIMOV, I. 132 (EN)
ASKIM, P. 106 (NO)
ASOCIACION INTERAMERICANA DE
  INGENIERIA SANITARIA 131 (PO)
ASOCIATIA STIINTIFICA A
  INGINERILOR... 143 (PO)
ASSOCIATION FOR COMPUTING MACHINERY
  43 (EN)
ASSOCIATION TECHNIQUE INTERNATIONALE...
  161 (PO)
ATLANTIC REFINING COMPANY 11 (EN)
AUDEL'S... 38, 137 (EN)
AUSSCHUSS FUER WIRTSCHAFTLICHE
  FERTIGUNG 76 (GE)
AUSTRALIAN INSTITUTE OF METALS
  91 (EN)
AUTOMOBILE CLUB DI MILANO 25 (IT)
AUTOMOBILE RESEARCH INSTITUTE 25 (JA)
AUTO-MOTO SAVEZ HRVATSKE 26 (PO)
AVEDON, D.M. 118 (EN)
AVIS, F.C. 47 (EN)
AYRENSCHMALZ, L. 82 (GE)

BABANI, B.B. 152 (PO)
BAHEL, E. 115 (GE)
BADER, O. 92 (FR)
BAKANOV, R.A. 101 (RU)
BAKER, C.C.T. 84 (EN)
BAKER, J.S. 157 (EN)
BAKO, E. 14 (HU)
BALLENTYNE, D.W.G. 29 (EN)
BANCROFT, R.W. 16 (EN)
BANK-WeKI, Z. 34 (PL)
BARANY, N. 73 (PO)
BARCELO,J.R. 36 (SP)
BARDET, G. 41 (PO)
BARES, K. 75 (OZ)
BARGIN, B.D. 56, 152 (PO)
BARKOV, A.S. 66 (RU)
BARNES, D.E. 108 (EN)
BARON, L.I. 104 (RU)
BARRET, W.J. 118 (EN)
BARRY, W.S. 16 (EN)
BASTEN, R. 45 (GE)
BATES, J,M.
  SEE HENDERSON, J.G. 92 (EN)
BATTEY, E.W. 71 (EN)

BAUDRY, H. 13 (FR)
BAUER, F.L. 45 (GE)
BAUER, R. 156 (GE)
BAULIG, H. 64 (PO)
BAUM, W.A. 96 (RU)
BAZANT, Z. 41 (PO)
BEAM, R.E. 148 (EN)
BEAUCHAMP, K.G. 55 (GE)
BECKER, E.R. 68 (EN)
BECKFORD, L.L. 16 (EN)
BECKIUS, K. 104 (SW)
BECKMAN, P. 136 (CZ)
BECKMANN, W. 112 (EN)
BEER, B. 140 (GE)
BELKINA, S.S. 107 (RU)
BELKIND, L.D. 79 (RU)
BELL TELEPHONE LABORATORIES 23,
  43 (EN)
BELLIENI, L. 41 (PO)
BELLISARIO, A. 95 (PO)
BELOIDVORSKII, IU.M. 62 (RU)
BENAMOU, M.
  SEE QUERE, H. 117 (FR)
BENDER, A.E. 60 (EN)
BENE, G.J. 110, 124 (PO)
BENES, K.
  SEE ZEMAN, O. 63 (CZ)
BENISLAWSKI, J. 70 (PO)
BENN, A.E. 68 (EN)
BENNETT, A.H. 113 (EN)
BENNETT, H. 29 (EN)
BERARD, H.
  SEE LANCELOT, E. 60 (FR)
BERG, A.I. 24 (RU)
BERGERON, T. 95 (FR)
BERGWEIN, K. 32 (GE)
BERINGER, C.C. 63 (GE)
BERKELEY, E.C. 43 (EN)
BERKENHOFF, G. 55 (GE)
BERLIN, R. 43 (EN)
BERNUY, J. 156 (FR)
BERRY, E. 38 (EN)
BERRY, W.T. 127 (EN)
BERSTEN, M.
  SEE LIPOWSKI, B. 39 (EN)
BERTIN, L. 63 (EN)
BERZOLARI, L. 85 (IT)
BES, J.. 157 (EN), 158 (GE),
  159 (RU/SP)
BESSERER, C.W. 16 (EN)
BESSERER, H.C.
  SEE BESSERER, C.W. 16 (EN)
BHANDARI, S. 142 (HI)
BIBBERO, R.J. 23 (EN)
BIESALSKI, E. 77 (PO)
BILLET, F.
  SEE FOUCHIER, J. 35 (PO)
BINCER, S. 152 (PO)
BINDER, R.
  SEE NOVAK, J. 147 (SL)
BIRKHOFF, C. 60 (GE)
BIZONY, M.T. 16 (EN)
BIZZARRI, L. 152 (IT)
BLACK, K. 140 (GE)
BLACKSHAW, H. 155 (EN)
BLASBERG ... 92 (GE)
BLUVSHTEIN, V.O. 15, 101 (RU)
BODE, A.W. 119 (GE)
BODENBENDER, H.G. 32 (GE)
BODNARSKII, M.S. 67 (RU)
BODSON, G. 39 (FR)
BOERME, E.T. 36 (SP)
BOERHAVE BEEKMAN, W. 161 (PO)
BOERNER, H.
  SEE LENK, G. 141 (GE)
BOTTARD, A. 151 (FR)
BOLL, L. 85 (PO)

KAI
)

173

176

UHLMANN, H. 156 (GE)
UNION INTERNATIONALE DES PRODUCTEURS.
   ET DISTRIBUTEURS... 58 (PO)
UNION OF INTERNATIONAL ASSOCIATIONS
   15 (PO)
UNION POUR LA COORDINATION DE LA
   PRODUCTION... 58 (PO)
UNION TECHNIQUE DE L'AUTOMOBILE...
   26 (PO)
UNITED ARAB REPUBLIC 132 (AR)
UNITED KINGDOM ATOMIC ENERGY AUTHORITY
   109 (EN)
UNITED NATIONS 19 (PO), 40 (FR), 49,62,
   74, 95 (PO), 108 (CH), 111, 136 (PO)
UNITED STATES STEEL CORPORATION 94 (PO)
U.S. ADVISORY GROUP ON ELECTRONIC PARTS
   53 (EN)
U.S. AERONAUTICAL CHART AND INFORMATION
   CENTER 28 (RU)
U.S. AERONAUTICAL CHART PLANT 27 (GE)
U.S. AGRICULTURAL STABILIZATION AND
   CONSERVATION SERVICE 44 (EN)
U.S. AIR COMMAND AND STAFF COLLEGE
   21 (SP)
U.S. AIR FORCE   17, 21 (EN)
U.S. AIR FORCE MISSILE TEST CENTER
   18 (EN)
U.S. AIR FORCE SCHOOL FOR LATIN
   AMERICA 21 (SP)
U.S. AIR FORCE SYSTEMS COMMAND 98 (EN)
U.S. AIR FORCE TERMINOLOGY CONTROL...
   98 (EN)
U.S. AIR TECHNICAL INTELLIGENCE CENTER
   20 (RU)
U.S. ARCTIC, DESERT, AND TROPIC
   INFORMATION CENTER 65 (EN)
U.S. ARMY. 500TH MILITARY INTELLIGENCE
   GROUP 96 (CH)
U.S. ARMY LANGUAGE SCHOOL 19 (FR),
   65 (CH), 96 (AR, BU, CH, CZ),
   97 (CZ,DA), 98 (EN), 99 (GE,GR,HU),
   100 (IN,IT,JA,KO,LI,NO,PL), 101 (PR,
   RO), 102 (RU, SP, SW, TH), 103 (TU,
   UK, VI)
U.S. ARMY MAP SERVICE 147 (RU)
U.S. ARMY MAP SERVICE, FAR EAST 27 (JA)
U.S. ARMY. ORDNANCE CORPS. 98 (EN),
   102 (RU)
U.S. ATOMIC ENERGY COMMISSION 109,
   111 (RU)
U.S. BUREAU OF PUBLIC ROADS 43 (SP)
U.S. BUREAU OF THE BUDGET 44 (EN)
U.S. BUSINESS AND DEFENSE SERVICES
   ADMINISTRATION 83 (PO)
U.S. CENTRAL AIR DOCUMENTS OFFICE
   96 (RU)
U.S. COMMAND AND GENERAL STAFF COLLEGE
   98 (EN)
U.S. CORPS OF ENGINEERS 68 (PO)
U.S. DEPT.OF AGRICULTURE. 39,60, 138
   (EN)
U.S. DEPT. OF DEFENSE 53-4, 98,
   118 (EN)
U.S. DEPT. OF HEALTH, EDUCATION AND
   WELFARE 98 (EN)
U.S. DEPT. OF LABOR 44 (EN)
U.S. DEPT. OF THE AIR FORCE 18,151 (EN)
U.S. DEPT. OF THE ARMY. 15-16, 28, 59
   (RU), 98 (EN), 99 (EO), 102 (RU)
U.S. DIVISION OF NAVAL HISTORY 105 (EN)
U.S. EMPLOYMENT SERVICE 139 (EN)
U.S. FEDERAL AVIATION AGENCY 12, 18 (EN)
U.S. FEDERAL CIVIL DEFENSE ADMINISTRATION
   98 (EN)
U.S. HYDROGRAPHIC OFFICE 66 (EN),
   112 (EN)
U.S. INTERAGENCY AUTOMATIC DATA
   PROCESSING COMMITTEE 44 (EN)
U.S. JOINT CHIEFS OF STAFF 12(EN),
   98 (EN)
U.S. LIBRARY OF CONGRESS 16, 22,
   134 (RU)
U.S. NATIONAL SCIENCE FOUNDATION 136(CH)

U.S. NAVAL ACADEMY 107 (PO, RU)
U.S. NAVY. HYDROGRAPHIC OFFICE 105 (EN)
U.S. OFFICE OF ORDNANCE RESEARCH 98 (EN)
U.S. PATENT OFFICE 70 (GE)
U.S.S.R. MINISTERSTVO SVIAZI 154 (PO,RU)
U.S. WHITE SANDS MISSILE RANGE 72 (EN)
URADRO NORMALISACI VACLAVSKE NAMESTI
   43 (CZ)
URIARTE Y LARRAONO, S.
   SEE EES, J. 159 (SP)
USLAN, S.D.
   SEE RIDER, J.F. 72 (EN)
USOVSKII, B.N. 61 (RU)
UVAROV, E.B. 133 (EN, FR), 134 (IT),
   135 (SP)
UVAROV, E.V. 36
   SEE CALLAHAM, L.I. 36 (RU)

VAAD HA-LASHON HA-IVRIT BE-ERETS-
   YISRAEL 33 (HE), 68 (PO)
VACLAVIK, J. 155 (SL)
VAGANOV, V.V. 161 (RU)
VALLANDRO, L. 146 (PR)
VAN MANSUM, C.J. 42 (PO)
VAN NOSTRAND'S ... 133 (EN)
VAN RENSSEN, S. 26 (PO)
VAN SCHOICKE, E. 81 (EN)
VARGA, J. 78 (PO)
VARMA, P. 33 (HI)
VARMA, R. 142 (HI)
VARNES, D.J. 63
   SEE STOKES, W.L. 63 (EN)
VASARHELYI, B. 159 (PO)
VASCONCELLOS, S.DE 42 (PR)
VASILEV, A.A. 20 (RU)
VASILEVSKAIA, Z.F. 161 (RU)
VASILIADI, H. 105 (GR)
VELART, W.
   SEE FUKSA, J. 110 (PO)
VELIMIROVIC, M. 111-12 (SC)
VERA, F. 86 (SP)
VEREIN DEUTSCHER EISENHUETTENLEUTE
   93 (GE)
VEREIN DEUTSCHER MASCHINENBAUANSTALT
   24 (GE)
VEREIN SCHWEIZERISCHER MASCHINEN-
   INDUSTRIELLER 70 (GE), 127 (PO)
VICENZA. SCUOLA PROFESSIONALE EDILE ...
   42 (PO)
VICKERY, B.C. 47 (EN)
VINCELETTE, M.H. 69 (FR)
VISSER, A. 154 (PO)
VISSER, A.D. 42 (PO)
VITRO CORP.OF AMERICA 44 (EN)
VOLODIN, N.V. 102 (RU)
VOLOSTNOVA, M.B. 67 (RU)
VOLPOVA, M.V. 131 (RU)
VON OSTERMANN, G.F. 49 (PO)
VORACEK, Z. 75 (CZ)
VORONTZOFF, A.N. 118 (FR)
VOSKOBOINIK, D.I. 111 (PO/RU)
VOTOCEK, E. 35 (PO)
VOTE, A. 146 (PO)
VUICH, T.M. 62 (RU)
VULETIN, A. 65 (SP)
VVEDENSKII, B.A. 126 (RU)

WACHA, I.
   SEE GRETSY, L. 142 (HU)
WADACHI, K. 95, 112 (JA)
WAGNER, F.S.JR. 47 (EN)
WAGNER, S.W. 45 (GE)
WALES. UNIVERSITY 148 (WE)
WALLACE, O. 98 (EN)
WALTHAR, R. 77, 89 (GE)
WANDERSLEB, H. 40 (GE)
WANG, CHU-HSI 84, 120 (CH)
WANG, YU-MING 131 (CH)
WANNER, G. 25 (GE)
WARREIT, I.A. 48 (EN)
WARRERN, A. 136 (DA)
WARSAW.PANSTWOWY INSTYTUT... 136 (PO)
WARTWODA, A. 143 (PL)
WATANABE, G. 64 (PO)
WEBEL, A. 141 (GE)

ADDENDUM

FOR UNI- AND BILINGUAL ENTRIES, REFERENCES ARE TO PAGE NUMBERS AND SUBJECT;
FOR MULTILINGUAL ENTRIES REFERENCES INCLUDE, IN ADDITION TO PAGE NUMBER AND
SUBJECT, THE SYMBOL PO (POLYGLOT) AND THE AUTHOR OR FIRST WORD OF THE TITLE.

182

THE NUMBERS FOLLOWING THE SUBJECT DESIGNATION INDICATE THE INCLUSIVE PAGES;
REFERENCES TO SPECIFIC ENTRIES INCLUDE, IN ADDITION TO PAGE NUMBERS, THE
LANGUAGE OF THE ENTRY AND THE AUTHOR'S NAME OR FIRST WORD OF THE TITLE.

TOPOGRAPHY, 27-8.
TORPEDOES, 105 (EN) THOMPSON.
TRADEMARKS, 68-71; 69 (EN) MICHEL;69 (FR)
BOUJU; (GE) DANIELS; 70 (GE) MIOSGA.
TRAFFIC ENGINEERING, 157-9; 157 (EN)
BAKER; BURKE; 158 (EN) NATIONAL;
STUFFLEBEAM; (FR) LA CIRCULATION; U.N.;
159 (PO) PERMANENT; POPOVIC; ROAD;
VASARHELYI; WORLD; (RU) KHAIKIN.
TRANSDUCERS, 50-60; 71-5.
TRANSFORMERS AND RECTIFIERS, 50-60; 50 (EN)
AIEE GR-15; 51 (EN) ASA C57.12.80;
53 (EN) MECHANICAL; 57 (PO) IEC-50-GR-10.·
TRANSISTORS, 50-60; 71-5; 148-55. SEE ALSO
SEMICONDUCTOR DEVICES.
TRANSPORTATION, 157-9. SEE ALSO AEROSPACE
(16-20); AUTOMOTIVE (25-7); INLAND
WATER (105-8); NAVAL (105-8); RAILROADS
(129-30); TRAFFIC ENGINEERING (148-55).
"TRONS" (ELECTRONICS), 50-60; 148-55;
53 (EN) JUPE; 54 (EN) WHITE; 55 (GE)
GOEDECKE.
TURBINE ENGINES, 16-20; 25-7; 105-8;
17 (EN) SWANBOROUGH; 19 (RU) AKADEMIIA,
NO.24; 77 (JA) JAPAN; 79 (RU)
AKADEMIIA, NO.21; NARTOV.
TYPE FONTS AND TYPE-SETTING, 127-9.

ULTRASONIC TESTING, 79-84; 83 (PO) INTL.
INSTITUTE; 84 (RU) ROBESON.
ULTRASONICS, 119-26.
UNITS OF MEASUREMENT, 71-5; 119-26;
71 (EN) ASA C61.1-1961; 72 (EN) CHILDS;
ISO; JERRARD; JONES; ZIMMERMAN; 73 (GE)
SACKLOWSKI; (IT) FERRARO; (PO) CLASON-
LEXICON; CUSSET; IEC; 74 (PO) IEC; U.N.;
75 (RU) SOKOLOV; U.S.

VACUUM PHYSICS AND TECHNOLOGY, 119-26;
120 (EN) AMERICAN VACUUM; BSI-B.S.2951;
125 (PO) THEWLIS; SEE ALSO ELECTRON
TUBES.
VACUUM TUBES SEE ELECTRON TUBES.
VALVES (MACHINERY), 75 (EN) ASME,NO.112;
BSI-B.S.2591; 76 (EN) FLUID.
VARNISH, 114-5.
VENEER, 160-1.
VIBRATION TESTING, 80-4; 80 (EN)
ASA S1.1-1960; 81 (EN) BSI-B.S.3015;
82 (JA) JAPAN.
VIDEO TAPES, 148-55; SEE ALSO AUDIO
EQUIPMENT
VOCATIONAL EDUCATION, 137 (EN) AMERICAN
VOCATIONAL; 141 (GE) WEFELMEYER.

WATER, 67-8; 95-6; 112-3; 131-2.
WATER CONSERVATION, 67-8.
WATER DESALINATION, 28-37.

WATER PURIFICATION, 28-37; 131-2; 36 (RU)
AKADEMIIA, NO.62, 38.
WATERPROOFING, 37-43; 37 (EN)
ASTM D1079-54.
WAVE RESEARCH, 65-7; 112-3;
112 (EN) WIEGEL; SEE ALSO RELEVANT
SUBJECTS.
WAVEGUIDES, 148-55; 149 (EN)
55 IRE 2.S1; 59 IRE 2.S1; 150 (EN)
MACLANACHAN; 152 (PO) BARGIN;
CLASON; 153 (PO) IEC-50-GR-62;
NORWAY,RTT-5; 154 (PO) RINT; (RU)
CLASON; 155 (SW) CLASON.

WATCHES SEE CHRONOMETRY.
WAXES, 28-37; 33 (GE) IVANOVSKY;
(HI) KAUSHAL.
WEATHER FORECASTING, 95-6.
WEAVING, 155-7; 155 (EN) BSI-
B.S.2020; PRITCHARD; ZIELINSKI;
156 (GE) LOHSE; MASCHEN; UHLMANN;
157 (PO) SCHLORMANN.
WEIGHTS AND MEASURES, 71-5;
119-26; SEE ALSO UNITS OF
MEASUREMENT.
WELDING RESEARCH AND TECHNOLOGY,
159-60.
WINDERS, 75-9.
WIRE-ROPE TRANSPORTATION, 157-9;
159 (PO) REMTA.
WIRES AND CABLES, 136-48.
WOOD PULP, 115-6; 160-1.
WOOD RESEARCH AND TECHNOLOGY,
160-1.
WOOL, 155-7; 155 (EN) BSI-B.S.2020;
156 (GE) HELLMICH; (IT) DIZIONARIO
TESSILE; 157 (PO) LINK; SKINNER.
WORK STUDY SEE TIME AND MOTION
STUDY.
WROUGHT IRON, 91-4; 91 (EN)
ASTM A81-60T.

XEROGRAPHY, 47-9; 127-9;
52 (EN) 60-IRE 28.S2.
X-RAY CRYSTALLOGRAPHY, 46-7 (PO)
INTERNATIONAL.
X-RAYS SEE RADIATION.

ZINC AND ALLOYS, 91-4; 93 (PO)
INTL. WROUGHT.

189

THE NATIONAL BUREAU OF STANDARDS

The National Bureau of Standards is a principal focal point in the Federal Government for assuring maximum application of the physical and engineering sciences to the advancement of technology in industry and commerce. Its responsibilities include development and maintenance of the national standards of measurement, and the provisions of means for making measurements consistent with those standards; determination of physical constants and properties of materials; development of methods for testing materials, mechanisms, and structures, and making such tests as may be necessary, particularly for government agencies; cooperation in the establishment of standard practices for incorporation in codes and specifications; advisory service to government agencies on scientific and technical problems; invention and development of devices to serve special needs of the Government; assistance to industry, business, and consumers in the development and acceptance of commercial standards and simplified trade practice recommendations; administration of programs in cooperation with United States business groups and standards organizations for the development of international standards of practice; and maintenance of a clearinghouse for the collection and dissemination of scientific, technical, and engineering information. The scope of the Bureau's activities is suggested in the following listing of its four Institutes and their organizational units.

Institute for Basic Standards. Electricity. Metrology. Heat. Radiation Physics. Mechanics. Applied Mathematics. Atomic Physics. Physical Chemistry. Laboratory Astrophysics.* Radio Standards Laboratory: Radio Standards Physics; Radio Standards Engineering.** Office of Standard Reference Data.

Institute for Materials Research. Analytical Chemistry. Polymers. Metallurgy. Inorganic Materials. Reactor Radiations. Cryogenics.** Office of Standard Reference Materials.

Central Radio Propagation Laboratory. ** Ionosphere Research and Propagation. Troposphere and Space Telecommunications. Radio Systems. Upper Atmosphere and Space Physics.

Institute for Applied Technology. Textiles and Apparel Technology Center. Building Research. Industrial Equipment. Information Technology. Performance Test Development. Instrumentation. Transport Systems. Office of Technical Services. Office of Weights and Measures. Office of Engineering Standards. Office of Industrial Services.

---

* NBS Group, Joint Institute for Laboratory Astrophysics at the University of Colorado.
** Located at Boulder, Colorado.

☆ U. S GOVERNMENT PRINTING OFFICE : 1964 O - 730-558

ABBREVIATIONS USED FOR NAMES OF LANGUAGES

AF	....	AFRIKAANS	IA	.... INTERLINGUA
AL	....	ALBANIAN		IRISH (SEE GAELIC)
AM	....	AMERICAN	IT	.... ITALIAN
	ANNAMESE (SEE		JA	.... JAPANESE
		VIETNAMESE)	KO	.... KOREAN
AR	....	ARABIC	LA	.... LATIN
AZ	....	AZERBAIJANI	LI	.... LITHUANIAN
BR	....	BURMESE		MALAY (SEE
BU	....	BULGARIAN		INDONESIAN)
CH	....	CHINESE	MO	.... MONGOLIAN
CR	....	CROATIAN	NO	.... NORWEGIAN
CZ	....	CZECH	PL	.... POLISH
DA	....	DANISH	PO	.... POLYGLOT
DU	....	DUTCH	PR	.... PORTUGUESE
EN	....	ENGLISH	RO	.... ROMANIAN
EO	....	ESPERANTO	RU	.... RUSSIAN
ES	....	ESTONIAN	SC	.... SERBOCROATIAN
FI	....	FINNISH	SL	.... SLOVAK
FR	....	FRENCH	SV	.... SLOVENIAN
GA	....	GAELIC	SP	.... SPANISH
GE	....	GERMAN	SW	.... SWEDISH
GR	....	GREEK	TH	.... THAI
HE	....	HEBREW	TU	.... TURKISH
HI	....	HINDI	UK	.... UKRAINIAN
HU	....	HUNGARIAN	VI	.... VIETNAMESE
IC	....	ICELANDIC	WE	.... WELSH
IN	....	INDONESIAN	WR	.... WHITE RUSSIAN